# JOHN WILLIS'

# THEATRE WORLD

## 1975–1976 SEASON

### VOLUME 32

CROWN PUBLISHERS, INC.
ONE PARK AVENUE
NEW YORK, N.Y. 10016

"Not So Long Ago"
(1920)

with Philip Merivale and Basil
Rathbone in "The Swan" (1923)

as Juliet
(1929)

"Three Sisters"
(1926)

"L'Aiglon"
(1934)

"The Cradle Song"
(1934)

with Joseph Schildkraut
in "The Cherry Orchard" (19

"Mary Stuart"
(1957)

with Una O'Connor in
"The Starcross Story"
(1954)

"The Seagull"
(1964)

2

1927        1945        1946        1975

# TO
## EVA LeGALLIENNE

*who for six decades has been an actress of consummate skill, a dauntless supporter of the classics, a creative and innovative producer-director, an heroic crusader for repertory, and who, justifiably, has earned immortal fame in the historical records of the American theatre.*

**"A CHORUS LINE"**

*Martha Swope Photos*

Winner of 1976 Pulitzer Prize, New York Drama Critics Circle
Award, 9 Antoinette Perry ("Tony") Awards, Drama Desk Award, and Special Theatre World Award

# CONTENTS

Dedication: Eva LeGallienne ................................................... 3

The Season in Review .......................................................... 6

Broadway Calendar:
    Productions that opened June 1, 1975 through May 31, 1976 ................... 8
    Productions from past seasons that played through this season ................ 60
    Productions from past seasons that closed during this season ................ 66

Off Broadway Calendar:
    Productions that opened June 1, 1975 through May 31, 1976 ................... 67
    The Actors Company ...................................................... 91
    American Place Theatre ................................................... 95
    Bil Baird Marionettes .................................................... 100
    Brooklyn Academy of Music ............................................... 101
    Chelsea Theater Center ................................................... 105
    Circle Repertory Theatre ................................................. 107
    The Classic Theatre ...................................................... 110
    Colonnades Theatre Lab ................................................... 111
    Counterpoint Theatre Company ............................................. 112
    The Cubiculo ............................................................ 113
    Dume Spanish Theatre .................................................... 115
    Equity Library Theatre ................................................... 116
    Joseph Jefferson Theatre Company ......................................... 121
    Manhattan Theatre Club .................................................. 122
    Negro Ensemble Company ................................................. 124
    New Dramatists Inc. ..................................................... 126
    New York Shakespeare Festival at Lincoln Center .......................... 128
    New York Shakespeare Festival at Public Theater .......................... 134
    Phoenix Theatre ......................................................... 138
    Playwrights Horizons .................................................... 143
    Public Players Inc. ...................................................... 146
    Roundabout Theatre ...................................................... 147
    Spanish Theatre Repertory ............................................... 150
    Theatre Off Park ........................................................ 151
    Productions from past seasons that played through this season ................ 152
    Productions from past seasons that closed during this season ................ 154

Productions that opened and closed before scheduled Broadway premier ............ 155

National Touring Companies .................................................... 158

Annual Shakespeare Festivals .................................................. 173

Professional Resident Companies in the United States ........................... 186

Award-Winning Productions: Pulitzer, Drama Critics Circle, "Tony" ................ 228

Theatre World Award Winners of 1975 - 1976 season ........................... 229

Theatre World Awards presentation party ....................................... 232

Theatre World Awardees of previous seasons .................................... 234

Biographies of this season's cast .............................................. 235

Obituaries from this season ................................................... 262

Index ....................................................................... 267

**EDITOR: JOHN WILLIS**

*Assistant Editor:* Don Nute

*Staff:* Alberto Cabrera, Fred Ortiz, Stanley Reeves, William Schelble, Paul Woodson

*Staff Photographers:* Joe Abeles, Bert Andrews, Ron Reagan, Van Williams

# THE SEASON IN REVIEW
## June 1, 1975–May 31, 1976

In addition to the exciting preparations for our American Bicentennial Celebration, the theatre season opened with the brightest prospects in over two decades. More backers were gambling on new productions, more actors were anxiously anticipating employment, and more productions were available than theatres to book them. However, almost immediately, dark clouds of union demands dimmed the optimistic horizon. On August 4, 1975, a new code went into effect for Off Off Broadway theatres and showcases. It would have annihilated a majority of houses where most experimental productions are staged, and where many performers have the opportunity to display and develop their talents. Instantaneously, there were loud protests of resentment from Actors Equity Association, and on Aug. 26 its members revoked the code. On September 18, Broadway's longest strike began. The musicians union forced all 9 Broadway musicals to close for 25 long days and nights. Plays without music and Off Broadway productions were not affected, but several new productions were postponed or cancelled. Although a settlement did not seem imminent, compromises were made, and on October 12 an agreement was reached that enabled theatres to re-open. The hits continued their sell-out business, but the shows doing marginal business had to struggle for survival. Theatrical advertising on television became an important factor in firing adrenalin back into Broadway's veins. At the season's conclusion, from the financial viewpoint, Broadway's box office receipts hit a record high (almost $71 million, according to *Variety's* statistical report), and the road had its second highest recorded grosses. In November, because of the unsavory atmosphere surrounding the Times Square area, producers, theatre owners and performers began a concerted effort to eradicate the mid-town peep shows, massage parlors, topless bars, loitering and soliciting. The League of New York Theatre Owners and Producers voted a levy on all New York and touring companies to promote this worthwhile project. They also accepted the general trend for an 8 o'clock curtain rather than last season's experimental 7:30 curtain.

From the creative and critical viewpoint, the season's quality was somewhat inconsistent. A surprising feature was the overwhelming number of revivals—due in part to the paucity of new playwrights who defected to the more lucrative tv "factories." Five of the revivals were produced at JFK Center in Washington especially for the bicentennial, and subsequently transferred to New York. They were "The Skin of Our Teeth" with Martha Scott, Alfred Drake, and a memorable characterization by Elizabeth Ashley; "Sweet Bird of Youth" with Christopher Walken and Irene Worth who received a "Tony" for best actress of the year; "The Royal Family" with Eva LeGallienne, George Grizzard, Sam Levene, and the scintillating Rosemary Harris; "Long Day's Journey into Night" with Zoe Caldwell, Jason Robards and Michael Moriarty; "The Heiress" with Jane Alexander and Richard Kiley. Other noteworthy revivals were "Death of a Salesman" with excellent performances by George C. Scott, Teresa Wright and James Farentino; "The Glass Menagerie" with Maureen Stapleton and Rip Torn; "The Lady from the Sea" with Vanessa Redgrave's Broadway debut; "Ah, Wilderness!" with Geraldine Fitzgerald, Richard Backus and Paul Rudd; and "Who's Afraid of Virginia Woolf?" with Colleen Dewhurst, Ben Gazzara, Maureen Anderman and Richard Kelton—superior in almost every respect to the original production. Musical revivals include "Very Good Eddie," "Hello, Dolly!," and "My Fair Lady" with commendable performances by Ian Richardson, Christine Andreas, Jerry Lanning and George Rose. The ever-popular Katharine Hepburn had a successful limited engagement in a less than mediocre English import, "A Matter of Gravity." Julie Harris again proved her great talent in the solo play about Emily Dickinson, "The Belle of Amherst." Richard Burton demonstrated his box office power by playing to SRO audiences for 12 weeks in last season's holdover, "Equus," and Liza Minnelli did likewise for 5 weeks in "Chicago" during Gwen Verdon's absence.

The outstandingly successful musicals were "Chicago" with gratifying performances by Gwen Verdon, Chita Rivera and Jerry Orbach, "Bubbling Brown Sugar" with show-stoppers Vivian Reed, Avon Long and Chip Garnett, "The Robber Bridegroom," and the incomparable "A Chorus Line." Another musical feature of the Broadway season was sold-out concerts by Paul Anka, Shirley MacLaine, and Frank Sinatra with Ella Fitzgerald and Count Basie. Several much-heralded and eagerly anticipated musicals were sadly disappointing failures: "Rockabye Hamlet," "Home Sweet Homer," "Treemonisha," "Rex," and "1600 Pennsylvania Avenue."

The Antoinette Perry (Tony) Award for best play went to "Travesties," a British import that also received the New York Drama Critics Circle citation. Its star, visiting artist John Wood, was voted a "Tony" as best actor for his bravura performance. Best actress and actor in a musical were Donna McKechnie of "A Chorus Line" and George Rose of "My Fair Lady." For best supporting performances, "Tonys" were awarded Shirley Knight of "Kennedy's Children," Edward Hermann of "Mrs. Warren's Profession," Kelly Bishop and Sammy Williams of "A Chorus Line." Special "Tonys" were presented George Abbott, Richard Burton, Circle in the Square's producers, and Washington, D.C.'s Arena Stage—the first "Tony" to a regional company. Alexander H. Cohen's televised production of the "Tony" presentations was again an exemplary format. New York Drama Critics Circle cited the dramatically powerful "Streamers" as best American play, and the visually opulent "Pacific Overtures" as best musical. The Pulitzer Prize, 9 "Tonys," 6 Drama Desk Awards, and a Special Theatre World Award went to the indisputably deserving "A Chorus Line." Since its Off Broadway premier last season, it has continuously played to capacity audiences.

Off Broadway again declined both quantitatively and qualitatively. Severe financial crises confronted most non-profit institutional companies, and necessitated appeals for support. The Brooklyn Academy of Music, the oldest performing arts center in the country, renovated and restored its Music Hall with a new name, Playhouse. It re-opened Dec. 2, 1975 with "Sweet Bird of Youth." To everyone's gratification, the Academy again imported the Royal Shakespeare Company who performed in its innovative and critically-praised "Henry V." Other notable Off Broadway productions include the superior revivals by The Acting Company and the Phoenix Company, Lincoln Center's "Trelawny of the 'Wells,'" "Hamlet," "Mrs. Warren's Profession" with Lynn Redgrave a perfect Vivie, "The Threepenny Opera" and "Streamers" with a memorable cast headed by Dorian Harewood and Paul Rudd, the Public Theater's "Jesse and the Bandit Queen" with Dixie Carter making an impressive debut, "Rich and Famous" with praiseworthy performers Anita Gillette, Ron Leibman and William Atherton, Equity Library Theatre's hit revival of "Follies," the delightful revue "Tuscaloosa's Calling. . . .," "Vanities," and Circle Repertory Theatre's "Knock Knock" that was transferred to Broadway. As always, Guy Lombardo beautifully produced another musical under the stars at Jones Beach, providing the usual enjoyable summer experience. This year it was "Oklahoma!"

In addition to the outstanding performers already mentioned, recognition should be given Danny Aiello, Lewis Arlt, Pamela Blair, Northern J. Callaway, John Cullum, Moses Gunn, Linda Hopkins, Ken Howard, Cleavon Little, Priscilla Lopez, Mako, Keith McDermott, Estelle Parsons, Anthony Perkins, Gilbert Price, Madeleine Renaud, Charles Repole, Rachel Roberts, Isao Sato, Virginia Seidel, Daniel Seltzer, John Shea, Carole Shelley, Donald Sinden, Nancy Snyder, Meryl Streep, Kristoffer Tabori, Donna Theodore, and Dick Anthony Williams.

As is endemic to every season, productions were born that deserved longer life, but failed to attract enough patrons to survive. Among this season's victims were the trilogy under the title "The Norman Conquests," "Lamppost Reunion," "The Poison Tree," and "Yentl" with a stellar performance by Tovah Feldshuh. In retrospect, it was a richly rewarding year for the "main stem of the Big Apple," as well as for the mainstream of theatre throughout the United States.

Donna McKechnie,
Robert LuPone
in "A Chorus Line"

John Wood
"Travesties"

# BROADWAY CALENDAR
## June 1, 1975 through May 31, 1976

Eva LeGallienne, Rosemary Harris
in "The Royal Family"

Christopher Walken,
Irene Worth
in "Sweet Bird of Youth"

Chita Rivera, Gwen Verdon
in "Chicago"

**FORTY-SIXTH STREET THEATRE**
Opened Tuesday, June 1, 1975.*
Robert Fryer and James Cresson present:

# CHICAGO

Book, Fred Ebb, Bob Fosse; Music, John Kander; Lyrics, Fred Ebb; Based on the play "Chicago" by Maurine Dallas Watkins; Directed and Choreographed by Bob Fosse; Settings, Tony Walton; Costumes, Patricia Zipprodt; Lighting, Jules Fisher; Musical Director, Stanley Lebowsky; Orchestrations, Ralph Burns; Dance Music Arrangements, Peter Howard; Sound, Abe Jacob; Hairstylist, Romaine Green; Produced in association with Martin Richards; Managerial Associate, Frank Scardino; Wardrobe Supervisor, Louise Van Dine; Assistant Conductor, Art Wagner; Production Assistant, Vicki Stein; Assistant-Choreographer, Tony Stevens; Assistant to Director, Kathryn Doby; Original Cast Album, Arista Records.

## CAST

| | |
|---|---|
| Velma Kelly | Chita Rivera†9 |
| Roxie Hart | Gwen Verdon†1 |
| Fred Casely | Christopher Chadman†2 |
| Sergeant Fogarty | Richard Korthaze |
| Amos Hart | Barney Martin†3 |
| Liz | Cheryl Clark |
| Annie | Michon Peacock†4 |
| June | Candy Brown†5 |
| Hunyak | Graciela Daniele†6 |
| Mona | Pamela Sousa |
| Martin Harrison | Michael Vita |
| Matron | Mary McCarty |
| Billy Flynn | Jerry Orbach |
| Mary Sunshine | M. O'Haughey |
| Go-to-Hell Kitty | Charlene Ryan†7 |
| Harry | Paul Solen |
| Aaron | Gene Foote†10 |
| The Judge | Ron Schwinn |
| Court Clerk | Gary Gendell†8 |

STANDBYS AND UNDERSTUDIES: Roxie, Lenora Nemetz; Matron, Mary Sunshine, Marsha Bagwell; Velma, Michon Peacock; Amos, Richard Korthaze; Dance Alternates, Hank Brunjes, Monica Tiller

MUSICAL NUMBERS: "All That Jazz," "Funny Honey," "Cell Block Tango," "When You're Good to Mama," "Tap Dance," "All I Care About,"."A Little Bit of Good," "We Both Reached for the Gun," "Roxie," "I Can't Do It Alone," "Chicago after Midnight," "My Own Best Friend," "I Know a Girl," "Me and My Baby," "Mister Cellophane," "When Velma Takes the Stand," "Razzle Dazzle," "Class," "Nowadays," "R.S.V.P." "Keep It Hot"

A musical vaudeville in two acts. The action takes place in the late 1920's in Chicago, Illinois.

*General Managers:* Joseph Harris, Ira Bernstein
*Press:* The Merlin Group, Cheryl Sue Dolby, Harriett Trachtenberg, Harold Lubin, Ron Harris
*Stage Managers:* Phil Friedman, Robert Corpora, Paul Phillips, Nick Malekos, Craig Jacobs

* Still playing May 31, 1976.
† Succeeded by: 1. Lenora Nemetz, Liza Minnelli during Miss Verdon's illness, 2. Gary Gendell, 3. Rex Everhart, 4. Joan Bell, 5. Karen G. Burke, Sally Neal, 6. Sandra Brewer, Candace Tovar, 7. Fern Fitzgerald, 8. Ross Miles, 9. Lenora Nemetz, 10. Lauren Giroux

*Martha Swope Photos*

**Top Left: Gwen Verdon, Jerry Orbach**

**Gwen Verdon, Chita Rivera**

Lenora Nemetz

Chita Rivera, Gwen Verdon
Above: Rex Everhart

9

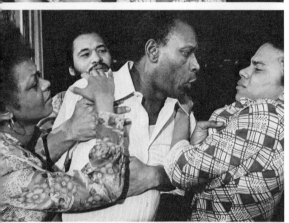

PALACE THEATRE
Opened Tuesday, June 10, 1975.*
The Negro Ensemble Company in cooperation with Woodie King, Jr., presents:

# THE FIRST BREEZE OF SUMMER

By Leslie Lee; Director, Douglas Turner Ward; Scenery, Edward Burbridge; Costumes, Mary Mease Warren; Lighting, Thomas Skelton; Production Administrator, Gerald S. Krone; Management Associates, Phyllis Restaino, Donald Tirabassi, Thelma Cooper; Production Assistant, Sandra L. Ross; Wardrobe Supervisor, Margaret Faison; Technical Director, Dik Krider

CAST

| | |
|---|---|
| Gremmar | Frances Foster |
| Nate Edwards | Charles Brown |
| Lou Edwards | Reyno |
| Aunt Edna | Barbara Montgomery |
| Milton Edwards | Moses Gunn |
| Hattie | Ethel Ayler |
| Lucretia | Janet League |
| Sam Greene | Carl Crudup |
| Briton Woodward | Anthony McKay |
| Reverend Mosely | Lou Leabengula Myers |
| Hope | Petronia |
| Joe Drake | Peter DeMaio |
| Gloria Townes | Bebe Drake Hooks |
| Harper Edwards | Douglas Turner Ward† |

UNDERSTUDIES: Jerry Cleveland, Bill Cobbs, Bebe Drake Hooks, Lou Leabengula Myers, Petronia, Roland Sanchez, Martha Short-Goldsen, Samm-Art Williams

A drama in two acts. The action takes place at the present time in a small city in the Northeast on a Thursday afternoon through Sunday night.

*General Management:* Dorothy Olim Associates
*Press:* Howard Atlee, Clarence Allsopp, Meg Gordean, Owen Levy
*Stage Managers:* Horacena J. Taylor, Jerry Cleveland

\* Closed July 20, 1975 after 48 performances and 5 previews.
† Succeeded by Samm-Art Williams

*Bert Andrews Photos*

**Left: Ethel Ayler, Charles Brown, Moses Gunn, Reyno Top: Ethel Ayler, Reyno**

Moses Gunn, Peter DeMaio

Frances Foster, Ethel Ayler, Barbara Montgomery

## CIRCLE IN THE SQUARE THEATRE

Opened Thursday, June 26, 1975.*
Circle in the Square Theatre (Theodore Mann, Artistic Director; Paul Libin, Managing Director) presents:

# DEATH OF A SALESMAN

By Arthur Miller; Director, George C. Scott; Scenery, Marjorie Kellogg; Costumes, Arthur Boccia; Lighting, Thomas Skelton; Incidental Music, Craig Wesson; Production Associate, E. J. Oshins; Hairstylist, Roberto Fernandez; Wardrobe Supervisor, Sydney Brooks; Production Assistants, Nancy Cook, Johnny Clontz, Gordon Bendall, Bernard Ferstenberg, Anne Oberbroeckling, Guy Martin, Jacqueline Jacobus, Rose Avallone

### CAST

| | |
|---|---|
| Linda Loman | Teresa Wright |
| Willy Loman | George C. Scott†1 |
| Happy | Harvey Keitel†2 |
| Biff | James Farentino |
| Bernard | Chuck Patterson |
| First Woman | Patricia Quinn |
| Charley | Dotts Johnson |
| Uncle Ben | Ramon Bieri |
| Howard Wagner | Pirie MacDonald |
| Jenny | Helen Harrelson |
| Stanley | Mordecai Lawner |
| Miss Forsythe | Bara-Cristin Hansen |
| Letta | Joanne Jonas |
| Second Woman | Julie Garfield |
| Second Waiter | Craig Wasson |

STANDBYS AND UNDERSTUDIES: Willy, Roy Poole; Linda, Helen Harrelson; Happy, Biff, Bruce Weitz; Howard, Stanley, Michael Durrell; Charley, Bernard, Arthur French; Miss Forsythe, Letta, Katherine De Hetre

A drama in two acts. The action takes place in Willy Loman's house, and in various offices he visits in New York City and Boston.

*Company Manager:* William Conn
*Press:* Merle Debuskey, Susan L. Schulman
*Stage Managers:* Randall Brooks, James Bernardi

* Closed Aug. 24, 1975 after limited engagement of 71 performances and 23 previews. For original production, see THEATRE WORLD, Vol. 5. Original cast included Lee J. Cobb, Mildred Dunnock, Cameron Mitchell, Arthur Kennedy.
† Succeeded by: 1. Roy Poole during Mr. Scott's illness, 2. Martin Sheen

*Inge Morath Photos*

**Top: Harvey Keitel, Teresa Wright, James Farentino, George C. Scott**

George C. Scott

**MARK HELLINGER THEATRE**

Opened Tuesday, September 9, 1975.*
Ken Marsolais with The Kennedy Center-Xerox American
Bicentennial Theatre presents:

# THE SKIN OF OUR TEETH

By Thornton Wilder; Director, Jose Quintero; Sets, Eugene Lee;
Costumes, Franne Lee; Lighting, Ken Billington; Produced by
Roger L. Stevens and Richmond Crinkley for Kennedy Center;
Wardrobe Supervisor, Kathleen Foster; Associate Producer, Scott/-
Bloom Productions Ltd.

### CAST

| | |
|---|---|
| Announcer/Professor/Mr. Tremayne | Alexander Reed |
| Sabina | Elizabeth Ashley |
| Mr. Fitzpatrick | F. J. O'Neil |
| Mrs. Antrobus | Martha Scott |
| Dinosaur | Roi Petersen |
| Mammoth/Monkey Man | Denny Dillon |
| Telegraph Boy/Assistant Announcer | Barry Livingston |
| Gladys | Janet Grey |
| Henry | Steve Railsback |
| Mr. Antrobus | Alfred Drake |
| Doctor/Fred Bailey | Lee Sherman |
| Judge | Joseph C. Davies |
| Homer/Announcer | Norman Michael Chase |
| Miss E. Muse/Conveener's Wife | Eda Seasongood |
| Miss T. Muse | Josephine Nichols |
| Miss M. Muse | Betty Lynd |
| Fortune Teller | Charlotte Jones |
| Defeated Candidate | Douglas Fisher |
| Hester | Yuye Fernandes |
| Ivy | Gertrude Jeannette |
| Chair Pushers | Philip Lindsay, Roi Petersen |
| Drum Majorettes | Betty Lynd, Kristina Callahan, Kate Kellery, Yuye Fernandes |
| Conveeners | Richard DeFabees, Joseph C. Davies, Douglas Fisher, J. F. Hall, Steven Kelly, Lee Sherman, Alexander Reed, Barry Livingston |

UNDERSTUDIES: Sabina, Misses Muse, Kristina Callahan; Antrobus, Alexander Reed; Mrs. Antrobus, Ivy, Eda Seasongood; Fortune Teller, Hester, Josephine Nichols; Henry, Richard DeFabees;
Tremayn, Philip Lindsay; Gladys, Kate Kellery; Fitzpatrick, Bailey,
J. F. Hall; Mammoth, Betty Lynd; Announcer, Douglas Fisher

A comedy in three acts. The action takes place at the present time
in a home in Excelsior, NJ., and on Atlantic City's boardwalk.

*General Manager:* Leonard Soloway
*Company Manager:* James Mennen
*Press:* Betty Lee Hunt, Maria Cristina Pucci, Bill Evans
*Stage Managers:* Martin Herzer, David Taylor, Steven Kelly,
Betty Lynd

* Closed Sept. 13, 1975 after 7 performances and 7 previews. Original production opened Nov. 18, 1942 with Tallulah Bankhead,
Florence Eldridge, Fredric March, Montgomery Clift and played
359 performances. See THEATRE WORLD, VOL. 12 for 1955
revival with Mary Martin, Helen Hayes, George Abbott that
played 22 performances.

*Richard Braaten Photos*

**Elizabeth Ashley, Charlotte Jones**

**Martha Scott Top: Elizabeth
Ashley, Alfred Drake**

## CIRCLE IN THE SQUARE

Opened Thursday, September 18, 1975.*
Circle in the Square (Theodore Mann, Artistic Director; Paul Libin, Managing Director) in association with the Long Wharf Theatre presents:

# AH, WILDERNESS!

By Eugene O'Neill; Director, Arvin Brown; Scenery, Steven Rubin; Costumes, Bill Walker; Lighting, Ronald Wallace; Production Associate, Johnny Clontz; Hairstylist, Roberto Fernandez; Wardrobe Supervisor, Sydney Brooks; Production Assistants, Gordon Bendall, Tom Smith, Jolly Nelson, Frank Storch, Nancy Shutter

### CAST

| | |
|---|---|
| Tommy Miller | Glenn Zachar |
| Mildred Miller | Christina Whitmore |
| Arthur Miller | Paul Rudd |
| Essie Miller | Geraldine Fitzgerald |
| Lily Miller | Teresa Wright |
| Sid Davis | John Braden |
| Nat Miller | William Swetland |
| Richard Miller | Richard Backus |
| David McComber | Ralph Drischell |
| Norah | Linda Hunt |
| Wint Selby | Sean G. Griffin |
| Belle | Suzanne Lederer |
| Bartender | Stephen Mendillo |
| Salesman | Don Gantry |
| Muriel | Swoosie Kurtz |

STANDBYS: Essie, Shirley Bryan; Arthur, Richard, Wint, Thomas Leopold; Belle, Mildred, Muriel, Norah, Alexandra Stoddart

A comedy in 3 acts and 7 scenes. The action takes place in the Miller home in a small Connecticut town on July 4, 1906.

*Company Manager:* William Conn
*Press:* Merle Debuskey, Susan L. Schulman
*Stage Managers:* Nina Seely, James Bernardi

* Closed Nov. 23, 1975 after limited engagement of 85 performances and 19 previews. Original production opened Oct. 2, 1933 at the Guild Theatre with George M. Cohan, Marjorie Marquis, Elisha Cook, Jr., and ran for 289 performances.

*Inge Morath, Sy Friedman Photos*

**Top: entire cast**

**Teresa Wright, John Braden
Above: Richard Backus, Swoosie Kurtz**

Ronald Dennis, Don Percassi, Priscilla Lopez,
Renee Baughman

**SHUBERT THEATRE**
Opened Sunday, October 19, 1975.*
Joseph Papp presents a New York Shakespeare Festival Production in association with Plum Productions:

# A CHORUS LINE

Conceived, Choreographed and Directed by Michael Bennett; Book, James Kirkwood, Nicholas Dante; Music, Marvin Hamlisch; Lyrics, Edward Kleban; Co-Choreographer, Bob Avian; Musical Direction and Vocal Arrangements, Don Pippin; Associate Producer, Bernard Gersten; Setting, Robin Wagner; Costumes, Theoni V. Aldredge; Lighting, Tharon Musser; Sound, Abe Jacob; Music Coordinator, Robert Thomas; Orchestrations, Bill Byers, Hershy Kay, Jonathan Tunick; Assistant to choreographers and dance captain, Baayork Lee; Wardrobe Mistress, Alyce Gilbert; Hairstylist, Harvey's Bazaar; Original Cast Album by Columbia Records

### CAST

| | |
|---|---|
| Roy | Scott Allen†16 |
| Kristine | Renee Baughman†1 |
| Sheila | Carole (Kelly) Bishop†17 |
| Val | Pamela Blair†2 |
| Mike | Wayne Cilento |
| Butch | Chuck Cissel |
| Larry | Clive Clerk |
| Maggie | Kay Cole†3 |
| Richie | Ronald Dennis†4 |
| Tricia | Donna Drake |
| Tom | Brandt Edwards |
| Judy | Patricia Garland†5 |
| Lois | Carolyn Kirsch†6 |
| Don | Ron Kuhlman†7 |
| Bebe | Nancy Lane†8 |
| Connie | Baayork Lee†9 |
| Diana | Priscilla Lopez†10 |
| Zach | Robert LuPone†11 |
| Mark | Cameron Mason |
| Cassie | Donna McKechnie†12 |
| Al | Don Percassi†13 |
| Frank | Michael Serrecchia |
| Greg | Michel Stuart†14 |
| Bobby | Thomas J. Walsh |
| Paul | Sammy Williams†15 |
| Vicki | Crissy Wilzak |

UNDERSTUDIES: Al, Mike, John Mineo; Paul, Richie, Chuck Cissel; Kristine, Connie, Maggie, Donna Drake; Don, Mark, Brandt Edwards; Cassie, Sheila, Carolyn Kirsch; Diana, Bebe, Carole Schweid; Larry, Greg, Bobby, Michael Serrecchia; Val, Judy, Crissy Wilzak; Zach, Clive Clerk

MUSICAL NUMBERS: "I Hope I Get It," "I Can Do That," "And. . . .," "At the Ballet," "Sing!," "Hello Twelve, Hello Thirteen, Hello Love," "Nothing," "Dance: Ten; Looks: Three," "The Music and the Mirror," "One," "The Tap Combination," "What I Did for Love"

A musical performed without intermission. The action takes place at an audition at the present time in this theatre.

*Company Managers:* Patricia Carney, Sally Campbell
*Press:* Merle Debruskey, Bob Ullman, Bruce Cohen
*Stage Managers:* Jeff Hamlin, Frank Hartenstein, Scott Allen

\* Still playing May 31, 1976. Cited as Best Musical by New York Drama Critics Circle; winner of Pulitzer Prize; received "Tony" for Best Musical, Best Book of a Musical, Best Score, Best Director of a Musical, Best Lighting, Best Choreographer, Best Actress in a Musical (Donna McKechnie), Best Featured Actress in a Musical (Carole (Kelly) Bishop), Best Featured Actor in a Musical (Sammy Williams); presented a Special Theatre World Award to every member of the creative staff and original cast.
†\*Succeeded by: 1. Cookie Vazquez, 2. Barbara Monte-Britton, 3. Lauree Berger, 4. Winston DeWitt Hemsley, 5. Sandahl Bergman, 6. Vickie Frederick, 7. David Thome, 8. Gillian Scalici, 9. Lauren Kayahara, 10. Carole Schweid, Rebecca York, 11. Joe Bennett, 12. Ann Reinking, 13. Bill Nabel, 14. Justin Ross, 15. George Pesaturo, 16. Danny Ruvolo, 17. Kathrynann Wright

*Martha Swope Photos*

**Top Left: Donna McKechnie, Carole (Kelly) Bishop,
Baayork Lee, Nancy Lane, Patricia
Garland, Renee Baughman, Kay Cole,
Priscilla Lopez, Pamela Blair, Robert LuPone**

Pamela Blair, Sammy Williams,
Cameron Mason Top: Chuck Cissel,
Thomas J. Walsh, Kelly Bishop, Clive Clerk,
Joe Bennett, Wayne Cilento

Ann Reinking, Joe Bennett

**THE LITTLE THEATRE**
Opened Thursday, October 16, 1975.*
Joe Garofalo presents:

# LAMPPOST REUNION

By Louis LaRusso II; Director, Tom Signorelli; Scenery, Robert U. Taylor; Lighting, Spencer Mosse; Costumes, Judy Dearing; Production Assistant, Tony Golden; Wardrobe Mistress, Marilyn Amaral; Associate Producer, Barry Singer

CAST

| | |
|---|---|
| Biggie | Danny Aiello |
| Mac | Frank Quinn† |
| Tommy | Frank Bongiorno |
| Jobby | George Pollock |
| Fred | Gabriel Dell |

STANDBYS: Biggie, Fred, Nick LaPadula; Tommy, Jobby, George Poulos; Mac, Ron Ryan

*General Manager:* Ashton Springer
*Company Manager:* Bob McDonald
*Press:* Max Eisen, Carl Samrock
*Stage Managers:* Paul Austin, Richard Lalli, Gary Stein

* Closed Dec. 21, 1975 after 76 performances.
† Succeeded by Tom Signorelli

**Right Top: Frank Bongiorno,
George Pollock, Gabriel Dell**

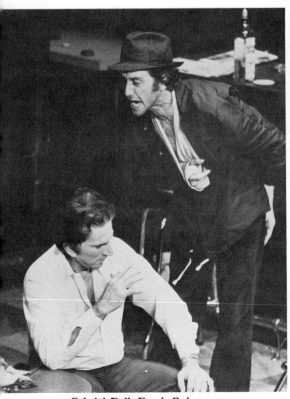

**Gabriel Dell, Frank Quinn**

**Gabriel Dell, Danny Aiello, Frank Quinn**

**BOOTH THEATRE**
Opened Monday, October 20, 1975.*
Joseph Papp presents a New York Shakespeare Festival Production of:

# THE LEAF PEOPLE

By Dennis J. Reardon; Director, Tom O'Horgan; Settings, John Conklin; Costumes and Makeup, Randy Barcelo; Lighting, John McLain; Sound, Roger Jay; Original Music, Xantheus Roh Leempoor; Associate Producer, Bernard Gersten; Assistant to director, Susan Elkind; Wardrobe Supervisor, Alfred Calamoneri

### CAST

The Fishbellies:

| | |
|---|---|
| First Interpreter | Grayson Hall |
| Second Interpreter | Anthony Holland |
| Shaughnessy (Shaw) | Tom Aldredge |
| Meatball | Ernesto Gonzalez |
| P. Sigmund Furth | Lane Smith |
| Steven | Ted LePlat |
| Michelle | Denise Delapenha |
| Anna Ames | Margaret Hall |

The Leaf People:

| | |
|---|---|
| Sutreeshay | Geanine-Michele Capozzoli |
| Gitaucho (Meesho) | Raymond J. Barry |
| The Sound (Keet) | Leon Morenzie |
| Leeboh | William Parry |
| Mayteemo | James Sbano |
| Monkey Man (Mututahsh) | Ernesto Gonzalez |
| Keerah | Denise Delapenha |
| Yawahlapeetee (Rubber Ball) | Joanna Featherstone |
| Kreetahshay (Chicken Mother) | Susan Batson |
| Green Father (Shay Tahndor) | Roy Brocksmith |
| Jeeshoom | Francisco Blackfeather |
| Kahleemshoht | Ron Capozzoli |
| Choolkahnoor | Jeffrey David-Owen |
| Lahbayneezh | Jelom Vieira |
| Treekah | Josevaldo Machado |
| Zhahbahroosh | Ric Lavin |
| Lohzhoodish | Soni Moreno |
| Lohmoheetet | Jeannette Ertelt |

UNDERSTUDIES: Ron Capozzoli, Jeffrey David-Owen, Jeannette Ertelt, Ric Lavin, Soni Moreno, William Parry, James Sbano

A drama in 2 acts and 16 scenes. The action takes place in early October of 1973 in the Amazon Rain Forest.

*Company Manager:* Maurice Schaded
*Press:* Merle Debuskey, Leo Stern
*Stage Managers:* Galen McKinley, William Schill, Ron Capozzoli

\* Closed Oct. 26, 1975 after 8 performances and 42 previews.

*Barry Kramer-Joseph Abeles Photos*

**Top: Joanna Featherstone, Tom Aldredge, Raymond Barry (R) Ted LePlat, Lane Smith, Margaret Hall**

**Susan Batson, Leon Morenzie**
**Above: Grayson Hall, Anthony Holland**

17

**URIS THEATRE**
Opened Tuesday, October 21, 1975.*
(Moved to Palace Theatre, Nov. 3, 1975)
Adela Holzer, James Nederlander and Victor Lurie present the
Houston Grand Opera Association Production of:

# TREEMONISHA

By Scott Joplin; Conceived and Directed by Frank Corsaro; Choreography, Louis Johnson; Orchestration and Music Supervision, Gunther Schuller; Conductor, Gunther Schuller; Sets and Costumes, Franco Colavecchia; Lighting, Nananne Porcher; Artistic Consultant, Vera Brodsky Lawrence; Presented by arrangement with the Dramatic Publishing Company; Assistant Director, David Drisin; Production Associate, Marion Kinsella; Wardrobe Mistress, Billie White; Assistant Choreographer and Dance Captain, James Thurston

### CAST

| | |
|---|---|
| Zodzetrick | Ben Harney |
| Ned | Willard White |
| Monisha | Betty Allen |
| | Matinees: Lorna Myers |
| Treemonisha | Carmen Balthrop |
| | Matinees: Kathleen Battle |
| Remus | Curtis Rayam |
| Andy | Kenneth Hicks |
| Lucy | Cora Johnson |
| Parson Alltalk | Edward Pierson |
| Simon | Raymond Bazemore |
| Cephus | Dwight Ransom |
| Luddud | Dorceal Duckens |

CHORUS: Earl L. Baker, Kenneth Bates, Barbara Christopher, Steven Cole, Ella Eure, Gregory Gardner, Melvin Jordan, Patricia McDermott, Janette Moody, Marion Moore, Vera Moore, Lorna Myers, Glover Parham, Patricia Pates, William Penn, Dwight Ransom, Cornel Richie, Patricia Rogers, Christine Spencer, Walter Turnbull, Gloria Turner, Peter Whitehead, Arthur Williams, Barbara Young

DANCERS: Clyde-Jacques Barrett, Thea Barnes, Dwight Baxter, Renee Brailsford, Karen Burke, Veda Jackson, Reggie Jackson, Julia Lema, Anita Littleman, Rick Odums, Dwayne Phelps, Ivson Polk, Mabel Robinson, Martial Roumain, Katherine Singleton, James Thurston, Bobby Walker, Pamela Wilson

An opera in two acts and three scenes. The action takes place on a plantation in Arkansas, northeast of Texarkana and three or four miles from the Red River.

MUSICAL NUMBERS: "The Bag of Luck," "The Corn-Huskers," "We're Goin' Around," "The Wreath," "The Sacred Tree," "Surprise," "Treemonisha's Bringing Up," "Good Advice," "Confusion," "Superstition," "Treemonisha in Peril," "Frolic of the Bears," "Wasp Nest," "The Rescue," "We Will Rest Awhile," "Going Home," "Aunt Dinah Has Blowed de Horn," "I Want to See My Child," "Treemonisha's Return," "Wrong Is Never Right," "Abuse," "When Villains Ramble Far and Near," "Conjuror's Forgiven," "We Will Trust You as Our Leader," "A Real Slow Drag"

*General Manager:* Nelle Nugent
*Company Manager:* John Scott
*Press:* Michael Alpert, Marilyn LeVine, Joshua Ellis, Warren Knowlton
*Stage Managers:* Ben Janney, Elizabeth Caldwell, Clinton Davis

\* Closed Dec. 14, 1975 after 64 performances and 6 previews.

**18** **Top: Carmen Balthrop, Curtis Rayam, also Right with Willard White, Betty Allen**

**Ben Harney, Dorceal Duckens, Kenneth Hicks, Carmen Balthrop Above: Willard White, Carmen Balthrop, Betty Allen**

AMBASSADOR THEATRE
Opened Wednesday, October 22, 1975.*
(Moved to Edison Theatre December 3, 1975)
Lee Apostoleris presents the Center Theatre Group/Mark Taper Forum & Lee Apostoleris production of:

## ME AND BESSIE

Conceived and Written by Will Holt and Linda Hopkins; Director, Robert Greenwald; Special Dance Sequences, Lester Wilson; Musical Director, Howlett Smith; Setting, Donald Harris; Costumes, Pete Menefee; Lighting, Tharon Musser; Assistant to producer, Monica Boscia; Music Coordinator, Earl Shendell; Sound, James Travers; Original Cast Album by Columbia Records.

### CAST

Bessie Smith.............................. Linda Hopkins
Man ...................................... Lester Wilson
Woman..................................... Gerri Dean
Understudies: Thomas M. Pollard, Alfre Woodard

MUSICAL NUMBERS: "I Feel Good," "God Shall Wipe All Tears Away," "Moan You Moaners," "New Orleans Hop Scop Blues," "Romance in the Dark," "Preach Them Blues," "A Good Man Is Hard to Find," "T'Ain't Nobody's Bizness If I Do," "Gimme a Pigfoot," "Put It Right Here," "You've Been a Good Ole Wagon," "Trombone Cholly," "Jazzbo Brown," "After You've Gone," "There'll Be a Hot Time in the Old Town Tonight," "Empty Bed Blues," "Kitchen Man," "Mama Don't 'Low," "Do Your Duty," "Fare Thee Well," "Nobody Knows You When You're Down and Out," "Trouble," "The Man's All Right"

A "musical evening" in two acts.

*General Manager:* Emanuel Azenberg
*Press:* Merlin Group, Sandy Manley, Elizabeth Rodman
*Stage Managers:* Martin Herzer, Bethe Ward

* Still playing May 31, 1975.

**Right: Linda Hopkins**

**Gerri Dean, Linda Hopkins, Lester Wilson**

## EUGENE O'NEILL THEATRE

Opened Thursday, October 23, 1975.*
Cheryl Crawford, Moe Septee, The Chelsea Theater with Mrs. Victor H. Potamkin present the Chelsea Theater Center of Brooklyn Production of:

# YENTL

By Leah Napolin and Isaac Bashevis Singer; Conceived and Directed by Robert Kalfin; Scenery, Karl Eigsti; Costumes, Carrie F. Robbins, Lighting, William Mintzer; Music, Mel Marvin; Associate Producer, Paul B. Berkowsky; Hairstylist, Kenneth Davis; Assistant Director, Philip Littell

### CAST

| | |
|---|---|
| Yentl | Tovah Feldshuh |
| Reb Todrus/Fulcha/Laibish/Cantor/ Messenger/Musician | Bernie Passeltiner |
| Rivka/Necheleh/Chambermaid | Mary Ellen Ashley |
| Lemmel/Yussel/Wedding Jester/Dr. Solomon/ Mohel/Musician | Leland Moss |
| Reb Nata/The Shamus/Zelig | Reuben Schafer |
| Nehemiah/Rabbi/Sheftel | Albert M. Ottenheimer |
| Mordecai/Feitl | Hy Anzell |
| Shmuel, Zisheh/Musician | Stephen DePietri |
| Moishe/Gershon/Chaim/Musician | David Eric |
| Dovid/Yitzhok/Musician | Michael James Stratford |
| Treitl/Reb Alter | Herman O. Arbeit |
| Avigdor | John V. Shea |
| Raizeleh/Avram | Robin Bartlett |
| Finkl/Berel | Diane Tarleton |
| Zelda-Leah/Shimmel | Madeline Shaw |
| Hadass | Lynn Ann Leveridge |
| Frumka | Natalie Priest |
| Pesheh | Blanche Dee |
| Yachna | Rita Karin |
| Zlateh | Elaine Grollman |

UNDERSTUDIES: Yentl, Robin Bartlett; Avigdor, Michael James Stratford; Hadass, Necheleh, Zelda-Leah, Raizelen, Chambermaid, Diane Tarleton; Yachna, Pesheh, Frumka, Mary Ellen Ashley; Reb Todrus, Mordecai, Herman O. Arbeit; Lemmel, Stephen DePietri; Messenger, Fulcha, David Eric; Reb Nata, Leland Moss; Zelig, Rabbi, Reb Alter, Bernie Passeltiner; Cantor, Sheftel, Feitl, Reuben Schafer; Zlateh, Rivka, Necheleh, Chambermaid, Madeline Shaw; Dovid, Shmuel, Chaim, Richard Manheim

A drama in two acts. The action takes place in the villages of Yanev, Zamosc, Bechev and Lublin, Poland in the year 1873.

*General Manager:* Paul B. Berkowsky
*Company Manager:* Gino Giglio
*Press:* Betty Lee Hunt, Maurice Turet, Maria Cristina Pucci, Bill Evans
*Stage Managers:* Clint Jakeman, Richard Manheim

\* Closed May 2, 1976 after 223 performances and 11 previews.

*Laura W. Pettibone Photos*

**Leland Moss, Bernie Passeltiner, Tovah Feldshuh**
**Top Right: John V. Shea, Tovah Feldshuh**

**Tovah Feldshuh**
**Above: Lynn Ann Leveridge, John V. Shea**

20

ANTA THEATRE
Opened Sunday, October 26, 1975.*
Barry M. Brown, Burry Fredrik, Fritz Holt, Sally Sears in association with Robert V. Straus present the American Bicentennial Theatre Production of:

# SUMMER BRAVE

By William Inge; Director, Michael Montel; Scenery, Stuart Wurtzel; Costumes, Donald Brooks; Lighting, David Segal; Dance Staging, Michel Stuart; Produced for the Kennedy Center and Xerox Corp. by Roger L. Stevens and Richmond Crinkley; Wardrobe Supervisor, Sydney Smith; Production Assistants, Allan Sobek, Jay Levy

### CAST

| | |
|---|---|
| Millie Owens | Sheila K. Adams |
| Newsboy | Bill Barrett |
| Bomber | Mark Kologi |
| Beano | Miles Chapin |
| Madge Owens | Jill Eikenberry |
| Alan Seymour | Peter Weller |
| Flo Owens | Nan Martin |
| Hal Carter | Ernest Thompson |
| Rosemary Sydney | Alexis Smith |
| Mrs. Helen Potts | Martha Greenhouse |
| Irma Kronkite | Patricia O'Connell |
| Christine Schoenwalder | Alice Drummond |
| Howard Bevans | Joe Ponazecki |

UNDERSTUDIES: Mrs. Potts, Flo, Irma, Alice Drummond; Howard, F. J. O'Neil; Madge, Millie, Christine, Stephanie Kurz; Alan, Hal, Richard DeFabees; Bomber, Beano, Bill Barrett; Newsboy, Jason La Padura

A drama in three acts. The action takes place in a small Kansas town in the early 1950's.

*General Management:* Marvin A. Krauss Associates
*Company Manager:* David Wyler
*Press:* Shirley Herz
*Stage Managers:* Dyanne Hochman, Jason LaPadura, Bill Barrett

* Closed Nov. 9, 1975 after 18 performances and 3 previews. This was William Inge's re-write of his Pulitzer-Prize play "Picnic."

*Richard Braaten, Bill Barrett Photos*

**Top: Nan Martin, Alexis Smith, Alice Drummond, Jill Eikenberry, Patricia O'Connell, Joe Ponazecki**

**Alexis Smith, Ernest Thompson**
**Above: Jill Eikenberry, Peter Weller, Nan Martin, Martha Greenhouse**

## ETHEL BARRYMORE THEATRE

Opened Thursday, October 30, 1975.*
David Merrick, Doris Cole Abrahams, Burry Fredrik in association with S. Spencer Davids and Eddie Kulukundis present the Royal Shakespeare Company Production of:

# TRAVESTIES

By Tom Stoppard; Director, Peter Wood; Scenery and Costumes, Carl Toms; Lighting, Robert Ornbo; Movement, William Chappell; Musical Supervision, Grant Hossack; Slide Drawings, Robert P. Vannutt; Wardrobe Mistress, Kathleen Foster; Production Assistant, Susan Cordon; Hairstylist, Tony Marrero

### CAST

| | |
|---|---|
| Tristan Tzara | Tim Curry |
| Cecily Carruthers | Beth Morris |
| James Joyce | James Booth |
| Gwendolen Carr | Meg Wynn Owen |
| Nadezhda Krupskaya | Frances Cuka |
| Vladimir Ilyich Ulyanov | Harry Towb |
| Henry Carr | John Wood |
| | Matinees: David Dukes |
| Bennett | John Bott |

UNDERSTUDIES: Henry, David Dukes; Tzara, Bill Biskup; Gwendolen, Cecily, Kate McGregor-Stewart; Joyce, John Bott; Lenin, Bennett, John Clarkson; Nadya, Lila Martin

A comedy in two acts. The action takes place in Zurich in 1917 in a section of the public library, and in the drawing room of Henry Carr's apartment.

*General Manager:* Helen L. Nickerson
*Company Manager:* John Caruso
*Press:* Solters & Roskin, Bud Westman
*Stage Managers:* Alan Hall, Bill Biskup

* Closed March 13, 1976 after 156 performances and 3 previews. Winner of "Tony," and New York Drama Critics Circle Awards for Best Play of the 1975–76 season. John Wood also received a "Tony" for Best Actor.

*Sophie Baker Photos*

**John Wood, John Bott**
**Top: John Wood**

**Frances Cuka, Harry Towb**

Meg Wynn Owen, Tim Curry, John Bott, James Booth, Beth Morris, John Wood
Top: Tim Curry, John Bott, John Wood

23

**JOHN GOLDEN THEATRE**
Opened Monday, November 3, 1975.*
Michael Harvey in association with Robert Colby presents:

# KENNEDY'S CHILDREN

By Robert Patrick; Director, Clive Donner; Designed by Santo Loquasto; Lighting, Martin Aronstein; Associate Producer, Ramon Getzov; Production Assistant, Christopher Cara; Wardrobe Supervisor, Arlene Konowitz

### CAST

| | |
|---|---|
| Wanda | Barbara Montgomery |
| Bartender | Douglas Travis |
| Sparger | Don Parker |
| Mark | Michael Sacks |
| Rona | Kaiulani Lee |
| Carla | Shirley Knight |

UNDERSTUDIES: Wanda, Rona, Carla, Giulia Pagano; Mark, Sparger, Douglas Travis; Bartender, Robert T. O'Rourke

A drama in two acts. The action takes place in a bar on the lower East Side of New York City, on a rainy February afternoon in 1974.

*General Manager:* Jay Kingwill
*Company Manager:* Robert Frissell
*Press:* David Powers, William Schelble
*Stage Managers:* Mark Wright, Robert T. O'Rourke

* Closed Jan. 4, 1976 after 72 performances and 5 previews. Shirley Knight received a 1976 "Tony" for Best Performance by a Featured Actress.

*Martha Swope Photos*

**Right: Kaiulani Lee, Shirley Knight, Barbara Montgomery**

**Barbara Montgomery, Don Parker, Douglas Travis, Shirley Knight, Kaiulani Lee, Michael Sacks**

Opened Thursday, November 6, 1975.*
Robert Cherin in association with Theatre Now, Inc. presents:

# HELLO, DOLLY!

Book, Michael Stewart; Based on play "The Matchmaker" by
ornton Wilder; Music and Lyrics, Jerry Herman; Director, Lucia
ctor; Dances Re-Created by Jack Craig from original choreogra-
y by Gower Champion; Settings, Oliver Smith; Lighting, John
eason; Costumes, Robert Pusilio; Musical Director, Al Cavaliere;
oduction Supervisor, Mitch Miller; Wardrobe Mistress, Kathleen
onnelly; Production Associate, Camille Ranson; Production Assis-
nt, Steven Goldstein; Assistant Conductor, Ben Payne

### CAST

| | |
|---|---|
| rs. Dolly Gallagher Levi | Pearl Bailey |
| nestina | Bessye Ruth Scott |
| mbrose Kemper | Howard Porter |
| orse | Kathy Jennings, Karen Hubbard |
| orace Vandergelder | Billy Daniels |
| mengarde | Karen Hubbard |
| ornelius Hackl | Terrence Emanuel |
| arnaby Tucker | Grenoldo Frazier |
| ene Molloy | Mary Louise |
| innie Fay | Chip Fields |
| rs. Rose | Birdie M. Hale |
| udolph | Jonathan Wynne |
| dge | Ted Goodridge |
| ourt Clerk | Ray Gilbert |

OWNSPEOPLE: Sally Benoit, Terry Gene, Pat Gideon, Ann Gi-
n, Birdie M. Hale, Karen Hubbard, Gwen Humble, Eulaula Jen-
ngs, Francie Mendenhall, Bessye Ruth Scott, Sachi Shimizu, Guy
llen, Don Coleman, Richard Dodd, Ray Gilbert, Charles Goed-
rtz, Ted Goodridge, Clark James, James Kennon-Wilson, Richard
axon, Charles Neal, Howard Porter, Jimmy Rivers, Ken Rogers,
avid Staller, Teddy Williams, Jonathan Wynne

NDERSTUDIES: Dolly, Birdie M. Hale; Vandergelder, Ted Goo-
idge; Irene, Pat Gideon; Cornelius, Jonathan Wynne; Minnie Fay,
wen Humble; Barnaby, Teddy Williams; Ermengarde, Eulaula
nnings; Ernestina, Mrs. Rose, Lisa Brown; Rudolph, Guy Allen;
mbrose, Ken Rogers; Clerk, Don Coleman; Dance Alternates, Ron
rofoot, Lisa Brown

USICAL NUMBERS: "I Put My Hand In," "It Takes a
oman," "Put on Your Sunday Clothes," "Ribbons Down My
ck," "Motherhood," "Dancing," "Before the Parade Passes By,"
legance," "Waiters Gallop," "Hello, Dolly!," "It Only Takes a
oment," "So Long, Dearie," Finale

A musical comedy in 2 acts and 15 scenes. The action takes place
Yonkers, and New York City.

*General Managers:* Theatre Now, Inc., William C. Cohen,
Edward H. Davis, Norman E. Rothstein
*Press:* Betty Lee Hunt Associates, Maria Cristina Pucci, Bill
Evans, Maurice Turet
*Stage Managers:* Kenneth Porter, Robert Vandergriff, Richard
Maxon

Closed Dec. 21, 1975 after limited engagement of 42 performances
and 3 previews. For original production with Carol Channing, see
THEATRE WORLD, Vol. 20.

**Top Right: Billy Daniels, Pearl Bailey
Below: Mary Louise, Grenoldo Frazier,
Chip Fields, Terrence Emanuel**

**Pearl Bailey (C)**

## ST. JAMES THEATRE
Opened Thursday, November 13, 1975.*
The Theatre Guild and Jonathan Conrow present:

# A MUSICAL JUBILEE

Written by Max Wilk; Director, Morton DaCosta; Musical Super
vision, Lehman Engel; Musical Director, John Lesko; Devised b
Marilyn Clark and Charles Burr; Associate Producer, Merle I
King; Dance Arrangements and Musical Continuity, Trude Rit
man; Orchestrations, Philip J. Lang, Hershy Kay, Elman Anderso
Scenery, Herbert Senn; Costumes, Donald Brooks; Lightin
Thomas Skelton; Choreography, Robert Tucker; Assistant to pr
ducer, William Dempsey; Assistant Conductor, Woody Kessler; E:
ecutive Assistant, Larusa Kay; Production Assistants, Jerr
MacLaughlin, William McCarthy, Mary Jane Gibbons, Jack Hoga
Wardrobe Supervisor, Sammy Alterman; Assistant to director, Jan
O'Morrison

### CAST

| | |
|---|---|
| Patrice Munsel | John Raitt † |
| Tammy Grimes | Dick Shawn † |
| Cyril Ritchard | Larry Ke |
| Lillian Gish | |

Steven Boockvor, Eric Brotherson, Marcia Brushingham, Igors Ga
von, Nana, David King, Jeanne Lehman, Bettye Malone, Estel
Munson, Julie Pars, Dennis Perren, Leland Schwantes, Craig Yat

UNDERSTUDIES: Raitt, Igors Gavon; Munsel, Estella Munso
Grimes, Jeanne Lehman; Shawn, David King; Ritchard, Eric Brot
erson; Kert, Craig Yates; Gish, Marcia Brushingham

MUSICAL NUMBERS: "Happy Days," "Whoa-Haw," "Lorena
"Sweet Betsy from Pike," "Skip to My Lou," "Hold on Abraham
"Bonnie Blue Flag," "Tipperary," "I Didn't Raise My Boy to Be
Soldier," "Mademoiselle from Armentieres," "Over There," "Batt
Hymn of the Republic," "Wien, Wien, You're Calling Me," "I'm i
Love with Vienna," "Der Shimmy," "I've Got Something," "O
The Women," "Gypsy Love," "And Her Mother Came Too," "Sor
of the Vagabonds," "Totem Tom Tom," "Serenade," "Violetta
"Moonstruck," "You Are Love," "I've Told Every Little Star
"Why Was I Born?," "The Best Things in Life Are Free," "The
Didn't Believe Me," "The Song Is You," "Something Seems Ting
Ingleing," "Yankee Doodle Tune," "We're Blasé," "Poor Litt
Rich Girl," "You Go to My Head," "Find Me a Primitive Man
"I Guess I'll Have to Change My Plans," "Sophisticated Lady
"Love Me or Leave Me," "Gilbert the Filbert," "At the Movin
Picture Ball," "The Green Eye of the Little Yellow God," "I Wann
Be Loved by You," "Miss Annabelle Lee," "How Jazz Was Born
"Ain't Misbehavin'," "I'm Just Wild about Harry," "Me and M
Shadow," "Sometime I'm Happy," "Great Day," "Lullaby
Broadway," "Lucky Day," "If You Knew Susie," "'S Wonderful
"Fascinating Rhythm," "Liza," "Where or When," "Hallelujah

A musical entertainment in two acts.

*General Manager:* Victor Samrock
*Press:* Joel Wolhandler Associates, Sol Jacobson
*Stage Managers:* William Dodds, Marnel Sumner, James Frashe

* Closed Jan. 1, 1976 after 92 performances and 2 previews.
† Succeeded by: 1. Igors Gavon, 2. David King

*Richard Braaten Photos*

Larry Kert, Cyril Ritchard, Patrice Munsel,
Dick Shawn, Tammy Grimes, John Rait, Lillian Gish

**Top Left: Dick Shawn, Lillian Gish, Tammy
Grimes, Patrice Munsel, Larry Kert**

**[M]DISON THEATRE**
Opened Monday, November 24, 1975.*
Rita Fredricks, Theatre Now, Inc., Norman Kean present:

# BOCCACCIO

Based on stories from "The Decameron" by Giovanni Boccaccio; [d]ramatization and Lyrics, Kenneth Cavander; Music, Richard [P]easlee; Director, Warren Enters; Musical Staging, Julie Arenal; [s]etting, Robert U. Taylor; Costumes, Linda Fisher; Lighting, Pa[t]ika Brown; Musical Director, Ken Bichel; Orchestrations and Ar[r]angements, Walt Levinsky, Richard Peaslee; Hairstylist Steve [A]tha; Wardrobe Mistress, Barbara Sibella

## CAST

| | |
|---|---|
| [P]eltramo/Egano | Michael Zaslow |
| [G]iletta/Abbess | Virginia Vestoff |
| [M]asetto/Ferondo | Armand Assante |
| [B]eatrice/Sister Teresa/Ferondo's Wife | Caroline McWilliams |
| [I]sabella/Sister Angelica | D'Jamin Bartlett |
| [A]libech/Sister Makaria | Jill Choder |
| [R]ustico/Brother Perdurabo/Leonetto | Munson Hicks |
| [A]nichino/Nuto/Abbot | Richard Bauer |

Standbys: Sheilah Rae, Michael Forella

[M]USICAL NUMBERS: Introduction, "Masetto's Song," "Nuns [S]ong," "God Is Good," "Now My Season's Here," "Only in My [S]ong," "Egano D'Galluzzi," "Men Who Have Loved Me," "In the [G]arden," "Lucky Anichino," "Pretend You're Living," "Devil in [H]ell," "She Doctor," "Lover Like a Blind Man," "If You Had [B]een," "Love Was Just a Game," "Madonna Isabella," "My Holy [P]rayer," "Hold Me Gently"

A musical in two acts. The action takes place at a villa outside [F]lorence in the year 1348.

*General Managers:* Theatre Now, Inc., Norman Kean
*Press:* Les Schecter Associates
*Stage Managers:* Ron Abbott, John Beven, Claudia Burk

Closed Nov. 30, 1975 after 7 performances and 48 previews.

*Kenn Duncan Photos*

**Top: Virginia Vestoff, Armand Assante,**
**[Ji]ll Choder, D'Jamin Bartlett, Caroline McWilliams**
**[?] Richard Bauer, Munson Hicks, D'Jamin Bartlett**

**(front) Richard Bauer, Caroline McWilliams,**
**(back) Munson Hicks, Michael Zaslow**

**MOROSCO THEATRE**
Opened Sunday, December 7, 1975.*
Robert Fryer, James Cresson, Michael Codron in associatior
with Martin Richards and Victor D'Arc present:

# THE NORMAN CONQUESTS

By Alan Ayckbourn; Director, Eric Thompson; Scenery and
Lighting, Robert Randolph; Costumes, Noel Taylor; Productior
Associate, Robert Linden; Wardrobe Supervisor, Louise Van Dine
Assistant to director, Richard Seff; Assistant to producers, Ror
Parker; Associate to General Managers, Nancy Simmons

### CAST

| | |
|---|---|
| Norman | Richard Benjamir |
| Annie | Paula Prentis |
| Tom | Ken Howard† |
| Sarah | Estelle Parson |
| Reg | Barry Nelsor |
| Ruth | Carole Shelley†2 |

STANDBYS: Norman, Donegan Smith; Annie, Donna Wandrey
Tom, Richard Altman; Sarah, Laura Stuart; Reg, Richard Self
Ruth, Elaine Hyman

A trilogy of comedies ("Table Manners," "Living Together,
"Round and Round the Garden"), each with two acts and fou
scenes. The action takes place on three separate nights over a week
end in an English country house at the present time. Each play ha
the same cast and is seen from a different viewpoint: from the dining
room, the living room, and the garden. They may be seen in any
order.

*General Managers:* Joseph Harris, Ira Bernstein
*Press:* Betty Lee Hunt, Maria Cristina Pucci, Bill Evans
*Stage Managers:* Milt Commons, Donegan Smith

* Closed June 19, 1976 after 225 performances and 3 previews.

† Succeeded by: 1. Don Murray, Richard Altman, 2. Elaine Hyma

Barry Nelson, Ken Howard, Estelle Parsons,
Richard Benjamin, Paula Prentiss, Carole Shelley

Top: Ken Howard, Carole Shelly (L) Richard Benja
Barry Nelson, Estelle Parsons

Carole Shelley, Barry Nelson, Richard Benjamin, Don Murray, Paula Prentiss, Estelle Parsons Top: (L) Estelle Parsons, Barry Nelson, (R) Richard Benjamin, Carole Shelley

**MARTIN BECK THEATRE**
Opened Tuesday, November 25, 1975.*
James M. Nederlander, Victor Lurie and Michael Codron present:

# HABEAS CORPUS

By Alan Bennett; Director, Frank Dunlop; Scenery and Costumes, Carl Toms; Lighting, Jennifer Tipton; Musical Arrangements, Dorothea Freitag; Dances, Riggs O'Hara; Production Associates, Sandra Mandel, Kim Sellon, Cathy Blaser; Wardrobe Supervisor, Rosalie Lahm; Hairstylist, Tiv Davenport

### CAST

| | |
|---|---|
| Arthur Wicksteed | Donald Sinden†1 |
| Mrs. Swabb | June Havoc |
| Mrs. Wicksteed | Rachel Roberts |
| Dennis Wicksteed | Kristoffer Tabori†2 |
| Constance Wicksteed | Jean Marsh |
| Canon Throbbing | Paxton Whitehead†3 |
| Sir Percy Shorter | Ian Trigger |
| Lady Rumpers | Celeste Holm |
| Felicity Rumpers | Constance Forslund |
| Mr. Shanks | Richard Gere |
| Mr. Purdue | Stephen D. Newman†4 |
| Patient | Leo Leyden†5 |

and the Hove Palm Court Trio

UNDERSTUDIES: Arthur, Canon, Stephen D. Newman; Mrs. Wicksteed, Mrs. Swabb, Lady Rumpers, Joyce Worsley; Constance, Felicity, Holly Villaire; Dennis, Shanks, Purdue, Tom Everett; Shorter, Leo Leyden

A comedy in two acts. The action takes place at the present time in a refined English seaside resort, in the Wicksteed's home, and on the West Pier.

*General Manager:* Nelle Nugent
*Company Manager:* James Turner
*Press:* Michael Alpert, Marilynn LeVine, Joshua Ellis
*Stage Managers:* Frank Bayer, Louis Pulvino

\* Closed Feb. 15, 1976 after 95 performances and 7 previews.
† Succeeded by: 1. Paxton Whitehead, 2. Mark Baker, 3. Stephen D. Newman, Kristoffer Tabori, 4. Tom Everett, 5. Joyce Worsley

*Martha Swope Photos*

**Top: Donald Sinden, Rachel Roberts**
**(R) Jean Marsh, June Havoc**

30

**Paxton Whitehead, Celeste Holm, Mark Baker,**
**Constance Forslund Above: Forslund, Sinden,**
**Kristoffer Tabori**

CIRCLE IN THE SQUARE THEATRE
Opened Thursday, December 18, 1975.*
Circle in the Square (Theodore Mann, Artistic Director; Paul
Libin, Managing Director) presents:

# THE GLASS MENAGERIE

By Tennessee Williams; Director, Theodore Mann; Scenery, Ming
Cho Lee; Costumes, Sydney Brooks; Lighting, Thomas Skelton;
Incidental Music, Craig Wasson; Production Associate, Atsumi
Iba; Wardrobe Supervisor, Virginia Merkel; Production Assis-
tants, Gordon Bendall, Sandy Caltabiano, Susan Elrod, Bernard
Rostenberg, Robin Groves, Sharon Kolberg, Jolly Nelson, Susan
Santiago, Tom Smith

### CAST

Amanda, the mother.....................Maureen Stapleton
Tom, her son...................................Rip Torn
Laura, her daughter ..................Pamela Payton-Wright
Jim, the gentleman caller......................Paul Rudd

STANDBYS AND UNDERSTUDIES: Amanda, Nancy Marchand; Tom, Jim, Marco St. John; Laura, Sharon Morrison

A drama in two acts. The action takes place in an alley in St. Louis
in the present time and in the past.

Company Manager: William Conn
Press: Merle Debuskey, Susan L. Schulman
Stage Managers: Randall Brooks, James Bernardi

Closed Feb. 22, 1976 after 77 performances and 23 previews. For
original production with Laurette Taylor, Eddie Dowling, Julie
Haydon and Anthony Ross, see THEATRE WORLD, Vol. 1. It
opened Mar. 31, 1945 at The Playhouse and ran for 563 performances. Revived Nov. 21, 1956 at City Center with Helen Hayes,
James Daly, Lois Smith and Lonny Chapman for 15 performances
(See THEATRE WORLD, Vol. 13). On May 4, 1965 it was
revived at the Brooks Atkinson Theatre for 176 performances
with Maureen Stapleton, George Grizzard, Piper Laurie and Pat
Hingle. (See THEATRE WORLD, Vol. 21)

*Inge Morath Photos*

**Right: Rip Torn, Maureen Stapleton**

**Top: Maureen Stapleton**

**Paul Rudd, Pamela Payton-Wright**

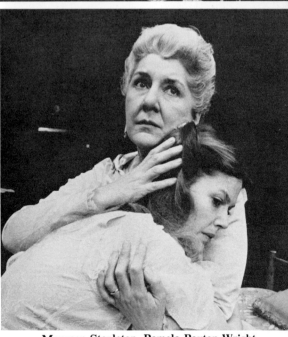

**Maureen Stapleton, Pamela Payton-Wright**

31

BOOTH THEATRE
Opened Sunday, December 21, 1975.*
David Merrick, Max Brown, Byron Goldman present t[
Goodspeed Opera House Production of:

# VERY GOOD EDDIE

Book, Guy Bolton; Based on a farce by Phillip Bartholoma[
Music, Jerome Kern; Lyrics, Schuyler Greene; Director, Bill Gi[
Dances and Musical Numbers Staged by Bill Gile; Musical Dire[
tion and Arrangements, Russell Warner; Scenery and Lighting, Fr[
Voelpel; Costumes, David Toser; Special Consultant, Alfred Simo[
Wardrobe Supervisor, Kathleen Foster; Hairstylist, Karol Coeyma[

## CAST

| | |
|---|---|
| Steward | James Hard[ |
| Mr. Dick Rivers | David Christma[ |
| Mme. Matroppo | Travis Hudso[ |
| Miss Elsie Lilly | Cynthia We[ |
| M. de Rougemont | Joel Cra[ |
| Mrs. Georgina Kettle | Spring Fairban[ |
| Mr. Eddie Kettle | Charles Repo[ |
| Mr. Percy Darling | Nicholas Wyma[ |
| Mrs. Elsie Darling | Virginia Seid[ |
| Al Cleveland | James Hard[ |
| Miss Lily Pond | Wendy You[ |
| Miss Chrystal Poole | Karen Crossle[ |
| Miss Carrie Closewell | Gillian Scalic[ |
| Miss Alwys Innit | Robin Herbe[ |
| Mr. Tayleurs Dumme | Russ Beasle[ |
| Mr. Dayr Thurst | Jon Engstro[ |
| Mr. Dustin Stacks | Larry McMilla[ |
| Mr. Rollo Munn | Hal Shar[ |

UNDERSTUDIES: Eddie, Jon Engstrom; Elsie, Robin Herber[
Steward, Joel Craig; Matroppo, Helon Blount; Rivers, de Roug[
mont, Russ Beasley; Percy, David Christman; Georgina, Jo-An[
Cifalo; Elsie, Wendy Young

MUSICAL NUMBERS: "We're on Our Way," "Some Sort [
Somebody," "Thirteen Collar," "Bungalow in Quogue," "Isn't [
Great to Be Married," "Good Night Boat," "Left All Alone Aga[
Blues," "Hot Dog!," "If You're a Friend of Mine," "Wedding Be[
Are Calling Me," "Honeymoon Inn," "I've Got to Dance," "Mo[
Love," "Old Boy Neutral," "Babes in the Wood," "Katy-did[
"Nodding Roses," Finale.

A musical in two acts and three scenes. The action takes place [
1913 on a Hudson River Dayliner, and in the Honeymoon Inn in t[
Catskill Mountains.

*General Manager:* Helen L. Nickerson
*Company Manager:* G. Warren McClane
*Press:* Max Eisen, Judy Jacksina, Warren Pincus
*Stage Managers:* Don Judge, Mark Potter, Pat Trott

* Still playing May 31, 1976.
† Succeeded by Jo-Ann Cifala

**Left: Joel Craig, Travis Hudson Top:**
**Charles Repole, Virginia Seidel**

Nicholas Wyman, Virginia Seidel,
Charles Repole, Spring Fairbank

entire cast

**Bette Henritze, Robert E. Thompson**
ight: Christine Andreas, Michael Allinson

EUM THEATRE
Opened Friday, December 26, 1975.*
Shepard Traube presents:

# ANGEL STREET

Patrick Hamilton; Director, Shepard Traube; Setting, Douglas
hmidt; Costumes, Patricia Adshead; Lighting, Leon DiLeone

### CAST

| | |
|---|---|
| Manningham | Dina Merrill |
| anningham | Michael Allinson |
| | Christine Andreas† |
| th | Bette Henritze |
| | Robert E. Thompson |

Understudies: Eleanor Tauber, Alfred Karl

ma in three acts. The action takes place in 1880 in a house
el Street in the Pimlico district of London.

*Manager:* Max Gendel
*Press:* Lenny Traube
*Stage Manager:* Rick Ralston

d Feb. 8, 1976 after 52 performances and 4 previews. Origi-
roduction with Judith Evelyn, Vincent Price, Leo G. Carroll
ed Dec. 5, 1941 and played 1293 performances. Revived Jan.
948 at City Center for 14 performances with Uta Hagen, Jose
er and Richard Whorf. (See THEATRE WORLD, Vol. 4)

ceeded by Christine Ebersole
*Bill Mitchell Photos*

**Michael Allinson, Dina Merrill**

**BILTMORE THEATRE**

Opened Sunday, December 28, 1975.*

R. Tyler Gatchell, Jr., Peter Neufeld in association with Barnard S. Straus present:

# MURDER AMONG FRIENDS

By Bob Barry; Director, Val May; Setting, Santo Loquasto; Costumes, Joseph G. Aulisi; Lighting, Jennifer Tipton; Associate Producers, Erv Tullman, Barry Potashnick; Production Supervisor, Pat Tolson; Hairstylist, Mr. Vincent of Enrico Caruso; Wardrobe Supervisor, Joe Busheme

### CAST

| | |
|---|---|
| Angela Forrester | Janet Leigh |
| Ted Cotton | Lewis Arlt |
| Palmer Forrester | Jack Cassidy |
| Gertrude Saidenberg | Jane Hoffman |
| Marshall Saidenberg | Richard Woods |
| Larry | Michael Durrell |

STANDBYS: Angela, Holland Taylor; Palmer, John Aniston; Larry, Andrew Bloch; Ted, Ted Shackelford

A mystery in two acts and four scenes. The action takes place at the present time in the Forrester townhouse throughout New Year's Eve.

*General Management:* Gatchell & Neufeld
*Company Manager:* James Mennen
*Press:* Betty Lee Hunt, Maria Cristina Pucci, Bill Evans
*Stage Manager:* Andrew Bloch

* Closed Jan. 11, 1976 after 17 performances and 8 previews.

**Top: Jack Cassidy, Lewis Arlt**

34  **Right: Cassidy, Janet Leigh Below: Leigh, Arlt**

**Lewis Arlt, Michael Durrell,
Jane Hoffman, Richard Woods**

Opened Monday, December 29, 1975.*
Michael Harvey and Harvey Frand present the Kennedy Center-Xerox Corporation Production of:

# SWEET BIRD OF YOUTH

By Tennessee Williams; Director, Edwin Sherin; Scenery, Karl
gsti; Costumes, Laura Crow; Lighting, Ken Billington; Wardrobe
pervisor, Cindy Chock; Produced in association with Brooklyn
cademy of Music

### CAST

| | |
|---|---|
| hance Wayne | Christopher Walken |
| rincess Kosmonopolis | Irene Worth |
| y | Flloyd Ennis |
| aid | Bunny Kacher |
| eorge Scudder | Christopher Bernau |
| atcher | Richard Kuss |
| oss Finley | Pat Corley |
| om Junior | Matthew Cowles |
| harles | Philip Lindsay |
| unt Nonnie | Eugenia Rawls† |
| eavenly Finley | Lisa Richards |
| iss Lucy | Cathryn Damon |
| uff | Tom Stechschulte |
| eckler | David Gale |
| olet | Linda Martin |
| otty | Lanny Flaherty |
| dna | Susan Kay Logan |
| ıd | Eric Loeb |
| en in bar | Richard Babcock, Frank Rohrbach |
| rooper | George Bamford |
| ıton Twirler | Alicia Enterline |

NDERSTUDIES: Chance, Christopher Bernau; Boss, Richard
uss; Miss Lucy, Aunt Nonnie, Violet, Edna, Bunny Kacher; Heav-
ly, Maid, Susan Kay Logan; Tom Junior, Tom Stechschulte;
atcher, Charles, Fly, Richard Babcock; Heckler, Scotty, Scudder,
ic Loeb; Man in bar, Dan Hild; Stuff, Bud, George Bamford

A drama in three acts and five scenes. The action takes place at
e present time in the Royal Palms Hotel, and Boss Finley's house
mewhere on the Gulf coast.

*General Manager:* Jay Kingwill
*Company Manager:* Albert Poland
*Press:* David Powers, William Schelble
*Stage Managers:* Mark Wright, Dan Hild

Closed Feb. 7, 1976 after 48 performances and 4 previews. For
original production, see THEATRE WORLD, Vol. 15. Paul
Newman and Geraldine Page were starred, and played 375 performances.
Succeeded by Elena Karam

*Richard Braaten, David Fishman Photos*

**Right: Lanny Flaherty, Christopher Walken,
Pamela Costello, Susan Logan, Cathryn Damon**

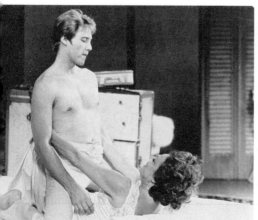

Christopher Walken, Irene Worth (also top right)

Irene Worth

HELEN HAYES THEATRE
Opened Tuesday, December 30, 1975.*
Barry M. Brown, Burry Fredrik, Fritz Holt, Sally Sears prese
the American Bicentennial Theatre Production of:

# THE ROYAL FAMILY

By George S. Kaufman and Edna Ferber; Director, Ellis Ra
Scenery, Oliver Smith; Costumes, Ann Roth; Lighting, John Gl
son; Original Music, Claibe Richardson; Produced for the Kenne
Center and Xerox Corp. by Roger L. Stevens and Richmond Cri
ley; Produced in association with the McCarter Theatre Compa
Wardrobe Supervisor, Clifford Capone; Hairstylist, Diane Stoke

### CAST

| | |
|---|---|
| Della | Rosetta LeN |
| Jo | John Rem |
| Hallboy | James C. Bu |
| McDermott | Sherman Ll |
| Herbert Dean | Joseph Mahe |
| Kitty Dean | Mary Louise Wilsor |
| Gwen Cavendish | Mary Layne |
| Perry Stewart | Forrest Buckn |
| Fanny Cavendish | Eva LeGallier |
| Oscar Wolfe | Sam Lev |
| Julie Cavendish | Rosemary Ha |
| Tony Cavendish | George Grizzar |
| Chauffeur | Miller L |
| Gilbert Marshall | Donald Bar |
| Hallboys | Miller Lide, Mark Fleischma |
| Gunga | James C. Bu |
| Miss Peake | Eleanor Phelp |

UNDERSTUDIES: Julie, Della, Kitty, Peake, Maria Cella
Fanny, Eleanor Phelps, Shirley Bryan; Tony, Perry, James C. Bu
Oscar, Gilbert, Herbert, Miller Lide; Gwen, Peake, Pat De Rou
Sandra LaVallee; Jo, McDermott, Mark Fleischman, John C. V
nema

A comedy in three acts. The action takes place in the dup
apartment of the Cavendishes in the East Fifties in New York du
1927–28.

*General/Company Manager:* David Lawlor
*Press:* Shirley Herz
*Stage Managers:* Helaine Head, Andre Love

* Closed July 18, 1976 after 233 performances. Original produc
  opened at the Selwyn Dec. 28, 1927 with Haidee Wright, A
  Andrews and Otto Kruger and played 345 performances. Revi
  at City Center Jan. 21, 1951 for 16 performances with E
  Griffies, Ruth Hussey, John Emery and Peggy Ann Garner. (
  THEATRE WORLD, Vol. 7). Ellis Rabb received a 1976 "To
  for Best Director.
† Succeeded by: 1. Richard Woods, 2. Peg Murray, 3. Ellen Fi
  4. Ellis Rabb, Richard Council, 5. John C. Vennema, Andre L
  6. Margot Stevenson, Maria Cellario

*Richard Braaten, Cliff Moore Photos*

**Left: James C. Burge, George Grizzard**
**Top: Rosemary Harris, Eva LeGallienne, Mary I**

**Rosemary Harris, Donald Barton**

**Ellis Rabb, Rosetta LeNoire, James Maher
Sam Levene, Mary Louise Wilson, Rosemar
Harris, Eva LeGallienne, Mary Layne**

PALACE THEATRE
Opened Sunday, January 4, 1976.*
The John F. Kennedy Center for the Performing Arts presents:

# HOME SWEET HOMER

Book, Roland Kibbee, Albert Marre; Music, Mitch Leigh; Lyrics, Charles Burr, Forman Brown; Book and Musical Staging, Albert Marre; Scenery and Lighting, Howard Bay; Costumes, Howard Bay, Ray Diffen; Musical Direction, Ross Reimueller; Orchestrations, Caryl Red; Choreographic Assistant, Michael Mann; Assistant to Director, Dwight Frye; Music Coordinator, Earl Shendell; Associate Conductor, Terrill Jory; Production Assistant, Kay Vance; Sound, Annie Will; Wardrobe Supervisor, Angelo Quillici; Hairstylists, Gloria Rivera, Wayne Herndon

## CAST

| | |
|---|---|
| Odysseus | Yul Brynner |
| Penelope | Joan Diener |
| Telemachus | Russ Thacker |

Penelope's Suitors:

| | |
|---|---|
| Antinous | Martin Vidnovic |
| Sokrates | Ian Sullivan |
| Mesippos | Bill Mackey |
| Eurymachus | Daniel Brown |
| Prokritos | Brian Destazio |
| Proteus | John Aristides |
| Helios | Bill Nabel |
| Xybos | Les Freed |
| King Alkinoos | Shev Rodgers |
| Nausikaa | Diana Davila |

Nausikaa's Handmaidens:

| | |
|---|---|
| Therapina | Suzanne Sponsler |
| Xantho | Cecile Santos |
| Hippodameia | Christine Uchida |
| Prux | Darel Glaser |
| Sikati Evdomi VII | P. J. Mann |

UNDERSTUDIES: Odysseus, Shev Rodgers; Penelope, Karen Shepard; Telemachus, Darel Glaser; Nausikaa, Suzanne Sponsler; Antinous, Daniel Brown; Alkinoos, Ian Sullivan; Swing, Linda Byrne

MUSICAL NUMBERS: "The Tales," "The Future," "The Departure," "Home Sweet Homer," "The Ball," "How Could I Dare to Dream," "I Never Imagined Goodbye," "Love Is the Prize," "Penelope's Hand," "He Will Come Home Again," "Did He Really Think," "I Was Wrong," "The Rose," "Tomorrow," "The Contest," "He Sang Songs"

A musical performed without intermission.

*General Managers:* Wolsk & Azenberg, Douglas C. Baker
*Press:* Betty Lee Hunt, Maria Cristina Pucci, Rugh Cage
*Stage Managers:* Patrick Horrigan, Gregory A. Hirsch

Closed Jan. 4, 1976 after one performance and 11 previews.

**Top: Shev Rodgers, Diana Davila,**
**Yul Brynner, Russ Thacker (also right)**

**Yul Brynner, Diana Davila Above: Joan Diener**

AMBASSADOR THEATRE
Opened Thursday, January 8, 1976.*
Emanuel Azenberg, William W. Bradley, Marvin A. Krauss
and Irving Siders present:

# THE POISON TREE

By Ronald Ribman; Director, Charles Blackwell; Settings, Marjorie Kellogg; Costumes, Judy Dearing; Lighting, Martin Aronstein; Production Manager, Henry Velez: Wardrobe Supervisor, Josephine Zampredi; Production Assistant, Michael Connors

## CAST

| | |
|---|---|
| Albert Heisenman | Danny Meehan |
| Walter Turner | Daniel Barton |
| Officer Lowery | Gene O'Neill |
| Officer DiSantis | Peter Masterson |
| Sgt. Coyne | Robert Symonds |
| Officer Lloyd | Charles Brown |
| Officer Friezer | Arlen Dean |
| Officer Rollock | Pat McNamara |
| Willy Stepp | Cleavon Little |
| Bobby Foster | Dick Anthony Williams |
| Benjamin Hurspool | Moses Gunn |
| Charles Jefferson | Northern J. Calloway |
| Smiling Man | Dennis Tate |

UNDERSTUDIES: Stepp, Hurspool, Arthur French; Foster, Charles Brown; DiSantis, Arlen Dean; Coyne, Heisenman, Frank Hamilton; Friezer, Rollock, Lowery, Steven Shaw; Jefferson, Lloyd, Turner, Charles Douglass

A drama in 2 acts and 10 scenes. The action takes place at the present time in a western state prison.

*General Manager:* Jose Vega
*Press:* Merle Debuskey, Leo Stern
*Stage Managers:* Robert St. Clair, Steven Shaw, Gene O'Neill
* Closed Jan. 11, 1976 after 5 performances and 2 previews.

*Barry Kramer-Joseph Abeles Photos*

**Right: Peter Masterson, Cleavon Little, Dick Anthony Williams Top: Danny Meehan, Daniel Barton, Gene O'Neill**

**Cleavon Little, Northern J. Calloway (top), Dick Anthony Williams**

**Moses Gunn, Peter Masterson, Dick Anthony Williams, Cleavon Little**

Opened Sunday, January 11, 1976.*

Harold Prince in association with Ruth Mitchell presents:

# PACIFIC OVERTURES

ook, John Weidman; Music and Lyrics, Stephen Sondheim; Di-
or, Harold Prince; Choreographer, Patricia Birch; Scenery, Bo-
Aronson; Costumes, Florence Klotz; Lighting, Tharon Musser;
hestrations, Jonathan Tunick; Musical Direction, Paul Gemig-
; Dance Music, Daniel Troob; Kabuki Consultant, Haruki
moto; Make-up and Wigs, Richard Allen; Masks and Dolls, E.
aylor; Sound, Jack Mann; Wardrobe Supervisor, Adelaide
rino; Assistant to director, Annette Brafman Meyers; Associate
ductor, Les Scott; Technical Supervisor, John J. Moore; Martial
Sequence, Soon-Teck Oh; Original Cast Album, RCA Records

## CAST

| | |
|---|---|
| ter/Shogun/Jonathan Goble | Mako |
| , First Councillor | Yuki Shimoda |
| jiro | Sab Shimono |
| nd Councillor/Old Man/French Admiral | James Dybas |
| un's Mother/Merchant/American Admiral | Alvin Ing |
| d Councillor/Samurai's Daughter | Freddy Mao |
| ama | Isao Sato |
| ate/Samurai/Storyteller/Swordsman | Soon-Teck Oh |
| ant/Commodore Perry | Haruki Fujimoto |
| rvers | Alvin Ing, Ricardo Tobia |
| erman/Wrestler/Lord of the South | Jae Woo Lee |
| Priest/Noble | Timm Fujii |
| dmother/Wrestler/Japanese Merchant | Conrad Yama |
| f/Samurai/Soothsayer/Warrior/ | |
| ian Admiral | Mark Hsu Syers |
| ns/Samurai/Noble | Ernest Abuba |
| ams/Lord of the South | Larry Hama |
| un's Wife | Freda Foh Shen |
| ician/Madam/British Admiral | Ernest Harada |
| t/Boy | Gedde Watanabe |
| un's Companion/Dutch Admiral | Patrick Kinser-Lau |
| | Timm Fujii, Patrick Kinser-Lau, Gedde Watanabe, Leslie Watanabe |
| rial Priest | Tom Matsusaka |
| sh Sailors | Timm Fujii, Patrick Kinser-Lau, Mark Hsu Syers |
| cians | Fusako Yoshida, Genji Ito |

VANTS, SAILORS, TOWNSPEOPLE: Susan Kikuchi, Diane
, Kim Miyori, Freda Foh Shen, Kenneth S. Eiland, Timm Fujii,
Ginza, Patrick Kinser-Lau, Tony Marinyo, Kevin Maung,
o Secretario, Mark Hsu Syers, Ricardo Tobia, Gedde Wata-
Leslie Watanabe

DERSTUDIES: Reciter, Jae Woo Lee; Tamate, Gedde Wata-
; Samurai, Storyteller, Freddy Mao; Swordsman, Abe, Ernest
a; Manjiro, Patrick Kinser-Lau; Kayama, Tom Matsusaka;
d Councillor, Ricardo Tobia; Third Councillor, Tony Marinyo

ICAL NUMBERS: "The Advantages of Floating in the Mid-
f the Sea," "There Is No Other Way," "Four Black Dragons,"
ysanthemum Tea," "Poems," "Welcome to Kanagawa,"
eone in a Tree," "Lion Dance," "Please Hello," "A Bowler
" "Pretty Lady," "Next"

musical in two acts. The action takes place in Japan in July of
and from then on.

*General Manager:* Howard Haines
*Company Manager:* Leo K. Cohen
*Press:* Mary Bryant, Randy Kaplan
*ge Managers:* George Martin, John Grigas, Carlos Gorbea

sed June 27, 1976 after 193 performances and 13 previews.
nner of 1976 "Tony's" for Best Scenic Design, Best Costumes.

*Van Williams, Martha Swope Photos*

**Top: Mako (c) Below: Patrick Kinser-Lau,
nest Harada, Mark Hsu Syers, Yuki Shimoda,
Alvin Ing, James Dybas**

Soon-Teck Oh      Haruki Fujimoto

Katharine Hepburn, Paul Harding

**BROADHURST THEATRE**
    Opened Tuesday, February 3, 1976.*
    Robert Whitehead, Roger L. Stevens, Konrad Mattha
present:

# A MATTER OF GRAVITY

  By Enid Bagnold; Director, Noel William; Scenery, Ben Edward
Costumes, Jane Greenwood; Lighting, Thomas Skelton; Productic
Assistants, Mark Potter, Katharine Allentuck; Wardrobe Superv
sor, Colin Ferguson; Hairstylist, Charles Lo Presto

## CAST

| | |
|---|---|
| Dubois | Charlotte Jor |
| Estate Agent | Robert Mobe |
| Mrs. Basil | Katharine Hepbu |
| Nicky | Christopher Ree |
| Shatov | Elizabeth Lawren |
| Herbert | Paul Hardi |
| Elizabeth | Wanda Bims |
| Tom | Daniel Tam |

UNDERSTUDIES: Dubois, Shatov, Maggie Task; Herbert, Rob
Moberly; Elizabeth, Kathleen Heaney; Estate Agent, Bill Becke

  A comedy in three acts. The action takes place in a room in
old English country house at the present time.

*General Manager:* Oscar E. Olesen
*Company Manager:* David Hedges
*Press:* Seymour Krawitz, Patricia McLean Krawitz
*Stage Managers:* Ben Strobach, Bill Becker

* Closed Apr. 10, 1976 after limited engagement of 79 perf
mances.

*Sy Friedman Photos*

**Top: Christopher Reeve, Katharine Hepburn,
Elizabeth Lawrence, Charlotte Jones, Wanda
Bimson, Daniel Tamm, Paul Harding**

SKOFF THEATRE

Opened Tuesday, February 17, 1976.*

Lester Osterman Productions and Joseph Kipness in Association with Martin Richards and Victor D'Arc, Marilyn Strauss
present:

# ROCKABYE HAMLET

Cliff Jones; Based on Shakespeare's play "Hamlet"; Direction
Choreography, Gower Champion; Co-Choreographer, Tony
ns; Scenery, Kert F. Lundell; Costumes, Joseph G. Aulisi;
ing, Jules Fisher; Sound, Abe Jacob; Swordplay, Larry Carpen-
Hairstylist, Make-up, Ted Azar; Musical Direction and Vocal
ngements, Gordon Lowry Harrell; Dance Music Arrange-
s, Douglas Katsaros; Assistant to director, Larry Carpenter;
al Effects, Robert Joyce; Wardrobe Master, Joe Busheme; Mu-
Coordinator, Eron Tabor; Associate Conductor, Bill Schneider

CAST

| | |
|---|---|
| tio | Rory Dodd |
| et | Larry Marshall |
| ius | Alan Weeks |
| ude | Leata Galloway |
| t | Meat Loaf |
| ius | Randal Wilson |
| lia | Beverly D'Angelo |
| es | Kim Milford |
| ncrantz | Christopher Chadman |
| lenstern | Winston DeWitt Hemsley |
| r | Irving Lee |
| ress/Honeybelle Huckster | Judy Gibson |

Standby: Philip Casnoff

LYTES, SWORDSMEN, NOBLES, COURTESANS:
ny Aguilar, Steve Anthony, Terry Calloway, Prudence Darby,
ge Giraldo, Larry Hyman, Kurt Johnson, Clinton Keen, Paula
, Joann Ogawa, Sandi Orcutt, Merel Poloway, Joseph Pugliese,
nda Raven, Michelle Stubbs, Dennis Williams

GERS: James Braet, Judy DeAngelis, B. G. Gibson, Judy Gib-
Pat Gorman, Suzanne Lukather, Bruce Paine, William Parry

DIES: Chet D'Elia, David Fredericks, David Lawson, Jeff Spi-
n

ICAL NUMBERS: "Why Did He Have to Die?," "The Wed-
," "That It Should Come to This," "Set It Right," "Hello-
," "Don't Unmask Your Beauty to the Moon," "If Not to
," "Have I Got a Girl for You," "Tis Pity, Tis True," "Shall We
e," "All My Life," "Something's Rotten in Denmark," "Den-
Is Still," "Twist Her Mind," "Gentle Lover," "Where Is the
on," "The Wart Song," "He Got It in the Ear," "It Is Done,"
Inight—Hot Blood," "Midnight Mass," "Hey!," "Sing Alone,"
ir Daddy's Gone Away," "Rockabye Hamlet," "All by Your-
"Rosencrantz and Guildenstern Boogie," "Laertes Coercion,"
e Last Blues," "Didn't She Do It for Love," "If My Morning
is," "Swordfight"

*General Manager:* Leonard Soloway
*Press:* Betty Lee Hunt, Maria Cristina Pucci, Bill Evans
*Stage Managers:* David Taylor, Bethe Ward, Tony Manzi

osed Feb. 21, 1976 after 7 performances and 21 previews.

*Kenn Duncan Photos*

**Top: Beverly D'Angelo, Larry Marshall**
**Below: Alan Weeks, Kim Milford**

**Judy Gibson, Larry Marshall**

**BILTMORE THEATRE**
Opened Tuesday, February 24, 1976.*
Terry Allen Kramer and Harry Rigby by arrangement with Circle Repertory Company present:

# KNOCK KNOCK

By Jules Feiffer; Director, Marshall W. Mason; Setting, John Lee Beatty; Costumes, Jennifer von Mayrhauser; Lighting, Dennis Parichy; Sound, Charles London, George Hansen; Assistant Director, John H. Davis; Production Assistant, Petder Lippman

## CAST

| | |
|---|---|
| Cohn | Daniel Seltzer |
| Abe | Neil Flanagan |
| Wiseman | Judd Hirsch† |
| Joan | Nancy Snyder |
| Messenger/Gambler/Judge/Joan's Voices | Judd Hirsch† |

A comedy in three acts. The action takes place at the present time in a small house in the woods.

*General Manager:* Leonard Soloway
*Press:* Henry Luhrman, Terry Lilly
*Stage Managers:* Dan Hild, Greg Taylor

*Closed May 23, 1976 after 104 performances. Opened Sunday, Jan. 18, 1976 at Circle Repertory Theatre with the same cast and played 48 performances before moving to Broadway. A new cast and production opened at the Biltmore on Wednesday, June 2, 1976.
† Succeeded by Leonard Frey

*Herbert Migdoll, Martha Swope Photos*

**Right: Judd Hirsch, Nancy Snyder, Neil Flanagan, Daniel Seltzer**
**Top: Flanagan, Seltzer**

Neil Flanagan, Daniel Seltzer

Nancy Snyder, Neil Flanagan, Daniel Seltzer

ANTA THEATRE
Opened Tuesday, March 2, 1976.*
J. Lloyd Grant, Richard Bell, Robert M. Cooper, Ashton Springer in association with Moe Septee, Inc., present the Media House Production of:

# BUBBLING BROWN SUGAR

Book, Loften Mitchell; Based on a concept by Rosetta LeNoire; Director, Robert M. Cooper; Musical Direction, Danny Holgate; Choreography and Musical Staging, Billy Wilson; Sets, Clarke Dunham; Costumes, Bernard Johnson; Lighting, Barry Arnold; Projections, Lucie D. Grosvenor, Clarke Dunham; Sound, Joel S. Fichman; Additional Music, Danny Holgate, Emme Kemp, Lillian Lopez; Choral Arrangements, Chapman Roberts; Hairstylists, Gene Sheppard, Stanley James; Production Supervisor, I. Mitchell Miller; Production Coordinator, Sharon Brown; Assistant to director, Kathleen Stanford-Grant; Assistant to choreographer, Dyann Robinson; Wardrobe Mistress, Linda Lee; Original Cast Album by H & L Records

### CAST

| | |
|---|---|
| Skip/Young Checkers | Lonnie McNeil |
| Bill/Time Man/Bumpy/M. C | Vernon Washington† |
| Ray/Young Sage | Newton Winters |
| Carolyn/Gospel Lady/Nightclub Singer | Carolyn Byrd |
| Norma | Karen Grannum |
| Gene/Gospel Lady's Son | Alton Lathrop |
| Helen | Dyann Robinson |
| Laura | Charlise Harris |
| Marsha/Young Irene | Vivian Reed |
| Tony/Waiter/Dutch | Anthony Whitehouse |
| Irene Paige | Josephine Premice |
| John Sage/Rusty | Avon Long |
| Checkers/Dusty | Joseph Attles |
| Jim/Nightclub Singer | Chip Garnett |
| Ella | Ethel Beatty |
| Judy/Dutch's Girl | Barbara Rubenstein |
| Charlie/Count | Barry Preston |
| The Solitunes | Alton Lathrop, Lonnie McNeil, Newton Winters |
| Chorus | Murphy Cross, Nedra Dixon, Emme Kemp, Stanley Ramsey |

STANDBYS AND UNDERSTUDIES: Sage, Vernon Washington; Irene, Gospel Lady, Nightclub Singer, Emme Kemp; Marsha, Young Irene, Karen Grannum; Checkers, Bill, Bumpy, MC, David Bryant; Jim, Stanley Ramsey; Judy, Murphy Cross; Tony, Charlie, Dutch, Count, E. Lynn Nickerson; Gospel Lady's Son, Millard Hurley; Dance Alternates, Carol Pennyfeather, Millard Hurley

MUSICAL NUMBERS: "Harlem '70," "Bubbling Brown Sugar," "That's What Harlem Is to Me," "Bill Robinson Specialty," "Harlem Sweet Harlem," "Nobody," "Goin' Back in Time," "Some of These Days," "Moving Uptown," "Strolling," "I'm Gonna Tell God All My Troubles," "His Eye Is on the Sparrow," "Swing Low, Sweet Chariot," "Sweet Georgia Brown," "Honeysuckle Rose," "Stormy Monday Blues," "Rosetta," "Sophisticated Lady," "In Honeysuckle Time When Emaline Said She'd Be Mine," "Solitude," "C'mon Up to Jive Time," "Stompin' at the Savoy," "Take the 'A' Train," "Harlem—Time," "Love Will Find a Way," "Dutch's Song," "Brown Gal," "Pray for the Lights to Go Out," "I Got It Bad," "Harlem Makes Me Feel!," "Jim, Jam, Jumpin' Jive," "There'll Be Some Changes Made," "God Bless the Child," "It Don't Mean a Thing"

A musical revue in 2 acts and 9 scenes. The action takes place in Harlem at the present time, and between 1920 and 1940.

*General Managers:* Ashton Springer, Susan Chase
*Company Manager:* Carolyne A. Jones
*Press:* Max Eisen, Barbara Glenn
*Stage Managers:* Sam Ellis, E. Lynn Nickerson

\* Still playing May 31, 1976.
† Succeeded by David Bryant

*Bert Andrews Photos*

**Right Center: Barbara Rubenstein, Barry Preston; Vivian Reed, Newton Winters, Lonnie McNeil**
**Top: Josephine Premice, Avon Long**

Josephine Premice, Avon Long, Vivian Reed, Joseph Attles, (top center) Chip Garnett

**CIRCLE IN THE SQUARE THEATRE**
Sundays, March 7 & 14, 1976.*
Circle in the Square (Theodore Mann, Artistic Director; P.
Libin, Managing Director) presents:

# GERALDINE FITZGERALD
## in
# SONGS OF THE STREET

Directed by Richard Maltby; Musical Direction, Stanley Wietr
chowski; Vocal Consultant, Andy Anselmo
A one-woman "informal concert."

*Press:* Merle Debuskey, Susan L. Schulman
*Stage Manager:* Randall Brooks

* Presented for two performances only.

**Left: Geraldine Fitzgerald**

**JOHN GOLDEN THEATRE**
Opened Saturday, March 13, 1976.*
Adela Holzer presents:

# ME JACK, YOU JILL

By Robes Kossez; Director, Harold J. Kennedy; Scenery and
Costumes, Lawrence King, Michael H. Yeargan; Lighting, Jane
Reisman; Special Effects, Ronald Vitelli, Neil Schatz; Hairstylist,
Rosalba; Assistant to director, Skipp Lynch; Wardrobe Supervisor,
Samuel Elterman

### CAST

| | |
|---|---|
| Bibi | Lisa Kirk |
| Annie | Barbara Baxley |
| Tessie | Sylvia Sidney |
| Young Man | Russ Thacker |

Standbys: Donna Pearson, Jeffrey Danneman

A "play of suspense" in two acts and three scenes. The action
takes place at the present time on the empty stage of a Broadway
theatre.

*General Manager:* Leonard A. Mulhern
*Company Manager:* David Relyea
*Press:* Michael Alpert, Marilynn LeVine, Joshua Ellis
*Stage Managers:* Tom Porter, Jeffrey Danneman

* Closed March 14, 1976 after 2 performances and 14 previews.

*Carl Samrock Photos*

**Above: Sylvia Sidney, also right with Lisa Kirk**

**Sylvia Sidney, Barbara Baxley, Russ Thacker**

Paul Sparer, Lee Wallace, Joseph Wiseman
Right: Joseph Wiseman (C), Richard Bauer (R)
(Also below)

YCEUM THEATRE
Opened Wednesday, March 17, 1976.*
Moe Septee presents:

# ALMEN OR THE MADNESS OF GOD

By Elie Wiesel; Stage Adaptation, Marion Wiesel; Director, Alan
hneider; Scenery, William Ritman; Costumes, Marjorie Slaiman;
ghting, Richard Nelson; Assistant Director, Susan Einhorn; Pro-
iction Supervisor, Sander Hacker; Wardrobe Supervisor, Cindy
nock; Hairstylist, Nino Raffaello; Production Assistant, Lee Mas-
odonato

### CAST

| | |
|---|---|
| almen | Richard Bauer |
| ne Rabbi | Joseph Wiseman |
| hairman of the Synagogue Council | Paul Sparer |
| embers of Synagogue Council: | |
| amuel | Edwin Bordo |
| ul | Sanford Seeger |
| lotke | Carl Don |
| haim | David Reinhardsen |
| ender | Warren Pincus |
| ne Doctor | David Margulies |
| spector from Ministry of Religious Affairs | Lee Wallace |
| ina | Polly Adams |
| ischa | Rodman Flender |
| lexei | David Little |
| antor | John B. Jellison |
| ommissar | Jack Hollander |
| irst Guard | Michael Haney |
| cond Guard | John B. Jellison |
| hird Guard | Irwin Atkins |
| cretary | Nancy Dutton |
| vron | Michael Gorrin |
| eige | Zviah Igdalsky |

NDERSTUDIES AND STANDBYS: Mischa, Jonathan Weisgal;
almen, Srul, John B. Jellison; Rabbi, Irwin Atkins; Chairman,
octor, Edwin Bordo; Inspector, Jack Hollander; Nina, Feige,
ancy Dutton; Alexei, David Reinhardsen; Avrom, Carl Don;
haim, Michael Haney; Commissar, Sanford Seeger

A drama in two acts. The action takes place in the late 1950's in
synagogue in a small town in Russia.

*General Manager:* Laurel Ann Wilson
*Company Manager:* Donald Tirabassi
*Press:* Max Eisen, Barbara Glenn, Judy Jacksina
*Stage Managers:* R. Derek Swire, Ted Harris, Michael Haney

Closed April 5, 1976 after 22 performances and 5 previews.

*Jack Hoffman Photos*

**David Little, Rodman Flender, Polly Adams,
Joseph Wiseman**

**CIRCLE IN THE SQUARE THEATRE**
Opened Thursday, March 18, 1976.*
Circle in the Square (Theodore Mann, Artistic Director; Paul
Libin, Managing Director) presents:

# THE LADY FROM THE SEA

By Henrik Ibsen; Translated by Michael Meyer; Director, Tony
Richardson; Scenery and Costumes, Rouben Ter-Arutunian; Light-
ing, Thomas Skelton; Music and Sound, Richard Peaslee; Produc-
tion Associate, Atsumi Kolba; Wardrobe Supervisor, Virginia
Merkel; Production Assistants, Gordon Bendall, Sandy Caltabiano,
Susan Elrod, Bernard Ferstenberg, Robin Groves, Sharon Kolberg,
Jolly Nelson, Susan Santiago, Tom Smith

### CAST

| | |
|---|---|
| Ballested | George Ede |
| Bolette | Kimberly Farr |
| Lyngstrand | Kipp Osborne |
| Hilde | Allison Argo |
| Dr. Wangel | Pat Hingle |
| Professor Arnholm | John Heffernan |
| Ellida | Vanessa Redgrave |
| The Stranger | Richard Lynch |

A drama in two acts. The action takes place during the summer
in a small town by a fjord in northern Norway.

*Company Manager:* William Conn
*Press:* Merle Debuskey, Susan L. Schulman
*Stage Managers:* Randall Brooks, James Bernardi

* Closed May 23, 1976 after limited engagement of 77 performances
and 23 previews.

*Inge Morath Photos*

### Right: Vanessa Redgrave, Pat Hingle, Richard Lynch Top: John Heffernan, Vanessa Redgrave, Kipp Osborne

George Ede, Kimberly Farr

Pat Hingle, Allison Argo, Kipp Osborne,
Kimberly Farr, John Heffernan, Vanessa Redgra

T. JAMES THEATRE
Opened Thursday, March 25, 1976.*
Herman Levin presents:

# MY FAIR LADY

Book and Lyrics, Alan Jay Lerner; Adapted from Bernard Shaw's "Pygmalion"; Music, Frederick Loewe; Director, Jerry Adler; Based on the original by Moss Hart; Choreography and Musical Numbers, Crandall Diehl; Based on original by Hanya Holm; Scenery, Oliver Smith; Costumes, Cecil Beaton; Lighting, John Gleason; Special Costume Assistant, W. Robert Lavine; Musical Director, Theodore Saidenberg; Musical Arrangements, Robert Russel Bennett, Phil Lang; Dance Music Arrangements, Trude Rittman; Wardrobe Master, Joseph Busheme; Production Assistant, Anne Tomfohrde; Assistant Conductor, R. Bennett Benetsky; Hair Supervisors, Vincent Prestia, Michael Fisher; Hairstylist, Ray Iagnocco

### CAST

| | |
|---|---|
| Buskers | Debra Lyman, Stan Pincus, Ernie Pysher |
| Mrs. Eynsford-Hill | Eleanor Phelps |
| Freddy Eynsford-Hill | Jerry Lanning |
| Eliza Doolittle | Christine Andreas†1 |
| Colonel Pickering | Robert Coote†2 |
| Henry Higgins | Ian Richardson |
| First Cockney | Kevin Marcum |
| Second Cockney | Jack Starkey |
| Third Cockney/Flunkey | William James |
| Fourth Cockney/Footman | Stan Page |
| Bartender/Footman | Kevin Lane Dearinger |
| Harry/Lord Boxington/Zoltan Karpathy | John Clarkson |
| Jamie/Ambassador | Richard Neilson |
| Alfred P. Doolittle | George Rose |
| Mrs. Pearce | Sylvia O'Brien |
| Mrs. Hopkins/Lady Boxington | Margaretta Warwick |
| Butler/Bartender | Clifford Fearl |
| Servants | Sonja Anderson, Lynn Fitzpatrick, Karen Gibson, Vickie Patik, Kevin Lane Dearinger |
| Mrs. Higgins | Brenda Forbes |
| Chauffeur | Jack Karcher |
| Constable | Timothy Smith |
| Flower Girl | Dru Alexandrine |
| Queen of Transylvania | Karen Gibson |
| Mrs. Higgin's Maid | Sonja Stuart |

SINGING ENSEMBLE: Sonja Anderson, Alyson Bristol, Lynn Fitzpatrick, Karen Gibson, Cynthia Meryl, Vickie Patik, Kevin Lane Dearinger, Clifford Fearl, William James, Kevin Marcum, Stan Page, Jack Starkey

DANCING ENSEMBLE: Dru Alexandrine, Sally Benoit, Marie Berry, Debra Lyman, Mari McMinn, Gina Ramsel, Catherine Rice, Sonja Stuart, Bonnie Walker, Richard Amrion, Jeremy Blanton, David Evans, Jack Karcher, Richard Maxon, Stan Pincus, Ernie Pysher, Rick Schneider, Timothy Smith

MUSICAL NUMBERS: "Street Entertainers," "Why Can't the English?" "Wouldn't It Be Loverly?," "With A Little Bit of Luck," "I'm an Ordinary Man," "Just You Wait," "The Rain in Spain," "I Could Have Danced All Night," "Ascot Gavotte," "On the Street Where You Live," "Embassy Waltz," "You Did It," "Show Me," "Get Me to the Church on Time," "A Hymn to Him," "Without You," "I've Grown Accustomed to Her Face"

UNDERSTUDIES AND STANDBYS: Higgins, Patrick Horgan; Eliza, Vickie Patik; Doolittle, John Clarkson; Pickering, Richard Neilson; Mrs. Higgins, Eleanor Phelps; Freddy, William James; Mrs. Pearce, Margaretta Warwick; Harry, Kevin Marcum; Jamie, Stan Page; Mrs. Hopkins, Cynthia Meryl; Mrs. Eynsford-Hill, Karen Gibson; Karpathy, Kevin Marcum

A musical in 2 acts and 18 scenes. The action takes place in London.

*General Manager:* Philip Adler
*Company Manager:* Malcolm Allen
*Press:* Seymour Krawitz, Patricia McLean Krawitz
*Stage Managers:* Nicholas Russiyan, Alisa Jill Adler, Robert O'Rourke

* Still playing May 31, 1976. George Rose received a 1976 "Tony" for Best Actor in a Musical. Original production opened Mar. 15, 1956 at the Mark Hellinger Theatre with Rex Harrison, Julie Andrews, Stanley Holloway, and Cathleen Nesbitt and ran for 2715 performances. (See THEATRE WORLD, Vol. 12)
† During illness played by: 1. Vickie Patik, 2. Eric Brotherson

*Sy Friedman Photos*

**George Rose**

**Christine Andreas**

**Top Right: Ian Richardson, Christine Andreas, also below with Robert Coote Center: Brenda Forbes, Jerry Lanning, Richardson, Andreas, Coote, Eleanor Phelps**

THE MUSIC BOX
Opened Thursday, April 1, 1976.*
Ken Marsolais and James Scott Productions, Inc., in associa-
tion with MPL, Ltd., present:

# WHO'S AFRAID OF VIRGINIA WOOLF?

By Edward Albee; Directed by Mr. Albee; Setting and Lightin
William Ritman; Costumes, Jane Greenwood; Produced by arran
ment with Richard Barr and Clinton Wilder; Assistant to produce
Jerry Sirchia; Assistant to director, Christopher Gore; Wardro
Supervisor, Fay Young

### CAST

| | |
|---|---|
| Martha | Colleen Dewhu |
| George | Ben Gazza |
| Honey | Maureen Anderm |
| Nick | Richard Kel |

STANDBYS: Martha, Betty Miller; George, James Karen; Hon
Katherine Bruce; Nick, Josef Warik

A comedy-drama in three acts. The action takes place at
present time in the home of George and Martha in a university tov

*General Manager:* Leonard Soloway
*Company Manager:* Terry Grossman
*Press:* Betty Lee Hunt, Maria Cristina Pucci
*Stage Managers:* Mark Wright, Wayne Carson

* Closed July 11, 1976 after 117 performances and three previe
Original production opened Oct. 13, 1962 at the Billy Rose T
atre and played 664 performances with Uta Hagen, Arthur H
George Grizzard and Melinda Dillon. (See THEATRE WORL
Vol. 19)

**Left: Richard Kelton, Colleen Dewhurst
Top: Richard Kelton, Ben Gazzara, Maureen
Anderman, Colleen Dewhurst**

Colleen Dewhurst, Ben Gazzara

Ben Gazzara, Colleen Dewhurst, Richard Kelto

**PALACE THEATRE**
Opened Monday, April 19, 1976.*
HMT Associates present:

# SHIRLEY MacLAINE
## with
## Shirley's Gypsies

Directed and Staged by Tony Charmoli; Musical Director, Donn Trenner; Music arranged or composed by Cy Coleman; Written by Fred Ebb; Additional Material, Bob Wells; Special Choreography, Alan Johnson; Lighting, Richard Winkler, Graham Large; Sound, Steve Wooley; Wardrobe Mistress, Sydney Smith; Recorded by Columbia Records

SHIRLEY'S GYPSIES: Jo Ann Lehmann, Gary Flannery, Adam Grammis, Larry Vickers

MUSICAL NUMBERS: "If My Friends Could See Me Now," "Personal Property," "Remember Me?," "Hey Big Spender," "I'm a Person Too," "Irma La Douce," "Gypsy in My Soul," "It's Not Where You Start," "Every Little Movement Has a Meaning All Its Own," "The Hustle," "Star," "I'm a Brass Band"

Performed without intermission.

*General Management:* Marvin A. Krauss Associates, David Wyler, Robert I. Goldberg
*Company Manager:* Bernard Lang
*Press:* Michael Alpert, Marilynn LeVine, Warren Knowlton, Carl Samrock, Jonas Halpern
*Stage Manager:* Earl Hughes

* Closed May 1, 1976 after 20 performances.

*Robin Platzer Photos*

**Shirley MacLaine (also above and left)**

**BROADHURST THEATRE**
Opened Tuesday, April 20, 1976.*
Steven Beckler and Thomas C. Smith present:

# THE HEIRESS

By Ruth and Augustus Goetz; Based on Henry James' novel, "Washington Square"; Director, George Keathley; Setting, Oliver Smith; Costumes, Ann Roth; Lighting, David F. Segal; Associate Producer, Ken Morse; Produced for the Kennedy Center by Roger L. Stevens and Richmond Crinkley; Technical Supervisor, Mitch Miller; Wardrobe Supervisor, Colin Ferguson; Hairstylist, J. Roy Helland

### CAST

| | |
|---|---|
| Maria | Sharon Laughlin |
| Dr. Austin Sloper | Richard Kiley |
| Lavinia Penniman | Jan Miner |
| Catherine Sloper | Jane Alexander |
| Elizabeth Almond | Dorothy Blackburn |
| Arthur Townsend | Roger Baron |
| Marian Almond | Cecilia Hart |
| Morris Townsend | David Selby |
| Mrs. Montgomery | Toni Darnay |
| Coachman | William Gibberson |

UNDERSTUDIES: Sloper, William Gibberson; Catherine, Marian, Sharon Laughlin; Lavinia, Diana Mathews, Toni Darnay; Morris, Roger Baron; Arthur, Coachman, Joe Lorden; Mrs. Almond, Mrs. Montgomery, Maria, Diana Mathews.

A drama in 2 acts and 7 scenes. The action takes place in the front parlor of Dr. Sloper's house in Washington Square, New York City, in 1850.

*General Manager:* Theatre Now., Inc., Edward H. Davis, William C. Cohen
*Press:* Betty Lee Hunt, Maria Cristina Pucci
*Stage Manager:* Joe Lorden

\* Closed May 9, 1976 after 23 performances and 5 previews. Original production opened Sept. 29, 1947 at the Biltmore and played 410 performances with Basil Rathbone, Wendy Hiller and Patricia Collinge. (See THEATRE WORLD, Vol. 4) Revived at City Center Jan. 25, 1950 for 15 performances with Basil Rathbone, Margaret Phillips, Edna Best and John Dall. (See THEATRE WORLD, Vol. 6)

*Richard Braaten Photos*

**Top: Richard Kiley**

**Richard Kiley, Jane Alexander**
**Above: David Selby, Jan Miner**

**Right: David Selby, Jane Alexander**

UNT-FONTANNE THEATRE
Opened Sunday, April 25, 1976.*
Richard Adler in association with Roger Berlind and Edward
R. Downe, Jr. presents:

# REX

Book, Sherman Yellen; Music, Richard Rodgers; Lyrics, Sheldon
Harnick; Director, Edwin Sherin; Choreography, Dania Krupska;
Orchestrations, Irwin Kostal; Musical Director, Jay Blackton;
Dance Arrangements, David Baker; Scenery and Costumes, John
Conklin; Lighting, Jennifer Tipton; Hairstylist, Bert Anthony;
Werner Sherer; Technical Supervisor, Mitch Miller; Wardrobe Su-
pervisor, Mariana Torres; Assistant to director, Christopher Adler;
Assistant to producers, Giselle Steiker; Original Cast Album by
RCA Records

## CAST

| | |
|---|---|
| Norfolk | Charles Rule |
| Cardinal Wolsey | William Griffis |
| Will Somers | Tom Aldredge |
| Henry VIII | Nicol Williamson |
| Mark Smeaton | Ed Evanko |
| Princess Mary | Glenn Close |
| Queen Catherine of England | Barbara Andres |
| Lady Jane Seymour | April Shawhan |
| Francis, King of France | Stephen D. Newman |
| English Herald | Danny Ruvolo |
| French Herald | Jeff Phillips |
| Queen Claude of France/Lady Margaret/Queen Katherine Parr of England | Martha Danielle |
| Anne Boleyn/Princess Elizabeth | Penny Fuller |
| Dauphin | Keith Koppmeier |
| Comus | Merwin Goldsmith |
| First Guard | Ken Henley |
| Lady in Waiting | Melanie Vaughan |
| Young Princess Elizabeth | Sparky Shapiro |
| Nurse | Lillian Shelby |
| Second Guard | Dennis Daniels |
| Thomas Cromwell | Gerald R. Teijelo |
| Katherine Howard | Valerie Mahaffey |
| Prince Edward | Michael John |

LADIES AND GENTLEMEN OF THE COURTS: Dennis Dan-
iels, Harry Fawcett, Paul Forrest, Pat Gideon, Ken Henley, Dawn
Herbert, Robin Hoff, Don Johanson, Jim Litten, Craig Lucas, Carol
Jo Lugenbeal, Valerie Mahaffey, G. Eugene Moose, Jeff Phillips,
Charles Rule, Danny Ruvolo, Lillian Shelby, Jo Speros, Gerald R.
Teijelo, Jr., Candace Tovar, John Ulrickson, Melanie Vaughan

SWORD AND MORRIS DANCERS: Dennis Daniels, Ken Henley, Don Johnson, Jim Litten, Jeff Phillips, Danny Ruvolo

UNDERSTUDIES: Henry, Stephen D. Newman; Anne Boleyn,
Martha Danielle; Somers, Jeff Phillips; Princess Elizabeth, Lady
Jane, Carol Jo Lugenbeal; Queen Catherine, Lillian Shelby; Princess
Mary, Lady Margaret, Pat Gideon; Queen Claude, Valerie Ma-
haffey; Queen Katherine Parr, Candace Tovar; Smeaton, Craig
Lucas; Comus, King Francis, Gerald R. Teijelo, Jr.; Wolsey, Charles
Rule; Prince Edward, Keith Koppmeier; Dauphin, Michael John

MUSICAL NUMBERS: "Te Deum," "No Song More Pleasing,"
"Where Is My Son?," "The Field of Cloth of Gold," "Basse Dance,"
"The Chase," "Away from You," "As Once I Loved You," "Eliza-
beth," "What Now?," "Christmas at Hampton Court," "Wee
Golden Warrior," "The Masque," "From Afar," "In Time"

A musical in 2 acts and 24 scenes. The action takes place during
the reign of Henry VIII of England until his death.

*General Managers:* Edward H. Davis, William C. Cohen
*Company Manager:* Leo K. Cohen
*Press:* Jeffrey Richards, James Storrow, Barbara Shelley
*Stage Managers:* Bob Bernard, Jack Timmers, Elise Warner

Closed June 5, 1976 after 48 performances and 14 previews.

*Martha Swope Photos*

**Top: Nicol Williamson**

**Below: Ed Evanko, Penny Fuller**

**Stephen D. Newman, Michael John, Tom Aldredge,
Nicol Williamson, Penny Fuller, Glenn Close**

## HARKNESS THEATRE
Opened Tuesday, April 27, 1976.*
Frederick Brisson in association with The Harkness Organization and Wyatt Dickerson presents:

# SO LONG, 174th STREET

Book, Joseph Stein; Based on his play "Enter Laughing"; From the novel by Carl Reiner; Music and Lyrics, Stan Daniels; Director Bert Shevelove; Choreography, Alan Johnson; Scenery, James Riley; Costumes, Stanley Simmons; Lighting, Richard Nelson; Hairstylist Ted Azar; Musical Direction, John Lesko; Orchestrations, Luther Henderson; Dance Music Arrangements, Wally Harper; Production Supervisor, Stone Widney; Wardrobe Supervisor, Agnes Farrell Production Assistant, Kim Beaty; Assistant Conductor, Wood Kessler; Assistant to director, Patrick Horrigan; Assistant to choreographer, Graziela Daniele

### CAST

| | |
|---|---|
| David | Robert Morse |
| Stage Manager | Joe Howard |
| Girl | Freda Soiffer |
| Barrymore/Waiter/Pike/Ziegfeld | Gene Varrone |
| Pope/Harry Hamburger | Robert Barr |
| King/Peabody | Richard Marr |
| Roosevelt | David Berk |
| Eleanor Roosevelt | Nancy Killmer |
| Mr. Foreman | Mitchell Jason |
| Wanda | Loni Ackerman |
| Marvin | Lawrence John Moss |
| Miss B | Sydney Blake |
| Don Baxter | Chuck Beard |
| Don Darwin | Michael Blue Aiken |
| Angela | Barbara Lang |
| Marlowe/Butler/Judge | George S. Irving |
| Papa | Lee Goodman |
| Soda Jerk/Man | James Brennan |

ENSEMBLE: Jill Cook, Nancy Killmer, Meribeth Kisner, Denise Mauthe, Rita Rudner, Freda Soiffer, Michael Blue Aiken, Chuck Beard, David Berk, Joe Howard, Richard Marr, William Swiggard

STANDBYS AND UNDERSTUDIES: David, James Brennan; Wanda, Rita Rudner; Swing Girl, Claudia Asbury; Swing Boy, Jack Magradey

MUSICAL NUMBERS: "David Kolowitz, the Actor," "It's Like," "Undressing Girls with My Eyes," "Bolero on Rye," "Whoever You Are," "Say the Words," "My Son the Druggist," "You Touch Her," "Men," "Boy Oh Boy," "Butler's Song," "Being with You," "If You Want to Break My Father's Heart," "So Long 174th Street," Finale

A musical performed without intermission. The action takes place at the present time and the late 1930's in New York City.

*General Manager:* Ralph Roseman
*Company Manager:* John A. Caruso
*Press:* Solters & Roskin, Bud Westman, Stanley F. Kaminsky, William Schelble
*Stage Managers:* Mortimer Halpern, Bryan Young, Jack Magradey

\* Closed May 9, 1976 after 16 performances and 6 previews.

*Martha Swope Photos*

**Robert Morse, also above with Loni Ackerman**

**Top: Lawrence John Moss, Robert Morse**
**Left: George S. Irving, Morse, Barbara Lang**

**LONGACRE THEATRE**
Opened Wednesday, April 28, 1976.*
Mike Merrick and Don Gregory present:

# THE BELLE OF AMHERST

By William Luce; Compiled by Timothy Helgeson; Director, Charles Nelson Reilly; Scenery and Lighting, H. R. Poindexter; Costumes, Theoni V. Aldredge; Hairstylist, Ray Iagnocco; Assistant to director, Timothy Helgeson; Assistants to producers, Rita Cocecchio, Joan DeYoung

### CAST
### JULIE HARRIS

A play in two acts based on the life and works of Emily Dickinson. The action takes place in the Dickinson home in Amherst, Massachusetts, between 1845 and 1886.

*General Manager:* James Awe
*Press:* Seymour Krawitz, Patricia McLean Krawitz, Ted Goldsmith
*Stage Managers:* George Eckert, Berny Baker

* Closed Aug. 8, 1976 after 116 performances and 1 preview to tour.

*Sy Friedman Photos*

**Julie Harris as Emily Dickinson**

**SAM S. SHUBERT THEATRE**
Sunday, May 2, 1976
Friends of the Theatre and Music Collection of the Museum of
the City of New York present:

# GEORGE ABBOTT
## ... A Celebration

Conceived and Produced by Anna Sosenko; Staged by Donald
Saddler; Lighting Design, Richard Winkler; Musical Direction, Co-
lin Romoff; Sound Design, Abe Jacob; Assistant to Miss Sosenko,
Donald Damask; Assistants to Mr. Saddler, Christopher Adler,
Mercedes Ellington; Wardrobe Supervisor, Marilyn Putnam; Pro-
duction Assistants, Paul Diaz, Merle Hubbard, Marvin Jenkins

### CAST

Richard Adler, Christine Andreas, Desi Arnaz, Elizabeth Ashley,
Alexandra Borrie, David James Carroll, Tim Cassidy, Betty Com-
den, Donald Correia, Howard DaSilva, Fred Ebb, Ed Evanko, Joey
Faye, Arlene Francis, Martin Gabel, Jack Gilford, Ben Grauer,
Adolph Green, June Havoc, Will Holt, Del Horstman, George S.
Irving, Anne Jackson, John Kander, Maria Karnilova, Garson Ka-
nin, Sam Levene, Shirley MacLaine, Liza Minnelli, Sono Osato,
Maureen O'Sullivan, Julian Patrick, Eddie Phillips, Barry Preston,
Harold Prince, Jerome Robbins, Donald Saddler, Alan Sanderson,
Stanley Simmonds, Roy Smith, Tim Smith, Jean Stapleton, Maureen
Stapleton, Jule Styne, David Thome, Eli Wallach, Walter Willison

A gala tribute honoring George Abbott's 63 years as a Broadway
producer, director, playwright and actor.

*Manager:* Victor Samrock
*Press:* Bob Ullman
*Stage Managers:* Edward Preston, Robert Schear, Jerry
O'Connell

*Robin Platzer Photos*

**Right: Liza Minnelli, George Abbott,
Shirley MacLaine
Above: George Abbott, Maureen Stapleton**

Helen Hayes

George Abbott, Jean Stapleton

54

MARK HELLINGER THEATRE
Opened Tuesday, May 4, 1976.*
Roger L. Stevens and Robert Whitehead present:

# 1600 PENNSYLVANIA AVENUE

Book and Lyrics, Alan Jay Lerner; Music, Leonard Bernstein; Directed, Choreographed and Staged by Gilbert Moses and George Faison; Scenery, Kert Lundell; Costumes, Whitney Blausen, Dona Granata; Lighting, Tharon Musser; Musical Director, Roland Gagnon; Orchestrations, Sid Ramin, Hershy Kay; Sound, John McClure; Hairstylist, Werner Sherer; Produced by arrangement with Saint Subber; Assistant Choreographer, Renee Rose; Production Coordinator, Doris Blum; Production Assistants, Katharine Allentuck, Jim Beloff; Wardrobe Supervisor, Josephine Zampedri; Assistant Conductor, Robert Rogers.

### CAST

| | |
|---|---|
| The President | Ken Howard |
| The President's Wife | Patricia Routledge |
| Lud | Gilbert Price |
| Seena | Emily Yancy |
| Little Lud | Guy Costley |
| Stage Manager | David E. Thomas |

The Thirteen Delegates:

| | |
|---|---|
| Massachusetts | Howard Ross |
| New York | Reid Shelton |
| Pennsylvania | Ralph Farnworth |
| New Hampshire | J. T. Cromwell |
| Rhode Island | Lee Winston |
| Connecticut | Richard Chappell |
| New Jersey | Walter Charles |
| Virginia | Edwin Steffe |
| North Carolina | John Witham |
| South Carolina | Richard Muenz |
| Delaware | Alexander Orfaly |
| Maryland | Raymond Cox |
| Georgia | Randolph Riscol |

The Staff:

| | |
|---|---|
| Henry | Raymond Bazemore |
| Rachel | Urylee Leonardos |
| Coley | Carl Hall |
| Toby | Janette Moody |
| Broom | Howard Ross |
| Jim | Cornel J. Richie |
| Sally | Louise Heath |

The British:

| | |
|---|---|
| Ordway | Walter Charles |
| Pimms | John Witham |
| Barker | Lee Winston |
| Glieg | Raymond Cox |
| Maitland | Alexander Orfaly |
| Ross | Edwin Steffe |
| Pratt | Richard Chappell |
| Scott | J. T. Cromwell |
| Budget | Richard Muenz |
| Cockburn | Reid Shelton |
| Rev. Bushrod | Bruce A. Hubbard |
| Auctioneer/Mr. Henry/Babcock | Lee Winston |
| James Hoban/Judge | Edwin Steffe |
| Royal Visitor | Randolph Riscol |
| Secretary of the Senate | Howard Ross |
| Senator Roscoe Condling | Reid Shelton |

UNDERSTUDIES: President, Richard Chappell; President's Wife, Beth Fowler; Lud, J. Edwards Adams; Seena, Louise Heath; Little Lud, Karl M. Horton; Swing Dancers, Leah Randolph, Marial Roumain.

SINGERS: Raymond Bazemore, Elaine Bunse, Nancy Callman, Richard Chappell, Walter Charles, Raymond Cox, J. T. Cromwell, Beth Fowler, Carl Hall, Louise Heath, Bruce A. Hubbard, Kris Karlowski, Urylee Leonardos, Joyce MacDonald, Janette Moody, Richard Muenz, Sharon Powers, Cornel J. Richie, Randolph Riscol, Martha Thigpen, Lee Winston

DANCERS: Jo-Ann Baldo, Clyde-Jacques Barrett, Joella Breedove, Allyne DeChalus, Linda Griffin, Bob Heath, Michael Lichefeld, Diana Mirras, Hector Jaime Mercado, Cleveland Pennington, Al Perryman, Renee Rose, Juliet Seignious, Thomas J. Stanton, Clayton Strange, Mimi B. Wallace

"A musical about the problems of housekeeping" in two acts. The action takes place at The White House in Washington, D. C.

*General Manager:* Oscar E. Olesen
*Company Manager:* James Walsh
*Press:* Seymour Krawitz, Patricia McLean Krawitz, Ted Goldsmith
*Stage Managers:* William Dodds, Marnel Sumner, Michael Turque

* Closed May 8, 1976 after 7 performances and 13 previews.

*Sy Friedman Photos*

**Top Right: Patricia Routledge, Ken Howard**
**Below: Ken Howard (C)**
**Bottom: Gilbert Price, Emily Yancy**

**AMBASSADOR THEATRE**
Opened Thursday, May 6, 1976.*

Under the sponsorship of L'Association Francaise D'Action Artistique of the Government of the French Republic, Le Treteau de Paris, Jean de Rigault in association with the French Institute/Alliance Francaise presents the Compagnie Renaud-Barrault in:

# DAYS IN THE TREES
## (Des Journees Entieres dans les Arbres)

By Marguerite Duras; Staged by Jean-Louis Barrault; Settings and Costumes, Atelier du Theatre d'Orsay; Lighting, Genevieve Soubirou; Sound, Carlos D'Alessio; Settings and Costumes Supervisor, Mason Arvold; Lighting Supervisor, Martin Aronstein; Wardrobe Master, Sam Elterman; Management, Seff Associates

### CAST

| | |
|---|---|
| The Mother | Madeleine Renaud |
| The Son (Jacques) | Jean-Pierre Aumont |
| Marcelle | Francoise Dorner |
| Bartender | Jean Martin |

A drama in 3 acts and 4 scenes performed in French. The action takes place at the present time during spring in Paris in a two room apartment, on the street, and in a nightclub.

*General Management:* McCann & Nugent
*Press:* Michael Alpert, Marilynn LeVine, Warren Knowlton, Carl Samrock, Randi Cone
*Stage Manager:* Dominique Ehlinger

* Closed May 15, 1976 after limited engagement of 12 performances.

*Ivan Farkas Photos*

**Madeleine Renaud, Jean-Pierre Aumont**

**Jean Martin, Francoise Dorner, Madeleine Renaud, Jean-Pierre Aumont**

**ETHEL BARRYMORE THEATRE**
Opened Thursday, May 13, 1976.*
Gladys Rackmil and Kennedy Center present:

# LEGEND

By Samuel Taylor; Director, Robert Drivas; Settings, Santo Loquasto; Costumes, Florence Klotz; Lighting, Thomas Skelton; Original Music, Dan Goggin; Title Song, Ronee Blakely; Production Supervisor, Larry Forde; Produced for the John F. Kennedy Center for the Performing Arts by Roger L. Stevens; Assistant to director, Tony DeSantis; Wardrobe Supervisor, Warren Morrill; Hairstylist, Lyn Quiyou; Production Assistants, Elicia Rinaldi, Stacey Ralph

### CAST

| | |
|---|---|
| Quince | Robert Anthony |
| Tumbleweed | James Carrington |
| Alkali | Ben Slack |
| Barney-One-Ball | Ron Max |
| Mahogany Brown | Chev Rodgers |
| Muley | Munson Hicks |
| Kettle-Belly | Bill McIntyre |
| William F. P. Morgan | George Dzundza |
| "Doc" Jesse Lymburner | F. Murray Abraham |
| Judah Lymburner | George Parry |
| Betsy-No-Name | Elizabeth Ashley |
| Virgil Biggers (Colorado) | Stephen Clarke |
| Frankie Scruggs | Wayne Maxwell |
| Freddie Scruggs | Sebastian Stuart |
| Lacy Underwood/McNally | J. J. Quinn |
| Clarence/A Stranger | Tom Flagg |

UNDERSTUDIES: Betsy, Tricia O'Neil; Doc, Robert Anthony; Virgil, James Carrington; Morgan, Ben Slack; Quince, Tumbleweed, Muley, Lacy Underwood, McNally, Clarence, Valentine Mayer; Alkali, Barney, Mahogany, Kettle-Belly, Frankie, Freddie, John Stewart; Stranger, J. J. Quinn; Judah, Donald Kehr

A romantic comedy in two acts. The action takes place somewhere in Western America, somewhere in the past.

*General Management:* Gatchell & Neufeld, Drew Murphy
*Press:* Betty Lee Hunt, Maria Cristina Pucci, Maurice Turet
*Stage Managers:* Valentine Mayer, John Stewart

\* Closed May 16, 1976 after 5 performances and 18 previews.

*Ron Reagan, Kramer-Abeles Photos*

**Top: Stephen Clarke, (R) Elizabeth Ashley,**
**F. Murray Abraham**

**Sebastian Stuart, Elizabeth Ashley**
**Above: Elizabeth Ashley**

57

**THE LITTLE THEATRE**
Opened Tuesday, May 18, 1976.*
Wayne Adams and Willard Morgan by special arrangement
with the Hartman Theatre Company present:

# THE RUNNER STUMBLES

By Milan Stitt; Director, Austin Pendleton; Set, Patricia Woodbridge; Costumes, James Berton Harris; Lighting, Cheryl Thacker

### CAST

| | |
|---|---|
| Amos | Morrie Piersol |
| Father Rivard | Stephen Joyce |
| Erna Prindle | Katina Commings |
| Toby Felker | James Noble |
| Sister Rita | Nancy Donohue |
| Mrs. Shandig | Sloane Shelton |
| Prosecutor | Craig Richard Nelson |
| Monsignor Nicholson | Joseph Mathewson |
| Louise | Marilyn Pfeiffer |

UNDERSTUDIES: David Lile for male roles; Monica Guglielmina
for Erna, Louise, Mrs. Shandig; Marilyn Pfeiffer for Sister Rita

A drama in two acts. The action takes place in a cell and court-
room in Solon, Michigan, during April of 1911.

*General Management:* Dorothy Olim Associates, Thelma Cooper,
Amy Idell Gitlin
*Press:* Howard Atlee, Clarence Allsopp, Becky Flora
*Stage Managers:* Peggy Peterson, David Lile

* Still playing May 31, 1976.

*Bert Andrews Photos*

**Above: Nancy Donohue, Stephen Joyce**
**Top: James Noble, Joyce,**
**(R) Katina Commings, Joyce**

**Craig Richard Nelson, Marilyn Pfeiffer**
**Above: Sloane Shelton, Stephen Joyce**

Opened Thursday, May 27, 1976.*

Emanuel Azenberg, Dasha Epstein, John Mason Kirby present:

# SOMETHING'S AFOOT

Book, Music, Lyrics by James McDonald, David Vos, Robert Gerlach; Additional Music, Ed Linderman; Directed and Choreographed by Tony Tanner; Scenery, Richard Seger; Costumes, Walter Watson, Clifford Capone; Lighting, Richard Winkler; Musical Director, Buster Davis; Orchestrator, Peter M. Larson; Production Associate, Peter Sanders; Music Coordinator, Earl Shendell; Sound, Robert Weeden; Wardrobe Supervisor, Sydney Smith

### CAST

| | |
|---|---|
| Lettie | Neva Small |
| Flint | Marc Jordan |
| Clive | Sel Vitella |
| Hope Langdon | Barbara Heuman |
| Dr. Grayburn | Jack Schmidt |
| Nigel Rancour | Gary Beach |
| Lady Grace Manley-Prowe | Liz Sheridan |
| Colonel Gillweather | Gary Gage |
| Miss Tweed | Tessie O'Shea |
| Geoffrey | Willard Beckham |

STANDBYS: Miss Tweed, Lady Grace, Lu Leonard; Gillweather, Grayburn, Flint, Clive, Bryan Hull; Nigel, Geoffrey, Sal Mistretta; Hope, Lettie, Meg Bussert

MUSICAL NUMBERS: "A Marvelous Weekend," "Something's Afoot," "Carry On," "I Don't Know Why I Trust You But I Do," "The Man with the Ginger Mustache," "Suspicious," "Legal Heir," "You Fell Out of the Sky," "Dinghy," "I Owe It All," "New Day"

A musical mystery in two acts. The action takes place during the late spring of 1935 in Rancour's Retreat: a country estate in the English lake district.

*General Manager:* Marvin A. Krauss
*Company Manager:* Robert Frissell
*Press:* Merlin Group, Sandra Manley, Harriett Trachtenberg, Ron Harris
*Stage Managers:* Marilyn Witt, Sal Mistretta

Closed July 18, 1976 after 61 performances and 13 previews.

*Ken Howard Photos*

**Right: Willard Beckham, Barbara Heuman**
**Top: Marc Jordan, Liz Sheridan, Gary Gage, Tessie O'Shea, Neva Small, Gary Beach, Barbara Heuman, Willard Beckham, Sel Vitella, Jack Schmidt**

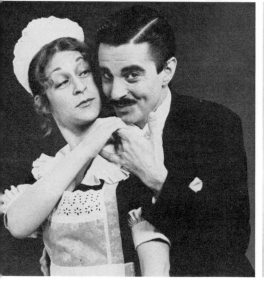

Neva Small, Gary Beach

Tessie O'Shea

**EDEN THEATRE**
Opened Monday, February 14, 1972*
(Moved June 7, 1972 to Broadhurst Theatre, November 21, 1972 to Royale Theatre) Kenneth Waissman and Maxine Fox in association with Anthony D'Amato present:

# GREASE

Book, Music and Lyrics, Jim Jacobs, Warren Casey; Director, Tom Moore; Musical numbers and dances staged by Patricia Birch; Musical Supervision and orchestrations, Michael Leonard; Musical Direction-Vocal and Dance Arrangements, Louis St. Louis; Scenery, Douglas W. Schmidt; Costumes, Carrie F. Robbins; Lighting, Karl Eigsti; Sound, Bill Merrill; Hairstyles, Jim Sullivan; Assistant to Producers, Barbara Jean Block; Production Assistants, Pinocchio Madrid, Carolyn Ciplet; Original Cast Album, MGM Records; General Management, Theatre Now Inc.; Production Supervisor, T. Schuyler Smith

### CAST

| | |
|---|---|
| Miss Lynch | Dorothy Leon†1 |
| Patty Simcox | Ilene Kristen†2 |
| Eugene Florczyk | Tom Harris†3 |
| Jan | Garn Stephens†4 |
| Marty | Katie Hanley†5 |
| Betty Rizzo | Adrienne Barbeau†6 |
| Doody | James Canning†7 |
| Roger | Walter Bobbie†8 |
| Kenickie | Timothy Meyers†9 |
| Sonny LaTierri | Jim Borelli†10 |
| Frenchy | Marya Small†11 |
| Sandy Dumbrowski | Carole Demas†12 |
| Danny Zuko | Barry Bostwick†13 |
| Vince Fontaine | Don Billett†14 |
| Johnny Casino | Alan Paul†15 |
| Cha-Cha DiGregorio | Kathi Moss |
| Teen Angel | Alan Paul†15 |

UNDERSTUDIES: Shelley Barre, Adele Paige, John Fennessy, Ted Wass, Frank Piegaro

MUSICAL NUMBERS: "Alma Mater," "Summer Nights," "Those Magic Changes," "Freddy, My Love," "Greased Lightnin'," "Mooning," "Look at Me, I'm Sandra Dee," "We Go Together," "Shakin' at the High School Hop," "It's Raining on Prom Night," "Born to Hand-Jive," "Beauty School Dropout," "Alone at a Drive-in Movie," "Rock 'n' Roll Party Queen," "There Are Worse Things I Could Do," "All Choked Up," Finale.

A rock musical in two acts and twelve scenes. The action takes place in the late 1950's.

*General Manager:* Edward H. Davis
*Press:* Betty Lee Hunt, Maria Cristina Pucci
*Company Managers:* Robb Lady, Camille Ranson
*Stage Managers:* Lynne Guerra, Michael Martorella, John Fennessy

* Still playing May 31, 1976. For original production, see THEATRE WORLD, Vol. 28.
† Succeeded by: 1. Sudie Bond, Ruth Russell, 2. Joy Rinaldi, Carol Culver, 3. Barrey Smith, Stephen Van Benschoten, Lloyd Alann, 4. Jamie Donnelly, Randee Heller, Rebecca Gilchrist, Mimi Kennedy, 5. Meg Bennett, Denise Nettleton, Marilu Henner, Char Fontane, Diane Stilwell, 6. Elaine Petricoff, Randee Heller, Livia Genise, 7. Barry J. Tarallo, 8. Richard Quarry, John Driver, Ray DeMattis, Michael Tucci, 9. John Fennessy, Jerry Zaks, Michael Tucci, 10. Matt Landers, Albert Insinnia, 11. Ellen March, Joy Rinaldi, Jill P. Rose, 12. Ilene Graff, Candice Earley, 13. Jeff Conaway, John Lansing, Lloyd Alann, 14. Jim Weston, John Holly, Walter Charles, 15. Bob Garrett, Philip Casnoff, Joe Rifici, Philip Casnoff, Frank Piegaro

**Top Right: Candice Earley (C)**

**Mimi Kennedy, Ellen March, Karren Dille**

Opened Monday, October 23, 1972.*
Stuart Ostrow presents:

# PIPPIN

Book, Roger O. Hirson; Music and Lyrics, Stephen Schwartz; Direction and Choreography, Bob Fosse; Scenery, Tony Walton; Costumes, Patricia Zipprodt; Lighting, Jules Fisher; Musical Direction, Rene Wiegert; Orchestrations, Ralph Burns; Dance Arrangements, John Berkman; Sound, Abe Jacob; Hair Styles, Ernest Adler, James Amaral; Original Cast Album, Motown Records; Wardrobe Supervisor, A. T. Karniewich

### CAST

Leading Player .......................... Ben Vereen†1
Pippin .............................. John Rubinstein†2
Charles ..................................... Eric Berry
Lewis ............................ Christopher Chadman†3
Fastrada ............................. Leland Palmer†4
Musician/Swordbearer ..................... John Mineo†5
The Head .......................... Roger Hamilton
Berthe .............................. Irene Ryan†6
Beggar ............................ Richard Korthaze†7
Peasant ................................ Paul Solen†8
Noble ................................ Gene Foote†9
Field Marshall .......................... Roger Hamilton
Catherine ........................... Jill Clayburgh†10
Theo .............................. Shane Nickerson†11

UNDERSTUDIES AND STANDBYS: Pippin, Dean Pitchford; Leading Player, Quitman Fludd III; Berthe, Dortha Duckworth; Catherine, Verna Pierce; Theo, Evan Turtz; Charles, Roger Hamilton; Gastrada, Patti D'Beck; Dance Alternates, Jill Owens, Roger Bigelow, Eileen Casey

MUSICAL NUMBERS: "Magic to Do," "Corner of the Sky," "Welcome Home," "War Is a Science," "Glory," "Simple Joys," "No Time at All," "With You," "Spread a Little Sunshine," "Morning Glow," "On the Right Track," "Kind of Woman," "Extraordinary," "Love Song," Finale

A musical in eight scenes, performed without intermission. The action takes place in 780 A.D. and thereabouts, in the Holy Roman Empire and thereabouts.

General Managers: Joseph Harris, Ira Bernstein
Company Manager: Nancy Simmons
Press: Solters/Roskin, Milly Schoenbaum, Nini Finkelstein
Stage Managers: Lola Shumlin, John H. Lowe III, Herman Magidson, Andy Keyser

Still playing May 31, 1976. For original production, see THEATRE WORLD, Vol. 29.
Succeeded by: 1. Northern Calloway, Samuel E. Wright, Irving Lee, Ben Harney, 2. Dean Pitchford, Michael Rupert, 3. Justin Ross, Jerry Colker, 4. Priscilla Lopez, Patti Karr, Antonia Ellis, 5. Ken Urmston, 6. Lucie Lancaster, Dorothy Stickney, Fay Sappington, 7. Larry Merritt, Roger Bigelow, Ken Miller, 8. Chet Walker, 9. Larry Giroux, Bryan Nicholas, 10. Betty Buckley, Joy Franz, 11. Douglas Grober

**Michael Rupert (C)**

**Michael Rupert, Joy Franz Top: Ben Harney (C)**

CORT THEATRE
Opened Tuesday, May 28, 1974.*
Edgar Lansbury, Joseph Beruh, Ivan Reitman present:

# THE MAGIC SHOW

Book, Bob Randall; Songs, Stephen Schwartz; Magic, Doug Henning; Direction and Dances, Grover Dale; Setting, David Chapman; Costumes, Randy Barcelo; Lighting, Richard Nelson; Musical Director, Stephen Reinhardt; Dance Arrangements, David Spangler; Assistant to Director, Jay Fox; Associate Producer, Nan Pearlman; Audio Design, Phil Ramone; Assistant to Producers, Jo Marie Wakefield; Wardrobe Supervisor, Virginia Sylvain; Production Assistants, Sam Cristensen, Darrell Jonas, Walter Wood

## CAST

| | |
|---|---|
| Manny | Robert LuPone†1 |
| Feldman | David Ogden Stiers†2 |
| Donna | Annie McGreevey†3 |
| Dina | Cheryl Barnes†4 |
| Cal | Dale Soules |
| Doug | Doug Henning†5 |
| Mike | Ronald Stafford |
| Steve | Loyd Sannes†6 |
| Charmin | Anita Morris†7 |
| Goldfarb | Sam Schacht |

STANDBYS AND UNDERSTUDIES: Doug, Jeffrey Mylett; Cal, Donna, Bailie Gerstein; Charmin, Dina, Sharron Miller; Feldman, Goldfarb, Garnett Smith; Mike, Steve, Robert Brubach; Manny, Jay Fox, Christopher Lucas

MUSICAL NUMBERS: "Up to His Old Tricks," "Solid Silver Platform Shoes," "Lion Tamer," "Style," "Charmin's Lament," "Two's Company," "Goldfarb Variations," "Doug's Act," "A Bit of Villainy," "West End Avenue," "Sweet, Sweet, Sweet," "Before Your Very Eyes"

A magic show with music performed without intermission.

*General Management:* Marvin A. Krauss Associates
*Company Manager:* Gary Gunas
*Press:* Gifford/Wallace, Tom Trenkle, Glenna Freedman
*Stage Managers:* Herb Vogler, Jay Fox, John Actman

* Still playing May 31, 1976. For original production, see THEATRE WORLD, Vol. 30.
† Succeeded by: 1. Clifford Lipson, 2. Kenneth Kimmins, Timothy Jerome, 3. Lisa Raggio, 4. Lynne Thigpen, 5. Jeffrey Mylett, Joseph Abaldo, during vacation, 6. T. Michael Reed, Christopher Lucas, 7. Loni Ackerman

**Doug Henning Top Right: Henning, Dale Soules, Timothy Jerome
Right Center: Cliff Lipson, Robert Brubach, Loni Ackerman, Ronald Stafford**

PLYMOUTH THEATRE
Opened Thursday, October 24, 1974.*
Kermit Bloomgarden and Doris Cole Abrahams in association
with Frank Milton present:

# EQUUS

By Peter Shaffer; Director, John Dexter; Scenery and Costumes,
John Napier; Lighting, Andy Phillips; Sound, Marc Wilkinson;
Mime, Claude Chagrin; American Supervision of Scenery and Lighting, Howard Bay; Costumes, Patricia Adshead; Production Assistant, Scott Rudin; Wardrobe Supervisor, Eric Harrison; Assistant to
the Director, Gabriel Oshen; American Supervision of Mime, Peter
Lobdell

## CAST

Martin Dysart ....................... Anthony Hopkins[1]
Alan Strang ............................. Peter Firth[2]
Nurse ................................. Mary Doyle[3]
Hesther Salomon ........................ Marian Seldes[4]
Frank Strang ........................... Michael Higgins[5]
Dora Strang ........................... Frances Sternhagen[6]
Horseman/Nugget ....................... Everett McGill[7]
Harry Dalton .......................... Walter Mathews[8]
Jill Mason ........................... Roberta Maxwell[9]
Horses .......... Gus Kaikkoen, Philip Kraus, Gabriel Oshen,
David Ramsey, John Tyrrell[10]

STANDBYS AND UNDERSTUDIES: Dysart, Alan Mixon; Da-
vid Leary; Alan, Thomas Hulce, Jacob Milligan, Dennis Erdman;
Frank, Don Plumley, Page Johnson; Dora, Hesther, Mary Doyle;
Jill, Nurse, Dale Hodges, Betsy Beard; Harry, Horseman, Philip
Kraus, Jeffrey David Pomerantz, William Wright; Horses, Michael
Wieben, Terence Burk

A Drama in two acts. The action takes place in Rokeby Psychiatric Hospital in Southern England at the present time.

*General Manager:* Max Allentuck
*Press:* John Springer Associates, Louis Sica
*Stage Managers:* Robert L. Borod, Nicholas Russiyan, Michael
Wieben, Barry Kearsley, Peter Lobdell, Brent Peek, William
Schill, Terence Burk

* Closed Sept. 11, 1976 after 781 performances and 10 previews.
Winner of 1975 Best Play awards from New York Drama Critics
Circle, "Tony," Drama Desk, New York Outer Critics, also
"Tony" and Drama Desk awards for Best Director. For original
production, see THEATRE WORLD, Vol. 31.
† Succeeded by: 1. Anthony Perkins, Richard Burton, 2. Thomas
Hulce, Jacob Milligan, Keith McDermott, 3. Catherine Byers, 4.
Louise Troy, 5. Page Johnson, 6. Marian Seldes, 7. David Combs,
William Wright, 8. Don Plumley, Page Johnson, Richard Neilson,
9. Jeanne Ruskin, Betsy Beard, 10. John David, Peter Lobdell,
Gary Faga, Jeffrey David Pomerantz, Gregory Salata, William
Wright, Terence Burk

*Van Williams Photos*

**Top Right: Anthony Perkins, Thomas Hulce,
Everett McGill Below: Keith McDermott,
Richard Burton**

Frances Sternhagen, Michael Higgins, Richard Burton

Anthony Perkins, Frances Sternhagen

**MAJESTIC THEATRE**
Opened Sunday, January 5, 1975.*
Ken Harper presents:

# THE WIZ

Book, William F. Brown; Based on L. Frank Baum's "The Wonderful Wizard of Oz"; Music and Lyrics, Charlie Smalls; Direction and Costumes, Geoffrey Holder; Setting, Tom H. John; Lighting, Tharon Musser; Orchestrations, Harold Wheeler; Musical Direction and Vocal Arrangements, Charles H. Coleman; Dance Arrangements, Timothy Graphenreed; Choreography and Musical Numbers Staged by George Faison; Wardrobe Supervisor, Yvonne Stoney; Assistant to Choreographer and Dance Captain, John Parks; Music Coordinator, Earl Shendell; Wigs, Stanley James; Original Cast Album by Atlantic Records.

### CAST

| | |
|---|---|
| Aunt Em | Tasha Thomas†1 |
| Toto | Nancy |
| Dorothy | Stephanie Mills |
| Uncle Henry | Ralph Wilcox†2 |
| Tornado | Evelyn Thomas†3 |
| Munchkins | Phylicia Ayers-Allen†4, Pi Douglass†5 Joni Palmer†6, Andy Torres†7, Carl Weaver |
| Addaperle | Clarice Taylor |
| Yellow Brick Road | Ronald Dunham, Eugene Little, John Parks †8, Kenneth Scott |
| Scarecrow | Hinton Battle |
| Crows | Wendy Edmead, Frances Morgan, Thea Nerissa Barnes |
| Tinman | Tiger Haynes |
| Lion | Ted Ross†9 |
| Kalidahs | Philip Bond†10, Pi Douglass†11, Rodney Green†12, Evelyn Thomas†13, Andy Torres†14 |
| Poppies | Lettie Battle †15, Leslie Butler, Eleanor McCoy†16, Frances Morgan, Joni Palmer†17 |
| Field Mice | Phylicia Ayers-Allen, Pi Douglass, Carl Weaver, Ralph Wilcox |
| Gatekeeper | Danny Beard†18 |
| The Wiz | Andre De Shields†19 |
| Evillene | Mabel King†20 |
| Lord High Underling | Ralph Wilcox†2 |
| Soldier Messenger | Carl Weaver |
| Winged Monkey | Andy Torres†21 |
| Glinda | Dee Dee Bridgewater†22 |

EMERALD CITY CITIZENS: Thea Nerissa Barnes, Pat Estwick, Leslie Butler, Wendy Edmead, Lois Hayes, Keith Harris, Alvin McDuffie, Frances Morgan, Claudia Lewis, Ronald Dunham, Rodney Green, Eugene Little, Kenneth Scott, Alwin Taylor

PIT SINGERS: Robert Benjamin, DeMarest Grey, Sam Harkness, Jozella Reed, Hanyse M. Singleton

UNDERSTUDIES: Tin Man, Kwame Johnson; Lion, Toney Watkins; Scarecrow, Carl Weaver; Addaperle, Evelline, Ruth Brisbane; Wiz, Kenneth Scott; Glinda, Janyse M. Singleton; Aunt Em, Deborah Burrell; Dorothy, Renee Harris, Pat Estwick

MUSICAL NUMBERS: "The Feeling We Once Had," "Tornado Ballet," "He's the Wizard," "Soon as I Get Home," "I Was Born on the Day before Yesterday," "Ease on down the Road," "Slide Some Oil to Me," "Mean Ole Lion," "Kalidah Battle," "Be a Lion," "Lion's Dream," "Emerald City Ballet," "So You Wanted to Meet the Wizard," "To Be Able to Feel," "No Bad News," "Funky Monkeys," "Everybody Rejoice," "Who Do You Think You Are?", "Believe in Yourself," "Y'All Got It!", "A Rested Body Is a Rested Mind," "Home"

A musical in 2 acts and 16 scenes, with a prologue.

*General Managers:* Emanuel Azenberg, Eugene V. Wolsk
*Manager:* Jose Vega
*Company Manager:* Susan Bell
*Press:* The Merlin Group, Sandra Manley, Elizabeth Rodman, Ron Harris
*Stage Managers:* Christopher Kelly, Bob Burland, Steven Shaw

\* Still playing May 31, 1976. For original production, see THEATRE WORLD, Vol. 31.
† Succeeded by: 1. Esther Marrow, 2. Al Fann, Toney Watkins, 3. Wendy Edmead, 4. Dyane Harvey, 5. Leslie Butler, 6. Lois Hayes, 7. Kwame Johnson, 8. Rodney Green, 9. James Wigfall, 10. Gregg Burge, 11. Keith Harris, 12. Alvin McDuffie, 13. Claudia Lewis, 14. Alwin Taylor, 15. Thea Nerissa Barnes, 16. Pat Estwick, 17. Lois Hayes, 18. Danny Beard, 19. Alan Weeks, 20. Edye Byrde, Theresa Merritt, 21. Keith Harris, 22. Deborah Burrell

*Martha Swope Photos*

Andre DeShields (c) Above: The Funky Monkey

**Top Right: Stephanie Mills, Hinton Battle, James Wigfall, Tiger Haynes (top)**

LVIN THEATRE
   Opened Tuesday, January 7, 1975.*
   Philip Rose, Gloria and Louis K. Sher present:

# SHENANDOAH

Book, James Lee Barrett, Peter Udell, Philip Rose; Music, Gary
eld; Lyrics, Peter Udell; Based on screenplay of same title by James
e Barrett; Scenery, C. Murawski; Lighting, Thomas Skelton; Cos-
mes, Pearl Somner, Winn Morton; Orchestrations, Don Walker;
usical Direction, Richard Parrinello; Dance Arrangements, Rus-
ll Warner; Choreography, Robert Tucker; Hairstylist, Werner
erer; Wardrobe Supervisor, Lee Decker; Production Assistant,
osemary Troyano; Original Cast Album by RCA Records

CAST

| | |
|---|---|
| harlie Anderson | John Cullum†7 |
| cob | Ted Agress |
| mes | Joel Higgins†1 |
| athan | Jordan Suffin |
| hn | David Russell |
| nny | Penelope Milford†2 |
| enry | Robert Rosen |
| obert (The Boy) | Joseph Shapiro†3 |
| ne | Donna Theodore |
| abriel | Chip Ford†4 |
| ev. Byrd | Charles Welch |
| m | Gordon Halliday |
| t. Johnson | Edward Penn |
| eutenant | Marshall Thomas |
| nkham | Charles Welch |
| arol | Casper Roos |
| orporal | Gary Harger |
| arauder | Gene Masoner |
| ngineer | Ed Preble†5 |
| onfederate Sniper | Craig Lucas†6 |

NSEMBLE: Tedd Carrere, Dennis Cooley, Stephen Dubov, Rich-
d Flanders, Kathleen Gordon, Gary Harger, David Cale Johnson,
obert Johanson, Sherry Lambert, Gene Masoner, Paul Myrvold,
an Ormond, Casper Roos, J. Kevin Scannell, Emily Bindiger, E.
llan Stevens, Marshall Thomas, Matt Gavin

NDERSTUDIES: Charlie, Edward Penn, Casper Roos; Jacob,
ene Masoner; Nathan, James, Paul Myrvold; John, Matt Gavin;
nny, Emily Bindiger; Henry, Dennis Cooley, Robert Johanson;
obert, Steve Grober; Anne, Kathleen Gordon; Gabriel, Donny
ooper; Byrd, Casper Roos; Sam, Richard Flanders; Johnson, Mar-
all Thomas; Lt., Tedd Carrere; Marauder, Tinkham, E. Allan
evens; Carol, J. Kevin Scannell; Engineer, Dan Ormond

USICAL NUMBERS: "Raise the Flag of Dixie," "I've Heard It
ll Before," "Pass the Cross to Me," "Why Am I Me," "Next to
ovin' I Like Fightin'," "Over the Hill," "The Pickers Are Comin',"
Meditation," "We Make a Beautiful Pair," "Violets and Silver-
lls," "It's a Boy," "Freedom," "Papa's Gonna Make It Alright,"
The Only Home I Know"

A musical in two acts with a prologue. The action takes place
uring the Civil War in the Shenandoah Valley of Virginia.

   General Manager: Helen Richards
      Press: Merle Debuskey, Leo Stern
Stage Managers: Steve Zweigbaum, Arturo E. Porazzi, Sherry
            Lambert

Still playing May 31, 1976. For original production, see THE-
ATRE WORLD, Vol. 31.
Succeeded by: 1. Wayne Hudgins, 2. Maureen Silliman, 3. Mark
Perman, 4. Bent Carter, David Vann, 5. E. Allan Stevens, 6.
Dennis Cooley, 7. William Chapman during vacation

*Friedman-Abeles Photos*

**Top Right: John Cullum, Donna Theodore**

**Donna Theodore, Chip Ford**

**BROOKS ATKINSON THEATRE**
Opened Thursday, March 13, 1975.*
Morton Gottlieb, Dasha Epstein, Edward L. Schuman, Palladium Productions present:

# SAME TIME, NEXT YEAR

By Bernard Slade; Director, Gene Saks; Scenery, William Ritman;
Costumes, Jane Greenwood; Lighting, Tharon Musser; Hairstylist,
Steve Atha; Associate producers, Ben Rosenberg, Warren Crane

CAST

Doris ................................... Ellen Burstyn†1
George ................................... Charles Grodin†2
          Standbys: Rochelle Oliver, Peter DeMaio

A comedy in two acts and six scenes. The action takes place in a
guest cottage of a country inn in Northern California from 1951 to
1975.

*General Manager:* Ben Rosenberg
*Company Manager:* Martin Cohen
*Press:* Solters & Roskin, Milly Schoenbaum
*Stage Managers:* Warren Crane, Kate Pollock

* Still playing May 31, 1976. For original production, see THE-
ATRE WORLD, Vol. 31.
† Succeeded by: 1. Joyce Van Patten, Loretta Swit, Sandy Dennis,
2. Conrad Janis, Ted Bessell

Joyce Van Patten, Conrad Janis

Ted Bessell, Sandy Dennis
Top: Loretta Swit, Ted Bessell

# BROADWAY PRODUCTIONS FROM OTHER YEARS THAT CLOSED THIS SEASON

| Title | Opened | Closed | Performances |
|---|---|---|---|
| Raisin | 10/18/73 | 12/8/75 | 847 |
| Candide | 3/8/74 | 1/4/76 | 740 |
| Absurd Person Singular | 10/8/74 | 3/6/76 | 591 |
| Sherlock Holmes | 1/12/75 | 1/4/76 | 479 |
| The Ritz | 1/20/75 | 1/4/76 | 398 |
| All Over Town | 12/29/74 | 7/20/75 | 233 |
| Rodgers & Hart | 5/13/75 | 8/16/75 | 108 |

# OFF BROADWAY PRODUCTIONS

**ELYSIAN PLAYHOUSE**
Opened Sunday, June 1, 1975.*
The Mufson Company presents:

## LAST OF THE RED HOT LOVERS

By Neil Simon; Director, Ken Mufson; Set, Shelly Gelfman;
Lighting, Joel Levine

### CAST

| | |
|---|---|
| Barney Cashman | Douglas Andros |
| Elaine Navazio | Faye Cameron |
| Bobbi Michele | Elizabeth Sanders |
| Jeanette Fisher | Madlyn Cates |

A comedy in three acts. The action takes place at the present time
in New York's East Thirties.

*Stage Manager:* Jeff Buchman

\* Closed June 15, 1975 after limited engagement of 15 performances.

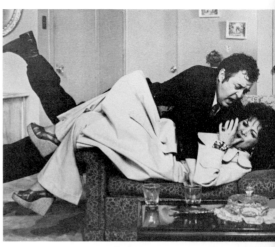

"Last of the Red Hot Lovers" (also left)

Pamela Burrell

Christopher Reeve

**STAGE 73**
Opened Tuesday, June 17, 1975.*
The Company Stage presents:

## BERKELEY SQUARE

By John L. Balderston; Director, Anthony Stimac; Set, David
Sackeroff; Costumes, Sydney Brooks, Dean H. Reiter; Lighting,
Clark W. Thornton; Music, Alan Rich; Coordinator, Joan M. Jeans;
Technical Director, Michael LaCourse; Assistant to producer, Alice
Gold; Wardrobe Supervisor, Virginia Merkel

### CAST

| | |
|---|---|
| Maid | Lynn Lobban |
| Tom Pettigrew | Munson Hicks |
| Kate Pettigrew | Robin Lane |
| Lady Anne Pettigrew | Beulah Garricks |
| Mr. Throstle | Peter Boyden |
| Helen Pettigrew | Claire Malis |
| Ambassador | Jonathan Moore |
| Mrs. Barwick | Lynne Hardy |
| Peter Standish | Christopher Reeve |
| Marjorie Frant | Joan Welles |
| Lord Stanley | Steve Lincoln |
| The Marquesa | Shanit Keter |
| Duchess of Devonshire | Pamela Burrell |
| Duke of Cumberland | James Brochu |

A play in three acts and seven scenes. The action takes place in
the morning room of a house of the Queen Anne period in Berkeley
Square, London, in the years 1784 and 1928.

*Press:* Anne Marie Borger
*Stage Managers:* Leslie Leonelli, Zoe Oka

\* Closed July 3, 1975 after limited engagement of 12 performances.
No photos available.

**JONES BEACH THEATRE**
Opened Friday, June 27, 1975.*
Guy Lombardo presents:

# OKLAHOMA!

Based on Lynn Riggs' play "Green Grow the Lilacs"; Book and Lyrics, Oscar Hammerstein 2nd; Music, Richard Rodgers; Director, John Fearnley; Choreographer, Robert Pagent; Scenery, John W. Keck; Costumes, Winn Morton; Lighting, Thomas Skelton; Musical Director, Jay Blackton; Entire production under the supervision of Arnold Spector; Wardrobe Mistress, Agnes Farrell; Assistant Conductor, Robert Stanley; Choral Director, Robert Monteil

### CAST

| | |
|---|---|
| Aunt Eller | Nancy Andrews |
| Curly | Thomas McKinney |
| Laurey | Judith McCauley |
| Ike Skidmore | Lee Cass |
| Slim | Stan Page |
| Will Parker | Harvey Evans |
| Jud Fry | Will Roy |
| Ado Annie Carnes | Patricia Masters |
| Ali Hakim | Bruce Adler |
| Gertie Cummings | Sherry Lambert |
| Andrew Carnes | John Dorrin |
| Cord Elam | Robert Pagent |
| Laurey in the ballet | Dru Alexandrine |
| Curly in the ballet | Jeremy Blanton |
| Jud in the ballett | Russell Anderson |

COWBOYS, FARMERS, TOWNSPEOPLE: Jean Busada, Mary-Pat Carey, Mona Elgh, Doris Galiber, Mickey Gunnersen, Sherry Lambert, Joyce McDonald, Kathleen Robey, Irma Rogers, Laurie Ann Scadura, Renee Spector, Dixie Stewart, Sara Swanson, Marsha Tamaroff, Candace Tovar, Deborah Dean Walker, Lisa Berg (Swing)
Russell Anderson, Baruch Blum, Donald Bonnell, Lawrence Scott Cahn, Peter Clark, Eugene Edwards, Paul Flores, Robert Monteil, Dale Muchmore, Michael Page, Stan Page, George Pesaturo, Rick Schneider, Timothy Smith, Ralph Vucci, Arthur Whitfield, Kevin Wilson, Edward Zimmerman, Tony Slez (Swing)

UNDERSTUDIES: Curly, Stan Page; Jud, Lee Cass; Laurey, Deborah Dean Walker; Will, Donald Bonnell; Aunt Eller, Irma Rogers; Ali, Robert Monteil; Ado Annie, Sherry Lambert: Cord, Tony Slez; Carnes, Peter Clark; Ike, Ralph Vucci; Slim, Kevin Wilson; Gertie, Candace Tovar

MUSICAL NUMBERS: Overture, "Oh, What a Beautiful Mornin'," "Surrey with the Fringe on Top," "Kansas City," "I Cain't Say No," "Many a New Day," "It's a Scandal! It's an Outrage!," "People Will Say We're in Love," "Pore Jud," "Lonely Room," "Out of My Dreams," "The Farmer and the Cowman," "All er Nothin'," "Oklahoma!, Finale

A musical in two acts. The action takes place in the Indian Territory, now Oklahoma, just after the turn of the century.

*Company Manager;* Sam Pagliaro
*Press:* Saul Richman, Fred Nathan
*Stage Managers:* Mortimer Halpern, Bernard Pollock, Stan Page, Tony Slez

* Closed Aug. 31, 1975

**Top: Harvey Evans (c)**

**Thomas McKinney, Judith McCauley**
**Above: Nancy Andrews, Patricia Masters**

LLY MUNK THEATRE
Opened Thursday, July 10, 1975.*
Moss Cooney and Pat Cooney present:

# THE LOVE DEATH PLAYS OF WILLIAM INGE

Director, Barbara Loden; Assistant to director, Ellen Sullivan
asey; Associate Producer, Barry Moss; Set, Kurt Lundell, Ronald
uBois; Costumes, Bessie Lou Kazoo; Lighting, Brett Landow-
ewis; Original Music, George Quincy; Sound, Stephen Gabis

## CAST

**ART I**
"Dialogue for Two Men"
erry ........................................ Jack Aaron
e .......................................... Lane Smith
"Midwestern Manic"
eorge ...................................... Morgan Donohue
arley Ffoulkes ............................ Lane Smith
arlene Ffoulkes .......................... Gayle Greene
ane ....................................... Judy Fields
"he Love Death"
ron ....................................... Lane Smith
The action takes place at the present time in New York.

Closed August 4, 1975 after limited engagement of 15 performances.
Opened Thursday, July 17, 1975.**

**ART II**
"Venus and Adonis"
ck/Gino ................................... Robert Giber
rs. Nell Fisher ........................... Janet Ward
"he Wake"
ther ...................................... Al Herter
ther ...................................... Janet Ward
ed ........................................ Joe Jamrog
on ........................................ Michael Nader
"he Star"
lia Richards .............................. Janet Ward
a ......................................... Molly McCarthy
The action takes place at the present time in New York.

*Press:* Michael Alpert, Anne Weinberg
*Stage Managers:* Winnie Whipple, Frank Levan

Closed August 4, 1975 after limited engagement of 12 performances.

*Peter Somogyi, Robertson Carricart Photos*

**Top Right: Judy Fields, Lane Smith**
**Below: Joe Jamrog, Michael Nader, Janet Ward**

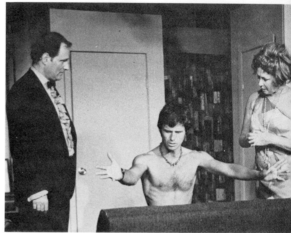

**entire cast of "Ivanov"**

CITY PLAYWORKS
Opened Thursday, August 14, 1975.*
ETC Theatre Company (Artistic Directors: Rae Allen, J. J.
Barry, Frank Bongiorno) in association with City Playworks
presents:

# IVANOV

By Anton Chekhov; Translated by Alex Szogyi; Director, Gus
Kaikkonen; Assistant Director, Linda Brumfield; Lighting, Richard
Winkler; Technical Director, James Larkin; Scenery, David George

## CAST

Nikolai Alexayevich Ivanov ................ William Sadler
Anna Petrovna ........................... Patricia Johnson
Matvyey Semyonovich .................. Warrington Winters
Pavel Kirilich Lyebedev ...................... Joe Endes
Zinaida Savishna ........................ Mary Ed Porter
Sasha ................................... Marilyn Pfeiffer
Yevgeny Kostantinovich Lvov ................ Ted Kubiak
Marfa Yegorovna Babakina .................. Susan Krebs
Dmitri Nikitich Kosich ................. Christopher Cara
Mikhail Mikhailovich Borkin ................ Robb Webb
Avdotya Nazarovna ................... Parker McCormick

A drama in four acts. The action takes place in 19th Century
Russia.

*Press:* Joshua Ellis
*Stage Manager:* David Semonin

* Closed Sept. 7, 1975 after 20 performances.

*Robb Webb Photos*

## ST. JOHN'S IN THE VILLAGE
Opened Thursday, August 14, 1975.*
Theater QED presents:

# MIME FOR A SUMMER NIGHT
# RICHARD MORSE
# PILAR GARCIA

Set, Carlos Delgado; Lighting, Lyn Corno; Technical Director, Mitchell Bogard; Costumes, Pamela Scofield; Assistant to Mr. Morse, Barbara Marks

*Stage Manager:* Mitchell Green

* Closed September 21, 1975 after limited engagement of 13 performances.

Opened Thursday, August 21, 1975.*
Theatre QED presents:

# SHAW FOR A SUMMER NIGHT

Director, Edward Townley; Assistant to director, Barbara Marks; Set, Carlos Delgado; Costume Coordinator, Shelly Friedman; Lighting and Technical Direction, Mitchell Bogard

### CAST

"Overruled"

| | |
|---|---|
| Mrs. Juno | Christine Lahti |
| Mr. Lunn | Thomas Wagner |
| Mrs. Lunn | Rasa Allen |
| Mr. Juno | Saylor Creswell |

The action takes place in 1912 in the garden of a seaside hotel.

"Village Wooing"

| | |
|---|---|
| A | Richmond Hoxie |
| B | Mary Shelley |

The action takes place aboard the Empress of Patagonia in January of 1932, and in a village shop in the Wiltshire Downs.

*Press:* Bud Westman, Sheldon Jacobs, Lyn Corno
*Stage Manager:* Mitchell Green

* Closed Sept. 20, 1975 after limited engagement of 12 performances

Pilar Garcia, Richard Morse

## ACTORS PLAYHOUSE
Opened Wednesday, September 17, 1975.*
Edith O'Hara in association with Lee Barton and Christophe Larkin presents:

# BOY MEETS BOY

Book, Bill Solly and Donald Ward; Music and Lyrics, Bill Soll; Director, Ron Troutman; Scenery and Lighting, David Sackero; Musical Direction and Vocal Arrangements, David Friedman; Music and Dance Arrangements, James Fradrich; Costumes, Share Buchs; Musical Numbers Staged by Robin Reseen; Piano, Jim Fradrich; Electric Keyboards, Dylan Hartman

### CAST

| | |
|---|---|
| Casey O'Brien | Joe Barre |
| Andrew | Paul Ratkevic |
| Guy Rose | David Galleg |
| Bellboy/Alphonse | Bobby Bowe |
| Reporters | Richard King, Bobby Reed, Dan Roun |
| Photographers | Jan Crean, Monica Grign |
| The Van Wagners | Bobby Bowen, Kathy Willing |
| Clarence Cutler | Raymond Wo |
| Lady Rose/Josephine LaRosa | Rita Gorde |
| Bruce | Bobby Re |
| Head Waiter | David Gui |
| Assistant Hotel Manager/Porter | Richard Ki |
| Rosita | Kathy Willing |
| Lolita | Mary-Ellen Hanl |
| Pepita | Jan Cre |

MUSICAL NUMBERS: "Boy Meets Boy," "Giving It Up f Love," "Me," "English Rose," "Marry an American," "It's a Bo Life," "Does Anybody Love You?," "You're Beautiful," "Let Dance," "Just My Luck," "It's a Dolly," "What Do I Care? "Clarence's Turn," Finale

A musical in two acts. The action takes place in London and Pa during December of 1936.

*General Manager:* Jim Payne
*Press:* Sol Jacobson, Lewis Harmon
*Stage Managers:* Gene Borio, David Guinn

* Still playing May 31, 1976.

*Joe Neumeyer Photos*

### Joe Barrett, David Gallegly

70

ANDAM THEATRE
Opened Thursday, September 11, 1975.*
Bari & Bennett Productions presents:

## M. GORKY: A PORTRAIT
### by
## MICHAEL A. DEL MEDICO

Written and Directed by Michael A. Del Medico; Production and
ostume Design, L. Bari; Lighting, Joy Lilly; Sound Technician, P.
randstein

Presented in four parts, each depicting another aspect of Gorky's
e from early childhood to his last years.

*General Manager:* J. Bennett

Closed Oct. 5, 1975 after limited engagement of 16 performances.
*Irene Fertik Photos*

ARYMOUNT MANHATTAN COLLEGE
Opened Friday, September 19, 1975.*
Marymount Manhattan College in association with BPS
presents:

## THE CAST AWAYS

Book and Direction, Anthony J. Stimac; Music, Don Pippin;
yrics, Steve Brown; Sets and Lighting, Clarke W. Thornton; Cos-
mes, Dean Reiter;Choreography, Gene Kelton; Musical Director,
, Bishop; Hairstylist, Vincent Prestia; Technical Director, Ken
erkel; Production Assistant, Rick Ladson

### CAST

| | |
|---|---|
| r. Warren/Jasper/Indian | Reid Shelton |
| rs. Warren/Christine | Marie Santell |
| r. Cooke/Jerry/Pendragon/General | Peter Boyden |
| rs. Cooke/LaRole | Patti Perkins |
| r. Lewis/Capt. Lenox | Dennis Howard |
| rs. Lewis/Adela | Sydney Blake |
| he Mate | Gibby Brand |
| rate Captain | Hank Berrings |

USICAL NUMBERS: "All the World's a Hold," "I Won't Love
Soldier Boy," "The Chase," "Let's Mop Up These Yankees and
o Back Home," "Bring Out Old Glory," "My Love," "She Would
a Soldier," "Whipperwill," "Call Back the Times," "If I Had
ings," "Isn't She," "This Dawn"

A pirate musical in two acts. The action takes place in 1819 in the
ld of a Barbary pirate ship somewhere in the Mediterranean.

*Stage Managers:* Clarke W. Thornton, Michael LaCourse

Closed Sept. 28, 1975 after limited engagement of 12 performances.

**Michael A. Del Medico**

**Peter MacLean, Valerie French, Eulalie Noble**

THEATRE DE LYS
Opened Monday, September 29, 1975.*
Rudi Golyn and Lee D. Sankowich present:

## FINN MACKOOL THE GRAND DISTRACTION

By Frank Hogan; Director, Lee D. Sankowich; Scenery, David
Chapman; Costumes, Jane Greenwood; Lighting, Richard Nelson;
Sound, Abe Jacob; Visual Projections, Jack Coddington; Wardrobe
Mistress, Evelyn Seubert; Technical Director, Jack Magnifico

### CAST

| | |
|---|---|
| Ossian | Michael J. Hume |
| Dark Marion | Valerie French |
| Mother Finn MacKool | Eulalie Noble |
| Vonner | Peter MacLean |
| Janna | Patti Walker |
| Father Finn MacKool | William Hickey |

A play in two acts and eight scenes.

*General Manager:* Leonard A. Mulhern
*Company Manager:* David Relyea
*Press:* Howard Atlee, Clarence Allsopp, Meg Gordean, Becky
Flora
*Stage Managers:* Paul Bennett, Lynn Gutter

* Closed Sept. 29, 1975 after one performance.

*Ken Howard Photos*

## EDEN THEATRE

Opened Sunday, October 12, 1975.*
Harry Rothpearl and Jewish Nostalgic Productions, Inc.,-
present:

# THE FIFTH SEASON

Adapted by Luba Kadison from the play of the same name by
Sylvia Regan; Music and Lyrics, Dick Manning; Director, Joseph
Buloff; Musical Director, Renee Solomon; Sets and Costumes, Jeff-
rey B. Moss; Lighting, Bob McCarthy; Yiddish Adaptation of Lyr-
ics, Isaac Dogim; Wardrobe Supervisor, Sylvia Friedlander;
Hairstylist, Jerry of Bergdorf's.

### CAST

| | |
|---|---|
| Mr. Katz | Elias Patron |
| Shelly | Gerri-Ann Frank |
| Laurie | Raquel Yossiffon |
| Perl | David Carey |
| Max Pincus | Joseph Buloff |
| Benny Goodwin | Stan Porter |
| Frances Goodwin | Evelyn Kingsley |
| Marty Goodwin | Gene Barrett |
| Miriam Oppenheim | Miriam Kressyn |
| Mr. Lewis | Jack Rechtzeit |
| Models | Franceska Fishler, Cathy Carnevale, Barbara Joan Frank |

MUSICAL NUMBERS: "Believe in Yourself," "My Son, the Doctor," "Goodbye," "The Fifth Season," "Friday Night," "Mom! You
Don't Understand!," "How Did This Happen to Me," "From Seventh Avenue to Seventh Heaven"

A musical in two acts and six scenes. The action takes place at the
present time in a Seventh Avenue fashion showroom.

*General Manager:* Seymour Rexite
*Press:* Max Eisen, Judy Jacksina, Barbara Glenn
*Stage Manager:* Jay S. Hoffman

**Top Right: Joseph Buloff, Miriam Kressyn**
**Below: Joseph Buloff, Stan Porter, Evelyn**
**Kingsley**

## THEATRE AT MAMA GAILS

Opened Wednesday, October 22, 1976.*
Theatre at Mama Gails presents:

# MEN WOMEN
## and Why It Won't Work

Book, June Siegel, Miriam Fond; Music, David Warrack; Lyrics,
June Siegel; Direction and Choreography, Miriam Fond; Musical
Direction and Arrangements, John R. Williams; Set, Dan Leigh;
Costumes, Danny Morgan; Lighting, Deanna Greenwood; Pro-
ducer, Charles Leslie; Pianist, John R. Williams

### CAST

| | |
|---|---|
| Elaine Desmond | Ann Hodapp |
| Art Desmond | Arne Gundersen |
| Jill Callen | Leila Holiday |
| Al Callen | Charles Maggiore |
| Phyllis Gelman | Gail Oscar |
| Herb Kessler | Garrett M. Brown |
| Kay Windsor | Barbara Lea |

MUSICAL NUMBERS: "What Do We Do?," "Weekend at the
Club," "Brand New Wall-to-Wall Day," "Desire under the Elms-
ford Country Club Oaks," "Temporary Woman Blues," "Let's
Spend an Hour," "Have a Career," "It's Great to Be Single Again,"
"Background Music," "Morris," "Wild Kingdom," "Capitalist Be-
guine," "Lonely Woman," "Men Are Never Lonely," "It's Love! So
What?," "It's Really Easy Baking Bread," "Best of Both Possible
Worlds," "People Are Up for Grabs," "Faceless Clock," "Million
Fountain," "Take Me—Find Me," Finale

A musical in 2 acts and 15 scenes. The action takes place at the
present time in the city and the suburbs.

*Stage Managers:* Greg Husinko, Walter Ditman

* Closed Nov. 8, 1975 after limited engagement of 12 performances

**Barbara Lea, Leila Holiday, Garrett M. Brown,**
**Ann Hodapp, Charles Maggiore, Gail Oscar,**
**Arne Gundersen**

Opened Wednesday, October 29, 1975.*
Elliot Martin presents the Playhouse Square Production of:

# CONVERSATIONS WITH AN IRISH RASCAL

Adapted from the works of Brendan Behan by Kathleen Kennedy
th David O. Frazier; Director, Joseph J. Garry

CAST

DAVID O. FRAZIER
GUSTI

"A musical biography" of Brendan Behan performed in two parts.

*General Manager:* Leonard A. Mulhern
*Associate Manager:* David Relyea
*Press:* Frank Goodman, Seymour Krawitz, Arlene Wolf
Goodman, Barbara Carroll
*Stage Manager:* Paul Bennett

Closed Nov. 9, 1975 after 13 performances.

*Foto Arts Photo*

**Right: Gusti, David O. Frazier**

NEW YORK THEATER ENSEMBLE
Opened Wednesday, November 5, 1975.*
The New York Theater Ensemble (Lucille Talayco, Artistc
Director) presents:

# TANIA

Book, Mario Fratti; Music and Lyrics, Paul Dick; Director, Ron
Nash; Assistant Director, Rudy Garza; Lighting, David Andrews;
Costumes, John Reid, Dianne Charbonneau; Piano, Zelig Sokoll

CAST

| | |
|---|---|
| Walter | Walter George Alton |
| Ann | Marcy Olive |
| Mizzie | Norah Foster |
| Cynthia | Cynthia Haynes |
| Helen | Lee Torchia |
| Cinque | Dennis Jones |
| Bob | Norman Lewis |
| Akki | Akki Onyango |
| Diana | Jane Kerns |
| Lee | Marsha Bonine |

MUSICAL NUMBERS: "To Start a Revolution," "There'll Come
a Day," "Fire and Joy," "The American Dream," "I Sing Woman,"
"Man in a Cage," "Hail Alma Mater," "The Wall," "The Shoot
Out"

A musical in two acts.

*Stage Manager:* John Wickman

* Closed Dec. 14, 1975 after 30 performances,

*Elise Sokoll Photo*

Cynthia Haynes (top), Dennis Jones,
Walter George Alton, Marsha Bonine

## STAGE 73

Opened Wednesday, November 5, 1975.*
Catherine Ellis presents:

# AND SO TO BED

By J. B. Fagan; Director, Eugenie Leontovich; Sets, Kristine Haugan; Costumes, Patricia Britton; Lighting, Barry Arnold; Musical Arrangements and Supervision, Jason McAuliffe; Hairstylist, Louis Guarascio; Assistant to director, Nora Peterson

### CAST

| | |
|---|---|
| Jacke | Michael Oakes |
| Samuel Pepys | David MacEnulty |
| Doll | Pawnee Sills |
| Mrs. Knight | Ellen Farran |
| Julia | Jane Altman |
| Pelling | Christopher Wynkoop |
| Pelham Humfrey | Jason McAuliffe |
| Mrs. Pierce | Laura May Lewis |
| Mrs. Knepp | Sharon Talbot |
| Mrs. Pepys | Catherine Ellis |
| Lettice | Cam Kornman |
| Prodgers | Randall Robbins |
| Charles II | John Bergstrom |

A comedy in three acts. The action takes place in London a few days after the close of the Diary in June of 1669.

*General Manager:* Ashton Springer
*Press:* David Powers, William Schelble
*Stage Managers:* Peter Lawrence, Michael Oakes

* Closed Nov. 9, 1975 after 7 performances and 9 previews.

*Bert Andrews Photo*

**David MacEnulty, Ellen Farran**

**Gail Cook, John Neville-Andrews, Darrell Ziegler**

### WONDERHORSE

Opened Thursday, November 6, 1975.*
Wayne Adams in association with Willard Morgan and Michael Condon presents the Alive Theatre Production of:

# THE HOMECOMING

By Harold Pinter; Directed and Designed by Jack Chandler; Lighting, Darrell Ziegler; Costumes, Betty Martin; Music Designed by Gary Burke, Dede Washburn; Production Coordinator, Ken Shelby

### CAST

| | |
|---|---|
| Lenny | John Neville-Andrews |
| Max | Jack Eric Williams |
| Sam | Tim Cahill |
| Joey | Darrell Ziegler |
| Teddy | Brad Russell |
| Ruth | Gail Cook |

A play in two acts. The action takes place at the present time in an old house in the north of London in late summer.

*Press:* Howard Atlee, Clarence J. Allsopp, Meg Gordean, Becky Flora
*Stage Manager:* Victor Amerling

* Closed Nov. 14, 1975 after 8 performances and 7 previews.

*Bill McDonough Photo*

Opened Wednesday, November 12, 1975.*
The Chelsea Theater Center of Brooklyn (Robert Kalfin, Artistic Director; Michael David, Executive Director; Burl Hash, Productions Director) and Peter Witt present:

# THE FAMILY

By Lodewijk de Boer; Translated by Albert Maurita; Director, Barry Davis; Scenery, Lawrence King; Costumes, Jeanne Button; Lighting, Daniel Flannery; Videography, Alan Shulman and Mediatrics; Assistant to director, Eric Bogosian; Video and Sound, Michael Schaefer; Original Theme composed and performed by L. Joyce Hitchcock; Wardrobe Mistress, Melissa Adzima

### CAST

Play 1
Doc ........................................ David Selby
Kil ......................................... Brent Spiner
Gina ....................................... Dale Soules
Cabot ...................................... Joe Palmieri
Brigit ...................................... Diane Kagan

In 2 acts and 4 scenes.

Play 2
Gina ....................................... Dale Soules
Kil ......................................... Brent Spiner
Brigit ...................................... Diane Kagan
Doc ........................................ David Selby
Man ........................................ Ed Preble

In 2 acts and 5 scenes.

UNDERSTUDIES: Doc, Kil, Richmond Hoxie; Brigit, Gina, Lynn Ritchie; Man, Edward Seamon

The action takes place in Amsterdam, Holland, a few years ago.

*Press:* Betty Lee Hunt Associates, Bill Evans
*Stage Managers:* Julia Gillett, M. S. Andrews

* Closed Nov. 30, 1975 after 23 performances and 14 previews.

*Laura W. Pettibone Photos*

**David Selby, Dale Soules, Brent Spiner**

**Ed Kuczewski, Prima Stephen**

Opened Friday, November 14, 1975.*
The Fantasy Factory presents:

# A MASS MURDER IN THE BALCONY OF THE OLD RITZ-RIALTO

Book, Ed Kuczewski; Music and Lyrics, Bill Vitale; Musical Direction, Vocal Arrangements, Orchestrations, Dance Music, Leon Odenz; Director, Bill Vitale; Choreography, Martin Rivera; Additional Staging, Teddy Kern; Setting, Elmon Webb, Virginia Dancy; Lighting, Rick Claflin; Costumes and Hairstyles, Reve Richards; Additional Orchestrations, James Fradrich; Sound, Danny O'Neil, Richard Foltz

### CAST

Joseph Adorante, Linda Andrews, Marc Castle, Louise Claps, Bruno Damon, Joyce Griffen, Michael Kemmerling, Ed Kuczewski, Ethel A. Morgan, Joy Venus Morton, Joan Neuman, David Noh, Oliver Rish, Martin Rivera, Bob Santucci, Ray Shelton, Prima Stephen, Claudia Tompkins, LizaGrace Vachon-Coco, Paul Vanase, Steve Wadley, Louis Zippin

MUSICAL NUMBERS: "Shadow Song," "Slumming," "Homely Woman," "42nd Street," "Popcorn and Piss," "Dope," "Dope Rag," "Dope Double Time," "Let's All Go to the Lobby," "Musical Chairs," "I Got Rhythm Too," "The Old Days," "Sung-Fu," "Pictures and an Exhibition," "Savin' Souls," "Time to Go Home, Vernon," "Anybody Wanna Buy a Little Love," "Pink Lady," "The Comic," "When You're Shot in the Movies"

A musical performed without intermission.

*Stage Managers:* Theodore Pappas, Garry Cavanagh, Larry Brumer

* Closed Dec. 21, 1975 after 20 performances.

*Ken Howard Photo*

**WESTSIDE THEATER**
Opened Sunday, November 23, 1975.*
The Chelsea Theater Center of Brooklyn (Robert Kalfin, Artistic Director; Michael David, Executive Director; Burl Hash, Productions Director) presents:

# BY BERNSTEIN

Conceived by Betty Comden and Adolph Green with Michael Bawtree, Norman L. Berman and the Chelsea Theater Center; Music, Leonard Bernstein; Lyrics, Leonard Bernstein, Comden and Green, John Latouche, Jerry Leiber, Stephen Sondheim; Written by Betty Comden and Adolph Green; Director, Michael Bawtree; Scenery and Costumes, Lawrence King, Michael H. Yeargan; Lighting, Marc B. Weiss; Vocal Arrangements and Musical Direction, Clay Fullum; Orchestrations, Thomas Pierson; Assisting Director, Norman L. Berman; Production Assistants, Amy Fripp, Cindee Mayfield

CAST

Jack Bittner
Margery Cohen
Jim Corti
Ed Dixon
Patricia Elliott
Kurt Peterson
Janie Sell
Understudy: David Horwitz

MUSICAL NUMBERS: "Welcome," "Gabey's Comin'," "Lonely Me," "Say When," "Like Everybody Else," "I'm Afraid It's Love," "Another Love," "I Know a Fellow," "It's Gotta Be Bad to Be Good," "Dream with Me," "Ringaroundarosy," "Captain Hook's Soliloquy," "The Riobamba," "The Intermission's Great,""Story of My Life," "Ain't Got No Tears Left," "The Coolie's Dilemma," "In There," "Spring Will Come Again," "Here Comes the Sun"

A musical entertainment in two parts.

*Press:* Betty Lee Hunt Associates, Bill Evans
*Stage Managers:* Fred Reinglas, David Horwitz

* Closed Dec. 7, 1975 after 17 performances and 40 previews.

*Laura W. Pettibone Photos*

**Margery Cohen, Ed Dixon, Jim Corti,
Janie Sell, Patricia Elliott, Kurt Peterson**

**PLAYERS THEATRE**
Opened Monday, December 1, 1975.*
Wayne Clark and Joseph Tiraco in association with Larry Pontillo present:

# GIFT OF THE MAGI

Based on O. Henry's short story; Book, Music and Lyrics Ronnie Britton; Director, M. T. Knoblauh; Musical Direction Arrangements, James Fradrich; Setting, Michael Dulin; Costum Neil Cooper; Lighting, Jerryn Michaels; Production Coordina David M. Clark; Musical Supervisor, Tom Roberts; Hairsty Wendy Kaplan

CAST

Her .................................... Mary Saund
Della .................................... Paige O'H
Jim .................................... Bill Ma
Him .................................... William Brockme

MUSICAL NUMBERS: "Magi Waltz," "There You Go Agai "The Gift," "Della's Desire," "Mr. James Dillingham Youn "Day after Day," "Kids Are Out," "Sullivan Street Flat," "Bea ful Children," "You'd Better Tell Her," "Washington Square," " Tomorrow," "Quiet Morning," "Brave You," "A Penny Save "I've Got Something Better," "Pretty Lady," "He Did It, She I It!," "Make Him Think I'm Still Pretty," Finale

A musical in two acts. The action takes place in Greenwich V lage, New York City, during December of 1906.

*General Manager:* Wayne Clark
*Press:* Betty Lee Hunt Associates, Ted Goldsmith
*Stage Manager:* Schorling Schneider

* Closed Jan. 4, 1976 after 40 performances and 16 previews.

*Kenn Duncan Photo*

**Paige O'Hara, Mary Saunders,
William Brockmeier, Bill March**

Opened Monday, December 1, 1975.*
(Moved Friday, December 26, 1975 to Westside Theater) Jerry Schlossberg, Arch Lustberg, Bruce Nelson present:

# TUSCALOOSA'S CALLING ME ...
## but I'm not going!

Written by Bill Heyer, Hank Beebe, Sam Dann; Music, Hank eebe; Lyrics, Bill Heyer; Costumes, Rome Heyer; Musical Direc- r, Jeremy Harris; Audio, Donald P. Smith; Designed by Charles Hoefler; Staged and Directed by James Hammerstein and Gui ndrisano; Associate Manager, David Relyea; Associate Production anager, Dave Okarski

CAST
Len Gochman †1
Patti Perkins
Renny Temple†2

USICAL NUMBERS: "Only Right Here in New York City," "I ig Myself," "Cold Cash," "Things Were Out," "Central Park on Sunday Afternoon," "New York from the Air," "The Old Man," Backwards," "Delicatessen," "Out of Towner," "Everything You ate Is Right Here," "Suburban Fugue," "Purse Snatch," "Poor," Grafitti," "Singles Bar," "New York '69," "Tuscaloosa's Calling e, But I'm Not Going."

A musical in two acts. The action takes place at the present time New York City.

*General Manager:* Leonard A. Mulhern
*Press:* Michael Alpert Associates, Warren Knowlton

Still playing May 31, 1976.
Succeeded by: 1. Ted Pritchard, Paul Kreppel, 2. Chip Zien

*Ken Howard Photos*

**Right: Patti Perkins, Renny Temple, Len Gochman**

**Paul Kreppel, Patti Perkins**

**Patti Perkins, Chip Zien, Ted Pritchard**

## GOOD SHEPHERD-FAITH PRESBYTERIAN CHURCH

Opened Thursday, December 4, 1975.*
The Comedy Stage Company presents:

# EVERYMAN
## and
# ACT WITHOUT WORDS i

Director, Tim Ward; Choreography, Hedy Weiss; Scenery, Alyse Newman; Costumes and Sculpture, Wendy Moore; Lighting, Tony Thompson

CAST

"Everyman" (Anonymous)

Messenger ......................... Betsy Julian Robinson
God/Confession ...................... Amandina Lihamba
Death ............................... Anne O'Sullivan
Everyman ............................. Michael Sears
Fellowship/Strength/Angel ........... James-Ivers O'Connor
Cousin/Five Wits ....................... Alice Barrett
Kindred/Discretion ..................... Otis Gustafson
Goods/Beauty ........................ Matthew Schuster
Good Deeds ............................. Sheila Ward
Knowledge ............................ John J. Barilla

The action takes place at the present time in Times Square, New York City.

"Act without Words I" by Samuel Beckett
Performed by Will Lebow
The Action takes place at the present time on a desert.

*Press:* Sheila Ward
*Stage Manager:* Paula Cohen

* Closed Dec. 21, 1975 after limited engagement of 12 performances.

*Susan Cook Photos*

"Everyman"

## CITY PLAYWORKS THEATRE

Opened Thursday, December 18, 1975.*
City Playworks presents:

# IN THE BOOM BOOM ROOM

By David Rabe; Director, Terry Grossman; Designed by Michael Hotopp and Paul DePass; Musical Supervisor, Marty Silvestri; Dance Sequences, Lynn Gannaway; Associate Producer, Christopher Cara; Executive Producer, Jonathan Sand

CAST

Chrissy ..................................... Corie Sims
Susan ...................................... Randy Danson
Harold/Eric/Guy/Al/The Man ................. Mike Scott
Ralphie .................................... Mark Kologi
Helen ...................................... Gloria Lord
Girls ...... Mary Ed Porter, Marilyn Pfeiffer, Linda Brumfield

A play in two acts. The action takes place in Philadelpbia in the mid 1960's.

*Press:* Joshua Ellis
*Stage Managers:* Harold Apter, Kathy Spear, Janie Maxwell

* Closed Dec. 28, 1975 after limited engagement of 8 performances.

*Robb Webb Photo*

**Mike Scott, Corie Sims**

## TOWN HALL

Opened Tuesday, January 6, 1976.*
Town Hall by arrangement with Arthur Cantor presents:

# EMLYN WILLIAMS
## AS
# CHARLES DICKENS

Mr. Williams, made up as Charles Dickens, reads from the works of Mr. Dickens.

*Press:* Dan Langan
*Production Supervisor:* Robert Crawley

* Closed Jan. 10 after limited engagement of 6 performances.

**Emlyn Williams**

## MARYMOUNT MANHATTAN THEATRE
Opened Wednesday, January 7, 1976.*
Charles Woodward presents:

# FROM SHOLOM ALEICHEM WITH LOVE

Adapted and Staged by Elliot Levine; Lighting, Rick Claflin; Technical Director, Terrence Byrne; Associate Producer, Jerry Irchia

with
### ELLIOTT LEVINE

An evening in English with the Jewish Mark Twain during 1915 in New York City. Performed in two acts.

*Press:* Betty Lee Hunt Associates

* Closed Feb. 1, 1976 after 32 performances.

**Elliot Levine**

**Pat Daniel**

## WOOD THEATRE
Opened Monday, January 12, 1976.*
Wood Theatre presents:

# ALLEY CATS

Written, Directed and Designed by Tom Coble.

with
### PAT DANIEL

A Dramatic monologue without intermission.

*Press:* Max Eisen
*Stage Manager:* Margie A. Phillips

*Charles Livingston Photo*

## ALL SOULS UNITARIAN CHURCH
Opened Thursday, January 22, 1976.*
The All Souls Players present:

# SOMEONE SORT OF GRANDISH

Conceived and Directed by Tran William Rhodes; Choreography, Kirby Lewellen; Lighting, Bill Pietrucha, Harry Blum; Projections-Photography, Mary Lumsden; Costumes, Hank Laurencelle

### CAST

| | |
|---|---|
| Dana Coen | Kathleen Roche-Zujko |
| Hester Lewellen | Monona Rossol |
| Kirby Lewellen | Allan Smith |
| Linda Lipson | Tina Tymus |
| Dick Pohlers | Gyle Waddy |
| Tran William Rhodes | Roger Whitmarsh |

A Musical Tribute to E. Y. (Yip) Harburg consisting of 59 songs spanning the career of the Broadway and Hollywood lyricist-librettist.

*Stage Manager:* Lou Pavone

* Closed January 26, 1976 after limited engagement of 6 performances.

**"Someone sort of Grandish"**

## HUNTER COLLEGE PLAYHOUSE
Saturday & Sunday, January 24–25, 1976.*
Frank Wicks and Hunter Arts Concert Bureau present:

# JUST BETWEEN US
## with
## PEGGY COWLES

Conceived and Adapted by Daniel Stein; Material by Daniel Stein, Ruth Draper, Thomas Hardy, Guy de Maupassant, Marietta Holley, and Vachel Lindsay

* Presented for two performances only.

**Peggy Cowles**

**Mike Kellin, Michael Egan, J. T. Walsh**
(also above)

80

## ST. CLEMENT'S THEATRE
Opened Monday, January 26, 1976.*
St. Clement's Theatre (Brian Murray, Artistic Director; Lawrence Goossen, Executive Producer) presents:

# AMERICAN BUFFALO

By David Mamet; Director, Gregory Mosher; Set, Leo Yoshimura; Lighting, Gary Porto; Costumes, Danny Mizell; Technical Coordinator, Jeffrey M. Jones; Coordinator, Jean Halbert; Wardrobe Mistress, Terry Rosario

### CAST

Donny Dubrow............................... Michael Egan
Walter Cole, "Teach"......................... Mike Kellin
Bobby...................................... J. T. Walsh

A play in two acts.

*Press:* Jean Halbert
*Stage Managers:* Lynn Gutter, Vicki Paul

* Closed Feb. 7, 1976 after limited engagement of 16 performances

*Rena Hansen Photos*

PROVINCETOWN PLAYHOUSE
Opened Thursday, January 29, 1976.*
The Peoples Performing Company presents:

# FIRE OF FLOWERS

Words and Lyrics, Peter Copani; Music, Christian Staudt, Bob
Tuthill, Lawrence Pitilli, David McHugh, Ed Vogel, Peter Copani;
Musical Director, Ed Vogel; Director, Don Signore; Set and Light-
ing, Richard Harper; Production Assistants, Bill Barry, Colleen
DeBlaise, Denise Bonenfant, Rafael Diaz, Al Simonds, Norma Si-
nore

CAST

Larry Campbell
Sylvia Miranda
Val Reiter
Gwen Sumter

MUSICAL NUMBERS: "Today Will Be," "Keep Hope Alive,"
"Poppy Fields," "A Special Man," "If Jesus Walked," "Instant
Hate," "One of Us," "I Need to Know," "In the Name of Love,"
"I'm Afire," "God Is in the People," "A Lover's Dream," "Who
Can Say?," "Strawberries, Pickles and Ice Cream," "Down on Me,"
"Blind Junkie," "Riot," "I Love the Sun," "Pairs of One," "Verily,
Verily," "More Than Love," "Make Them Hate," "Street Jesus,"
"L'America Ha Fato Per Te," "Love Comes and Goes," "Drug
Free," "Wait and See," "When We Are Together"

*Press:* Lewis Harmon
*Stage Manager:* John Copani

Closed Feb. 29, 1976 after 38 performances and 17 previews.

*Gary Wheeler Photo*

Top Right: (front) Larry Campbell, Sylvia Miranda
(back) Gwen Sumter, Val Reiter

THEATRE DE LYS
Opened Tuesday, February 10, 1976.*
Adela Holzer presents:

# CRACKS

By Martin Sherman; Director, Tony Giordano; Music, Carlos
Holzer; Scenery, Peter Larkin; Costumes, Randy Barcelo; Lighting,
Marc B. Weiss; Associate Manager, David Relyea; Production As-
sistant, Rosemarie Schieffer; Wardrobe Supervisor, Judy Mauer;
Hairstylist, Karol Coeyman

CAST

Gideon .................................. Christopher Lloyd
Maggie ...................................... Meg Myles
Sammy ..................................... Victor Garber
Nadine ...................................... Gale Garnett
Clay ....................................... Donald Linahan
Jade .................................. Mary Elaine Monti
Roberta .................................. Louis Giambalvo
Irene ......................................... Jane Lowry
Rick ....................................... Jeremy Lucas

UNDERSTUDIES: Gideon, Jeremy Lucas; Irene, Maggie, Nadine,
Susanne Wasson

A comedy performed without intermission. The action takes place
at the present time in Rick's house in Southern California on a
summer evening.

*General Manager:* Leonard A. Mulhern
*Company Manager:* Paul B. Berkowsky
*Press:* Michael Alpert, Marilynn LeVine, Warren Knowlton,
Joshua Ellis, Randi Cone

* Closed Feb. 10, 1976 after one performance.

*Sy Friedman Photo*

(front) Christopher Lloyd, Gale Garnett, Jeremy Lucas,
Louis Giambalvo, (back) Jane Lowry, Meg Myles,
Victor Garber, Mary Elaine Monti, Donald Linahan

**PERFORMING GARAGE**
Opened Tuesday, February 10, 1976.*
(Moved April 15, 1976 to Provincetown Playhouse)
The Ridiculous Theatre Company presents:

# CAPRICE

Written and Directed by Charles Ludlam; Set, Bobjack Callejo; Lighting, Richard Currie; Costumes, Edward Avedisian, Arthur Brady, Mario Montez, Suzanne Peters, Roy Finamore, Georg Osterman, Mary Brecht; Choreography, Ethyl Eichelberger

CAST

| | |
|---|---|
| Claude Caprice | Charles Ludlam |
| Adrian | John D. Brockmeyer |
| TaTa | Adam MacAdam |
| Harry Feinschmecher | Lola Pashalinski |
| Zuni Feinschmecher | Black-Eyed Susan |
| Twyfford Adamant | Bill Vehr |
| Copelias | Georg Osterman |
| Scrub Woman/La Fleur/Bertha | Ethyl Eichelberger |
| Ballerinas | Ekathrina Sobechanskaya, Tamara Karpova, Claudette Caprichovna, Flossie Flanagan |

A comedy in two acts.
*General Management:* New Arts Management
*Press:* Alan Eichler
*Stage Manager:* Richard Gibbs

* Closed April 25, 1976 after 45 performances.

*John Stern Photo*

**Black-Eyed Susan, Charles Ludlam**

**ACTORS STUDIO**
Opened Thursday, March 18, 1976.*
The Actors Studio presents:

# ECONOMIC NECESSITY

By John Hopkins; Director, Arthur Sherman; Executive Producer, Carl Schaeffer; Technical Director, Eric R. Cowley; Coordinator, Alan Mandell; Lighting, Paul Kaine; Set, Sally Loc Costumes, Francie Trotta; Assistant to director, Heath r Gubr

CAST

| | |
|---|---|
| Audrey | Sandra Sea |
| Barry | Michael H |
| Christine | Maxmillia Schei |
| Dennis | Geoffrey Hc |
| Eric | Joseph Ra |
| Frank | J. J. Qu |
| Gerry | Nick La Pac |
| Harriet | Carlin Gl |
| Ian | Paul Glea |
| Jessica | Ann Wedgewc |
| Ken | Michael Ha |

A play in two acts.
*Production Manager:* Deedee Wehle
*Press:* Lee Pucklis
*Stage Manager:* Howard Meadow

* Closed April 4, 1976 after limited engagement of 12 performan

*Mallory Jones Photo*

**Sandra Seacat, Geoffrey Horne**

CRCLE IN THE SQUARE THEATRE
Opened Monday, February 16, 1976.*
Jack Schlissel, Joseph Kipness, Steven Steinlauf present:

# THE PRIMARY ENGLISH CLASS

By Israel Horovitz; Director, Edward Berkeley; Associate Pro-
cer, Irving Welzer; Scenery, Fredda Slavin; Lighting, Andrea
Wilson; Costumes, Patricia McGourty; Production Supervisor,
na Antaramian; Production Assistant, Alan Lifschitz

### CAST

| | |
|---|---|
| iednik | Tom Kubiak |
| tumiera | Richard Libertini |
| Poubelle | Jean-Pierre Stewart |
| anslator | Rogert Picardo |
| ulleimer | Sol Frieder |
| rs. Pong | Lori Tan Chinn |
| anslator | Christine Von Dohln |
| ko Kazukago | Atsumi Sakato |
| bbie Wastba | Diane Keaton† |

NDERSTUDIES: Debbie, Christine Von Dohln; Patumiera, La
ubelle, Mulleimer, Robert Picardo

A comedy performed without intermission. The action takes place
the present time in a classroom at night.

General Manager: Jay Kingwill
Assistant General Manager: Mark Bramble
Press: Solters & Roskin, Milly Schoenbaum, Bud Westman
Stage Manager: Robert Schear

Closed May 16, 1976 after 104 performances.
Succeeded by Jill Eikenberry

*Ken Howard Photos*

**Atsumi Sakato, Jean-Pierre Stewart, Diane Keaton, Richard Libertini, Sol Frieder**
**Top Right: Jill Eikenberry**

## THE THEATRE

Opened Thursday, March 20, 1976.*
New York Theater Strategy presents:

# SHE WHO WAS HE

By Rosalyn Drexler; Director, William Prosser; Music, John Herbert McDowell; Choreographer, Joe Goode; Set, Robert Franklin; Costumes, Carole Steinke, Kathi Horne; Lights, Michael Watson; Technical Director, Gary Grill

### CAST

| | |
|---|---|
| Tumbler/Dancer | Edward Bartonn |
| Amon Ra/Tutmose I | Lawrence Gallegos |
| Ahmose | Gretel Cummings |
| Priest | Dale Fuller |
| Hathor | Yvonne Dell |
| Hatshepsut | Roxana Stuart or Margaret Harrington |
| Nemra/Dancer | Richard Thorne |
| Sheeshonk/Dancer/Set | Bill Kirkpatrick |
| Tutmose II | Tazewell Thompson |
| Kinnor | Ken Fitch |
| Singer | Carol Grant |
| Senmut | Amlin Gray |
| Sekmet/Dancer | Andrea Borak |
| Isis | Ann Freeman |
| Tutmose III | Gabriel Gribetz |
| Young Soldier | Cameron Duncan |
| Hand Maidens | Jana Fontana, Lenora May |
| Dancers | Candice Christakos, Mary Dunnavant |
| Percussionist | Daniel Wallack |

A drama in two acts. The action takes place in Egypt.

*Press:* Alan Eichler
*Stage Managers:* Timothy Gabbert, John Buonassissi, Dorothy Silver

* Closed April 4, 1976 after limited engagement of 12 performances.

**Roxana Stuart**

**David Clennon, Howard E. Rollins, Jr.**

THEATRE DE LYS
Opened Sunday, March 28, 1976.*
Paul B. Berkowsky, Woodie King, Jr. and Lucille Lorte present:

# MEDAL OF HONOR RAG

By Tom Cole; Director, David Chambers; Setting, Raymond C Recht; Lighting, Marshall S. Spiller; Costumes, Carol Oditz; Wardrobe Mistress, Rebecca Howard; Assistant to director, Clay Stevenson; Production Assistant, Kevin B. Berkowsky

### CAST

| | |
|---|---|
| Doctor | David Clennon |
| Dale Jackson (D.J.) | Howard E. Rollins, Jr |
| Military Guard | John Robert Yate |

A drama performed without intermission. The action takes place in an office of the Valley Forge Army Hospital, Valley Forge, PA on the afternoon of April 23, 1971.

*General Manager:* Paul B. Berkowsky
*Press:* Merlin Group, Sandra Manley, Elizabeth Rodman
*Stage Managers:* Dan Early, John Robert Yates

* Closed May 2, 1976 after 41 performances.

*Arlene Spiller Photo*

**WESTSIDE THEATER**
Opened Monday, March 22, 1976.*
The Chelsea Theater Center, The Lion Theatre Company, and
Playwrights Horizons present:

# VANITIES

By Jack Heifner; Director, Garland Wright; Scenery, John Arnone; Lighting, Patrika Brown; Costumes, David James; Wardrobe
Mistress, Gertrude Sloan

CAST

Kathy.................................... Jane Galloway
Mary..................................... Susan Merson
Joanne ....................................... Kathy Bates

A play in three acts. The action takes place in a gymnasium in
1963, a sorority house in 1968, and a garden apartment in 1974.

*Press:* Betty Lee Hunt, Maria Cristina Pucci
*Stage Manager:* Ginny Freedman

* Still playing May 31, 1976.

*Laura W. Pettibone Photos*

**Right: Jane Galloway, Susan Merson, Kathy Bates**

**Kathy Bates, Jane Galloway, Susan Merson**

## DIPLOMAT CABARET THEATRE

Opened Friday, April 2, 1976.*
Jolandrea Music Inc. in association with Gail Davis, Parker
Willson, Edmund Gaynes presents:

## LE BELLYBUTTON

Book, Music, Lyrics, and Direction by Scott Mansfield; Choreography, Katherine Hull, Louise Quick; Designed by David Chapman; Lighting Associate, Richard Winkler; Costume Associate, Ben Gutierrez-Soto; Orchestrations and Musical Direction, Ken Werner; Additional Sketch Material, Johnathan Copley, Joel Scott; Assistant Director, Alan Fox; Production Consultant, Gail Davis; Assistant to producers, Jane Hershcopf; Assistant Musical Director, Donald Oliver; Wardrobe Mistress, Fern Laurie

### CAST

Marilyn Chambers      Alan Lee Kootsher
Thommie Bush      Billy Padgett
Jessie Hill      Paulette Sanders
Adrienne Frimet      Jim Sbano
Larry Kingery      Alan Scott
Debbie Kinney      Suzanne Walker

A musical in two acts.

*General Manager:* Malcolm Allen
*Press:* Henry Luhrman, Terry Lilly
*Stage Managers:* Alan Fox, Lee Triplett

* Closed April 25, 1976 after 28 performances.

*Jerome Yulesman Photos*

**Right: Marilyn Chambers, Thommie Bush,
Adrienne Frimet, Larry Kingery, Suzanne Walker
Above: Debbie Kinney, Marilyn Chambers,
Suzanne Walker**

**Lisa Hall, Norman Weiler, William Fredericks,
Margo Lacey, Jonathan Jones**

## BILLY MUNK THEATRE

Opened Monday, April 12, 1976.*
Marc Hamerman presents:

## I KNOCK AT THE DOOR

By Sean O'Casey; Adapted by Paul Shyre; Music and Lyrics, P
Dick; Director, Ron Nash; Music Director, Sal Sicari; Costum
John Reid; Associate Producer, Robert Pace

### CAST

Mother . . . . . . . . . . . . . . . . . . . . . . . . . . . . . . . . . . Margo La
Johnny . . . . . . . . . . . . . . . . . . . . . Jonathan Howard Jc
Narrator/Cabman . . . . . . . . . . . . . . . . . . . . . . . . . Richard Ia
Nurse/Ella . . . . . . . . . . . . . . . . . . . . . . . . . . . . . . . . . Lisa F
Doctor/Conductor/Archie/Mr. Story/Cabman/
Harry Tait . . . . . . . . . . . . . . . . . . . . . . . . . . . William Freder
Father/Old Man/Clergyman/Slogan . . . . . . . . . . . . Kevin Hur
Narrator/Aunt/Woman in hospital/Woman at
Wake/Jenny . . . . . . . . . . . . . . . . . . . . . . . . . . . . Susan J. Ba
One-eyed      Man/Murphy/Cabman/Mich
George Middleton/Rev. Hunter . . . . . . . . . . . . Norman We

MUSICAL NUMBERS: "The Last Shake o' the Bag," "At
Annual Vice-Regal Ball," "Ounce of Cavendish Cut Plug," "
Love Goes Down," "Prepare Ye Now for the World to Con
"Same Way Home," "Little Boy Blue," "Cock Robin," "There
a Funny Man," "White Bum," "An Irish Ireland," "Why Are
Weepin', Jenny?," "My Country's Call," "Ay, Michael, O,
chael," "Soliloquy on a Sunny Wedding Morn," "The Brook"

A musical in two acts.

*Stage Managers:* JW Roberts, Pat Sullivan

* Closed April 14, 1976 after limited engagement of four pe
mances.

**TY CENTER 55th STREET THEATER**
Opened Thursday, April 15, 1976.*
Artists Consultants presents:

# MONTY PYTHON LIVE!

American Scenic Supervision, Karl Eigsti; Sound, Abe Jacob;
ghting Designer, John Gleason; Wardrobe Supervisor, Ann Good-
; Production Coordinators, Charles Knode, Anne Henshaw

### CAST

Terry Gilliam
Terry Jones
John Cleese
Eric Idle
Graham Chapman
Michael Palin
with Neil Innes, Carol Cleveland

A British comedy revue in two acts.

*General Manager:* Theatre Now, Inc.
*Company Manager:* Robert Frissell
*Press:* Wartoke Concern, Jane Friedman
*Stage Managers:* Molly Kirkland, Frank Marino

Closed May 2, 1976 after limited engagement of 22 performances
and 2 previews.

*Martha Swope Photos*

## ASTOR PLACE THEATRE

Opened previews Tuesday, April 20, 1976.*
Labor Arts Community Services Committee in association with
Stuart White presents:

# I PAID MY DUES

Book and Lyrics, Eric Blau; Music Arrangements, Musical Direction, David Frank; Director, George Allison Elmer; Sets and Costumes, Don Jensen; Lighting, Jeff Davis; Assistant Conductor, Bob Stecko; Production Assistant, Dell Setzer

### CAST

Joe Morton

| | |
|---|---|
| Christopher Cable | James Robinson |
| Tom Demenkoff | Edward Rodriguez |
| Jacqueline Reilly | Wendy Wolfe |
| Linda Rios | Zenobia |

Alternates: Lynnie Godfrey, Alphanzo Harrison

MUSICAL NUMBERS: "I Paid My Dues," "In Good Old Colony Times," "Whiskey in the Jar," "Yankee Doodle," "Fate of John Burgoyne," "Battle of Trenton," "Young Ladies in Town," "Yankee Doodle Dandy-O," "Johnny Has Gone for a Soldier," "Blow Ye Winds," "Cape Cod Girls," "Haul on the Bow Line," "Erie Canal," "Frozen Logger," "Santy Anno," "Praties They Grow Small," "Shenandoah," "John Henry," "Doney Gal," "Red Iron Ore," "My Sweetheart's the Mule in the Mine," "Railroad Bill," "A Cowboy's Life," "The Cowboys," "Zum Gali, Gali," "Drill Ye Tarriers, Drill," "Wade in the Water," "Go Down Moses," "This Train," "Oh! Freedom," "Take This Hammer," "When I'm Gone," "Pick a Bale of Cotton," "Many Thousands Gone," "Tenting Tonight," "John Brown's Body," "Battle Hymn of the Republic," "Solidarity Forever," "Dark as a Dungeon," "Sixteen Tons," "Union Maid," "Which Side Are You On," "Talking Union," "The Scabs Crawl In," "Hinky Dinky Parlez Vous," "On the Line," "You've Got to Go Down," "Roll the Union On," "Casey Jones," "Hold the Fort," "We Shall Not Be Moved," "Goin' Down the Road," "Beans, Bacon and Gravy," "Soup Song," "Brother Can You Spare a Dime?," "Let's Have Another Cup of Coffee," "When the Red Red Robin," "I Want to Be Happy," "Agent 008," "Violet Eyes," "Ballad of Mervyn Schwartz," "Nosotros Venceremos," "A Man's a Man for All That"

A musical celebration of labor in two acts.

*General Manager:* Lily Turner
*Press:* Seymour Krawitz, Ted Goldsmith, Patricia McLean Krawitz
*Stage Manager:* James Nisbet Clark

* Closed May 23, 1976 after 20 performances.

*Bert Andrews Photos*

**Christopher Gable, Jacqueline Reilly, James Robins[**
**Edward Rodriguez, Tom Demenkoff,**
**Wendy Wolfe, Linda Rios, Zenobia**
**Above: Linda Ross, Joe Morton**

## TRUCK AND WAREHOUSE THEATRE
Opened Tuesday, April 20, 1976.*
R. Paul Evans and Otto Grun, Jr. present:

# WOMEN BEHIND BARS

By Tom Eyen; Director, Ron Link; Designed by Sturgis Warr[
Lighting, Michael Lodick; Production Assistant, Trey Luckenba[
Title Song, Tom Eyen; Sung by Larry Paulette

### CAST

| | |
|---|---|
| Matron | Div[ |
| Louise | Sweet Willi[ |
| Blanche | Lori Saveri[ |
| Jo-Jo | Beverly Bon[ |
| Cheri | Brenda Bergr[ |
| Gloria | Ellie Sch[ |
| Ada | Jana Schnei[ |
| Guadalupe | Vira Color[ |
| Mary-Eleanor | Lisa Jane Per[ |
| Granny | Virginia Ba[ |

A comedy performed without intermission. The action takes pl[
in the Women's House of Detention between 1952 and 1960.

*Company Manager:* Jerry Sandusky
*Press:* Alan Eichler, Tony Kavanaugh

* Still playing May 31, 1976.

*Glenn Capers Photos*

**Ellie Schadt, Jana Schmeider, Divine,**
**Brenda Bergman, Lisa Jane Persky**

88

## THEATRE FOUR

Opened Monday, April 26, 1976.*
Norman Stephens and Primavera Productions Ltd. in association with Max Weitzenhoffer present:

# TICKLES BY TUCHOLSKY

Original Material, Kurt Tucholsky; Translated and Adapted by Louis Golden, Harold Poor; Conceived and Directed by Moni Yakim; Music Arranged and Conducted by Wolfgang Knittel; Sets, Don Jensen; Lights, Spencer Mosse; Costumes, Christina Giannini; Production Coordinator, George Allison Elmer; Assistant to director, Kathleen Gargan; Wardrobe Mistress, Betty Martin

### CAST

Helen Gallagher
Joe Masiell
Jana Robbins
Joseph Neal
Jerry Jarrett
Understudy: Susan Waldman

MUSICAL NUMBERS AND SKETCHES: "The Song of Indifference," "Rising Expectations," "Tickles," "Christmas Shopping," "Brown Shirted Cowboy," "German Evening," "Transition," "Lovers," "Waldemar," "Compromise Soft Shoe," "Come Avec!," "How to Get Rich," "King's Regiment," "Lullaby," "Verdun," "War against War," "Waiting," "Follow Schmidt," "Anna Louisa," "Lamplighters," "Heartbeat," "It's Your Turn," "25 Points," "I'm Out," "General! General!," "To You I Gave My All," "Now That Things Are Rough," "Testimony," "Over the Trenches," Epilogue

A "cabaret musical" in two acts.

*General Manager:* Lily Turner
*Company Manager:* Donald Joslyn
*Press:* Merlin Group, Sandra Manley, Harriett Trachtenberg, Ron Harris
*Stage Managers:* Phillip Price, Steve Helliker

* Closed May 9, 1976 after 16 performances and 24 previews.

*Bert Andrews Photos*

**Jerry Jarrett,**    **Joe Masiell, Jana Robbins**
**Helen Gallagher**    **Top: Jerry Jarrett,**
**Joseph Neal,**
**Helen Gallagher, Joe Masiell**

## EDISON THEATRE

Opened Tuesday, May 4, 1976.*
Norman Kean presents:

# A KURT WEILL CABARET

Conceived and Directed by Will Holt; Musical Direction, William Cox

### CAST

WILL HOLT & DOLLY JONAH

MUSICAL NUMBERS: "Alabama Song," "Ballad of the Easy Life," "Barbara Song," "Moritat," "Mahagonny Duet," "Tango Ballade," "Pirate Jenny," "Recruiting Song," "Benares Song," "Denn Wie Man Sich Bettet," "Caesar's Death," "Johnny Johnson," "My Ship," "Speak Low," "Jenny Made Her Mind Up," "September Song," "It Never Was You," "Mandalay Song," "Sailor's Tango," "Surabaya Johnny," "Bilboa Song," Finale

A musical cabaret in two acts.

*Company Manager:* Maria Di Dia
*Press:* Les Schecter Associates
*Stage Manager:* Sam Stickler

* Closed May 25, 1976 after limited engagement of 3 performances.

*Bert Andrews Photos*

**Dolly Jonah, Will Holt**

89

**VAN DAM THEATRE**
Opened Monday, May 10, 1976.*
John Rothman Productions Ltd. in association with the Direct
Theatre and Dorothy Ames presents:

## TITANIC
### and
## DAS LUSITANIA SONGSPIEL

Director, Peter Mark Schifter; Sets and Costumes, Ernie Smith;
Lighting, Mitchell Kurtz; Accompanist, Jack Gaughan; Production
Associate, David Geronemus

CAST

"Das Lusitania Songspiel":
The Theatre Songs of Bertolt Breck
Christopher Durang
Sigourney Weaver

"Titanic" by Christopher Durang
Victoria Tammurai . . . . . . . . . . . . . . . . . Kate McGregor-Stewart
Richard Tammurai . . . . . . . . . . . . . . . . . . . . . . Stefan Hartman
Teddy Tammurai . . . . . . . . . . . . . . . . . . . . . Richard Peterson
Lidia . . . . . . . . . . . . . . . . . . . . . . . . . . . . . Sigourney Weaver
The Captain . . . . . . . . . . . . . . . . . . . . . . . . . . . . Jeff Brooks
Higgins . . . . . . . . . . . . . . . . . . . . . . . . . . . . . Ralph Redpath

*Manager:* Jerry Arrow
*Press:* Betty Lee Hunt, Maria Cristina Pucci, Fred Hoot
*Stage Managers:* Peter Schifter, Chris Durang, Anne Hoffman,
Kimberly Meyers

* Closed May 16, 1976 after 7 performances and 7 previews.

*Laura W. Pettibone Photos*

**Right: Kate McGregor-Stewart, Richard Peterson,
Ralph Redpath, Sigourney Weaver, Stefan
Hartman in "Titanic" Top: Sigourney Weaver,
Christopher Durang in "Das Lusitania
Songspiel"**

Lee Nagrin, Margaret Beals, Brook Myers

**THERESA L. KAUFMANN CONCERT HALL**
Opened Sunday, May 23, 1976.*
Impulses Arts Inc. in association with the 92 Street Y
YWHA presents:

## STINGS

Based on "Ariel," the final poems of Sylvia Plath; Created,
rected and Choreographed by Margaret Beals; Scenery, Jim Mea
Costumes, Sally Ann Parsons; Lighting, Edward M. Greenb
Sound, Antony Giovanetti

CAST

Margaret Beals
Brooke Myers
Lee Nagrin

POEMS: "Tulips," "Elm," "Couriers," "Applicant," "Lady L
rus," "Duet," "Ariel," "Trio," "Lesbos," "A Birthday Prese
"Daddy," "Edge," "Words."

Performed without intermission.

*Management:* Bruce Michaels, Neil Fleckman
*Stage Manager:* Richard Tauber

* Closed May 27, 1976 after limited engagement of 4 performan

*Suzanne Opton Photo*

# THE ACTING COMPANY

John Houseman, Artistic Director
Margot Harley, Producing Director
Porter Van Zandt, Executive Director

ARKNESS THEATRE
Opened Tuesday, October 7, 1975.*
The Acting Company presents:

## THE ROBBER BRIDEGROOM

Book and Lyrics, Alfred Uhry; Based on novella by Eudora
elty; Composed and Arranged by Robert Waldman; Director,
erald Freedman; Choreography, Donald Saddler; Settings, Doug-
 W. Schmidt; Costumes, Jeanne Button; Lighting, David F. Segal;
chnical Director, Richard Elkow; Wardrobe Supervisor, Karen L.
ert; Hairstylist, Steve Atha

### CAST

| | |
|---|---|
| mie Lockhart | Kevin Kline |
| ke Fink | Norman Snow |
| emment Musgrove | David Schramm |
| at | Robert Bacigalupi |
| ttle Harp | J. W. Harper |
| g Harp | Anderson Matthews |
| le Nunnery | Brooks Baldwin |
| m Plymale | Richard Ooms |
| ly Brenner | Nicolas Surovy |
| hn Oglesby | Roy K. Stevens |
| nie Summers | Peter Dvorsky |
| rman McLaughlin | Michael Tolaydo |
| ome | Mary Lou Rosato |
| samund | Patti LuPone |
| at's Mother | Glynis Bell |
| rie | Sandra Halperin |
| ven | Elaine Hausman |
| eenie Sue Stevens | Cynthia Dickason |
| ddler | Alan Kaufman |

NDERSTUDIES: Jamie, Mike, Nicolas Surovy; Little Harp, Nor-
an Snow; Clemment, Richard Ooms; Goat, Brooks Baldwin;
ome, Glynis Bell; Rosamund, Sandra Halperin; Goat's Mother,
aine Hausman; Airie, Raven, Cynthia Dickason; Alternate Big
arp, Benjamin Hendrickson

USICAL NUMBERS: "With Style," "The Real Mike Fink,"
he Pricklepear Bloom," "Nothin' Up," "Deeper in the Woods,"
iches," "Love Stolen," "Poor Tied Up Darlin'," "Goodbye
ome," "Sleepy Man"

A country-folk musical performed without intermission. The ac-
n takes place in legendary Mississippi.

*Company Manager:* Mannie Kladitis
*Press:* Gifford/Wallace, Tom Trenkle
*Stage Managers:* Howard Crampton-Smith, San Clester, Jo
Mayer

Closed Oct. 18, 1975 after limited engagement of 15 performances
and 1 preview.

*Diane Gorodnitzki Photos*

**Top Right: David Schramm, Patti LuPone,
Kevin Kline Below: Kevin Kline, Nicolas Surovy,
Patti LuPone**

Patti LuPone, Kevin Kline

**HARKNESS THEATRE**
Opened Tuesday, October 21, 1975.*
The Acting Company presents:

# EDWARD II

By Christopher Marlowe; Director, Ellis Rabb; Music and Sour
Bob James; Costumes, Nancy Potts; Settings, Douglas W. Schmie
Lighting, David F. Segal.

## CAST

Gaveston ................................ Peter Dvors
Beggar I ............................ Anderson Matthe
Beggar II .......................... Cynthia Dickas
Beggar III .......................... Roy K. Steve
King Edward II ......................... Norman Sno
Lancaster ........... Benjamin Hendrickson or Kevin Kli
Elder Mortimer .......................... Richard Oor
Young Mortimer ..................... Sam Tsoutsouv
Kent, brother of Edward II .............. David Schram
Warwick ................................ Brooks Baldw
Bishop of Coventry ..................... Michael Tolay
Archbishop of Canterbury ................ Nicolas Suro
Queen Isabella ........................ Mary-Joan Neg
Lady Margaret ......................... Elaine Hausm
Baldock ................................ J. W. Harp
Spencer ............................ Robert Bacigalu
Leicester ............................. Michael Tolay
Price Edward, later Edward III .......... Patti LuPor
Abbott ................................ Richard Oor
Matrevis ............................... Roy K. Steve
Berkeley .............................. Brooks Baldw
Gurney ............................ Anderson Matthe
Lightborn ........... Kevin Kline or Benjamin Hendrickse
Ladies-in-waiting ........ Cynthia Dickason, Sandra Halper
Attendants .............. Cynthia Dickason, Peter Dvorsk
Sandra Halperin, J. W. Harper, Elaine Hausman, Anders
Matthews, Richard Ooms, Roy K. Stevens, Micha
Tolay

UNDERSTUDIES: Prince Edward, Sandra Halperin; Margar
Cynthia Dickason; Isabella, Mary Lou Rosato; Leicester, Cante
bury, Matrevis, Gurney, Bishop, Beggar, Attendant, Gerald G
tierrez; Young Mortimer, Lancaster, Lightborn, J. W. Harpe
Gaveston, Attendant, Kevin Kline; Spencer, Anderson Matthew
Edward II, David Schramm; Baldock, Roy K. Stevens; Elder Mor
mer, Warwick, Abbott, Alternate Lancaster, Lightborn, Kev
Kline

Performed with one intermission.

*Company Manager:* Mannie Kladitis
*Press* Gifford/Wallace, Tom Trenkle
*Stage Managers:* Howard Crampton-Smith, Sam Clester, Jo
Mayer

* Closed Oct. 25, 1976 after limited engagement of 8 performanc
and 1 preview in repertory.

*Diane Gorodnitzki Photos*

**Top Left: Mary-Joan Negro,
Norman Snow, Peter Dvorsky**

**Norman Snow, Patti LuPone, Mary-Joan Negro**

**MARKNESS THEATRE**
 Opened Tuesday, October 28, 1975.*
 The Acting Company presents:

# THE TIME OF YOUR LIFE

By William Saroyan; Director, Jack O'Brien; Settings, Douglas
W. Schmidt; Costumes, Nancy Potts; Lighting, David F. Segal;
Technical Director, Richard Elkow; Wardrobe Supervisor, Karen L.
Sifert; Lighting Associate, Timmy Harris; Hairstylist, S. A. Moore

### CAST

| | |
|---|---|
| Newsboy | Elaine Hausman |
| Joe | Nicolas Surovy |
| Arab | Richard Ooms |
| Drunkard | Anderson Matthews/Michael Tolaydo |
| Nick | Benjamin Hendrickson |
| Willie | Michael Tolaydo/Sam Tsoutsouvas |
| Tom | Norman Snow |
| Kitty Duval | Patti LuPone |
| Harry | Brooks Baldwin |
| Dudley | Robert Bacigalupi |
| Wesley | Gerald Gutierrez |
| Lorene/Killer's Sidekick | Glynis Bell |
| Blick | J. W. Harper |
| Mary L | Mary Lou Rosato |
| Krupp | Roy K. Stevens |
| McCarthy | Kevin Kline |
| Kit Carson | David Schramm |
| Sailor | Anderson Matthews |
| Killer | Cynthia Dickason |
| Elsie | Sandra Halperin |
| Society Lady | Mary-Joan Negro |
| Society Gentleman | Peter Dvorsky |

UNDERSTUDIES: Joe, David Schramm; Kitty, Sandra Halperin;
Nick, Roy K. Stevens; Kit, J. W. Harper; Arab, Dudley, Michael
Tolaydo; Krupp, Harry, Anderson Matthews; Elsie, Cynthia Dicka-
son; Blick, Sam Tsoutsouvas; McCarthy, Peter Dvorsky; Mary L,
Mary-Joan Negro; Tom, Wesley, Kevin Kline; Society Lady, Killer,
Glynis Bell

A drama in three acts. The action takes place in Nick's Pacific
Street Saloon, Restaurant and Entertainment Palace at the foot of
Embarcadero in San Francisco during an afternoon and night in
October of 1939.

*Company Manager:* Mannie Kladitis
*Press:* Gifford/Wallace, Tom Trenkle
*Stage Managers:* Howard Crampton-Smith, Sam Clester, Jo
Mayer

Closed November 1, 1975 after limited engagement of 8 performances and 1 preview in repertory.

**Top Right: Patti LuPone, Norman Snow**

**Patti LuPone**

Mary-Joan Negro, Patti LuPone, Mary Lou Rosato

HARKNESS THEATRE
Opened Tuesday, November 4, 1975.*
The Acting Company presents:

# THE THREE SISTERS

By Anton Chekhov; Translated by Tyrone Guthrie and Leon
Kipnis; Director, Boris Tumarin; Musical Direction, Gerald
tierrez; Dances Staged by Elizabeth Kee; Settings, Douglas
Schmidt; Costumes, John David Ridge; Lighting, David F. Se
Hairstylist, Jonn Quaglia

## CAST

| | |
|---|---|
| Olga | Mary Lou Ros |
| Masha | Mary-Joan Ne |
| Irina | Patti LuP |
| Baron Tusenbach | Norman Sn |
| Chebutykin, Military Doctor | David Schra |
| Captain Solyony | Sam Tsoutsou |
| Dounyasha | Elaine Hausn |
| Anfisa (Nyanya) | Glynis |
| Ferapont | Roy K. Stev |
| Colonel Vershinin | Peter Dvo |
| Andrey Prozorov | Benjamin Hendrick |
| Fyodor Kulygin | Richard O |
| Natasha | Sandra Halp |
| Lt. Fedotik | Nicolas Sur |
| Lt. Rode | Michael Tola |
| Members of the Prozorov Household | Brooks Baldw |

Cynthia Dickason, Anderson Matthews, J. W. Ha

UNDERSTUDIES: Olga, Glynis Bell; Natasha, Dounya
Cynthia Dickason; Masha, Mary Lou Rosato; Irina, Anfisa, Ela
Hausman; Rode, Solyony, Robert Bacigalupi; Fedotik, Gerald
tierrez; Chebutykin, J. W. Harper; Baron, Colonel, Kevin Kl
Fyodor, Nicolas Surovy; Ferapont, Michael Tolaydo; Andrey, S
Tsoutsouvas

A drama in four acts performed with one intermission. The ac
takes place in the Prozorov home in a provincial town of Russi
the turn of this century.

*Company Manager:* Mannie Kladitis
*Press:* Gifford/Wallace, Tom Trenkle
*Stage Managers:* Howard Crampton-Smith, Sam Clester, Jo
Mayer

* Closed Nov. 8, 1975 after 8 performances and 1 preview in re
tory.

Top: David Schramm, Patti LuPone,
Gerald Gutierrez, Benjamin Hendrickson, Norman

# AMERICAN PLACE THEATRE

Wynn Handman, Director
Julia Miles, Associate Director
Twelfth Season

...ERICAN PLACE THEATRE
Opened Sunday, November 16, 1975.*
The American Place Theatre presents:

## GORKY

...y Steve Tesich; Director, Dennis Rosa; Music, Mel Marvin;
...ics, Steve Tesich; Scenery, David Jenkins; Costumes, Shadow;
...hting, Roger Morgan; Orchestrations, Mel Marvin; Ken Guil-
...tin; Technical Director, Henry Millman; Wardrobe Mistress,
...la III; Assistant Director, Douglas Cloud; Production Assistant,
...hael St. John; Costume Associate, Hugh Sherrer

### CAST

| | |
|---|---|
| ...ky | Philip Baker Hall |
| ...tor/Gypsy/Matthew | Richard Ramos |
| ...ndma/Peasant | Lilia Skala |
| ...ndpa/Peasant | Fyvush Finkel |
| ...stage Speaking Patient/Gavrillo | Stuart Pankin |
| ...x (Gorky as a boy) | John Gallogly |
| ...ther/Peasant/Electric Lady | Tanny McDonald |
| ...ky | Caroline Kava |
| ...st/Nikita/Stalin | Lloyd Battista |
| ...xim (Gorky as a young man) | Douglas Clark |
| ...sant/Party Man | J. Kevin Scannell |
| ...liapin/Cement Man | Monte Jaffe |
| ...sant Woman | Jacque Dean |
| ...sant Girl/Dancer | Diane Duffy |
| ...ing Peasant/Dancer | Robert Petersen |

... play in two acts. The action takes place in Old Russia during
... revolution days and into Soviet Union.

*Press:* David Roggensack
*Stage Managers:* Franklin Keysar, Mary E. Baird

...losed Nov. 30, 1975 after 48 performances.

*Martha Holmes Photos*

**Top Right: Tanny McDonald, J. Kevin Scannell,
Monte Jaffe, Douglas Clark, John Gallogly**

**Philip Baker Hall, John Gallogly,
Lloyd Battista, Douglas Clark**

**John Gallogly, Philip Baker Hall, Douglas Clark**

**AMERICAN PLACE THEATRE**
Opened Monday, December 8, 1975.*
Seff Associates Limited presents Le Treteau de Paris (Je
Rigault, Executive Director) Production of:

# PHEDRE

By Racine; Director, Michel Hermon; Scenery, Michel Har
tumes, Michel Hermon; Masks, Jean Herbin; Lighting, Pollux
Administrator, Francisco De Castro

CAST

| | |
|---|---|
| Hippolyte | Didier |
| Theramene | Olivie |
| Oenone | Anita Plessner or Miche |
| Phedre | Jeanne |
| Aricie/Ismene | Lawrence |
| Thesee | Michel H |

A tragedy in five acts performed with one intermission. The
takes place in Trezene, city of Peloponnesus.

*Stage Manager:* Roland Hergault

\* Closed Dec. 14, 1975 after limited engagement of 8 perform
in French.

MERICAN PLACE THEATRE
Opened Sunday, February 15, 1976.*
The American Place Theatre presents:

# VERY NIGHT WHEN THE SUN GOES DOWN

By Phillip Hayes Dean; Director, Gilbert Moses; Scenery, Kert
ndell; Lighting, Richard Nelson; Costumes, Judy Dearing;
und, Jerry Kornbluth; Music Arranged and Adapted by Howard
berts; Hymns performed by the Metropolitan AME Church
oir; Technical Director, Henry Millman; Wardrobe Mistress,
ula III

### CAST

| | |
|---|---|
| eeky Pete | Joe Seneca |
| ood | Frank Adu |
| ldonia | Marge Eliot |
| etty Eddie | Roscoe Orman |
| llerina | Marki Bey |
| ean Sam | Les Roberts |
| richo | Norman Matlock |
| ckeyed Rose | Billie Allen |

A drama in two acts. The action takes place in the recent past in
oloch, Michigan.

*Press:* David Roggensack
*Stage Managers:* Franklin Keysar, Mary E. Baird

Closed Feb. 22, 1976 after 46 performances.

*Martha Holmes Photos*

**Right: Frank Adu, Marki Bey**

**Richard Ward, Roscoe Orman, Marge Elliot, Marki Bey, Joe Seneca, Billie Allen,
Norman Matlock**

**AMERICAN PLACE THEATRE**
Opened Sunday, April 18, 1976.*
The American Place Theatre presents:

# THE OLD GLORY
## A Trilogy

By Robert Lowell; Scenery, John Wulp; Costumes, Willa Kim;
Lighting, Neil Peter Jampolis; Technical Director, Henry Millman;
Wardrobe Mistress, Jody Mayer

### CAST

**ENDECOTT AND THE RED CROSS**
Directed by Brian Murray; Music, Herbert Kaplan; Choreography,
Eileen Lawlor

| | |
|---|---|
| Assawamset | Manu Tupou |
| Thomas Morton | Jerome Dempsey |
| Merry Mount Men | James Cromar, George Hall, Rene Mainguy, Colter Rule |
| Indians | Frank Askin, George Simson, Gerard Wagner |
| Assawamset's Daughter | Joan Jacklin |
| Mr. Blackstone | Richard Clarke |
| Man with stag's head | Andre Bishop |
| Edward | Noah Manne |
| Edith | Elisabeth Price |
| Indian Whore | Gloria Rossi |
| Sergeant | Thomas O'Rourke |
| Private | Bruce Bouchard |
| Soldiers | James Cromar, Rene Mainguy, Robert Rigley |
| Drummer | George Simson |
| Governor Endecott | Kenneth Harvey |
| Standard Bearer | Josh Clark |
| Man with wolf's head | Colter Rule |
| Palfrey | J. T. Walsh |
| Man dressed as witch | George Hall |
| Merry Mount Woman | Barbara Le Brun |
| Bear | Rene Mainguy |
| Merry Mount Girl | Sallyanne Tackus |
| Executioner | Frank Askin |

The action takes place in the 1630's at Merry Mount, the settlement of Thomas Morton, near Wollaston, Massachusetts.

**MY KINSMAN, MAJOR MOLINEUX**
Director, Brian Murray; Music, Herbert Kaplan

| | |
|---|---|
| Ferryman | Manu Tupou |
| Boy | Scott Sorrell |
| Robin | Josh Clark |
| First Redcoat | Rene Mainguy |
| Second Redcoat | Colter Rule |
| First Barber | Thomas O'Rourke |
| Tavern Keeper | J. T. Walsh |
| Second Barber | Bruce Bouchard |
| Clergyman | George Hall |
| Prostitute | Gloria Rossi |
| Colonel Greenough | Jerome Dempsey |
| Man in periwig | Richard Clarke |
| Watchman | J. T. Walsh |
| Major Molineux | Kenneth Harvey |
| Citizens of Boston | Frank Askin, Andre Bishop, James Cromar, Joan Jacklin, Barbara LeBrun, Noah Manne, Elisabeth Price, Robert Rigley, George Simson, Sallyanne Takcus, Gerard Wagner |

The action takes place in Boston just before the American Revolution.

**Top Right: Paul Benjamin, John Getz,
Roscoe Lee Browne, Nicolas Coster in "Benito
Cereno"**

**BENITO CERENO**
Director, Austin Pendleton
Associate Director, John Parks

| | |
|---|---|
| Captain Amasa Delano | Nicolas Coster |
| John Perkins | John Getz |
| Don Benito Cereno | Alan Mixon |
| Babu | Roscoe Lee Browne |
| Arufal | Paul Benjamin |
| Francesco | Darryl Croxton |
| American Sailors | Bill Conway, Mark A. French, Steven Pally, Stephen Lawrence Smith, Daniel Stern, Peter Gelblum, Peter Lown |
| Negro Slaves | Make Bray, Edythe Davis, Sandra Harris, Gregory Jackson, Llewellyn Jones, Bob Long, Gavin Moses, Jarett Smithwrick, Sidney Strong, Anthony Way |

The action takes place about the year 1800, aboard the ships
President Adams and the San Domingo.

*Press:* David Roggensack
*Stage Managers:* Franklin Keysar, Mary E. Baird, Peter
Schneider, Samuel Miller

* Closed May 23, 1976 after 54 performances to appear in Amsterdam and Paris.

*Martha Holmes Photos*

Noah Manne, Kenneth Harvey, Elisabeth Price, Thomas O'Rourke, Bruce Bouchard in
"Endecott and the Red Cross" Top: "My Kinsman, Major Molineux"

99

**BIL BAIRD THEATER**
Opened Sunday, November 2, 1975.*
The American Puppet Arts Council (Arthur Cantor, Executi▮
Producer) presents:

## BIL BAIRD'S MARIONETTES
### Tenth Season

ALICE IN WONDERLAND: Book, A. J. Russell; Music, J▮
Raposo; Lyrics, Sheldon Harnick; Scenery, Howard Mandel; Ligh▮
ing, Peggy Clark; Designed and Produced by Bil and Susanna Bair▮
Artistic Associate, Frank Sullivan; Director, Paul Leaf; Based on t▮
book by Lewis J. Carroll

#### PUPPETEERS

| | |
|---|---|
| Olga Felgemacher | Rebecca Bond▮ |
| William Tost | Steven Widerma▮ |
| Peter Baird | Brian Stashi▮ |

and the singing voices of Mary Case, George S. Irving, Sheld▮
Harnick, Rose Marie Jun, Ivy Austin, Margery Gray, William To▮
Bil Baird

* Closed January 18, 1976 after 87 performances. On January 2▮
  1976 "Winnie the Pooh" opened and played 111 performance▮
  closing April 30, 1976.

WINNIE THE POOH: By A. A. Milne; Adapted by A. J. Russe▮
Music, Jack Brooks; Lyrics, A. A. Milne, Jack Brooks; Director, ▮
Baird; Scenery, Howard Mandel; Lighting, Peggy Clark; Music▮
Director, Arranger, Alvy West; Designed and Produced by Bil a▮
Susanna Baird; Production Manager, Douglas Gray

*General Manager:* Henry Senber
*Assistant General Manager:* Debbie Lepsinger
*Press:* C. George Willard

*Nat Messik Photos*

**Fish Footman in "Alice in Wonderland"**
**Top: "Winnie-the-Pooh"**

# BROOKLYN ACADEMY OF MUSIC

Harvey Lichtenstein, Executive Director
Judith E. Daykin, General Manager

BROOKLYN ACADEMY PLAYHOUSE
Opened Wednesday, December 3, 1975.*
The Brooklyn Academy of Music presents the Kennedy Center-
Xerox Corporation American Bicentennial Theatre Production
of:

## SWEET BIRD OF YOUTH

(see Broadway Calendar page 31)
Closed December 14, 1975 after limited engagement of 16 performances. Re-opened on Broadway Monday, Dec. 29, 1975.

BROOKLYN ACADEMY PLAYHOUSE
Opened Tuesday, December 16, 1975.*
The Brooklyn Academy of Music presents the Kennedy Center-
Xerox Corporation American Bicentennial Theatre Production
of:

## THE ROYAL FAMILY

(see Broadway Calendar page 32)
Closed Dec. 18, 1975 after limited engagement of 16 performances. Re-opened on Broadway Tuesday, December 30, 1975.

*Richard Bratten Photos*

**Christopher Walken, Irene Worth in "Sweet Bird of Youth" Top: Mary Layne, Rosemary Harris, Sam Levene, Eva LeGalliene, Joseph Maher, Mary Louise Wilson, George Grizzard**

## BROOKLYN ACADEMY OPERA HOUSE

Opened Wednesday, January 28, 1976.*
The Brooklyn Academy of Music presents the Kennedy Center-Xerox Corporation American Bicentennial Theatre Production of:

# LONG DAY'S JOURNEY INTO NIGHT

By Eugene O'Neill; Director, Jason Robards; Scenery, Ben Edwards; Costumes, Jane Greenwood; Lighting, Ken Billington; Production Supervisor, Jack Hofsiss; Wardrobe Supervisor, Walter Rivera; Hairstylist, Steve Atha; Assistant Director, Lois O'Connor

### CAST

| | |
|---|---|
| James Tyrone | Jason Robards |
| Mary Cavan Tyrone | Zoe Caldwell |
| James Tyrone, Jr | Kevin Conway |
| Edmund Tyrone | Michael Moriarty |
| Cathleen | Lindsay Crouse |

STANDBYS AND UNDERSTUDIES: Tyrone, Ernest Graves; Mary, Carol Teitel; Tyrone, Jr., Paul Thomas; Edmund, W. T. Martin; Cathleen, Dyanne Hochman

A drama in three acts and five scenes. The action takes place in the living room of the Tyrones' summer home on an August day and night in 1912.

*General Manager:* Edmonstone Thompson, Jr.
*Company Manager:* Bill Liberman
*Press:* Charles Ziff, Kate MacIntyre, Deborah Ann Williams
*Stage Managers:* Murray Gitlin, Dyanne Hochman, W. T. Martin

* Closed Feb. 8, 1976 after limited engagement of 16 performances.

*Richard Braaten Photos*

**Kevin Conway, Michael Moriarty, Zoe Caldwell, Jason Robards**
**Top Right: Jason Robards, Zoe Caldwell**

ROOKLYN ACADEMY OPERA HOUSE
Opened Wednesday, April 21, 1976.*
The Brooklyn Academy of Music by arrangement with the
Governors of the Royal Shakespeare Theatre, Stratford-upon-
Avon, England, presents the Royal Shakespeare Company
(Trevor Nunn, Artistic Director and Chief Executive) in:

# HENRY V

By William Shakespeare; Director, Terry Hands; Designed by
rrah; Music, Guy Woolfenden; Lighting, Stewart Levition;
und, Keith Clarke; Wardrobe Mistress, Carol Deary; Wardrobe
pervisor, Walter Rivera; Assistant to director, Ian Judge

### CAST

| | |
|---|---|
| orus | Emrys James |

e English:

| | |
|---|---|
| chbishop of Canterbury | Jeffery Dench |
| shop of Ely | Trevor Peacock |
| ng Henry V | Alan Howard |
| mphrey Duke of Gloucester | Stephen Jenn |
| omas Duke of Clarence | Anthony Naylor |
| ke of Exeter | Philip Brack |
| rl of Cambridge | Barrie Rutter |
| rd Scroop | Charles Dance |
| Thomas Grey | Arthur Whybrow |
| rl of Westmoreland | Reginald Jessup |
| rporal Bardolph | Tim Wylton |
| rporal Nym | Philip Dunbar |
| cient Pistol | Richard Moore |
| y | Peter Bourke |
| stress Quickly | Brenda Bruce |
| wer | Jeffrey Dench |
| iellen | Trevor Peacock |
| acmorris | Barrie Rutter |
| ny | Ken Stott |
| lliams | Charles Dance |
| tes | Arthur Whybrow |
| urt | Richard Derrington |
| Thomas Erpingham | Reginald Jessup |

e French:

| | |
|---|---|
| ng Charles VI | Clement McCallin |
| uphin | Geoffrey Hutchings |
| tharine | Carolle Rousseau |
| ke of Orleans | Philip Dunbar |
| nstable of France | Bernard Brown |
| ntjoy | Oliver Ford-Davies |
| onsieur le Fer | Tim Wylton |
| ice | Yvonne Coulette |
| ench Bishop | Oliver Ford-Davies |

Presented in two acts.

*Stage Managers:* Tim Richards, Anne Bonehill, David Hendry
*Press:* Charles Ziff, Kate MacIntyre, Kay Green

Closed May 9, 1976 after limited engagement of 23 performances.
Two performances of "Hollow Crown" were given at matinees
May 1 and May 8, 1976. The cast consisted of Jeffery Dench,
Oliver Ford-Davies, Brenda Bruce, Richard Moore, Bill Home-
wood. (No photos available)

**Top Right: Alan Howard Below: Philip Brack,
Stephen Jenn, Alan Howard, Anthony Naylor**

**Richard Moore, Tim Wylton, Philip Dunbar**

## BROOKLYN ACADEMY/LEPERCQ SPACE

Opened Thursday, May 6, 1976.*
The Brooklyn Academy of Music presents the Mabou Mines production of:

# THE RED HORSE ANIMATION

Text and Direction by Lee Breuer; Music, Philip Glass; Lighting Design, Jene Highstein

CAST

JoAnne Akalaitis
Ruth Maleczech
David Warrilow

The process and procedure of a creative act—animating an image of a red horse.

*Press:* Charles Ziff, Kate MacIntyre, Clint Brownfield

* Closed May 9, 1976 after limited engagement of 4 performances.

**Top Right: David Warrilow, JoAnne Akalaitis, Ruth Maleczech in "The Red Horse Animation"**

## BROOKLYN ACADEMY/OPERA HOUSE

Opened Tuesday, May 25, 1976.*
The Brooklyn Academy of Music presents the Warsaw Slav Cultural Center (E. J. Czerwinski, Artistic Director) production of:

# DANTE

Written, Directed and Designed by Jozef Szajna; Based on Dante's "The Divine Comedy"; Music, Krzysztof Penderecki; Projections, Kazimierz Urbanski

CAST

| | |
|---|---|
| Dante | Tomasz Marzec |
| Beatrice | Anna Milewsl |
| Charon | Antoni Pszonia |
| Maria | Aleksandra Karzynsl |
| Magdalene | Ewa Szykulsl |
| Francesca | Ewa Kozlowsl |
| Jacob | Zygmunt Maciejews |
| John/The Damned | Tadeusz Wludars |
| Judas | Jozef Wieczor |
| Pope/Clotho | Wanda Lothe-Stanislawsl |
| Cardinal/Atropos | Helena Norowi |
| Monk/Lachesis/Megaera | Krystyna Kolodziejcz |
| Medusa | Ewa Pok |
| Megaera | Krystyna Kc |
| Fury/Monk II | Krystyna Chmielewsl |
| Cerberus | Gustaw Kr |
| Penitent | Stanislaw Brud |
| The Chosen | Eugeniusz Priwiezience |

* Closed May 30, 1976 after limited engagement of 7 performanc

Opened Tuesday, June 1, 1976.*

# REPLIKA

Conceived and Directed by Jozef Szajna; Music, Bogusl Schaffer

CAST

Ewa Kozlowska
Irena Jun
Stanislaw Brudny
Antonia Pszoniak
Jozef Wieczorek

A wordless odyssey through the holocaust, depicting the indo table spirit of man, tempered by the inhumanity directed against h by himself.

*Press:* Charles Ziff, Kate MacIntyre, Clint Brownfield

* Closed June 6, 1976 after limited engagement of 7 performanc

**"Dante"**

# CHELSEA THEATER CENTER OF BROOKLYN

Robert Kalfin, Artistic Director
Michael David, Executive Director
Burl Hash, Productions Director

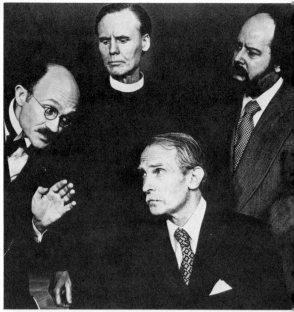

BROOKLYN ACADEMY OF MUSIC
Opened Wednesday, November 26, 1975.*
Chelsea Theater Center of Brooklyn presents:

## ICE AGE

By Tankred Dorst in cooperation with Ursula Ehler; English version, Peter Sander; Director, Arne Zaslove; Setting, Wolfgang Roth; Costumes, Ruth Morley; Lighting, Daniel Flannery; Technical Director, James Burke; Production Coordinator, Ginny Freedman

CAST

| | |
|---|---|
| Old Man | Roberts Blossom |
| Fragile Lady | Anne Ives |
| Cleaning Lady/Diva | Sonia Zomina |
| Gardener/Man with camera | Curt Williams |
| Spinster | Eleanor Cody Gould |
| Major's Widow | Frances Pole |
| Oswald | Nicholas Hormann |
| Prof. Jenssen | Jerrold Ziman |
| Male Assistant | Robert Einenkel |
| Female Assistant | Janice Fuller |
| Paul | George Morfogen |
| Holm/Man in mask | Larry Swansen |
| Reich/Fat Man in mask | K. Lype O'Dell |
| Bank Director/Blind Man | Gary Allen |
| Vera | Ruth Hunt |
| Woman in wheelchair | Frances Bay |
| Soldier | William Robertson |
| Berend | Charles Mayer |
| Dirk | Renos Mandis |
| Christian | Roger DeKoven |

UNDERSTUDIES: Frances Bay (Vera, Fragile Lady, Major's Widow, Cleaning Lady), Roger DeKoven (Old Man), Robert Einenkel (Reich, Paul, Oswald); K. Lype O'Dell (Cook), Curt Williams (Christian, Jenssen, Berend), Jerrold Ziman (Bank Director, Holm), Sonia Zomina (Spinster)

A drama in two acts. The action takes place at an old people's home and the adjoining park in Norway during 1947 and 1948.

*General Manager:* William Craver
*Press:* Joel Wald, Betty Lee Hunt Associates
*Stage Managers:* Sherman Warner, Bob Jaffe

Closed Dec. 14, 1975 after 32 performances.

*Laura W. Pettibone Photos*

**Top Right: Gary Allen, Larry Swansen,
K. Lype O'Dell, Roberts Blossom**

**Roger DeKoven, Roberts Blossom**

**BROOKLYN ACADEMY OF MUSIC**
Opened Thursday, March 4, 1976.*
Chelsea Theater Center of Brooklyn presents:

# THE BOSS

By Edward Sheldon; Director, Edward Gilbert; Settings, Lawrence King; Costumes, Carrie F. Robbins; Lighting, William Mintzer; Assistant to director, Charles Conwell; Music Consultant, Mel Marvin; Hairstylist, Paul Huntley

## CAST

| | |
|---|---|
| James D. Griswold | Allan Frank |
| Donald Griswold | Gregory Abels |
| Emily Griswold | Louise Shaffer |
| Mitchell | John Genke |
| Lawrence Duncan | Dennis Lipscomb |
| Michael R. Regan | Andrew Jarkowsky |
| Davis | Richard K. Sanders |
| Mrs. Cuyler | Pamela Burrell |
| Gates | John Eames |
| "Porky" McCoy | Tom-Patrick Dineen |
| Scanlan | Chris Carrick |
| Archbishop Sullivan | Igors Gavon |
| A Cook | Pamela Burrell |
| French Maid | Catherine Henry Lamm |
| Lieutenant of Police | John Genke |
| Police Officers | Chris Carrick, Chip Lucia |

UNDERSTUDIES: Allan Frank (Gates), Igors Gavon (Inspector), John Genke (Davis, Regan, Archbishop), Catherine Henry Lamm (Emily, Mrs. Cuyler), Dennis Lipscomb (Scanlan), Chip Lucia (Donald, Duncan, Porky), Richard K. Sanders (Mitchell)

A drama in four acts performed with one intermission. The action takes place in one of the Eastern lake-ports during 1910 and 1911.

*General Manager:* William Craver
*Press:* Joel Wald
*Stage Managers:* Bob Jaffe, Joseph Kavanagh

* Closed March 14, 1976 after 24 performances. Re-opened in Queens Playhouse for 16 performances.

*Laura W. Pettibone Photos*

**Louise Shaffer, Andrew Jarkowsky**

**Tom-Patrick Dineen, Andrew Jarkowsky
Top: Louise Shaffer, Chris Carrick, Andrew Jarkowsky**

# CIRCLE REPERTORY COMPANY

Marshall W. Mason, Artistic Director
Jerry Arrow, Executive Director
Seventh Season

CIRCLE REPERTORY COMPANY THEATRE
Opened Thursday, June 12, 1975.*
Circle Repertory Company presents:

## SPRING'S AWAKENING

By Frank Wedekind; Director, Jan P. Eliasberg; Set, Tracy Killam; Costumes, Faye Fingesten; Lighting, David Kissel; Original
Music, Tom Aronis; Technical Director, Bob Yanez

CAST

| | |
|---|---|
| Wendla | Lisa Pelikan |
| Mrs. Bergmann | Jo-Anne Belanger |
| Melchior | Arthur Marcus |
| Lammermeier | Kevin Geer |
| Moritz | Kenneth Norris |
| Ernst | Van Gosse |
| Hans | Charles T. Harper |
| Martha | Kate Schaefer |
| Thea | Cynthia Crumlish |
| Mrs. Gabor | Natalie Priest |
| Ilse | Deborah Offner |
| Rev. Sonnenstich | William Robertson |
| Judge Gabor | Thomas Barbour |
| Man in the mask | Roger McIntyre |

A play in three acts. The action takes place in Germany in 1892

Company Manager: Barbara Darwall
Press: Sharon Madden
Stage Managers: Susana Meyer, Anne Fishel

Closed June 15, 1975 after limited engagement of 5 performances.
No photos available.

CIRCLE REPERTORY COMPANY THEATRE
Opened Wednesday, June 25, 1975.*
Circle Repertory Company presents:

## NOT TO WORRY

By A. E. Santaniello; Director, Lanford Wilson; Setting, John Lee
Beatty; Costumes, Jennifer von Mayrhauser; Lighting, Dennis Pa-
richy; Sound, Chuck London, George Hansen; Technical Director,
Bob Yanez; Production Coordinator, Marshall Oglesby

CAST

| | |
|---|---|
| Larry | Brad Dourif |
| Tony | Rob Thirkield |
| Ruth | Teri Keane |

A play in two acts and five scenes. The action takes place at the
present time in a garden apartment in the French Quarter of New
Orleans, LA.

Company Manager: Barbara Darwall
Press: Sharon Madden
Stage Managers: Walter Wood, Cathy Rennich, Sarah Rodman

Closed July 13, 1975 after limited engagement of 20 performances.

*Michael Zettler Photo*

**Top Right: Rob Thirkield, Brad Dourif in
"Not to Worry" Below: Lisa Pelikan, Neil
Flanagan, Helen Stenborg in
"The Elephant in the House"**

CIRCLE REPERTORY COMPANY THEATRE
Opened Sunday, November 2, 1975.*
Circle Repertory Company presents:

## THE ELEPHANT IN THE HOUSE

By Berrilla Kerr; Director, Marshall W. Mason; Setting, John Lee
Beatty; Costumes, Jennifer von Mayrhauser; Lighting, Dennis Parichy; Original Music, Jonathan Hogan; Sound, Charles London,
George Hansen; Assistant Director, Steven Gomer; Technical Director, Earl R. Hughes

CAST

| | |
|---|---|
| Mary Elizabeth Adams | Helen Stenborg |
| Francesca | Lisa Pelikan |
| Mr. Johnson | Neil Flanagan |
| Timothy | Terence Foley |
| Molly | Conchata Ferrell |
| Jenny | Stephanie Gordon |
| Horace | Rob Thirkield |
| Gwenyth | Henrietta Bagley |

and Sugar, Cowboy, Cha-Cha and Apache

A play in two acts. The action takes place at the present time in
Mary Elizabeth Adams' house in New York City.

Company Manager: Dennis Purcell
Press: Rima Corben
Stage Managers: Susana Meyer, Dave Clow

* Closed Nov. 23, 1976 after limited engagement of 25 performances
and 7 previews.

*Marc Sadoux Photos*

**CIRCLE REPERTORY COMPANY THEATRE**
Opened Sunday, December 14, 1975.*
Circle Repertory Company presents:

# DANCING FOR THE KAISER

By Andrew Colmar; Director, Marshall Oglesby; Settings, Atkin Pace; Costumes, Jennifer von Mayrhauser; Lighting, Dennis Parichy; Choreography, Gilda Mullette; Sound, George Hansen, Charles London; Assistant Director, Carla Granat;

### CAST

| | |
|---|---|
| Douglas North Wicksteed | Douglass Watson |
| Walter Skendal | Peter Burnell |
| Willimot | Hy Mencher |
| Lional Buckmaster | Tom McDermott |
| Erica Kroonenberg | Jacqueline Bertrand |
| Martha Willow | Joanna Miles |
| Mrs. Willow | Maryellen Flynn |
| Rev. Father Bernard Buller | George Hall |
| Leo Kroonenberg | Peter Walker |
| Sir Osmon Pryor | Peter Murphy |
| Maurice | Hy Mencher |
| Annie | Patricia Roberts |
| Judge Sweet | George Hall |
| Court Clerk | Hy Mencher |
| Dr. Alfred Brey | Tom McDermott |
| The Man | Jean-Pierre Stewart |

A drama in two acts. The action takes place in London in 1918.

*Company Manager:* Dennis Purcell
*Press:* Rima Corben
*Stage Managers:* Richard Kilberg, Robin Tagliente

* Closed Jan. 4, 1976 after limited engagement of 25 performances and 7 previews.

*Marc Sadoux Photos*

### Top Right: Peter Murphy, Peter Burnell

**Peter Walker, Joanna Miles**

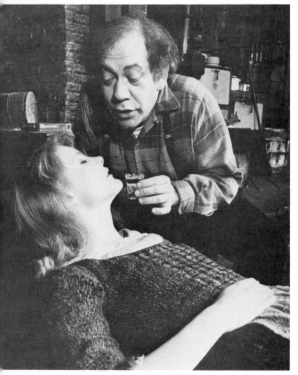

**Nancy Snyder, Daniel Seltzer**

**CIRCLE REPERTORY COMPANY THEATRE**
Opened Sunday, January 18, 1976.*
Circle Repertory Company presents:

# KNOCK KNOCK

By Jules Feiffer; Director, Marshall W. Mason; Setting, John L Beatty; Costumes, Jennifer von Mayrhauser; Lighting, Dennis P richy; Sound, Charles London, George Hansen; Technical Dire tors, Earl Hughes, Robert Yanez; Assistant to director, Steve Gomer

### CAST

| | |
|---|---|
| Cohn | Daniel Seltz |
| Abe | Neil Flanag |
| Wiseman | Judd Hirs |
| Joan | Nancy Snyd |
| Joan's Voices and other apparitions | Judd Hirs |

A comedy in three acts. The action takes place at the present tir in a small house in the woods.

*Company Manager:* Dennis Purcell
*Press:* Rima Corben
*Stage Manager:* Dan Hild

* Closed Feb. 22, 1976 after 41 performances and 7 previews move to Broadway. (See Broadway Calendar page 37)

*Herbert Migdoll Photos*

**RCLE REPERTORY COMPANY THEATRE**
Opened Wednesday, March 10, 1976.*
Circle Repertory Company presents:

# WHO KILLED RICHARD CORY?

By A. R. Gurney, Jr.; Director, Leonard Peters; Setting, Joan
enchak; Costumes, Gary Jones; Lighting, Arden Fingerhut; Mu-
al Director, Charles L. Greenberg; Choreography, Bridget Leices-
Assistant to director, Steve Steisel; Wardrobe Mistress, Cathy
ney

CAST

| | |
|---|---|
| hard Cory | Bruce Gray |
| ward/Joe/Chip | Roger Chapman |
| stitute/Librarian/Emily | Jane Hallaren |
| ce/Louise/Bessie | Sharon Madden |
| se/Charlotte/Grandmother | Patricia O'Connell |
| ie/Mrs. Baker/Richard's Mother | Joyce Reehling |
| die/Richard's Father/Anarchist | Larry Rosler |
| ctor/William/Chester | M. Jonathan Steele |
| nk/Rev. Davis/Ted Babcock | Robb Webb |

A drama in two acts.

*Company Manager:* Dennis Purcell
*Press:* Rima Corben, Marlyn Baum
*Stage Managers:* Marjorie Horne, Amy Schecter

Closed March 18, 1976 after 23 performances and 9 previews.

*Ken Howard Photo*

Bruce Gray (c)

CIRCLE REPERTORY COMPANY THEATRE
Opened Wednesday, May 5, 1976.*
Circle Repertory Company presents:

# SERENADING LOUIE

By Lanford Wilson; Director, Marshall W. Mason; Setting, John
Lee Beatty; Costumes, Jennifer von Mayrhauser; Lighting, Dennis
Parichy; Assistant to Director, John Sheehan; Artistic Staff Assis-
tant, Daniel Irvine; Administrative Staff Assistant, Marlyn Baum

CAST

| | |
|---|---|
| Mary | Tanya Berezin |
| Carl | Edward J. Moore |
| Gabrielle | Trish Hawkins |
| Alex | Michael Storm |

A play in two acts. The action takes place at the present time in
a suburban home north of Chicago during late October.

*Company Manager:* Dennis Purcell
*Press:* Rima Corben, Marlyn Baum
*Stage Managers:* Dave Clow, Amy Schecter

* Closed May 30, 1976 after limited engagement of 33 performances
and 7 previews.

*Gerry Goodstein Photos*

aya Berezin, Trish Hawkins, Edward J. Moore,
Michael Storm, also Right Center

# THE CLASSIC THEATRE

Nicholas John Stathis, Producer

**CENTRAL PRESBYTERIAN CHURCH**
November 12–30, 1975 (16 performances)

MARY TUDOR by Victor Hugo; Director, Maurice Edwards; Sets, James Cuomo; Costumes, Maryanne White; Music, George Prideaux; Lights, Howard Wallowitz; Technical Director, Terry Hunter; Stage Managers, Valerie Laura Imbarrato, Ron Cappa. CAST: Linda Barnhurst, Russell Costen, John Getz, Elek Hartman, Toni Kalem, Robert Milton, Norman Sample, Ron Cappa, Dan Hall, Tom Jarus, Lloyd Kay, Ron Piretti

**HAIK & ALICE KAVOOKJIAN AUDITORIUM**
January 18–February 3, 1976 (12 performances)

BADVI HAMAR (For the Sake of Honor) by Alexandre Shirvanzade; Translation, Nishan Parlakian; Director, Maurice Edwards; Sets, Tony Giovanetti; Costumes, Ruth Thomason; Lights, Annie Rech, Diana Conkling, Betsey McKearnan; Props, Renee Dodge; Stage Manager, Valerie L. Imbarrato. CAST: David Kerman, Elia Braca, Dan Lutzky, Michael Hardstark, Wende Sherman, Miriam Guttman-Iranyi, Dan Rubinate, Vincent Millard, Lawrence Harbison, Annie Rech

**CENTRAL PRESBYTERIAN CHURCH**
March 28–April 11, 1976 (12 performances)

THE APOCALYPSE ACCORDING TO J - J (ROUSSEAU) by Mario Apollonio (World Premiere); Translated by Anne Paolucci; Director, Maurice Edwards; Sets and Lights, Tony Giovanetti; Costumes, John Ahrens; Music, Joseph Albano; Choreography, Carin Molnar; Technical Assistants, Renee Dodge, Anthony Borovicka; Stage Manager, D. Jule Oliver. CAST: John Michalski (Jean-Jacques Rousseau), Joseph Frisari, Annette Hunt, Tom Jarus, Ellen Kelly, Jillian Lindig, Robert Milton, Wendy Nute, Emile Van der Noot, Craig Wyckoff, Loyola Boys Choir (Rona Klinghoffer, Director)

**CLASSIC THEATRE**
April 22–May 9, 1976 (12 performances)

A REPORT TO AN ACADEMY by Franz Kafka; Adapted, Designed and Directed by Gerd Staub; Lighting, Technical Adviser, Anthony Borovicka; Assistant to director, Matthias Boettrich; Stage Manager, Terry Hunter; Press, Alan Eichler. CAST: Henry Bal Robert Milton, Linda Barnhurst

*Ann Blackstock Photos*

**Ron Piretti, Lloyd Kaye in "Mary Tudor"**

**Henry Bal in "A Report to the Academy"**

**Robert Milton, John Merensky, and above: Wendy Nute in "The Apocalypse according to J.**

110

# COLONNADES THEATRE LAB

Michael Lessac, Artistic Director-Producer
Tom V. V. Tammi, Associate Artistic Director
Louisa Anderson, Administrative Director

COLONNADES THEATRE LAB
Opened Tuesday, December 2, 1975.*
Colonnades Theatre Lab presents;

## SECOND WIND

By David Morgan; Director, Michael Lessac; Composer, Joseph
Blunt; Sets and Projections, Robert U. Taylor; Lighting, Joe Ka-
minsky; Costumes, Joan Ferenchak, Donato Moreno; Sound, Gary
Harris; Technical Director, Robert H. Rickner; Wardrobe Master,
Mike Fiorentine

### CAST

| | |
|---|---|
| ne ......................... | Jacqueline Cassel |
| vor ......................... | Louis Giambalvo |
| h ......................... | Charlie Stavola |
| s. Galbraith ......................... | Sherrill Wainer |

*Stage Managers:* Michael Boonstra, Patricia Hannigan

Closed Jan. 18, 1976 after limited engagement of 15 performances
in repertory.

Opened Tuesday, December 2, 1975.*

## CINEMA SOLDIER

By Paavo Tammi; Director, Tom Tammi; Musical Arrangements,
Alexandra O'Karma, Miriam Moses; Lighting, Joe Kaminsky;
Graphics, Carol Banever

### CAST

| | |
|---|---|
| dier ......................... | Rhea Perlman |
| nes ......................... | Ruth Wallman |
| ltz ......................... | Ellene Winn |
| nist ......................... | Alexandra O'Karma |

*Press:* Ruth Wallman
*Stage Managers:* Michael Boonstra, Louisa Anderson

Closed Jan. 18, 1976 after limited engagement of 14 performances
in repertory.

**Top Right: Ruth Wallman, Rhea Perlman,
Ellene Winn in "Cinema Soldier"**

COLONNADES THEATRE LAB
Opened Thursday, December 4, 1975.*
Colonnades Theatre Lab presents:

## A MONTH IN THE COUNTRY

By Ivan Turgenev; Adaptation, David Morgan; Director, Michael
Lessac; Music Coordinator, Joseph Blunt; Sets, Robert U. Taylor;
Costumes, Donato Moreno, Joan Ferenchak; Sound, Gary Harris

### CAST

| | |
|---|---|
| Adam Ivanitch Schaff ......................... | Bob Byrd |
| Anna Semyonovna ......................... | Marian Baer |
| Lizaveta Bogdanovna ......................... | Sherrill Wainer |
| Natalya Petrovna ......................... | Alexandra O'Karma |
| Mihail Alexandritch Rakitin ............. | Tom V. V. Tammi |
| Kolya ......................... | Sima Chalfy |
| Alexei Nicolaitch Beliayev ............... | Edward Edwards |
| Mattvei ......................... | Charlie Stavola |
| Ignaty Illyitch Shpigelsky ................. | Bill E. Noone |
| Vera Alexandrovna ......................... | Jacqueline Cassel |
| Arkady Sergeitch Yslaev ................... | John Hammil |
| Katya ......................... | Linda Swenson |
| Afanasy Ivanitch Bolshintsov ............. | Louis Giambalvo |

*Press:* Ruth Wallman
*Stage Managers:* Michael Boonstra, Patricia Hannigan

* Closed Jan. 14, 1976 after 14 performances in repertory.

COLONNADES THEATRE LAB
Opened Tuesday, December 9, 1975.*
Colonnades Theatre Lab presents:

## REFLECTIONS

By David Morgan; Based on story by Oscar Wilde; Director,
Michael Lessac; Music, Miriam Moses; Sets, Robert U. Taylor;
Lighting, Joe Kaminsky; Costumes, Joan Ferenchak; Sound, Gary
Harris; Choreographic Assistant, Bill E. Noone; Pianist, Elvira
Steinberg

### CAST

| | |
|---|---|
| The Reflection ......................... | Jacqueline Cassel |
| The Narrator ......................... | Peter Scolari |
| The Infanta ......................... | Deborah Davison |
| The Duchess ......................... | Sherrill Wainer |
| The King ......................... | Tom V. V. Tammi |
| Yuval ......................... | John Hammil |
| Nada ......................... | Portia Patterson |
| Vita ......................... | Rhea Perlman |
| The Hunter ......................... | Charlie Stavola |
| The Dwarf ......................... | Louis Giambalvo |

*Press:* Ruth Wallman
*Stage Managers:* Michael Boonstra, Jim Palmer

* Closed Jan. 16, 1976 after 16 performances in repertory.

*Diane Gorodnitzki Photos*

**Jacqueline Cassel, Edward Edwards
in "A Month in the Country"**

# COUNTERPOINT THEATRE COMPANY

Howard Green, Artistic Director
Gonzalo Madurga, Associate Artistic Director
Paulene Reynolds, Managing Director

**COUNTERPOINT THEATRE**

October 3 - 20, 1975 (12 performances)

MISS JULIE and THE STRONGER by August Strindberg; Director, Gonzalo Madurga; Costumes, Ernesto Leston; Scenery, Minda Chipurnoi; Lighting, James Singlar; Stage Managers, Fred Berry, Darleen Bever. CAST: "The Stronger" - Paulene Reynolds (Miss Y), Linda Geiser (Mrs. X) Howard Green (Waiter), "Miss Julie" - Howard Green (Jean), Linda Geiser (Kristin), Paulene Reynolds (Julie)

November 21 - December 15, 1975 (16 performances)

CHILDREN OF DARKNESS by Edwin Justus Mayer; Director, Howard Green; Scenery, Minda Chipurnoi; Costumes, Ernesto Leston; Lighting, Ronald Daley; Assistant to director, Darleen Bever; Technical Director, George Coleman; Sound, Gary Tims. CAST: George Salerno (Mr. Snap), George Coleman (First Bailiff), Carl Brown (Cartwright), Don Marletto (Fierce), Tom Leo (Jonathan), Donald Berry (Count), Marina Stefan (Laetitia), Fred Berry (Second Bailiff), Jeremy Brook (Wainwright)

January 16 - February 2, 1976 (12 performances)

A CHEKHOV PORTFOLIO by Anton Chekhov; Director, Howard Green; Scenery, Lighting, George Coleman; Costumes, Carol D. Wahlquist; Production Assistant, Darleen Bever; Stage Managers, Fred Berry, Rawle Brome, Cindy Russell, Gary Tims. CAST: "The Harmfulness of Tobacco" - Ed Crowley (Lecturer), "The Brute" - Tom Leo (Luka), Annie Kravat, Paulene Reynolds (Mrs. Popov), James Himelsbach (Smirnov), "Summer in the Country" - Tom Leo (Murashkin), Don Marlette (Tolkachov), "Swan Song" - Sam Gray (Vassily), Don Marlette (Nikita)

March 5-22, 1976 (12 performances)

ROCKET TO THE MOON by Clifford Odets; Director, Joel Friedman; Lighting, Deborah Lynne Helitzer; Costumes, Ernesto Leston; Technical Director, George Coleman; Company Manager, Fred Berry; Stage Managers, Rawle Brome, Gareth Tims. CAST: Howard Green (Ben), Sylvia Gassell (Belle), Tanny McDonald (Cleo), John J. Martin (Phil), Sam Gray (Prince), Len Auclair (Frenchy), Elek Hartman (Wax)

April 23 - May 10, 1976 (12 performances)

THE REHEARSAL by Jean Anouilh; Director, Howard Green; Scenery and Lighting, George L. Coleman; Costumes, Ernesto Leston; Stage Manager, Cindy Russell. CAST: Elek Hartman (Damiens), Linda Geiser (Countess), Geoffrey Webb (Count), Rebecca Darke (Hortensia), Gonzalo Madurga (Hero), Rod Britt (Villebosse), Elaine Kilden (Lucile)

**Linda Geiser, Paulene Reynolds in "Miss Julie"**

**Right: Sam Gray, Donald Marlette in "A Chekhov Portfolio" Above: Marina Stefan, Carl Brown, Donald Berry, George Salerno, Tom Leo in "Children of Darkness"**

**Gonzalo Madurga, Elaine Kilden in "The Rehearsal"**

**Howard Green, Tanny McDonald in "Rocket to the Moon"**

# THE CUBICULO

Philip Meister, Artistic Director
Elaine Sulka, Managing Director
John Dudich, Publicity Director

THE CUBICULO
September 18 - October 11, 1975 (12 performances)

THE MEMOIRS OF CHARLIE POPS by Joseph Hart; Director, John Bettenbender; Scenery, Joseph Miklojcik; Lighting and Projections, Michael Tomko; Sound, William Motyka; Costumes, Vickie McLaughlin; Technical Adviser, Priscilla Travis; Stage Managers, Donna Miklojcik, Tom Iovanne. CAST: Frank Ammirati (Charlie Pops), Keith Kermizian (Robert), Ann Rottman (Anna), Robin Siegel (Mary), Fred Sirasky (Coolie), Edward Yanowitz (John), Rita Bascari (Jeannie), Brian Connors, William Mastrosimone (Two Men), Italian Ladies: Sherry Akselrod, Esther Blanchford, Mary Ann Michaels, Wendy Lyon, Yasmin Vargas

September 25 - 28, 1975 (4 performances)

WEEKS by Nancy Heikin; Songs, Nancy Heikin; Lighting, Tammy Temptation; Stage Manager, Nicki Nelki. CAST: Susan Topping (Inner), Michael Haynes (Herr Guitar), Nancy Heikin (Outer)

October 23 - November 8, 1975 (12 performances)

SURVIVING THE BARBED WIRE CRADLE by Francine Storey; Director, Dana Roberts; Stage Manager, Lawrence Harbison; Lighting, Curt Ostermann; Assistant Stage Manager, Geraldine Kedrick; Art Director, Kenneth G. Beck. CAST: Janice Kay Young (Maureen), Jen Jones (Nanna), John Camera (The Man)
TERRIBLE JIM FITCH by James Leo Herlihy; Director, Dana Roberts; Stage Manager, Lawrence Harbison CAST: Mary Ed Porter (Sally), Richard Zobel (Jim)

November 12 - 22, 1975 (8 performances)

A GOOD OLD-FASHIONED REVUE conceived and directed by Les Barkdull; Scenery, Michael Hotopp, Paul dePass; Lighting, Randy Becker; Costumes, Al Sardella; Musical Direction, John Franceschina; Musical Staging, Judy Haskell; Stage Managers, Lee Cotterell, Barbara Ramsey; Press, Alan Eichler. CAST: Carleton Carpenter, Sue Lawless, Gordon Ramsey, Harold Davis Ann Hodapp

November 14 - 30, 1975 (12 performances)

PEOPLE FROM DIVISION STREET by Studs Terkel; Adapted by Alexandra Devon; Director, MacIntyre Dixon; Assistant to director, Philip Visco; Producer, Pegasus Productions; Associate Producer-Stage Manager, Carole McPhee; Lighting, Howard Kessler; Scenery, Michael deSouza. CAST: MacIntyre Dixon, Saundra MacDonald, Gail Ryan, Jay Bonnell, Owen Hollander, Beverly Wideman, Jeanne Schlegel, Philip Visco

December 4 - 21, 1975 (12 Performances)

BOXES by Gary Martin; Director, Gene Becker; Sets, Leon Munier; Lighting, Rafe Scheinblum; Costumes, Dianne Huffman; Assistant Director, Ronnie Asbell; Technical Director, Randy Becker; Stage Managers, Jill Harwood, Geri Silk. CAST: "Benson and Cissy" - Darrie Lawrence (Cissy), Mark Curran (Benson), Ron Harrington (Moriarity), Bilo Bryant (Wanda), "Boxes Going to Salem" - Margot Hastings (Annette), Michael Kolba (Sam), Ron Harrington (Carlos), "Two See beside the Sea"-Don Welch (Jon), Ron Welch (Don)

*Conrad Ward Photos*

**Top Right: Carleton Carpenter in
"Good Old-Fashioned Revue"
Below: Raymond Stough,
Mary Ellen Mathews in "Holy Ghosts"**

**Sally Mercer, Jeffrey DeMunn in "Founding Father"**

## THE CUBICULO

January 28 - February 8, 1976 (12 performances)

THE HOME by Kent Anderson and Bengt Bratt; Translated from the Swedish by Yvonne Sandstroem; Adapted and Directed by Bob Horen; Choreography, Louanna Gardner; Music, Don Arrington; Designed by Jay B. Keene; Stage Managers, David Rosenberg, Philip Hirsch, Mary Jo Robertiello. CAST: Pat Carmichael (Dagny), Suzanne Granfield (Jenny), Gwendolyn Brown (Matilda), Ann Freeman (Svea), Lee Billington (Charlotte), Fred Carmichael (Hjalmar), Peter Murphy (Nils), Kenneth L. Chomont (Albin), Edwin Young (Johan), John Merensky (Nurse Siv), Gary Swartz (Nurse Gunnel), K. T. Baumann (Anette).

January 28, 1976 (1 performance)

DUETS OF DRAMA PRESENTED BY the Inscape Company, (Jacqueline Berger, Roseann Sheridan, Artistic Directors); Technical Director, Randy Becker; Art Design, Lighting, Marian Bruhns; Poetry and Narration, Marianne Wrobleski. CAST: "I Hate the Situation More Than I Love You" by Jacqueline Berger: William Van Hunter (Burt), Roseann Sheridan (Norma) "Kiss the World Goodbye" by Jack Hollander; Director, William Van Hunter: Michael McCarthy (Charles), Roseann Sheridan (Violet), Jacqueline Berger (Joanne), William Van Hunter (George), Tim Silver (Milton), Gil Tores (Leo)

February 19- March 7, 1976 (12 performances)

HOLY GHOSTS by Romulus Linney; Director, John Olon-Scrymgeour; Scenery and Lighting, Jane Thurn; Music Coach, Janet Siegal; Stage Manager, Deborah Teller. CAST: Susan Berger (Nancy), Guy Boyd (Coleman), Robert Baines (Rogers), John Wilkerson (Obediah), Charles Harper (Virgil), Frank Rohrbach (Orin), Martin Treat (Howard), Dolores Kenan (Lorena), Josephine Nichols (Mrs. Wall), Mary Ellen Mathews (Muriel), Curt May (Billy), Ric Lavin (Obediah Sr.), Robert Milton (Carl), Elaine Sulka (Bonnie), Raymond Stough (Cancer Man)

THE BEDBUG by Vladimir Mayakovsky; Adapted and Directed by John Merensky; Designed by Joe Phillips; Lighting, Paul Harkins; Music, Joseph Hardin; Movement, Francine Storey; Artistic Director, Philip Meister; Stage Manager, Jim Singlar; Presented by The Cubiculo Playmakers. CAST: Karen Bernhard, Kenneth Freeman, Joseph Hardin, Dolores Kenan, Ron Klein, Bill Maloney, Sally Mercer, John Merensky, Jim Singlar, Francine Storey

"The Bedbug"    *Pictures of People Ph*

April 5 - 25, 1976 (12 performances)

DR. HERO by Israel Horovitz; Director, Lee Rachman; Scen Trueman Kelley; Lighting, Bradley G. Richart; Sound, Bob J Program Coordinators, John Dudich, Dinah Carlson; Stage M ager, Barbara Alpert. CAST: Anthony Mark, Leah Brecher, M Keeler, Nancy Mette, Bob Perry, Alan Rosenberg

April 22 - May 9, 1976

FOUNDING FATHER by Amlin Gray; Director, Consta Clarke; Set, Ted Enik; Lighting, Paul Harkins; Costumes, ( Franks; Technical Director, John Moran; Stage Manager, C Kuypers; Special Consultant, Mary E. Devine. CAST: Jeffrey Munn (Aaron Burr), Karen Bernhard (Margaret), Perrin Fe (Leroy), Ed Powell (Robinson), Ed Crowley (Harmon), Irving M man (James), Sally Mercer (Theodosia), John Merensky (Gide Jeffrey Herman (Marques), Ed Powell (John Marshall), Richm

Hoxie (George Hay)

May 11 - 16, 1976 (5 performances)

CLYTEMNESTRA by Elaine Sulka; Director, Philip Meister; ( tumes, Sharon Hollinger; Setting, Marie McKim; Music and So John Franceschina; Movement, Francine Storey; Lighting, Will Lambert; Stage Manager, Kirk Wolfinger; Technical Director, B ley G. Richart. CAST: Joanna Merlin (Clytemnestra), Cynthia I low (Electra), Irene Frances Kling, Darrie Lawrence, Je Schlegel (Voci/Furies), Women: Eliza DeCroes, Ann Freen Willi Kirkham, Amy Margaret Samuelson, Marilynn Winb Grace Woodard

May 20 - 30, 1976 (8 performances)

OH SPEAKIES by Sandro Key-Aberg; Translated from Swedis Goran Prinyz-Pahlson and Brian Rothwell; Adapted and Dire by Bob Horen; Choreography, Louanna Gardner; Lights and V als, Jay Keene; Production Supervisor, David Rosenberg; S Manager, Carmalita Fuentes. CAST: K. T. Baumann, Julia Cu Suzanne Granfield, Douglas Maxwell, Frank Vohs, Edwin Yo

May 25 - 30, 1976 (8 performances)

STAUF by Michael Sahl and Eric Salzman; Composed and Dire by Mr. Sahl and Mr. Salzman; Presented by the Quog Music The (Eric Salzman, Artistic Director; Richard Green, Executive Di tor); Choreography, Anne Sahl; Scenery, Christina Weppner; ( tumes, Sally Ann Parsons; Tape, Laurie Spiegel; Lighting, Winberry; Stage Manager, Andrew Bates; Keyboards, Michael S Jordan Kaplan. CAST: William Parry (Stauf), Denise Delape (Margarita), Gerrianne Raphael (Kali), Michael Best (Dr. Jo Peggy Levine, David Barney (Dancers)

**Joanna Merlin, Cynthia Darlow in "Clytemnestra"**

# DUME SPANISH THEATRE

Herberto Dume, Producer-Artistic Director
Enrique Gomez, Public Relations

JME SPANISH THEATRE
June 13 - 29, 1975 (15 performances)

MALENTENDIDO by Albert Camus; Produced and Directed
Herberto Dume; Sets, Guido Betancourt; Costumes, Serge Pinc-
ey; Lighting, Wilfredo Zagal; Hairstylist, Julio Ambros; Make-up,
lando Zaragoza; Assistant Director, Wilfredo Zagal. CAST: En-
ue Gomes (Jesus), Isabel Segovia (Marta), Sol (La Madre), Idalia
az (Maria), Rafael Delgado (El Viejo)

October 10 - November 9, 1975 (23 performances)

NTA CAMILA DE LA HABANA VIEJA by Jose R. Brene;
duced and Directed by Herberto Dume; Sets, Guido Betancourt;
stumes, Serge Pinckney; Assistant Director, Juan Carlos Gi-
nez. CAST: Mercedes Enriquez (Camila), Antonieta Blanco
ica), William Perez (Nico), Emma Vilvas (Antonia), Mateo
mez (Pirey), Israel Ramos (Bocachula), Esther Rivera (Madrina),
lia Diaz (Leonor), Teresa Pernas (Jacinta), Emilio Rodriguez
odoro)

November 19 - December 7, 1975 (15 performances)

SENORITA JULIA by August Strindberg; Produced and Di-
ted by Herberto Dume; Sets, Guido Betancourt; Costumes, Serge
ckney; Assistant Director, Juan Carlos Gimenez; Make-up, Ro-
do Zaragoza. CAST: Teresa Yenque (Cristina), Manuel Yesckas
an), Isabel Segovia (Julia), Belinda Roger (Criada), Juan Carlos
menez (Criado)

January 30 - February 29, 1976 (15 performances)

JRLESQUE and LA RELACION by Lorenzo Piriz-Carbonell;
s, Guido Betancourt; Costumes, Serge Pinckney; Assistant Direc-
, Juan Carlos Gimenez; General Director, Herberto Dume.
ST: "Burlesque" Patricia Rodriguez (Lina), Manuel Yesckas
ony), "La Relacion" Teresa Yenque (Rosa), Freddy Valle (Brian)

April 2 - May 30, 1976 (29 performances)

NOCHE DE LOS ASESINOS by Jose Triana; Director, Her-
to Dume; Sets, Guido Betancourt; Costumes, Serge Pinckney;
ke-up Rolando Zaragoza; Stage Manager, Mario Castillo. CAST:
via Brito (Cuca), Manuel Yesckas (Lalo), Teresa Yenque (Beba)

*Rafael Llerena Photos*

**Top Right: Mercedes Enriquez,**
**William Perez in "Santa Camila ..."**
**Below: Teresa Yenque,**
**Freddy Valle in "Le Relacion"**

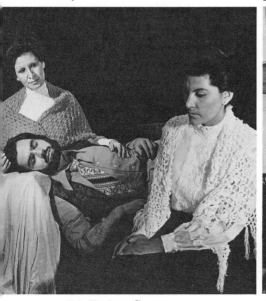

**Sol, Enrique Gomez,**
**Isabel Segovia in "El Malentendido"**

**Isabel Segovia, Manuel Yesckas in "La Senorita Julia"**

# EQUITY LIBRARY THEATRE

George Wojtasik, Managing Director
Lynn Montgomery, Production Director
Ann B. Grassilli, Producer ELT Informals

**EQUITY LIBRARY THEATRE**
Opened Thursday, October 16, 1975.*
Equity Library Theatre presents:

## THE PURSUIT OF HAPPINESS

By Lawrence Langner and Armina Marshall Langner; Director,
Tisa Ching; Costumes, Susan Sigrist; Set, John Barker; Music, Louis
Stewart; Lighting, Pat Stern; Hairstylist, J. Alexander

### CAST

| | |
|---|---|
| Meg | Grace Woodard |
| Mose | Peter Yoshida |
| Capt. Aaron Kirkland | Alvin Lum |
| Colonel Sherwood | Gus Fleming |
| Prudence | Deborah Moldow |
| Comfort | Lilah Kan |
| Max | Peter Julian |
| Thad | Dennis Sakamoto |
| Rev. Banks | Stan Kahn |

A comedy in 2 acts and 4 scenes. The action takes place in the
parlor of the Kirkland farm in Westville, Connecticut.

*Press:* Lewis Harmon, Sol Jacobson
*Stage Managers:* Laurence Rothenberg, Nancy T. Finn

* Closed Oct. 26, 1975 after limited engagement of 14 performances.

**Top Right: Dennis Sakamoto,
Stan Kahn, Alvin Lum, Deborah Moldow**

**EQUITY LIBRARY THEATRE**
Opened Thursday, November 6, 1975.*
Equity Library Theatre presents:

## TENDERLOIN

Book, George Abbott, Jerome Weidman; Based on novel by Samuel Hopkins Adams; Music, Jerry Bock; Lyrics, Sheldon Harnick;
Director, Robert Brink; Choreographer, Rick Atwell; Musical Direction and Dance Arrangements, Bill Grossman; Vocal Arrangements, Bill Grossman, Thomas Helm; Assistant Musical Director,
Thomas Helm; Settings, James Steere; Lighting, Jeffrey Schissler;
Costumes, Mimi Berman Maxmen

### CAST

| | |
|---|---|
| Tommy | Brad Blaisdel |
| Nita | Sherry Rooney |
| Lt. Schmidt | Jim Hillgartner |
| Rev. Brock | Stan Page |
| Gertie | Beverly Hart |
| Maggie | Sally Mitchel |
| Margie | Adrienne Del Mont |
| Bridget | Elaine Rinehar |
| Terence | Steven Rotblat |
| Richard | Craig Schaefe |
| Angela | Amanda Castl |
| Jessica | Suzanne Fore |
| Laura | Pamela McLernon |
| Ellington | William Perle |
| Purdy | Richard Rossomm |
| Joe Kovack | Alan Abram |
| Martin | Michael Makma |
| Rooney | Marcus Smyth |
| Nellie | Deborah Geffne |
| Sgt. Becker | Douglass Wenric |
| Jake | Jerry Colke |
| Frye | Neal Thompso |
| Liz | Janice Ehrlic |
| Deacon | Michael Zeke Zaccar |
| Lillie | Betsy Lapk |

MUSICAL NUMBERS: "Bless This Land," "Little Old New
York," "Dr. Brock," "Artificial Flowers," "What's in It for You,"
"Reform," "I Wonder What It's Like," "Tommy, Tommy,"
"Lovely Laurie," "Picture of Happiness," "Shame Dance," "Dea
Friend," "Army of the Just," "Money Changes Hands," "Goo
Clean Fun," "My Miss Mary," "My Gentle Young Johnny," "Th
Trial," "Tenderloin Celebration," "Nobody Cares," Epilogue

A musical in 2 acts and 18 scenes. The Action takes place on th
Island of Manhattan in the latter part of the 19th Century.

*Press:* Lewis Harmon, Sol Jacobson
*Stage Managers:* Robert Bennett, Nancy Harrington, Amy F.
Leveen

* Closed Nov. 23, 1975 after limited engagement of 22 perfor
mances.

*Gary Wheeler Photo*

**Adrienne Del Monte, Sherry Rooney,
Beverly Hartz, Sally Mitchell**

# ANOTHER LANGUAGE

By Rose Franken; Director, Leonard Peters; Set, Calvin Church-man; Lighting, Todd Lichtenstein; Costumes, Dennis O'Connor; Assistant to director, Bob Dixon; Hairstylist, J. Alexander; Wardrobe Mistress, Linda Kavy

CAST

| | |
|---|---|
| Mrs. Hallam | Mildred Dana |
| Mr. Hallam | Warrington Winters |
| Harry Hallam | James Doerr |
| Helen Hallam | Nicki Kaplan |
| Walter Hallam | Mel Boudrot |
| Grace Hallam | June Squibb |
| Paul Hallam | Robert Bonds |
| Etta Hallam | Marjorie Lovett |
| Victor Hallam | Ron Frazier |
| Stella Hallam | Margaret Whitton |
| Jerry Hallam | Dennis Boutsikaris |

A play in 3 acts. The action takes place in the Hallams' home during October in the early 1930's.

*Press:* Lewis Harmon, Sol Jacobson
*Stage Managers:* Mary Burns, Marge Pfleiderer

* Closed Dec. 14, 1975 after limited engagement of 14 performances.

*Gary Wheeler Photo*

**Marjorie Lovett, Nicki Kaplan, June Squibb**

# PANAMA HATTIE

Music and Lyrics, Cole Porter; Book, Herbert Fields, B. G. DeSylva: Adaptation, Charles Abbott, Fredric Dehn; Director, Charles Abbott; Musical Direction, Eileen LaGrange; Choreography, Roger Braun; Musical Numbers Staged by Charles Abbott, Roger Braun; Vocal and Dance Arrangements, Eileen LaGrange; Sets, Philipp Jung; Lighting, Emily Jefferson; Costumes and Hairstyles, Mimi Berman Maxmen; Assistant Musical Director, Thomas Helm

CAST

| | |
|---|---|
| Skat | Robert Browning |
| Windy | Terrance McKerrs |
| Woozy | Michaeljohn McGann |
| Mac | Christopher Wynkoop |
| Florrie | May Keller |
| Hattie Maloney | Mary Ellen Ashley |
| Leila Tree | Lynn Martin |
| Nick Bullett | Michael Davis |
| Geraldine Bullett | Diana Barrows |
| Vivien Budd | Douglas Hayle |
| Whitney Randolph/Admiral Tree | Christopher Wynkoop |
| Sea Biscuit | Nick |

PANAMANIANS, GUESTS, SAILORS: Robert Longbottom (Bootblack/M.P.), Vernon Spencer (Bootblack/Captain/Conga Drummer), Donn Hollander (Father/Announcer), Martha Deering (Mother/Senorita), Mark Barrows (Son), K. K. Preece (Vendor/Girl with ice cubes), Steve Belin (Newsboy/Messenger/Henry), Robert Lintner (Waiter), Sue Anne Gershenson (Girl on beach/Girl with leis), J. Thomas Wierney (Boy on beach/Conga Drummer), Rick DeFilipps (Stranger/Guard), Karen Keller (Mrs. Foxcroft/Girl with Cards), Marilyn Firment (Guest/Girl with smile), Linda Madama (Senorita/Girl with pinatas), Dione Messina (Girl with two ribs)

MUSICAL NUMBERS: "A Stroll on the Plaza," "Visit Panama," "My Mother Would Love You," "I've Still Got My Health," "Make It Another Old Fashioned," "Let's Be Buddies," "Don't Look at Me That Way," "Who Would Have Dreamed Dance," "I'm Throwing a Ball Tonight," "Fiesta," "So Near and Yet So Far," "I've Got You under My Skin," "Fresh as a Daisy," "You Said It," "Join It Right Away," Finale

A musical in 2 acts and 12 scenes. The action takes place in Panama City

*Press:* Sol Jacobson, Lewis Harmon
*Stage Managers:* Eve Sorel, Rona Cappa, P. Steven Shlansky

* Closed February 1, 1976 after limited engagement of 22 performances.

**Douglas Hayle, Diana Barrows,
Michael Davis, Mary Ellen Ashley**

## EQUITY LIBRARY THEATRE

Opened Thursday, February 12, 1976.*
Equity Library Theatre presents:

# MISSOURI LEGEND

By E. B. Ginty; Director, Thom Molyneaux; Scenery, Marla Schweppe; Lighting, Timothy Galvin; Costumes, Paula Davis; Musical Direction, Earl Wentz; Additional Music and Lyrics, Earl Wentz, Thom Molyneaux

### CAST

| | |
|---|---|
| Billy Gashade | Earl Wentz |
| Aunt Belle | Jeanne Schlegel |
| Frank Howard | Todd Drexel |
| Jim Cummins | Peter Looney |
| Charlie Johnson | Michael Cutt |
| Bob Johnson | Michael Oakes |
| Mrs. Howard | Sofia Landon |
| Thomas Howard | Bill Tatum |
| Martha | Jody Hingle |
| Widow Weeks | Susanne Marley |
| Hosea "Pop" Hickey | Bill Wiley |
| Sam | James Galvin |
| George | Ray Rantapaa |
| Asa | Michael Zeke Zaccaro |
| Jenny | Annie O'Neill |
| Trapper's Wife | Georgia Southcotte |
| Police Commissioner Gregg | Harry Carlson |
| The Reverend | Ray Rantapaa |

A play in 2 acts and 6 scenes. The action takes place in Missouri in March in the past.

*Press:* Sol Jacobson, Lewis Harmon
*Stage Managers:* Ed Oster, Amy F. Leveen, Tom Nagle

* Closed Feb. 22, 1976 after limited engagement of 14 performances.

*Gary Wheeler Photo*

**Sofia Landon, Harry Carlson, Bill Tatum**

## EQUITY LIBRARY THEATRE

Opened Thursday, March 4, 1976.*
Equity Library Theatre presents:

# MAGGIE FLYNN

Book, Music, Lyrics, Hugo Peretti, Luigi Creatore, George I Weiss; Book in collaboration with Morton DaCosta; Based on ide by John Flaxman; Conceived, Directed, Staged by William Koc Musical Concept and Direction, Thomas Helm; Scenery and Ligh ing, Richard B. Williams; Costumes, Susan Tsu; Assistant to dire tor, Joanne Benson; Wardrobe Mistress, Shelly Friedman

### CAST

Austin Colyer (O'Brian, Ed Waters, Jenkins, Ambassador), Deb rah Combs (Mary O'Cleary, Mrs. Schultz), Paul A. Corma (Timmy, Schultz), Mike Dantuono (Farraday, Chauncey), Be Glenn (Maggie Flynn), Richard Halpern (Carter, O'Rourke, W liam, Piedmont, Opdyke), Mark Hattan (O'Reilly, Mulligan, Sg Andrew, Efram, O'Shaughnessy), Parks Hill (Walter, Logan, W Jefferson, Senator Savage), Linda Kampley (Hyacinth, Molly, M Van Horn, Mrs. Parkington), Nita Novy (Jenny, Violet, Mrs. V Stock, Mrs. Opdyke), Ian O'Connell (O'Leary, O'Shea, Sebastia Bob Jefferson, Gen. Parkington), Paula Parker (Tessie, Pansy, M Humperdink, Bearded Lady, Mrs. Savage), Ross Petty (Phine Flynn), Bill Roberts (Sprague Sgt., Suggins, Erasmus, Donnell Cathy Roskam (Gladys, Chrysanthemum, Mrs. Vanderhoff)

MUSICAL NUMBERS: "Overture of Coming Attractions," "Co Morning Montage," "Nice Cold Morning," "Hot Morning Mor age," "Any Other Way," "Maggie Flynn," "Learn How to Laugh "Look around Your Little World," "Thank You Song," "I Wo Let It Happen Again," "Homeless Children," "How about a Bal "They're Never Gonna Make Me Fight," "Pitter Patter," "I Works!," "Why Can't I Walk Away?," "Game of War," "Le Drink to That," "Mr. Clown"

A musical in 2 acts and 14 scenes. The action takes place in t Irish Bowery of New York City in 1863.

*Press:* Lewis Harmon, Sol Jacobson
*Stage Managers:* Ellen Zalk, R. Bruce Martin, Camille Monte

* Closed March 21, 1976 after limited engagement of 22 perfo mances.

*Gary Wheeler Photo*

**Mark Hattan, Richard Halpern, Bette Glenn, Ian O'Connell, Paul Corman, Parks Hill**

## EQUITY LIBRARY THEATRE
Opened Thursday, April 1, 1976.*
Equity Library Theatre presents:

# THE RIMERS OF ELDRITCH

By Lanford Wilson; Director, Cyprienne Gabel; Scenery, John C. Jackson; Costumes, Joyce Aysta; Lighting, Patrika Brown; Associate Scenic Designer, Kenneth A. Shewer; Wardrobe Mistress, Maggie Raywood

### CAST

| | |
|---|---|
| Judge-Preacher | Kender Jones |
| Wilma Atkins | Virginia Downing |
| Martha Truit | Joan G. Gilbert |
| Nelly Windrod | Martha Miller |
| Mary Windrod | Rose Lischner |
| Robert Conklin | Daniel Landon |
| Trucker | Robert Einenkel |
| Cora Groves | Ruth Livingston |
| Walter | Richard Harmel |
| Eva Jackson | Amy Wright |
| Josh Johnson | Timothy Wallace |
| Skelly Mannor | William Robertson |
| Peck Johnson | Wally Duquet |
| Evelyn Jackson | Edith Greenfield |
| Mavis Johnson | Shirley Bodtke |
| Patsy Johnson | Valli Hanley |
| Lena Truit | Deborah Savadge |

A play in two acts. The action takes place at the present time in Eldritch, a small former mining town in the Middle West with a population of about 70.

*Press:* Lewis Harmon, Sol Jacobson
*Stage Managers:* Amy Pell, David Rosenberg

* Closed April 11, 1976 after limited engagement of 14 performances.

*Gary Wheeler Photo*

**Top Right: Amy Wright, Daniel Landon
in "The Rimers of Eldritch"**

**Randy Hugill, Kaylyn Dillehay, Nancy Salis,
George F. Maguire, Eleanor Barbour in
"Follies"**

## EQUITY LIBRARY THEATRE
Opened Thursday, May 6, 1976.*
Equity Library Theatre presents:

# FOLLIES

Book, James Goldman; Music and Lyrics, Stephen Sondheim; Director, Russell Treyz; Musical Direction, Jim Coleman; Choreography, John Montgomery; Scenery, John M. Falabella; Costumes, Donna Meyer; Lighting, Victor En Yu Tan; Hairstylist, J. Alexander Scafa; Wardrobe Mistresses, Shelly Friedman, Lynda Kavy; Assistant Choreographer, Barbara Beck; Headdresses, J. Douglas James

### CAST

| | |
|---|---|
| Sally Durant Plummer | Lois Ann Saunders |
| Roscoe | Andrew Roman |
| Phyllis Rogers Stone | Joan Ulmer |
| Benjamin Stone | George F. Maguire |
| Buddy Plummer | Jack Finnegan |
| Dimitri Weissman | Donald C. Moore |
| Stella Deems | Ileane Gudell |
| Max Deems | Joshua Michaels |
| Hattie Walker | Sarah Philips Felcher |
| Solange La Fitte/Vanessa | Lucille Patton |
| Young Phyllis | Eleanor Barbour |
| Young Sally | Sara Louise |
| Young Buddy | Randy Hugill |
| Young Ben | Richard Cooper Bayne[1] |
| Vincent | Alan Gilbert |
| Heidi Schiller | Lynn Archer [2] |
| Carlotta Campion | Barbara Lea |
| Emily Whitman | Virginia Barton |
| Theodora Whitman | Emile Julian |
| Young Heidi | Robbi Curtis |
| Kevin/Young Vincent | Michael Perrier |
| Young Vanessa | Nancy Salis |
| Young Stella | Kaylyn Dillehay[3] |

MUSICAL NUMBERS: "Beautiful Girls," "Don't Look at Me," "Waiting for the Girls Upstairs," "Listen to the Rain on the Roof," "Ah Paris!," "Broadway Baby," "The Road You Didn't Take," "Bolero D'Amour," "In Buddy's Eyes," "Who's That Woman," "I'm Still Here," "Too Many Mornings," "The Right Girl," "One More Kiss," "Could I Leave You?," "Loveland," "You're Gonna Love Tomorrow," "Love Will See Us Through," "The God-God-Why-Don't-You-Love-Me Blues," "Losing My Mind," "The Story of Lucy and Jessie," "Live, Laugh, Love"

A musical in two acts. The action takes place at a party on the stage of the Weissman Theatre on an evening in May of 1971.

*Press:* Lewis Harmon, Sol Jacobson
*Stage Managers:* Joel Grynheim, Victor A. Gelb, Mark Dennis Mellender

* Closed May 30, 1976 after limited engagement of 30 performances.
† Succeeded by: 1. Kurt Johnson, 2. Margaret Goodman, 3. Spence Ford

*Gary Wheeler Photo*

LINCOLN CENTER LIBRARY & MUSEUM
Monday, Tuesday Wednesday, October 20 - 22, 1975.
Equity Library Theatre presents:

# BRAINWASHED
## and
# WITNESS

By Florence Stevenson; Director, Michael Dennis Moore; Scenery, John Schak; Lighting, Candy Dunn; Stage Manager, Cindy Horton

CAST

"Brainwashed"
| | |
|---|---|
| Carol | Patricia Carter |
| Eb | Dana Gladstone |
| Harry | Franz Jones |
| Agnes | Lee Kheel |
| Bunny | Madonna Young |

"Witness"
| | |
|---|---|
| Freddie | Hattie Crystal |
| Ursula | Julia Curry |
| Dave | Dana Gladstone |
| Ziggy | Wayne Harding |
| Betty | Joelle Pacht |
| Joe | Bill Weylock |

LINCOLN CENTER LIBRARY & MUSEUM
Monday, Tuesday, Wednesday, December 8 - 10, 1975
Equity Library Theatre Presents:

# THANKSGIVING
## and
# JULY 2

By Stan Kaplan; Director, Francis Carmine Miazga; Lighting, Dan Bartlett; Stage Manager, Jaqui Oringer

CAST

"Thanksgiving"
| | |
|---|---|
| Maryanne | Suzanne Foster |
| Martin | Paul Meacham |
| Max | Lou Miranda |
| Mother Huff | Valerie Morrell |
| Father Huff | Sid Paul |
| Johnny | Alan Spitz |

"July 2"
| | |
|---|---|
| Tony | Robert Coluntino |
| Ben | Paul Meacham |
| Monk | Lou Miranda |
| Mike | Sid Paul |
| Big Al | Nick Quinault |
| Sammy | Alan Spitz |
| Tommy | Bill Tatum |

LINCOLN CENTER LIBRARY & MUSEUM
Monday, Tuesday, Wednesday, January 26 - 28, 1976
Equity Library Theatre Informals presents:

# SEPARATE CHECKS, PLEASE

By Harry Cauley, Sally-Jane Heit; Music and Lyrics, Shirley Grossman

CAST

Sally-Jane Heit
Harry Cauley

LINCOLN CENTER LIBRARY & MUSEUM
Monday, Tuesday, Wednesday, February 23 - 25, 1976
Equity Library Theatre Informals presents:

# THE LILY AND THE ROSE

Arranged by Nina Polan; Director, Steven D. Nash; Stage Managers, Judy Goldstein, Annabel Brigleb, Sunny Baker

CAST

| | |
|---|---|
| James Higgins | Nina Polan |
| Tom Jarus | Forbesy Russel |
| Heidi Mefford | Neil Seme |

LINCOLN CENTER LIBRARY & MUSEUM
Monday, Tuesday, Wednesday, March 22-24, 1976
Equity Library Theatre Informals presents:

# HOLE IN THE WALL
## and
# CLICK

By Stan Hart; Director, Richard Harden; Designed by Patrick Mann; Stage Manager, Robert Foose

CAST

| "Hole in the Wall" | "Click" |
|---|---|
| Sam Assaid | Sam Assaid |
| Tony Aylward | Beth Dixon |
| Linda Cook | Woody Eney |
| Andy Rohrer | Toby Nelson |

LINCOLN CENTER LIBRARY & MUSEUM
Monday, Tuesday, Wednesday, April 19-21, 1976
Equity Library Theatre Informals present:

# THE VIRGIN AND THE UNICORN

By Oscar Mandel; Director, Michael Martorella; Set, David Murdock; Costumes, Karen Seitz; Music, Jack Biser; Stage Managers, Jim Pentecost, Anabel Brigleb

CAST

| | |
|---|---|
| Sir Ralf | Norman Bein |
| Baron | Avrom Bere |
| Peter | Jack Bise |
| Earl | John Edward Dale |
| Margaret | Kathleen Hube |
| Clotilda | Gwen Humbl |
| Leofa | Leon Spelma |

LINCOLN CENTER LIBRARY & MUSEUM
Monday, Tuesday, Wednesday, May 17-19, 1976
Equity Library Theatre Informals present:

# NAOMI

By Nell Branyon; Directed by the author; Set, Jerry Simeone; Lighting, Anne L. Peters; Costumes, Sally Krell; Stage Manager, Joanne Benson

CAST

| | |
|---|---|
| Michael | Jim Burnet |
| Naomi | Gina Collen |
| Sheriff | Bill DaPrat |
| Harold Burns | John Fowle |
| Floosie | Marian Haraldson |
| Sally | Margaret Kitching |
| Luanna | Meg Sargen |
| Mrs. Bonely | Louise Shelton |
| Grandma | Marion Well |

# JOSEPH JEFFERSON THEATRE COMPANY

Cathy Roskam, Executive Director
Connie Alexis, General Manager

**LITTLE CHURCH AROUND THE CORNER**

October 23–November 8, 1975 (12 performances)

THUNDER ROCK by Robert Ardrey; Director, William Koch; Set, Richard Williams; Lighting, Robby Monk; Costumes, John Scheffler; Sound, Gerald Weinstein; Assistant to director, Paul Berry; Stage Manager, Joanne Benson. CAST: Bill Tatum (Streeter), Tracey Walter (Nonny), Richard Marr (Inspector), Reathel Bean (Charleston), Paul Meacham (Captain), William Koch (Briggs), Frank Miazga (Dr. Kurtz), Nita Novy (Melanie), Suzanne Osborne (Miss Kirby), Madeleine Gorman (Anne Marie), Peter Aldo (Cassidy)

December 2–13, 1975 (12 performances)

THE WOOING OF LADY SUNDAY by Ted Pezzulo; Set, Cliff Simon; Lighting, Francis Roefaro; Costumes, A. Christina Giannini; Stage Managers, David Rosenberg, Karen E. Nothmann. CAST: Henry Ferrentino (Briglio), Marjorie Austrian (Concetta), Susan Walker (Domenica), Frank Cascio (Benvenuto), Jason Howard (Agnello), Josh Milder (Giuseppe), Jennifer Thompson (Tommasino), Rachael Milder (Chiarina), Rifka Milder (Giuseppina), Kate Shapiro (Iolanda), Justine Grubar (Carmela), Jevan Damadian (Antonio)

APRIL FISH by Ted Pezzulo; other credits above. CAST: Jason Howard (Anselmo), Jo Flores Chase (Assunta), Richard Zavaglia (Fortunato), Dwight Marfield (Umberto), Marianne Muellerleile (Abbatella), Rachael Milder (Giovannina), Stephanie Satie (Nicolina), Michael Brindisi (Pasquale), Antonio Pandolfo (Pietro), Hope W. Sacharoff (Filomena), Maurice Braddell (Padre)

February 11–28, 1976 (12 performances)

MORNING'S AT SEVEN by Paul Osborn; Director, Cathy Roskam; Sets, Gerald Weinstein, Costumes, Cindy Polk; Lighting, Robby Monk; Sound, Fred Garrett, Bill Stallings; Press, Marion Fredi Towbin; Stage Managers, Evan Canary, Joanne Benson; Wardrobe Mistress, Rachael Milder; Production Coordinator, Evan Canary. CAST: William Robertson (Theodore), Anita Bayless (Cora), Rose Lischner (Aaronetta), Frances Pole (Ida), William LaPrato (Carl), I. W. Klein (Homer), Melanie Hill (Myrtle), Eleanor Cody Gould (Esther), George Lloyd (David)

May 5–22, 1976 (12 performances)

JOHN by Philip Barry; Director, Cyril Simon; Set, Kenneth Shewer; Lighting, Jennifer Herrick Jebens; Costumes, Susan Hilferty; Hairstylist, Patrik D. Moreton; Music, Wendy Erdman; Costume Mistress, Cindy Polk; Sound, Debbie Carter; Assistant to director, Missy Powell; Press, Marion Fredi Towbin; Stage Managers, Evan Canary, Toby Bellin, Marilyn Modlin. CAST: David Rasche (Joel), Richard Cox (Hanan), James Carruthers (Antipas), Elizabeth Hubbard (Herodias), Oz Tortora (Pete), Stanton Coffin (Nathaniel), Duane Morris (Simon), Robert Shockley (Andrew), Paul Ruben (Dan), Armand Assante (John), Joel Parsons (James), Tom Bair (Ethan), Sylvester Rich (Zebedee), Natalia E. Chuma (Salome), Charles C. Timm (Dancing Master), Davidson Garrett (Servant), Allan Warren (Warden)

*Ambur Hiken, Mike Uffer Photos*

**Top Right: Bill Tatum, Reathel Bean in
"Thunder Rock" Below: "April Fish" and "The
Wooing of Lady Sunday"
Right Center: Rose Lischner,
William Robertson in "Morning's at Seven"**

**Elizabeth Hubbard, Armand Assante
in "John"**

# MANHATTAN THEATRE CLUB

Lynne Meadow, Artistic-Executive Director
Managing Director, Barry Grove; Associate Director, Thomas Bullard; Press, Daniel Caine; Technical Director, William D. Anderson; Assistant to Managing Director, Pat Bartolotta; Administrative Assistant, Lorie Barber; Technical Assistants, Ron Woods, Frank Kelly; Staff Assistants, Sylvia Hollander, Frances Burdock; Cabaret Directors, Thomas Bullard, Stephen Pascal

Laura Esterman, Dick Latessa,
Dan Hedaya in "Golden Boy"

## MANHATTAN THEATRE CLUB

October 23–November 9, 1975 (12 performances)

RUBY'S PLACE with Book by Richard Beeson Johnson; Music and Lyrics, Elli Faye; Musical Direction and Arrangements; Staged by Andre De Shields. CAST: Sarah Harris, Lawrence John Moss, Alaina Reed, Andre De Shields

October 23–November 9, 1975 (12 performances)

SEA MARKS by Gardner McKay; Director, Steven Robman; Scenery, Marjorie Kellogg; Costumes, Kenneth M. Yount; Lighting, Arden Fingerhut. CAST: Edwin J. McDonough (Colm Primrose), Veronica Castang (Timothea Stiles)

October 24–November 9, 1975 (12 performances)

GOLDEN BOY by Clifford Odets; Director, Lynne Meadow; Settings, John Lee Beatty; Costumes, Vittorio Capecce; Lighting, William D. Anderson; Sound, George Hansen, Charles London; Assistant to director, Zane Weiner; Stage Manager, Michael Heaton. CAST: Dick Latessa (Tom), Laura Esterman (Lorna), Jerry Zaks (Joe), Dan Hedaya (Tokio), Frank Hamilton (Carp), Michael Kell (Siggie), Paul Lipson (Bonaparte), Erica Weingast (Anna), Joel Colodener (Frank), Jerrold Ziman (Roxy), Clarence Felder (Eddie), Larry Guardino (Pepper), Bob DeFrank (Mickey), Danny Sewell (Drake), Vic Polizos (Barker)

November 13–30, 1975 (12 performances)

MARVIN'S GARDEN with Music by Mel Marvin; Director, David Chambers; Lyrics, Moose 100, Ron Whyte, David Chambers. CAST: Donna Emmanuel, Robert Montgomery, Richard Ryder, Dale Soules, Donovan Sylvest, Mary Wright

November 13–23, 1975 (12 performances)

THE BASEMENT by Harold Pinter; Director, David Kerry Heefner; Settings, Sandi Marks; Lighting, Patricia Moeser; Costumes, Louis Pshena; Sound, George Hansen; Stage Managers, Katherine Talbert, Neil Broat; Production Assistant, Lee Pucklis. CAST: John C. Vennema (Law), James Hummert (Stott), Patricia Gorman (Jane); A SLIGHT ACHE by Harold Pinter; Same staff as preceding. CAST: Kathleen Betsko (Flora), James Hummert (Edward), John C. Vennema (Matchseller)

December 4–21, 1975 (12 performances)

LIFE CLASS by David Storey; Director, Robert Mandel; Setting, Marjorie Kellogg; Lighting, Arden Fingerhut; Costumes, Jennifer von Mayrhauser; Stage Managers, Marjorie Horne, Amy Schecter. CAST: Kevin Conway (Allott), David Wilson (Warren), William Carden (Saunders), Veronica Castang (Stella), Lenny Baker (Mathews), Dale Hodges (Brenda), Christopher Curry (Carter), Swoosie Kurtz (Catherine), Keith McDermott (Mooney), Toni Kalem (Gillian), John Ramsey (Abercrombie), William Roerick (Foley), Peter DeMaio (Phillips)

December 4–21, 1975 (11 performances)

A MUSICAL EVENING WITH FRED COFFIN AND DOROTHEA JOYCE

December 4–21, 1975 (15 performances)

GEOGRAPHY OF A HORSE DREAMER by Sam Shepard; Director, Jacques Levy; Settings, T. Winberry; Costumes, Kenneth M. Yount; Lighting, Frank R. Kelly; Sound, Carol Waaser; Assistant to director, Nancy Tribush; Stage Managers, Sari Weisman, Stephen Radosh. CAST: Rick Warner (Cody), Robert Lesser (Santee), J. Zakkai (Beaujo), John Mitchell (Fingers), Gordon Hammett (Doctor), Paul Andor (Walter), Ronald F. Toler (Jasper), Lee Jines (Jason)

*Ken Howard Photos*

**Right Center: David Leary,
Robert Christian in "The Blood Knot"**

**Keith McDermott, Lenny Baker,
Kevin Conway in "Life Class"**

MANHATTAN THEATRE CLUB

December 19, 1975 (1 performance)

OOD TIME DOLLY DEE by John Vari; Director, Alfred Chris-
. CAST: Alan Fleisig (Narrator), Jo Flores Chase (Dolly Dee),
on Nute (Sonny), Madeleine Gorman (Fitzy), Dennis Drew
udge), Tom Coppola (Little Willie)

February 4–21, 1976 (12 performances)

KANDER & EBB CABARET: An evening of songs by John
ander and Fred Ebb; Conceived and Directed by Seth Glassman;
usical Director, Richard DeMone. CAST: Carl Barone, Tommy
eslin, Channing Case, Kay Cummings, Linda Glick, Suzanne
erjat

February 4–22, 1976 (15 performances)

ATRICK HENRY LAKE LIQUORS by Larry Ketron; Director,
onald Roston; Set and Costumes, Ernie Smith; Lighting, John
isondi; Sound, George Hansen, Charles London; Stage Managers,
my Schecter, Frances Murdock; Production Assistant, Kevin Con-
ant. CAST: Jay Devlin (James), James Hilbrandt (Horace), Ed
eamon (Mickey), Regina Baff (Sandra), Christine Lavren (Louise),
onna Emmanuel (Ann), Vic Polizos (Gary), Mark Metcalf (Leif),
oni Kalem (Floral), George Brice (Customer), Frank Saracino
Customer)

February 12–March 6, 1976 (18 performances)

HE BLOOD KNOT by Athol Fugard; Director, Thomas Bullard;
cenery, Pat Woodbridge; Costumes, Kenneth M. Yount; Lighting,
rden Fingerhut; Stage Managers, Katherine Talbert, Joe Millett;
roduction Assistant, Kevin Constant. CAST: David H. Leary
Morris), Robert Christian (Zachariah)

February 26–March 14, 1976 (12 performances)

ONGS FROM PINS AND NEEDLES by Harold Rome; Directed
nd Choreographed by Marc Gass; Musical Director, Jez Davidson.
AST: Scott Bodie, Cynthia Bostick, Margery Cohen, Jonathan
Iadary, Margaret Warncke

March 3–21, 1976 (15 performances)

HE VOICE OF THE TURTLE by John van Druten; Director,
ilianne Boyd; Scenery, Bill Groom; Costumes, Danny Mizell;
ighting, Patricia Moeser; Stage Managers, Ian McColl, Stacy Scott.
AST: Susan Sharkey (Sally), Julie Garfield (Olive), Munson Hicks
Bill)

March 3–21, 1976 (15 performances)

N EVENING OF SHOLOM ALEICHEM: Stories from the
orks of Sholom Aleichem; Director, Richard Maltby, Jr.; Cos-
umer, Pegi Goodman. CAST: Murray Horwitz in a solo perfor-
ance.

March 18–April 4, 1976 (12 performances)

HE SON by Gert Hofmann; Translated by Jon Swan; Director,
tephen Pascal; Set and Lighting, Raymond Recht; Costumes, Vit-
orio Capecce; Stage Managers, Katherine Talbert, Robert Epstein.
AST: Tanya Berezin (Mrs. Nickel), Andrew Bloch (Karlemann),
. Zakkai (Councilman, Station Attendant, Shopkeeper, Landlord),
iane Barry (Secretary, Shopkeeper's Wife, Fanny), Gail Kellstrom
Traveler, Monika), Reed Birney (Traveler, Customer), Robert Ep-
ein (Traveler), Elaine Bromka (Waitress, Lucretia)

March 31–April 18, 1976 (15 performances)

EARLY BELOVED by John Raymond Hart; Director, Paul
chneider; Scenery, Vittorio Capecce; Costumes, Margo Bruton El-
ow; Lighting, Paul Kaine; Sound, George Hansen, Charles Lon-
on; Dialect Coach, Gordon A. Jacoby; Stage Managers, David M.
verard, Nona Pipes. CAST: Margaret Ladd (Nora), Suzanne Col-
ns (Cathleen), Barbara eda-Young (Joanna), Judith L'Heureux
Deirdre), Robert B. Silver (David), Larry Bryggman (Christian),
obert McIlwaine (Peter), James Rebhorn (Frank), Nancy Reardon
Bridget), Joseph Daly (Owen)

April 8–18, 1976 (12 performances)

EVILS AND DIAMONDS: a one-woman show of song and po-
try by Stephanie Cotsirilos.

April 21–May 16, 1976 (28 performances)

N THE WINE TIME by Ed Bullins; Director, Robert Macbeth;
ettings, Steven Rubin; Costumes, Grace Williams; Lighting, Spen-
er Mosse; Sound, Sonny Morgan; Stage Managers, Mark Paquette,
vy McCray. CAST: Robert Christian (Cliff), Loretta Greene (Lou),
alvin Alexis (Ray), Marilyn Randall (Bunny), Flow Wiley (Doris),

John Heard, Laura Esterman in "The Pokey"

Martha Short-Goldsen (Miss Minny), Otis Young-Smith (Red),
Walter Steele (Bama), Dana Manno (Beatrice), Jenny Gooch (Tiny),
Richard Gant (Silly Willy), Steve Sheahan (Policeman)

April 21–May 1, 1976 (9 performances)

CRACKED TOKENS: a comedy-improvisation group featuring
Robert Fraina, Joanna Lipari, Pam Moller, John Slavin, Mary
Steenburgen

April 22–May 9, 1976 (10 performances)

SONGS OF QUINCY-BURCH with Lynn Gerb

MANHATTAN THEATRE CLUB

May 5–23, 1976 (14 performances)

A NOEL COWARD CABARET: Conceived and Directed by Gary
Pearle; Musical Director, Steven Blier. CAST: George Lee Andrews
and Marti Morris

May 5–22, 1976 (15 performances)

THE POKEY by Stephen Black; Director, Lynne Meadow; Settings,
Raymond Recht; Costumes, Margo Bruton Elkow; Lighting, William D. Anderson; Stage Managers, David M. Everard, Robert Epstein. CAST: Laura Esterman (Young Woman), John Heard (Young
Man)

May 13–June 6, 1976 (16 performances)

JAZZ BABIES: Written, Directed and Choreographed by Marc
Jordan Gass; Musically Arranged and Directed by Jez Davidson;
Conceived by Marc Gass and Jez Davidson; Stage Manager, Chris-
topher Pitney. CAST: Cynthia Bostick, Herb Downer, Joel Eagon,
Susan Edwards, Frank Juliano

May 18–June 6, 1976 (15 performances)

TRANSFORMATIONS by Anne Sexton; Music, Conrad Susa; Di-
rector, David Shookhoff; Musical Director, Benton Hess; Scenery,
Pat Woodbridge; Costumes, Ken Holamon; Lighting, Spencer
Mosse; Stage Manager, David S. Rosenkak. CAST: Karen Clauss,
Patricia Deckert, Tonio Di Paolo, Jonathan Rigg, Thomas A. Rowe,
Raymond Sambolin, John Shackelford, Carolyn Weber

May 26–June 6, 1976 (15 performances)

LIFE IS LIKE A MUSICAL COMEDY: Songs by George M.
Cohan; Conceived and Directed by Jack Allison; Musical Director,
Anthony Zaleski; Stage Manager, Liz Plonka. CAST: Alice Cannon,
Melanie Chartoff, David Dyer, Wayne Scherzer, Barbara Worthing-
ton

May 28–June 12, 1976 (13 performances)

THE HUMAN VOICE: Music by Francis Poulenc; Text, Jean Cocteau; English Version, Joseph Machlis; Director, Thomas Bullard;
Musical Director, Ethan Mordden; Sets, Vittorio Capecce; Costumes, Ann Wolff; Lights, John Gisondi; Stage Manager, Rena
Rockoff. CAST: Linda Phillips or Judith James

# THE NEGRO ENSEMBLE COMPANY

Dougals Turner Ward, Artistic Director
Robert Hooks, Executive Director
Frederick Garrett, Administrative Director

**ST. MARK'S PLAYHOUSE**
Opened Wednesday, March 3, 1976.*
The Negro Ensemble Company presents:

## EDEN

By Steve Carter; Director, Edmund Cambridge; Scenery, Pamela S. Peniston; Costumes, Edna Watson; Lighting, Sandra L. Ross; Technical Director, Dik Krider; Assistant, George Scott; Wardrobe Mistress, Marzetta Jones

### CAST

| | |
|---|---|
| Eustace | Samm-Art Williams |
| Nimrod | Nate Ferrell |
| Solomon | Laurence Fishburne 3d |
| Aunt Lizzie | Barbara Montgomery |
| Agnes. | Ramona King |
| Annetta | Shirley Brown |
| Florie | Ethel Ayler |
| Joseph Barton | Graham Brown |

UNDERSTUDIES: George Campbell, Dean Irby, Sheryl-Lee Ralph, Lea Scott

A drama in 3 acts and 9 scenes. The action takes place in the Bartons' apartment on the upper West Side of New York City during 1927.

*Company Manager:* Frederick Garrett
*Press:* Howard Atlee, Clarence Allsopp
*Stage Manager:* Clinton Turner Davis

\* Closed May 9, 1976 after 79 performances. Moved May 16, 1976 to Theatre DeLys and still playing May 31, 1976. Laurence Fishburne 3d was succeeded by George Campbell, James Warden, Jr.

*Bert Andrews Photos*
**Right: Ramona King, Shirley Brown**
**Top: Ethel Ayler, Graham Brown**

**Shirley Brown, Samm-Art Williams**

**James Warden, Jr., Graham Brown**

**ST. MARK'S PLAYHOUSE**
Opened Wednesday, May 19, 1976.*
The Negro Ensemble Company presents:

# LIVIN' FAT

By Judi Ann Mason; Director, Douglas Turner Ward; Scenery and Costumes, Mary Mease Warren; Lighting, Sandra L. Ross; Title Song Composed and Arranged by Jothan Callins; Lyrics, Douglas Turner Ward; Sung by Hattie Winston; Production Assistant, Ron Lewis; Technical Director, Dik Krider; Assistant, George Scott; Wardrobe Supervisor, Ali Davis.

### CAST

| | |
|---|---|
| Big Mama | Minnie Gentry |
| Mama | Frances Foster |
| Daddy | Wayne Elbert |
| Candy | Joyce Sylvester |
| David Lee | Dean Irby |
| Boo | Frankie Faison |

Understudies: Charles Brown, Rosanna Carter

A comedy in 2 acts and 5 scenes. The action takes place at the present time in the front room of the Carter family in the black quarters section of a southern city.

*Company Manager:* Frederick Garrett
*Press:* Howard Atlee, Clarence Allsopp
*Stage Manager:* Horacena J. Taylor

Closed July 18, 1976 after 69 performances.

*Bert Andrews Photos*

**Top: Frances Foster, Wayne Elbert, Dean Irby**
**Below: Dean Irby, Joyce Sylvester, Frankie Faison**

**Frankie Faison, Dean Irby**
**Top: Wayne Elbert, Frances Foster**

# THE NEW DRAMATISTS INC.

Chairman, L. Arnold Weissberger; President, Mary K. Frank; Program Director, Jeff Peters; Workshop Coordinator, Stephen Harty; Administrative Assistant, Kathleen Mucciolo; Technical Director, Clay Coyle

Thursday, June 5, 1975

THE WOLVES AND THE LAMBS by Frieda Lipp. CAST: Roger Serbagi (Wayne), Nancy Franklin (Cynthia), Douglas Cowgill (Steven), Eren Özker (Louise), Kate Williamson (Amy), Bill Weylock (Joseph), Arthur Hammer (Prosecutor), Bette Howard (Marianne), Lawrence Watson (Lester), Jim Horn (Deputy/Guard/Officer/Judge)

June 11 & 12, 1975

HALFWAY TREE BROWN by Clifford Mason; Director, Stan Lachow; Stage Manager, Everett Johns; Technician, Maureen Bryan. CAST: Robin Braxton (Elizabeth), Sandi Franklin (Hyacinth), Richard Ward (Edward), Wendell Brown (Winston), Jorge Johnson (Derrick), Ingrid Wang (Yvonne), Clifford Mason (Richard), Dorothi Fox (Enid), Herb Rice (Buddu/Photographer), Roy Thomas (Calypsonian/Governor General), Sundra Jean Williams (Mae), Ernest Thomas (Rastus), Faizul Khan (Babu/Isaacs), Derrel Edwards (David), Arthur Hammer (Englishman), Sam Singleton (Minister)

June 19 & 20, 1975

THE CORRIDOR by Diane Kagan; Production and Lighting Design, Meryl Joseph; Music Direction, Herbert Kaplan; Stage Manager, Peter Abode; Sound, Bruce Lazarus. CAST: Anna Minot (Woman), Joseph Warren (Man), Lisa Richards (Emissary)

September 14, 1975

THE ENCHANTED HUDSON by Eric Thompson. CAST: Edmond Lyndeck (Paul), Joan Shepard (Mary), Jeanne Ruskin (Ann)

September 23–27, 1975 (5 performances)

NEVER A SNUG HARBOUR by David Ulysses Clarke; Director, Tom Ligon; Lighting, Gregg Marriner; Sound, Katharine Clarke; Costumes, David James; Stage Manager, Roger Pippin. CAST: Joseph Regalbuto (Will), Richard Brestoff (Gwylim), Robert Boardman (Teddy), Paul Andor (Simon), Nora Dunfee (Mary), Peter Dee (Charlie), Tom Bair (Joe), Katherine Clark (Ellen), Joseph Jamrog (Jack)

*Jeff Peters Photos*

Barbara Coggin in "Father Uxbridge Wants to M

# THE NEW DRAMATISTS INC.

October 7–11, 1975 (5 performances)

THE LAST CHRISTIANS by Jack Gilhooley; Director, Clint Atkinson; Set, Kevin Golden; Lighting, Stephen Ommerle; Managers, Stephen Ommerle, Peter Abode; Production Assis Barbara Nivelt. CAST: Alan Brasington (Caiaphas), Robert Ly (Herod), Steve Vinovich (Rev. Sykes), Marianne Muellerleile ( Trudy), Libby Lyman (Mrs. Young), Joseph Alaskey (Harri Nick Francesco (P. P.), William Russ (J. J.), Nancy Ba (Veronica), Terrence Hopkins (Judas), Joseph Daly (Jedediah) ane Stilwell (Dummy), Lillah McCarthy (Aurelia)

October 21–25, 1975 (5 performances)

THE WOLVES AND THE LAMBS by Frieda Lipp; Dire Christopher Adler; Lighting, Gregg Marriner; Stage Mana Roger Pippin, Barbara Alpert. CAST: Mervyn Gaines, Jr. (Wa Edith Greenfield (Cynthia), Peter Anlyan (Steven), Lane Bir (Louise), Beth Holland (Amy), Stephan Weyte (Caravella), D Clarke (Alexander), Lawrence Wall (Authority), Beatrice W (Marianne), Laurence Watson (Lester)

November 4–7, 1975 (5 performances)

SISTER SADIE by Clifford Mason; Director, Mr. Mason; Assi to director, Angela Lee; Set and Lighting, Guy J. Smith; Manager, Haskell V. Anderson III; Production Assistant, Ba Nivelt. CAST: Virginia Capers (Sadie), Ernest Harden, Jr. (B Fred Morsell (Fish), Ellwoodson Williams (Horse), Henry Hay (Moe), Maurice Watson (Blue), Maurice Sneed (Squeeze), Smithwrick (Popsey), Dorothi Fox (Lula), Andrea Frierson metta)

November 18–22, 1975 (5 performances)

FATHER UXBRIDGE WANTS TO MARRY by Frank Gag Director, Mr. Gagliano; Set, Robert Steinberg; Lighting, Porto; Sound and Music, James Reichert; Costumes, Ariel; Manager, Gary Porto; Sound, George Patterson. CAST: Ba Coggin (Mrs. Green), Steve Vinovich (Norden), Bill McIntyre ther Uxbridge), Valerie Mahaffey (Angel), Robert Christian (O

**Joseph Daly, Lillah McCarthy, Robert Lydiard, Steve Vinovich, Diana Stilwell in "The Last Christians"**

## NEW DRAMATISTS INC.

December 9–13, 1975 (5 performances)

THE ENCHANTED HUDSON by Eric Thompson; Director, Tom Molyneaux; Set, Clay Coyle; Lighting, Chuck Ferrand; Stage Managers, Larry Lorberbaum, Mike Maines. CAST: Ellen Cameron (Mary), Bernard Pollock (Paul), Marina Thompson (Child), Barbra Cohen (Ann), Carrie Rubio (Mimu), Haskell V. Anderson III (Sabari), William Preston (Grandfather), Rocko Cinelli (Chief), Anne Ruskin (Organist), Natives: Jamie Farbman, Nick Fransco, Jody Hingle, Nicki Stephens

January 14–16, 1976 (3 performances)

THE BEACH CHILDREN by John von Hartz; Director, Ronald Roston; Stage Manager, Sari Weisman. CAST: Maia Danziger (Sherry), Mark Metcalf (Jimmy), Roger Omar Serbagi (Max), Nancy Franklin (Margaret), Martin Marinaro (Domingo), Tanny McDonald (Alma), Gil Rogers (Antonio)

January 19, 1976

AMOUREUSE by Anne and Stuart Vaughan; From the French play by Georges de Porto-Riche. CAST: Donald Madden (Dr. Feraud), Sharon Laughlin (Germaine), Louis Turenne (Pascal), Lauda Barrett (Catherine), Barbara Caruso (Mme. de Chazal), Angela Wood (Mme. Henriet), Ann Thompson (Madelein)

January 28, 1976

A NICE GIRL LIKE YOU by Aldo Giunta; Stage Manager, Peter Rozik. CAST: Tony Wein (Anne), Ben Slack (Fatso), Bob Resnikoff (Sam), Joe Ragno (Charley), Tucker Smallwood (Wade)

February 17–19, 1976 (3 performances)

THE ELUSIVE ANGEL by Jack Gilhooley; Director, Peter Maney; Stage Manager, Mark Oberman. CAST: Tracey Walter (Carlin), Amy Wright (Mary), Graham Beckel (Slick), Jayne Haynes (Jo Peep), Lillah McCarthy (Lucy), James Handy (Ken)

February 27, 1976

APRIL by John Wolfson; Stage Directions read by John Yates. CAST: Laura Ilene (Melody), Norman Evans (Mankowitz), Sam Schoumado (Arnold), Harry Browne (Buddy), Gladys Smith (April), John Yates (Val), Richie Allan (Waldo), Richard Niles (Steve), Ozzie Tortora (Poletti), John LaGioia (Dominick), Faith Catlin (Diane), Bill Roulet (Huong)

Amy Wright, Tracey Walter in "The Elusive Angel"

March 5, 1976

THE FAR-OFF SWEET FOREVER by Conn Fleming; Stage Manager, John Mintun. CAST: Maurice Copeland (Patton), Mark Metcalf (Banner), Karen Shallo (Mable), Ed Genest (Dr. Phipps/Preacher), Barbara Coggin (Oma), Townspeople: Sharon Brewer, Tom Keever, Katie Mucciolo, Greg Willis

March 8–11, 1976 (3 performances)

THE MAN WHO DREW CIRCLES by Barry Berg; Director, Cliff Goodwin. CAST: David Dukes (Harold), Elizabeth Reavey (Vanessa), Richard Greene (Norman), Nancy Franklin (Brenda), Richard DeFabees (Ted), Anna Minot (Miriam)

March 16 & 17, 1976 (2 performances)

A SAFE PLACE by C. K. Mack. CAST: Douglas Stark (Arthur), Bette Marshall (Elizabeth), Toni Kalem (Nadia), Beatrice Winde (Besse), Stuart Vaughan (Henry), Amy Wright (Jennifer), Jayne Haynes (Heidi), Linda Lodge (Charlie), Donna Gabel (Anna/Florence)

April 2, 1976

EVEN THE WINDOW IS GONE by Gene Radano; Director, Shan Covey CAST: Jack Aaron (Paul), Julia Barr (Bonnie), Laura Esterman (Shirley), Jeanne Kaplan (Mother), Susan Marshall (Carmella), Mary Moon (Florence), Harvey Siegel (Mel), Lou Tiano (Sal)

April 20–24, 1976 (6 performances)

THE RESURRECTION OF JACKIE CRAMER by Frank Gagliano; Music, Raymond Benson; Director, J. Ranelli; Set and Lighting, Robert Steinberg; Musical Direction and Performed by Raymond Benson; Stage Manager, Gary Porto. CAST: David Berman (Jackie Cramer), Mary Testa (Mom), Jerry McGee (Pop), Kenith Bridges (Father Bodoni), Nancy Foy (Susie), Joseph White (Remo), Jane MacDonald (Chorus), Phylis Frelich (Benjy), Board of Directors: Joel Brooks, Mike Dantuono, Doug Holsclaw, Marion Lindell

May 5, 1976

THE HOUSE OF SOLOMON by Allen Davis III. CAST: Paul Lipson (Joseph Solomon), Ruth Jaroslow (Rachel), Nancy Marchand (Esther), Wil Albert (Ted) Paul Sparer (Danny), Alba Oms (Felicia)

May 13, 1976

LUST by Steven Somkin; Director, Rhoda Feuer. CAST: Betty Russell, (Madeleine), Linda Bernstein (Adele), Frederic Major (Bernard), Peter Flood (Richard), Myra Turley (Dora), Paul Merrill (Charles), Victor DeRose (Bobby), Nicholas Levitin (Auctioneer), Bidders: Murray Cantor, Belle Weiss

Virginia Capers, Fred Morsell in "Sister Sadie"

127

# NEW YORK SHAKESPEARE FESTIVAL AT LINCOLN CENTER

Joseph Papp, Producer
Bernard Gersten, Associate Producer

**VIVIAN BEAUMONT THEATER**
Opened Wednesday, October 15, 1975.*
The New York Shakespeare Festival presents:

## TRELAWNY OF THE 'WELLS'

By Sir Arthur Wing Pinero; Director, A. J. Antoon; Scenery, David Mitchell; Costumes, Theoni V. Aldredge; Supervised by Hal George; Lighting, Ian Calderon; Music, Peter Link; Wardrobe Supervisor, James McGaha; Production Assistants, Daniel Koetting, Bonnie Christensen; Assistant to director, Jane Paley; Hairstylist, J. Roy Helland

### CAST

| | |
|---|---|
| Mrs. Mossop | Helen Verbit |
| Mr. Ablett | Merwin Goldsmith |
| Mr. Tom Wrench | Michael Tucker |
| Miss Imogen Parrot | Meryl Streep |
| Mr. James Telfer | Jerome Dempsey |
| Mr. Ferdinand Gadd | John Lithgow |
| Mr. Augustus Colpoys | Ben Slack |
| Mrs. Telfer (Violet Sylvester) | Anita Dangler |
| Miss Avonia Bunn | Sasha von Scherler |
| Miss Rose Trelawny | Marybeth Hurt |
| Mr. Arthur Gower | Mandy Patinkin |
| Sarah | K. T. Baumann |
| Clara De Foenix | Ann McDonough |
| Captain DeFoenix | Jeffrey Jones |
| Justice William Gower | Walter Abel |
| Miss Trafalger Gower | Aline MacMahon |
| Charles | Walt Gorney |
| O'Dwyer (Stage Manager) | Christopher Hewett |
| Mr. Denzil | Jerry Mayer |
| Miss Brewster | Suzanne Collins |
| Mr. Hunston | Tom Blank |

UNDERSTUDIES: Wrench, Arthur, Tom Blank; Justice, Telfer, Charles, Thomas Barbour; Clara, K. T. Baumann; Avonia, Imogen, Sara, Suzanne Collins; Gadd, O'Dwyer, Jeffrey Jones; Augustus, Ablett, Captain, Jerry Mayer; Rose, Ann McDonough; Trafalgar, Mrs. Telfer, Mrs. Mossop, Elsa Raven

A comedy in four acts performed with one intermission. The action takes place in New York City around the turn of the century.

*Press:* Merle Debuskey, Faith Geer
*Stage Managers:* Louis Rackoff, Richard S. Viola

* Closed Nov. 23, 1975 after 47 performances and 14 previews.

*Barry Kramer-Joseph Abeles Photos*

**Walter Abel, Aline MacMahon**

Marybeth Hurt, Michael Tucker, Sasha von Sche
John Lithgow Top: Mandy Patinkin,
Michael Tucker, Marybeth Hurt

VIVIAN BEAUMONT THEATER
Opened Wednesday, December 17, 1975.*
New York Shakespeare Festival presents:

# HAMLET

By William Shakespeare; Director, Michael Rudman; Scenery, Santo Loquasto; Costumes, Hal George; Lighting, Martin Aronstein; Music, John Morris; Production Assistant, Frank Di Filia; Fight Sequences, Erik Fredricksen

CAST

| | |
|---|---|
| Claudius | Charles Cioffi |
| Gertrude | Jane Alexander |
| Hamlet | Sam Waterston |
| Polonius/First Gravedigger | Larry Gates |
| Laertes | James Sutorius |
| Ophelia | Maureen Anderman |
| Horatio | George Hearn |
| Voltmand | James Gallery |
| Rosencrantz | David Ackroyd |
| Guildenstern | John Heard |
| Marcellus/ A. Murderer | Richard Brestoff |
| Francisco/Player Queen.; | David Naughton |
| Bernardo/Priest/Dumb Show Murderer | Stephen Lang |
| Reynaldo | Erik Fredricksen |
| Second Gravedigger | Jack R. Marks |
| Fortinbras/Dumb Show King | Mandy Patinkin |
| Captain to Fortinbras/Dumb Show Queen | Hannibal Penney, Jr |
| Ghost of Hamlet's Father | Robert Burr |
| Osric | Bruce McGill |
| Player King | James Hurdle |
| Player Queen | David Naughton |
| Prologue/Apprentice Actor | Nancy Campbell |
| Company Manager | Vance Mizelle |
| Technical Director | Ernest Austin |
| Stagehands | Michael Cutt, Ronald Hunter, Reginald Vel Johnson, Jack R. Marks, David Howard |

ENSEMBLE: Ernest Austin, Richard Brestoff, Michael Cutt, Erik Fredricksen, David Howard, Ronald Hunter, Reginald Vel Johnson, Henson Keys, Stephen Lang, Jack R. Marks, Vance Mizelle, Bruce McGill, David Naughton, Richard Sanders

A drama in two acts.

*General Manager:* Robert Kamlot
*Press:* Merle Debuskey, Faith Geer
*Stage Managers:* D. W. Koehler, Michael Chambers

Closed Jan. 25, 1976 after 47 performances and 14 previews.

*George E. Joseph Photos*

**Right: Sam Waterston,
and top with Jane Alexander**

**George Hearn, Sam Waterston**

**Maureen Anderman, Larry Gates**

**MITZI E. NEWHOUSE THEATER**
Opened Thursday, January 22, 1976.*
New York Shakespeare Festival presents:

# THE SHORTCHANGED REVIEW

By Michael Dorn Moody; Director, Richard Southern; Scene
Marsha L. Eck; Costumes, Hilary M. Rosenfeld; Lighting, Che
Thacker; Sound, Samuel E. Platt; Music, Clouds; Assistant to dir
tor, Gwen Jennings; Wardrobe Master, Al Calamoneri

### CAST

| | |
|---|---|
| Ed Squall | Herbert Br |
| Nicky Shannigan | Mason Ada |
| Vanessa Sloat | Tricia Bo |
| Jane Sloat Shannigan | Virginia Ves |
| Darrell Shannigan | T. Mir |
| Peter Cope | William R |

UNDERSTUDIES: Raleigh Bond (Nicky, Ed), Robert Burke (D
rell, Peter), Mia Dillon (Vanessa), Janet Sarno (Jane)

A drama in two acts. The action takes place during 1975
suburban New York.

*Production Manager:* Andrew Mihok
*Press:* Merle Debuskey, Faith Geer
*Stage Managers:* Louis Rackoff, Zoya Wyeth

* Closed Feb. 29, 1976 after 46 performances.

*Kramer-Abeles Photos*

**Left: Virginia Vestoff, Herbert Braha, Mason Ad**

**Virginia Vestoff, Mason Adams**

**T. Miratti, Tricia Boyer**

Ron Randell, Lynn Redgrave, Philip Bosco,
Ruth Gordon, Milo O'Shea, Edward Herrmann

VIAN BEAUMONT THEATER
Opened Wednesday, February 18, 1976.*
New York Shakespeare Festival presents:

# MRS. WARREN'S PROFESSION

By Bernard Shaw; Director, Gerald Freedman; Settings, David
itchell; Costumes, Theoni V. Aldredge; Lighting, Martin Aron-
in; Assistant to director, John Seidman; Hairstylist, J. Roy Hel-
d; Technical Director, Mervyn Haines, Jr.

### CAST

| | | |
|---|---|---|
| vie Warren | ............................ | Lynn Redgrave |
| aed | ........................................ | Ron Randell |
| rs.Kitty Warren | ......................... | Ruth Gordon |
| George Crofts | ......................... | Philip Bosco |
| ank Gardner | ......................... | Edward Herrmann |
| v. Samuel Gardner | ...................... | Milo O'Shea |

NDERSTUDIES: John Carpenter (Gardner, Crofts), Donna
acson (Vivie), Edmund Lyndeck (Praed), John Schak (Frank)

A drama in four acts, performed with one intermission. The action
es place during 1894 in a summer cottage garden in Haslemere,
rrey, England, in the rectory garden, and Honoria Fraser's cham-
s in Chancery Lane, London.

*Press:* Merle Debuskey, Faith Geer
*Stage Managers:* Mary Porter Hall, John Beven

Closed Apr. 4, 1976 after 55 performances and 14 previews.

*Sy Friedman Photos*

Edward Herrmann, Lynn Redgrave

**Dorian Harewood, Paul Rudd**

**MITZI E. NEWHOUSE THEATER**
Opened Wednesday, April 21, 1976.*
New York Shakespeare Festival presents:

# STREAMERS

By David Rabe; Director, Mike Nichols; Setting, Tony Walt
Costumes, Bill Walker; Lighting, Ronald Wallace; Production
sistant, Kathy Talbert; Wardrobe Master, Al Calamoneri; Prod
tion Supervisor, Jason Steven Cohen

### CAST

| | |
|---|---|
| Martin | Michael |
| Richie | Peter Ev |
| Carlyle | Dorian Harewoo |
| Billy | Paul Rud |
| Roger | Terry Alexar |
| Sgt. Rooney | Kenneth McMi |
| Sgt. Cokes | Dolph Sv |
| M. P. Officer | Arlen Dean Sny |
| Hinson | Les Rob |
| Clark | Mark Me |
| M. P. | Miklos Hor |

UNDERSTUDIES: Miklos Horvath (Clark, Hinson, M.P.),
chael Kell (Richie), Mark Metcalf (Billy), Les Roberts (Car
Roger), Arlen Dean Snyder (Rooney, Cokes)

A drama in two acts. The action takes place in 1965 in an a
barracks in Virginia.

*General Manager:* Robert Kamlot
*Production Manager:* Andrew Mihok
*Press:* Merle Debuskey, Faith Geer
*Stage Managers:* Nina Seely, Miklos Horvath

\* Still playing May 31, 1976.
† Succeeded by: 1. Kene Holliday, 2. Mark Metcalf, Peter W
*Martha Swope Photos*

**Top: Kenneth McMillan, Dolph Sweet,
Terry Alexander, Peter Evans, Paul Rudd**

VIVIAN BEAUMONT THEATER
Opened Saturday, May 1, 1976.*
New York Shakespeare Festival presents:

# THREEPENNY OPERA

By Bertolt Brecht and Kurt Weill; Translated by Ralph Manheim and John Willett; Director, Richard Foreman; Scenery, Douglas W. Schmidt; Costumes, Theoni V. Aldredge; Lighting, Pat Collins; Wardrobe Supervisor, Elonzo Dann; Sound, Joseph Dungan; Hairstylists, J. Roy Helland, Kathy Jones; Assistant to producers, Marian Lebowitz, Peggy Marks

### CAST

| | |
|---|---|
| Ballad Singer | Roy Brocksmith |
| Mack the Knife | Raul Julia |
| Jenny Towler | Ellen Greene |
| Jonathan Peachum | C. K. Alexander |
| Samuel | Tony Azito |
| Charles Filch | Ed Zang |
| Mrs. Peachum | Elizabeth Wilson |
| Matt | Ralph Drischell |
| Polly Peachum | Caroline Kava |
| Jake | William Duell |
| Bob | K. C. Wilson |
| Ned | Rik Colitti |
| Jimmy | Robert Schlee |
| Walt | Max Gulack |
| Tiger Brown | David Sabin |
| Smith | Glenn Kezer |
| Lucy Brown | Blair Brown |
| Whores | Penelope Bodry, Nancy Campbell, Gretel Cummings, Brenda Currin, Mimi Turque |

BEGGARS AND POLICEMEN: Pendleton Brown, M. Patrick Hughes, George McGrath, Rick Petrucelli, John Ridge, Craig Rupp, Armin Shimerman, Jack Eric Williams, Ray Xifo

UNDERSTUDIES: Keith Charles (Mack), Tony Azito (Ballad Singer), Penelope Bodry (Polly, Lucy), Pendleton Brown (Walt), Gretel Cummings (Mrs. Peachum), Ralph Drischell (Peachum), Frank di Filia (Ensemble Swing), Glenn Kezer (Tiger), Liza Kirchner (Ensemble Swing), George McGrath (Samuel, Bob), John Ridge (Matthew), Craig Rupp (Jimmy, Smith), Armin Shimerman (Filch, Ned), Mimi Turque (Jenny), Jack Eric Williams (Ballad Singer), Ray Xifo (Jake)

A musical in three acts. The action takes place in London at the time of Queen Victoria's Coronation, re-arranged in Brecht's imagination.

General Manager: Robert Kamlot
Production Manager: Andrew Mihok
Press: Merle Debuskey, Faith Geer
Stage Managers: D. W. Koehler, Michael Chambers, Frank Di Filia

Still playing May 31, 1976

*Kramer-Abeles Photos*

Right: Raul Julia, Ellen Greene Top: C. K. Alexander, Elizabeth Wilson, Caroline Kava

Raul Julia, Caroline Kava, David Sabin

Raul Julia, Blair Brown

# NEW YORK SHAKESPEARE FESTIVAL PUBLIC THEATER

Joseph Papp, Producer
Bernard Gersten, Associate Producer

**PUBLIC THEATER/OTHER STAGE**
Opened Sunday, November 2, 1975.*
The New York Shakespeare Festival presents:

## JESSE AND THE BANDIT QUEEN

By David Freeman; Director, Gordon Stewart; Setting, Richard J. Graziano; Costumes, Hilary M. Rosenfeld; Lighting, Arden Fingerhut; Wardrobe Mistress, Sue Gandy

### CAST

Belle .......................... Pamela Payton-Wright†1
Jesse ................................. Kevin O'Connor†2
Understudies: Judith Light, Tracey Walter

The play takes place in Missouri, Kansas, and the Indian Territories from just after the Civil War until the early 1880's.

*Press:* Bob Ullman, Bruce Cohen, Eileen McMahon
*Stage Managers:* Penny Gebhard, Miklos Horvath

\* Closed Feb. 29, 1976 after 155 performances.
† Succeeded by: 1. Dixie Carter, 2. Barry Primus

*Barry Kramer-Joseph Abeles Photos*

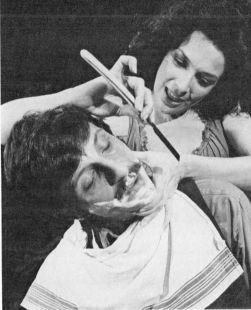

**Dixie Carter, Barry Primus** Top Right:
Kevin O'Connor, Pamela Payton-Wright

**Dixie Carter, Barry Primus, also above**

Opened Friday, December 26, 1975.*
New York Shakespeare Festival presents:

# SO NICE, THEY NAMED IT TWICE

By Neil Harris; Director, Bill Lathan; Scenery, Lighting and Vi-
al Format, Clarke Dunham; Projections, Lucie D. Grosvenor;
und, Gerald Dellasala; Wardrobe, Saidah Nelson

### CAST

| | |
|---|---|
| be | Bill Jay |
| etty | Veronica Redd |
| oris | Dianne Kirksey |
| r. Harris | Nick Smith |
| Irs. Jones | Joanna Featherstone |
| o Go Dancer | Nadyne Spratt |
| eggie | Neil Harris |
| unn | J. W. Smith |
| enrietta | Starletta DuPois |
| itty | Robbie McCauley |
| arry | Brent Jennings |
| ee | Taurean Blacque |
| erry | Alfre Woodard |
| liji | Allen Ayers |
| ountry Bill | Hank Ross |
| assersby | War Hawk Tanzania, Cheryl Jones, Hank Frazier |

NDERSTUDIES: Gerry Black (Abe), Hank Frazier (Gunn, Miji,
ountry Bill), Nadyne Spratt (Kitty, Terry), War Hawk Tanzania
eggie, Lee, Larry), Cheryl Jones (Doris, Henrietta), Sundra Jean
illiams (Betty, Mrs. Jones)

A play in two acts. The action takes place at the present time in
ew York City.

*General Manager:* Robert Kamlot
*Press:* Merle Debuskey, Bob Ullman, Bruce Cohen
*Stage Managers:* Martha Knight, Toby MacBeth

Closed Jan. 4, 1976 after 8 performances.

*Kramer-Abeles Photo*

**Neil Harris, Dianne Kirksey**

**John Ferraro, Michael Moran,
David Laden, Larry Pine**

PUBLIC THEATER/MARTINSON HALL
Opened Wednesday, January 21, 1976.*
New York Shakespeare Festival presents:

# JINXS BRIDGE

By Michael Moran; Conceived, Directed and Designed by members of The Manhattan Project (Andre Gregory, Artistic Director);
Lighting, Victor En Yu Tan; Special Effects, Arthur Muhleisen

### CAST

| | |
|---|---|
| Ghost of Capt. Ogden Leroy Jinxs | Tom Costello |
| Charlie | John P. Holms |
| Mendelsohn Wilkes Jinxs | Tom Costello |
| Alvin Dimple | Himself |
| Carl | Michael Moran |
| Maeve Zant | Kate Weiman |
| Vito Benelli | John Ferraro |
| Elmo Durke | Larry Pine |
| Fred E. Metzman | David Laden |
| Maria Louise Bianci | Angela Pietropinto |

A play in 2 acts and 5 scenes. The action takes place in a room
under a bridge over the Harlem River at the present time.

*Production Manager:* Carlos Esposito
*Company Manager:* Victoria Berning

*Press:* Bob Ullman, Bruce Cohen, Eileen McMahon

* Closed Feb. 15, 1975 after 31 performances.

**PUBLIC/NEWMAN THEATER**
Opened Thursday, February 19, 1976.*
New York Shakespeare Festival presents:

## RICH AND FAMOUS

By John Guare; Director, Mel Shapiro; Musical Direction and Arrangements, Herbert Kaplan; Music and Lyrics, John Guare; Setting, Dan Snyder; Costumes, Theoni V. Aldredge; Lighting, Arden Fingerhut; Production Assistant, Jory Johnson; Wardrobe Mistress, Melissa Adzima; Production Supervisor, Jason Steven Cohen; Technical Director, Mervyn Haines, Jr.

### CAST

Bing Ringling ......................... William Atherton
All Other Characters ........... Ron Leibman, Anita Gillette

A comedy performed without intermission. The action takes place on the opening night of Bing Ringling's first produced play.

*General Manager:* Robert Kamlot
*Production Manager:* Andrew Mihok
*Press:* Merle Debuskey, Bob Ullman, Bruce Cohen
*Stage Managers:* Peter von Mayrhauser, Jean Weigel

* Closed April 25, 1976 after 120 performances.

*Martha Swope Photos*

**Ron Leibman, William Atherton,
Anita Gillette (also above)**

PUBLIC/ANSPACHER THEATER
Opened Thursday, February 12, 1976.*
New York Shakespeare Festival presents:

# APPLE PIE

Libretto, Myrna Lamb; Music, Nicholas Meyers; Director, Joseph
app; Design, David Mitchell; Costumes, Timothy Miller; Lighting,
at Collins; Musical Direction, Liza Redfield; Paintings, Richard
indner; Visuals, Thom Lafferty, David Mitchell; Movement, Lynne
'eber; Associate Producer, Bernard Gersten; Assistant to director,
ndy Lopata; Production Assistant, Jonathan Sheffer; Assistant
onductor, Bill Grossman; Wardrobe Mistress, Jackie Carhart

CAST

ise .............................. Stephanie Cotsirilos
he Mirror ......................... Ilsebet Anna Tebesli
other Marlene ...................... Lucille Patton
reicher .............................. Spain Logue
merican ............................ Robert Polenz
octor ............................. Joseph Neal
ss ............................... John Watson
arshall ........................... Robert Guillaume†
arry/Father ........................ Lee Allen

NDERSTUDIES: Harry/Father, Virgil Curry; Streicher, Will
harpe Marshall; Marshall, Ra Joe Darby; Lise, Marlene, Mirror,
orothea Joyce

USICAL NUMBERS: "Yesterday Is Over," "I'm Lise," "Waltz
Lise's Childhood," "Father's Waltz," "Men Come with Guns,"
Hundsvieh," "Mother's March," "The Trial," "Marshall's Blues,"
Counterman," "America, We're in New York," "Victim Dream,"
Stockboy Blues," "Too Much Motet," "Mating Dance," "Love
cene," "The Doctor," "Lise Dear," "The Wedding," "Gun Scene,"
Harry's Rag," "Freedom Anthem," "Reified Expression," "Break-
p Rag," "Marshall's Reply," "Survival Song," "Final Judgment"

A musical work performed without intermission.

*General Manager:* Robert Kamlot
*Press:* Bob Ullman, Bruce Cohen, Eileen McMahon
*Stage Managers:* Richard S. Viola, Jane E. Neufeld

Closed March 21, 1976 after 72 performances.
Succeeded by Alan Weeks

*Sy Friedman Photos*

Stephanie Cotsirilos, Lee Allen, Robert Guillaume
Top: Spain Logue, Stephanie Cotsirilos,
Lucille Patton, John Watson, Ilsebet Anna Tebesli,
Joseph Neal, Robert Rolenz, Lee Allen

PUBLIC/MARTINSON THEATER
Opened Wednesday, March 24, 1976.*
The New York Shakespeare Festival presents:

# WOYZECK

By Georg Buchner; Completed by Mira Rafalowicz; Director,
Leonardo Shapiro; Lighting, Nicholas Wolff Lyndon; Costumes,
Patricia McGourty; Design Coordinator, Ronald Antone; Music,
Peter Golub; Production Manager, DeLoss Brown

CAST

Drum Major/Grandmother/Cop ................. Ray Barry
Idiot ..................................... James Carrington
Woyzeck ................................... Joseph Chaikin
Child/Doctor/Soldier ........................ Jake Dengel
Captain/Barker/Soldier/Student/Pawnbroker ...... Ron Faber
Andres/Old Man/Soldier/Student/Child . Christopher McCann
Marie ..................................... Jane Mandel
Announcer/Servant/Soldier/Student ........ Arthur Strimling
Margaret/Monkey/Horse/Kathy/Child ..... Maria Zakrzewski

* Closed Apr. 25, 1976 after 35 performances.

*Nathaniel Tileston Photo*

Maria Zakrzewski, Joseph Chaikin, Ray Barry,
Jake Dengel, Ron Faber, Arthur Strimling

Tony Musante, Roy Poole, Meryl Streep

## PHOENIX THEATRE

T. Edward Hambleton, Managing Director
Marilyn S. Miller, Executive Director
Daniel Freudenberger, Producing Director

### THE PLAYHOUSE
Opened Monday, January 26, 1976.*
The Phoenix Theatre presents

## 27 WAGONS FULL OF COTTON

by Tennessee Williams
and

## A MEMORY OF TWO MONDAYS

by Arthur Miller
Scenery and Lighting, James Tilton; Costumes, Albert Wolsk
Production Manager, Robert Beard; Production Assistant, Barba
Carrellas

### CAST

"27 Wagons Full of Cotton"

| | |
|---|---|
| Jake Meighan | Roy Poo |
| Flora Meighan | Meryl Stre |
| Silva Vicarro | Tony Musar |

UNDERSTUDIES: Jake, Rex Robbins; Flora, Fiddle Viraco
Silva, Joel Colodner

The action takes place on the front porch of the Meighan's cotta
near Blue Mountain, Mississippi.

"A Memory of Two Mondays"

| | |
|---|---|
| Bert | Thomas Hu |
| Raymond | Pierre Epste |
| Agnes | Alice Drummo |
| Patricia | Meryl Stre |
| Gus | Roy Poo |
| Jim | Leonardo Cimi |
| Kenneth | John Lithg |
| Larry | Tony Musar |
| Frank | Joe Grif |
| Jerry | Joel Colodr |
| William | Calvin Ju |
| Tom | Rex Robb |
| Mechanic | Clarence Fel |
| Mr. Eagle | Ben Kap |

UNDERSTUDIES: Bert, Kenneth, Joel Colodner; Gus, Jim, B
Kapen; Raymond, Larry, Clarence Felder; Patricia, Linda Carls
Agnes, Fiddle Viracola; Tom, Joe Grifasi

The action takes place in the shipping room of a large auto pa
warehouse in Manhattan.

*General Manager:* Marilyn S. Miller
*Press:* Gifford/Wallace, Tom Trenkle
*Stage Managers:* Jonathan Penzner, Peter DeNicola

* Closed March 21, 1976 after 40 performances in repertory an
previews.

*Van Williams Photos*

**Top Left: Roy Poole, Meryl Streep**

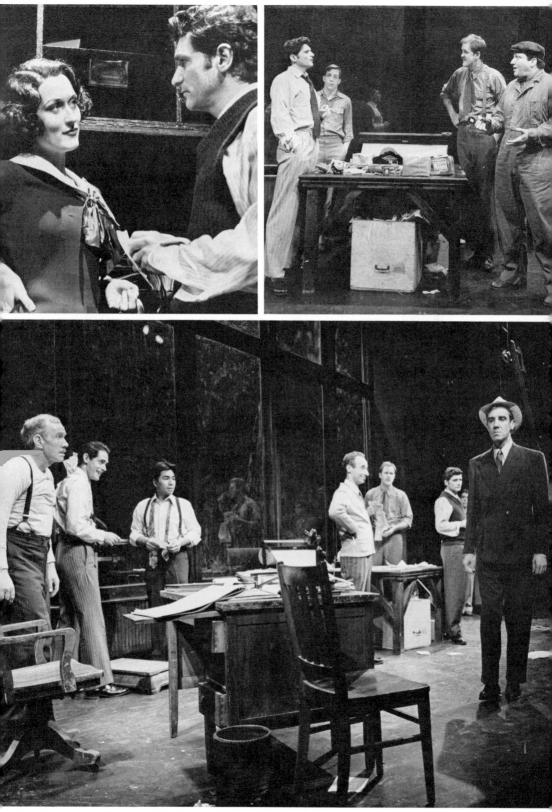

Roy Poole, Joel Colodner, Calvin Jung, Pierre Epstein, John Lithgow, Tony Musante, Thomas Hulce, Rex Robbins Top: (L) Meryl Streep, Tony Musante (R) Tony Musante, Thomas Hulce, John Lithgow, Clarence Felder

139

Opened Tuesday, January 27, 1976.*

The Phoenix Theatre presents:

# THEY KNEW WHAT THEY WANTED

By Sidney Howard; Director, Stephen Porter; Production Manager, Robert Beard; Production Assistant, Barbara Carrellas; Wardrobe Supervisor, Helen McMahon; Hairstylist, J. Roy Helland

CAST

| | |
|---|---|
| Joe | Barry Bostwick |
| Father McKee | Leonardo Cimino |
| Ah Gee | Calvin Jung |
| Tony | Louis Zorich |
| The R. F. D. | Ben Kapen |
| Amy | Lois Nettleton |
| Angelo | Clarence Felder |
| Giorgio | Joel Colodner |
| The Doctor | Rex Robbins |

UNDERSTUDIES: Tony, Clarence Felder; Amy, Linda Carlson; Joe, Joel Colodner; Father McKee, Doctor, Pierre Epstein

A drama in three acts. The action takes place in Tony's farmhouse in the Napa Valley, California.

*General Manager:* Marilyn S. Miller
*Press:* Gifford/Wallace, Tom Trenkle
*Stage Managers:* Jonathan Penzner, Peter DeNicola

* Closed March 6, 1976 after 23 performances in repertory.

*Van Williams Photos*

**Barry Bostwick, Lois Nettleton, Louis Zorich Top Right: Lois Nettleton, Louis Zorich**

THE PLAYHOUSE
Opened Monday, April 12, 1976.*
The Phoenix Theatre presents:

## SECRET SERVICE

By William Gillette; Director, Daniel Freudenberger; Scenery and Lighting, James Tilton; Costumes, Clifford Capone; Audio, David Rapkin; Musical Director, Arthur Miller; Hairstylist, Lyn Quiyou; Production Assistant, Barbara Carrellas; Wardrobe Supervisor, Helen McMahon

### CAST

| | |
|---|---|
| Wilfred Varney | Don Scardino |
| Martha | Louise Stubbs |
| Mrs. Varney | Alice Drummond |
| Edith Varney | Meryl Streep |
| Jonas | David Harris |
| Lt. Maxwell | Frederick Coffin |
| Capt. Thorne | John Lithgow |
| Caroline Mitford | Marybeth Hurt |
| Benton Arrelsford | Charles Kimbrough |
| Cpl. Matson | Joe Grifasi |
| Pvt. Eddinger | Stuart Warmflash |
| Cavalry Orderly | Moultrie Patten |
| Henry Dumont | Lenny Baker |
| Lt. Allison | Jonathan Penzner |
| Lt. Foray | Rex Robbins |
| Telegraph Messenger | Hansford Rowe |
| Sgt. Wilson | Jeffrey Jones |
| Maj. Gen. Harrison Randolph | Roy Poole |
| Banjo, Autoharp, Harmonica | Arthur Miller |

UNDERSTUDIES: Gwendolyn Brown (Mrs. Varney, Edith), Stuart Warmflash (Wilfred), Ann McDonough (Caroline), Rex Robbins (Thorne), Frederick Coffin (Benton), Jeffrey Jones (Maxwell, Dumont), Joe Grifasi (Foray), Moultrie Patten (Randolph, Allison)

A play in 2 acts and 4 scenes. The action takes place during 1864 in General Varney's house on Franklin Street in Richmond, VA, and in the War Department's telegraph office.

*General Manager:* Marilyn S. Miller
*Production Manager:* Robert Beard
*Press:* Gifford/Wallace, Tom Trenkle
*Stage Managers:* Jonathan Penzner, Peter DeNicola

* Closed May 2, 1976 after 13 performances in repertory with "Boy Meets Girl."

*Van Williams Photos*

John Lithgow, Meryl Streep

**Top: Marybeth Hurt, John Lithgow**
**ght: Meryl Streep, Alice Drummond, Charles Kimbrough**

**THE PLAYHOUSE**
Opened Tuesday, April 13, 1976.*
The Phoenix Theatre presents:

# BOY MEETS GIRL

By Bella and Sam Spewack; Director, John Lithgow; Scenery and Lighting, James Tilton; Costumes, Clifford Capone; Audio, David Rapkin; Musical Director, Arthur Miller

## CAST

| | |
|---|---|
| Robert Law | Lenny Baker |
| Larry Toms | Frederick Coffin |
| J. Carlyle Benson | Charles Kimbrough |
| Rosetti | Rex Robbins |
| Mr. Friday (C. F.) | Roy Poole |
| Peggy | Ann McDonough |
| Miss Crews | Alice Drummond |
| Rodney Bevan | Don Scardino |
| Green/Announcer | Joe Grifasi |
| Slade | Moultrie Patten |
| Susie | Marybeth Hurt |
| Studio Nurse | Gwendolyn Brown |
| Young Man | Stuart Warmflash |
| Studio Officer | David Harris |
| Cutter | Arthur Miller |
| Hospital Nurse | Louise Stubbs |
| Major Thompson | Jeffrey Jones |

UNDERSTUDIES: Joe Grifasi (Law), Moultrie Patten (Larry, Thompson), Jeffrey Jones (Benson, Rosetti), Stuart Warmflash (Bevan, Slade), Ann McDonough (Susie), Gwendolyn Brown (Miss Crews), Louise Stubbs (Peggy), David Harris (Green), Hansford Rowe (Friday).

A comedy in 3 acts and 7 scenes. The action takes place in the Royal Studios in Hollywood, CA, in the past.

*Production Manager:* Robert Beard
*Press:* Gifford/Wallace, Tom Trenkle
*Stage Managers:* Jonathan Penzner, Peter DeNicola

\* Closed May 1, 1976 after 10 performances in repertory with "Secret Service."

*Van Williams Photos*

**Top: Charles Kimbrough, Lenny Baker, also Right with Rex Robbins, Frederick Coffin**

**Alice Drummond, Charles Kimbrough, Marybeth Hurt, Lenny Baker, Roy Poole Above Baker, Kimbrough, Joe Grifasi**

# PLAYWRIGHTS HORIZONS, INC.

Robert Moss, Executive Director
Philip Himberg, Producing Director
Associate Producer, Joan Lowell; Fiscal Manager, Jim Swaine;
Technical Directors, Charles Tyndall, Mary Calhoun; Associate
Technical Director, Christie Heiss; Program Administrator, Ira
Schlosser; Literary Manager, Andre Bishop

**PLAYWRIGHTS HORIZONS**
June 19–22, 1975 (4 performances)

TWELFTH NIGHT by William Shakespeare; Director, Garland
Wright; Set, Jemima; Stage Managers, Robert Tomlin, Eric Segal;
Produced in association with The Lion Theatre Company. CAST:
Garland Wright, Jack Heifner, John Arnone, William Metzo, Rob-
ert Machray, Gene Nye, John Guerrasio, Sharon Laughlin, Wanda
Bimson, Janice Fuller, Bill Karnowsky, Randy Goldsborough

June 22–29, 1975 (10 performances)

MISSISSIPPI MOONSHINE by Jim Magnuson; Director, Leland
Moss; Set, Jim Stewart; Costumes, Susan Dennison; Lights, Jeremy
Lewis; Stage Manager, Christie Heiss. CAST: Mike Burke, Mary
Carter, Kathleen Chalfant, Kelly Fitzpatrick, David Gallagher, Jane
Galloway, Laurie Heinemann, Gil Robbins, John Ross, Ken Tigar,
Ron Van Lieu, Horton Willis

June 24–27, 1975 (3 performances)

SWAN DIVE by Frederick Kirwin; Director, Caymichael Patten;
Lights, Charles Tyndall; Stage Manager, Georgie Fleenor. CAST:
Maria Cellario, Christopher Pitney, Rozanne Ritch

June 27–30, 1975 (4 performances)

GETTING GERTIE'S GARTER by Willson Collison and Avery
Hopwood; Director, Robert Moss; Sets and Lights, Richard Wil-
iams; Costumes, Hugh Sherrer; Stage Manager, Connie Alexis; Produced in association with the Joseph Jefferson Theatre Company.
CAST: Carole Doscher, Peter Simpson, Cathy Roskam, Maria Cellario, Robert McFarland, Dana Gladstone, Douglas Travis, Linda
Robbins, Dameon Fayad

September 25–October 12, 1975 (14 performances)

CLAIR AND THE CHAIR by Marsha Sheiness; Director, Hillary
Wyler; Lights, Arden Fingerhut; Stage Manager, Kent Rigsby.
CAST: Linda Barry, Jane Cook, Lisa Bryon, Arthur DeMaio
PROFESSOR GEORGE by Marsha Sheiness; Director, Miss Shei-
ness; Stage Manager, David Rosenberg. CAST: Steve Pomerantz,
Alice Elliott, Maria Callario, Paul Lieber, Robert Burke, Victoria
Boothby

October 2–9, 1975 (7 performances)

THE IMPORTANCE OF BEING EARNEST by Oscar Wilde;
Director, Paul Cooper; Sets, Hope Auerbach; Costumes, Lorri
Schneider; Lights, Cheryl Thacker; Stage Manager, Christie Heiss.
CAST: Ron Johnston, Peter Bartlett, Gene Nye, Margaret Gwenver,
Jayne Haynes, Kathleen Gray, Alice White, Robert Einenkel

**"A Report to the Stockholders"**

**PLAYWRIGHTS HORIZONS**
October 16–November 2, 1975 (13 performances)

A QUALITY OF MERCY by Roma Greth; Director, Anita Khan-
zadian; Sets, Cliff Simon; Costumes, Louise Herman; Lights, James
Chaleff; Sound, Joe Lazarus; Stage Manager, Ian McColl. CAST:
Andy Backer, Sheila Coonan, Elizabeth Perry, Fran Myers, Kathy
Bates, John Martinuzzi

October 23–30, 1975 (7 performances)

THE MIKADO by Gilbert and Sullivan; Director, Barry Keating;
Musical Director, Larry Garner; Associate Director, Pat LaVelle;
Sets, Frank Kelly; Costumes, Bosha Johnson, Cynthia Ann Geis;
Lights, James Chaleff; Stage Manager, Adrien Birnbaum. CAST:
Sebastian Russ, Ira Siff, Barry Keating, Tom Cipolla, Vance Mizelle,
Chuck Richie, Martha Thigpen, Leslie Middlebrook, Cyndee Szym-
kowicz, Marjorie Minnis, Lauren Shub, Maura Stevens, Deborah
Packard, Linda Creamer, Bernard Mantel, Robert B. Whittemore,
Craig Sturgis, Charles Ryan

November 6–23, 1975 (14 performances)

THE LYMWORTH MILLIONS by David Shumaker; Director,
Alfred Gingold; Sets, Joe Lazarus; Costumes, Louise Herman;
Lights, John Gisondi; Stage Manager, Marjie Klein. CAST: George
Mirabella, Mary Jennings Dean, Cathy Roskam, Peter Coffeen,
Brian Meister, Lynda Myles, Andy Backer

November 17–21, 1975 (5 performances)

GLANCE OF A LANDSCAPE by Stephen Yaffee; Director, William Shorr; Set, Tony Straiges; Lights, Tony Santoro; Stage Manager, Barbara Murphy. CAST: Kent Rigsby, Tom Cuff, Robert J.
Herron, Peter Evans, Lee Wilkof, Randall Merrifield, Alan Rosenberg, Christine Jansen, Frank Spencer

November 25–December 14, 1975 (13 performances)

REPORT TO THE STOCKHOLDERS by Kevin O'Morrison; Director, Robert H. Livingston; Music, Louis Schere; Set and Lighting,
Clarke Dunham; Costumes, Allen Munch; Stage Manager, Lewis
Pshena. CAST: Ron Comenzo, Peter Dompe, Hugh L. Hurd, Robbee Jones, Dolores Kenan, John Lack, J. Frank Lucas, James Pritchett, Michael Sklaroff, Paulette Sinclair, Chris Weatherhead

December 4–11, 1975 (8 performances)

JULIUS CAESAR by William Shakespeare; Director, Paul
Schneider; Sets, David Sackeroff; Costumes, Greg Etchison; Lights,
Paul Kaine; Stage Managers, Katherine Mylenki, Ellen Zalk. CAST:
John Archibald, Neal Arluck, Ralph Byers, Pierre Epstein, Steven
Gilborn, Tony Giardina, Robert Grillo, Charles Harper, Steven
Pamela Lewis, Pinocchio Madrid, Jeff Maron, Tom McCready,
Charles Morey, Claude Peters, Jack Pettey, Peter Reznikoff, John
Shearin, James Shearwood, Robert Silver

December 4–6, 1975 (5 performances)

MATT, THE KILLER by Howard Pflanzer; Director, Paul Cooper;
Stage Manager, Cindy S. Tennenbaum. CAST: Dan Deitch, Richard
Allert, Alison Mills, Janis Dardaris, Elliot Burtoff, Harold Cherry,
Stan Edelman

**Douglas Travis, Maria Cellario in
"Getting Gertie's Garter"**

## PLAYWRIGHTS HORIZONS

December 17, 1975–January 4, 1976 (10 performances)

WINNER TAKE ALL by Meir Zvi Ribalow; Director, Michael Heaton; Stage Manager, Marjie Klein. CAST: Linda Carlson, Paul Geier, Lin Shaye

December 18–28, 1975 (9 performances)

GUY GAUTHIER'S EGO PLAY by Guy Gauthier; Director, Kent Wood; Sets, Minda Chipurnoi; Costumes, Danny Morgan; Lights, Gail Kennison; Stage Manager, Ira Schlosser. CAST: Robert Burke, Laurie Copland, Sheldon Feldner, Paul Lieber

January 8–18, 1976 (8 performances)

MISALLIANCE by George Bernard Shaw; Director, Robert Moss; Sets, Frank Kelly; Costumes, Susan Sudert; Lights, John Gisondi; Stage Manager, Amy Chase. CAST: Richard Ryder, Peter Simpson, Carolyn Kruse, Victoria Boothby, Gil Robbins, Douglas Fisher, Peter Brouwer, Jane Sanford, Keith McDermott

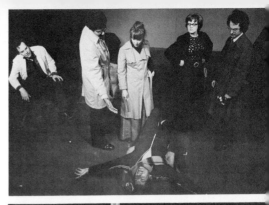

January 15–February 1, 1976 (13 performances)

VANITIES by Jack Heifner; Director, Garland Wright; Sets, John Arnone; Costumes, David James; Lights, Tony Santoro; Stage Manager, Charles Kopelman; Produced in association with the Lion Theatre Co. CAST: Jane Galloway, Susan Merson, Kathy Bates

January 29–February 7, 1976 (11 performances)

OCEAN WALK by Philip Magdalany; Director, Michael Flanagan; Sets, John Gisondi; Costumes, Marya Ursin; Lights, Paul Kaine; Stage Managers, Ted Snowdon, Steve Burdick. CAST: Geraldine Court, Claire Malis, T. Richard Mason, John Martinuzzi, Rex Stallings, John Shearin

February 6–15, 1976 (9 performances)

THE CHEKHOV COMEDIES by Anton Chekhov; Directors, Jonathan Alper, Dennis Pearlstein, Kent Wood, Robert Moss, Philip J. Himberg; Composer, Jeremiah Murray; Sets, Chris Thomas; Lights, David George; Costumes, Louise Herman; Stage Managers, Ian McColl, Marjie Klein. CAST: Anthony Baksa, Patrick Beatey, Kenneth Bell, Victoria Boothby, Jim Broaddus, Mary Louise Burke, Larry Carr, Mike Champagne, Samuel Chapin, Richert Easley, Dameon Fayad, Lucy Lee Flippen, Donna Gabel, Madeline Gorman, Ron Lindbloom, Tony Pandolfo, Don Paul, Linda Phillips, Susan Varon, David Washburn

February 11–15, 1976 (7 performances)

THE TEACHER'S ROOM by Howard Pflanzer; Director, Carol Corwen; Stage Manager, Cindy Tennenbaum. CAST: Leonard Di Sesa, Robert McFarland, Sharon Spitz, William Hart, Robert Barger, Hal Studer, Rick Petrucelli, Billie Lou Watt

**"Misalliance" Top Right: "The Teacher's Room"**
**Below: "Guy Gauthier's Ego Play"**

**"Winner Take All"**
**Above: "Oceanwalk"**

## PLAYWRIGHTS HORIZONS

February 19–28, 1976 (13 performances)

THE PUBLIC GOOD by Susan Dworkin; Director, Leonard Peters; Sets, Steve Duffy, Costumes, Ruth A. Wells; Lights, John Gisondi; Stage Managers, Patricia Wingerter, Steven Steisel, Mary Burns. CAST: Patricia Triana, Robert Bonds, Earl Hindman, Dennis Tate, Martin Shakar, Andrew Bloch, Robert Manuel, Jim Weiss, June Squibb, Marsha Wischhusen, Anne Murray, Sharron Shayne, Lise Cherylyn Collins, Avner Reyer, A. D. Cannon

February 26–March 13, 1976 (13 performances)

THE SPELLING BEE by Marsha Sheiness; Director, Harold Scott; Sets, John Scheffler; Costumes, Kenneth M. Yount; Lights, Arden Fingerhut; Stage Managers, David Rosenberg, Linda Robin Morris. CAST: Joel Brooks, Chevi Colton, Robyn Goodman, Patricia Stewart, Christopher Curry, McLin Crowell, Amelia Haas, John Wylie

March 17–28, 1976 (14 performances)

THE BOSS by Edward Sheldon; Director, Edward Gilbert; Set, Lawrence King; Costumes, Carrie F. Robbins; Lights, William Mintzer; Stage Manager, Bob Jaffe. CAST: Allan Frank, Gregory Abels, Louise Shaffer, John Genke, Dennis Lipscomb, Andrew Jarowsky, Richard K. Sanders, Pamela Burrell, John Eames, Tom-Patrick Dineen, Chris Carrick, Igors Gavon, Chip Lucia, Catherine Henry Lamm

March 17–21, 1976 (6 performances)

UP by Iris Rosofsky; Director, Anita Khanzadian; Stage Manager, David Thalenberg. CAST: Edwin Owens, Janice Fuller, Mary Carter, Eddy Jones, Cynthia Frost

April 1–18, 1976 (13 performances)

PERCHED ON A GABARDINE CLOUD by Steven Braunstein; Director, Frank Cento; Sets and Lights, David George; Costumes, Greg Etchison; Stage Manager, Ian McColl. CAST: Rex D. Hays, Alan Braunstein, K. T. Baumann, Liesha Gullison, Geena Goodwin, Don Paul, Joel Simon, Robert C. Brandt, Kate Weiman

April 1–25, 1976 (12 performances)

TWO FOR THE SEESAW by William Gibson; Director, Michael Keaton; Set, John Gisondi; Costumes, Louise Klein; Lights, William D. Anderson; Stage Manager, Marjie Klein. CAST: Lin Shaye, John Cunningham

April 22–May 1, 1976 (11 performances)

MAGRITTE SKIES by Yale M. Udoff; Director, Richard Place; Sets, John W. Jacobsen; Costumes, Greg Etchison; Lights, Spencer Mosse; Stage Manager, Iris Olshin. CAST: Chevi Colton, Mark Lenard, Tobias Haller, Faith Catlin

## PLAYWRIGHTS HORIZONS

April 29–May 9, 1976 (11 performances)

GEORGE WASHINGTON SLEPT HERE by George S. Kaufman and Moss Hart; Director, Paul Cooper; Lights, William J. Plachy; Costumes, Louise Klein; Stage Managers, Ellen Zalk, Camille Monte. CAST: Elaine Bromka, Michael Burke, Mary Carter, Jerome Collamore, Louis Cruz, Carmelita Fuentes, Margaret Gwenver, Bob Horen, Greg Johnson, Joan Lowell, Bob Luciano, William Robertson, Douglas Stark, Dai Stockton, Louise Williams, Ellen Murray

May 13–22, 1976 (12 performances)

THE CASEWORKER by George Whitmore; Director, Leland Moss; Sets, Christopher Hacker; Costumes, Susan Dennison; Lights, Jeffrey Schissler; Sound, Harry Itkowitz; Stage Manager, Bruce Conner. CAST: William Schilling, Tony Campisi, Chuck McCaughan, Mary Carter

May 27–June 5, 1976 (12 performances)

CAKES WITH THE WINE by Edward M. Cohen; Directed by the author; Sets, Greg Etchison; Costumes, Louise Herman; Lights, Tony Santoro; Stage Manager, Peter DeLaurier. CAST: Nita Reiter, Helen Hanft, Jake Dengel, Anna Shaler, Rodman Flender, Willy Switkes, Arn Weiner, Warren Pincus, Stan Edelman, Charles Kopelman

**Top Right: "Perched on a Gabardine Cloud"**
**Below: "Magritte Skies"**

**"Cakes with the Wine"**
**Above: "George Washington Slept Here"**

# PUBLIC PLAYERS, INC.

J. Perry McDonald, Producer-Director

### CENTRAL ARTS THEATRE
Saturday, September 20, 1975

ONCE IN A LIFETIME by Moss Hart and George S. Kaufman; Director, J. Perry McDonald; Assistant Director, Gary Knight; Music John Kander, Stephen Sondheim, Guiseppe Verdi; Sound, Joseph Bly; Sets and Lighting, Charles McDonough. CAST: Jim Hackett (George), Nancy Frangione (May), Rod Britt (Jerry), Andrew C. Dinan (Porter/Ernest), Dana Smith (Helen), Erika Fox (Susan), Candace Coulston (Phyllis), Jo Ann Havrilla (Florabel), Peggy Cooper (Mrs. Walker), Dolph Browning (Herman)

December 4–7, 1975 (4 performances)

RING ROUND THE MOON by Jean Anouilh; Director, J. Perry McDonald; Pianist, Eliott Finkle. CAST: Charles McDonough (Hugo), Dolph Browning (Joshua), John Sheehan (Frederic), Jamy Rand (Diana), J. R. Horne (Messerschmann), Nancy L. Green (Lady India), Andrew C. Dinan (Patrice), Marguerite Hunt (Mme. Desmortes), Carol de Onis (Capulet), Andrew Natzke (Romainville), Nancy Frangione (Isabelle), Peggy Cooper (Her Mother)

January 22–February 1, 1976 (8 performances)

LA RONDE by Arthur Schnitzler; English Version, Eric Bentley; Producer-Director, J. Perry McDonald; Associate Producer, Iris Grossman; Assistant to producers, Ellen Kaplan; Lighting, Ricki Klein; Set, Charles McDonough; Costumes, Max Navarre; Stage Manager, Andrea Larson. CAST: Nancy Frangione (Whore), Gerard Surerus (Soldier), Nancy L. Green (Parlor Maid), John Sheehan (Young Gentleman), Barbara Myers (Young Wife), Jim Hackett (Husband), Mary Ann Renz (Little Miss), Bernard Tato (Poet), Peggy Cooper (Actress), Mark M. Kelly (Count)

March 11–21, 1976 (12 performances)

A MIDSUMMER NIGHT'S DREAM by William Shakespeare; Director-Producer, J. Perry McDonald; Assistant Director, Iris Grossman; Lighting, Ricki Klein; Set, Charles McDonough; Costumes, Max Navarre; Audio, Joe Bly; Press, Fern Alvins; Stage Manager, Amy Corenthal. CAST: Peggy Cooper (Hippolyta), Alan Coates (Theseus), Edward Sager (Egeus), Mary Ann Renz (Hermia), John Sheehan (Demetrius), Gerard Surerus (Lysander), Nancy Frangione (Helena), Andrew C. Dinan (Peter Quince), Jim Hackett (Bottom), Mark M. Kelly (Flute), Bobby Sheridan (Snout), Elbert Dinkins (Snug), K. W. Geoffries (Starveling), Pat Pell (Puck), Dorothy Fielding (Titania), Richard Ryder (Oberon)

*Frank Derbas, Ron Schwinn Photos*

**Top Right: cast of "La Ronde"**
**Below: "Ring Round the Moon"**

**Dorothy Fielding**

**"A Midsummer Night's Dream"**

146

# ROUNDABOUT THEATRE COMPANY

Gene Feist, Producing Director
Michael Fried, Executive Director
Tenth Season

ROUNDABOUT THEATRE/STAGE TWO
Opened Wednesday, June 4, 1975.*
The Roundabout Theatre Company presents:

## A MUSICAL MERCHANT OF VENICE

Book, William Shakespeare; Music, Jim Smith; Lyrics, Tony Tanner; Director, Tony Tanner; Set, Sandro LaFerla; Costumes, Dwayne Moritz; Lights, Lewis Mead; Associate Producer, David Guc; Production Associates, Diane Factor, Mark McKenna; Manager, Leslie H. Magerman

### CAST

| | |
|---|---|
| Lorenzo | Gary Beach |
| Antonio | Rudy Hornish |
| Portia | Cara-Duff McCormick |
| Jessica | Mary Ann Robbins |
| Shylock | Danny Sewell |
| Duke | Albert Verdesca |
| Arragon | Sel Vitella |
| Gratiano | John Thomas Waite |
| Nerissa | Phylis Ward |
| Bassanio | Mark Winkworth |
| Chorus | Michael Bright, Linda diDario, Nancy Donovan, Jack Godby, Sara Maylond, Theresa Saldana |

*Press:* Gerald Siegal
*Stage Manager:* Charles Repole

* Closed June 13, 1975 after limited engagement of 12 performances.

Sara Lou Cooper, Wyman Pendleton, Deborah Mooney, Bill Newman, Katharine Stanton, Robin Rose, Michael Storm, Livia Genise, Lou Meade, Eda Reiss Merin, Nancy Donovan in "Summer and Smoke"

Deborah Mooney, Michael Storm

ROUNDABOUT THEATRE/STAGE ONE
Opened Monday, October 6, 1975.*
Roundabout Theatre Company presents:

## SUMMER AND SMOKE

By Tennessee Williams; Director, Gene Feist; Set, Holmes Easley; Lighting, Ian Calderon; Costumes, Christina Giannini; Sound, T. Richard Fitzgerald; Score, Philip Campanella; Sculpture, Debra Schechter; Hairstylist, Paul Huntley; Technical Director, Lewis Mead; Production Supervisor, Ian Calderon; Assistant Producers, Steve Evans, David Guc

### CAST

| | |
|---|---|
| Mrs. Winemiller | Sara Lou Cooper |
| Rev. Winemiller | Wyman Pendleton |
| Alma Winemiller | Debra Mooney |
| Dr. John Buchanan, Jr. | Michael Storm |
| Rosa Gonzales | Livia Genise |
| Nellie Ewell | Robin Pearson Rose |
| Chloe | Katharine Stanton |
| Roger Doremus | William Newman |
| Dr. John Buchanan, Sr. | Edward Holmes |
| Mrs. Bassett | Eda Reiss Merin |
| Rosemary | Nancy Donovan |
| Dusty | Lewis Mead |
| Gonzales | John Seitz |
| Archie Kramer | Howard Schechter |

A drama in two acts. The action takes place in the town of Glorious Hill, Miss., at the turn of the century.

*General Manager:* Mary Beth Carroll
*Company Manager:* Barbara Price
*Production Manager:* James Grant
*Press:* Gerald Siegal, Valerie Warner
*Stage Manager:* Douglas F. Goodman

* Closed Oct. 9, 1975 after 40 performances and 24 previews.

*Martha Swope Photos*

**ROUNDABOUT THEATRE/STAGE TWO**
Opened Thursday, December 4, 1975.*
Roundabout Theatre Company and McGraw-Lyttle Productions present:

# DEAR MR. G

By Donna de Matteo; Director, Gene Feist; Set, Holmes Easley; Costumes, Christina Giannini; Lighting, Dan Koetting, Ian Calderon; Assistant to director, Diane Factor; Wardrobe, Samantha S. Hamilton

CAST

| | |
|---|---|
| Tommy Giordano | Antony Ponzini |
| Marlene Giordano | Karen Leslie |
| Louis "Squint" Polaski | Chip Zien |
| Roscoe Nigera | Frank Nastasi |
| Carmella Giordano | Mildred Clinton |

A comedy in two acts. The action takes place at the present time in the home of Mr. and Mrs. Thomas Giordano in a suburban town in Queens, N. Y.

*Company Manager:* Barbara Price
*Press:* Gerald Siegal, Valerie Warner
*Stage Manager:* J. R. Grant

* Closed Jan. 4, 1976 after 37 performances and 9 previews.

*Martha Swope Photos*

**Right: Mildred Clinton, Frank Nastasi,
Anthony Ponzini, Karen Leslie,
Chip Zien Top: Karen
Leslie, Chip Zien, Anthony Ponzini**

**Anthony McKay, Sam McMurray, Sonny Fox,
Stephen Keep, Nancy Addison, Barbara
Britton, Marian Clarke**

**ROUNDABOUT THEATRE/STAGE ONE**
Opened Tuesday, January 6, 1976.*
Roundabout Theatre Company presents:

# CLARENCE

By Booth Tarkington; Director, Gene Feist; Set, Holmes Easley; Costumes, Christina Giannini; Lighting, Ian Calderon; Musical Supervision, Philip Campanella; Hairstylist, Paul Huntley; Technical Director, Lewis Mead; Wardrobe, Rozanne Myers

CAST

| | |
|---|---|
| Mrs. Martyn | Lorraine Spritzer |
| Mr. Wheeler | Sonny Fox |
| Mrs. Wheeler | Barbara Britton |
| Bobby Wheeler | Sam McMurray |
| Cora Wheeler | Nancy Addison |
| Violet Pinney | Marian Clarke |
| Clarence | Stephen Keep |
| Della | Carolyn Lagerfelt |
| Dinwiddie | John Neville-Andrews |
| Hubert Stem | Anthony McKay |

A comedy in four acts, presented with two intermissions. The action takes place during 1919 in Mr. Wheeler's office in New York and the living room of his home in Englewood, N.J.

*Production Manager:* James Grant
*Press:* Gerald Siegal, Valerie Warner
*Stage Manager:* Douglas F. Goodman

* Closed Feb. 15, 1976 after 48 performances and 16 previews.

*Martha Swope Photos*

## ROUNDABOUT THEATRE/STAGE ONE
Opened Monday, April 26, 1976.*
Roundabout Theatre Company presents:

# THE CHERRY ORCHARD

By Anton Chekhov; Director, Robert Mandel; Set, Holmes Easley; Costumes, Christina Giannini; Lighting, Arden Fingerhut; Music, Robert Dennis; Choreography, Pennye Stahlnecker; Hairstylist Robert Baker; Technical Director, Lewis Mead; Technical Coordinator, James Grant; Assistant to director, Craig LaPlount; Wardrobe Mistress, Nette Reynolds

### CAST

| | |
|---|---|
| Lopahin | Paul Benedict |
| Dunyasha | Regina Baff |
| Epihodov | Roy K. Stevens |
| Firs | Fred Stuthman |
| Madame Ranevskaya | Kim Hunter |
| Anya | Patricia Conwell |
| Varya | Verna Bloom |
| Charlotta | Sudie Bond |
| Gaev | William Roerick |
| Pishtchik | Kurt Knudson |
| Yasha | Christopher Curry |
| Trofimov | Stephen Keep |
| A Wayfarer | Michael Kolba |
| Station Master | Paul Pape |
| Post Office Clerk | Mark Blum |

A drama in four acts performed with one intermission. The action takes place in Russia during 1904 on the country estate of Madame Ranevskaya.

*General Manager:* Mary Beth Carroll
*Stage Manager:* Douglas F. Goodman

Closed May 23, 1976 after 32 performances and 24 previews.

*Martha Swope Photos*

**Right: Paul Benedict, William Roerick, Stephen Keep, Fred Stuthman, Verna Bloom, Kim Hunter, Patricia Conwell Top: Verna Bloom, Kim Hunter, William Roerick**

**Jon Benson, William Preston, Georgia Southcotte**

Opened Thursday, May 6, 1976.*
Roundabout Theatre Company presents:

# LOVE AND INTRIGUE

By Friedrich von Schiller; Translated by Frederick Rolf; Director, Gavin Cameron-Webb; Costumes, Carol David; Technical Advisers, Ron Antone, James R. Grant, Dan Koetting, Lewis Mead

### CAST

| | |
|---|---|
| Miller | William Preston |
| Mrs. Miller | Georgia Southcotte |
| Worm | Jon Benson |
| Louisa Miller | Shelley Wyant |
| Baron Ferdinand Walter | John Shearin |
| Chancellor, Baron Walter | Frank Hamilton |
| Lord Chamberlain Stork | Chris Tenney |
| Sophy | Carol David |
| Lady Milford | Kate Weiman |
| Steward | Roger DeKoven |
| Attendants | Chip Keys, Steve Satterfield |

A play in three acts. The action takes place during 1784 in a dukedom in Germany in the Millers' house, the chancellor's palace, and Lady Milford's mansion.

*Stage Manager:* Cameron A. Thompson

* Closed May 23, 1976 after 12 performances.

*Anastasia Nicole Photo*

## SPANISH THEATRE REPERTORY COMPANY

Gilberto Zaldivar, Producer

**GRAMERCY ARTS THEATRE**

May 29, 1975–May 31, 1976 (49 performances)

LOS SOLES TRUNCOS by Rene Marques; Director, Rene Buch; Designs, Robert Federico; Production Assistant, Braulio Villar. CAST: Mirtha Cartaya, Vivian Deangelo, Haydee Zambrana

July 20, 1975–May 25, 1976 (53 performances)

PASOS Y ENTREMESES: 4 one-act plays directed by Francisco Morin; Designer, Robert Federico; Costumes, Ofelia Gonzalez; Technician, William Stiegel. "La Caratula" by Lupe de Rueda, with Tony Diaz, Sadel Alamo, Jean Cacharel, "Las Aceitunas" by Lupe de Rueda, with Braulio Villar, Phyllis Balzaretti, Maria Norman, Vivian Deangelo, Ofelia Gonzalez, Sadel Alamo, Tony Diaz, "Los Habladores" by Miguel de Cervantes, with Sadel Alamo, Tony Diaz, Jean Cacheral, Raoul Alphonse, Braulio Villar, Rene Sanchez, Regina Suarez, Ofelia Gonzalez, Eduardo Barrios, Omar Restrepo, "El Viejo Celoso" by Miguel de Cervantes, with Phyllis Balzaretti, Regina Suarez, Maria Norman, Rene Sanchez, Alfonso Manosalvas, Braulio Villar, Sadel Alamo, Tony Diaz

October 9–19, 1975 (10 performances)

LA REVOLUCION by Isaac Chocron; Director, Roman Chalbaud; Lighting and Assistant to director, Elias Perez Borjas; Costumes, Anibal Soto, Afiche, John Lange. CAST: Rafael Briceno, Jose Ignacio

November 13, 1975–May 31, 1976 (44 performances)

DONA ROSITA, LA SOLTERA by Federico Garcia Lorca; Director, Rene Buch; Designer, Robert Federico; Costumes, Maria Ferreira; Assistant Director, Tony Diaz; Musical Director, Juan Viccini; Visual Effects, Skip Ronglin; Pianist, Zenaida Manfugas. CAST: Alfonso Manosalvas, Lolina Gutierrez, Ofelia Gonzalez, Amelia Bence, Virginia Rambal, Tony Diaz, Raoul Alphonse, Phyllis Balzaretti, Luisa Leschin, Nereida Mercado, Braulio Villar, Graciela Mas, Xonia Benguria, Vivian Deangelo, Maria Norman, Haydee Zambrana, Nidia Pulles, Jose Rodriguez, Rene Sanchez, Orlando Nunez, Felipe Paredes, Rafael Gorbea, Tony Diaz

**Top Right: Virginia Rambal, Maria Norman in "Los Soles Truncos" Below: Tony Diaz, Sadel Alamo in "La Caratula"**

December 5–22, 1975 (9 performances)

LA COMPANIA DE MARIONETAS DE BOGOTA directed Jaime Manzur, with Alfonso Aranguren, Francisco Piedrahita, M tha Ulloa, Pedro Nel Lopez, Victoria Londono, Esther Giraldo

February 18–April 25, 1976 (6 performances)

LOS SOLES TRUNCOS by Rene Marques; Translated by Cha Pilditch; Designer, Robert Federico; Director, Rene Buch; Prod tion Assistant, Braulio Villar. CAST: Virginia Rambal, Luisa L chin, Phyllis Balzaretti, Maria Norman

**GRAMERCY ARTS THEATRE**

March 13–May 31, 1976 (53 performances)

LA MALQUERIDA by Jacinto Benavente; Director, Rene Bu Scenery and Lights, Robert Federico; Costumes, Maria Ferre Rafael Martinez. CAST: Ofelia Gonzalez, Alfonso Manosalvas, V ian Deangelo, Maria Norman, Rene Sanchez, Jose Rodriguez, T Diaz, Alberto Tore, Regina Suarez, Braulio Villar, Sadel Alar Tony Diaz, Lolina Gutierrez, Bela Aguirre, Maria Meulener, Phy Balzaretti, Luisa Leschin, Haydee Zambrana, Jean Cacheral, Ra Gorbea, Tony Diaz, Eduardo Aranco, Jorge Amud

April 4–12, 1976 (5 performances)

NINO ROGER IN HOMBRE, GRITO Y GUITARRA Rodolfo C. Quebleen; Music, Gaudencio Thiago de Mello.

April 24–May 31, 1976 (12 performances)

AMOR DE DON PERLIMPLIN CON BELISA EN SU JARD by Federico Garcia Lorca; Director, Christopher Martin; Assist to director, Tony Diaz; Production Assistant, Braulio Villar; C tume Coordinator, Ofelia Gonzalez; Lighting, Robert Feder CAST: Alfonso Manosalvas, Vivian Deangelo, Ofelia Gonzal Lolina Gutierrez, Tony Diaz, Sadel Alamo, Raoul Alphon Braulio Villar, Omar Restrepo

*Gerry Goodstein Photos*

**Amelia Bence, Alfonso Monosalvas in "Dona Rosita, la Soltera"**

# THEATRE OFF PARK

Martin deMaat, Executive Director
Patricia Peate, Associate Director
Monica May, Artistic Consultant

MMUNITY CHURCH

September 23–October 4, November 10–23, 1975 (24 performances)

IOKING PISTOLS by Don Kvares; Director, Ernest Martin; Set,
ff Simon; Lighting, Robby Monk; Sound, Jerry Kornbluth, A &
udio Visual; Stage Managers, Zoa and Phillip Becker. CAST:
uglas Andros (Woody), Monica May (Edie)

January 12–26, 1976 (12 performances)

ARIES OF ADAM AND EVE adapted from Mark Twain by
ry Allyn-Raye; Director, Miss Allyn-Raye; Costumes, Ann
rt; Stage Manager, Laurie Leffingwell. CAST: Eve Packer (Eve),
y Sorrels (Adam)

March 7–20, 1976 (12 performances)

E PIMIENTA PANCAKES by Sally Dixon Wiener; Adapted
m O. Henry; Director, Monica May; Designer, Gary Weathers-
; Associate Producer, Evelyn Bunn; Assistant to director, Sylvia
dford; Stage Managers, Alvin Ho, David Bosboom, Lee Pucklis,
da Harris; Production Assistant, Susan Greenbaum; Music and
ics, Sally Dixon Wiener; Musical Arrangements, Vernon Jerni-
. CAST: Ned Austin (Uncle Emsley), Vernon Jernigan (Vern),
c Marshall (Judson), Don Paul (Jackson), Celia Weston (Wil-
a)

WBOYS #2 by Sam Shephard; Director, David Avcollie; Asso-
te Producer, Phillip Becker. CAST: Vincent Ferro (Chet), Marty
vy (Stu)

May 23–June 13, 1976 (12 performances)

IALL WAR ON MURRAY HILL by Robert Sherwood; Direc-
, Frank Marino; Set, Bill Michaelovitch; Lighting, John Gleason;
stumes, Anne deVelder; Stage Managers, Judy Binus, Mark Sick.
ST: Keith Aldrich (Judah), Michael Clarke (Mullet), Dottie Dee
san), Woody Eney (Robert), James A. Farley III (Soldier),
ayne Flower (Messenger), Paul Haskins (Gen. Howe), Wanda
n Jones (Amelie), Lars Kampmann (Von Donop), Anna Law-
ce (Daisy), Lou Miranda (Maj. Clove), Robert E. Quigley (Fred-
ck), Linda Selman (Mary), Richard Vernon (Galway)

*Mike Uffer, Gerard Barnier Photos*

**Monica May, Douglas Andros in "Smoking Pistols"**

**Eric Marshall, Don Paul, and right center, Celia Weston, Ned Austin, Eric Marshall
in "The Pimienta Pancakes"**

151

**SULLIVAN STREET PLAYHOUSE**
Opened Tuesday, May 3, 1960.*
Lore Noto presents:

# THE FANTASTICKS

Book and Lyrics, Tom Jones; Suggested by Edmond Rostand's "Les Romanesques"; Music, Harvey Schmidt; Director, Word Baker; Original Musical Direction and Arrangements, Julian Stein; Designed by Ed Wittstein; Associate Producers, Sheldon Baron, Dorothy Olim, Robert Alan Gold; Assistant to the producer, Thad Noto; Production Assistant, John Krug; Original Cast Album, MGM Records

### CAST

| | |
|---|---|
| The Narrator | David Brummel†1 |
| The Girl | Sarah Rice†2 |
| The Boy | Ralph Bruneau†3 |
| The Boy's Father | Lore Noto |
| The Girl's Father | Sy Travers†4 |
| The Actor | Evan Thompson†5 |
| The Man Who Dies | Jack Fogarty†6 |
| The Mute | Paul W. Francis†7 |
| At the piano | William F. McDaniel |
| At the harp | Pattee Cohen |

MUSICAL NUMBERS: Overture, "Try to Remember," "Much More," "Metaphor," "Never Say No," "It Depends on What You Pay," "Soon It's Gonna Rain," "Rape Ballet," "Happy Ending," "This Plum Is Too Ripe," "I Can See It," "Plant a Radish," "Round and Round," "They Were You," Finale

A musical in two acts.

*Press:* David Powers
*Stage Managers:* Ned Levy, Anthony Rasemus

* Still playing May 31, 1976. For original production see THE-

† Succeeded by: 1. David Rexroad, Roger Brown, 2. Cheryl Horne, Betsy Joslyn, 3. Bruce Cryer, 4. Arthur Anderson, David Vogel, 5. Seamus O'Brien, Anthony Rasemus, 6. James Cook, 7. Tom Flagg, John Thomas Waite

**Top Right: Roger Brown (top), Arthur Anderson, Betsy Joslyn, Lore Noto, John Thomas Waite, Bruce Cryer, James Cook**

**Seamus O'Brien, James Cook**

**Arthur Anderson, Bruce Cryer, Betsy Joslyn, Lore Noto**

LLAGE GATE
Opened Tuesday, January 8, 1974.*
Phil Oesterman presents:

# LET MY PEOPLE COME

Music and Lyrics, Earl Wilson, Jr.; Music Arranged and Con-
cted by Billy Cunningham; Choreography, Ian Naylor; Lighting,
ntaur Productions; Produced and Directed by Phil Oesterman;
oduction Assistant, Neal Haynes; Wardrobe Coordinator, Diane-
rie Lemon; Associate Music Director, Norman Bergen; Original
st Album by Libra Records

### CAST

| | |
|---|---|
| nne Baron† | Judy Gibson |
| bin Charin | Jo Ann Lehmann |
| y Colbert | Edwina Lewis |
| ven Alex-Cole | James Morgan |
| rraine Davidson | Michael Poulos |
| rl Deese | Jim Rich |
| rty Duffy | Tuesday Summers |

CT I: "Opening Number," "Mirror," "Whatever Turns You On,"
ive It to Me," "Giving Life," "The Ad," "Fellatio 101," "I'm
y," "Linda Georgina Marilyn & Me," "Dirty Words," "I Believe
y Body"
CT II: "The Show Business Nobody Knows," "Take Me Home
th You," "Choir Practice," "And She Loved Me," "Poontang,"
ome in My Mouth," "The Cunnilingus Champion of Company
" "Doesn't Anybody Love Anymore," "Let My People Come"

*General Management:* Jay Kingwill
*Company Manager:* Mark Bramble
*Press:* Saul Richman, Fred Nathan
*Stage Managers:* Duane F. Mazy, Ray Colbert

Closed July 4, 1976 after 1167 performances to move to Broadway. For original production, see THEATRE WORLD, Vol. 30.
During the season, the following succeeded various members of
the cast: James Bryan, Scott Farrell, Yvette Freeman, Bob Jockers, Empress Kilpatrick, Barry Pearl, Rocky Suda, Dean Tait,
Terri White, Irma Kaye

*Ken Howard Photos*

**Top Right: Carl Deese, Joanne Baron, Jim Rich**

**Terry White, Edwina Lewis**

**Scott Farrell, Empress Kilpatrick**

**CHERRY LANE THEATRE**
Opened Monday, May 17, 1971.*
(Moved August 10, 1971 to Promenade Theatre)
Edgar Lansbury, Stuart Duncan, Joseph Beruh present:

# GODSPELL

Based on the Gospel according to St. Matthew; Music and Lyrics, Stephen Schwartz; Conceived and Directed by John-Michael Tebelak; Lighting, Barry Arnold; Costumes, Susan Tsu, Reet Pell; Production Supervisor, Nina Faso; Musical Director, Bob Christianson; Associate Producer, Charles Haid; Musical Arrangement and Direction, Stephen Schwartz; Musical Supervision, Steve Reinhardt; Set, Fred Gallo; Original Cast Album by Bell Records

### CAST

| | |
|---|---|
| Kerin Blair | Howard Sponseller |
| Bruce Connelly | Melinda Tanner |
| Elizabeth Lathram | Ed Trotta |
| Bobby Lee | Jaison Walker |
| Marilyn Pasekoff | Valerie Williams |

Alternates: Nancy McCall, Douglas Walker

MUSICAL NUMBERS: "Tower of Babble," "Prepare Ye the Way of the Lord," "Save the People," "Day by Day," "Learn Your Lessons Well," "Bless the Lord," "All for the Best," "All Good Gifts," "Light of the World," "Turn Back, O Man," "Alas for You," "By My Side," "We Beseech Thee," "On the Willows," Finale

A musical in two acts and sixteen scenes.

*General Manager:* Al J. Isaac
*Company Manager:* Gail Bell
*Press:* Gifford/Wallace, Tom Trenkle
*Stage Managers:* Michael J. Frank, Tom Demenkoff

\* Closed June 13, 1976 after 2118 performances to move to Broadway.

## OFF-BROADWAY PRODUCTIONS FROM OTHER YEARS THAT CLOSED THIS SEASO|

| Title | Opened | Closed | Performance. |
|---|---|---|---|
| The Hot l Baltimore | 3/22/73 | 11/30/75 | 112( |
| Diamond Studs | 1/14/75 | 8/3/75 | 23; |
| National Lampoon Show | 2/21/75 | 6/29/75 | 18( |
| Rubbers/Yanks 3 Detroit 0 | | | |
| Top of the Seventh | 5/16/75 | 9/21/75 | 14; |
| Be Kind to People Week | 3/23/75 | 6/14/75 | 10( |
| Bluebeard | 4/18/75 | 6/22/75 | 4; |
| The Taking of Miss Janie | 5/4/75 | 6/15/75 | 4; |
| Harry Outside | 5/11/75 | 6/8/75 | 3( |

# PRODUCTIONS THAT OPENED AND CLOSED BEFORE
# SCHEDULED BROADWAY PREMIER

## THE RED DEVIL BATTERY SIGN

y Tennessee Williams; Director, Edwin Sherin; Scenery, Robin
gner; Costumes, Ruth Wagner; Lighting, Marilyn Rennagel;
sic, Sidney Lippman; Musical Arrangements and Supervision,
ace Diaz, Robert Colby; Sound, Robert Maybaum; Wardrobe
ervisor, Kathleen Foster; Hairstylist, Tony Marrero; Production
sistant, Penny Franks; Presented by David Merrick, Doris Cole
rahams, Robert Colby; Opened at the Shubert Theatre in Boston,
., Monday, June 16, 1975 and closed there June 28, 1975.

### CAST

| | |
|---|---|
| man downtown | Claire Bloom |
| n at the bar | Pat Corley |
| arlie the barman | John Ramsey |
| g Del Rey | Anthony Quinn |
| o | Frank C. Martinez |
| Nina | Annette Cardona |
| la | Katy Jurado |
| Cabe | Stephen McHattie |
| ummer | Alfred Karl |
| tel Manager | Tom Noel |
| armacist | Will Hussung |
| st Policeman | Pat Corley |
| ond Policeman | John Ramsey |

E KING'S MEN: Agustin Bustamente, Paul Cohen, Juan De
ctis, Dick Dia, Ford Harrison, Paul La Tirenta, Frank C. Marti-
, Emilio Prados, San Rainone

DERSTUDIES: King, Alfred Karl; Woman, Lee Terry; Perla,
nne Kaplan; McCabe, Drummer, Charlie, Mitchell McGuire; La
na, Sandra Gallardo; Man, Manager, Pharmacist, Eugene Stuck-
nn

A drama in two acts and ten scenes. The action takes place in
llas, Texas, shortly after the John F. Kennedy assassination.

*General Manager:* Helen L. Nickerson
*Company Manager:* Gino Giglio
*Press:* Solters & Roskin, Stanley F. Kaminsky
*Stage Managers:* Marnel Summer, Eugene Stuckmann

*No production photographs taken.*

## TRUCKLOAD

Music, Louis St. Louis; Lyrics, Wes Harris; Book, Hugh Wheeler;
Direction and Choreography, Patricia Birch; Scenery, Douglas W.
Schmidt; Costumes, Carrie F. Robbins; Lighting, John Gleason;
Sound, Robert Minor; Orchestrations, Michael Gibson, Bhen Lan-
zaroni; Vocal Arrangements, Flamin' Mama Music/Carl Hall; As-
sistant to director, James Dybas; Wardrobe Supervisor, Josephine
Zampedri; Production Assistants, Francis Tobin, Roz Monahan;
Associated Conductor, Richard Weinstock; Music Coordinator,
Earl Shendell; Presented by Adela Holzer, The Shubert Organiza-
tion, Dick Clark. Opened Saturday, September 6, 1975 at the Ly-
ceum Theatre, NYC, and closed there Sept. 11, 1975.

### CAST

| | |
|---|---|
| Driver | Louis St. Louis |
| Heustis | Kelly Ward |
| Bonnie | Ilene Graff |
| Horace | Donny Burks |
| Amelia | Laurie Prange |
| Glory | Cheryl Barnes |
| Darleen | Sherry Mathis |
| Leon | Doug McKeon |
| Lee Wu | Kenneth S. Eiland |
| Whitfield | Ralph Strait |
| Rosa | Deborah Allen |
| Ricardo | Jose Fernandez |
| Carlos | Rene Enriquez |
| and The All Nite Drivers | |

UNDERSTUDIES: Darleen, Rosa, Chris Callan; Driver, Bob
Christianson: Leon, Fred Fields; Glory, Andrea Frierson; Amelia,
Bonnie, Laura Michaels; Horace, Anthony William Perkins; Heus-
tis, Whitfield, John Scoullar

MUSICAL NUMBERS: "Truckload," "Find My Way Home:"
"Cumbia/Wedding Party:" "Step-Mama," "Look at Us," "Standing
in this Phonebooth," "Amelia's Theme," "I Guess Everything Will
Turn Out All Right," "Rest Stop," "Boogie Woogie Man," "Ricardo's Lament," "Hash House Habit," "Dragon Strikes Back," "Bonnie's Song," "Our Out Your Soul," "There's Nothing Like Music,"
"Hello Sunshine."

A musical performed without intermission. The action takes place
last night on any open road.

*General Manager:* Emanuel Azenberg
*Managers:* Jose Vega, John M. Kirby
*Press:* Betty Lee Hunt Associates, Maria Cristina Pucci, Bill
Evans, Maurice Turet
*Stage Managers:* T. Schuyler Smith, William H. Batchelder, Lani
Sundsten

**Sherry Mathis, Louis St. Louis, and top right,
Donny Burks in "Truckload"**

# SOUVENIR

By George Axelrod and Peter Viertel; Director, Gerald Freedman; Scenery, William Pitkin; Costumes, Theoni V. Aldredge; Lighting, Martin Aronstein; Sound, Pia Gilbert; Production Manager, Mitchell Erickson; Production Assistants, William R. Goulding, Peter T. Kulok; Wardrobe Master, Elonzo Dann; Presented by Arthur Cantor and E. E. Fogelson in association with Eric Friedheim. Opened Wednesday, Oct. 29, 1975 at the Shubert Theatre in Century City, CA., and closed there Nov. 9, 1975.

## CAST

| | |
|---|---|
| Julie's Stand-in | Jillian Lindig |
| Jack's Stand-in | Bryce Holman |
| Fritz Tauber | John Carpenter |
| Mark Sanders | Tony Musante |
| Assistant Director | Joseph Hill |
| Camera Operator | Bruce Brighton |
| Jack Robson | Edward Easton |
| Eunice Blaustein | Donna Isaacson |
| Julie Stevens | Deborah Kerr |
| William (Swanee) Swanson | Edmund Lyndeck |
| Ben | Laurence Hugo |
| Larry Stevens | Reno Roop |
| Edith | Emmy Nance Grise |
| French Bellboy | Gary Farr |
| Italian Bellboy | John Michalski |
| Guy Holstein | Arthur Ed Forman |
| Rick Townsend | Art Burns |

STANDBYS AND UNDERSTUDIES: Julie, Jillian Lindig; Mark, Art Burns; Ben, Joseph Hill; Swanee, John Carpenter; Larry, John Michalski; Jack, Bryce Holman; Fritz, Arthur Ed Forman; Rick, Gary Farr; Guy, Bruce Brighton

A romantic comedy in two acts. The action takes place at the present time in Hollywood.

*Company Manager:* Ronald Bruguiere
*Press:* Stanley F. Kaminsky, C. George Willard
*Stage Managers:* Charles Kindl, Richard Delahanty

*Eric Skipsey Photos*

Tony Musante, Deborah Kerr

Deborah Kerr, Laurence Hugo
Top: Tony Musante, Deborah Kerr

# WEEKEND WITH FEATHERS

By Romeo Muller; Director, Morton DaCosta; Scenery, James
milton; Costumes, Gloria Gresham; Lighting, Thomas Skelton;
sistant to director, Janet O'Morrison; Wardrobe Supervisor,
elma Davis; Presented by Don Saxon, Don Kaufman, Lesley
vage. Opened Saturday, April 10, 1976 at the Shubert Theatre in
w Haven, CT., and closed at the Playhouse Theatre, Wilmington,
., Apr. 24, 1976.

### CAST

tel Bellhop ............................ Nick Malekos
llie Burroughs ................. Cara Duff-MacCormack
nny Stone ........................ Donald O'Connor
tel Maid ............................ Gloria Irizarry
arky ................................. Robert R. Kaye
r. Warhol ............................ Truman Gaige
ary "Feathers" Jones ...................... Lee Meredith
    Understudies: Vince O'Brien, Jeramie Rain

A comedy in two acts and four scenes. The action takes place at
e present time in a large over-priced hotel suite in midtown Man-
ttan, N.Y.

*General Manager:* Hal Grossman
*Company Manager:* Morry Efron
*Press:* Marvin Kohn, Michael Sean O'Shea
*Stage Managers:* Ben D. Kranz, Jeramie Rain

*Sy Friedman Photos*

**Right: Donald O'Connor, Lee Meredith**

**Donald O'Connor, Cara Duff-MacCormick**          **Donald O'Connor, Truman Gaige**

157

## ALL OVER TOWN

By Murray Schisgal; Director, Dustin Hoffman; Scenery, Oliv
Smith; Costumes, Albert Wolsky; Lighting, John Gleason; Produc
tion Supervisor, Frank Marino; Wardrobe Supervisor, Carl Rose
thal; Assistant to director, Theresa Curtin; Hairstylist, Pa
Huntley; Presented by Adela Holzer; Opened Tuesday, August 1
1975 at the Shubert in Chicago, IL., and closed Sept. 27, 1975 at th
Fisher in Detroit, MI. For original NY production, see THEATR
WORLD, Vol. 31.

### CAST

| | |
|---|---|
| Sybil Morris | Mary Neal |
| Dr. Lionel Morris | Thomas Ton |
| Beebee Morris | Constance Bac |
| Millie | Beth Hatt |
| Charles Kogan | Philip Poli |
| Col. Martin Hopkins | William LeMasse |
| Lewis | Ron O'Ne |
| Louie | Chip Zi |
| Michael Boyssan | Arn Wein |
| Jackie Boyssan | Marie Tomm |
| Laurent | Albert Sande |
| Philomena Hopkins | Sarah Salt |
| Demetrius | Leon Spelma |
| Harold P. Hainesworth | Pi Dougla |
| Francine | Barbara Slotni |
| Maharishi Bahdah | Kurt Knudso |
| Detective Peterson | Arn Wein |
| Detective Kirby | Fredric Sto |

UNDERSTUDIES: Lewis, Hainsworth, Mel Johnson, Jr.; Loui
Charles, Laurent, Fredric Stone; Sybil, Millie, Jackie, Barbara Slo
nick; Beebee, Philomena, Kate Webster; Dr. Morris, Hopkins, M
chael, Kurt Knudson

A comedy in 2 acts and 5 scenes. The action takes place at th
present time in the Morris family's duplex apartment on Manha
tan's Upper East Side.

*General Management:* Theatre Now, Inc., Edward H. Davis,
William Court Cohen
*Company Manager:* Donald Antonelli
*Press:* Michael Alpert, Fred Weterick
*Stage Managers:* Michael Mortorella, Leon Spelman, Mel
Johnson, Jr.

**Chip Zien, Ron O'Neal, Beth Hattub, Thomas Toner, William LeMassena**
**Top Left: Ron O'Neal, Beth Hattub, Thomas Toner**

# CHARLEY'S AUNT

By Brandon Thomas; Director, James Higgins; Settings and
~~lighting~~, Leo B. Meyer; Presented by Jane Friedlander, Saul No-
~~ck~~; Opened Monday, May 10, 1976 at Power Center, Ann Arbor,
~~MI~~, and closed June 26, 1976 at the Performing Arts Center, Mil-
~~waukee~~, WI.

### CAST

| | |
|---|---|
| ~~Ja~~ck Chesney | Robert Doyen |
| ~~B~~rassett | Carle Bensen |
| ~~C~~harley Wykeham | Paul Anderson |
| ~~Lo~~rd Fancourt Babberley | Roddy McDowall |
| ~~K~~itty Verdun | Joanna Hall |
| ~~Am~~my Spettigue | Ann Potts |
| ~~Co~~l. Sir Francis Chesney | James Higgins |
| ~~St~~ephen Spettigue | Vincent Price |
| ~~D~~onna Lucia d'Alvadorez | Coral Browne |
| ~~El~~a Delahay | Isabel Grandin |

~~U~~NDERSTUDIES: Spettigue, Carle Bensen; Babberley, Charley,
~~Ja~~ck Brassett, Barry Smith; Donna Lucia, Amy, Ela, Kitty, Liz
~~P~~olick

A comedy in three acts. The action takes place at Oxford in 1892,
~~an~~d in the drawing room of Spettigue's house.

*Company Manager:* Irving Sudrow
*Press:* Howard Atlee, Clarence Allsopp, Meg Gordean, Becky
Flora
*Stage Managers:* Mark Krause, Barry Smith

**Vincent Price, Coral Browne, Roddy McDowall (also top right)**

# A CHORUS LINE

Conceived, Choreographed and Directed by Michael Benne[]
Book, James Kirkwood and Nicholas Dante; Music, Marvin Ha[]
lisch; Lyrics, Edward Kleban; Setting, Robin Wagner; Costum[]
Theoni V. Aldredge; Lighting, Tharon Musser; Sound, Abe Jac[]
Co-Choreographer, Bob Avian; Orchestrations, Bill Byers, Hers[]
Kay, Jonathan Tunick; Music Coordinator, Robert Thomas; Mu[]
Direction and Vocal Arrangements, Don Pippin; Internation[]
Company Music Director, Ray Cook; Associate Producer, Berna[]
Gersten; Presented by the New York Shakespeare Festival in asso[]
ation with Plum Productions; Assistant Conductor, Patrick H[]
land; Wardrobe Master, Darrell Reed. Opened Monday, May []
1976 at the Royal Alexandra Theatre, Toronto, Canada, and s[]
playing May 31, 1976.

## CAST

| | |
|---|---|
| Paul | Tommy Agui[] |
| Kristine | Christine Bark[] |
| Al | Steve Bauma[] |
| Vicki | Nancy Dafg[] |
| Tom | Mark Dov[] |
| Maggie | Jean Fras[] |
| Frank | Troy Gar[] |
| Val | Mitzi Hamilt[] |
| Zach | Eivind Haru[] |
| Mike | Jeff Hysl[] |
| Diana | Loida Igles[] |
| Greg | Andy Keys[] |
| Bobby | Ron Kurows[] |
| Connie | Jennifer Ann L[] |
| Lois | Wendy Mansfie[] |
| Judy | Yvette Mathe[] |
| Richie | A. William Perki[] |
| Larry | T. Michael Re[] |
| Butch | Ken Roge[] |
| Cassie | Sandy Rove[] |
| Mark | Timothy Sc[] |
| Roy | Donn Simio[] |
| Sheila | Jane Summerha[] |
| Bebe | Miriam Wel[] |
| Tricia | Nancy Wo[] |
| Don | Ronald You[] |

For musical numbers, see Broadway Calendar, page 14.

*General Manager:* Emanuel Azenberg
*Company Manager:* Maurice Schaded
*Press:* Gino Empry
*Stage Managers:* Martin Herzer, David Taylor, Michael Austi[]

**Jean Fraser, Mark Dovey, Miriam Welch, Ronald Young, Jane Summerhays, Eivind Harum, Sandy Roveta, Ron Kurowski, Yvette Mathews, Troy Garza, Christine Barker, A. William Perkins Top Left: Sandy Roveta, Jane Summerhays, Ron Kurowski, Miriam Welch, Yvette Mathews, A. William Perkins Below: Steve Baumann, Christine Barker, Wendy Mansfield, Timothy Scott, Tommy Aguilar, Loida Iglesias**

160

# A CHORUS LINE

onceived, Choreographed and Directed by Michael Bennett; k, James Kirkwood, Nicholas Dante; Music, Marvin Hamlisch; cs, Edward Kleban; Setting, Robin Wagner; Costumes, Theoni Aldredge; Lighting, Tharon Musser; Sound, Abe Jacob; Co-reographer, Bob Avian; Orchestrations, Bill Byers, Hershy Kay, than Tunick; Music Coordinator, Robert Thomas; Music Di-on and Vocal Arrangements, Don Pippin; Musical Direction, ur Rubinstein; Associate Conductor, Tom Hancock; Associate ucer, Bernard Gersten; Presented by the New York Shake-re Festival in association with Plum Productions; Opened nesday, July 7, 1976 at the Shubert in Los Angeles.

## CAST

| | |
|---|---|
| tine | Renee Baughman |
| . | Pamela Blair |
| . | Tim Cassidy |
| k | Paul Charles |
| gie | Kay Cole |
| e | Don Correia |
| ie | Ronald Dennis |
| y | Patricia Garland |
| g | Andy Keyser |
| . | Ron Kuhlman |
| . | Nancy Lane |
| nie | Baayork Lee |
| na | Priscilla Lopez |
| h | Robert LuPone |
| sie | Donna McKechnie |
| ci | Mary Ann O'Reilly |
| by | Scott Pearson |
| . | Don Percassi |
| la | Charlene Ryan |
| ry | Roy Smith |
| ch | Sam Tampoya |
| . | Danny Taylor |
| nk | Claude R. Tessier |
| . | Sammy Williams |
| . | Lee Wilson |
| ia | Rebecca York |

or musical numbers, see Broadway Calendar, page 14.

*General Manager:* Emanuel Azenberg
*Company Managers:* Peter Neufeld, Douglas C. Baker
*Press:* Merle Debuskey, Judi Davidson
*ge Managers:* Jeff Hamlin, Patricia Drylie, Frank Hartenstein, Andy G. Bew

**Donna McKechnie, Charlene Ryan Top Right: Pamela Blair, Sammy Williams, Donna chnie, Robert LuPone, Charlene Ryan, Priscella Lopez**

**Don Correia Above: Donna McKechnie**

# DON'T BOTHER ME, I CAN'T COPE

By Micki Grant; Conceived and Directed by Vinnette Carroll; Choreography, Edmond Kresley; Choral Director, Micki Grant; Musical Director, George Broderick; Producer, Tom Mallow; Associate Producer, James Janek; Musical Arrangements, Danny Holgate; Production Supervisor, Roger Franklin; Presented by American Theatre Productions; Opened Sept. 17, 1975 in Hamilton, Ont., Can., and closed Feb. 1, 1976 in Brockville, Ont., Can. For original NY production, see THEATRE WORLD, Vol. 28.

## CAST

| | |
|---|---|
| Bardell Conner | Bobby London |
| Clinton Derricks | Robert Melvin |
| Michel DeSilva | Nat Morris |
| Sheila Ellis | Steiv Semien |
| Elaine Holloman | Jacqueline Smith-Lee |
| Sally Johnson | Charlaine Woodard |

MUSICAL NUMBERS: "I Gotta Keep Movin'," "Harlem Intro," "Lock Up the Dog," "Harlem Street," "Lookin' Over from Your Side," "Don't Bother Me, I Can't Cope," "Children's Rhymes," "Billie Holliday Blues," "Ghetto Life," "You Think I Got Rhythm?," "Time Brings about a Change," "So Little Time," "Thank Heaven for You," "Show Me That Special Gene," "My Love's So Good," "Men's Dance," "They Keep Comin'," "My Name Is Man," "All I Need," "Questions," "Love Mississippi," "It Takes a Whole Lot of Human Feeling," "Good Vibrations," "Prayer," "Sermon," "Fighting for Pharoah," "Universe in Mourning," "We Gotta Keep Moving'"

A "musical entertainment" in two acts.

*General Manager:* James Janek
*Company Manager:* Robert Ossenfort
*Press:* Howard Atlee, Clarence Allsopp
*Stage Managers:* Robert Bruce Holley, Steiv Semien

*Bert Andrews Photos*

**Prudence Darby (C) Top Right: Elaine Holloman**

# EQUUS

By Peter Shaffer; Director, John Dexter; Scenery and Costumes, John Napier; Lighting, Andy Phillips; Sound, Marc Wilkinson; Mime, Claude Chagrin; Production Supervisor, Robert Borod; Presented by Kermit Bloomgarden, Doris Cole Abrahams in association with Frank Milton; Opened Tuesday, Nov. 18, 1975 at the Wilbur, Boston, MA, and still playing May 31 1976. For original NY production see THEATRE WORLD, Vol. 31.

### CAST

Martin Dysart ............................ Brian Bedford
Alan Strang ............................... Dai Bradley
Nurse ..................................... Mary Hara
Hesther Salomon ......................... Sheila Smith
Frank Strang ..................... Humbert Allen Astredo
Dora Strang ........................... Delphi Lawrence
Horseman/Nugget ..................... Richard Marshall
Harry Dalton ........................... Danny Sewell
Jill Mason ............................... Penelope Willis
Horses .......... Joseph Capelli, Mark Hanks, Tom Rolfing,
Patrick Watkins, Mark Shannon†

UNDERSTUDIES: Dysart, Humbert Allen Astredo; Alan, Dennis Erdman; Frank, Danny Sewell; Dora, Hesther, Mary Hara; Jill, Nurse, Dorothy French; Harry, Joseph Cappelli; Horseman/Nugget, Tom Rolfing

A drama in two acts. The action takes place in Rokeby Psychiatric Hospital in Southern England at the present time.

*General Manager:* Max Allentuck
*Company Manager:* John Bloomgarden
*Press:* John Springer, Louis Sica, Harry Davies
*Stage Managers:* Nicholas Russiyan, Robert L. Borod, Mark Shannon, Dorothy French

† Succeeded by Michael Paliotti

*Van Williams Photos*

**Top: Brian Bedford, Dai Bradley,
Richard Marshall Right: Dai Bradley,
Delphi Lawrence, Humbert Allen Astredo**

**Dai Bradley, Penelope Willis
Above: Brian Bedford, Sheila Smith**

Ed Nelson as Harry S. Truman

## GIVE 'EM HELL HARRY!

By Samuel Gallu; Director, Peter H. Hunt; Scenic Design, Ja
Hamilton; Presented by Samuel Gallu and Thomas J. McErla
Technician, John Lucas; Coordinator, Bambi Dudley; Opened S
17, 1975 at the Robinson Auditorium in Little Rock, AR., a
closed Apr. 27, 1976 in Portland, OR.

CAST

ED NELSON

A play in two acts, based on the life and times of President Ha
S. Truman.

*Company Manager:* Jo Rosner
*Press:* Robert W. Jennings
*Stage Manager:* Martha Knight, succeeded by Leanna Lenha

# KENNEDY'S CHILDREN

By Robert Patrick; Director, Clive Donner; Designed by Santo
Loquasto; Lighting, Martin Aronstein; Presented by Michael Har-
rin association with Robert Colby; Associate Producer, Ramon
Rzov; Tour Direction, Theatre Now, Inc.; Opened Friday, March
1976 in San Francisco, CA, in Marines' Memorial Theatre, and
sed May 29, 1976 in the Studebaker Theatre in Chicago, IL.

### CAST

| | |
|---|---|
| nda | Bobo Lewis†1 |
| tender | K. C. Kelly |
| rger | Don Parker†2 |
| rk | Michael Sacks†3 |
| na | Kaiulani Lee†4 |
| rla | Shirley Knight†5 |

UNDERSTUDIES: Jane Sanford (Wanda, Rona, Carla), K. C.
lly (Mark, Sparger), Ernest Austin (Bartender)

A drama in two acts. The action takes place in a bar on the lower
st Side of New York City on a rainy February afternoon in 1974.

General Manager: Jay Kingwill
Company Manager: Donald Antonelli
Press: Alan Edelson, Beverly Snyder
Stage Managers: Murray Gitlin, Ernest Austin

Succeeded by: 1. Barbara Rush, Shelley Winters, 2. Farley
Granger, 3. Al Freeman, Jr., 4. Sally Kirkland, 5. Ann Wedgeworth

*Ken Howard Photos*

**Right: Al Freeman, Jr., Farley Granger,
Shelley Winters**

**Sally Kirkland, Shelley Winters, Ann Wedgeworth**

# MAN OF LA MANCHA

Book, Dale Wasserman; Music, Mitch Leigh; Lyrics, Joe Darion; Direction and Choreography, Joe Lorden; Musical Director, Milt Setzer; Associate Producer, James Janek; Designed by Associat Theatrical Designers, Ltd.; Costume Coordinator, Darrell Re Producer, Tom Mallow; Assistant Conductor, Jene Citronbau Wardrobe Supervisor, Darrell Reed; Production Assistant, Richa Martini; Opened Tuesday, Jan. 15, 1976 in Kalamazoo, MI, a closed Apr. 4, 1976 in Paramus, NJ. For original NY productio see THEATRE WORLD, Vol. 22.

### CAST

| | |
|---|---|
| Don Quixote (Cervantes) | David Atkins |
| Sancho | Mark R |
| Aldonza | Alice Eva |
| Innkeeper | Frederic Ma |
| Padre | Walter Bloc |
| Dr. Carrasco | Christopher M |
| Antonia | Melanie Ler |
| Barber/Paco | Donald Tar |
| Pedro, Head Muleteer | David Brumm |
| Anselmo | Richard Re |
| Housekeeper/Maria | Louise Armstro |
| Jose/Mule | Hector Merca |
| Tenorio/Horse | Luis Monte |
| Juan | Mark Hollid |
| Fermina | Donna Ni |
| Captain of Inquisition | Michael J. St |
| Moorish Dancer | Donna Ni |
| Guitarist | Robin Pols |
| Guards and Inquisitors | John Hemmer, Jacquil |
| | Rohrbacker, Charles Sho |

UNDERSTUDIES: Quixote, Michael Stone; Aldonza, Mela Lerner; Sancho, Donald Tango; Innkeeper, David Brummel; Barb Richard Reece; Padre, Anselmo, Mark Holliday; Captain, Pe John Hemmer; Antonia, Housekeeper, Maria Fermina, Moor Dancer, Jacquiline Rohrbacker; Swing, Glen McClaskey; Carras David Brummel

MUSICAL NUMBERS: "Man of La Mancha," "It's All the Sam "Dulcinea," "I'm Only Thinking of Him," "I Really Like Him "What Does He Want of Me," "Little Bird," "Barber's Son "Golden Helmet of Mambrino," "To Each His Dulcinea," " Quest," "The Combat," "The Dubbing," "The Abduction," "Mo ish Dance," "Aldonza," "Knight of the Mirrors," "A Little G sip," "The Psalm"

A musical performed without intermission. The action takes pl in a dungeon in Seville at the end of the 16th Century, and in imagination of Cervantes.

*General Manager:* James Janek
*Company Manager:* L. Liberatore
*Press:* Fred Weterick
*Stage Managers:* Jack Welles, Charles Shores, John Hemme

*Bert Andrews Photos*

**Top Left: David Atkinson**
**Below: Alice Evans, Mark Ross**

David Atkinson, Mark Ross

# NATIONAL SHAKESPEARE COMPANY

Artistic Director, Philip Meister; Managing Director, Elaine Ilka; Tour Director, Mary Spector; Scenery, Jane Thurn; Costumes, Sharon Hollinger; Lighting, Bob Lampel; Technical Director, Mustafa Kadaster; Opened Friday, Oct. 3, 1975 in Glen Falls, NY, and closed Apr. 22, 1976 in West Long Branch, NJ.

## CAST

"Much Ado about Nothing" by William Shakespeare;
directed by Philip Meister

| | |
|---|---|
| Leonato | William A. Leone |
| Borachio | Bert Kruse |
| Beatrice | Vivienne Lenk |
| Hero | Nancy Hammill |
| Don Pedro | Richard Boddy |
| Benedick | John Camera |
| Don John | Julian Bailey |
| Claudio | K. C. Kizziah |
| Dogberry | Philip W. Shaw |
| Verges | Granvill Marsh |
| Francis Seacole | Peter Umbras |
| Friar Francis | Julian Bailey |

"Macbeth" by William Shakespeare;
directed by Neil Flanagan

| | |
|---|---|
| Witch | Nancy Hammill |
| Duncan | Philip W. Shaw |
| Malcolm | Bert Kruse |
| Seyton | Granvill Marsh |
| Donalbain | K. C. Kizziah |
| Ross | William A. Leone |
| Macbeth | T. Louis Weltz, Julian Bailey |
| Banquo | Julian Bailey, Peter Umbras |
| Macduff | John Camera |
| Old Siward | Richard Boddy |
| Lady Macbeth | Vivienne Lenk |

"The Tempest" by William Shakespeare;
directed by Mario Siletti

| | |
|---|---|
| Miranda | Nancy Hamill |
| Prospero | Richard Boddy |
| Ariel | Vivienne Lenk |
| Caliban | Joe Dalton Lauck, John Camera |
| Ferdinand | K. C. Kizziah |
| Gonzalo | William A. Leone |
| Alonso | Julian Bailey |
| Sebastian | Philip W. Shaw, Bert Kruse |
| Antonio | Peter Umbras |
| Trinculo | Granvill Marsh |
| Stephano | Philip W. Shaw |
| Mariner | Mustafa Kadaster |

*Company Manager:* Richard Boddy
*Press:* John Dudich
*Stage Managers:* Peter Umbras, K. C. Kizziah, Mustafa Kadaster

**Top Right: Nancy Hammill, Richard Boddy in "Much Ado about Nothing" Below: T. Louis Weltz, Nancy Hammill, Julian Bailey in "Macbeth"**

**Vivian Lenk, Philip W. Shaw, Joe Dalton Lauck in "The Tempest"**

# NEW YORK THEATRE COMPANY

Artistic Director, Philip Meister; Managing Director, Elaine Sulka; Tour Director, Mary Spector; Assistant Tour Director, Ellen Davidow; Sets, Joan Fernacek; Costumes, Sharon Hollinger; Musical Director, Ross Allen; Stage Manager, Kirk Wolfinger

## CAST

"The Fantasticks"—Book and Lyrics, Tom Jones; Music, Harvey Schmidt

| | |
|---|---|
| Mute | Kirk Wolfinger |
| Hucklebee | David Clark |
| Amy Bellamy | Mary Helen Fisher |
| Luisa | Marilynn Winbush |
| Matt | Gary T. Colombo |
| El Gallo | Lawrence Raiken |
| Henry | Kirk Wolfinger |

Opened Jan. 28, 1976 in Kings Point, NY, and closed Apr. 6, 1976 in Lawrenceville, NJ

"Spoon River Anthology"
Book and Music, John Franceschina

David Clark
Gary T. Colombo
Mary Helen Fisher
Lawrence Raiken
Marilynn Winbush
Kirk Wolfinger

Opened Feb. 1, 1976 in Marion, IL., and closed Apr. 13, 1976 in Washington, PA.

**Gary T. Colombo, Kirk Wolfinger, Marilynn Winbush, Lawrence Raiken, David Clark, Mary Helen Fisher in "Spoon River Anthology" Top Right: David Clark, Mary Helen Fisher in "The Fantasticks"**

# RAISIN

Based on Lorraine Hansberry's "A Raisin in the Sun"; Book, [R]obert Nemiroff, Charlotte Zaltzberg; Music, Judd Woldin; Lyrics, [R]obert Brittan; Directed and Choreographed by Donald McKayle; [As]sistant, Dorene Richardson; Scenery, Robert U. Taylor; Cos[tum]es, Bernard Johnson; Lighting, William Mintzer; Musical Direc[tor-]Conductor, Margaret Harris; Orchestrations, Al Cohn, Robert [Fr]edman; Vocal Arrangements, Howard Roberts, Joyce Brown; [Da]nce Arrangements, Judd Woldin; Incidental Arrangements, [Do]rothea Freitag; Production Supervisor, Nate Barnett; Dance Su[per]visor, Zelda Pulliam; Producer, Robert Nemiroff; Associate Pro[duc]ers, Sydney Lewis, Jack Friel; Executive Associates, Irving [We]lzer, Will Mott, Charles Briggs; Technical Adviser, Mitch Miller; [Wa]rdrobe Supervisor, Betty D'Aloia; Hairstylists, Stanley James, [Mi]chael Smith; Associate Conductor, Frank Anderson; Opened [Tu]esday, Dec. 9, 1975 at the Playhouse, Wilmington, DE, and still [tou]ring May 31, 1976. For original NY production, see THEATRE [WO]RLD, Vol. 30.

## CAST

| | |
|---|---|
| [U]sher | Le-Von Campbell |
| [Pul]tim | Loretta Abbott |
| [Ru]th Younger | Mary Seymour |
| [Tra]vis Younger | Darren Green |
| [M]rs. Johnson | Sandra Phillips |
| [Wa]lter Lee Younger | Autris Paige |
| [Bea]neatha Younger | Arnetia Walker |
| [Le]na "Mama" Younger | Virginia Capers |
| [Ba]r Girl | Zelda Pulliam |
| [Bo]bo Jones | Irving Barnes |
| [Wil]lie Harris | Walter P. Brown†1 |
| [Jo]seph Asagai | Milton Grayson |
| [Pa]stor | Roderick Sibert†2 |
| [Pa]stor's Wife | Kay Barnes |
| [Ca]rl Lindner | Stacy McAdams |

[PE]OPLE OF THE SOUTHSIDE: Eddie Jordan, Le-Von Campbell, [Re]nee Warren, Zelda Pulliam, Irving Barnes, Lacy Phillips, H. [Do]uglas Berring, Vanessa Shaw, Corliss Taylor, Kay Barnes, [Ch]arles E. Grant, Bonita Jackson, Cleveland Pennington, Roderick [Sib]ert

[U]NDERSTUDIES: Walter, Asagai, Nate Barnett; Ruth, Vanessa [Sh]aw; Beneatha, Zelda Pulliam; Lena, Sandra Phillips; Mrs. John[so]n, Kay Barnes; Lindner, Will Mott; Willie, Bobo, Roderick Sibert; [Tr]avis, Lacy Phillips; Pastor, Irving Barnes; Walter, Asagai, H. [Do]uglas Berring

[M]USICAL NUMBERS: Prologue, "Man Say," "Whose Little An[gr]y Man," "Runnin' to Meet the Man," "A Whole Lotta Sunlight," ["B]ooze," "Alaiyo," "African Dance," "Sweet Time," "You Done [Ri]ght," "He Come Down This Morning," "It's A Deal," "Sidewalk [Tr]ee," "Not Anymore," "Measure the Valleys"

A musical in two acts. The action takes place in the 1950's in [Ch]icago, Illinois.

*General Manager:* John Corkill
*Company Manager:* Kimo Gerald
*Press:* Arlene Shattil, Max Eisen
*Stage Managers:* Anthony Neely, Bert Wood, Stacy McAdams

Succeeded by: 1. Gregg Baker, 2. Isaac Clay

**Top Right: Darren Green, Autris Paige, Mary Seymour, Virginia Capers, Arnetia Walker Below: Clinton Keen, Loretta Abbott, Irving Barnes, Zelda Pulliam, Autris Paige, Renee Warren, Chuck Thorpes**

Sandra Phillips, Virginia Capers, Mary Seymour

169

# THE ROCKY HORROR SHOW

Book, Music and Lyrics, Richard O'Brien; Director, Mich
Amarino; Musical Director, Steven Applegate; Set, George Barc
Costumes, Mary Piering; Lighting, Fred Kopp; Presented by D
Enterprises; Opened Tuesday, February 3, 1976 at Montgom
Playhouse, San Francisco, CA, and still touring May 31, 1976. F
original NY production, see THEATRE WORLD, Vol. 31.

### CAST

| | |
|---|---|
| Dr. Frank N. Furter | David Jar |
| Rocky Horror | Bill Tac |
| Janet Weiss | Sharon Widn |
| Brad Majors | Robert Reyn |
| Riff-Raff | Buddy K |
| Magenta/Trixie | Vikki D'Ora |
| Columbia | Kelli White |
| Eddie/Dr. Scott | Emil Bor |
| Narrator | Richard C |
| Back-up Singer | Kelly St. Jc |

MUSICAL NUMBERS: "Science Fiction," "Wedding Son
"Over at the Frankenstein Place," "Sweet Trnasvestite," "T
Warp," "Sword of Damocles," "Charles Atlas Song," "What E
Happened to Saturday Night," "Eddie's Teddy," "Once in Awhi
"Planet Shmanet Janet," "It Was Great When It All Began," "Su
Heroes," Finale

A rock musical in 2 acts and 17 scenes.

*Press:* Carol Orsborn
*Stage Managers:* David Rubin, Richard Gee

*Barry Kelsall Photos*

Vikki D'Orazzi Top: David
James, Emil Borelli

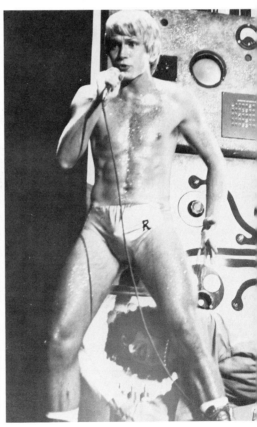

**Bill Tackey**

170

# SHERLOCK HOLMES

By Arthur Conan Doyle and William Gillette; Director, Warren
[I]nters; Scenery and Costumes, Carl Toms; Lighting, Neil Peter
[I]mpolis; Music Arranged by Michael Lankester; Production Asso-
[ci]ates, Cathy Blaser, Sandra Mandel; Wardrobe Supervisor, Billie
[W]hite; Hairstylist, Tiv Davenport; Scenery and Costumes super-
[vi]sed by Mason Arvold; Theme Music, Irving Joseph; The Royal
[S]hakespeare Company's Production is presented by James Neder-
[la]nder, Shubert Organization, Kennedy Center Productions, Adela
[H]olzer, Eddie Kulukundis and Victor Lurie; Opened Jan. 14, 1976
[at] the O'Keefe Center, Toronto, Can., and closed May 22, 1976 at
[th]e Shubert in Chicago, IL. For original NY production, see THE-
TRE WORLD, Vol. 31.

### CAST

| | |
|---|---|
| [M]adge Larrabee | Valerie French |
| [Jo]hn Forman | Neil Hunt |
| [Ja]mes Larrabee | Dalton Dearborn |
| [Th]erese | Alexandra Stoddart |
| [Si]dney Prince | Geoff Garland |
| [A]lice Faulkner | Diana Kirkwood |
| [Sh]erlock Holmes | Robert Stephens† |
| [P]rofessor Moriarty | Alan Sues |
| [Jo]hn | Richard Lederer |
| [A]lfred Bassick | Charles Berendt |
| [Bi]lly | Jeffrey Hillock |
| [D]r. Watson | Ronald Bishop |
| [Ji]m Craigin | Alvah Stanley |
| [Th]omas Leary | Henry Leon Baker |
| ["Li]ghtfoot" McTague | John Seitz |
| [P]arsons | Richard Lederer |
| [Si]r Edward Leighton | John C. Vennema |
| [C]ount von Stalburg | George Ebeling |
| [N]ewsboy | Brian Brownlee |
| [L]ondoners ... Michael Connolly, Tiv Davenport, Vivien Ferrara |
| [Vi]olin | Paul Childs |

A mystery in 2 acts and 5 scenes. The action takes place in London
1891.

*General Manager:* Nelle Nugent
*Company Manager:* Fred J. Cuneo
*Press:* Michael Alpert, Horace Greeley McNab, Marilynn
LeVine, Joshua Ellis
*Stage Managers:* Paul Bengston, Elizabeth Caldwell, Jeffrey
Hillock, Brian Brownlee

**Top: Leonard Nimoy, Diana Kirkwood**
**Right: Leonard Nimoy, Alan Sues**

**Robert Stephens**

# SNOOPY!!!

Based on the comic strip "Peanuts" by Charles M. Schulz; Book, Warren Lockhart, Arthur Whitelaw, Michael L. Grace; Music, Larry Grossman; Lyrics, Hal Hackady; Director, Arthur Whitelaw; Choreography, Marc Breaux; Designed by David Graden; Lighting, Ken Billington; Musical Direction and Vocal Arrangements, Lawrence J. Blank; Production Assistant, Richard Otto; Pianists, Larry Blank, Jon Olson; Wardrobe Supervisor, Rita Yovino; Presented by Arthur Whitelaw, Michael L. Grace, Susan Bloom, Warren Lockhart in association with Charles M. Schulz Creative Associates; Opened Tuesday, Dec. 9, 1975 at the Little Fox Theatre, San Francisco, CA, and closed July 5, 1976 in Marin County, CA.

## CAST

| | |
|---|---|
| Charlie Brown | James Gleason |
| Linus | Jimmy Dodge |
| Sally | Randi Kallan |
| Lucy | Janell Pulis |
| Peppermint Patty | Pamela Myers |
| Snoopy | Don Potter |
| Woodstock | Cathy Cahn |

Understudies; Rhoda Butler Blank, John Forman

MUSICAL NUMBERS: "The World according to Snoopy," "Sit Up! Lie Down! Roll Over! Play Dead!," "Woodstock's Theme," "Edgar Allan Poe," "I Know Now," "The Vigil," "Clouds," "Where Did That Little Dog Go?," "Daisy Hill," "Friend," "It was a Dark and Stormy Night," "Wishy-Washy," "Poor Sweet Baby," "Don't Be Anything Less Than Everything You Can Be," "The Big Bow-Wow!," "Just One Person"

"A musical entertainment" in two acts.

*General Manager:* Peter H. Russell
*Press:* Suzy Strauss, Kevin Kaiser
*Stage Managers:* John Anderson, John Forman

**Right: Jimmy Dodge Top: Don Potter**

**Sammy Cahn**

# WORDS AND MUSIC

Director, Jerry Adler; Musical Director, Richard Leon Gowns, Anne Fogarty; Associate Producer, James Janek; Produc tion Supervisor, Jack Welles; Production Assistant, Mary B Tour Management, American Theatre Productions; Opened Fri September 26, 1975 in Ann Arbor, MI, and closed January 11, 1 in Los Angeles, CA. For Original NY production, see THEAT WORLD, Vol. 30.

## CAST

SAMMY CAHN
Martha Danielle
Sydnee Devitt
Paul Eichel
Standby: William James

An evening of songs written by Sammy Cahn. Presented in parts.

*General Manager:* James Janek
*Company Manager:* Stanley J. Brody
*Press:* Horace Greeley McNab
*Stage Manager:* William James

*Bert Andrews Photos*

## LABAMA SHAKESPEARE FESTIVAL

Anniston, Alabama
July 18–August 23, 1975

Artistic Director, Martin L. Platt; Associate Director, Bruce
ard; Stage Managers, Melissa Taylor, Lissa LeGrand; Assistant
Director, Kathryn Dell; Set Design and Technical Direction, Joel
ehr; Costume Design, Alan Armstrong; Costumer, Lynn Em-
rt; Assistant Technical Director, Alan Prendergast; Property
stress, Paula Drucker; Lighting, Alan Prendergast; Production
sistants, Margaret Jones, Kathy Chandler, Sam Hitchcock, Jack
riakos, Laurence Feldman, Michael Stedham, Mary Ann O'Neal,
my Hensleigh; Wardrobe, Rose Mary Etheridge, Hi Bedford,
dra Fuller, Barry Sellers, Deborah Bunson; Original Music com-
ed and conducted by Martin L. Platt and Bruce Hoard

### COMPANY

arles Antalosky, Michael Burt, Kathryn Dell, Bruce Hoard,
ckson Lane, Joseph Larrea, Lissa LeGrand, Randye Lordon,
ster Malizia, Joseph Mauck, William F. Miller, Norman Neil,
d Osterhoff, Sebastian Richards, Robert Rieben, Robin Robinson,
egory Schroeder, Elizabeth Schuette, Ronald S. Sopyla, Michael
dham, Beth Taffee, Melissa Taylor, Mark Varian, Jennifer
rner, Ronald Wainscott, Steve Wise

### PRODUCTIONS

ne Tempest," "Richard II," "Twelfth Night," "Fitting for La-
" by Feydeau translated by Peter Meyer, "Ralph Roister Dois-
"

*Glenn Andrews, Jr. Photos*

**"Richard II"**

# AMERICAN SHAKESPEARE THEATRE

Stratford, Connecticut
May 17–August 31, 1975
Twenty-first Season

Artistic Director, Michael Kahn; Managing Director, William Stewart; Production Manager, Lo Hardin; Stage Managers, Stephen Nasuta, Arthur Karp; Assistant Director, Larry Carpenter; Wardrobe Mistress, Helen McMahon; Hairstylist, Steve Atha; Production Assistant, Michael Novak; Music Director and Conductor, Allan Lewis; Press, Thomas O'Connor, Seymour Krawitz; President of the Board, Konrad Matthaei; Directors, Anthony Page, Michael Kahn; Scenery, David Jenkins, John Conklin; Costumes, Jane Greenwood, Lawrence Casey; Lighting, Ken Billington; Movement, Liz Thompson; Fights Staged by Rod Colbin; Choreography, Elizabeth Keen; Business Manager, Donald Bundock.

## COMPANY

Gregg Almquist, David Arnstein, Richard Backus, Sally Backus, Laurinda Barrett, Robert Beseda, Powers Boothe, Frank Borgman, Morris Carnovsky, Richard Dix, Tom Everett, Geraldine Fitzgerald, John Glover, Grayce Grant, Fred Gwynne, Eileen Heckart, Bette Henritze, Michael Houlihan, William Larsen, Julia MacKenzie, Donald Madden, Kate Mulgrew, E. E. Norris, Wyman Pendleton, Briain Petchey, Sarah Peterson, Lee Richardson, Jack Ryland, Michele Shay, Marshall Shnider, Theodore Sorel, Alvah Stanley, Charles Sweigart, Maria Tucci, Janet White, Luke Yankee

## REPERTOIRE

"King Lear" by William Shakespeare; Director, Anthony Page. "The Winter's Tale" by William Shakespeare; Director, Michael Kahn; "Our Town" by Thornton Wilder; Director, Michael Kahn.

*Martha Swope Photos*

**William Larsen, Eileen Heckart, Richard Backus, Kate Mulgrew, Lee Richardson, Geraldine Fitzgerald, (front), Victoria Nuland, Todd Alechnowicz in "Our Town" Top Left: Morris Carnovsky, Michele Shay in "King Lear" Below: Bette Henritze, Maria Tucci, Donald Madden in "The Winter's Tale"**

Gerard E. Moses in "Timon of Athens"

# CHAMPLAIN SHAKESPEARE FESTIVAL

Burlington, Vermont
July 9–August 30, 1975
Seventeenth Season
Director, Edward J. Feidner; Associate Producer, George B.
Bryan; Stage Manager, Andrew Mack; Costumes, Polly Smith; Designer, Lisa M. Devlin; Technical Director, Alan Campbell; Assistant Director, James Wimsatt; Business Manager, Barbara Phillips;
Press, Peter Kurth; Sound, Nadine Maleski; Musical Director, Steven A. Freeman; Technical Assistants, W. Bradford Walker, John
Patton; Choreographer, Ruthmary O'Brien.

## COMPANY

Tom Carlisle, Jeffrey DeMunn, Jon Farris, Dennis Lipscomb, Rita
Litton, Gerard E. Moses, Robert Odsley, Armin Shimerman, Marcus Smythe, Sarah Brooke, Susan Dunlop, Margaret Klenck, Sara
O'Neil, Claude Albert Saucier, Susan Selig, Charles Touers, Jonathan Bourne, Peter DeLorenzo, Brooke Gladstone, David S. Godkin, Kevin Meconi, Ciel Metoyer, Greg Patnaude, John Patton,
Craig Purinton, Sally Faye Reit, Jose Angel Santana, Ed Tracy

## REPERTOIRE

"Timon of Athens" by William Shakespeare; Director, Edward J.
Feidner; "Much Ado about Nothing" by William Shakespeare; Director, John Milligan; "Our Town" by Thornton Wilder; Director,
Edward J. Feidner

Robert Ousley, Thomas Carlisle, Marcus Smythe
in "Much Ado about Nothing"

# GLOBE OF THE GREAT SOUTHWEST

Odessa, Texas
June 20–August 24, 1975

Seventh Season

Founder-Producer-Director, Charles David McCally; Business Manager, Bert Coleman; Technical Director, Gregory Wurz; Press, Wanda Snodgrass; Chairman of the Board, Jim Reese; Costumes, Cathleen Gregory Runge; Sets, D. Arthur Runge; Stage Managers, Steve Linn, Michael Ward, Evan Lee, Gwen Griffith, Michael Rowan, Greta Reese, Ruthmary Turnham; Original Music, Michael Morrison; Choreographers, James Kelley, Chikita Wallace; Guest Director, Michael Finlayson

## COMPANY

Wayne Alexander, James Bottom, Dennis Arthur Runge, Steven Linn, Michael Ward, James Kelley, Jeffrey G. Forward, Barry S. Eisenberg, Evan Lee, Criss Bramlet, Matthew Pearl, Alice Altvater, Michael Morrison, Chikita Wallace, Kathleen Gregory Runge, Morris Brown, Charles Benton, Casey Childs, Ruthmary Turnham, Thomas Taylor, Veronica Newell, Peggy McCracken, Jon Shapiro, James M. Rymer, Jr., Steve Bland, Art Berggren, Greta Reese, Joe Durham, Gwendolyn Griffith, Steve McGuire, Lindie Nichols, Brett Elise McCally, Fred Cowles

## REPERTOIRE

"Much Ado about Nothing" by William Shakespeare; Director, Michael Finlayson; "Dames at Sea" by George Haimsohn and Robin Miller; Director, Charles David McCally; "Troilus and Cressida" by William Shakespeare; Director, Michael Finlayson; "The Life of Christ" by Regina Walker McCally; Adapted from the Four Gospels; Director, Charles David McCally

**"As You Like It" Top Right: "Dames at Sea"**

# THE GLOBE PLAYHOUSE

Los Angeles, California
August 22, 1975–May 16, 1976
Producing Organization, The Shakespeare Society of America; Executive Producer-Founder, R. Thad Taylor; Artistic Director, DeVeren Bookwalter; Associate Producers, Robert Epstein, James Farquharson, Thom Shields; Directors, DeVeren Bookwalter, Shannon Eubanks, Martin Platt; Sets, Roger Hampton, Steven Sassen; Costumes, Alan Armstrong, Kathleen Bishop, Shannon Eubanks, Gerri Grammer, B. Jaye Schooley; Lighting, Rob Esselstein, Lewis Martin, Douglas J. Oliver; Music and Sound, James Farquharson, Chris Kuhni

## PRODUCTIONS AND CASTS

CYRANO DE BERGERAC with DeVeren Bookwalter (Cyrano), Adair Jameson (Roxana), Jefferson Watts (Christian), Gary Bass, Paul Bordman, James Boller, Stefan Cotner, Alfred Dennis Shannon Eubanks, Herb Fitch, Frank Geraci, Charles Goldman, Richard Grady, William Gunther, Roger Hampton, Patricia Harvey, Colin Jameson, David Kinne, Jerry Marymont, Karen McLaughlin, Norrine Philips, Gloria Reese, Augie Tribach. This production was the recipient of three awards from the Los Angeles Drama Critics Circle: Distinguished Production, Distinguished Direction, Distinguished Performance (DeVeren Bookwalter). During the season it was returned to the repertoire with the following replacements in the cast: Gloria Dorcy, Ann Driscoll, Edward Dullaghan, B. J. Grogan, Stevie Ann Mitchell, Jon Palo, Michael Ross-Oddo, Raynor Scheine, Steven Schwartz, Bradley Thrush

HAMLET with DeVeren Bookwalter (Hamlet), Shannon Eubanks (Ophelia), Amelia Lauren (Gertrude), Herb Fitch (Claudius), Charles Goldman (Polonius), Stefan Cotner, Gloria Dorcy, Edward Dullaghan, Ray Van Goeye, Richard Grady, William Gunther, Roger Hampton, Odysseus Llowell, Jerry Marymont, Norrine Philips, Robert Redding, Michael Ross-Oddo, Raynor Scheine, Steven Schwarts, Bradley Thrush, Jefferson Watts

LOVE'S LABOURS LOST with James Scott (Berowne), Kres Mersky (Rosaline), Daniel Arden, Richard Baker, Kathleen Bishop, David Bulasky, Stefan Cotner, Michael Endy, William Frankfarter, Paul Fredrix, Dan Gilvezan, Ann Greer, Charles Hutchins, Thomas Mahard, Kim Sudol, Jennifer Varner, Erik White

KING RICHARD III with DeVeren Bookwalter (Richard), Alfred Rossi (Buckingham), Sarah Boulton, Bronia Dearle, Craig Fisch, John Flynn, Ann Greer, Richard Guilfoyle, William Gunther, Roger Hampton, Don Higdon, Jerry Marymont, John Megna, Karen McLaughlin, Norrine Philips, Mark Pint, Anne Potts, Michael Ross-Oddo, Raynor Scheine, Robert Schenk, Steven Schwartz, John Sherwood, Cal Thomas, Bradley Thrush

CYMBELINE with Anne Potts (Imogen), Richard Baker (Posthumus), Steven Schwartz (Cloten), Jay Bell, Sarah Boulton, Christiana Bramlet, Robert Chapel, Tina Deane, Gregory Elliot, William Forward, William Frankfather, Ed Garrabrandt, Frank Geraci, Richard Guilfoyle, William Hargreaves, David Meyers, James O'Kleshen, James Ralston

*James Saterlie, Ralph Bien Photos*

**Karen McLaughlin, Deveren Bookwalter in "Richard III" Top Right: Bookwalter, Charles Goldman, Adair Jameson in "Cyrano de Bergerac"**

**Shannon Eubanks, Deveren Bookwalter in "Hamlet"**

# GREAT LAKES SHAKESPEARE FESTIVAL

Lakewood, Ohio
Lawrence Carra, Producer-Director
July 3–October 11, 1975
Administrative Director, Mary Bill; Press, William Rudman; S
Warner Blake; Costumes, Michael Olich; Lighting, Frederic Y
ens; Stage Managers, J. P. Valente, Harold Warren; Guest Directc
Jean Gascon for "The Miser," Tad Danielewski for "The Winte
Tale"

## COMPANY

Robert Allman, Michael R. Boyle, Gregory Lehane, Keith Mack
Tom Mardirosian, Erika Petersen, James Selby, Billie Anita Stewa
Edward Stevlingson, John Straub, Patrick Watkins, David Willian
Susan Willis, Kate Young

## PRODUCTIONS

"As You Like It" and "The Winter's Tale" by William Shakespa
"The Miser" by Moliere, "Our Town" by Thornton Wilder, "1
Frogs" by Shevelove/Sondheim, freely adapted from Aristopha

*Joseph Karabinus, William Goddard Photos*

**Left: Robert Allman, John Straub in "The Frogs**
**Top: Patrick Watkins, Kate Young, James**
**Selby, Billie Anita Stewart in "As You Like It"**

Erika Petersen, Keith Mackey, Gregory
Lehane in "The Frogs"

Edward Stevlingson, Tom Mardirosian
in "The Miser"

178

# NATIONAL SHAKESPEARE FESTIVAL

Old Globe Theatre
San Diego, California
June 3–September 14, 1975
Twenty-sixth Season

Producing Director, Craig Noel; General Manager, Robert McGlade; Art Director, Peggy Kellner; Press, William B. Eaton; Stage Directors, Ellis Rabb, Jack O'Brien, Diana Maddox; Costumes, Edguard Johnson, Steven Rubin; Lighting, John McLain; Composers, Cathy MacDonald, Conrad Susa; Sound, Charles Richmond, Dan Dugan; Stage Managers, Tom Corcoran, Diana Clarke

## COMPANY

Frank Adams, Ronnie B. Baker, Joseph Bird, Katherine Donohoe Brecka, Forrest Buckman, Patrick Carroll, Hal Chidnoff, Andrew Cole, Tom DeMastri, Patrick Ferguson, Christopher Foster, Lew Horn, David Jensen, Mary Ann Jensen, John-Frederick Jones, Toni Joy, Barry Kraft, Mary Layne, Jason Lee, Ronald Long, Sindy McKay, Richard Marion, Patrick McMinn, Marian Mercer, David Meyers, Danna Mongoven, Susan Mosher, Thomas M. Nahrwold, Pam Navarre, D. Michael Nowicki, Terrence O'Connor, Ellis Rabb, Tom Ramirez, Larry St. John, Patrick B. Sammon, Susan Saunders, Holly Schoonover, Norman Simpler, Mimi Smith, Michael Staetter, David Ogden Stiers, Valeda Turner, Carl Weintraub, G Wood, Vikki Young

## PRODUCTIONS

"The Tempest," "Much Ado about Nothing," "Measure for Measure" by William Shakespeare, "Godspell" by Stephen Schwartz

*Bill Reid Photos*

**Top: Tom DeMastri, Ellis Rabb in "The Tempest"**

**Right: Barry Kraft, Mary Layne, G Wood, Marian Mercer, John Frederick Jones in "Much Ado about Nothing" Below: Terrence O'Connor, Patrick Duffy in "Measure for Measure"**

**David Meyers, Larry St. John in "Godspell"**

# NEW JERSEY SHAKESPEARE FESTIVAL

Madison, N. J.
June 24–November 16, 1975
Eleventh Season
Artistic Director, Paul Barry; Guest Director ("Uncle Vanya").
Davey Marlin-Jones; Press, Ellen Barry; Stage Managers, John
Starr, Gary C. Porto; Scenery, David M. Glenn; Costumes, Gay
Beale Smith, Dean H. Reiter; Lighting, Gary C. Porto; Assistant
Producer, Tom Borsay; Administrative Assistant, Rose Pancirov;
Musical Director, Brian Lynner; Press Assistants, Pam Wright,
Carol Saville

### COMPANY

Humbert Allen Astredo, Ellen Barry, Paul Barry, Robertson Car-
ricart, Kevin Cotter, Kathy Dyas, Robert Foley, Clarence Felder,
Richard Graham, David Howard, J. C. Hoyt, Alan Jordan, Lloyd
Kay, Daryn Kent, Tarina Lewis, Robert Machray, Ron Mangravite,
Susanne Marley, William Preston, Naomi Riseman, Dale Robinette,
Edward Rudney, Margery Shaw, Ronald Steelman, Eric Tavaris, Y
Yve York

Barbara Adinaro, Barbi Alison, Sue Arsenault, Dean Barclay, Sue
Barr, Geoffrey M. Brandt, Jim Bender, Alexander H. Berkeley,
Leona Beth, Susan Bewley, Susan Bloodworth, Vincent Borelli, Bet-
tina R. Carter, Mark L. Churchill, Carol Craddock, Patrick Crea,
Matthew Connors, Anne-Marie Czaykowski, Robert D'Aprile,
Linda Ann Davis, Bethany DeCof, Linda Della-Grotte, Robert De-
siderio, Jeffrey Dighton, Richard H. Dorfman, Camelia Drew, De-
bra L. Dumas, Ted Gargiulo, Gail Gordon, Michael Hegedus, Mark
S. Herb, Cynthia Hodin, Sheri L. Johnson, Rose H. Jung, Stephen
P. Katz, Rick Kirsch, Douglas Kisley, Jeffrey H. Klotz, David
Krafchick, Perry Kroeger, Sarah Fairfax Lansden, William LaRosa,
James Lawrence, Susan Levine, Robert Jeffrey Levitt, Brian Lynner,
Druce McDaniel, Carol Millstein, Garry Morris, Scott Nangle, Sa-
sha Nanus, Gary Pannullo, Rush Pearson, Roger I. Pellaton, Faye
Pollock, David Porter, Deborah Putnam, Leslie H. Raff, Ramon
Ramos, John Rathburn, Bruce Rayvid, Douglas E. Richardson,
Nancy K. Rieth, Jose Rivera, Amy Rosenberg, Tiana Jo Schlitten,
Mary Schmidt, Jan Ian Schwartz, Jo Sennett, S. R. Serafin, Camille
Shawnasey, John Shepherd, Ronald Skorton, Dick St. George, Neil
Stadtmore, Artie Stern, Rawle Titus, Stewart Turner, Debbie Wax-
man, R. E. Wertheim, Haig Zakian

### PRODUCTIONS

"Henry IV, Part I," "Henry IV, Part II," "Two Gentlemen of
Verona" by William Shakespeare, "John Brown's Body" by Stephen
Vincent Benet, "That Championship Season" by Jason Miller, "Un-
cle Vanya" by Anton Chekhov, "Sweet Bird of Youth" by Tennessee
Williams, "The Lady's Not for Burning" by Christopher Fry

*Blair Holley, Rich Towlen, Lee Tanner Photos*

**Right: "Sweet Bird of Youth"**
**Above: "Uncle Vanya" Top: "Henry IV, Part II"**

**Margery Shaw, Paul Barry in "The Lady's
Not for Burning"**

**Eric Tavaris in "Two Gentlemen of Verona"**

# NEW YORK SHAKESPEARE FESTIVAL

Delacorte Theater-Central Park
New York, N.Y.
June 18–August 24, 1975
Nineteenth Season
Producer, Joseph Papp; Associate Producer, Bernard Gersten; Produced in association with the City of New York; Production Manager, Andrew Mihok; Assistant to producer, Gail Merrifield; Press, Merle Debuskey, Bob Ullman, Norman L. Berman; Production Associate, Meir Zvi Ribalow; Music Coordinator, Herbert Harris

June 18–July 19, 1975

## HAMLET

By William Shakespeare; Director, Michael Rudman; Setting, Santo Loquasto; Costumes, Albert Wolsky; Lighting, Martin Aronstein; Fight Sequences, Erik Fredericksen; Percussion Score, Herbert Harris; Danish Anthem, Norman L. Berman; Stage Managers, Jason Steven Cohen, Louis Rackoff; Technical Coordinator, David Manwaring; Wardrobe Master, James McGaha; Production Assistant, Frank Difilia

CAST

Robert Burr (Claudius/Ghost), Ruby Dee (Gertrude), Sam Waterston (Hamlet), Larry Gates (Polonius/First Gravedigger), John Lithgow (Laertes/Player King), Andrea Marcovicci (Ophelia), James Cahill (Horatio), James Gallery (Voltemand), Douglas Stender (Rosencrantz/2nd Gravedigger), John Heard (Guildenstern/Priest), Mark Metcalf (Marcellus/Dumb Show King), Richard Brestoff (Francisco), Bruce McGill (Reynaldo), Franklyn Seales (Fortinbras/Player Queen), Hannibal Penney, Jr. (Captain/Dumb Show Queen), Stephen Lang (Prologue), Vance Mizelle (Company Manager), Ernest Austin (Technical Director), Aides to the King: Richard Brestoff, Graham Beckel, Ray Munro, Cleveland O'Neal III, John Rowe, Stage Hands: Michael Cutt, Reggie Johnson, Jack R. Marks, Ken Marshall, Peter Van Norden, Nancy Campbell (Apprentice Actor)

*Friedman-Abeles Photos*

August 6–24, 1975

## THE COMEDY OF ERRORS

By William Shakespeare; Director, John Pasquin; Music, Peter Link; Setting and Costumes, Santo Loquasto; Lighting, Martin Aronstein; Choreography, Elizabeth Keen; Stage Managers, Richard S. Viola, Peter von Mayrhauser; Technical Coordinator, David Manwaring; Wardrobe Master, Alfred Calamoneri; Production Assistant, Frank DiFilia

CAST

Ted Danson (Bodyguard), Peter Iacangelo (Bodyguard), Leonardo Cimino (Egeon), John Seitz (Solinus), Laurie Faso (Merchant), Paul Kreppel (Merchant), Don Scardino (Antipholus), Michael Tucker (Dromio of Syracuse), Larry Block (Dromio of Ephesus), June Gable (Adriana), Blair Brown (Luciana), John Christopher Jones (Antipholus of Ephesus), Danny DeVito (Balthazar), Susan Peretz (Luce), Pierre Epstein (Angelo), Linda Lavin (Courtesan), Jeffrey Jones (Dr. Pinch), Anita Dangler (Emilia), Townspeople: Maggie Askew, Roxanne Hart, Terri King, Charles McCaughan, Thom McCleister, Harlan Schneider, Kas Self

*Friedman-Abeles Photos*

op Right: **Robert Burr, Ruby Dee, Sam Waterston in "Hamlet" Below: Sam Waterston, Andrea Marcovicci in "Hamlet"**

Don Scardino, June Gable, John Christopher Jones in "Comedy of Errors"

# OREGON SHAKESPEARE FESTIVAL

Ashland, Oregon
February 14–April 12, June 14–September 21, 1975
Fortieth Season

Founder-Consultant, Angus L. Bowmer; Producing Direct
Jerry Turner; General Manager, William Patton; Scenery, Richa
L. Hay; Costumes, Jeannie Davidson; Lighting, Steven A. Ma
Directors, James Edmondson, Will Huddleston, Jon Jory, Andr
Stanley; Production Coordinator, Pat Patton; Technical Director,
Duncan MacKenzie; Choreographer, Judith Kennedy; Music Dire
tor, Jack Ashworth; Stage Managers, James Verdery, Peter Alle
Dennis Bigelow, Jeffrey Hirsch; Hairstylists, Candy Neal, Dia
Gates; Press, Joan Olson, Kathy Glaser, Sally White

## COMPANY

Bruce Abbott, Adrienne Alexander, Denis Arndt, Jack Ashwor
Larry R. Ballard, Alan Blumenfeld, Carmi Boushey, David L. Bc
shey, Jeff Brooks, John A. Caldwell, Joseph De Salvio, James Da
iels, Ted D'Arms, Randi Douglas, le Clanche du Rand, Jam
Edmondson, Joseph H. Feldman, Michael Keys Hall, David Ha
Christine Healy, Keith Herritt, Michael J. Hill, Michael Horto
Will Huddleston, William M. Hurt, Katherine James, Philip
Jones, Wayne Lee, E. Bonnie Lewis, David Marston, Eric Boc
Miller, Michael Kevin Moore, William Moreing, Barry Mulhollar
Mark D. Murphey, Allen Nause, Gayle Stuwe Neuman, Steve Ne
comb, Todd Oleson, Brad O'Neil, Judd Parkin, JoAnn Johns
Patton, Kristin Ann Patton, Pat Patton, Shirley Patton, Mack Ra
sey, Todd Reichenbach, Rebecca Robbins, Neil A Savage, Pe
Silbert, Jean Smart, Mary Turner, William Turner, Leslie Velt
Mark Wardenburg, Cal Winn

## PRODUCTIONS

"Winter's Tale," "Charley's Aunt," "Oedipus the King," "The P
rified Forest," "Romeo and Juliet," "All's Well That Ends Wel
"Henry VI," "Long Day's Journey into Night"

*Hank Kranzler Photos*

**Top: Christine Healy, Mark Murphey in
"Romeo and Juliet" Left: "All's Well That Ends
Well"**

**"The Winter's Tale"
Above: "Romeo and Juliet"**

# SHAKESPEAREAN THEATER OF MAINE

Monmouth, Maine
June 26–August 31, 1975
Artistic Director, Earl McCarroll; Guest Director, Beatrice MacLeod; Sets, Ursula Beldon; Costumes, Joyce Aysta; Lighting, Paul Gallo; Business Manager, Paul Wycisk; Stage Manager, James J. Thesing.

## COMPANY

Lee McClelland, Robert De Lany, Laverne Light, William Meisle, Ronald Parady, Bob Burrus, John H. Fields, Jo Anne Jameson, Robert Johanson, Peter Webster, Herman Tuider, Barbara Selden, Robert Bell, William R. Brown, Lawrence Cappiello, Tom Graff, Richard Haverinen, Nina Jones, Nicholas Kaledin, Cheryl Moore, Robert Nadir, Michael O'Brien, Polly Penn, Kathryn Meisle

## PRODUCTIONS

"The Tempest," "The Comedy of Errors," "Androcles and the Lion," "Dark Lady of the Sonnets," "King Lear"

*Harry Marshall Photos*

**Right: Peter Michael Webster, Robert Johanson in "The Tempest"**

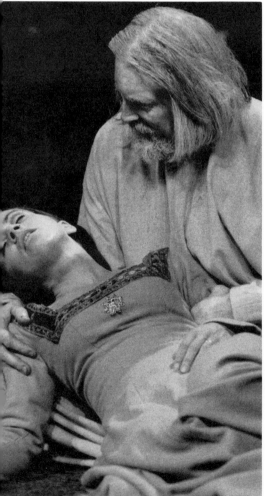

**Lee McClelland, John H. Fields in "King Lear"**

**"A Comedy of Errors"**

## STRATFORD FESTIVAL OF CANADA

Stratford, Ontario
June 9–October 11, 975
Twenty-third Season

Artistic Director, Robin Phillips; Director/Festival Stage, William Hutt; Directors, Bill Glassco; David Jones, Jan Rubes, David Toguri, John Wood; General Manager, Bruce Swerdfager; Business Manager, Gerald Corner; Company Manager, Barry MacGregor; Executive Producer, John Hayes; Design, Daphne Dare; Production Manager, Jack Hutt; Technical Director, Robert Scales; Press, Anne Selby, Douglas Allan, Richard Wolfe; Directors of Music, Alan Laing, Raffi Armenian; Fencing Master, Patrick Crean; Stage Managers, Jack Merigold, Vincent Berns, Nora Polley, Colleen Stephenson, R. Lorne McFarland, Catherine McKeehan, Peter Roberts, David Walsh, Thomas Schweitzer, Penelope Ritco, Wardrobe Mistress, Eleanor Nickless; Production Assistant, Heather Kitchen

### COMPANY

Mia Anderson, Bob Baker, Keith Batten, Rod Beattie, Brian Bedford, Pat Bentley-Fisher, Mervyn Blake, Geoffrey Bowes, Daniel Buccos, Barbara Budd, Jackie Burroughs, Graeme Campbell, J. Kenneth Campbell, J. Winston Carroll, Douglas Chamberlain, Mare Connors, Richard Curnock, Eric Donkin, Martin L. Donlevy, Mary Lou Fallis, Denise Fergusson, Michael Fletcher, Pat Galloway, Gale Garnett, John C. Goodin, Lewis Gordon, Diane Grant, Max Helpmann, Martha Henry, Meg Hogarth, Bernard Hopkins, Linda Huffman, Don Junkin, Peter Hutt, John Innes, Terence Kelly, Tom Kneebone, Jan Kudelka, Larry Lamb, Sheena Larkin, Michael Liscinsky, Barry MacGregor, Stephen Macht, Frank Maraden, Mart Maraden, Richard Monette, Robert G. More, William Needles, Robin J. Nunn, Blaine Parker, Richard Partington, Nicholas Pennell, Jack Roberts, Stephen Russell, Melody Ryane, John Sweeney, Robert Vigod, Ian Wallace, Richard Whelan, Kathleen Widdoes, Leslie Yeo

### PRODUCTIONS

"Saint Joan," "Twelfth Night," "Measure for Measure," "Trumpets and Drums," "The Comedy of Errors," "Two Gentlemen of Verona," "The Crucible," "Fellowship," "Kennedy's Children," "Oscar Remembered," "The Importance of Being Earnest"

*Robert C. Ragsdale Photos*

**Left: Brian Bedford, Geoffrey Bowes, Richard Monette, Martha Henry in "Measure for Measure" Above: Jackie Burroughs, Nicholas Pennell, Gale Garnett in "A Comedy of Errors" Top: Tom Kneebone, Pat Galloway in "Saint Joan"**

**William Hutt, Kathleen Widdoes<br>in "Measure for Measure"**

**Mia Anderson, Nicholas Pennell<br>in "Two Gentlemen of Verona"**

184

**Dennis Lipscomb, Betsy Palmer, Alice Elliott**
**Right: David MacEnulty, Betsy Palmer in "As**
**You Like It"**

# THEATRE VENTURE '76

Beverly, Massachusetts
May 3–28, 1976
Managing Director, Stephan Slane; Resident Manager, Theda Taylor; Press, Peter Downs; Stage Manager, Henry Banister; Production Staff, Michael Neelon, Nancy Jean Schertler; Directors, Ada Brown Mather, Russell Treyz; Sets, Eve Lyon; Costumes, Mary Aiello Bruce; Lighting, Theda Taylor; Musical Director, Ken Collins

### COMPANY

David Brummel, Deborah Combs, Martin Meredith, Richard Kinter, Jack Honor, David MacEnulty, George Cavey, J. Kenneth Campbell, Michael Kane, David Licht, Alice Elliott, Betsy Palmer, Dennis Lipscomb, Stephen Foster, Christopher Wynkoop, Thomas Barbour, Virgil Roberson, Tom Klunis, Kathleen Forbes, Shanly Heffelfinger, Jason Metaxas, Michael Finnerty, Dan Kirsch

### PRODUCTIONS

"As You Like It," "The Fantasticks"

*Peter Downs Photos*

**Martin Meredith, Jack Honor, Deborah Combs**
**in "The Fantasticks"**

# PROFESSIONAL RESIDENT COMPANIES

*(Failure to meet deadline necessitated several omissions)*

## ACT: A CONTEMPORARY THEATRE

Seattle, Washington
June 1, 1975–May 31, 1976
Artistic Director, Gregory A. Falls; General Manager, Andrew M. Witt; Press, Edna K. Hanna, Louise Mortenson; Assistant to General Manager, Warren Sklar; Musical Director, Stan Keen; Directors, Greg Falls, James Higgins, Robert B. Loper, Jack Sydow, M. Burke Walker, Eileen MacRae Murphy; Costumes, Donna Eskew, Sally Richardson; Lighting, Al Nelson, Phil Schermer; Technical Director, Michael Lowther; Stage Managers, Eileen MacRae Murphy, Sandy Cruse, Michael Weholt

### COMPANY

Barbara Bercu, Jay Fernandez, William L. Kux, James W. Monitor, Maryann M. Nagel, Ruth Kidder, A. C. Weary, Richard Watson, Donald Ewer, Henry Hoffman, James Higgins, Rod Pillous, Richard Arnold, Tobias Andersen, Alvin Lee Sanders, Edwin Bordo, Ben Tone, Dean Gardner, John Horn, Kurt Garfield, Richard Blackburn, Jane Bray, Tom Spiller, Joseph Edward Meek, Steven W. Herrmann, Kurt Beattie, Daryl Anderson, Bill Myers, Robert Deitrich, Ann H. Topping, Gregory Elliot, Eric Augusztiny, Ivars Mikelson, Tanny McDonald, C. W. Armstrong, Randy Johnstad, David McMahan, D. H. Panchot, Mada Stockley, John Aylward, Patricia Murray, Clayton Corzatte, Frederick Coffin, Robert Donley, Vern Taylor, William C. Witter, Gail Hebert, Henry Kendrick, Glenn Buttkus, Joe Fields, Brian Avery, Eve Robert, G Wood, Leon Bibb, Gail Nelson, Stan Keen

### PRODUCTIONS

"Sleuth," "The Resistible Rise of Arturo Ui," "When You Comin' Back, Red Ryder?," "Of Mice and Men," "Oh Coward!," "Contact: Fred Coffin," "We Three," "The Christmas Show," "Fire," "Absurd Musical Revue for Children," "See the Players," and *World Premiere* of "Quiet Caravans" by Barry Dinerman, with Sylvia Gassell, Ben Tone, Marjorie Nelson, John Renforth, Susan Ludlow

*Greg Gilbert Photos*

**Right: "When You Comin' Back, Red Ryder?"**
**Above: "Of Mice and Men"**

**Henry Hoffman, Don Ewer**
**in "Sleuth"**

**Ben Tone, Sylvia Gassell**
**in "Quiet Caravans"**

# ACTORS THEATRE OF LOUISVILLE

Louisville, Kentucky
October 16, 1975–May 23, 1976

Producing Director, Jon Jory; Administrative Director, Alexan-
er Speer; Associate Director, Trish Pugh; Assistant Administrative
irector, Stewart Slater; Directors, Clifford Ammon, Ray Fry, Eliz-
eth Ives, Jon Jory, Charles Kerr, Christopher Murney, Adale
Brien, Michael Thompson; Set Designers, Paul Owen, Anne A.
ibson, Grady Larkins, Kurt Wilhelm; Costumes, Kurt Wilhelm;
ghting, Geoffrey T. Cunningham, Vincent Faust, Paul Owen;
roperty Master, Stephen McDowell; Technical Directors, Joseph
agey, Jeffrey Hill; Costumiere, Mary Lou Owen; Stage Managers,
izabeth Ives, Don Johnson, Kimberly Francis Kearsley, Lewis
osen, David Rosenak

## COMPANY

arah Atkins, Jim Baker, Eric Booth, Leo Burmester, Bob Burrus,
'illiam Cain, Barry Corbin, Jean DeBaer, Randi Douglas, Earle
dgerton, Lee Anne Fahey, John H. Fields, Robert Forster, Ray
ry, Michael Gross, Allan Gruet, John Hancock, James Harris,
atharine Houghton, Ken Jenkins, Don Johnson, Victor Jory, Mi-
ael Kevin, Susan Cardwell Kingsley, Marsha Korb, Jack Lan-
on, Jeremy Lawrence, Lauren Levian, Beverly May, Vaughn
cBride, John Meadows, Adale O'Brien, Ardeth Pappas, C. C. H.
ounder, Dennis Predovic, Pamela Reed, Peter Silbert, Michael
hompson

## PRODUCTIONS

Arms and the Man," "The Hot l Baltimore," "Ten Little Indians,"
Oedipus the King," "Scapino!," "The Last Meeting of the White
lagnolia," "The Sunshine Boys," "Dear Liar," "Sea Horse" *World
remiere* of "Scott and Zelda," and *American Premiere* of Maro-
itz' "Measure for Measure"

*David S. Talbott Photos*

**Top Right: Robert Forster, Adale O'Brien
in "The Sea Horse"**

"The Hot l Baltimore"
Above: "Measure for Measure"

Victor Jory, Peter Silbert in "The Last Meeting
of the Knights of the White Magnolia"

187

## ALLEY THEATRE

Houston, Texas
October 18, 1975–May 30, 1976

Producing Director, Nina Vance; Director, Beth Sanford; Se █
William Trotman; Costumes, Barbara A. Cox; Lighting, Jonatha █
Duff; Sound, Paul Dupree; Technical Director, William C. Lin █
strom; President, McClelland Wallace; Press, Bob Feingold, Marg █
ret Genovese; Managing Director, Iris Siff; Business Manager, B █
Halbert; Production Associate, H. Wilkenfeld; Staff Directors, B █
Leonard, Beth Sanford, William Trotman; Company Manager, B █
Leonard; Stage Managers, Bettye Fitzpatrick, George Anderso █
Rutherford Cravens, Trent Jenkins

### COMPANY

John Adams, Cal Bedford, Mimi Carr, Roderick Cook, Rutherfo █
Cravens, Philip Davidson, Carl Davis, James Edmonson, Haske █
Fitz-Simons, Brenda Forbes, Larry Ford, Wayne Gagne, Craig █
Gardner, Russell Gold, Dale Helward, John Houser, Stephen Isbe █
George Jackson, Rodger McDonald, Margo McElroy, Mark Mu █
phy, Jim Nolan, Rand Porter, Rex Rabold, Richard Reed, Richa █
Rorke, Tony Russel, Greg Ryan, Dwight Schultz, Daniel Therriau █
Concetta Tomei, Ben Wolf, David Wurst, Leslie Yeo, Bettye Fitz █
trick, Robert Symonds, Bella Jarret, Lyle Talbot

### PRODUCTIONS

"Indians," "The Cocktail Party," "The Front Page," "The La █
Meeting of the Knights of the White Magnolia," "Old Times, █
"Juno and the Paycock," "The Show-Off," "Scenes from America █
Life," "Tiny Alice," "Purgatory," "The Harmful Effects of T █
bacco," "A Christmas Carol"

*Dome City Photos*

**Top Left: Bettye Fitzpatrick, Mark Murphey,
Leslie Yeo, Cristine Rose in "Juno and the
Paycock" Below: William Troutman, Brenda Forb █
Roderick Cook in "The Cocktail Party"
Center: Dwight Schultz, Bella Jarret in "Tiny Alic █**

**Lyle Talbot, Tony Russel
in "The Front Page"**

**Dale Helward in "Indians"**

# AMERICAN CONSERVATORY THEATRE

San Francisco, California
October 4, 1975–May 22, 1976
Tenth Season

General Director, William Ball; Executive Producer, James B. McKenzie; Executive Director, Edward Hastings; Development Director, Edith Markson; Conservatory Director, Allen Fletcher; Production Director, Benjamin Moore; General Manager, Charles Dillingham; Press, Cheryle Elliott; Stage Directors, William Ball, Allen Fletcher, Edward Hastings, Jon Jory, Laird Williamson; Sets and Costumes, Robert Blackman, Greg Bolton; Lighting, F. Mitchell Dana; Sound, Bartholomeo Rago; Wardrobe Supervisor, Cathy Edwards; Stage Managers, James Haire, James L. Burke, Julia Fletcher, Raymond Gin, Christian Leigh

## COMPANY

Hope Alexander-Willis, Candace Barrett, Joseph Bird, Ray Birk, Earl Boen, Ronald Boussom, Joy Carlin, Megan Cole, Nicholas Cortland, Daniel Davis, Peter Donat, Franchelle Stewart Dorn, Barbara Dirickson, Sabin Epstein, Janice Garcia, Lou Ann Graham, Ross Graham, Nathan Haas, Charles Hallahan, Rick Hamilton, Harry Hamlin, Lawrence Hecht, Elizabeth Huddle, Charles H. Hyman, Daniel Kern, Michael Keys-Hall, Anne Lawder, Deborah May, Fredi Olster, William Paterson, Ray Reinhardt, Stephen Schnetzer, Sandra Shotwell, Anna Deavere Smith, Francine Tacker, Anthony S. Teague, Sydney Walker, Marrian Walters, Al White, J. Steven White, Laird Williamson, James R. Winkler, Daniel Zippi

Frank Abe, Wayne Alexander, Jane Bolton, Cynthia Burch, Traber Burns, Kraig Cassity, Charles Coffey, Linda Connor, William Ferriter, Gina Franz, Bruce Gerhard, Bennet Guillory, Barta Heiner, Gregory Itzin, Delores Mitchell, William Peck, Susan Pellegrino, Peter Schuck, Caroline Smith, Katharine Stapleton, Mary Lou Stewart

## PRODUCTIONS

"Tiny Alice," "The Matchmaker," "Desire under the Elms," "The Merry Wives of Windsor," "Equus," "Peer Gynt," "The Taming of the Shrew" and *World Premieres* of "General Gorgeous" by Michael McClure, and "This Is (An Entertainment)" by Tennessee Williams

*William Ganslen, Hank Kranzler Photos*

**Top: Nicholas Cortland in "General Gorgeous"**
**Right: Peter Donat, Janice Garcia, Daniel Zippi in "Equus" Below: Hope Alexander-Willis, Nicholas Cortland in "Tiny Alice"**

**Earl Boen, Ray Reinhardt, James R. Winker in "This Is (An Entertainment)" Above: "The Merry Wives of Windsor"**

189

# ARENA STAGE

## Washington, D.C.

Producing Director, Zelda Fichandler; Executive Director, Thomas C. Fichandler; Associate Producer, George Touliatos; Assistant Executive Director, Alton Miller; Directors, Edward Payson Call, David Chambers, John Dillon, Zelda Fichandler, Martin Fried, Norman Gevanthor, Gene Lesser, Tom Moore, John Pasquin, Alan Schneider, Douglas C. Wager; Set Designers, John Lee Beatty, Karl Eigsti, Grady Larkins, Ming Cho Lee, Santo Loquasto; Costumes, Gwynne Clark, Carol Luiken, Marjorie Slaiman; Lighting, Robert Crawley, Allen Hughes, Hugh Lester, William Mintzer; Composer, Robert Dennis; Music Adapter, Vance Sorrells; Stage Managers, Jay Allison, John D. Charlesworth, Robert Crawley, Michael S. Mantel, Gully Stanford, Douglas C. Wager; Technical Director, Henry R. Gorfein; Staff for Living Stage: Director, Robert Alexander; Assistant Director, Rebecca Rice; Musical Director, Joan Berliner; Stage Manager, Bob Alexander; Production Assistant, Roberta Gasbarre; Director's Assistant, Pamela Horner.

## COMPANY

Tony Abatemarco, Barry Alexander, Jason Alexander, Jay Allison, Stanley Anderson, John Barrett, Richard Bauer, Gary Bayer, Ned Beatty, Sudie Bond, Nancy Boykin, Peggy Lee Brennan, James Broderick, Russell Carr, Barbara Caruso, Leslie Cass, Howland Chamberlain, Neil Churgin, Liam Clark, William Clark, Carolyn Coates, Hal Corley, Christopher Councill, Jan Cremeans, Terrence Currier, Leora Dana, Regina David, MacIntyre Dixon, le Clanche du Rand, Conchata Ferrell, David Garrison, Grayce Grant, Valorie Gear, Mark Hammer, Dorothea Hammond, Bob Harper, Edward Herrmann, John Hollis, Bella Jarrett, Chris Johnstone, Jeffrey Jones, Pat Karpen, Danny Kelly, Linn Klitzkie, David Leary, Bob Leslie, Kathleen Lindsey, Marilyn McIntyre, Howard Marsden, Norman Martin, Steve Mellor, Michael Mertz, Alexander Metcalf, Mark Metcalf, Michael Miller, Michael Joyce Miller, Gene S. Minkow, Bill Moor, Achim Nowak, Gilbert Oakley, Theresa O'Rourke, Joan Pape, Ron Parker, Tony Pasqualini, Robert Pastene, Daniel Pollack, Ray Procter, Robert Prosky, Richard Ramos, Jack Ryland, David Schaeffer, Scott Schofield, Lane Smith, Phyllis Somerville, Vance B. Sorrells, Robert Stattel, Deborah Ann Stern, Barbara Tarbuck, Joy Tauber, Glenn Taylor, James Tolkan, Lily Tomlin, Eric Vickland, Douglas C. Wager, Mary Lou Walton, Lloyd Webber, Jon Weinberg, Bruce Weitz, Eric Weitz, Dianne Wiest, Eleanor D. Wilson, Halo Wines, Howard Witt, Victoria Wood, Max Wright, Wendell W. Wright.

## PRODUCTIONS

"Long Day's Journey into Night," "An Enemy of the People," "Once in a Lifetime," "Heartbreak House," "What the Babe Said," "Total Recall," "Madmen," "Waiting for Godot," "Busy Dyin'," "Death of a Salesman," "The Front Page," "Our Town," and *PREMIERES* of Istvan Orkeny's "The Tot Family" and a new version of Ray Bradbury's "Dandelion Wine."

*Alton Miller Photos*

**Right: "The Tot Family" Above: "Cabrona"
Top: Leora Dana, Mark Metcalf, Stanley
Anderson, James Broderick in
"Long Day's Journey into Night"**

**Dianne Wiest, Robert Pastene
in "Heartbreak House"**

**James Tolkan, Norman Martin
in "Dandelion Wine"**

# ASOLO STATE THEATER

Sarasota, Florida
June 1, 1975–May 31, 1976

xecutive Director, Richard G. Fallon; Artistic Director, Robert
ne; Managing Director, Howard J. Millman; Sets, Rick Pike;
nting, Martin Petlock; Costumes, Catherine King, Flozanne
n; Technical Director, Victor Meyrich; Press, Edith N. Anson;
e Managers, Marian Wallace, Stephanie Moss

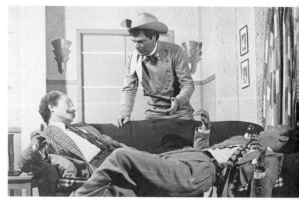

## COMPANY

tha J. Brown, Burton Clarke, Bernerd Engel, Max Gulack, Ste-
n Johnson, Henson Keys, William Leach, Philip LeStrange, Bar-
a Reid, Robert Murch, Bette Oliver, Joan Rue, Robert Strane, Isa
mas, Bradford Wallace, Ken Costigan, Kelly Fitzpatrick, James
gartner, David S. Howard, Pamela Lewis, Dennis Michaels,
queline Hammond, Steven Ryan, Stephen Van Benschoten, Ritch
kley, Katherine Rao, Ralph Clanton, Bob Horen, Gerald
mby, William Jay

vis Agrell, Dottie Dee, Pat Hurley, Barry Klassel, Thomas
mby, Anne Sandoe, Alan Smith, Cathy S. Chappell, Nora Ches-
Janice Clark, Jim Crisp, Jr., John Gray, Stephen Joseph, David
iat, Clark Niederjohn, Patricia Oetken, Frederic-Winslow Oram,
na Pelc, Robert Stallworth, Romulus E. Zamora, Linda Burn-
n, Fred Davis, Molly DePree, Bill Herman, Peter Ivanov, Beth
cks, Paul Murray, Steven J. Rankin, Deborah Unger, John C.
ll

EST ARTISTS: S. C. Hastie, John Dillon, Paxton Whitehead,
Hoskins, Salli Parker, William Woodman, Erskine Caldwell,
n Ulmer, Holmes Easley, Joseph Nieminski, Nick Hall, Bennet
eryt, Jim Chestnutt, Neal Kenyon, Peter Harvey, Eberle Thomas,
n Scheffler, Bella Spewack

## PRODUCTIONS

bacco Road," "The Sea," "Heartbreak House," "Guys and
lls," "Tartuffe," "There's One in Every Marriage," "King Lear,"
he Patriots," "The New York Idea," "Hogan's Goat," "Boy
ets Girl," "A Streetcar Named Desire," "Look Homeward, An-
" and *World Premieres* of "Trolls and Bridges" by Jon Caulkins
d Sandie Hastie, "Going Ape" by Nick Hall, "The Quibbletown
cruits" by Eberle Thomas, "Win with Wheeler," by Lee Kal-
im, "1776 . . . And All That Jazz" by Neal Kenyon

*Gary Sweetman Photos*

**Right: Robert Murch, Ralph Clanton in
"The Patriots" Above: Steven Ryan, Martha J.
own, Barbara Reid in "A Streetcar Named Desire"
Top Right: "Boy Meets Girl"**

**Dennis Michaels, Bradford Wallace
in "Going Ape"**

**William Leach, Barbara Reid
in "Tobacco Road"**

# BARTER THEATRE

Abingdon, Virginia
April 1–October 31, 1975
Artistic Director-Manager, Rex Partington; Director, Owen Phillips; Business Manager, Pearl Hayter; Administrative Director, Ruth Carr; Press, Lucy Bushore, Patricia Bailey; Designer, Bennet Averyt; Costumes, Cynthia Doty, George Carr Garnett; Lights, Michael Dalzell, Richard Marsters; Technical Director, Clayton Austin; Sound, Tony C. Partington; Stage Managers, Peter Dowling, Michael Mantel

## COMPANY

Eric Conger, Tiina Cartmell, Mary Carney, Joseph P. Edens, Gwyllum Evans, Holly Cameron, George Hosmer, Margaret Lunsford, Katharine Manning, Gale McNeeley, Peggity Price, Robert E. Rutland, Jr.

GUEST ARTISTS: David Darlow, Joe Costa, George Black, Herbert DuVal, Kenneth Frankel, John E. Going, Yolande Bryant, Rai Helsing, Gloria Hayen Herman, Cleo Holladay, Gloria Maddox, Charles Maryan, John W. Morrow, Jr., Amy Nathan, Steve Novelli, John Spencer

## PRODUCTIONS

"The Devil's Disciple," "The Diary of Anne Frank," "The Beaux' Stratagem," "The Male Animal," "Broadway," "Light Up the Sky," "Biography," "Sleuth," "Two on an Island," "The America Experiment," "La Ronde," "Subreal"

*Eric Conger Photos*

**Left: John W. Morrow, Jr., Mary Carney in "Diary of Anne Frank," Below: "Broadway" Top Left: "The Devil's Discipline"**

"The Beaux' Strategem"

Cleo Holladay, Gale McNeeley
in "Biography"

192

# CALIFORNIA ACTORS THEATRE

Los Gatos, California
October 17, 1975–May 29, 1976
Second Season
Artistic Director, Peter Nyberg; Executive Director, Sheldon Kleinman; Producing Director, James Dunn; Directors, Peter Nyberg, James Dunn, John Reich, Milton Lyon, Jack Bender; Sets, Ronald E. Krempetz, Ralph Fetterly, Russell Pyle, Steven T. Howell, Peter Nyberg; Costumes, Marcia Frederick, Gini Vogel; Lighting, Ray Garrett; Press, Barbara Carpenter; Technical Director, Stephen F. Cherry; Stage Managers, Frank Silvey, Earl Frounfelter, Robert Steiger

### COMPANY

Martin Ferrero, Bonnie Gallup, Wesley Goddard, David Goldmund, Kit Gross, Michael Hill, Karen Hensel, Dan Johnson, Sarita Johnson, Lee Kopp, Dakin Matthews, Brian McGreen, Thomas Menz, Gregory Meecham, Sandy McCallum, John Napierala, Peter Nyberg, Victor Pappas, Joan Pirkle, Roxann Pyle, Tom Ramirez, Carolyn Reed, Carl Reggiardo, Alice Rorvik, Peggy Schoditsch, Kurtwood Smith, Robert Steiger, Paul Ventura, Gary Voss, Vernon Weddle

### PRODUCTIONS

"Our Town," "Earnest in Love," "The Imaginary Invalid," "Three Sisters," "Enrico IV," "What Price Glory?," "A Midsummer Night's Dream," and *World Premiere* of "A Very Gentle Person" by Hans Steinkellner

*H. J. Susser Photos*

**Top: "Earnest in Love"**
**Below: "The Imaginary Invalid"**
**Right: "What Price Glory?" Top:**
**"The Three Sisters"**

**"A Very Gentle Person"**
**Above: "Our Town"**

193

# CENTER STAGE

Baltimore, Maryland
December 3, 1975–June 27, 1976
Artistic Coordinator, Stan Wojewodski, Jr.; Managing Director,
Peter W. Culman; Press, Jonathan D. Rogers, Hillary Aidus; Stage
Managers, Michael McMahon, Julia Gillett

## PRODUCTIONS AND CASTS

TARTUFFE by Moliere; Director, Jacques Cartier; Sets, David
Jenkins; Costumes, Nancy Potts; Lighting, Roger Morgan. CAST:
Peter Vogt, Vivienne Shub, Hillary Aidus, Jane House, Trish Haw-
kins, Davis Hall, Christine Baranski, George Ede, Terrance O'-
Quinn, Henry Thomas, John Eames, Stan Wojewodski, Jr., Michael
A. Cook, Joseph Snair.

BUSY BEE GOOD FOOD ALL NIGHT DELICIOUS and BOR-
DERS *(World Premiere)* by Charles Eastman; Sets and Costumes,
Kurt Lundell; Lighting, Roger Morgan. CAST: "Busy Bee . . .":
George Ede, Ruth Gilbert, Davis Hall, "Borders": Helen Hanft,
Trinity Thompson, Peter Vogt

DREAM ON MONKEY MOUNTAIN by Derek Walcott; Direc-
tor, Albert Laveau; Choreography, Carol LaChapelle; Musical Di-
rector, Andrew Beddeau; Set, Eugene Lee; Costumes, Robert
Wojewodski; Lighting, Roger Morgan. CAST: Obba Babatunde,
Anthony Chisholm, Charles Grant-Green, Sam Singleton, David
Pendleton, Clayton Corbin, Marilyn Donnenberg, Sullivan Walker,
Malonga Auguste Casquelourd, Luther Fontaine, Randy Grant, Ha-
zel Bryant, Lynette Laveau, Paula Moss, Aramide Pamela Rice,
Michelle Summers

OLD TIMES by Harold Pinter; Director, Stan Wojewodski, Jr.; Set,
Peter Harvey; Costumes, Elizabeth Palmer; Lighting, Ian Calderon.
CAST: Patricia Gage, George Taylor, Lois Markle

THE CHERRY ORCHARD by Anton Chekhov; Director, Jacques
Cartier; Set and Costumes, John Jensen; Lighting, Gilbert V. Hems-
ley, Jr. CAST: Patricia Gage, Patricia Pearcy, Tana Hicken, Henry
Thomas, George Morfogen, Stan Wojewodski, Jr., Paul C. Thomas,
Anita Keal, Yusef Bulos, Christine Baranski, John Eames, Ronald
Frazier, Joseph Snair, Jay Stone, Justin White, Timothy Wolfe

THE REAL INSPECTOR HOUND by Tom Stoppard; Director,
Stan Wojewodski, Jr.; Sets, Peter Harvey; Costumes, Liz Covey;
Lighting, Ian Calderon. CAST: Henry Thomas, Paul C. Thomas,
Paddy Croft, Lee Corbet, Christine Baranski, Patricia Gage, John
Wylie, Dan Szelag

BLACK COMEDY by Peter Shaffer; Director, Stan Wojewodski,
Jr.; Sets, Peter Harvey; Costumes, Liz Covey; Lighting, Ian Cald-
eron. CAST: Andrew Rohrer, Christine Baranski, Paddy Croft,
John Wylie, Charles O. Lynch, Paul C. Thomas. Patricia Gage, Dan
Szelag

*Richard Anderson, Anston-Worthington Photos*

**Top Right: "The Cherry Orchard"**
**Below: "Dream on Monkey Mountain"**

**Trinity Thompson, Helen Hanft in**
**"Busy Bee Good Food All Night Delicious"**

# CENTER STAGE THEATRE

Austin, Texas
September 1975–May 1976
Artistic Director-Manager, Ken Johnson; Assistant Manager, Laine Leibick; Press, Diane Bertram; Technical Directors, Bob Sertner, Michel Jaroschy; Costumes, Maggie Cox, Mary Lou Stephens

## COMPANY

Barbara Amaral, Sandy Leibick, Kim Quillin, Jon Rice, Patti Davis, Melanie Guilbeault, Benjamin Wear, Diane Bertram, Jeff Broyles, Susie Higley, Scott Maynig, Susan Bruton, John Huddleston, Rob Wilds, Brent Thomas, John Bernardoni, Oliver Handley, Ann Armstrong, Adrienne Blalock, Jim Carpetas, Ben Carssons, Bill Chamberlain, Tom Cloutier, Michael Cosentino, Bill Dick, Larry Fitzgerald, Diana Goodman, Patricia Harris, Bruce Kalman, Dorothea Kiker, Glenn Long, Richard McDowell, David Pearson, Karol Phelan, Wanda Pierce, Arthur Rankin, Alison Smith, Allan Stephens, Rex Voland, Jim Baggett, Charles Baumhauer, Dale Bearden, Christine Beato, Jeffrey Benkoe, Sally Bull, James Childs, Maggie Cox, Therese Dean East, Barton Faulks, Bill Johnson, Royce Gehrels, Laura Grayson, Rod Grayson, Sherie Hartle, Karen Sue Hastings, Donald Janda, Peter Lawson, Peter Malof, Duncan McGann, Randy Reece, John Ross, Mack Waldrip, Chris Weismann

## PRODUCTIONS

"Macbeth," "West Side Story," "Godspell," "That Championship Season," "Man of La Mancha"

*Ken Johnson Photos*

**Top Right: Bill Dick, Karol Phelan in
"Man of La Mancha"**

**Below: Sandy Leibick, Barbara
Amaral in "West Side Story"**

**Kim Quillin, Jon Rice in "Godspell"**

**Oliver Handley in "That Championship Season"**

Marge Redmond, Simon Oakland
in "The Shadow Box"

# CENTER THEATRE GROUP

MARK TAPER FORUM
Los Angeles, California
July 1, 1975–June 30, 1976
Artistic Director, Gordon Davidson; General Manager, Willia
P. Wingate; Associate Director, Edward Parone; Director Forum
Laboratory, Robert Greenwald; Director Improvisational Thea
Project, John Dennis; Press, Richard Kitzrow, Leigh Charlton, A
thony Sherwood, Thomas Brocato; Lighting, Tharon Musser; Pr
duction Manager, John DeSantis; Technical Director, Rob
Calhoun; Stage Managers, Don Winton, Madeline Puzo, Richa
Serpe, Chuck Linker

## PRODUCTIONS AND CASTS

ONCE IN A LIFETIME by Moss Hart, George S. Kaufman; Dir
tor, Edward Parone; Designers, Jim Newton, Pete Menefee, Thar
Musser. CAST: Jayne Meadows Allen, Janell Buff, Helen Pa
Camp, Judy Cassmore, Gordon Connell, Nathan Cook, Lisa Cutl
Dennis Dugan, Wayne C. Dvorak, Antonia Ellis, Stefan Fisch
Aileen Fitzpatrick, Lorry Goldman, Dody Goodman, Harc
Gould, John D. Gowans, David Himes, Jerry Hoffman, Richa
Lenz, Terry Lumley, Joseph G. Medalis, Louisa Moritz, Char
Thomas Murphy, Julie Payne, Marcia Rodd, Arnold Soboloff, Ga
Stephens, Patricia Sturges, Britt Swanson, Donald Torres, Shar
Ullrick, Rick Vartorella

TOO MUCH JOHNSON by William Gillette; Adapted by Bu
Shevelove; Director, Gordon Davidson; Designers, Robert Zent
Tom Rasmussen, H. R. Poindexter. CAST: Mary Carver,
Checco, Frank Geraci, Rose Gregorio, Cynthia Harris, David Hu
man, William Katt, Zale Kessler, Laurence Luckinbill, Simon Oa
land, Brad Rearden, Marge Redmond, Tom Rosqui, Joe Zaloon

in repertory with

THE SHADOW BOX (World Premiere) by Michael Cristofer; D
rector, Gordon Davidson; Designers, Robert Zentis, Tom Ra
mussen, H. R. Poindexter. CAST: Mary Carver, Rose Gregor
Cynthia Harris, David Huffman, Laurence Luckinbill, Simon Oa
land, Brad Rearden, Marge Redmond, Tom Rosqui

THE DUCHESS OF MALFI by John Webster; Director, Howa
Sackler; Designers, Paul Sylbert, Dorothy Jeakins, John Gleaso
CAST: Eileen Atkins, G. W. Bailey, Jeff Bergqvist, Olivia Co
Marlin Charles, Kermit Christman, Edgar Daniels, Tony De Fon
Robin Gammell, Rick Garr, Henry Hoffman, Byron Jennings, Sal
Kemp, Zale Kessler, Philip Larson, Charles O. Lynch, Herta Wa
Byron Webster, G Wood, Ken Zimmerman

ASHES (American Premiere) by David Rudkin; Director, Edwa
Parone; Designers, Sally Jacobs, Julie Weiss, F. Mitchell Dar
CAST: Andra Akers, Michael Cristofer, Tyne Daly, Janet Johnso
James Ray

CROSS COUNTRY (World Premiere) by Susan Miller; Directc
Vickie Rue; Designers, Sally Jacobs, Julie Weiss, F. Mitchell Dan
CAST: Frances Lee McCain, Ron Rifkin, Robin Strasser, Shar
Ullrick

AND WHERE SHE STOPS NOBODY KNOWS (World Premier
by Oliver Hailey; Director, Gordon Davidson; Designers, Mar
Champion, Sally Jacobs, Julie Weiss, F. Mitchell Dana. CAST: F
leen Brennan, Lou Gossett
in repertory with

THREE SISTERS by Anton Chekhov; Translated by Micha
Heim; Director, Edward Parone; Designers, Sally Jacobs, F. Mitc
ell Dana. CAST: Marc Alaimo, Michael Cristofer, Tyne Daly, L
Gossett, Barra Grant, Warren Hammack, David Himes, Janet Joh
son, Laurie Kennedy, Berry Kroeger, Frances Lee McCain, Jam
Ray, Ron Rifkin, Pearl Shear, Delos V. Smith, Jr., David Ogd
Stiers, Richard Warrick

*Steven Keull Photos*

**Left Center: "Three Sisters"**
**Above: Ron Rifkin, Sharon Ullrick,**
**Frances Lee McCain, Robin**
**Strasser in "Cross Country"**
**Top: Marcia Rodd, Dennis Dugan,**
**Jayne Meadows, Harold**
**Gould, Charles Thomas Murphy in**
**"Once in a Lifetime"**

## IMPROVISATIONAL THEATRE PROJECT

...ector, John Dennis; Manager, Michael Lonergan; Stage Man-...r, Ron Rudolph; Writer, Doris Baizley; Designers, Charles Ber-...er, Dawn Chiang, Joe Tompkins; Music, Harry Aguado; Lyrics, ...ris Baizley, Harry Aguado. CAST: Nathan Cook, Brenda Davis, ...reen Hennessy, Hal Landon, Jr., Michael McNeilly, Eric Neu-...l, Rick Vartorella, Bruce French

## FORUM/LABORATORY

...ector, Robert Greenwald; Managers, Michael Lonergan, Doug-... G. Burns; Production Managers, Erik Brenmark, Ron Rudolph; ...ge Managers, Michael Castle, Arni Fishbaugh, Richard Lewis, ...phen Rich, Ron Rudolph, Estela Scarlata, Cathy Zheutlin

...IE GREAT POTATO FAMINE by Daniel Wray, Brendan Noel ...ard; Director, Richard M. Johnson; Designers, Ron Rudolph, ...uise Hayter; Music, Steven Wells, Ray Doyle. CAST: Blanche ...onte, Judy Chaikin, Maryellen Clemons, Duncan Gamble, Sindy ...wke, Kay Howell, Drew Lobenstein, John Megna, Tony Papen-...s, E. A. Sirianni, David Stifel, Steven Wells, Terry Wolf

...AMONDS IN THE ROUGH by Jeremy Blahnik, David Cope-..., Vickie Rue. CAST: Herb Foster, Barra Grant, Henry Hoffman, ...rk Jenkins, Julie Payne, Carolyn Reed, Robin Strasser, Sharon ...rick, Rick Vartorella

...DIPUS AT COLONUS by Sophocles; Director, Sally Jacobs; ...signers, Julie Weiss, Ron Rudolph, Steven Wells. CAST: Andrew ...le, Joe Hudgins, Philip Larson, Ralph Lev Mailer, Julie Payne, ...n Roddick, Gene Rosen, Benjamin Stewart, Kate Woodville

...O SEE THE ELEPHANT by Elizabeth Clark; Director, Liebe ...ay; Designers, Ellyn Gersh, Durinda Wood, Susie Helfond; Mu-..., Cris Williamson. CAST: Terri Carson, E. Marcy Dicterow, ...rol-Lynn Fillet, Janet Johnson, Frances Lee McCain, Belita ...oreno, Shirley Slater, Sharon Ullrick, Cris Williamson, Carrie ...vetz

...ECTRA by Robert Montgomery; Director, Joseph Chaikin; ...amaturg, Mira Rafalowicz; Designers, Gwen Fabricant, Arden ...ngerhut. CAST: Shami Chaikin, Tina Shepard, Paul Zimet

...IE COMMON GARDEN VARIETY by Jane Chambers; Direc-..., Gwen Arner; Designers, Robert Zentis, Durinda Wood. CAST: ...ne Gee Byrd, Mary Jackson, Marc McClure, Ann O'Donnell, ...tsy Slade

...CK STREET by Joan Tewkesbury; Directed by author; Design-..., Erik Brenmark, Louise Hayter, Pamela Cooper; Musical Direc-..., Tony Berg; Music, Tony Berg, Albert Greenberg, Melissa ...urphy, Ted Neeley, Allan Nichols. CAST: Paul Ainsley, Tony ...rg, Ed Buck, Hannah Dean, Bob DoQui, Tom Eden, Scott Glenn, ...ariette Hartley, Joan Hotchkis, Lee Jones-DeBroux, Johnn Ray ...cGhee, John Megna, Melissa Murphy, Ted Neeley, Craig Richard ...lson, Julie Newmar, Paul Potash, Cristina Raines, Rod Rimmer, ...san Tyrrell, Herve Villechaize, Joe Zaloom

...PROOTED by Humberto Robles-Arena; English Adaptation, ...vero Perez; Director, Margarita Galban; Designers, Estela Scar-...a, Jason Shubb. CAST: Linda Dangcil, Ronald Joseph Godines, ...fael Lopez, Julio Medina, Drew Michaels, Karmin Murcelo, Car-...en Zapata

*Steven Keull Photos*

**Top: Michael Cristofer, Tyne Daly in "Ashes"**
**Right: Lou Gossett, Eileen Brennan in "And**
**Where She Stops Nobody Knows"**
**Below: "Colonel Montana"**
**(Improvisational Theatre)**

**Mariette Hartley, Susan Tyrrell in "Jack Street"**
**Above: "The Common Garden Variety"**

197

# CINCINNATI PLAYHOUSE IN THE PARK

Cincinnati, Ohio
October 21, 1975–May 30, 1976
Producing Director, Michael Murray; General Manager, Robert W. Tolan; Guest Directors, Israel Hicks, John Going, Michael Bawtree; Stage Manager, J. P. Valente; Sets, Neil Peter Jampolis, Eric Head; Costumes, Annie Peacock Warner; Press, Lanni Johnston; Assistant to Producing Director, Jerri Roberts; Production Manager, Richard Lukaszewicz

## PRODUCTIONS AND CASTS

DEATH OF A SALESMAN with Sam Gray, Paul Vincent, Richard Kline, Dorothy Stinnette, Robert Beatey, David Stanley Luman, William Myers, Joseph Regalbuto, Diane Danzi, Paul Forste, Georgia Neu, Pat VanOver, David Dreyfoos

RELATIVELY SPEAKING with Leah Chandler, Jo Henderson, Robert Nichols, Douglas Jones

THE LITTLE FOXES with Robert Baines, George Brengel, Louis Edmonds, Jan Farrand, Jo Henderson, Bryan Hull, Robert Johnson, Julia McKenzie, Randall Merrifield, Beatrice Winde

WHAT THE BUTLER SAW with I. M. Hobson, Linda Alper, Philip Anglim, Eric House, Jeanette Landis, Ronald Steelman

THE CONTRAST with Lynn Milgrim, I. M. Hobson, Philip Anglim, Jim Broaddus, Lisa Hemphill, Tom Mardirosian, Fred McCarren, Monica Merryman, Pamela Rohs, Claudia Zahn

WHERE'S CHARLEY? with Adrienne Angel, Dennis Bailey, George Brengel, Dan Diggles, Lee Roy Reams, I. M. Hobson, Sally Mitchell, Marti Rolph, Paul Forste, Keith Mackey, Linda Poser, Linda Lauter, James Braet, Neal Thompson, Bernardo Hiller, Peggy Neeson, Kathryn Cordes, Laura Liebman

*Sandy Underwood Photos*

**Right: "What the Butler Saw" Top: Beatrice Winde, Robert Baines in "The Little Foxes"**

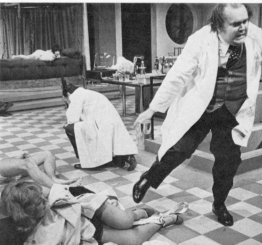

**Jo Henderson, Robert Nichols in
"Relatively Speaking"**

**Marti Rolph, Dan Diggles
in "Where's Charley?"**

# CLEVELAND PLAY HOUSE

Cleveland, Ohio
October 17, 1975–May 2, 1976

Director, Richard Oberlin; Associate Director, Larry Tarrant; Press, Ric Wanetik, Paula Bond; Administrative Coordinator, Nelson Isekeit; Scenic Director, Richard Gould; Assistant Director, Robert Snook; Directors, Jonathan Farwell, Richard Halverson, Paul Lee, Evie McElroy, Richard Oberlin, Robert Snook, Larry Tarrant; Production Coordinator, Larry Tarrant; Designers, Richard Gould, Eugene Hare, Barbara Leatherman, Tim Zupancic; Technical Director, Barbara Leatherman; Costumes, Diane Dalton

## COMPANY

Robert Allman, Norm Berman, Sharon Bicknell, John Buck, Jr., Daniel Desmond, Jo Farwell, Jonathan Farwell, June Gibbons, Richard Halverson, Dana Hart, Dee Hoty, Allen Leatherman, Paul Lee, Andrew Lichtenberg, Lizbeth Mackay, Evie McElroy, Spencer McIntyre, David Meyer, Ralph Neeley, Richard Oberlin, Dale Place, Leslie Rapp, Howard Renensland, Jr., James Richards, Dennis Romer, Tedd Rubinstein, Frederic Serino, George Cecil Simms, Robert Snook, Bonnie Sosnowsky, J. D. Sutton

GUEST ARTISTS: Ken Albers, Jean Arthur, Yolande Bavan, David Berman, Jonathan Bolt, George Brengel, Joel Brooks, Victor Caroli, Clayton Corzatte, Mike Dantuono, Carolelinda Dickey, Marji Dodrill, Kenneth Dolin, Melvin Douglas, Ben Evett, Mark Gardner, George Gould, Margaret Hilton, Lee Karnes, Earl Keyes, Greg Krizman, Jerome Lawrence, Robert E. Lee, Vaughn McBride, Christina Moore, Edith Owen, Tony Phelan, J. Ranelli, Ellen Renensland, Ray Walston, William Paterson, William Rhys

## PRODUCTIONS

"First Monday in October" *(World Premiere)* by Robert E. Lee and Jerome Lawrence, "The Prague Spring" by Lee Kalcheim, "Bingo" *(American Premiere)* by Edward Bond, "Caesar and Cleopatra," "Abigail Adams: The Second First Lady" by Edith Owen, "Relatively Speaking" by Alan Ayckbourn, "Dr. Jekyll and Mr. Hyde" *(World Premiere)* by Paul Lee, "The Dark at the Top of the Stairs" by William Inge, "A Profile of Benjamin Franklin" by William Patterson, "Get-Rich-Quick Wallingford" by George M. Cohan, "The Last Meeting of the Knights of the White Magnolia" by Preston Jones, "Of Mice and Men" by John Steinbeck, "Scapino" by Frank Dunlop and Jim Dale, "The World of Carl Sandburg" by Norman Corwin

*James Fry Photos*

**Right: "Dr. Jekyll and Mr. Hyde"**
**Above: "Get-Rich-Quick Wallingford"**
**Top: "First Monday in October" (Melvyn Douglas and Jean Arthur guest stars)**

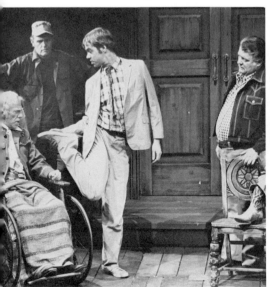

**Ray Walston, David Meyer in "The Last Meeting of the Knights of the White Magnolia"**

**Yolande Bavan, Clayton Corzatte in "Caesar and Cleopatra"**

# COMPANY THEATRE

Los Angeles, California
September 1975–June 1976

## COMPANY

Alan Abelew, Arthur Allen, David Alperin, Polita Barnes, Pe⊓ Bergren, Dierdre Berthrong, Laurel Bogen, Gar Campbell, Wa⊓ Carlisle, Larry Cohen, Jim Cypherd, William Dannevik, Jam⊓ DiAngelo, Stephen Downs, Andy Dworkin, Milton Earl Forre⊓ Myrna Gawryn, Susan Gelb, Harvey Gold, Barbara Grover, D⊓ Grace, Donald Harris, Nora Heflin, Nancy Hickey, Debbie Jam⊓ Lisa James, Lori Landrin, Gil Laurence, Paul Linke, Lance Larse⊓ Sandra Morgan, Bebe Marks, Constance Mellors, Kathi McGinn⊓ Marcina Motter, Liz Palmer, Andrew Parks, Louie Piday, Mars⊓ Polekoff, Jerry Pojawa, Michael Prichard, Roxann Pyle, Russ⊓ Pyle, Dennis Redfield, Jack Rowe, Carol Rusoff, Billy Schaffne⊓ Sally Schulte, Trish Soodik, Michael Stefani, Diane Uchima, B⊓ Walter, Lisette Williams, Dan Wyman

## PRODUCTIONS

"Mirror Mirror" *(World Premiere)* adaptation of Pierre Marivau⊓ "La Dispute" by Louie Piday, "Salt" by Mort Goldberg, "Tw⊓ McClures Sunnyside Up: 'The Pink Helmet,' 'The Masked Choir'⊓ *(World Premiere)* by Michael McClure

*Roger Marshutz Photos*

**Left: Milton Earl Forrest, Andrew Parks, Paul Linke in "The Pink Helmet" Above: Constance Mellors, Louie Piday in "The Masked Choir"**

# CLARENCE BROWN THEATRE

Knoxville, Tennessee
Director, Ralph G. Allen; Director of Productions, Anthony Quayle; General Manager, Julian Forrester; Associate Directors, Thomas Cooke, Fred Fields, Albert Harris, Wandalie Henshaw, Robert Washburn; Design, Robert Cothran; Technical Director, Robert Field; Company Manager, Janice Stanton; Wardrobe Mistress, Malou Flato; Assistant to General Manager, Elise Adams; Stage Managers, Kenneth Leavee, Waller Barret Smith, Maria Alexandra Wozniak; Costumes, Marianne Custer

## COMPANY

Catherine Byers, Barbara Caruso, Jay Doyle, Bernard Engel, Paul A. Foley, Richard Galuppi, Jack Gwillim, Wandalie Henshaw, Earle Hyman, Frederic Major, Harriet Nichols, Anthony Quayle, Susan Ringwood, Douglas Stender, Eric Schneider, Barry Smith, Cynthia Woll, Maria Alexandra Wozniak, Richard Bowden, David Fox-Brenton, Kenneth Gray, Walter Barrett Smith

Elise Adams, Linda Benemann, Bill Duncan, Doug Eckert, John Ferguson, Warren Gaffney, John Gann, Stephen Martin, Laurie Metter, Jeff Moore, Terry Morris, Sam O'Donnell, Dwight Percy, Judy Rye, Chris Smith, Lemmie Smith, Lee Toombs, Ronny Venable

## PRODUCTIONS

"Everyman," "Macbeth," "Rip Van Winkle"

**Andrew McHenry, Anthony Quayle in "Rip Van Winkle"**

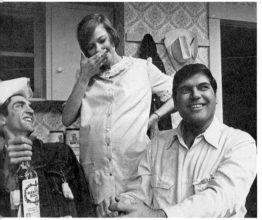

# DALLAS THEATER CENTER

Dallas, Texas
October 7, 1975–August 14, 1976

Managing Director, Paul Baker; Assistant Director, Mary Sue Jones; Administrative Assistant, Judith Davis; Press, Lynn Trammell; Guest Directors, Robin Lovejoy, David Healy, Dolores Ferro; Stage Directors, Ken Latimer, Judith Davis, Paul Baker; Sets, Koichi Aoki, John Henson, Mary Sue Jones, Sam Nance, Virgil Beavers; Costumes, Diana Devereaux, Kathleen Latimer, Randolf Larson, Gina Taulane, Susan A. Haynie; Lighting, Robert Duffy, Robyn Flatt, Allen Hibbard, Sam Nance, Randy Moore; Stage Managers, Bryant J. Reynolds, Randy Bonifay, Gina Taulane, Steve Lovett, Nick Dalley, Carolyn Pines, Steve Wallace

## COMPANY

Koichi Aoki, Linda Blase, Judith Davis, John Figlmiller, Robyn Flatt, Martha Robinson Goodman, John Henson, Allen Hibbard, Preston Jones, Mary Sue Jones, Kathleen Latimer, Ken Latimer, Fritz Lennon, John Logan, Rebecca Logan, Steven Mackenroth, Ryland Merkey, Norma Moore, Randy Moore, Louise Mosley, Sam Nance, Sally Netzel, Patti O'Donnell, Mona Pursley, Bryant J. Reynolds, Synthia Rogers, Glenn Allen Smith, John R. Stevens, Randolph Tallman, Jacque Thomas, Matt Tracy, Lynn Trammell

## PRODUCTIONS

"The Amorous Flea" by Jerry Devine and Bruce Montgomery, "Promenade, All!" by David V. Robison, "Saturday, Sunday, Monday" by Eduardo de Filippo, "Manny" *(World Premiere)* by Randolph Tallman, Steven Mackenroth, Glenn Allen Smith, "A Place on the Magdalena Flats" *(World Premiere)* by Preston Jones, "Much Ado about Nothing" by William Shakespeare, "Stillsong" *(World Premiere)* by Sallie Laurie

*Linda Blase Photos*

Top: "A Place on the Magdalena Flats"
Below: "Saturday Sunday Monday" Right: "Manny"

Quinn Mathews, Judith Davis, Ted Bowlin,
William George in "Stillsong"

201

Renate Walker in
**"The Song of the Whip-Poor-Will"**
Left: **"The Adding Machine"** Top: **"In Abraham's Bosom"**

## DETROIT REPERTORY THEATRE

Detroit, Michigan
November 1975–June 1976
Artistic Director, Bruce E. Millan; Executive Director, Doroth
J. Brown; Press, Betty DuPuis; Sets, Bruce E. Millan, John Kno
Zubek Kachadoorian; Lighting, Dick Smith; Costumes, Marian
Hoad; Sound, Jack Slater; Assistant Director, Jesse Newton

### COMPANY

Willie Hodge, Kwabena Caworrie, Charles Haynie, John W. Hard
William Boswell, Mark Murri, Joyce Williams, Myrenna Ha
thorne, Robert Williams, Barbara Busby, Yolanda Williams, Cher
Lemans, Michael Joseph, Colleen Davis, Jack Slater, Darlene Blac
burn, Jobai Burke, Charles R. Roseborough, Betty Dupuis, Ter
Wilks, Jesse Newton, Myrenna Hawthorne, Ruthe Palmer, Ma
Palmer, Frenchy Hodges, Dee Andrus, John Hardy, Renate Walk
Fred Bennett

### PRODUCTIONS

"In Abraham's Bosom" by Paul Green, "The Song of the Whi
Poor-Will" *(World Premiere),* "The Adding Machine" by Eln
Rice, "Morning's at Seven" by Paul Osborn

**Barbara Busby, Jesse Newton
in "Morning's at Seven"**

# DRURY LANE NORTH THEATRE

Lincolnshire, Illinois
May 27, 1975–June 20, 1976
Producer, Richard S. Kordos; Press, Bill Wilson, Aaron D. Cush-
man Associates; Stage Managers, Ernie Lane, Paul Ferris; Technical
Directors, Bill Biltgen, Pat Nesladek; Costumes, Susan Gayford,
Susan Clare; Props, Michael Zemenick, Paul Ferris, Jeffrey Harris,
William Derl-Davis

## PRODUCTIONS AND CASTS

THE FOURPOSTER by Jan de Hartog; Director, Tony Mockus;
Set, William B. Fosser. CAST: Leonard Nimoy, Ann Eggert

BORN YESTERDAY by Garson Kanin; Director, Leland Ball; Set
William B. Fosser. CAST: Elke Sommer, Art Kassul, Frank Miller,
Don Marston, David Morrison, Fern Persons, Joe Shea, Paul A.
Ferris, Dianne Hosken, Michael Zemenick, John Kettermaster, Jon
Robb, Fred Michaels

THE CONFIDENCE GAME by Tom Sharkey; Director, Vernon
R. Schwartz; Set, William Fosser. CAST: Brooke Tucker, John
Burns, Douglas Weiss, Forrest Tucker, Jeannette Leahy, David Carl
Starwalt, Sandra Weygandt, Denise Latella, Joe Bell

MY THREE ANGELS by Sam and Bella Spewack; Director, Dick
Sasso; Set, William B. Fosser. CAST: Jack Goring, Vera Ward,
Wesley Pfenning, Geraldine Power, Chuck Connors, Dick Sasso,
David Whitaker, Tom Elrod, Al Nuti, Mark Ullius, B. J. Jones

SUNDAY IN NEW YORK by Norman Krasna; Director, Dick
Sasso; Set, Vernon R. Schwartz. CAST: Brad Bisk, Sandra Dee,
Owen Sullivan, B. J. Jones, Fred Michaels, Dianne Hosken

LAST OF THE RED HOT LOVERS by Neil Simon; Director, Alba
Oms. CAST: Sheila MacRae, Jack Heller

UNDER PAPA'S PICTURE by Joe Connelly and George Tibbles;
Director, Brooks West; Set, Jeffrey Harris. CAST: Clay Taylor,
David Rupprecht, Gloria Lynn, Esther Sutherland, Eve Arden, J. J.
Butler, Brooks West, Barbara A. Harris, Nikki Zelaya

*David H. Fishman Photos*

**Right: Eve Arden, David Rupprecht,
Gloria Lynn in "Under Papa's Picture" Above: Owen
Sullivan, Brad Bisk, B. J. Jones, Sandra Dee in
"Sunday in New York" Top: Dick Sasso,
Chuck Connors, David Whitaker in
"My Three Angels"**

**Ann Eggert, Leonard Nimoy
in "The Fourposter"**

**Jack Heller, Sheila MacRae
in "Last of the Red Hot Lovers"**

## FOLGER THEATRE GROUP

Washington, D.C.
October 7, 1975–June 27, 1976

Producer, Louis W. Scheeder; General Manager, Larry Ver
Company Manager, Mary Ann de Barbieri; Press, Pat Bailey; Te
nical Director, Thom Shovestull; Stage Managers, David M. Lev
Dorothy Maffei, Pamela Horner; Lighting, Betsy Toth; Assistan
producer, Jonathan Alper

### PRODUCTIONS AND CASTS

THE COLLECTED WORKS OF BILLY THE KID *(Ameri
Premiere)* by Michael Ondaatje; Music, Desmond McAnuff; Di
tor, Louis W. Scheeder; Set, David Chapman; Costumes, Ra
Barcelo; Lighting, Hugh Lester. CAST: Allan Carlsen, Guy Bo
Mark Robinson, Sandy Faison, Albert Malafronte, Anne Sto
Brad Sullivan, Richard Greene

THE COMEDY OF ERRORS by William Shakespeare; Direc
Jonathan Alper; Music, William Penn; Set, Stuart Wurtzel; C
tumes, Bob Wojewodski; Lighting, Arden Fingerhut. CAST: Al
Malafronte, Paul Milikin, Edward Young, Donald Warfield, M
Champagne, Peter Riegert, Deborah Darr, Kathleen Doyle, M
shall Lee Shnider, Sherry Nehmer, Richard Vernon, Timothy J
kins, Edward Henry, Joanne Hrkach, Charles Montgomery, J
Hansen, Dianne Bye, Tracy Davis, Kurt K. Feuer, Rea Ros
Sunny Schnitzer

MEDAL OF HONOR RAG *(World Premiere)* by Tom Cole; Di
tor, David Chambers; Set, Raymond C. Recht; Costumes, C
Oditz, Deborah Walther; Lighting, Betsy Toth. CAST: David C
non, Howard E. Rollins, Jr., David M. Levine

HENRY V by William Shakespeare; Director, Lous W. Schee
Music, William Penn; Set, Raymond C. Recht; Costumes, I
Wojewodski; Lighting, Arden Fingerhut. CAST: Tony M. Ab
marco, Patrick Beatey, Mike Champagne, David Cromwell, Cl
ent Fowler, Jeremy Gage, Joanne Hrkach, Kathleen Ireton, Rich
Kline, Charles Montgomery, Charles Morey, Antonino Pande
Terrance O'Quinn, Rea Rosno

ALL'S WELL THAT ENDS WELL by William Shakespeare;
rector, Jonathan Alper; Music, William Penn; Set, Raymond
Recht; Costumes, Bob Wojewodski; Lighting, Arden Finger
CAST: Carla Meyer, Mark Winkworth, Etain O'Malley, Clen
Fowler, Jo Spiller, Michael Houlihan, Albert Corbin, Robert Ha
Kurt K. Feuer, Jim Brady, Tri Garraty, Barry MacMillan, Da
Cromwell, Licia Colombi, Mary Carney

*Joe B. Mann Photos*

**Left: Joanne Hrkach, Richard Kline in
"Henry V" Above: Etain O'Malley,
Albert Corbin in "All's Well That Ends Well"
Top: Marshall Lee Shnider,
Mike Champagne, Peter Riegert in
"Comedy of Errors"**

**Howard E. Rollins, Jr.
in "Medal of Honor Rag"**

**David Clennon
in "Medal of Honor Rag"**

## FORD'S THEATRE

Washington, D.C.
September 19, 1975–June 27, 1976
Executive Producer, Frankie Hewitt; General Manager, Maury
Sutter; Press, Alma Viator, Wayne Knickel; Assistant to producer,
Nora Lee

### PRODUCTIONS AND CASTS

ARE YOU NOW OR HAVE YOU EVER BEEN by Eric Bentley;
Director, William Devane; Set, Barry Robinson; Lighting, Robert
Bye; Stage Manager, Haig Shepherd. CAST: Tom Bower, Beeson
Carroll, Jeff David, Wynn Irwin, John Lehne, Heidi Mefford, Allan
Miller, Byron Morrow, Stephen Roberts, Ed Rombola, Martin Sha-
ar, David Spielberg, Charles Weldon, M. Emmet Walsh

YOUR ARMS TOO SHORT TO BOX WITH GOD by Vinnette
Carroll adapted from the Book of Matthew; Music and Lyrics, Alex
Bradford; Orchestrations, Billy Taylor; Sets and Costumes, William
Schroder; Lighting, Gilbert Hemsley, Jr; Choreographer, Talley
Beatty; Director, Vinnette Carroll. CAST: Lamar Alford, Salome
Bey, Alex Bradford, Sharon Brooks, Maryce Carter, Billy Dorsey,
Thomas Jefferson Fouse, Jr., Cardell Hall, Delores Hall, William
Hardy, Jr., Jan Hazell, Aisha Khabeera, Michele Murray, Stanley
Perryman, Zola Shaw, Alwin Taylor

I HAVE A DREAM adapted by Josh Greenfeld; Conceived and
Directed by Robert Greenwald; Setting, Donald Harris; Costumes,
Terence Tam Soon; Lighting, Martin Aronstein; Associate Pro-
ducer, Pat Lang; Stage Managers, David Clive, Janyce Ann Wagner.
CAST: Billy Dee Williams, Judyann Elder, Marion Ramsey

ELEANOR by Arlene Stadd; Director, Michael Kahn; Set, Ed Wittstein; Costumes, Jane Greenwood; Lighting, John McLain; Stage
Manager, Lo Hardin. CAST: Eileen Heckart as Eleanor Roosevelt

**Top: Alwin Taylor, Michelle Murray in
"Your Arms Too Short to Box with God"
Right: "Are You Now or Have You Ever Been"
Below: Billy Dee Williams in "I Have a Dream"**

**Eileen Heckart in "Eleanor"**

# GOODMAN THEATRE CENTER

Chicago, Illinois
October 9, 1975–June 13, 1976
Fiftieth Season
Artistic Director, William Woodman; Managing Director, John Economos; Technical Director, Joseph E. Bates; Press, Rhona Schultz, Ron Christopher; Stage Managers, Peter Dowling, Joseph Drummond, James Greek, James T. McDermott; Stage 2 Coordinator, Gregory Mosher; Sets, Richard Oates; Wardrobe Mistress, Ruth Rinklin; Business Manager, Janet Wade

## PRODUCTIONS AND CASTS

### MAINSTAGE
OUR TOWN by Thornton Wilder; Director, George Keathley. CAST: Tony Mockus, George Womack, Bruce Powell, Nesbitt Blaisdell, Avril Gentles, Jane Groves, David-James Carroll, Janet Locker, Dennis MacNeille, Harriet Hall, Wiley Harker, Robert Blackburn, Jane MacIver, Glenn Kovacevich, Jane Almquist, Don Marston, William Munchow, Scott Larsson, John Bryson Le-Grande, James H. Eckhouse, Timothy J. Murray, Edgar Meyer

BENITO CERENO by Robert Lowell; Director, Michael Montel. CAST: Tony Mockus, Thomas A. Stewart, Gus Kaikkonen, Robert Guillaume, Paul Butler, Lenard Norris, Frank Barrett, Tricia Borha, Geoffrey Clark, Isaac Clay, Karen Ghoston, Frank Rice, Avis LaVelle Sampson, Lionel Smith, William Vines, Steven Williams, Fred Eberle, Mark Hutter, Thomas McKeon, Adrian Smith, Timothy Smith, Mike Genovese, Tony Gillotte, John Heitmanek

MOURNING BECOMES ELECTRA by Eugene O'Neill; Director, William Woodman. CAST: Nesbitt Blaisdell, Murray Nash, Jane MacIver, Brina Rodin, Rosemary Murphy, Laura Esterman, Judith Ivey, Thomas A. Stewart, Robert Murch, Tony Mockus, Tony Lincoln, Brina Rodin, Mike Genovese, Ben Masters, Dennis Kennedy

THE LAST MEETING OF THE KNIGHTS OF THE WHITE MAGNOLIA by Preston Jones; Director, Harold Stone. CAST: Earl Sydnor, Frank Hamilton, Douglas Fisher, Jack Wallace, Gordon Oas-Heim, Chet Carlin, John Wardwell, W. H. Macy, Brad O'Hare

OUR FATHER'S FAILING (World Premiere) by Israel Horovitz; Director, John Dillon. CAST: Dominic Chianese, Joseph Leon, Lawrence Pressman, Lanna Saunders

THE DEVIL'S DISCIPLE by George Bernard Shaw; Director, William Woodman. CAST: Pat Fraser, Wesley Ann Pfenning, Eugene J. Anthony, Robert Murch, Allison Giglio, Michael Tezla, Tony Lincoln, Judy Herbst, Leonard Kraft, Diane Jean Ciesla, Kenneth Welsh, J. J. Johnston, Don Marston, Brian Murray, Tom Birk, Robert Garcia, Tony Gillotte, Ira Goldstein, Tom McKeon, Larry Palmissano, Chris Reynolds, Tim Samuelson, Dan Shapiro, David Wirth

### STAGE 2
AMERICAN BUFFALO (World Premiere) by David Mamet; Director, Gregory Mosher. CAST: J. J. Johnston, Bernard Erhard, William H. Macy

THREE PLAYS OF THE YUAN DYNASTY by June Pyskacek; Translated by Liu Jung-en. CAST: Dan Ziskie, Keith Szarabajka, Felicity LaFortune, Michael Tezla, Glenn Kovacevich, Marge Kotlisky

CHICAGO by Sam Shepard; Director, Dennis Zacek. CAST: Jim Jacobs, Mark Nutter, Arlene Schulfer, Sara Asher, Warren Leming, Jeanette Goldberg, Dan Ziskie

THE LOCAL STIGMATIC by Heathcote Williams; Director, Gary Houston. CAST: Jim Jacobs, Warren Leming, Leonard Kraft, Dan Ziskie

DANDELION WINE by Ray Bradbury; Arranged and Adapted by Peter John Bailey; Director, William Woodman. CAST: Scott Stevens, Scott Larsson, Tom McDonald, Danny Goldring, Don Marston, Cordis Fejer, Jane MacIver, Nesbitt Blaisdell, Fern Persons

STATUES and THE BRIDGE AT BELHARBOUR (World Premiere) by Janet L. Neipris; Director, Gregory Mosher. CAST: Mike Genovese, Judith Ivey

*Terry Shapiro Photos*

**Top Right: Lawrence Pressman, Joseph Leon in "Our Father's Failing" Below: Mike Genovese, Judith Ivey in "The Bridge at Belharbour"**

**"American Buffalo" Above: "Chicago"**

# HARTFORD STAGE COMPANY

Hartford, Connecticut
September 19, 1975–June 20, 1976

Producing Director, Paul Weidner; Managing Director, Jessica L. Andrews; Press, Dave Skal; Business Manager, Alan Toman; Technical Director, Paul Daniels; Directors, Roderick Cook, Irene Lewis, Charles Turner, Paul Weidner; Sets, Marjorie Kellogg, Hugh Hanwehr, Santo Loquasto; Costumes, Claire Ferraris, Linda Fisher, Caley Summers; Lighting, Ian Calderon, David Chapman, Arden Fingerhut, Peter Hunt; Stage Managers, Fred Hoskins, Gary Lamagna, Fred Mills, Craig Watson

## COMPANY

Leon Alexander, Ray Aranha, Joan Astley, Samuel Barton, Gertrude Blanks, Elaine Bromka, Bette Carole, Myra Carter, Rosanna Carter, Dalton Cathey, Frances Chaney, Bill Clemons, Roderick Cook, Cynthia Crumlish, Humphrey Davis, David Downing, Femi Euba, Gary Evans, Al Freeman, Jr., Kimberly Gaisford, Edmond Genest, Alan Gifford, Ted Graeber, Elaine Graham, Charles Grant-Greene, Lois Holmes, Jeffrey Horowitz, Chequita Jackson, Jerry Jarrett, William Jay, Jennifer Jestin, Mel Johnson, Jr., Charles Kaufman, Gary Lamagna, Will Lee, Leroy Lessane, Richard Lieberman, Anne Lynn, Pirie MacDonald, Maura McGeary, Jeffrey B. McLaughlin, Clarkston McPhee, James Maloney, Paul Marin, Joseph Mascolo, Macon McCalman, Candy Minor, Anita Morris, Neil Napolitan, David O. Petersen, David Peterson, Larry Ross, Marco St. John, Seret Scott, Anne Shrosphire, Geddeth Smith, Josef Sommer, Regina Stivender, Count Stovall, Margaret Thomson, Edgar Wilcock, Paul Woodard

## PRODUCTIONS

"Awake and Sing!" by Clifford Odets, "All Over" by Edward Albee, "Oh Coward!" by Noel Coward and Roderick Cook, "The Estate" by Ray Aranh (World Premiere), "Dream on Monkey Mountain" by Derek Walcott, "Born Yesterday" by Garson Kanin, "Way Back When ..." (World Premiere) by Ray Aranha, "Striptease" by Slawomir Mrozek, "Workman! Whoever You Are...." (World Premiere)

*David Robbins Photos*

**Right: "The Estate" Above: "Awake and Sing!"
Top: "Born Yesterday"**

**Myra Carter
in "All Over"**

**Dalton Cathey, Kimberly Gaisford,
Roderick Cook in "Oh Coward!"**

207

# HARTMAN THEATRE COMPANY

Stamford, Connecticut
November 5, 1975–May 16, 1976
First Season
Producing Directors, Del and Margot Tenney; Managing Director, Daniel B. Miller; Press, Steve Rothman; Business Manager, Stanley D. Silver; Production Manager, Roger Meeker; Sets, Robert VerBerkmoes, John Wright Stevens; Costumes, Rachel Kurland; Lighting, John McLain; Music Director, Barbara Damashek; Guest Director, John Beary.

## PRODUCTIONS AND CASTS

THE GOVERNMENT INSPECTOR by Nikolai Gogol; Director, Byron Ringland. CAST: Bob Balaban, William Bogert, J. Robert Dietz, Bernard Frawley, Haskell Gordon, George S. Irving, Eren Ozker, Austin Pendleton, Sloane Shelton, Joseph Sommer, David Tabor, Byron Ringland, Patrick Collins, Mark Segal, Rosalyn R. Farinella, Stephen Stabler, Jim Dirlam, Florence Fox, Florence Phillips, George W. Vollano, Bob Callahan, Bill O'Brien, Skip Wolfe, Scott Thomas, Ed Rice, Christian Ericson, Scott Silver, Larry Silbert, Jasper Wellington, John Vichiola, Jack Mason, Mike Lehrman, Nadya Grushetzka Sheehan, Elsa Bastone, Wendell McCombas, Jeanne Harker, Jan Mason, Madlyn O'Neil, Charlotte Smith, Anne Wilcox

THE HOSTAGE by Brendan Behan; Director, John Beary. CAST: Jane Clarke, Greg Kolb, Mark Segal, Bernard Frawley, Sasha von Scherler, Carmel O'Brien, Lark Lee Tyrrell, Leann Enos, Marilynn May, Carole Cortese, Robert Armistead, Patrick Collins, Robert Donley, Gary F. Martin, Eren Ozker, William Bogert, Morgan Redmond, J. Robert Dietz, Susan Stevens, Peter Rogan, David MacNeill, Ed Rice, Gina Dunlap, Kathleen Collins, Ken Perlman

THE RUNNER STUMBLES (*World Premiere*) by Milan Stitt; Director, Austin Pendleton. CAST: Morrie Piersol, Stephen Joyce, Katina Commings, James Noble, Nancy Donohue, Sloane Shelton, William Bogert, Bernard Frawley, Eren Ozker

TOM JONES by Henry Fielding; Adapted and Directed by Larry Arrick. CAST: Stephen Berenson, George Bliss, Roy Brocksmith, Eric Christiansen, J. Robert Dietz, Jill Eikenberry, Kathy Falk, Rosalyn Farinella, Bernard Frawley, Joan Friedman, Haskell Gordon, Victoria Hawken, Shami Jones, Ruth Landowne, Libby Moyer, James Naughton, James Noble, Rico Peterson, Charles Pistone, Teri Ralston, Shellie Sclan, Anne Scurria, Barbara Sieck, Joy Smith, Susan Strickler, Mark Taylor, Margot Tenney, Molly Thompson, Courtney Tucker, Tim Warren

JOAN OF LORRAINE by Maxwell Anderson; Director, Alan Arkin. CAST: Adam Arkin, Matthew Arkin, Deborah Arnold, Roy Brocksmith, Eric R. Christiansen, Patrick Collins, Barbara Dana, Kurt Garfield, Michael Granger, John Horn, Robert Lesser, Ed Rice, Alex Rocco, Anne Scurria, Nikos Valance, Irving Harrison Vincent, Tony Arkin, Sam Luneeta, Tom Gould

AN EVENING OF TENNESSEE WILLIAMS directed by Del Tenney. CAST: Margot Tenney, Louis Turenne, Peter Gatto, Greg Kolb, Sandy Martin, Dennis Cooney

CATCH-22 by Joseph Heller; Director, Larry Arrick. CAST: Robert Balaban, George Martin, T. Richard Mason, Ed Rice, Louis Turenne, David Ackroyd, Betty Gordon, James Brick, Michael Tucker, Ed Hall, Molly Thompson, Barbara Sieck, John Olesen, Courtney Tucker

STAG AT BAY by Charles MacArthur and Nunnally Johnson; Director, Stephen Rothman. CAST: Alan Brooks, William Leach, Judith Light, Henson Keys, John Ulmer, Alfred Drake, Dick Shawn, Heidi Mefford, Joy Smith, Anne Scurria, Marilyn Hase, Joan Friedman, Rosalyn Farinella, Jillian Lindig, Barbara Dana

*David Robbins Photos*

**Right Center: Stephen Joyce, Nancy Donohue in "The Runner Stumbles" Above: T. Richard Mason, George Martin, Louis Turenne in "Catch-22" Top: Sloane Shelton, Austin Pendleton, Erin Ozker in "The Government Inspector"**

**Barbara Dana in "Joan of Lorraine"**

# HIPPODROME THEATRE

San Francisco, California
June 1, 1975–May 31, 1976

BULLSHOT CRUMMOND by Ron House, Diz White, Alan Shearman, John Neville-Andrews, Derek Cunningham; Producers, Ron House, Jonathan Gardner, Alan Shearman, Diane White in association with Gil Adler and Jack Temchin; General Manager, Jonathan Gardner; Stage Manager, Russell Haney. CAST: Alan Shearman, Ron House, Louisa Hart, Diz White, Mark Blankfield, John Achorn, Brandis Kemp, Joyce Harris, Mitch Kreindel

EL GRANDE DE COCA COLA by Ron House, Diz White, Alan Shearman, John Neville-Andrews; Produced by Low Moan Spectacular and American Conservatory Theatre; Designed by Michael Garrett; Stage Managers, Russell Haney, Michael Wolf. CAST: Ron House, James Howard Laurence, Jonathan Gardner, Janet McGrath, Diz White

**Top Right: Diz White, Alan Shearman in
"Bullshot Crummond"
Below: "That Championship
Season"**

# INDIANA REPERTORY THEATRE

Indianapolis, Indiana
October 16, 1975–May 7, 1976

Producing Director, Benjamin Mordecai; Artistic Director, Edward Stern; Administrative Director, James A. Clark; Press, Gayle Gordon; Directors, John Abajian, Jack L. Davis, Bernard Kates, Edward Stern; Sets, Keith Brumley; Costumes, Sherry Lynn Mordecai, Florence L. Rutherford; Lighting, Jody Boese, Allen Cornell, Timothy K. Joyce, Carl Roetter; Technical Directors, Richard Archer, Ed Collins; Stage Managers, Jody Boese, Leslie Robinson, Walter Schoen, Robert Stevenson

### PRODUCTIONS AND CASTS

THAT CHAMPIONSHIP SEASON with John C. Capodice, Robert Elliott, John Grassilli, Alfred Hinckley, Robert Scogin

THE CARETAKER with John Grassilli, Bernard Kates, Robert Scogin

ARMS AND THE MAN with Linda Atkinson, Jack L. Davis, Jack Donner, Robert Elliott, Donald Ewer, Priscilla Lindsay, Steven Ryan, Dee Victor

LONG DAY'S JOURNEY INTO NIGHT with Edward Binns, Elizabeth Franz, Priscilla Lindsay, T. Richard Mason, Steven Ryan

THE SEA HORSE with Susan Riskin, Steven Ryan

THE ENVOI MESSAGES (World Premiere) by Louis Phillips, with Henry Kaimu Bal, Rosanna Carter, Barry Cullison, Brenda Currin, Jack L. Davis, Maxwell Glanville, Delia Hattendorf, Bernard Kates, Duncan Larson, Chenault Lillard, Robert Machray, Lou Malandra, Robert Scogin, Linda Selman, Jeffrey V. Thompson, Loretta Yder

THE REAL INSPECTOR HOUND with John Abajian, John Guerrasio, Carol Gustafson, Delia Hattendorf, Bernard Kates, Robert Machray, Gun-Marie Nilsson, Robert Scogin

BLACK COMEDY with John Abajian, Carol Gustafson, Delia Hattendorf, Bernard Kates, Robert Machray, Gun-Marie Nilsson, Robert Scogin, Edward Stevlingson

THE TAVERN with John Abajian, Jody Boese, Jack L. Davis, John Guerrasion, Carol Gustafson, Paul Ilg, Carol Mayo Jenkins, Bernard Kates, Robert Machray, Gun-Marie Nilsson, Robin Pearson Rose, Robert Scogin, Edward Stevlingson, Jeremiah Sullivan, Jeffery V. Thompson

THE MAN WITH THE FLOWER IN HIS MOUTH with Shelley Joyce, Bernard Kates, Robert Scogin

*Joe McGuire Photos*

**Right Center: "Long Day's Journey into Night"**

**Jeremiah Sullivan, Carol Mayo Jenkins,
Bernard Kates in "The Tavern"**

## INNER CITY REPERTORY THEATRE

Los Angeles, California
October 1, 1975–June 30, 1976
Executive Director, C. Bernard Jackson; Press, John C. Thorpe; Sets and Costumes, Terence Tam Soon; Sets and Lighting, William Grant III; Assistant Directors, Fred Beauford, Jeanne Joe, Betty Muramoto; Producers, Virginia Bernache, Nikki Sanz, Virginia Wing

### COMPANY

Ray Adams, Lonnie Bradford, Roger Brown, Gloria Calomee, Danny de la Paz, Paris Earl, Edloe, Talya Ferro, Jessye Hageman, Jeanne Joe, Michael Johnson, Barbara O. Jones, Kutee, Lynn Kuratomi, Frank Michael Liu, Yolanda Marquez, Rosemary Martinez, Michael McKnight, Reginald Montgomery, Steve Reed, Nikki Sanz, Gloria Scott, Marilyn Tokuda, Les Tuckcho, Dan Turner, A. J. Walker, Violette Winge, and *Guest Artists* Beah Richards, Carmen Zapata

### PRODUCTIONS

"Maggie D. Mouse Meets De Dirdy Rat Fink," "Piano Bar," "Free Southern Theatre," "El Teatro Campesino," "Voices Inc.," "Langston Hughes Said," "A Black Woman Speaks," and *World Premiere* of "B/C" written by C. Bernard Jackson

**Below: Reggie Montgomery, Jeanne Joe, Steve Reed in "Piano Bar" Right: A. J. Walker, Michael Harris in "Maggie D. Mouse Meets de Dirty Rat Fink"**

**Susan Rich, Scott Duncan, Jamie Leo, Christopher Amato in "Sweetbird"**

## IOWA THEATER LAB

Baltimore, Maryland
September 15, 1975–June 30, 1976
Director, Ric Zank; Associate Director, Christopher Amato; A ministrative Director, Gillian Richards

### COMPANY

| | |
|---|---|
| Christopher Amato | Jamie L |
| Scott Duncan | Barry Mein |
| Rocky Greenberg | Susan R |
| George Kon | Steffen Sa |
| Helen Szablya | |

### PRODUCTIONS

"The Naming," "Dancer without Arms," "Moby Dick," and *Wo Premieres* of "Sweetbird," and "Judas-Pax"

*Ric Zank Photos*

**Top: Carmen Zapata in "B/C"**

# JOHN F. KENNEDY CENTER FOR THE PERFORMING ARTS

Washington, D.C.
July 9, 1975–May 31, 1976
Chairman, Roger L. Stevens; Executive Director, Martin Fein-stein; Press, Frank Cassidy, Lawrence Weiner Associates; American Bicentennial Theatre Productions presented by The Kennedy Center and Xerox Corporation; Produced by Roger L. Stevens and Rich-mond Crinkley

## PRODUCTIONS AND CASTS

THE SKIN OF OUR TEETH by Thornton Wilder; Director, Jose Quintero. See Broadway Calendar page 11.

THE SCARECROW by Percy MacKaye; Director, Austin Pendle-ton; Sets, John Conklin; Costumes, Carrie Robbins; Lighting, John Gleason; Incidental Music, Arthur B. Rubinstein; General Manager, Edmonstone Thompson, Jr.; Stage Managers, Franklin Keysar, Pat De Rousie, Kimothy Cruse; Wardrobe Supervisor, Louise Allen; Production Assistant, Frances K. Quigley. CAST: Barbara Baxley (Goody), Leonard Frey (Dickon), Susan Sharkey (Rachel), Kimothy Cruse (Ebenezer), Ralph Byers (Richard), King Donovan (Merton), William Atherton (Lord Ravensbane), Sloane Shelton (Cynthia), Peter Bosche (Micah), Frank Hamilton (Bugby), Patricia Fay (Mistress Dodge), John Wardwell (Dodge), Jon Richards (Rev. Todd), Joseph Mathewson (Rev. Rand).

SUMMER BRAVE by William Inge; Director, Michael Montel. See Broadway Calendar page 20.

SWEET BIRD OF YOUTH by Tennessee Williams; Director, Ed-win Sherin. See Broadway Calendar, page 31.

THE ROYAL FAMILY by George S. Kaufman and Edna Ferber; Director, Ellis Rabb. See Broadway Calendar page 32.

LONG DAY'S JOURNEY INTO NIGHT by Eugene O'Neill; Di-rector, Jason Robards; Set, Ben Edwards; Costumes, Jane Green-wood; Lighting, Ken Billington; General Manager, Edmonstone Thompson, Jr.; Stage Managers, Murray Gitlin, Dyanne Hochman, W. T. Martin; Assistant Director, Lois O'Connor. CAST: Jason Robards (James Tyrone), Zoe Caldwell (Mary Tyrone), Walter McGinn (James, Jr.) was succeeded by Kevin Conway, Michael Moriarty (Edmund), Lindsay Crouse (Cathleen).

RIP VAN WINKLE adapted by Joshua Logan and Ralph Allen from Washington Irving's story and from plays attributed to John Kerr, Charles Burke and Dion Boucicault; Director, Joshua Logan; Sets, Robert Cothran; Costumes, Marianne Custer; Lighting, David F. Segal; Traditional Airs adapted by Trude Rittmann; Musical Supervision, Susan Romann; Technical Director, David Nash; Pro-duction Supervisor, Jack Hofsiss; Company Manager, Janice Stan-ton. CAST: Anthony Quayle (Rip Van Winkle), Annie McGreevey (Dame Van Winkle), Bernerd Engel (Diedrich), Richard Galuppi (Nicholas), Jay Doyle (Von Brummel), Andrea McHenry (Tina), Fred Van Winkle (Brom), Ronald Venable (Casper), Michael Petro (Vedder), Deborah Fezelle (Tina), Maria Wozniak (Martha), David Fox-Brenton (Cyrus), Mary Armour, Susan Glaze, Shaun Helton, Billy Jayne Jacoby, Susan Jayne Jacoby, Rex James, Nancy Johnston Smith, Richard Spivey, Patrick Woliver

THE HEIRESS by Ruth and Augustus Goetz; Director, George Keathley. See Broadway Calendar page 47.

A TEXAS TRILOGY: three full-length plays in repertory by Pres-ton Jones; Director, Alan Schneider; Assistant Director, Joan Thorne; Costumes, Jane Greenwood; Produced by Robert White-head and Roger L. Stevens; General Manager, Oscar E. Olesen; Stage Managers, Mitchell Erickson, Charles Kindl, Stephen Nasuta; Hairstylist, Steve Atha; Production Assistant, Lee Mastrodonato.

CASTS:

LU ANN HAMPTON LAVERTY OBERLANDER with Kate Wilkinson (Claudine), Diane Ladd (Lu Ann), James Staley (Billy Bob), Graham Beckel (Skip), Everett McGill (Dale), Patrick Hines (Red), Walter Flanagan (Rufe), Thomas Toner (Olin), Baxter Harris (Corky), Josh Mostel (Milo), Kristin Griffin (Charmaine)

THE LAST MEETING OF THE KNIGHTS OF THE WHITE MAGNOLIA with John Marriott (Ramsey), Walter Flanagan (Rufe), Thomas Toner (Olin), Patrick Hines (Red), Henderson For-sythe (L. D.), Fred Gwynne (Colonel), Graham Beckel (Skip), Paul O'Keefe (Lonnie), Josh Mostel (Milo)

THE OLDEST LIVING GRADUATE with Kristin Griffith (Mar-tha Ann), Patricia Roe (Maureen), Fred Gwynne (Colonel), Ralph Roberts (Mike), Lee Richardson (Floyd), Henderson Forsythe (Clarence), William Le Massena (Maj. Ketchum), Paul O'Keefe (Whopper), Kate Wilkinson (Claudine)

*Richard Braaten Photos*

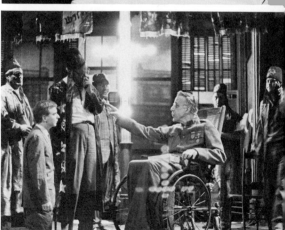

Fred Gwynne in "The Last Meeting of the Knights of the White Magnolia" Above: Patrick Hines, Diane Ladd in "Lu Ann Hampton Laverty Oberlander" Top: "The Scarecrow"

# LONG WHARF THEATRE

New Haven, Connecticut
October 17, 1975–June 11, 1976
Artistic Director, Arvin Brown; Executive Director, M. Edgar Rosenblum; Administrative Associate, Alison Harris; Press, Rosalind Heinz; Stage Directors, Arvin Brown, Kenneth Frankel, Waris Hussein, Peter Levin, Mike Nichols; Sets, Kenneth Foy, David Jenkins, Marjorie Kellogg, Steven Rubin, Tony Walton; Costumes, Linda Fisher, Jania Szatanski, Bill Walker; Lighting, Jamie Gallagher, Judy Rasmuson, Ronald Wallace; Stage Managers, Anne Keefe, Nina Seely, Clint Spencer

PRODUCTIONS AND CASTS

ARTICHOKE *(World Premiere)* by Joanna Glass. CAST: Emery Battis, Louis Beachner, Colleen Dewhurst, James Greene, Brian Murray, Rex Robbins, Ellin Ruskin

THE SHOW-OFF by George Kelly. CAST: William Atherton, Emery Battis, Joyce Ebert, Clarence Felder, Tom Martin, Jan Miner, James Noble, Leon Russom, Susan Sharkey

WHAT EVERY WOMAN KNOWS by J. M. Barrie. CAST: Emery Battis, Blair Brown, Mildred Dunnock, Joyce Ebert, Sean Griffin, Christopher Lloyd, Stephen Mendillo, William Swetland

STREAMERS *(World Premiere)* by David Rabe. CAST: Peter Evans, Joe Fields, John Heard, Herbert Jefferson, Jr., Michael Kell, Kenneth McMillan, Stephen Mendillo, Michael-Raymond O'Keefe, Ron Siebert, Dolph Sweet

ON THE OUTSIDE by Thomas Murphy and Noel O'Donoghue, and ON THE INSIDE by Thomas Murphy *(American Premieres)* CAST: "On the Outside": Jarlath Conroy, Lance Davis, James Greene, Michael Houlihan, Swoosie Kurtz, Suzanne Lederer, Stephen McHattie, "On the Inside": Frank Converse, Don Gantry, Sean Griffin, Bara-Cristin Hansen, James Hummert, Dorothy Lyman, Linda McGuire, Elizabeth Parrish, Ellin Ruskin

THE HOUSE OF MIRTH by Edith Wharton, adapted by John Tillinger. CAST: Emery Battis, Fran Brill, Joyce Ebert, Mary Fogarty, Victor Garber, James Greene, Bara-Cristin Hansen, George Hearn, James Hummert, Ben Kapen, Dorothy Lyman, Linda McGuire, Elizabeth Parrish, Paul Rosson, Susan Sharkey, Douglas Stender, William Swetland, Fiddle Viracola

DAARLIN' JUNO a new musical adaptation of Sean O'Casey's "Juno and the Paycock" by Richard Maltby, Jr. and Geraldine Fitzgerald, with music by Marc Blitzstein. CAST: Emery Battis, Joel Colodner, Jarlath Conroy, Joyce Ebert, James Ferrier, Geraldine Fitzgerald, Victor Garber, James Greene, Sean Griffin, Ruby Holbrook, Suzanne Lederer, Milo O'Shea, Elizabeth Parrish, Fiddle Viracola

*William L. Smith Photos*

**Right: Emery Battis, Milo O'Shea in "Darlin' Juno" Above: Stephen McHattie, James Greene in "On the Outside"**

**Colleen Dewhurst, Brian Murray in "Artichoke" Top Right: "Streamers"**

**Fran Brill, Joyce Ebert in "The House of Mirth"**

# MANITOBA THEATRE CENTRE

Winnipeg, Manitoba, Canada
October 17, 1975–May 15, 1976
Artistic Director, Len Cariou; General Manager, Gregory Poggi; Press, Max Tapper; Production Manager, Dwight Griffin; Technical Director, Kent McKay; Sets and Costumes, Mark Negin, Raymond C. Recht, Taras Korol, Doug McLean, Peter Wingate, Lawrence Schafer, James R. Bakkon; Lighting, Robert R. Scales, Raymond C. Recht, Bill Williams, Gil Wechsler

## PRODUCTIONS AND CASTS

CYRANO DE BERGERAC by Edmond Rostand; Director, Jean Gascon. CAST: Len Cariou, Frank Adamson, Joseph Bahr, Robert Benson, Jay Brazeau, Doreen Brownstone, Claude Dorge, Alexe Duncan, Erik Fredricksen, Marilyn Gardner, Fran Gebhard, David Gillies, Ralph Glass, Harvey Harding, Catherine Harris, Roland Hewgill, David Hurband, Susan Kapilow, Daniel V. Koren, Jack Medley, Louis Negin, Harry Nelken, Sharon Noble, Gilles Paquin, Dixie Seatle, Alf Silver, Howard Storey, Max Tapper, Robin Ward

THE PRICE by Arthur Miller; Director, Robert Bilheimer. CAST: Robert Benson, Roland Hewgill, Milton Selzer, Angela Wood

THE COLLECTED WORKS OF BILLY THE KID by Michael Ondaatje; Director, Arif Hasnain. CAST: Guy Bannerman, Claude Bede, Trudy Cameron, Larry Davis, Patricia Hamilton, Peter Jobin, Des McAnuff, Douglas Millar

A CHRISTMAS CAROL by Charles Dickens; Adapted by David Ball and David Feldshuh; Director, Robert Bilheimer. CAST: Jay Brazeau, Christopher Britton, Doreen Brownstone, David Calderisi, Alexe Duncan, David Gillies, Ralph Glass, Susan Kapilow

EQUUS by Peter Shaffer; Director, Edward Gilbert. CAST: Zoe Alexander, Len Cariou, Ian Deakin, Cliff Gardner, Fran Gebhard, Patricia Hamilton, Jack Mather, Gwen Thomas, Robin Ward

BEYOND WORDS by the Canadian Mime Theatre. CAST: Adrian Pecknold, Harro Maskow, Robin Patterson, Paulette Hallich, Larry Lefevbre

COMPANY by Stephen Sondheim and George Furth; Director, Dean Regan; Musical Director, Victor Davies. CAST: Evelyne Adnerson, Marilyn Boyle, Scot Denton, Roger Dressler, Janis Dunning, Cliff Gardner, Particia Hamilton, Tabby Johnson, Barbara Lawlor, Lynn Marsh, Brian McKay, Nora McLellan, Scott Walker, Steve Weston

ENDGAME by Samuel Beckett; Director, Robert Bilheimer. CAST: Roland Hewgill, David Calderisi, Christopher Britton, Doreen Brownstone

OF MICE AND MEN by John Steinbeck; Director, Len Cariou. CAST: Bob Aaron, Frank Adamson, Martin Doyle, Erik Fredricksen, Cliff Gardner, David Gillies, Delroy Lindo, John-Peter Linton, Janis Nickleson, Scott Walker

CREEPS by David Freeman; Director, Robert Bilheimer. CAST: Aaron Schwartz, Jay Brazeau, Joe Horvath, Christopher Britton, Guy Bannerman, Fran Gebhard, Brian Richardson

PRIVATE LIVES by Noel Coward; Director, Frances Hyland. CAST: Zoe Alexander, Doreen Brownstone, David Calderisi, Clare Coulter, Robin Ward

*Gerry Kopelow Photos*

**Right Center: Len Cariou as Cyrano de Bergerac
Above: "Company" Top: Doreen
Brownstone, Christopher Britton in "Endgame"**

**Ian Deakin, Len Cariou in "Equus"**

213

# McCARTER THEATRE COMPANY

Princeton, N. J.
October 9, 1975–April 4, 1976
Producing Director, Michael Kahn; General Manager, Edward A. Martenson; Producing Manager, Mark S. Krause; Press, Norman Lombino, David Wynne; Business Managers, Louise Bayer, Marsha Senack; Technical Director, Mitchell Kurtz; Guest Directors, Kenneth Frankel, Ellis Rabb; Sets, John Conklin, David Jenkins, Marjorie Kellogg, Kert Lundell, Oliver Smith, Paul Zalon; Costumes, Jeanne Button, Lawrence Casey, Jane Greenwood, Ann Roth; Lighting, L. B. Achziger, John Gleason, John McLain; Stage Managers, Suzanne Egan, Helaine Head, Arthur Karp

### COMPANY

John Arnone, George Axler, Richard Backus, Sally Backus, Donald Barton, Powers Boothe, Frank Borgman, John Christian Browning, Forrest Buckman, James C. Burge, Morris Carnovsky, David Chandler, Curt Dawson, Richard Dix, Conrad Fowkes, Richard Gere, Steven Gilborn, George Grizzard, Jack Gwillim, Sarah-Jane Gwillim, Rosemary Harris, David Haskell, Bette Henritze, Barton Heyman, Pat Hingle, Michael Houlihan, Joseph Jamrog, Elaine Kerr, Philip Kerr, Jerry Lanning, William Larsen, Paul Larson, Mary Layne, Eva LeGallienne, Rosetta LeNoire, Richard Lenz, Barbara Lester, Sam Levene, Miller Lide, Karl Light, Sherman Lloyd, Joan Lorring, Larry C. Lott, Joseph Maher, Carol Morley, Gabor Morea, Mary Joan Negro, Deborah Offner, Kristin Paulus, Wyman Pendleton, Sarah Peterson, Eleanor Phelps, John Remme, David Rounds, Martin Rudy, Chris Sarandon, Anne Sheldon, Marshall Shnider, Drew Snyder, Josef Sommer, Theodore Sorel, Ian Trigger, Maria Tucci, Steve Vinovich, Kate Wilkinson, Mary Louise Wilson

### PRODUCTIONS

"A Grave Undertaking" *(World Premiere)* by Lloyd Gold, directed by Michael Kahn, "The Royal Family" by George S. Kaufman and Edna Ferber, "Section Nine" *(American Premier)* by Philip Magdalany, directed by Michael Kahn, "The Heiress" by Ruth and Augustus Goetz, "Awake and Sing" by Clifford Odets, "The Winter's Tale" by William Shakespeare

*Cliff Moore Photos*

**Right: Maria Tucci,**
**David Haskell in "The Winter's Tale"**
**Above: Morris Carnovsky (1) in**
**"Awake and Sing!" Top: Jerry Lanning,**
**Richard Lenz, Drew Snyder in "Section Nine"**

**Maria Tucci, Richard Backus**
**in "The Heiress"**

**Chris Sarandon, Deborah Offner**
**in "A Grave Undertaking"**

# MEADOW BROOK THEATRE

Rochester, Michigan
October 9, 1975–May 16, 1976

Artistic Director, Terence Kilburn; Managing Director, David
obert Kanter; Sets, Peter Hicks; Costumes, Mary Lynn Bonnell;
age Managers, R. Joseph Mooney, Robert Neu, James Corrigan;
usiness Manager, Vincent L. Ammann; Guest Directors, Anthony
ockus, Michael Montel, Charles Nolte; Guest Designers, Tom
ston, Lance Brockman, Larry A. Reed, Nancy Thompson

## COMPANY

ark Addy, Dan C. Bar, Mary Benson, Rolfe Bergsman, James
orrigan, J. L. Dahlmann, Fred Fonner, Cheryl Giannini, Robert
rossman, William Halliday, John Hammond, Elizabeth King,
ennis MacMath, Mark McKinney, Marianne Muellerleile, Patricia
iveri, James D. O'Reilly, Elisabeth Orion, John L. Peakes, Su-
nne Peters, F. Jackson Reilly, Melanie Resnick, Richard Riehle,
amona Santiago, Laurie Schirner, Thomas C. Spackman, Eric
avaris, Fred Thompson, James Winfield

UEST ARTISTS: Curtis J. Armstrong, Burneice Avery, Terence
aker, Evalyn Baron, Stephen Berger, Peter Brandon, Nancy Cole-
an, Donald Ewer, Patricia Gage, Demene Hall, John Hallow,
lly Holliday, William LeMassena, Mae Marmy, Kent Martin,
rri McRay, Edgar Meyer, Donald C. Moore, Michele Mullen,
illip Piro, David Schurmann, Max Showalter, Guy Stockwell,
even Sutherland, Marie Wallace, Joseph Warren

## PRODUCTIONS

"A Midsummer Night's Dream," "Witness for the Prosecution,"
"Arms and the Man," "The Little Foxes," "Relatively Speaking,"
"Under Milk Wood," "Born Yesterday," and *World Premiere* of
"Yankee Ingenuity"

*Walt Bromley Photos*

**Right: "The Little Foxes"**
**Above: "Under Milk Wood"**
**Top: "Yankee Ingenuity"**

Susanne Peters, Mae Marmy, Donald C. Moore,
Eric Tavaris in "Arms and the Man"

Marie Wallace, Guy Stockwell
in "Born Yesterday"

215

# MILWAUKEE REPERTORY THEATER

Milwaukee, Wisconsin
September 12, 1975–May 30, 1976
Artistic Director, Nagle Jackson; Managing Director, Sara O'
Connor; Press, Michael Krawczyk, Denise Masnica; Directors,
Barry Boys, Montgomery Davis, John Dillon, Nagle Jackson, Rob
ert Lanchester, William McKereghan, John Olon-Scrymgeour, Paul
Weidner; Sets and Lighting, Christopher M. Idoine, R. H. Graham;
Costumes, Elizabeth Covey, Ellen M. Kozak; Stage Manager, Fre
dric H. Orner

## COMPANY

Tom Blair, Robert Dawson, Leslie Geraci, Rose Herron, Robert
Ingham, Robert Lanchester, John Mansfield, Durward McDonald,
William McKereghan, Daniel Mooney, James Pickering, Penelope
Reed, Stephen Stout, Jeffrey Tambor

GUEST ARTISTS: Ray Aranha, Glenn Close, Peggy Cowles,
Elaine Dale, Daniel Davis, Jill Heavenrich, Josephine Nichols, Rich
ard Risso, Jessie Saunders, Ruth Schudson, Seret Scott, Sirin Der
rim Trainer, Beatrice Winde, Mary Wright

## PRODUCTIONS

"King Lear," "Democracy," "School for Wives," "My Sister, My
Sister," "Happy Days," "Out at Sea," *American Premieres* of "The
Visions of Simone Machard" by Bertolt Brecht, "Fanshen" by Da
vid Hare, *World Premieres* of "Never a Snug Harbor" by David
Ulysses Clarke, "Out" by Robert Ingham and Penelope Reed

*Sorgel-Lee-Riordan Photos*

**Left: "Democracy" Top: "King Lear"**

**"Never a Snug Harbor"**
**Above: "My Sister, My Sister"**

**"The Visions of Simone Machard"**
**Above: "School for Wives"**

216

"The Last Meeting of the Knights
of the White Magnolia"
Above: Susan Borneman, Steve
Ryan in "Born Yesterday"
Right: "Much Ado about Nothing"
Below: Meg Myles, Steve Ryan
in "A Streetcar Named Desire"

# MISSOURI REPERTORY THEATRE

Kansas City, Missouri

Producing Director, Patricia McIlrath; Staff Directors, James Asd, Francis J. Cullinan; Production Manager, David Dannenbaum; echnical Director, Alan Kibbe; Costumes, Vincent Scassellati; Sets, ax A. Beatty, G. Philippe de Rosier; Lighting, Joseph Appelt, Curt terman; Sound, James Coleman; Stage Managers, John Maddin, Ron Durbian, Joyce McBroom, Joseph dePauw

## COMPANY

amwell Fletcher, Meg Myles, Susan Borneman, Richard C. own, John Q. Bruce, Jr., Al Christy, Lynn Cohen, Liza Cole, John thran, Jr., Robert Elliott, Marla Frumkin, Michael LaGue, Hart Levitt, John Maddison, Walter Rhodes, Leslie Robinson, Steve an, Steve Scearcy, Henry Strozier, Gloria P. Terrell, Eberle omas, Ronetta Wallman, Von H. Washington, Ron Durbian, Art ison, Jeannine Hutchings

## PRODUCTIONS

orn Yesterday," "The Cherry Orchard," "Much Ado about othing," "The Last Meeting of the Knights of the White Maglia," "A Streetcar Named Desire," "In the Well of the House," he Rainmaker," "The Morgan Yard"

"The Morgan Yard" Above: Bramwell Fletcher,
Von H. Washington in "In the Well of the
House"

# OKLAHOMA THEATER CENTER

Oklahoma City, Oklahoma
October 1, 1975 - April 18, 1976
Artistic Director, Lyle Dye, Jr.; Business Director, Russ Walton; Pat Cacy; Technical Director, Roger Drummond; Wardrobe Master, Jim Hampton; Directors, Jeanie Miller, Lyle Dye, Paul Nutt, JoAnn Muchmore, Lee Hicks, Eugene Jacobson, Roberta Sloan, Jeanne Adams Wray, Garry Charter, David McElroy, Judith McElroy; Sets, Dale Hall, Steve Estes, David Pape, Sheldon Wilhelm, Chris VanZandt, Roger Drummond; Lighting, Dell Unruh, Steve Estes, David Pape, Sheldon Wilhelm, Chris VanZandt, Roger Drummond, Keith Jones, Dan Diamond; Costumes, Vicki Holden, Charlotte Stratton, Jim Hampton, Judi McElroy; Musical Director, John Robinson; Choreographer, Cheri Ingram.

## PRODUCTIONS AND CASTS

THE STAR SPANGLED GIRL with Kerry Robertson, Steven Schmidt, David DeBatto

INHERIT THE WIND with Dean Eikleberry, Tammy Wheat, Melissa J. Clifton, Vernon Wall, Mark Goodwin, Jeffery Spelman, Rusty Plumbtree, John Chandler, Mary S. Patterson, Shana Ledet, Pepper Twyford, Christopher VanZandt, Lance Reese, Mike Blakely, Steven B. Tesney, Susan Arleen Winters, Timmy Hoch, Michael Blackmore, T. J. Sommers, John C. Pickard, Jr., John B. Doolin, Florene Merrit Garner, Scotty Dallas, Eric Schoaff, Clyde Martin, Kent Rulon, Dale Bassler, Paul Toles, Helen Overpeck, Steve Higgins, Bruce Meyers, Kenneth Hamilton, Ira McLaughlin, John Amick, Rick DeSpain, Roy Dunlap, James F. Robbinson, David Taylor, Bill Snyder, Dan Murphy, Jack Sterling Pratt, Timothy Aschmann, Richard Sinclair, Hugh A. Baysinger, Curtis Michener, Dana Rojas

YOU'RE A GOOD MAN, CHARLIE BROWN with Curtiss Clayton, Dana Carnett, David M. Scott, Judith McElroy, Brian Tidwell, Lara Teeter

U. S. A. with Richard Darby, Terry Schenk, Harry Parker, Dusty Presler, Linda Magbee, Sue Long

MARY, MARY with Jim Smith, Cheri Ingram, Thomas Sheehan, Richard Sinclair, Patricia Cacy

THE DIARY OF ANN FRANK with Eric Schoaff, Cecilia Bristow, Joan Pickard, Vernon Wall, Tom Brown, Mary Gordon Taft, Marilyn Morris, Dawn Kutz, Robert Wootten, Charles Unger

CATCH ME IF YOU CAN with T. A. Minton, John Thompson, Richard B. Darby, Joyce Bishop, Clyde Martin, Phoebee Revelle, Harry Revelle, Jr.

WHEN YOU COMIN' BACK, RED RYDER? with J. Shane McClure, Suzan Ott, David Earl Hodges, John Webb, Joan Pickard, Rodger W. Smith, Daniel J. Christiaens, Melody Brook

THE LAST MEETING OF THE KNIGHTS OF THE WHITE MAGNOLIA with Steve Higgins, John Patterson, Les Chick, Roy E. Dunlap, David Earl Hodges, James F.     Jinson, John B. Doolin, Richard B. Doolin, Richard C. White, Marvin G. Shawn

THE HOT L BALTIMORE with David Taylor, Melody Brook, Eleanora Woodruff, Vicki S. Holden, John C. Pickard, Jr., Gloria Barton, John Chandler, Clayton Barnes, Pepper Twyford, Steve Huntress, Larry Bailey, Sally Unger, Les Chick, Rusty Plumbtree

*Pat Cacy, Dave Stanton Photos*

Top: "Inherit the Wind" Right: "Diary of Anne Frank"
Below: "When You Comin' Back, Red Ryder?"

"The Hot l Baltimore" Above: "The Last Mee[t]
of the Knights of the White Magnolia"

218

# PHILADELPHIA DRAMA GUILD

Philadelphia, Pennsylvania
November 4, 1975 - March 18, 1976

Artistic Director, Douglas Seale; Managing Director, James B. [
...]ydberg; Chairman of the Board, Elkins Wetherill; President, [
...]ney S. Bloom; Artistic-Administrative Coordinator, Lillian Stein[
...]g; Sets, John Kasarda; Costumes, Jane Greenwood, David [
...]arles; Lighting, Spencer Mosse; Press, James E. McCormick; [
...]ge Directors, Douglas Seale, Richard Maltby, Jr., Brian Murray; [
...]ge Managers, Gerald Nobles, Rusty Swope; Technical Director, [
...]n Trumpler

## PRODUCTIONS AND CASTS

[TH]E ROYAL FAMILY by George S. Kaufman and Edna Feber. [CA]ST: Lois De Banzie, Russell Leib, Terrence Markovich, Eric [...]ler, Rogert Gerringer, Catherine Wolf, Carolyn Younger, Wil[...]n Buell, Betty Leighton, Joseph Leon, Louise Troy, John Glover, [...]k Viola, William LeMassena, Maureen Garrett

[TH]E GLASS MENAGERIE by Tennessee Williams. CAST: Ger[ald]ine Fitzgerald, James Valentine, Margaret Ladd, Edward Albert

[TH]E BIRTHDAY PARTY by Harold Pinter. CAST: William Pres[to]n, Betty Leighton, John Glover, Ann Crumb, Leonard Frey, Rob[ert] Gerringer

[H]EDDA GABLER by Henrik Ibsen. CAST: Betty Leighton, Bar[ba]ra Lester, James Valentine, Roberta Maxwell, Swoosie Kurtz, [Ro]bert Gerringer, John Glover

[TH]E MISER by Moliere. CAST: Thom Christopher, Lu Ann Post, [A]lan Carlsen, Robert Gerringer, Russell Leib, William Buell, [Lo]uise Troy, John Glover, Ann Crumb, Peter Sauer, Susan Keller, [Wi]lliam Preston, Eric Uhler, Douglas Seale

*James McCormick Photos*

**Right: Roberta Maxwell,
James Valentine in "Hedda Gabler"
Above: Robert Gerringer,
Leonard Frey in "The Birthday Party"
Top: James Valentine, Geraldine Fitzgerald
in "The Glass Menagerie"**

**William LeMassena, Louise Troy
in "The Royal Family"**

**Robert Gerringer, John Glover
in "The Miser"**

219

# PITTSBURGH PLAYHOUSE

Pittsburgh, Pennsylvania
February 3 - 21, 1976
Producer, Mark Lewis; Assistant to producer, Carole Berger; Director, Jose Ferrer; Set, Oren Parker; Lighting, Hank Graff; Sound, Jack Givens; Costumes, Mary M. Turner; Press, Leo Carlin; Production Coordinator, Janus Purins; Stage Manager, Jean Kahl

## PRODUCTION AND CAST

THE INTERVIEW (*World Premiere*) by Tom Thomas. CAST: Jose Ferrer, Michael Wager, Dennis Sakamoto, James Prescott

Season was curtailed because of financial problems.

*Guild Photographers Photos*

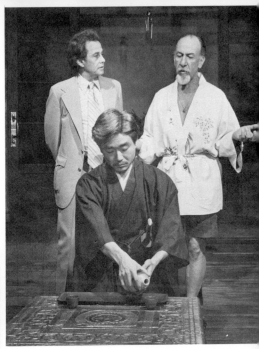

**Michael Wager, Dennis Sakamoto, Jose Ferrer
in "The Interview"**

# PITTSBURGH PUBLIC THEATER

Pittsburgh, Pennsylvania
September 17 - December 21, 1975
First Season
General Director, Ben Shaktman; Business Manager, Dolo Logue; Press, Joel Warren; Administrative Coordinator, Marie N gent-Head; Stage Directors, Ben Shaktman, John Going; Sets, Pe Wexler, David Chapman; Costumes, Whitney Blausen, David Cha man; Lighting, Peter Wexler, Bernard J. Brannigan; Stage Mana ers, Margaret Peckham, Michael V. Murphy; Production Manag Bernard J. Brannigan; Wardrobe Mistress, Renee Banks; Scer Artist, Joseph Bock; Costume Coordinator, Ann Watson

## PRODUCTIONS AND CASTS

THE GLASS MENAGERIE by Tennessee Williams. CAST: Da Snell, Carol Teitel, Amy Wright, Steve Simpson

ONE FLEW OVER THE CUCKOO'S NEST by Dale Wasserma CAST: Ralph Roberts, Edward Lee Talmadge, Jake Turner, Ca Mayo Jenkins, Amy Wright, Michael Thompson, Steve Simps Albert Corbin, Thomas Carson, John Long, Vic Kleman, Tom A kins, Tony Aylward, Wayne Darby Cook, Christine Hulter, Mich V. Murphy, Katherine Clarke, Leonard R. Tolbert, Renee Y. Bar

TWELFTH NIGHT by William Shakespeare. CAST: Dvida Bloo Fred Bright, Jake Turner, Steve Simpson, Daniel Booth, Mark Connolly, Pamela Brook, Albert Corbin, Thomas Carson, Jeane Landis, Michael Flanagan, John Long, Christine Hulter, Leona Nimoy, Don Wadsworth, Michael V. Murphy, Daniel Booth, F Bright, Fritz Kupfer

*Jack Weinhold Photos*

**Left Center: Ralph Roberts, Tom Atkins in "Or
Flew over the Cuckoo's Nest"**

**Carol Teitel, David Snell, Amy Wright
in "The Glass Menagerie"**

# PROFESSIONAL PERFORMING COMPANY

Chicago, Illinois
March - May 1976
Producer, H. Adrian Rehner; Artistic Coordinators, Jack Montmery, Lenard Norris; Set Designer and Director, Jack Montgomy; Costumes, Leon Natker; Lighting, James Highland; Stage anagers, Michael Smith, Denise Gilchrist; Press, Jimmie Barquillo

### PRODUCTION AND CAST

NDROCLES AND THE LION by George Bernard Shaw. CAST: C. Coleman, Robert Cunningham, Madelyn Dowell, Theodore reene, Anna Grose, Charles Lee, Randy Lindsay, Jonathon Lind-y, James Lloyd, Mary Mabry, Eva McCann, Dennis McCoy, Al-rt McGhee, Michael Perkins, Ann Ricks, Valerie Rodgers, orothy Singleton, Gayle Tolbert, Glen Washington, Paulette Wil-ms

*Ray Hasch Photos*

"Androcles and the Lion"

# STAGE I THEATRE LAB

Boston, Massachusetts
October 10, 1975 - May 24, 1976
Artistic Director, Kaleel Sakakeeny; Managing Director, David L. Archer; Lighting, Debra Margolis

### COMPANY

Wendie Flagg, Deirdre O'Connell, Joseph Pilato, Paul Knill, Deborah Desnoo, Michael Fulginetti, Steven Snow

### PRODUCTIONS

"The Hamlet Syndrome," and *Premieres* of "The Arrangers," "Gertrude og Ophelia," "Masques," "Icarus"

*Warren Goldberg Photos*

Michael Fulginitti in "Icarus" Right Center: Wendie Flagg, Dierdre O'Connell in "Gertrude og Ophelia"

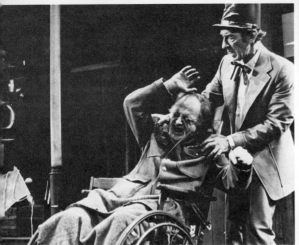

**Robert Donley, John Wylie in "The Last Meeting of the Knights of the White Magnolia" Right: Farley Granger, Margaret Hall in "Private Lives" Above: Harry Groener, James Cahill in "Cyrano de Bergerac"**

## SEATTLE REPERTORY THEATRE

Seattle, Washington
October 22, 1975 - April 1, 1976
Thirteenth Season
Artistic Director, Duncan Ross; Producing Director, Peter Donnelly; Assistant Artistic Director, Arne Zaslove; Costumes, Lewis D. Rampino, Donna Eskew; Sets, Eldon Elder, John Lee Beatty, Jerry Williams, Robert Dahlstrom; Technical Director, Floyd Hart; Lighting, Steven A. Maze, Phil Shermer, Richard Devin, Cynthia Hawkins, Jim McKie; Guest Directors, Harold Scott, Clayton Corzatte, Robert Patrick; Production Manager, Marc Rush; Stage Managers, Jay Moran, Rod Pilloud; Press, Shirley Dennis, Marnie Andrews; Assistant to Producing Director, Jeff Bentley; Company Manager, Charles Younger

### COMPANY

Richard E. Arnold, John Aylward, Andy Backer, Kurt Beattie, Jon Peter Benson, Rafic Bey, Alan Brandon, Henry Butler, David Boushey, Katherine Bruce, Marck Buchan, Gerald Burgess, Genn Buttkus, James Cahill, James Carruthers, Dorothy Chace, Michael Christensen, Jerome Collamore, David Connell, Bill Cobbs, Edwin Cooper, Lee Corbet, Ted D'Arms, Roger DeKoven, Robert Donley, Katherine Ferrand, Loren Foss, John Gilbert, Wesley Grant, Margaret Hall, Maureen Hawkins, Gardner Hayes, Eric Helland, Margaret Hilton, Michael Keenan, Jean Marie Kinney, Zoaunne LeRoy, Madeleine LeRoux, Nick Lewis-Jones, Susan Ludlow, Michael Medeiros, Dean Melang, Marilyn Meyers, Marjorie Nelson, John Newton, Douglas Nigh, Frances Peter, Demetra Pittman, Robin Reeds, Joseph Regalbuto, Gary Reineke, John Renforth, Gil Rogers, William Rongstad, Kimberly Ross, Lucy Rush, Alvin Lee Sanders, Phil Shallat, Robert Sevra, Eric Sinclair, Sharon Spelman, James Staley, Paul C. Thomas, Deems Urquhart, Earl Christopher Williams, Dan Winston, Max Wright, John Wylie, Alan Zampese

GUEST ARTISTS: Jeannie Carson, Farley Granger

### PRODUCTIONS

"Cyrano de Bergerac," "Jumpers," "Seven Keys to Baldpate," "The Last Meeting of the Knights of the White Magnolia," "The Madwoman of Chaillot," "Private Lives," "Benito Cereno," "Entertaining Mr. Sloane," "Kennedy's Children," "The Collected Works of Billy the Kid," and *World Premiere* of "Made for TV"

*Greg Gilbert Photos*

**Marjorie Nelson in "Made for TV"
Above: "Benito Cereno"**

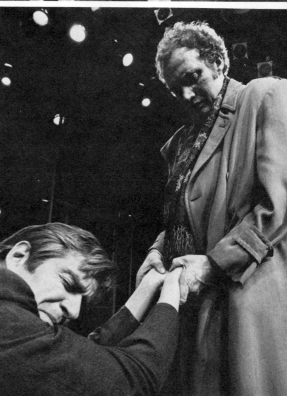

...tricia Cray, David Gale in "Serenading Louie" Above: "The Balcony" Right: Robert ...astene, Gwyllum Evans in "Ah, Wilderness!"

## STAGE/WEST

West Springfield, Massachusetts
November 15, 1975 - April 25, 1976
...rtistic Director, Rae Allen; Managing Director, Stephen E.
...s; General Manager, Susan B. Hutton; Press, Sally Fuller; Stage
...nagers, James Riggs, Barbara Dilker; Designers, Laurence King,
...rles Stockton, Eugene Warner, Marc B. Weiss, Fredda Slavin;
...tumes, Sigrid Insull; Lighting, Ron Wallace, Jamie Gallagher,
...y Rasmuson; Directors, Rae Allen, Martin Fried, Edward Berke-
...John Milligan, Tom Crawley, Marjorie Sigley

### COMPANY

...ham Beckel, Yusef Bulos, Thomas Carson, Tom Crawley, Pa-
...a Cray, Gwyllum Evans, David Gale, Phillip Littell, Jane
...vry, Jerry Mayer, Lillah McCarthy, Michael Miller, John Milli-
... John O'Creagh, Elizabeth Parrish, Robert Pastene, Chris
...nilly, John Ryan, Franklyn Seales, James Secrest, Nancy Sellin,
...cy Snyder, Barbara Tarbuck, Janis Young

...es Cass, Dan Eaton, David Gosselin, Lisa Grayton, Madonna T.
...agher, A. J. Morin, Leigh Plakias, Betsy Tucker, Tommy N.
...ker, Jr.

### PRODUCTIONS

..., Wilderness!," "The Tempest," "The Balcony," "The Country
...," "Design for Living," "Serenading Louie," "Christopher Co-
...bus," "Hugo"

*Paramount Commercial Studios Photos*

**Right Center: Michael Miller, John Ryan
in "The Country Girl"**

**Nancy Snyder, Graham Beckel
in "Ah, Wilderness!"**

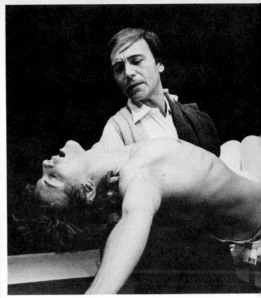

# STUDIO ARENA THEATRE

Buffalo, N. Y.
October 10, 1975 - May 23, 1976
Eleventh Season

Executive Producer, Neal DuBrock; Associate Producer, Gin▮
Sileika; Press, Blossom Cohan, Brian T. Whitehill; Production Cc▮
dinator, Tom Pechar; Producers' Assistant, Jane Abbott; St▮
Managers, John Philip Luckacovic, Brennan Roberts, Donald W▮
ters, Jean E. Russ; Production Assistant, Jean Bernecky; Techni▮
Directors, Jim Crossley, Daniel Dour; Wardrobe, Diane R. Scha▮
Claudia Lynch; Props, Ronald Schroeder, Carl John; Sound, Ri▮
ard Menke; Sets, Frank J. Boros; David F. Segal

## PRODUCTIONS AND CASTS

BUTLEY by Simon Gray; Director, Richard Barr. CAST: T▮
Tanner, Katherine Bruce, Peter Burnell, Nancy Cushman,
Herndon, Andrea Stonorov, Bill VandeSande·

SCAPINO! by Frank Dunlop and Jim Dale; Director, Grover D▮
CAST: John Christopher Jones, John Abajian, Julia Barr, A▮
Benjamin, Nicholas Cosco, Denny Dillon, David Johns, Neal Kl▮
Mordecai Lawner, Tom Mardirosian, Albert Sanders, James S▮
mour, Rick Wessler, Shelley Wyant

A DOLL'S HOUSE by Henrik Ibsen; Director, Stephen Po▮
CAST: Betsy Palmer, James Cahill, Don Gantry, Betty Lutes, ▮
nie McInerney, Patricia O'Connell, Patricia Weber, Bishop ▮
Justin DeBlase, Chelsey DiStefano, Adam Martin

EQUUS by Peter Shaffer; Director, Paul Giovanni. CAST: Jerem▮
Sullivan, Laurinda Barrett, Elizabeth Brown, Kermit Brown, C▮
Mayo Jenkins, Jonathan Howard Jones, Jim Oyster, Peggy Whit▮
Ben Fuhrman, Roger Sewall, Lawrence Smith, Richard Tabor, D▮
Tucker, Norman Weiler

THE MAGIC SHOW by Stephen Schwartz, Bob Randall, D▮
Henning; Director, Jay Fox. CAST: Joseph Abaldo, Richard Ba▮
trino, Serhij Bohdan, Gwendolyn Coleman, Connie Day, W. P. ▮
mak, Anthony Inneo, Rose Anna Mineo, John-Ann Washing▮
Rick Wessler

A LITTLE NIGHT MUSIC by Stephen Sondheim and H▮
Wheeler; Director, Tony Tanner. CAST: Rosemary Prinz, Will▮
Chapman, Paula Laurence, David Holliday, Alan Brasing▮
Karen Good, Gail Johnston, Jay Lowman, Leila Martin, Sarah R▮
Howard Shalwitz

REPLIKA conceived and directed by Jozef Szajna. CAST: ▮
Kozlowska, Irena Jun, Stanislaw Brudny, Antoni Pszoniak, J▮
Wieczorek

*Greenberg, Wrazen and May Photos*

**Top: Jeremiah Sullivan, Jonathan Howard Jone▮**
**"Equus" Left: Tony Tanner, Peter Burnell**
**in "Butley" Below: Betsy Palmer,**
**Don Gantry in "A Doll's House"**

"Replika" Above: "Scapino!"

224

# TRINITY SQUARE REPERTORY COMPANY

Providence, Rhode Island
October 14, 1975 - May 2, 1976

irector, Adrian Hall; Administrator, G. David Black; Press,
on Simon, Patricia Schwadron; Musical Director, Richard
ming; Sets, Eugene Lee, Robert D. Soule; Lights, Mark Rippe,
Custer; Costumes, James Berton Harris, Betsey Potter; Techni-
irector, Douglas Smith; Production Coordinator, David Ward;
e Managers, William Radka, Beverly Andreozzi; Stage Direc-
Adrian Hall, Word Baker, Vincent Dowling

### COMPANY

rt Black, William Cain, Robert J. Colonna, Timothy Crowe,
am Damkoehler, Lane Davies, Timothy Donahue, John Gar-
Peter Gerety, Brad Gott-Lin, Tom Griffin, Ed Hall, Zina Jas-
Richard Jenkins, David C. Jones, Melanie Jones, Richard
anaugh, Richard Kneeland, Marguerite Lenert, Howard Lon-
Mina Manente, George Martin, Derek Meader, Barbara Meek,
Miterko, Nancy Nichols, Barbara Orson, Bonnie Sacks, Wil-
Sadler, Margo Skinner, Cynthia Strickland, Danie Von Bargen,
Weaver, Ricardo Wiley

### PRODUCTIONS

o Gentlemen of Verona," "Another Part of the Forest," "The
e Foxes," and *Premieres* of "Cathedral of Ice" by James Sche-
"Bastard Son" by Richard Lee Marks, "Eustace Chisholm and
Works" by Adrian Hall and Richard Cumming from a novel by
s Purdy

*Dana Duke, William L. Smith, Roger Birn Photos*

**Right: "Two Gentlemen of Verona"**
**Top: "Another Part of the Forest"**

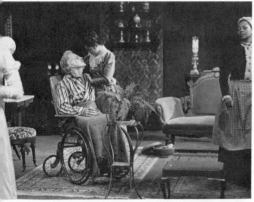

**"Eustace Chisholm and the Works"**
**Above: "The Little Foxes"**

**"Bastard Son"**

# VIRGINIA MUSEUM THEATRE REPERTORY COMPANY

Richmond, Virginia
October 22, 1975 - March 27, 1976
Artistic Director, Keith Fowler; General Manager, Loraine Sl.
Stage Directors, Keith Fowler, James Kirkland, Ken Letner, T
Markus; Music Director, William Stancil; Choreographer,
Horne; Designers, Robert Franklin, Richard Norgard, T
Straiges, Frederick Norman Brown, Don Pasco; Lighting, James
Block, Michael Watson; Stage Managers, Rachael Lindhart, D
Flinchum; Press, Fred Haseltine, Michael P. Hickey

## COMPANY

David Addis, Nico Boccio, Sarah Brooke, Alan Brooks, Mel C
Jim Cyrus, Dottie Dee, Ron Duncan Maury Erickson, Doug F
chum, Spence Ford, Alan Gilbert, Prudence Wright Holmes, De
Howard, Marie Goodman Hunter, Earle Hyman, James Kirkla
Marjorie Lerstrom, Carl Blackwell Lester, Ken Letner, Racl
Lindhart, Heather MacRae, Carmen Mathews, Milledge Mos
Lynda Myles, Kathy O'Callaghan, Lype O'Dell, Maureen O'Ke.
David Pichette, Stan Picus, William Pitts, Roger Rathburn, Bart
Redmond, Walter Rhodes, Dino Shorte, William Stancil, Su
Streater, John Wylie, Eloise Zeigler

## PRODUCTIONS

"Guys and Dolls," "Sherlock Holmes in Scandal in Bohemia,"
Member of the Wedding," "The Crucible," "The Emperor Jon
"The Contrast," and *Premiere* of "Children" by A. R. Gurney

*Virginia Museum Theatre Photos*

**Left: Carmen Mathews, Lynda Myles
in "Children"**

**Earle Hyman
in "The Emperor Jones"**

**Nico Boccio, Carl Blackwell Lester, also
above in "Guys and Dolls"**

Cuervo, Dan Hamilton, Carmen de Lavallade in "General Gorgeous" Right: Eugene Troobnick, Norma Brustein, Tom Hill, stine Estabrook in "Walk the Dog, Willie" Right: ugene Troobnick, Paul Schierhorn, Linda Lavin, Alvin Epstein in "Dynamite Tonite!" Below: Philip Kerr, Victor Garber, Stephen Rowe in "Don Juan"

## YALE REPERTORY THEATRE

New Haven, Connecticut
October 4, 1975–May 15, 1976

irector, Robert Brustein; Associate Director, Alvin Epstein; aging Director, Robert J. Orchard; Business Manager, Abigail on; Press, Jan Geidt; Designers, Michael H. Yeargan, Tony ges; Lighting, William B. Warfel; Production Supervisor, John ert Hood; Technical Directors, Bronislaw Sammler, George say; Stage Managers, Frank S. Torok, James F. Ingalls; Assis- Managing Directors, Mark Rosenthal, Michael Sheehan; Stage ctors, Alvin Epstein, Robert Brustein, Walt Jones, Ron Daniels, rence Kornfeld; Designers, Tony Straiges, Michael Yeargan, di Ettinger, David Lloyd Gropman, Ursula Belden; Costumes, k Brown, Tony Straiges, Suzanne Palmer, Michael Yeargan, ne Button, Annette Beck; Lighting, William Warfel, Stephen ody, Lewis Folden, Donald Bondy Lowy, Steve Pollock, Lloyd iford, III, Paul Gallo; Choreographer, Carmen de Lavallade; ductors, Gary Fagin, Paul Schierhorn

### COMPANY

da Atkinson, Richard Bey, James Brick, Norma Brustein, Rob- Brustein, Joseph Capone, Alma Cuervo, Andrew Davis, Carmen Lavallade, Randall Duk Kim, Alvin Epstein, Christine Esta- ok, Victor Garber, Jeremy Geidt, Anne Gerety, Joseph Grifasi, Hamilton, Laurie Heineman, Tom Hill, Philip Kerr, Linda in, Charles Levin, Jonathan Marks, John Neville-Andrews, Ste- D. Nowicki, Lynn Oliver, Peter Phillips, Barry Primus, Marcell enblatt, Stephen Rowe, Kenneth Ryan, Paul Schierhorn, Jeremy th, Eugene Troobnick, Paula Wagner, Frederick Warriner

### PRODUCTIONS

Midsummer Night's Dream" by William Shakespeare, "Don n" a version of Moliere's play by Kenneth Cavander, "Dynamite ite!" by Arnold Weinstein, William Bolcom, "Bingo: Scenes of ney and Death" by Edward Bond, "General Gorgeous" by Mi- el McClure and Paul Schierhorn, "Troilus and Cressida" by iam Shakespeare, and World Premiere of "Walk the Dog, Wil- by Robert Auletta, with music and sound by Carol Lees

*Eugene Cook, Bruce Siddons, Julie Haber Photos*

Anne Gerety, Jeremy Geidt, Alvin Epstein in "Bingo: Scenes of Money and Death"  227

# PULITZER PRIZE PRODUCTIONS

1918–Why Marry?, 1919– No award, 1920–Beyond the Horizon, 1921–Miss Lulu Bett, 1922–Anna Christie, 1923–Icebound, 1924–Hell-Bent fer Heaven, 1925–They Knew What They Wanted, 1926–Craig's Wife, 1927–In Abraham's Bosom, 1928–Strange Interlude, 1929–Street Scene, 1930–The Green Pastures, 1931–Alison's House, 1932–Of Thee I Sing, 1933–Both Your Houses, 1934–Men in White, 1935–The Old Maid, 1936–Idiot's Delight, 1937–You Can't Take It with You, 1938–Our Town, 1939–Abe Lincoln in Illinois, 1940–The Time of Your Life, 1941–There Shall Be No Night, 1942–No award, 1943–The Skin of Our Teeth, 1944–No award, 1945–Harvey, 1946–State of the Union, 1947–No award, 1948–A Streetcar Named Desire, 1949–Death of a Salesman, 1950–South Pacific, 1951–No award, 1952–The Shrike, 1953–Picnic, 1954–The Teahouse of the August Moon, 1955–Cat on a Hot Tin Roof, 1956–The Diary of Anne Frank, 1957–Long Day's Journey into Night, 1958–Look Homeward, Angel, 1959–J. B., 1960–Fiorello!, 1961–All the Way Home, 1962–How to Succeed in Business without Really Trying, 1963–No award, 1964–No award, 1965–The Subject Was Roses, 1966–No award, 1967–A Delicate Balance, 1968–No award, 1969–The Great White Hope, 1970–No Place to Be Somebody, 1971–The Effect of Gamma Rays on Man-in-the-Moon Marigolds, 1972–No award, 1973–That Championship Season, 1974–No award, 1975–Seascape, 1976–A Chorus Line

# NEW YORK DRAMA CRITICS CIRCLE AWARDS

1936–Winterset, 1937–High Tor, 1938–Of Mice and Men, Shadow and Substance, 1939–The White Steed, 1940–The Time of Your Life, 1941–Watch on the Rhine, The Corn is Green, 1942–Blithe Spirit, 1943–The Patriots, 1944–Jacobowsky and the Colonel, 1945–The Glass Menagerie, 1946–Carousel, 1947–All My Sons, No Exit, Brigadoon, 1948–A Streetcar Named Desire, The Winslow Boy, 1949–Death of a Salesman, The Madwoman of Chaillot, South Pacific, 1950–The Member of the Wedding, The Cocktail Party, The Consul, 1951–Darkness at Noon, The Lady's Not for Burning, Guys and Dolls, 1952–I Am a Camera, Venus Observed, Pal Joey, 1953–Picnic, The Love of Four Colonels, Wonderful Town, 1954–Teahouse of the August Moon, Ondine, The Golden Apple, 1955–Cat on a Hot Tin Roof, Witness for the Prosecution, The Saint of Bleecker Street, 1956–The Diary of Anne Frank, Tiger at the Gates, My Fair Lady, 1957–Long Day's Journey into Night, The Waltz of the Toreadors, The Most Happy Fella, 1958–Look Homeward Angel, Look Back in Anger, The Music Man, 1959–A Raisin in the Sun, The Visit, La Plume de Ma Tante, 1960–Toys in the Attic, Five Finger Exercise, Fiorello!, 1961–All the Way Home, A Taste of Honey, Carnival, 1962–Night of the Iguana, A Man for All Seasons, How to Succeed in Business without Really Trying, 1963–Who's Afraid of Virginia Woolf?, 1964–Luther, Hello, Dolly!, 1965–The Subject Was Roses, Fiddler on the Roof, 1966–The Persecution and Assassination of Marat as Performed by the Inmates of the Asylum of Charenton under the Direction of the Marquis de Sade, Man of La Mancha, 1967–The Homecoming, Cabaret, 1968–Rosencrantz and Guildenstern Are Dead, Your Own Thing, 1969–The Great White Hope, 1776, 1970–The Effect of Gamma Rays on Man-in-the-Moon Marigolds, Borstal Boy, Company, 1971–Home, Follies, The House of Blue Leaves, 1972–That Championship Season, Two Gentlemen of Verona, 1973–The Hot l Baltimore, The Changing Room, A Little Night Music, 1974–The Contractor, Short Eyes, Candide, 1975–Equus, The Taking of Miss Janie, A Chorus Line, 1976–Travesties, Streamers, Pacific Overtures

# AMERICAN THEATRE WING
# ANTOINETTE PERRY (TONY) AWARD PRODUCTIONS

1948–Mister Roberts, 1949–Death of a Salesman, Kiss Me, Kate, 1950–The Cocktail Party, South Pacific, 1951–The Rose Tattoo, Guys and Dolls, 1952–The Fourposter, The King and I, 1953–The Crucible, Wonderful Town, 1954–The Teahouse of the August Moon, Kismet, 1955–The Desperate Hours, The Pajama Game, 1956–The Diary of Anne Frank, Damn Yankees, 1957–Long Day's Journey into Night, My Fair Lady, 1958–Sunrise at Campobello, The Music Man, 1959–J. B., Redhead, 1960–The Miracle Worker, Fiorello! tied with Sound of Music, 1961–Becket, Bye Bye Birdie, 1962–A Man for All Seasons, How to Succeed in Business without Really Trying, 1963–Who's Afraid of Virginia Woolf?, A Funny Thing Happened on the Way to the Forum, 1964–Luther, Hello, Dolly!, 1965–The Subject Was Roses, Fiddler on the Roof, 1966–The Persecution and Assassination of Marat as Performed by the Inmates of the Asylum of Charenton under the Direction of the Marquis de Sade, Man of La Mancha, 1967–The Homecoming, Cabaret, 1968–Rosencrantz and Guildenstern Are Dead, Hallelujah, Baby!, 1969–The Great White Hope, 1776, 1970–Borstal Boy, Applause, 1971–Sleuth, Company, 1972–Sticks and Bones, Two Gentlemen of Verona, 1973–That Championship Season, A Little Night Music, 1974–The River Niger, Raisin, 1975–Equus, The Wiz, 1976–Travesties, A Chorus Line

# 1976 THEATRE WORLD AWARD WINNERS

**DANNY AIELLO**
of "Lamppost Reunion"

**CHRISTINE ANDREAS**
of "My Fair Lady"

**DIXIE CARTER**
of "Jesse and the Bandit Queen"

**CHIP GARNETT**
of "Bubbling Brown Sugar"

**TOVAH FELDSHUH**
of "Yentl"

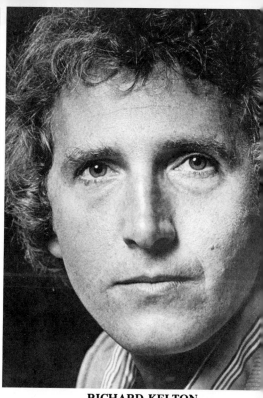

**RICHARD KELTON**
of "Who's Afraid of Virginia Woolf?"

**CHARLES REPOLE**
of "Very Good Eddie"

**VIVIAN REED**
of "Bubbling Brown Sugar"

**VIRGINIA SEIDEL**
of "Very Good Eddie"

**DANIEL SELTZER**
of "Knock Knock"

**JOHN V. SHEA**
of "Yentl"

**MERYL STREEP**
of "27 Wagons Full of Cotton"

**1976 THEATRE WORLD AWARDS PARTY, Thursday, May 27, 1976:** Top: Jerry Lanning, Maureen Anderman, Colleen Dewhurst, Ben Gazzara, Anthony Perkins, Julie Harris; Ian Richardson; John Cullum, Estelle Parsons, Christopher Walken, Catherine Burns, Gilbert Price Below: Dixie Carter, John Cullum; John, Jennifer and Rosemary Harris Ehle; Ben Gazzara; Richard Kelton, Colleen Dewhurst, Second row from bottom: Vivian Reed, Gilbert Price; Angela Lansbury (L); Anthony Perkins; Carole Schweid, Chuck Cissel, Donna Drake, Marvin Hamlisch, Kelly Bishop, Edward Kleban, Tharon Musser (front), Bottom Row: John V. Shea; Russ Thacker, Joel Grey, Charles Repole; Virginia Seidel; Chip Garnett, Estelle Parsons

Top: Danny Aiello, Rosemary Harris; Angela Lansbury; Julie Harris, Below: Meryl Streep; Daniel Seltzer; Maureen Anderman; Tovah Feldshuh, Anthony Perkins, Second row from bottom: D'Jamin Bartlett (L), Paul Rudd (C); Tovah Feldshuh; Meryl Streep (L), William Atherton (R); Bottom: Stewart Klein, Vivian Reed; Jerry Lanning; Christine Andreas; Christopher Walken, Catherine Burns

*Howard Gray, Ron Reagan, Van Williams Photos*

**Marlon Brando**  **Julie Andrews**  **Robert Redford**  **Julie Harris**  **George C. Scott**

# PREVIOUS THEATRE WORLD AWARD WINNERS

**1944–45:** Betty Comden, Richard Davis, Richard Hart, Judy Holliday, Charles Lang, Bambi Linn, John Lund, Donald Murphy, Nancy Noland, Margaret Phillips, John Raitt

**1945–46:** Barbara Bel Geddes, Marlon Brando, Bill Callahan, Wendell Corey, Paul Douglas, Mary James, Burt Lancaster, Patricia Marshall, Beatrice Pearson

**1946–47:** Keith Andes, Marion Bell, Peter Cookson, Ann Crowley, Ellen Hanley, John Jordan, George Keane, Dorothea MacFarland, James Mitchell, Patricia Neal, David Wayne

**1947–48:** Valerie Bettis, Edward Bryce, Whitfield Connor, Mark Dawson, June Lockhart, Estelle Loring, Peggy Maley, Ralph Meeker, Meg Mundy, Douglass Watson, James Whitmore, Patrice Wymore

**1948–49:** Tod Andrews, Doe Avedon, Jean Carson, Carol Channing, Richard Derr, Julie Harris, Mary McCarty, Allyn Ann McLerie, Cameron Mitchell, Gene Nelson, Byron Palmer, Bob Scheerer

**1949–50:** Nancy Andrews, Phil Arthur, Barbara Brady, Lydia Clarke, Priscilla Gillette, Don Hanmer, Marcia Henderson, Charlton Heston, Rick Jason, Grace Kelly, Charles Nolte, Roger Price

**1950–51:** Barbara Ashley, Isabel Bigley, Martin Brooks, Richard Burton, James Daly, Cloris Leachman, Russell Nype, Jack Palance, William Smothers, Maureen Stapleton, Marcia Van Dyke, Eli Wallach

**1951–52:** Tony Bavaar, Patricia Benoit, Peter Conlow, Virginia de Luce, Ronny Graham, Audrey Hepburn, Diana Herbert, Conrad Janis, Dick Kallman, Charles Proctor, Eric Sinclair, Kim Stanley, Marian Winters, Helen Wood

**1952–53:** Edie Adams, Rosemary Harris, Eileen Heckart, Peter Kelley, John Kerr, Richard Kiley, Gloria Marlowe, Penelope Munday, Paul Newman, Sheree North, Geraldine Page, John Stewart, Ray Stricklyn, Gwen Verdon

**1953–54:** Orson Bean, Harry Belafonte, James Dean, Joan Diener, Ben Gazzara, Carol Haney, Jonathan Lucas, Kay Medford, Scott Merrill, Elizabeth Montgomery, Leo Penn, Eva Marie Saint

**1954–55:** Julie Andrews, Jacqueline Brookes, Shirl Conway, Barbara Cook, David Daniels, Mary Fickett, Page Johnson, Loretta Leversee, Jack Lord, Dennis Patrick, Anthony Perkins, Christopher Plummer

**1955–56:** Diane Cilento, Dick Davalos, Anthony Franciosa, Andy Griffith, Laurence Harvey, David Hedison, Earle Hyman, Susan Johnson, John Michael King, Jayne Mansfield, Sarah Marshall, Gaby Rodgers, Susan Strasberg, Fritz Weaver

**1956–57:** Peggy Cass, Sydney Chaplin, Sylvia Daneel, Bradford Dillman, Peter Donat, George Grizzard, Carol Lynley, Peter Palmer, Jason Robards, Cliff Robertson, Pippa Scott, Inga Swenson

**1957–58:** Anne Bancroft, Warren Berlinger, Colleen Dewhurst, Richard Easton, Tim Everett, Eddie Hodges, Joan Hovis, Carol Lawrence, Jacqueline McKeever, Wynne Miller, Robert Morse, George C. Scott

**1958–59:** Lou Antonio, Ina Balin, Richard Cross, Tammy Grimes, Larry Hagman, Dolores Hart, Roger Mollien, France Nuyen, Susan Oliver, Ben Piazza, Paul Roebling, William Shatner, Pat Suzuki, Rip Torn

**1959–60:** Warren Beatty, Eileen Brennan, Carol Burnett, Patty Duke, Jane Fonda, Anita Gillette, Elisa Loti, Donald Madden, George Maharis, John McMartin, Lauri Peters, Dick Van Dyke

**1960–61:** Joyce Bulifant, Dennis Cooney, Nancy Dussault, Robert Goulet, Joan Hackett, June Harding, Ron Husmann, James MacArthur, Bruce Yarnell

**1961–62:** Elizabeth Ashley, Keith Baxter, Peter Fonda, Don Galloway, Sean Garrison, Barbara Harris, James Earl Jones, Janet Margolin, Karen Morrow, Robert Redford, John Stride, Brenda Vaccaro

**1962–63:** Alan Arkin, Stuart Damon, Melinda Dillon, Robert Drivas, Bob Gentry, Dorothy Loudon, Brandon Maggart, Julienne Marie, Liza Minnelli, Estelle Parsons, Diana Sands, Swen Swenson

**1963–64:** Alan Alda, Gloria Bleezarde, Imelda De Martin, Claude Giraud, Ketty Lester, Barbara Loden, Lawrence Pressman, Gilbert Price, Philip Proctor, John Tracy, Jennifer West

**1964–65:** Carolyn Coates, Joyce Jillson, Linda Lavin, Luba Lisa, Michael O'Sullivan, Joanna Pettet, Beah Richards, Jaime Sanchez, Victor Spinetti, Nicolas Surovy, Robert Walker, Clarence Williams III

**1965–66:** Zoe Caldwell, David Carradine, John Cullum, John Davidson, Faye Dunaway, Gloria Foster, Robert Hooks, Jerry Lanning, Richard Mulligan, April Shawhan, Sandra Smith, Lesley Ann Warren

**1966–67:** Bonnie Bedelia, Richard Benjamin, Dustin Hoffman, Terry Kiser, Reva Rose, Robert Salvio, Sheila Smith, Connie Stevens, Pamela Tiffin, Leslie Uggams, Jon Voight, Christopher Walken

**1967–68:** Pamela Burrell, Sandy Duncan, Julie Gregg, Bernadette Peters, Alice Playten, Brenda Smiley, David Birney, Jordan Christopher, Jack Crowder, Stephen Joyce, Michael Rupert, Russ Thacker

**1968–69:** Jane Alexander, David Cryer, Ed Evanko, Blythe Danner, Ken Howard, Lauren Jones, Ron Leibman, Marian Mercer, Jill O'Hara, Ron O'Neal, Al Pacino, Marlene Warfield

**1969–70:** Susan Browning, Donny Burks, Catherine Burns, Len Cariou, Bonnie Franklin, David Holliday, Katharine Houghton, Melba Moore, David Rounds, Lewis J. Stadlen, Kristoffer Tabori, Fredricka Weber

**1970–71:** Clifton Davis, Michael Douglas, Julie Garfield, Martha Henry, James Naughton, Tricia O'Neil, Kipp Osborne, Roger Rathburn, Ayn Ruymen, Jennifer Salt, Joan Van Ark, Walter Willison

**1971–72:** Jonelle Allen, Maureen Anderman, William Atherton, Richard Backus, Adrienne Barbeau, Cara Duff-MacCormick, Robert Foxworth, Elaine Joyce, Jess Richards, Ben Vereen, Beatrice Winde, James Woods

**1972–73:** D'Jamin Bartlett, Patricia Elliott, James Farentino, Brian Farrell, Victor Garber, Kelly Garrett, Mari Gorman, Laurence Guittard, Trish Hawkins, Monte Markham, John Rubinstein, Jennifer Warren, Alexander H. Cohen (Special Award)

**1973–74:** Mark Baker, Maureen Brennan, Ralph Carter, Thom Christopher, John Driver, Conchata Ferrell, Ernestine Jackson, Michael Moriarty, Joe Morton, Ann Reinking, Janie Sell, Mary Woronov, Sammy Cahn (Special Award)

**1974–75:** Peter Burnell, Zan Charisse, Lola Falana, Peter Firth, Dorian Harewood, Joel Higgins, Marcia McClain, Linda Miller, Marti Rolph, John Sheridan, Scott Stevensen, Donna Theodore, Equity Library Theatre (Special Award)

Richard Aaron

Naola Adair

Lloyd Alann

Dru Alexandrine

Arthur Anderson

# BIOGRAPHIES OF THIS SEASON'S CAST

**AARON, JACK.** Born May 1, 1933 in NYC. Attended Hunter Col., Actors Workshop. OB in "Swim Low Little Goldfish," "Journey of the Fifth Horse," "The Nest," "One Flew Over the Cuckoo's Nest," "The Birds," "The Pornographer's Daughter," "Love Death Plays."

**AARON, RICHARD.** Born Apr. 27, 1946 in Brookline, MA. Graduate Suffolk U., Brandeis U. Debut OB 1972 in "The Lady's Not for Burning," followed by "One Cent Plain," Bdwy 1975 in "Candide."

**ABEL, WALTER.** Born June 6, 1898 in St. Paul, MN. Attended AADA. Made Bdwy debut in 1918 in "A Woman's Way," subsequently appearing in, among others, "Forbidden," "Back to Methuselah," "Square Peg," "As You Like It," "The Enemy," "Taming of the Shrew," "Hangman's House," "Beyond the Horizon," "Skidding," "The Seagull," "Mourning Becomes Electra," "When Ladies Meet," "Invitation to a Murder," "Merrily We Roll Along," "Wingless Victory," "Mermaids Singing," "Parlor Story," "Biggest Thief in Town," "Wisteria Trees," "The Long Watch," "Pleasure of His Company," "Night Life," "90 Day Mistress," "Saturday Sunday Monday," "Trelawny of the Wells."

**ABELS, GREGORY.** Born Nov. 6, 1941 in Jersey City, NJ. Studied with Stella Adler. Debut 1970 OB in "War of the Roses," followed by "Macbeth," "Phobus," "Oedipus at Colonus," "I Love Thee Freely," "Veil of Infamy," "The Moss."

**ABRAHAM, F. MURRAY.** Born Oct. 24, 1939 in Pittsburgh, Pa. Attended U. Tex. OB bow 1967 in "The Fantasticks," followed by "An Opening in the Trees," "Fourteenth Dictator," "Young Abe Lincoln," "Tonight in Living Color," "Adaptation," "Survival of St. Joan," "The Dog Ran Away," "Fables," "Richard III," "Little Murders," "Scuba Duba," "Where Has Tommy Flowers Gone?," "Miracle Play," "Blessing," Bdwy debut "The Man In The Glass Booth" (1968), followed by "6 Rms Riv Vu," "Bad Habits," "The Ritz," "Legend."

**ABRAMS, ALAN.** Born Mar. 16, 1950 in Boston, MA. Graduate Boston U. Bdwy debut 1975 in ELT's "Tenderloin."

**ABUBA, ERNEST.** Born Aug. 25, 1947 in Honolulu, HI. Attended Southwestern Col. Bdwy debut 1976 in "Pacific Overtures."

**ACKERMAN, LONI.** Born Apr. 10, 1949 in NYC. Attended New School. Bdwy debut 1968 in "George M!," followed by "Dames at Sea" (OB), "No, No, Nanette," "So Long 174th Street," "Magic Show."

**ACKROYD, DAVID.** Born May 30, 1940 in Orange, NJ. Graduate Bucknell, Yale. Bdwy debut 1971 in "Unlikely Heroes" followed by "Full Circle," "Hamlet" (LC).

**ADAIR, NAOLA.** Born in Chicago, IL. Graduate Whittier Col. and Portland State U. Debut 1975 OB in "Flux."

**ADAMS, MASON.** Born Feb. 26, 1919 in NYC. Graduate UWisc. Has appeared in "Get Away, Old Man," "Public Relations," "Career Angel," "Violet," "Shadow of My Enemy," "Tall Story," "Inquest," "Trial of the Catonsville 9," "Sign in Sidney Brustein's Window," "Meegan's Game" (OB), "Shortchanged Review" (LC).

**ADAMS, MOLLY.** Born in Portchester, NY. Graduate Smith College. Debut 1973 OB in "Older People," followed by "Hot l Baltimore."

**ADAMS, POLLY.** Born in Nashville, TN. Graduate Stanford U., Columbia U. Bdwy debut 1976 in "Zalmen, or the Madness of God."

**ADAMS, SHEILA K.** Born June 24, 1950 in Omaha, NE. Attended AADA. Bdwy debut 1973 in "A Little Night Music," followed by "Summer Brave."

**AGRESS, TED.** Born Apr. 20, 1945 in Brooklyn, NY. Attended Adelphi U. Bdwy debut 1965 in "Hello, Dolly!" followed by "Dear World," "Look Me Up" (OB), "Shenandoah."

**AIELLO, DANNY.** Born June 20, 1935 in NYC. Debut OB 1975 in "Wheelbarrow Closers," followed by "Lamppost Reunion" for which he received a Theatre World Award.

**ALANN, LLOYD.** Born Aug. 15, 1952 in The Bronx, NY. Attended Lehman Col. Bdwy debut 1975 in "Grease."

**ALDREDGE, TOM.** Born Feb. 28, 1928 in Dayton, O. Attended Dayton U., Goodman Theatre. Bdwy bow 1959 in "The Nervous Set," followed by "UTBU," "Slapstick Tragedy," "Everything in the Garden," "Indians," "Engagement Baby," "How the Other Half Loves," "Sticks and Bones," "Where's Charley?," "Leaf People," "Rex," OB in "The Tempest," "Between Two Thieves," "Henry V," "The Premise," "Love's Labour's Lost," "Troilus and Cressida," "Butter and Egg Man," "Ergo," "Boys In the Band," "Twelfth Night," "Colette," "Hamlet," "The Orphan," "King Lear," "Iceman Cometh."

**ALEXANDER, C. K.** Born May 4, 1920 in Cairo, Egypt. American U. graduate. Bdwy debut 1946 in "Hidden Horizon," followed by "The Happy Time," "Flight into Egypt," "Mr. Pickwick," "Can-Can," "Fanny," "The Matchmaker," "La Plume de Ma Tante," "Rhinoceros," "Carnival," "Tovarich," "Poor Bitos," "Ari," OB in "The Dragon," "Corruption in the Palace of Justice," "Justice Box," "Threepenny Opera."

**ALEXANDER, JANE.** Born Oct. 28, 1939 in Boston, MA. Attended Sarah Lawrence, UEdinburgh. Bdwy debut 1968 in "The Great White Hope" for which she received a Theatre World Award, followed by "6 Rms Riv Vu," "Find Your Way Home," "Hamlet" (LC), "The Heiress."

**ALEXANDER, TERRY.** Born Mar. 23, 1947 in Detroit, MI. Wayne State U. graduate. Bdwy debut 1971 in "No Place to Be Somebody" OB in "Rashomon," "Glass Menagerie," "Breakout," "Naomi Court," "Streamers."

**ALEXANDRINE, DRU.** Born Apr. 23, 1950 in Cheshire, Eng. Studied at Royal Ballet School. Bdwy debut 1973 in "Pajama Game," followed by "My Fair Lady" (1976).

**ALLEN, DEBORAH.** Born Jan. 16, 1950 in Houston, TX. Graduate Howard U. Debut OB 1972 in "Ti-Jean and His Brothers," Bdwy 1973 in "Raisin."

**ALLEN, GARY.** Born Sept. 4, 1942 in Camden, TN. Attended Memphis State U., Goodman Theatre. Bdwy debut 1975 OB in "Ice Age."

**ALLEN, SCOTT.** Born Aug. 29, 1948 in Morristown, NJ. Attended Union Col., Upsala Col., AMDA. Bdwy debut 1975 in "A Chorus Line."

**ALLINSON, MICHAEL.** Born in London; attended Lausanne U., RADA. Bdwy bow 1960 in "My Fair Lady," followed by "Hostile Witness," "Come Live with Me," "Coco," "Angel Street," OB in "Importance of Being Earnest," "Staircase."

**ALTMAN, JANE.** Born Sept. 7 in Philadelphia, Pa. Temple U. graduate. Debut OB in "Importance of Being Earnest," followed by "Taming of the Shrew," "Candida," "A Doll's House," "Magda," "The Three Musketeers," "And So to Bed."

**ANDERMAN, MAUREEN.** Born Oct. 26, 1946 in Detroit, MI. Graduate U. Mich. Bdwy debut 1970 in ASF's "Othello," followed by "Moonchildren" for which she received a Theatre World Award, "An Evening with Richard Nixon and. . . .," "The Last of Mrs. Lincoln," "Seascape," "Hamlet" (LC), "Who's Afraid of Virginia Woolf?"

**ANDERSON, ARTHUR.** Born Aug. 29, 1922 in Staten Island, NY. Attended AmThWing. Made Bdwy debut 1937 in "Julius Caesar," followed by "Shoemakers' Holiday," "1776," OB in "Winkelberg," "The Doctor's Dilemma," "Zoo Story," "American Dream," "Gallows Humor," "The Rivals," "Fantasticks."

**ANDREAS, CHRISTINE.** Born Oct. 1, 1951 in Camden, NJ. Bdwy debut 1975 in "Angel Street," followed by "My Fair Lady" for which she received a Theatre World Award.

**ANDRES, BARBARA.** Born Feb. 11, 1939 in NYC. Graduate of Catholic U. Bdwy debut 1969 in "Jimmy," followed by "The Boy Friend," "Rodgers and Hart," "Rex."

**ANTHONY, ROBERT.** Born May 10, 1941 in Newark, NJ. Attended Boston U., AADA. Off Bdwy in "Jerico-Jim Crow," "Bugs and Veronica," "Dirty Old Man," "Hamlet," "Othello," "Scuba Duba," "Salome," on Bdwy in "Man in the Glass Booth," "Butterflies Are Free," "Legend."

**ARBEIT, HERMAN.** Born Apr. 19, 1925 in Brooklyn, NY. Attended CCNY, HB Studio, Neighborhood Playhouse. Debut 1959 OB in "The Golem," followed by "Awake and Sing," "A Delicate Balance," "Yentl the Yeshiva Boy," Bdwy 1975 in "Yentl."

**ARGO, ALLISON.** Born Dec. 23, 1953 in Richmond, VA. Debut OB 1974 in "Neighbors," followed by Bdwy 1976 in "Lady from the Sea."

**ARLT, LEWIS.** Born Dec. 5, 1949 in Kingston, NY. Graduate Carnegie Tech. Bdwy debut 1975 in "Murder among Friends."

**ASHLEY, ELIZABETH.** Born Aug. 30, 1939 in Ocala, FL. Attended Neighborhood Playhouse. Bdwy debut 1959 in "The Highest Tree," followed by "Take Her, She's Mine" for which she received a Theatre World Award, "Barefoot in the Park," "Ring Round the Bathtub," "Cat on a Hot Tin Roof," "The Skin of Our Teeth," "Legend."

Armand Assante

Regina Baff

Roger Baron

K. T. Baumann

Michael Beirne

ASHLEY, MARY ELLEN. Born June 11, 1938 in Long Island City, NY. Queens College graduate. Bdwy debut 1943 in "The Innocent Voyage," followed by "Bobino," "By Appointment Only," "Annie Get Your Gun," "Yentl," OB in "Carousel," "Yentl the Yeshiva Boy," "Polly," "Panama Hattie" (ELT).

ASSANTE, ARMAND. Born Oct. 4, 1949 in NYC. Attended AADA. Debut OB 1971 in "Lake of the Woods," followed by "Yankees 3, Detroit O," "Rubbers," "Boccacio."

ATHERTON, WILLIAM. Born July 30, 1947 in New Haven, CT. Carnegie Tech graduate. Debut 1971 OB in "House of Blue Leaves," followed by "Basic Training of Pavlo Hummel," "Suggs" for which he received a Theatre World Award, "Rich and Famous," Bdwy 1972 in "The Sign in Sidney Brustein's Window."

ATTLES, JOSEPH. Born Apr. 7, 1903 in Charleston, SC. Attended Harlem Musical Conservatory. Bdwy bow in "Blackbirds of 1928," followed by "John Henry," "Porgy and Bess," "Kwamina," "Tambourines to Glory," "The Last of Mrs. Lincoln," "Bubbling Brown Sugar," OB in "Jerico-Jim Crow," "Cabin in the Sky," "Prodigal Son," "Day of Absence," "Cry of Players," "King Lear," "Duplex."

AUMONT, JEAN-PIERRE. Born Jan. 5, 1913 in Paris. Attended Ntl. Sch. of Dramatic Art. Bdwy debut 1942 in "Rose Burke," followed by "My Name Is Aquilon," "Heavenly Twins," "Second String," "Tovarich," "Camino Real" (LC), "Murderous Angels" (OB), "Days in the Trees."

AZITO, ANTONIO. Born July 18, 1948 in NYC. Attended Juilliard. Debut OB 1971 in "Red, White and Black," followed by "Players Project," "Secrets of the Citizens' Correction Committee," "Threepenny Opera."

BACIGALUPI, ROBERT. Born Oct. 21, 1949 in San Francisco, CA. Juilliard graduate. Debut 1975 in "The Robber Bridegroom," followed by "Edward II," "The Time of Your Life."

BACKUS, RICHARD. Born Mar. 28, 1945 in Goffstown, NH. Harvard graduate. Bdwy debut 1971 in "Butterflies Are Free," followed by "Promenade, All!" for which he received a Theatre Award, "Studs Edsel" (OB), "Ah Wilderness."

BAFF, REGINA. Born Mar. 31, 1949 in The Bronx, NY. Attended Western Reserve, Hunter Col. Debut 1969 OB in "The Brownstone Urge," followed by "Patrick Henry Lake Liquors," "The Cherry Orchard," Bdwy in "Story Theatre," "Metamorphosis," "Veronica's Room."

BAILEY, PEARL. Born Mar. 28, 1918 in Newport News, VA. Bdwy debut 1946 in "St. Louis Woman," followed by "Arms and the Girl," "House of Flowers," "Hello, Dolly!"

BAKER, LENNY. Born Jan. 17, 1945 in Boston, MA. Graduate Boston U. Debut OB 1969 in "Frank Gagliano's City Scene," followed by "The Year Boston Won the Pennant," "The Time of Your Life," "Summertree," "Early Morning," "Survival of Joan," "Gallery," "Barbary Shore," "Merry Wives of Windsor," "Pericles," "Secret Service," "Boy Meets Girl," Bdwy 1974 in "Freedom of the City."

BAKER, MARK. Born Oct. 2, 1946 in Cumberland, Md. Attended Wittenberg U., Carnegie-Mellon U., Neighborhood Playhouse, AADA. Debut 1971 OB in "Love Me, Love My Children," Bdwy bow 1972 in "Via Galactica," followed by "Candide" for which he received a Theatre World Award, "Habeas Corpus."

BAMFORD, GEORGE. Born Nov. 6, 1944 in Dundalk, MD. Attended Frostberg State Col., AADA, Peabody Cons. Debut OB 1973 in "Anna K," followed by 'The Kid," "Killer's Head," "Yanks 3, Detroit O," "Sweet Bird of Youth."

BARBOUR, ELEANOR. Born Jan. 23, 1945 in NYC. Graduate Hofstra U. Debut OB 1976 in "Follies."

BARON, JOANNE. Born Feb. 3, 1953 in New Haven, CT. Attended UConn, Neighborhood Playhouse. Appeared OB in "pops!," "Bah Humbug."

BARON ROGER. Born Nov. 22, 1946 in Chicago, IL. Graduate Northwestern U. Bdwy debut 1976 in "The Heiress."

BARRETT, BILL. Born Oct. 25, 1950 in Jersey City, NJ. Graduate Commonwealth U. Bdwy debut 1975 in "Summer Brave." OB in "The Fifth," "Brick and the Rose," "Absence of Heroes," "Touch," "Fool's Delight," "Leander Stillwell."

BARRETT, JOE. Born Nov. 30, 1950 in Webster, NY. Graduate URochester. Debut 1975 OB in "Boy Meets Boy."

BARROWS, DIANA. Born Jan. 23, 1967 in NYC. Bdwy debut 1975 in "Cat on a Hot Tin Roof," followed by "Panama Hattie" (ELT).

BARRY, ROBERT. Born Mar. 17, 1943 in Spring Valley, NY. Graduate Rockland Com. Col. Debut OB 1971 in "Stag Movie," followed by "The Drunkard," "Alligator Man," "Brass Butterfly," "So Long 174th Street."

BARTLETT, D'JAMIN. Born May 21 in NYC. Attended AADA. Bdwy debut 1973 in "A Little Night Music" for which she received a Theatre World Award, OB in "The Glorious Age," "Boccacio."

BARTON, DANIEL. Born Jan. 23, 1949 in Buffalo, NY. Attended Buffalo State, Albany State. Bdwy debut 1976 in "The Poison Tree."

BARTON, DONALD. Born May 2, 1928 in Eastland, TX. Attended UTex. Credits include "Design for a Stained Glass Window," "Paint Your Wagon," "Wonderful Town," "Goldilocks," "Much Ado about Nothing," "The Royal Family."

BATES, KATHY. Born June 28, 1948 in Memphis, TN. Graduate Southern Methodist U. Debut OB 1976 in "Vanities."

BATTISTA, LLOYD. Born May 14, 1937 in Cleveland, OH. Graduate Carnegie Tech. Bdwy debut 1966 in "Those That Play the Clowns," followed by "The Homecoming," OB in "The Flame and the Rose," "Murder in the Cathedral," "The Miser," "Gorky."

BAUER, BRUCE. Born July 5, 1944 in Santa Monica, CA. Attended Santa Monica Col. Bdwy bow 1975 in "The Ritz."

BAUMANN, K. T. (formerly Kathryn) Born Aug. 13, 1946 in The Bronx, NY. Attended Neighborhood Playhouse. Bdwy debut 1967 in "The Prime of Miss Jean Brodie," followed by "The Penny Wars," OB in "Lemon Sky," "Effect of Gamma Rays . . . ," "Trelawny of the Wells."

BAXLEY, BARBARA. Born Jan. 1, 1925 in Porterville, CA. Attended Pacific Col., Neighborhood Playhouse. Bdwy debut 1948 in "Private Lives," followed by "Out West of Eighth," "Peter Pan," "I Am a Camera," "Bus Stop," "Camino Real," "Frogs of Spring," "Oh, Men! Oh, Women!," "Flowering Peach," "Period of Adjustment," "She Loves Me," "Three Sisters," "Plaza Suite," "Me Jack, You Jill," OB in "Brecht on Brecht," "Measure for Measure," "To Be Young, Gifted and Black," "Oh, Pioneers."

BAYNE, RICHARD COOPER. Born Feb. 25, 1949 in Brooklyn, NY. Graduate NYU. Bdwy debut 1971 in "Hair," followed by "Seesaw," "Rachael Lily Rosenbloom," OB in "The Boy Friend," "Follies."

BEACH, GARY. Born Oct. 10, 1947 in Alexandria, VA. Graduate NC Sch. of Arts. Bdwy bow 1971 in "1776," followed by "Something's Afoot," OB in "Smile, Smile, Smile," "What's a Nice Country. . . . ," "Ionescopade."

BEARD, CHARLES. Born July 24, 1945 in Lake Charles, LA. Attended Butler U. NY debut 1968 in "West Side Story" (LC), followed by "Carnival" (CC), "Gantry," "So Long 174th Street," OB in "Dark of the Moon."

BECKHAM, WILLARD. Born Nov. 6, 1948 in Hominy, OK. Graduate Cleveland Inst. of Music. Debut OB 1972 in "Crazy Now," Bdwy 1974 in "Lorelei," followed by "Something's Afoot."

BEDFORD, BRIAN. Born Feb. 16, 1935 in Morley, Eng. Attended RADA. Bdwy bow 1960 in "Five Finger Exercise," followed by "Lord Pengo," "The Private Ear," "The Knack" (OB). "The Astrakhan Coat," "The Unknown Soldier and His Wife," "Seven Descents of Myrtle," "Jumpers," with APA in "Misanthrope," "Cocktail Party," and "Hamlet," "Private Lives," "School for Wives."

BEIRNE, MICHAEL. Born Apr. 23, 1943 in Endicott, NY. Graduate NYU, Harvard, Neighborhood Playhouse. Bdwy bow 1968 in "Hallelujah Baby," followed by "Cactus Flower," "The Ritz."

BELL, GLYNIS. Born July 30, 1947 in London. Attended Oakland U, AADA. Debut 1975 OB in "The Devils," followed by "The Time of Your Life," "The Robber Bridegroom," "Three Sisters."

BELL, JOAN. Born Feb. 1, 1935 in Bombay, Ind. Studied at Sylvia Bryan Stage Sch. Bdwy debut 1963 in "Something More," followed by "Applause," "Chicago."

BELLOMO, JOE. Born Apr. 12, 1938 in NYC. Attended Manhattan Sch. of Music. Bdwy bow 1960 in "New Girl in Town," followed by CC's "South Pacific" and "Guys and Dolls," OB in "Cindy," "Fantasticks."

BENJAMIN, RICHARD. Born May 22, 1938 in NYC. Graduate Northwestern U. Bdwy bow 1966 in "Star Spangled Girl" for which he received a Theatre World Award, followed by "Little Black Book," "Norman Conquests."

BENNETT, MEG. Born Oct. 4, 1948 in Los Angeles, CA. Graduate Northwestern U. Debut OB 1971 in "Godspell," Bdwy 1972 in "Grease."

BEREZIN, TANYA. Born Mar. 25, 1941 in Philadelphia, Pa. Attended Boston U. Debut OB 1967 in "The Sandcastle." Member of Circle Rep. Theatre Co. from 1969, and has appeared in "Three Sisters," "Great Nubula in Orion," "him," "Amazing Activity of Charlie Contrare," "Battle of Angels," "Mound Builders," "Serenading Louie."

| orothy Blackburn | Mark Blum | Verna Bloom | Edwin Bordo | Maureen Brennan |

**BERK, DAVID.** Born July 20, 1932 in NYC. Graduate Manhattan Sch. of Music. Debut OB 1958 in "Eloise," followed by "Carnival" (CC), "So Long 174th Street."

**BERRY, ERIC.** Born Jan. 9, 1913 in London. Graduate RADA. NY debut 1954 in "The Boy Friend," followed by "Family Reunion," "The Power and the Glory," "Beaux Stratagem," "Broken Jug," "Pictures in the Hallway," "Peer Gynt," "Great God Brown," "Henry IV," "The White House," "White Devil," "Charley's Aunt," "The Homecoming" (OB), "Capt. Brassbound's Conversion," "Pippin."

**BERTRAND, JACQUELINE.** Born June 1, 1937 in Quebec City, Can. Attended Neighborhood Playhouse, LAMDA. Debut OB 1957 in "Madwoman of Chaillot," followed by "Geranium Hat," "Rhuy Blas," "Command Performance," "The Elizabethans," "Tovarich," "Dancing for the Kaiser."

**BILLINGTON, LEE.** Born July 15, 1932 in Madison, WI. Attended UWisc. Bdwy debut 1969 in "But Seriously," OB in "Dance of Death," "3 by O'Neill," "Our Town," "Capt. Brassbound's Conversion," "Henry VIII," "Boy with a Cart," "Epicoene," "The Homecoming."

**BISHOP, KELLY** (formerly Carole) Born Feb. 28, 1944 in Colorado Springs, CO. Bdwy debut 1967 in "Golden Rainbow," followed by "Promises, Promises," "On the Town," "Rachel Lily Rosenbloom," "A Chorus Line."

**BITTNER, JACK.** Born in Omaha, NE. Graduate UNeb. Has appeared OB in "Nathan the Wise," "Land of Fame," "Beggar's Holiday," "Rip Van Winkle," "Dear Oscar," "What Every Woman Knows," "By Bernstein."

**BLACKBURN, DOROTHY.** Born in Buffalo, NY. Bdwy debut 1924 in "New Brooms," followed by "Sweet Land of Liberty," "Pick-up Girl," "Desk Set," "Auntie Mame," "Desert Incident," "Passage to India," "Loves of Cass McGuire," "Harvey," "The Heiress," OB in "Nigh Named Today," "The Father."

**BLAIR, PAMELA.** Born Dec. 5, 1949 in Arlington, VT. Attended Ntl. Acad. of Ballet. Made Bdwy debut in 1972 in "Promises, Promises," followed by "Sugar," "Seesaw," "Of Mice and Men," "Wild and Wonderful," "A Chorus Line," OB in "Ballad of Boris K."

**BLAISDELL, BRAD.** Born Mar. 15, 1949 in Baltimore, MD. NY debut OB 1975 in ELT's "Tenderloin."

**BLAKE, SYDNEY.** Born Feb. 4, 1951 in Rome, Italy. Graduate Smith Col. Debut OB 1971 in "One Flew over the Cuckoo's Nest," followed by "El Grande de Coca Cola," "Fashion," "So Long 174th Street."

**BLOCK, LARRY.** Born Oct. 30, 1942 in NYC. Graduate URI. Bdwy bow 1966 in "Hail Scrawdyke," followed by "La Turista," OB in "Eh?," "Fingernails Blue as Flowers," "Comedy of Errors" (CP).

**BLOOM, VERNA.** Born Aug. 7 in Lynn, MA. Graduate Boston U. Bdwy debut 1967 in "Marat/Sade," followed by OB "Kool Aid," "The Cherry Orchard."

**BLUM, MARK.** Born May 14, 1950 in Newark, NJ. Graduate UPa., UMinn. Debut 1976 OB in "The Cherry Orchard."

**BOBBIE, WALTER.** Born Nov. 18, 1945 in Scranton, Pa. Graduate UScranton, Catholic U. Bdwy bow 1971 in "Frank Merriwell," followed by "Grass Harp," "Grease," "Drat!" (OB), "Tricks."

**BOGERT, WILLIAM.** Born Jan. 25, 1936 in NYC. Yale graduate. Bdwy in "Man for All Seasons," "Hamlet," "Star Spangled Girl," "Cactus Flower," "Sudden and Accidental Re-education of Horse Johnson," OB in "Country Wife," "Taming of the Shrew," "Henry V," "Love's Labour's Lost," "A Gun Play," "The Real Inspector Hound," "Conflict of Interest," "Killdeer," "Rubbers," "Yankees 3 . . ."

**BOND, SUDIE.** Born July 13, 1928 in Louisville, KY. Attended Rollins Col. OB in "Summer and Smoke," "Tovarich," "American Dream," "Sandbox," "Endgame," "Theatre of the Absurd," "Home Movies," "Softly and Consider the Nearness," "Memorandum," "Local Stigmatic," "Billy," "New York! New York!," "The Cherry Orchard," Bdwy in "Waltz of the Toreadors," "Auntie Mame," "The Egg," "Harold," "My Mother, My Father and Me," "The Impossible Years," "Keep It in the Family," "Quotations from Chrmn. Mao Tse-Tung," "American Dream," "Forty Carats," "Hay Fever," "Grease."

**BONDS, ROBERT.** Born Feb. 27, 1933 in Pasadena, CA. Attended LACC. Debut 1975 OB in ELT's "Another Language."

**BOOCKVOR, STEVE.** Born Nov. 18, 1942 in NYC. Attended Queens Col., Juilliard. Bdwy debut 1966 in "Anya," followed by "A Time for Singing," "Cabaret," "Mardi Gras," "Jimmy," "Billy," "The Rothschilds," "Follies," "Over Here," "The Lieutenant," "Musical Jubilee."

**BORDO, ED.** Born Mar. 3, 1931 in Cleveland, OH. Graduate Allegheny Col., LAMDA. Bdwy bow 1964 in "The Last Analysis," followed by "Inquest," "Zalmen or the Madness of God," OB in "The Dragon," "Waiting for Godot," "Saved."

**BORRELLI, JIM.** Born Apr. 10, 1948 in Lawrence, MA. Graduate Boston Col. NY Debut OB 1971 in "Subject to Fits," followed by "Grease."

**BOSCO, PHILIP.** Born Sept. 26, 1930 in Jersey City, NJ. Graduate Catholic U. Credits: "Auntie Mame," "Rape of the Belt," "Ticket of Leave Man" (OB), "Donnybrook," "Man for All Seasons," "Mrs. Warren's Profession," with LCRep in "The Alchemist," "East Wind," "Galileo," "St. Joan," "Tiger at the Gate," "Cyrano," "King Lear," "A Great Career," "In the Matter of J. Robert Oppenheimer," "The Miser," "The Time of Your Life," "Camino Real," "Operation Sidewinder," "Amphitryon," "Enemy of the People," "Playboy of the Western World," "Good Woman of Setzuan," "Antigone," "Mary Stuart," "Narrow Road to the Deep North," "The Crucible," "Twelfth Night," "Enemies," "Plough and the Stars," "Merchant of Venice," and "A Streetcar Named Desire."

**BOSTWICK, BARRY.** Born Feb. 24, 1945 in San Mateo, CA. Graduate Cal-Western, NYU. Bdwy debut with APA in "War and Peace," followed by "Pantagleize," "Misanthrope," "Cock-a-Doodle Dandy," "Hamlet," "Grease," OB in "Salvation," "Colette," "Soon," "Screens," "They Knew What They Wanted."

**BOTT, JOHN.** Born Mar. 28, 1923 in Douglas, Isle of Man. Bdwy debut 1974 in "Sherlock Holmes," followed by "Travesties."

**BOUTSIKARIS, DENNIS.** Born Dec. 21, 1952 in Newark, NJ. Graduate Hampshire Col. Debut 1975 OB in ELT's "Another Language."

**BOWEN, BOBBY.** Born Apr. 8, 1949 in New Haven, CT. Graduate R.I. Sch. of Design. Debut in 1975 OB in "Boy Meets Boy."

**BOYER, TRICIA.** Born Apr. 14, 1953 in Hagerstown, MD. Attended Mary Baldwin Col., AADA. Debut 1976 OB in "The Shortchanged Review."

**BRAHA, HERBERT.** (formerly Herb Simon) Born Sept. 18, 1946 in Hyannis, MA. Attended Carnegie Tech. Debut 1971 OB in "Godspell," followed by "The Shortchanged Review."

**BREMSETH, LLOYD.** Born July 27, 1948 in Minneapolis, MN. Attended UMinn. Debut OB 1968 in "Kiss Rock," followed by "Klara," "Sweet Shoppe Myriam," "Kiss Now," "Godspell."

**BRENNAN, MAUREEN.** Born Oct. 11, 1952 in Washington, DC. Attended UCincinnati. Bdwy debut 1974 in "Candide" for which she received a Theatre World Award.

**BROCHU, JAMES.** Born Aug. 16, 1946 in NYC. Graduate St. Francis Col, AADA. Debut OB 1968 in "Endecott and the Red Cross," followed by "Taming of the Shrew," "Unfair to Goliath," "Skye," "To Be or Not To Be," "Greenwillow," "Berkeley Square."

**BROCKSMITH, ROY.** Born Sept. 15, 1945 in Quincy, IL. Debut OB 1971 in "Whip Lady," followed by "The Workout," "Beggar's Opera," "Polly," "Threepenny Opera," Bdwy 1975 in "The Leaf People."

**BROOKES, JACQUELINE.** Born July 24, 1930 in Montclair, NJ. Graduate UIowa, RADA. Bdwy debut in 1955 in "Tiger at the Gates," followed by "Watercolor," "Abelard and Heloise," OB in "The Cretan Woman" for which she received a Theatre World Award, "The Clandestine Marriage," "Measure for Measure," "Duchess of Malfi," "Ivanov," "Six Characters in Search of an Author," "An Evening's Frost," "Come Slowly, Eden," "The Increased Difficulty of Concentration" (LC), "The Persians," "Sunday Dinner," "House of Blue Leaves," "A Meeting by the River," "Owners," "Hallelujah," "Dream of a Blacklisted Actor," "Knuckle."

**BROTHERSON, ERIC.** Born May 10, 1911 in Chicago, IL. Attended UWisc. Bdwy debut 1937 in "Between the Devil," followed by "Set to Music," "Lady in the Dark," "My Dear Public," "Gentlemen Prefer Blondes," "Room Service," "The Hot Corner," "Musical Jubilee," "My Fair Lady."

**BROWN, CANDY A.** Born Aug. 19 in San Rafael, CA. Attended MacAlester Col. Bdwy debut 1969 in "Hello, Dolly," followed by "Purlie," "Pippin," "Chicago."

**BROWN, CHRISTOPHER J.** Born in Port Chester, NY. Emerson Col. and Yale graduate. Bdwy debut 1975 in "The Ritz."

**BROWN, DANIEL.** Born June 9, 1947 in Little Rock, AR. Graduate LSU. Debut 1972 OB in "Absolutely Time!," followed by "Secret Life of Walter Mitty," "Be Kind to People Week," Bdwy 1976 in "Home Sweet Homer."

**Shirley Brown**  **Terence Burk**  **Pamela Burrell**  **Miles Chapin**  **Mary Carter**

BROWN, GRAHAM. Born Oct. 24, 1924 in NYC. Graduate Howard U. OB in "Widower's Houses," "The Emperor's Clothes," "Time of Storm," "Major Barbara," "Land Beyond the River," "The Blacks," "Firebugs," "God Is a (Guess What?)," "An Evening of One Acts," "Man Better Man," "Behold! Cometh the Vanderkellans," "Ride a Black Horse," "Great MacDaddy," "Eden," on Bdwy in "Weekend," "Man in the Glass Booth," "The River Niger," "Pericles," "Black Picture Show" (LC).

BROWN, GWENDOLYN. (formerly Gwen Saska) Born Sept. 9, 1939 in Mishawaka, IN. Northwestern and Columbia graduate. Debut 1969 OB in "Geese," followed by "Macbeth," "In the Boom Boom Room," "Secret Service," "Boy Meets Girl."

BROWN, SHIRLEY. Born Oct. 5, 1953 in Cincinnati, OH. Attended UCinn. Debut 1976 OB in "Eden."

BROWN, WALTER P. Born Apr. 18, 1926 in Newark, NJ. Attended Bklyn Cons of Music. Bdwy bow in "Porgy and Bess," followed by "Fiorello!," "The Advocate," CC's "Guys and Dolls" and "South Pacific," "Kelly," "Hello, Dolly," "Raisin."

BROWNE, HARRY. Born Aug. 21, 1952 in Flemington, NJ. Graduate Boston U. Debut 1975 OB in "Down by the River Where the Waterlilies are Disfigured," followed by "The Hot l Baltimore."

BROWNING, ROBERT. Born Apr. 30, 1942 in Syracuse, NY. Graduate Carnegie Tech, Purdue. Bdwy debut 1970 in "Candida," followed by OB's "Speed Gets the Poppys," "Panama Hattie" (ELT).

BROWNING, SUSAN. Born Feb. 25, 1941 in Baldwin, NY. Graduate Penn State. Bdwy bow 1963 in "Love and Kisses," followed by "Company" for which she received a Theatre World Award, "Shelter," "Goodtime Charley," OB in "Jo," "Dime A Dozen," "Seventeen," "Boys from Syracuse," "Collision Course," "Whiskey," "As You Like It," "Removalists."

BRUMMEL, DAVID. Born Nov. 1, 1942 in Brooklyn. Bdwy debut 1973 in "The Pajama Game," followed by "Cole Porter," "Fantasticks."

BRUNEAU, RALPH. Born Sept. 22, 1952 in Phoenix, AZ. Graduate UNotre Dame. Debut 1974 OB in "The Fantasticks."

BRUNO, JEAN. Born Dec. 7, 1926 in Bklyn. Attended Hofstra Col., Feagin School. Bdwy debut 1960 in "Beg, Borrow or Steal," followed by "Midgie Purvis," "Music Man," "Family Affair," "Minnie's Boys," "The Lincoln Mask," "Lorelei," OB in "All That Fall," "Hector," "Hotel Paradiso," "Pidgeons in the Park," "Ergo," "Trelawny of the Wells," "Song for the First of May."

BRYAN, WAYNE. Born Aug. 13, 1947 in Compton, CA. Graduate UCal. Bdwy debut 1974 in "Good News," followed by "Rodgers and Hart."

BRYDON, W. B. Born Sept. 20, 1933 in Newcastle, Eng. NY debut 1962 in "The Long, the Short and the Tall," followed by "Live Like Pigs," "Sgt. Musgrave's Dance," "The Kitchen," "Come Slowly Eden," "The Unknown Soldier and His Wife," "Moon for the Misbegotten," "The Orphan," "Possession," Bdwy in "The Lincoln Mask," "Ulysses in Nighttown."

BRYNNER, YUL. Born June 15, 1915 in Sakhalin Island, Japan. Bdwy debut 1946 in "Lute Song," followed by "The King and I," "Home Sweet Homer."

BUCKLEY, BETTY. Born July 3, 1947 in Big Spring, TX. Graduate TCU. Bdwy debut 1969 in "1776," followed by "Pippin," OB in "Ballad of Johnny Pot," "What's a Nice Country Like You Doing in a State Like This?," "Circle of Sound."

BURGE, JAMES. Born Dec. 3, 1943 in Miami, FL. Graduate U Okla., Wayne State U. Bdwy bow 1970 in "Grin and Bare It," followed by "The Royal Family."

BURK, TERENCE. Born Aug. 11, 1947 in Lebanon, IL. Graduate S.IL.U. OB in "Religion," "The Future," "Sacred and Profane Love," Bdwy debut 1976 in "Equus."

BURNELL, PETER. Born Apr. 29, 1950 in Johnstown, NY. OB in "Henry IV," "Antony and Cleopatra," "The Tempest," "Macbeth," "Olathe Response," "Ubu Roi/Ubu Bound," "Dancing for the Kaiser," Bdwy debut 1974 in "In Praise of Love" for which he received a Theatre World Award.

BURR, ROBERT. Born in Jersey City, NJ. Attended Colgate U. Has appeared in "Cradle Will Rock," "Mr. Roberts," "Romeo and Juliet," "Picnic," "The Lovers," "Anniversary Waltz," "Top Man," "Remains to Be Seen," "The Wall," "Andersonville Trial," "A Shot in the Dark," "A Man for All Seasons," "Luther," "Hamlet," "Bajour," "White Devil," "Royal Hunt of the Sun," "Dinner at 8," "King John," "Henry VI," "Love Suicide at Schofield Barracks," "Wild and Wonderful."

BURRELL, PAMELA. Born Aug. 4, 1945 in Tacoma, WA. Bdwy debut 1966 in "Funny Girl," followed by "Arms and the Man" (OB) for which she received a Theatre World Award, "Where's Charley?," "Berkeley Square" (OB), "The Boss" (BAM)

BURSTYN, ELLEN. Born Dec. 7, 1932 in Detroit, MI. Attended Actors Studio. Bdwy debut 1957 (then known as Ellen McRae) in "Fair Game," followed by "Same Time, Next Year."

BURTON, RICHARD. Born Nov. 10, 1925 in Pontrhydyfen, S. Wales. Attended Exeter Col., Oxford. Bdwy debut 1950 in "The Lady's Not for Burning" for which he received a Theatre World Award, followed by "Legend of Lovers," "Time Remembered," "Camelot," "Hamlet," "Equus."

BUTLER, RHODA. Born July 25, 1949 in Sanford, ME. Attended Centenary Col. Debut OB 1974 in "Fashion," Bdwy 1974 in "Candide," followed by "Goodtime Charley."

BYERS, CATHERINE. Born Oct. 7 in Sioux City, IA. Graduate UIowa, LAMDA. Bdwy debut 1971 in "The Philanthropist," followed by "Don't Call Back," "Equus," OB in "Petrified Forest," "All My Sons."

BYRDE, EDYE. Born Jan. 19, 1929 in NYC. Bdwy debut 1975 in "The Wiz."

CAHILL, JAMES. Born May 31, 1940 in Brooklyn. Bdwy debut 1967 in "Marat/deSade," OB in "The Hostage," "The Alchemist," "Johnny Johnson," "Peer Gynt," "Timon of Athens," "An Evening for Merlin Finch," "The Disintegration of James Cherry," "Crimes of Passion," "Rain," "Screens," "Total Eclipse," "Entertaining Mr. Sloane," "Hamlet."

CALDWELL, ZOE. Born Sept. 14, 1933 in Melbourne, Aust. Attended Methodist Ladies Col. Bdwy debut 1965 in "The Devils," followed by "Slapstick Tragedy" for which she received a Theatre World Award, "The Prime of Miss Jean Brodie," "The Creation of the World and Other Business," OB in "Colette," "Dance of Death," "Long Day's Journey into Night."

CANNING, JAMES J. Born July 2, 1946 in Chicago, IL. Graduate DePaul U. Debut 1972 in "Grease."

CAPERS, VIRGINIA. Born Sept. 22, 1925 in Sumter, SC. Attended Juilliard. Bdwy debut 1973 in "Raisin."

CAPOZZOLI, GEANINE MICHELE. Born Nov. 8, 1966 in Pittsburg, PA. Bdwy debut 1975 in "The Leaf People."

CAPOZZOLI, RON. Born Feb. 8, 1947 in Pittsburgh, PA. Studied at Pittsburgh Playhouse, HB Studio. Debut 1974 OB in "Sgt. Pepper's Lonely Hearts Club Band," Bdwy 1975 in "The Leaf People."

CARLSON, HARRY. Born Oct. 20, 1926 in Ashland, PA. Graduate Penn State U. Debut 1960 OB in "Here Come the Clowns," followed by "Missouri Legend" (ELT), 1963 in "Luther."

CARPENTER, CARLETON. Born July 10, 1926 in Bennington, VT. Attended Northwestern U. Bdwy bow 1944 in "Bright Boy," followed by "Career Angel," "Three to Make Ready," "Magic Touch," "John Murray Anderson's Almanac," "Hotel Paradiso," "A Box of Watercolors," "Hello, Dolly!," OB in "A Stage Affair," "Boys in the Band," "Lyle," "Dylan," "Greatest Fairy Story Ever Told," "Good Old Fashioned Revue."

CARTER, DIXIE. Born May 25, 1939 in McLemoresville, TN. Graduate Memphis State U. Debut 1963 OB in "The Winter's Tale," followed by LC's "Carousel," "Merry Widow," "The King and I," "Sextet," "Jesse and the Bandit Queen" for which she received a Theatre World Award.

CARTER, MARY. Born Oct. 3, 1938 in Washington, DC. Attended Peabody Cons. Debut 1969 OB in "The Glorious Ruler," followed by "Why Hanna's Skirt Won't Stay Down," "Two by John Ford Noonan."

CASSIDY, JACK. Born Mar. 5, 1927 in Richmond Hills, NY. Bdwy debut 1943 in "Something for the Boys," followed by "Sadie Thompson," "Around the World," "Inside U.S.A.," "Small Wonder," "Music in My Heart," "Alive and Kicking," "Wish You Were Here," "Sandhog" (OB), "Shangri-La," "Beggar's Opera" (CC), "She Loves Me," "Fade Out-Fade In," "It's Superman!," "Maggie Flynn," "The Mundy Scheme," "Murder among Friends."

CELLARIO, MARIA. Born June 19, 1948 in Buenos Aires, Arg. Graduate Ithaca Col. Bdwy debut 1975 in "The Royal Family."

CHANNING, CAROL. Born Jan. 31, 1921 in Seattle, Wash. Attended Bennington Col. Bdwy debut 1941 in "No for an Answer," followed by "Let's Face It," "Proof through the Night," "Lend an Ear" for which she received a Theatre World Award, "Gentlemen Prefer Blondes," "Wonderful Town," "The Vamp," "Show Girl," "Hello Dolly!," "Four on a Garden," "Lorelei."

CHAPIN, MILES. Born Dec. 6, 1954 in NYC. Studied at HB Studio. Debut 1974 OB in "Joan of Lorraine," Bdwy 1975 in "Summer Brave."

| Roger Chapman | Zan Charisse | Rik Colitti | Deborah Combs | Jeff Conaway |

**CHAPMAN, ROGER.** Born Jan. 1, 1947 in Cheverly, MD. Graduate Rollins Col. Debut 1976 OB in "Who Killed Richard Cory?"

**CHARIN, ROBIN.** Born July 18 in New Jersey. Attended Boston U. Debut 1974 OB in "Let My People Come."

**CHARISSE, ZAN.** Born Nov. 14, 1951 in NYC. Debut 1971 OB in "Look Me Up," Bdwy bow 1974 in "Gypsy" for which she received a Theatre World Award.

**CHARLES, WALTER.** Born Apr. 4, 1945 in East Stroudsburg, PA. Graduate Boston U. Bdwy debut 1973 in "Grease," followed by "1600 Pennsylvania Avenue."

**CHINN, LORI.** Born in Seattle, WA. Bdwy debut 1970 in "Lovely Ladies, Kind Gentlemen," OB in "Coffins for Butterflies," "Hough in Blazes," "Peer Gynt," "King and I," "Children," "Secret Life of Walter Mitty," "Bayou Legend," "The Primary English Class."

**CHODER, JILL.** Born Dec. 14, 1948 in Pittsburg, PA. Attended NYU. Bdwy debut 1962 in "Bye Bye Birdie," followed by "Stop the World. . . .," "The Roar of the Greasepaint," OB in "Best Foot Forward," "Your Own Thing," "Boccaccio."

**CHRISTIAN, ROBERT.** Born Dec. 27, 1939 in Los Angeles. Attended UCLA. OB in "The Happening," "Hornblend," "Fortune and Men's Eyes," Boys in the Band," "Behold! Cometh the Vanderkellans," "Mary Stuart," "Narrow Road to the Deep North," "Twelfth Night," "The Past Is the Past," "Going through Changes," "Black Sunlight," "Terraces," "Blood Knot," Bdwy in "We Bombed in New Haven," "Does a Tiger Wear a Necktie?," "An Evening with Richard Nixon," "All God's Chillun."

**CHRISTMAS, DAVID.** Born May 2, 1942 in Pasadena, Ca. Attended Pasadena City Col., HB Studio. Bdwy debut 1970 in "Grin and Bare It," followed by "Very Good Eddie," OB in "Butter and Egg Man," "Dames at Sea," "Give My Regards to Broadway."

**CILENTO, WAYNE.** Born Aug. 25, 1949 in The Bronx, NY. Graduate State U. Brockport. Bdwy in "Irene," "Rachel Lily Rosenbloom," "Seesaw," "A Chorus Line."

**CINKO, PAULA.** Born Dec. 14, 1950. Debut 1972 OB in "A Quarter for the Ladies Room." Bdwy debut 1974 in "Good News," followed by "Candide."

**CIOFFI, CHARLES.** Born Oct. 31, 1935 in NYC. Graduate UMinn. OB in "A Cry of Players," "King Lear," "In the Matter of J. Robert Oppenheimer," "Antigone," "Whistle in the Dark," "Hamlet" (LC).

**CISSEL, CHUCK.** Born Oct. 3, 1948 in Tulsa, OK. Graduate UOkla. Bdwy debut 1971 in "Purlie," followed by "Lost in the Stars," "Via Galactica," "Don't Bother Me, I Can't Cope," "A Chorus Line."

**CLARK, JOSH.** Born Aug. 16, 1955 in Bethesda, MD. Attended NC Sch. of Arts. Debut 1976 in "The Old Glory."

**CLARKE, RICHARD.** Born Jan. 31, 1933 in Eng. Graduate UReading. With LCRep in "St. Joan," "Tiger at the Gates," "Cyrano de Bergerac," Bdwy debut 1970 in "Conduct Unbecoming," OB in "Old Glory."

**CLARKSON, JOHN.** Born Jan. 19, 1932 in London. Graduate Oxford U. NY debut OB 1971 in "Murderous Angels," followed by "An Evening with Ma Bell," "Staircase," Bdwy (1973) in "No Sex Please, We're British," "My Fair Lady."

**CLAY, LOUISE.** Born Mar. 3, 1938 in Lafayette, La. LSU graduate. Bdwy debut 1966 in "Marat/deSade," followed by "Mike Downstairs," OB in "Rondelay," "The Hot l Baltimore."

**CLOSE, GLENN.** Born Mar. 19, 1947 in Greenwich, CT. Graduate William & Mary Col. Bdwy debut 1974 with Phoenix Co. in "Love for Love," "Member of the Wedding," and "Rules of the Game," followed by "Rex."

**COATES, CAROLYN.** Born Apr. 29, 1930 in Oklahoma City, OK. Attended UCLA. OB in "The Innocents," "The Balcony," "Electra," "The Trojan Women" for which she received a Theatre World Award, "A Whitman Portrait," "Party on Greenwich Avenue," "Club Bedroom," "A Scent of Flowers," "Effect of Gamma Rays on Man-in-the-Moon Marigolds," LCRep's "Country Wife," "Condemned of Altona," "Caucasian Chalk Circle," and "Disintegration of James Cherry," Bdwy in "Death of Bessie Smith," "American Dream," "Fire!," "All Over."

**COFFIN, FREDERICK.** Born Jan. 16, 1943 in Detroit, MI. Graduate UMich. Debut 1971 OB in "Basic Training of Pavlo Hummel," followed by "Much Ado about Nothing," "King Lear," "As You Like It," "Boom Boom Room," "Merry Wives of Windsor," "Secret Service," "Boy Meets Girl," Bdwy bow 1975 in "We Interrupt This Program."

**COHEN, MARGERY.** Born June 24, 1947 in Chicago, IL. Attended UWisc, UChicago. Bdwy debut 1968 in "Fiddler on the Roof," followed by "Jacques Brel Is Alive. . . .," OB in "Berlin to Broadway," "By Bernstein."

**COLE, KAY.** Born Jan. 13, 1948 in Miami, Fl. Bdwy debut 1961 in "Bye Bye Birdie," followed by "Stop the World I Want to Get Off," "Roar of the Greaspaint . . .," "Hair," "Jesus Christ Superstar," "Words and Music," "Chorus Line," OB in "The Cradle Will Rock," "Two if by Sea," "Rainbow," "White Nights," "Sgt. Pepper's Lonely Hearts Club Band."

**COLITTI, RIK.** Born Feb. 1, 1934 in NYC. Graduate USCal. Deput OB 1961 in "Montserrat," followed by "One Flew over the Cuckoo's Nest," "Gandhi," "The Queen and the Rebels," "Threepenny Opera," Bdwy bow 1975 in "The Ritz."

**COLKER, JERRY.** Born Mar. 16, 1955 in Los Angeles, CA. Attended Harvard. Deput 1975 OB in "Tenderloin."

**COLLENS, GINA.** Born in Hollywood, CA. Attended UCLA, USCal. Bdwy deput 1966 in "The Rose Tattoo," followed by "Naomi" (OB).

**COLLINS, PAUL.** Born July 25, 1937 in London. Attended City and State Col. in Los Angeles. OB in "Say Nothing," "Cambridge Circus," "The Devils," Bdwy in "Royal Hunt of the Sun," OB in "A Minor Adjustment."

**COLLINS, STEPHEN.** Born Oct. 1, 1947 in Des Moines, IO. Graduate Amherst Col. Bdwy debut 1972 in "Moonchildren," followed by "No Sex Please, We're British," "The Ritz," OB in "Twelfth Night," "More Than You Deserve," "Macbeth" (LC), " Last Days of British Honduras."

**COLLINS, SUZANNE.** Born in San Francisco, CA. Graduate USan Francisco. Deput 1975 OB in "Trelawny of the Wells."

**COLODNER, JOEL.** Born May 1, 1946 in Brooklyn, NY. Graduate Cornell U, SMU. Bdwy debut 1973 with CC Acting Co. in "Three Sisters," "Beggar's Opera," "Measure for Measure," OB in "Do I Hear a Waltz?," "A Memory of Two Mondays," "They Knew What They Wanted."

**COLTON, CHEVI.** Born In NYC. Attended Hunter Col. OB in "Time of Storm," "Insect Comedy" (CC). "The Adding Machine," "O Marry Me," "Penny Change," "The Mad Show," "Jacques Brel Is Alive. . . .," "Bits and Pieces," "Spelling Bee," Bdwy in "Cabaret."

**COLUMBUS, TOBIE.** Born May 14, 1951 in Detroit, MI. Graduate Wayne State U. Debut OB 1974 in "Let My People Come."

**COLYER, AUSTIN.** Born Oct. 29, 1935 in Brooklyn, NY. Attended SMU. Has appeared in "Darwin's Theories," "Let It Ride," "Maggie Flynn," CC revivals of "Brigadoon," "Music Man," and "How to Succeed. . . .," "Jimmy," "Desert Song," OB in "Show Me Where the Good Times Are," "Maggie Flynn."

**COMBS, DAVID.** Born June 10, 1949 in Reno, NV. Graduate UNev., Wayne State U. Bdwy debut 1975 in "Equus."

**COMBS, DEBORAH.** Born July 2, 1951 in Tucson, AZ. Attended UOkla., AMDA. Deput 1974 OB in "The Boy Friend," followed by "Maggie Flynn" (ELT).

**CONAWAY, JEFF.** Born Oct. 5, 1950 in NYC. Attended NYU. Bdwy debut 1960 in "All the Way Home," followed by "Grease."

**CONNELLY, R. BRUCE.** Born Aug. 22, 1949 in Meriden, CT. Graduate S. Conn. State Col. Deput 1975 OB in "Godspell."

**CONNOLLEY, DENISE.** Born Nov. 19, 1951 in Brooklyn, NY. Attended HB Studio. Debut 1974 OB in "Let My People Come."

**CONWAY, KEVIN.** Born May 29, 1942 in NYC. Debut 1968 OB in "Muzeeka," followed by "Saved," "Plough and the Stars," "One Flew over the Cuckoo's Nest," "When You Comin' Back, Red Ryder?," "Long Day's Journey into Night," on Bdwy in "Indians," "Moonchildren," "Of Mice and Men."

**CONWELL, PATRICIA.** Born Aug. 17, 1951 in Mexico City, Mex. Graduate Incarnate Word Col. Deput 1974 OB in "Pericles" (NYSF), followed by Bdwy bow in "Love for Love" (1974), "The Cherry Orchard"(OB).

**COOLEY, DENNIS.** Born May 11, 1948 in Huntington Park, Ca. Attended Northwestern U Bdwy debut 1970 in "Hair," followed by "Jesus Christ Superstar," "Creation of the World and Other Business," "Where's Charley?", "Shenandoah"

**COONEY, DENNIS.** Born Sept. 19, 1938 in NYC. Attended Fordham U. OB in "Whisper to Me," "Every Other Girl" for which he received a Theatre World Award, "In a Summer House," LCR's "Tiger at the Gates," and "Cyrano de Bergerac," on Bdwy in "Ross," "Love and Kisses," "Lion in Winter," "The Last of Mrs. Lincoln," "Sherlock Holmes."

**COOTE, ROBERT.** Born Feb. 4, 1909 in London. Bdwy debut 1953 in "The Love of Four Colonels," followed by "Dear Charles," "My Fair Lady" (1956, 1976), "Jockey Club Stakes."

**Richard Council**    **Lindsay Crouse**    **Jack Davidson**    **Toni Darnay**    **Richard DeFabee**

**COPELAND, JOAN.** Born June 1, 1922 in NYC. Attended Bklyn Col., AADA. Debut 1945. OB in "Romeo and Juliet," followed by "Othello," "Conversation Piece," "Delightful Season," "End of Summer," Bdwy in "Sundown Beach," "Detective Story," "Not for Children," "Handful of Fire," "Something More," "The Price," "Two by Two," "Pal Joey."

**CORMAN, PAUL A.** Born Apr. 22, 1946 in Dallas, TX. Graduate Antioch Col., NYU. Debut 1976 in "Maggie Flynn."

**COSTER, NICOLAS.** Born Dec. 3, 1934 in London. Attended Neighborhood Playhouse. Bdwy bow 1960 in "Becket," followed by "90 Day Mistress," "But Seriously," "Twigs," OB in "Epitaph for George Dillon," "Shadow and Substance," "Thracian Horses," "O, Say Can You See," "Happy Birthday, Wanda June," "Naomi Court.," "Old Glory."

**COUNCIL, RICHARD.** Born Oct. 1, 1947 in Tampa, Fl Graduate UFla. Debut OB 1973 in "Merchant of Venice," followed by "Ghost Dance," "Look We've Come Through," "Arms and the Man.", Bdwy 1975 in "The Royal Family."

**COURT, GERALDINE.** Born July 28, 1942 in Binghamton, NY. Attended AADA. Debut 1968 OB in "Possibilities," followed by "Medea," "Lower Depths," "Midsummer."

**COWLES, MATTHEW.** Born Sept. 28, 1944 in NYC. Attended Neighborhood Playhouse. Bdwy bow 1966 in "Malcolm," "Sweet Bird of Youth," OB in "King John," "The Indian Wants the Bronx," "Triple Play," "Stop, You're Killing Me!," "The Time of Your Life," "Foursome," "Kid Champion."

**CRAIG, JOEL.** Born Apr. 26 in NYC. Attended Brandeis U. Bdwy debut 1961 in "Subways are for Sleeping," followed by "Nowhere to Go but Up," "Hello, Dolly!," "Follies," "Out of This World" (OB), "Cyrano," "Very Good Eddie."

**CROMWELL, J. T.** Born Mar. 4, 1935 in Ann Arbor, MI. Graduate UCinn. Bdwy bow 1965 in "Half a Sixpence," followed by "Jacques Brel Is Alive . . ." (OB), "1600 Pennsylvania Avenue."

**CRONIN, JANE.** Born Apr. 4, 1936 in Boston, MA. Attended Boston U. Bdwy debut 1965 in "Postmark Zero," OB in "Bald Soprano," "One Flew over the Cuckoo's Nest," "Hot 1 Baltimore."

**CROSSLEY, KAREN.** Born May 20 in Cleveland, OH. Attended Case Western Reserve. Bdwy debut 1975 in "Very Good Eddie."

**CROUSE, LINDSAY ANN.** Born May 12, 1948 in NYC. Graduate Radcliffe. Bdwy debut 1972 in "Much Ado about Nothing," followed OB by "The Foursome," "Fishing," "Long Day's Journey into Night."

**CROXTON, DARRYL.** Born Apr. 5, 1946 in Baltimore, MD. Attended AADA. Appeared OB in "Volpone," "Murder in the Cathedral," "The Taking of Miss Janie," "Volpone," "Old Glory," Bdwy debut 1969 in "Indians."

**CULLUM, JOHN.** Born Mar. 2, 1930 in Knoxville, TN. Graduate U. Tenn. Bdwy bow 1960 in "Camelot," followed by "Infidel Caesar," "The Rehearsal," "Hamlet," "On A Clear Day You Can See Forever" for which he received a Theatre World Award, "Man of LaMancha," "1776," "Vivat! Vivat Regina!," "Shenandoah," OB in "Three Hand Reel," "The Elizabethans," "Carousel," "In the Voodoo Parlor of Marie Leveau," "The King and I" (JB).

**CURRY, CHRISTOPHER.** Born Oct. 22, 1948, in Grand Rapids, MI. Graduate UMich. Debut 1974 OB in "When You Comin' Back, Red Ryder?" followed by "The Cherry Orchard," "Spelling Bee."

**CURTIS, ROBBI.** Born Sept. 4, 1943 in Boston, MA. Graduate Emmanuel Col. Debut 1976 OB in ELT's "Follies."

**CWIKOWSKI, BILL.** Born Aug. 4, 1945 in Newark, NJ. Graduate Monmouth and Smith Cols. Debut 1972 OB in "Charlie the Chicken," followed by "Summer Brave," "Desperate Hours," "Mandragola," "Two by John Ford Noonan."

**DAMON, CATHRYN.** Born Sept. 11 in Seattle, WA. Bdwy debut 1954 in "By the Beautiful Sea," followed by "The Vamp," "Shinbone Alley," "A Family Affair," "Foxy," "Flora, The Red Menace," "UTBU," "Come Summer," "Criss-Crossing," "A Place for Polly," "Last of the Red Hot Lovers," OB in "Boys from Syracuse," "Secret Life of Walter Mitty," "Show Me Where The Good Times Are," "Effect of Gamma Rays on Man-in-the-Moon Marigolds," "Siamese Connections," "Prodigal," "Down by the River . . .," "Sweet Bird of Youth."

**DANA, LEORA.** Born Apr. 1, 1923 in NYC. Attended Barnard Col., RADA. Bdwy debut 1947 in "Madwoman of Chaillot," followed by "Happy Time," "Point of No Return," "Sabrina Fair," "Best Man," "Beekman Place," "The Last of Mrs. Lincoln," "The Women," "Mourning Pictures," OB in "In the Summer House," "Wilder's Triple Bill," "Collision Course,""Bird of Dawning Singeth All Night Long," "Increased Difficulty of Concentration," "Place without Mornings," "Rebel Women."

**DANA, MILDRED.** Born Apr. 3 in Milford, MA. Attended AADA, NYU. Debut 1975 OB in "Another Language."

**DANGLER, ANITA.** Born Sept. 26 in NYC. Attended NYU. Bdwy debut 1956 in "Affair of Honor," followed by "The Hostage," APA's "Right You Are," "You Can't Take It with You" and "War and Peace," "Hamlet" (CP), "Cyrano," "Comedy of Errors" (CP), "Trelawny of the Wells."

**DANIELE, GRACIELA.** Born Dec. 8, 1939 in Buenos Aires. Bdwy debut 1964 in "What Makes Sammy Run?" followed by "Here's Where I Belong," "Promises, Promises," "Follies," "Chicago."

**DARNAY, TONI.** Born Aug. 11 in Chicago, IL. Attended Northwestern U. Debut 1942 OB in "Name Your Poison," followed by "When the Bough Breaks," "Nocturne in Daylight," "The Gold Watch," "Possibilities," Bdwy 1944 in "Sadie Thompson," followed by "Affair of Honor," "Life with Father" (CC), "The Women," "Molly," "The Heiress."

**DARZIN, DAINA.** Born Jan. 10, 1953 in Spokane, WA. Attended Carnegie-Mellon U. Debut OB 1974 in "Let My People Come."

**DAVIDSON, JACK.** Born July 17, 1936 in Worcester, MA. Graduate Boston U. Debut 1968 OB in "Moon for the Misbegotten," followed by "Battle of Angels," "Midsummer Night's Dream," "Hot 1 Baltimore," Bdwy 1972 in "Capt. Brassbound's Conversion."

**DAVIDSON, LORRAINE.** Born Oct. 11, 1945 in Boston, MA. Attended HB Studio. Debut OB 1974 in "Let My People Come."

**DAVIES, JOSEPH C.** Born June 29, 1928 in Chariton, IA. Attended Mich. State Col., Wayne U. Debut 1961 OB in "7 at Dawn," followed by "Jo," "Long Voyage Home," "Time of the Key," "Good Soldier Schweik," "Why Hanna's Skirt Won't Stay Down," "Ghandi," Bdwy debut 1975 in "The Skin of Our Teeth."

**DAVILA, DIANA.** Born Nov. 5, 1947 in NYC. Bdwy debut 1967 in "Song of the Grasshopper," followed by "The Prime of Miss Jean Brodie," "Two Gentlemen of Verona," "Home Sweet Homer," OB in "What the Butler Saw," "The Refrigerators," "People Are Living There," "Last Analysis," "The Seducers."

**DAWSON, CURT.** Born Dec. 5, 1941 in Kansas. RADA graduate. Debut OB 1968 in "Futz," followed by "Boys in the Band," "Not Now, Darling," "White Nights," "Enter a Free Man," Bdwy 1975 in "Absurd Person Singular."

**DEAN, JACQUE.** Born Jan. 21 in Washington, DC. Attended UMd., HB Studio. Debut 1961 OB in "Little Mary Sunshine," followed by "Gorky," "Mata Hari," Bdwy in "The Student Gypsy," "Lolita My Love," "Coco," "Dear World," "I'm Solomon," "Drat! The Cat!," "I Had a Ball."

**DEARINGER, KEVIN LANE.** Born Nov. 23, 1951 in Versailles, KY. Graduate UKy. Bdwy debut 1976 in "My Fair Lady."

**DE BEER, GERRIT.** Born June 17, 1935 in Amsterdam. Bdwy debut 1965 in "Pickwick," followed by "Illya Darling," "Zorba," "Pajama Game," "All Over Town."

**DEE, BLANCHE.** Born Jan. 18, 1936 in Wheeling, WV. Graduate Bklyn. Col. Debut 1967 OB in "Rimers of Eldritch," followed by "Tom Paine," "Sunset," "Yentl the Yeshiva Boy," Bdwy in "Grin and Bare It," "Yentl."

**DEE, RUBY.** Born Oct. 27, 1923 in Cleveland, OH. Graduate Hunter Col. Bdwy debut 1946 in "Jeb," followed by "Anna Lucasta," "Smile of the World," "Long Way Home," "Raisin in the Sun," "Purlie Victorious," OB in "World of Sholom Aleichem," "Boesman and Lena," "Wedding Band," "Hamlet."

**DEERING, MARTHA.** Born Mar. 6, 1949 in Worcester, MA. Graduate Carnegie-Mellon U. Bdwy debut 1972 in "Jesus Christ Superstar," followed by "Where's Charley?," OB in "Inner City," "Panama Hattie" (ELT).

**DeFABEES, RICHARD.** Born Apr. 4, 1947 in Englewood, NJ. Georgetown U. graduate. Debut 1973 OB in "Creeps," Bdwy 1975 in "The Skin of Our Teeth."

**DeFILIPPS, RICK.** Born Apr. 16, 1950 in Binghamton, NY. Attended AMDA. Debut 1976 OB in "Panama Hattie" (ELT).

**DEITCH, DAN.** Born Oct. 26, 1945 in San Francisco, CA. Graduate Princeton, Harvard, LAMDA. Bdwy debut 1972 in "Grease," OB in "Troilus and Cressida."

**DeKOVEN, ROGER.** Born Oct. 22, 1907 in Chicago, ILL. Attended UChicago, Northwestern, Columbia. Bdwy bow 1926 in "Juarez and Maximilian," followed by "Mystery Man," "Once in a Lifetime," "Counsellor-at-Law," "Murder in the Cathedral," "Eternal Road," "Brooklyn U.S.A.," "The Assassin," "Joan of Lorraine," "Abie's Irish Rose," "The Lark," "Hidden River," "Compulsion," "Miracle Worker," "Fighting Cock," OB in "Deadly Game," "Steal the Old Man's Bundle," "St. Joan," "Tiger at the Gates," "Walking to Waldheim," "Cyrano de Bergerac," "An Enemy of the People," "Ice Age."

| | | | | |
|---|---|---|---|---|
| **Kaylyn Dillehay** | **Ed Dixon** | **Jamie Donnelly** | **William Duell** | **Virginia Downing** |

**DELL, GABRIEL.** Born Oct. 7, 1930 in Barbadoes, BWI. On Bdwy in "Dead End," "Tickets, Please," "Ankles Aweigh," "Prisoner of Second Ave," CC's "Can-Can," "Wonderful Town," and "Oklahoma!," "Marathon '33," "Anyone Can Whistle," "Sign in Sidney Brustein's Window," "Luv," "Something Different," "Fun City," "Lamppost Renuion." OB in "Chocolates," "Adaptation," "Where Do We Go from Here?"

**DeMAIO, PETER.** Born in Hartford, Conn. Attended New School, Julliard. Debut OB 1961 in "Threepenny Opera," followed by "Secret Life of Walter Mitty," "Dark of the Moon," "Welcome to Black River," "Last Breeze of Summer," Bdwy in "Billy," "Indians," "The Changing Room."

**DEMAS, CAROLE.** Born May 16, 1940 in Bklyn. Attended UVt., NYU. OB in "Morning Sun," "The Fantasticsk," "How to Steal an Election," "Rondelay," Bdwy debut 1965 in "Race of Hairy Men," followed by "Grease."

**DEMPSEY, JEROME.** Born Mar. 1, 1929 in St. Paul, MN. Toledo U-graduate. Bdwy bow 1959 in "West Side Story," followed by "The Deputy," "Spoford," "Room Service," "Love Suicide at Schofield Barracks," OB in "Cry of Players," "Year Boston Won the Pennant," "The Crucible," "Justice Box," "Threlawny of the Wells," "The Old Glory."

**DENGEL, JAKE.** Born June 19, 1933 in Oshkosh, WI. Graduate Northwestern U. Debut OB in "The Fantasticks," followed by "Red Eye of Love," "Fortuna," "Abe Lincoln in Illinois," "Dr. Faustus," "An Evening with Garcia Lorca," "Shrinking Bride," APA's "Cock-a-Doodle Dandy" and "Hamlet," "Where Do We Go from Here?," "Woyzeck," Bdwy in "Royal Hunt of the Sun," "The Changing Room."

**DENNIS, RONALD.** Born Oct. 2, 1944 in Dayton. OH. Debut OB 1966 in "Show Boat," followed by "Of Thee I Sing," "Moon Walk," "Please Don't Cry," Bdwy 1975 in "A Chorus Line."

**DENNIS, SANDY.** Born Apr. 27, 1937 in Hastings, NE. Bdwy debut 1957 in "The Dark at the Top of the Stairs," followed by "Burning Bright" (OB), "Face of a Hero," "Complaisant Lover," "A Thousand Clowns" for which she received a Theatre World Award, "Any Wednesday," "Daphne in Cottage D," "How the Other Half Loves," "Let Me Hear You Smile," "Absurd Person Singular," "Same Time Next Year."

**de PIETRI, STEPHEN.** Born Apr. 5, 1952 in NYC. Graduate Tufts U. Debut OB 1974 in "Yentl the Yeshiva Boy," Bdwy 1975 in "Yentl."

**DeSHIELDS, ANDRE.** Born Jan. 12, 1946 in Baltimore, MD. Graduate U Wisc. Bdwy debut 1973 in "Warp," followed by "Rachel Lily Rosenbloom," "The Wiz," OB in $"2008½."

**DEWHURST, COLLEEN.** Born in Montreal, Can. Attended Downer Col., AADA. Bdwy debut 1952 in "Desire under the Elms," followed by "Tamburlaine the Great," "Country Wife," "Caligula," "All the Way Home," "Great Day in the Morning," "Ballad of the Sad Cafe," "More Stately Mansions," "All Over," "Mourning Becomes Electra," "Moon for the Misbegotten," "Who's Afraid of Virginia Woolf?," OB in "Taming of the Shrew," "The Eagle Has Two Heads," "Camille," "Macbeth," "Children of Darkness" for which she received Theatre World Award, "Antony and Cleopatra" (CP), "Hello and Goodbye," Good Woman of Setzuan" (LC), "Hamlet" (NYSF).

**DIENER, JOAN.** Born Feb. 24, 1934 in Cleveland, O. Attended Sarah Lawrence Col. Bdwy debut 1948 in "Small Wonder," followed by "Season in the Sun," "Kismet" for which she received a Theatre World Award, "Cry for Us All," "Man of La Mancha," "Home Sweet Homer."

**DILLEHAY, KAYLYN.** Born Dec. 1, 1954 in Oklahoma City, OK. Attended Tex. Christian U., OkCityU. Debut 1976 OB in ELT's "Follies"

**DILLON, DENNY.** Born May 18, 1951 in Cleveland, O. Graduate Syracuse U. Bdwy debut 1974 in "Gypsy," followed by "The Skin of Our Teeth."

**DIXON, DIANNE OYAMA.** Born Mar. 24, 1954 in Nashville, TN. Stephens Col. graduate. Debut 1975 OB in "The Taking of Miss Janie."

**DIXON, ED.** Born Sept. 2, 1948 in Oklahoma. Attended OklaU. Bdwy in "Student Prince," "No, No, Nanette," OB in "By Bernstein."

**DIXON, MacINTYRE.** Born Dec. 22, 1931 in Everett, MA. Graduate Emerson Col. OB in "Quare Fellow," "Plays for Bleecker St.," "Stewed Prunes," "Cat's Pajamas," "Three Sisters," " 3 X 3," "Second City," "Mad Show," "Meeow!," "Lotta," "Rubbers," Bdwy in "Xmas in Las Vegas," "Cop-Out," "Story Theatre," "Metamorphoses," "Twigs," "Over Here."

**DION, CARL.** Born Dec. 15, 1916 in Vitebsk, Russia. Attended Western Reserve U. Bdwy debut 1954 in "Anastasia," followed by "Romanoff and Juliet," "Dear Me, the Sky Is Falling," "The Relapse," "The Tenth Man," "Zalmen," OB in "Richard III," "Twelfth Night," "Winterset," "Arms and the Man." "Between Two Thieves," "He Who Gets Slapped," "Jacobosky and the Colo-

**DONNELLY, JAMIE.** Bdwy debut 1965 in "Flora the Red Menace," followed by "You're a Good Man, Charlie Brown," (OB), "George M!," "Rodgers and Hart," "Rocky Horror Show."

**DONOHUE, NANCY.** Born Nov. 2, 1938 in Orange, NJ. Graduate Conn. Col. Bdwy debut 1964 in "Never Too Late," followed by OB "Canadian Gothic," "Prometheus Bound," "Little Eyolf," "The Runner Stumbles."

**DOUGLASS, PI.** Born in Sharon, CT. Attended Boston Conserv. Bdwy debut 1969 in "Fig Leaves Are Falling," followed by "Hello, Dolly!," "Georgy," "Purlie," "Ari," "Jesus Christ Superstar," "Selling of the President," "The Wiz," OB in "Of Thee I Sing."

**DOWNING, DAVID.** Born July 21, 1943 in NYC. OB in "Days of Absence," "Happy Ending," "Song of the Lusitanian Bogey," "Ceremonies in Dark Old Men," "Man Better Man," "The Harangues," "Brotherhood," "Perry's Mission," "Rosalee Pritchett," "Dream on Monkey Mt.," "Ride a Black Horse," "Ballet behind the Bridge," "Please Don't Cry and Say No," "Richard III," Bdwy in "Raisin."

**DOWNING, VIRGINIA.** Born Mar. 7, in Washington, DC. Attended Bryn Mawr. OB in "Juno and the Paycock," "Man with the Golden Arm," "Palm Tree in a Rose Garden," "Play with a Tiger," "The Wives," "The Idiot," "Medea," "Mrs. Warren's Profession," "Mercy Street," "Thunder Rock," "Pygmalion," "The First Week in Bogota," "Rimers of Eldritch," Bdwy in "Father Malachy's Miracle," "Forward the Heart," "The Cradle Will Rock," "A Gift of Time," "We Have Always Lived in the Castle."

**DRAKE, ALFRED.** Born Oct. 7, 1914 in NYC. Graduate Brooklyn Col. Bdwy bow 1935 in "The Mikado," followed by "White Horse Inn," "Babes in Arms," "Two Bouquets," "One for the Money," "Two for the Show," "Straw Hat Revue," "Out of the Frying Pan," "As You Like It," "Yesterday's Magic," "Oklahoma!," "Sing Out, Sweet Land," "Beggar's Holiday," "The Cradle Will Rock," "Joy to the World," "Kiss Me, Kate," "The Liar," "The Gambler," "The King and I," "Kismet," "Kean," "Lorenzo," "Hamlet," "Those That Play the Clowns," "Song of the Grasshopper," "Gigi," "The Skin of Our Teeth."

**DRISCHELL, RALPH.** Born Nov. 26, 1927 in Baldwin, NY. Attended Carnegie Tech. OB in "Playboy of the Western World," "The Crucible," "The Balcony" "Time of Vengeance," "Barroom Monks," "Portrait of the Artist . . . ," "Abe Lincoln in Illinois," "The Caretaker," "A Slight Ache," "The Room," "Year Boston Won the Pennant," "Time of Your Life," "Camino Real," "Operation Sidewinder," "Beggar on Horseback," "Threepenny Opera," Bdwy in "Rhinoceros," "All in Good Time," "Rosencrantz and Guildenstern Are Dead," "The Visit," "Chemin de Fer," "Ah, Wildnerness."

**DRIVAS, ROBERT.** Born Nov. 20, in Chicago. Bdwy debut 1958 in "The Firstborn," followed by "One More River," "The Wall," "Lorenzo," "Irregular Verb to Love," "And Things That Go Bump in the Night," "The Ritz," OB in "Mrs. Dally Has a Lover" for which he received a Theatre World Award, "Sweet Eros," "Where Has Tommy Flowers Gone," "Breeze from the Gulf."

**DRUMMOND, ALICE.** Born May 21, 1929 in Pawtucket, RI. Attended Pembroke Col. OB in "Royal Gambit," "Go Show Me a Dragon," "Sweet of You to Say So," "Gallows Humor," "American Dream," "Giants' Dance," "Carpenters," "Charles Abbott & Son," "God Says There Is No Peter Ott," "Enter a Free Man," "Memory of Two Mondays," "Secret Service," "Boy Meets Girl," Bdwy debut 1963 in "Ballad of the Sad Cafe," followed by "Malcolm," "The Chinese," "Thieves," "Summer Brave."

**DUELL, WILLIAM.** Born Aug. 30, in Corinth, NY. Attended Ill. Wesleyan, Yale. OB in "Portrait of the Artist . . . ," "Barroom Monks," "Midsummer Night's Dream," "Henry IV," "Taming of the Shrew," "The Memorandum," "Threepenny Opera," Bdwy in "A Cook for Mr. General," "Ballad of the Sad Cafe," "Ilya, Darling," "1776."

**DUFF-MacCORMICK, CARA.** Born Dec. 12 in Woodstock, Can. Attended AADA. Debut 1969 OB in "Love Your Crooked Neighbor," followed by "The Wager," "Macbeth" (LC), "A Musical Merchant of Venice," Bdwy 1972 in "Moonchildren" for which she received a Theatre World Award, followed by "Out Cry."

**DUKES, DAVID.** Born June 6, 1945 in San Francisco, CA. Attended Mann College. Bdwy debut 1971 in "School for Wives," followed by "Don Juan," "The Play's the Thing," "The Visit," "Chemin de Fer," "Holiday," "Rules of the Game," "Love for Love," "Travesties," OB in "Rebel Women."

**James Dybas**

**Leslie Easterbrook**

**Brandt Edwards**

**Wendy Edmead**

**Gary Faga**

**DURNING, CHARLES.** Born Feb. 28, 1933 in Highland Falls, NY. Attended Columbia, NYU. Bdwy in "Poor Bitos," "Drat! The Cat!," "Pousse Cafe," "Happy Time," "Indians," "That Championship Season," "Knock Knock," OB in "Two by Saroyan," "Child Buyer," "Album of Gunther Grass," "Huui, Huui," "Invitation to a Beheading," "Lemon Sky," "Henry VI," "Happiness Cage," "Hamlet," "Boom Boom Room," "Au Pair Man."

**DURRELL, MICHAEL.** Born Oct. 6, 1939 in Brooklyn, NY. Attended Boston U. OB 1961 in "Worm in the Horseradish," "Butterfly Dream," "Phedre," "MacBird," "A Maid's Tragedy," APA's "Cherry Orchard," "Pantagleize," "Misanthrope," "Cock-a-Doodle Dandy," and "Hamlet," "Nuts," Bdwy 1973 in "Emperor Henry IV," "Murder among Friends."

**DUTTON, NANCY.** Born Aug. 12, 1952 in Long Island, NY. Boston U. graduate. Bdwy debut 1976 in "Zalmen, or the Madness of God."

**DVORSKY, PETER.** Born Aug. 27, 1948 in Komarno, Czech. Antioch Col. graduate. Debut OB 1972 in "School for Scandal," "Lower Depths," Bdwy in "Three Sisters" (1973), "Beggar's Opera," "Measure for Measure," "Edward II," "The Time of Your Life," "The Robber Bridegroom."

**DYBAS, JAMES.** Born Feb. 7, 1944 in Chicago, IL. Bdwy debut 1965 in "Do I Hear a Waltz?," followed by "George M!," "Via Galactica," "Pacific Overtures."

**EAMES, JOHN.** Born Oct. 8, 1924 in Hartford, CT. Graduate Carnegie-Mellon U. Debut 1959 OB in "Leave It to Jane," followed by "The Boss," Bdwy 1972 in "1776."

**EARLEY, CANDICE.** Born Aug. 18, 1950 in Ft. Hood, TX. Attended Trinity U. Bdwy debut 1971 in "Hair," followed by "Jesus Christ Superstar," "Grease."

**EASTERBROOK, LESLIE.** Born July 29, 1949 in Los Angeles, CA. Stephens Col. graduate. Bdwy debut 1976 in "California Suite."

**EASTON, EDWARD.** Born Oct. 21, 1942 in Moline , IL. Graduate Lincoln Col., UIll., Neighborhood Playhouse. Debut 1967 OB in "Party on Greenwich Avenue," followed by "Middle of the Night," "Summer Brave."

**EDE, GEORGE.** Born Dec. 22, 1931 in San Francisco, CA. Bdwy debut 1969 in "A Flea in Her Ear," followed by "Three Sisters," "The Changing Room," "The Visit," "Chermin de Fer," "Holiday," "Love for Love," "Rules of the Game," "Member of the Wedding," "Lady from the Sea."

**EDMEAD, WENDY.** Born July 6, 1956 in NYC. Graduate NYCU. Bdwy debut 1974 in "The Wiz."

**EDWARDS, BRANDT.** Born Mar. 22, 1947 in Holly Springs, MS. Graduate UMiss. NY debut 1975 off and on Bdwy in "A Chorus Line."

**EGAN, MICHAEL.** Born Aug. 24, 1926 in Washington, PA. Graduate Bucknell U. Bdwy debut 1956 in "The Great Sebastians," followed by "Luther," "A Cry of Players," "The Incomparable Max," "The Ritz," OB in "The Real Inspector Hound," "Drums in the Night," "Duck Variations." "American Buffalo."

**EHRLICH, JANICE.** Born Sept. 6, 1947 in Elizabeth, NJ. Graduate WVa. U., Neighborhood Playhouse. Debut 1975 OB in "Tenderloin."

**EINENKEL, ROBERT.** Born Feb. 23, 1944 in NYC. Graduate Queens Col., UMich., Yale. Debut OB 1970 in "AC/DC," followed by "Screens," "Kaspar," "Self-Accusation," "The Importance of Being Earnest," "Rimers of Eldritch," "Ice Age."

**ELLIOTT, PATRICIA.** Born July 21, 1942 in Gunnison, CO. Graduate U. Colo., London Academy. Debut with LCRep 1968 in "King Lear," and "A Cry of Players," followed OB in "Henry V," "The Persians," "A Doll's House," "Hedda Gabler," "In Case of Accident," "Water Hen," "Polly," "But Not for Me," "By Bernstein," Bdwy bow 1973 in "A Little Night Music" for which she received a Theatre World Award.

**ELLIS, ANTONIA.** Born Apr. 30, 1944 in Newport, Isle of Wight. Bdwy debut 1975 in "Pippin."

**ENEY, WOODY.** Born June 8, 1937 in Canberra, Aust. Attended RADA. Debut OB 1974 in "The Desperate Hours," followed by "Click."

**ENGSTROM, JON.** Born in Fresno, CA. Bdwy debut 1971 in "No, No, Nanette," "The Pajama Game," "Very Good Eddie."

**ENNIS, FLLOYD.** Born June 29, 1926 in Philadelphia, PA. Studied with Stella Adler. Debut 1961 OB in "The Octoroon," followed by "Kid Champion," "Sweet Bird of Youth."

**ENSERRO, MICHAEL.** Born Oct. 5, 1918 in Soldier, PA. Attended Allegheny Col., Pasadena Playhouse. Bdwy in "Me and Molly," "Passion of Josef D," "Song of the Grasshopper," "Mike Downstairs," "Camino Real," "Saturday Sunday Monday," OB in "Penny Change," "Fantasticks," "The Miracle," "The Kitchen," "Rome, Rome," "The Jar."

**ENTEN, BONI.** Born Feb. 20, 1947 in Baltimore, MD. Attended TCU. Bdwy debut 1965 in "Roar of the Greasepaint," followed by "Rocky Horror Show," "Pal Joey," OB in "You're a Good Man, Charlie Brown," "Oh! Calcutta!," "Salvation," "The Real Inspector Hound."

**EPSTEIN, PIERRE.** Born July 27, 1930 in Toulouse, France. Graduate UParis, Columbia. Bdwy bow 1962 in "A Shot in the Dark," followed by "Enter Laughing," "Bajour," "Black Comedy," "Thieves," "Fun City," OB in "Incident at Vichy," "Threepenny Opera," "Too Much Johnson," "Second City," "People vs. Ranchman," "Promenade," "Cakes with Wine," "Little Black Sheep," "Comedy of Errors," "A Memory of Two Mondays," "They Knew What They Wanted."

**ERIC, DAVID.** Born Feb. 28, 1949 in Boston, MA. Graduate Neighborhood Playhouse. Debut OB 1971 in "Ballad of Johnny Pot," followed by "Love Me, Love My Children," Bdwy in "Yentl" (1975), "Shenandoah."

**ESPEL, PAUL.** Born Aug. 17, 1947 in Clarksburg, WV. Graduate Villanova U., Neighborhood Playhouse. Bdwy debut 1975 in "The Ritz."

**ESTERMAN, LAURA.** Born Apr. 12, in NYC. Attended Radcliffe, London's AMDA. Debut 1969 OB in "The Time of Your Life" (LCR), followed by "Pig Pen," "The Carpenters," "Ghosts," "Waltz of the Toreadors," "MacBeth (LC)," "The Seagull," "Rubbers," "Yanks 3, Detroit O," "Golden Boy," Bdwy 1974 "God's Favorite."

**EVANKO, ED.** Born in Winnipeg, Can. Studied at Bristol Old Vic. Bldwy debut 1969 in "Canterbury Tales" for which he received a Theatre World Award, OB in "Love Me, Love My Children," "Leaves of Grass." "Rex."

**EVERHART, REX.** Born June 13, 1920 in Watseka, IL. Graduate UMo., NYU. Bdwy bow 1955 in "No Time for Sergeants," followed by "Tall Story," "Moonbirds," "Tenderloin," "Matter of Position," "Rainy Day in Newark," "Skyscraper," "How Now Dow Jones," "1776," "The Iceman Cometh," "Chicago."

**EVERSON, JOHN.** Born May 21, 1947 in Dawson, MN. Graduate UWisc. Bdwy debut 1974 in "Grease," followed by "The Ritz."

**FAGA, GARY.** Born Nov. 23, 1953 in Brooklyn, NY. Attended Bklyn Col. Debut OB 1975 in "Hustlers," followed by "Dance with Me," Bdwy 1976 in "Equus."

**FAIRBANK, SPRING.** Born Mar. 15, 1941 in Chicago, IL. Attended New Eng. Conserv. Debut 1968 in "My Fair Lady" (CC), followed by "Oh, Lady, Lady" (ELT), Bdwy 1975 in "Very Good Eddie."

**FANN, ALBERT.** Born Feb. 21, 1933 in Cleveland. OH. Attended Cleveland Inst. of Music. Debut 1970 OB in "King Heroin," Bdwy 1975 in "The Wiz."

**FARENTINO, JAMES.** Born Feb. 24, 1938 in Brooklyn, NY. Attended AADA. Bdwy debut 1961 in "Night of the Iguana," followed by "Death of a Salesman," OB in "Days and Nights of Beebee Fensternaker," "In the Summer House," LC's "Streetcar Named Desire," for which he received a Theatre World Award.

**FARR, KIMBERLY.** Born Oct. 16, 1948 in Chicago. UCLA graduate. Bdwy debute 1972 in "Mother Earth," followed by "The Lady from the Sea," OB in "More than You Deserve," "The S.S. Benchley," "At Sea with Benchley."

**FASO, LAURIE.** Born Apr. 11, 1946 in Buffalo, NY. Graduate Denison U., Carnegie Tech. Debut OB 1974 in "Godspell," followed by "The Glorious Age," "Comedy of Errors" (CP)

**FEARL, CLIFFORD.** Born in NYC. Graduate Columbia U. Bdwy debut 1950 in "Flahooley," followed by "Three Wishes for Jamie," "Two's Company," "Kismet," "Happy Hunting," "Oh, Captain," "Redhead," "Let It Ride," "110 in the Shade," "Ben Franklin in Paris," "Mame," "La Plume de Ma Tante," "Dear World," "Jimmy," "My Fair Lady."

**FELDER, CLARENCE.** Born Sept. 2, 1938 in St. Matthews, SC. Debut OB 1964 in "The Room," followed by "Are You Now or Have You Ever Been," Bdwy 1969 in "Red, White and Maddox," "Love for Love," "Rules of the Game," "Golden Boy," "A Memory of Two Mondays," "They Knew What They Wanted."

**FELDSHUH, TOVAH.** Born Dec. 27 in NYC. Graduate Sarah Lawrence Col. Bdwy debut 1973 in "Cyrano," followed by "Drefus in Rehearsal," "Rodgers and Hart," "Yentl" for which she received a Theatre World Award, OB in "Yentl the Yeshiva Boy," "Straws in the Wind."

**Conchata Ferrell**   **Jack Finnegan**   **Niki Flacks**   **Timm Fujii**   **Julie Garfield**

**FERNANDES, YUYE.** Born Nov. 9, 1948 in Wareham, MA. Graduate Smith Col. Debut OB 1970 in "Pig," followed by "Silver Queen," "La Gente," "Inner City," "Three Musketeers," Bdwy in "Scapino" (1974), "Skin of Our Teeth."

**FERRELL, CONCHATA.** Born Mar. 28, 1943 in Charleston, WV. Graduate Marshall U. Debut 1973 OB in "The Hot l Baltimore," "The Sea Horse" for which she received a Theatre World Award, "Battle of Angels," "Elephant in the House," "Wine Untouched."

**FIELDS, JUDY.** Born in Louisville, KY. Graduate Georgetown Col., Northwestern U. Debut 1973 OB in "Summer Brave," followed by "Love Death Plays."

**FINEMAN, VIVIAN.** Born June 23, 1951 in Philadelphia, PA. Debut OB 1973 in "Call Me Madam," followed by "Panama Hattie."

**FINKEL, FYVUSH.** Born Oct. 9, 1922 in Brooklyn, NY. Bdwy debut 1970 in "Fiddler on the Roof," OB in "Gorky."

**FINNEGAN, JACK.** Born Mar. 21, 1927 in NYC. Attended AADA AmTh-Wing. Debut 1961 OB in "Follies of 1910," followed by "Follies" (ELT).

**FIRTH, PETER.** Born Oct. 27, 1953 in Bradford, Eng. Bdwy debut 1974 in "Equus" for which he received a Theatre World Award.

**FITCH, ROBERT.** Born Apr. 29, 1934 in Santa Cruz, CA. Attended U Santa Clara. Bdwy debut 1961 in "Tenderloin," followed by "Do Re Mi," "My Fair Lady" (CC), "Girl Who Came to Supper," "Flora the Red Menace," "Baker Street," "Sherry," "Mack and Mabel," "Henry, Sweet Henry," "Mame," "Promises, Promises," "Coco," "Lorelei," OB in "Lend an Ear," "Half-Past Wednesday," "Anything Goes," "Crystal Heart," "Broadway Dandies," "One Cent Plain."

**FITZGERALD, GERALDINE.** Born Nov. 24, 1914 in Dublin, Ire. Bdwy debut 1938 in "Heartbreak House," followed by "Sons and Soldiers," "Doctor's Dilemma," "King Lear," "Hide and Seek," "Ah, Wilderness," OB in "Cave Dwellers," "Pigeons," "Long Day's Journey into Night," "Everyman and Roach."

**FITZPATRICK, LYNN.** Born in Philadelphia, PA. Graduate Ohio Dominican Col. Bdwy debut 1972 in "Ambassador," followed by "You Never Know" (OB), "My Fair Lady."

**FLACKS, NIKI.** Born Apr. 7, 1943 in Daytona Beach, Fl Attended Northwestern, UMinn. Bdwy debut 1966 in "Dinner at 8," followed by "Private Lives," "Candide."

**FLAGG, TOM.** Born Mar. 30, 1949 in Canton, OH. Attended Kent State U., AADA. Debut 1975 OB in "The Fantasticks," followed by "Give Me Liberty."

**FLANAGAN, NEIL.** Born May 3, 1934 in Springfield, IL. Debut 1966 OB in "Fortune and Men's Eyes," followed by "Haunted Host," "Madness of Lady Bright," "Dirtiest Show in Town," "The Play's the Thing," "As You Like It," "Hedda Gabler," "Design for Living," "him," "Partnership," "Down by the River . . . ," "Lisping Judas," "Elephant in the House," Bdwy in "Sheep on the Runway," "Secret Affairs of Mildred Wild," "Knock Knock."

**FLEISCHMAN, MARK.** Born Nov. 25, 1935 in Detroit, MI. Attended UMich Bdwy debut 1955 in "Tonight in Samarkand," followed by "A Distant Bell," "The Royal Family," "What Every Woman Knows," "Lute Song," "The Beautiful People," "Big Fish, Little Fish."

**FLIPPIN, LUCY LEE.** Born July 23, 1943 in Philadelphia, PA. Graduate Northwestern U. Debut OB 1970 in "The Playground," followed by "Shoestring Revue," "Rip Van Winkle," "Midsummer Night's Dream," "Rebirth and Celebration of the Human Race."

**FLYNN, MARYELLEN.** Born Aug. 22, 1940 in Boston, MA. Attended Fordham U., AADA. Debut 1963 OB in "Pullman Car Hiawatha," followed by "Babes Don't Cry Anymore," "Guimpes and Saddles," "Hot l Baltimore," "Battle of Angels," "Dancing for the Kaiser."

**FOGARTY, JACK.** Born Oct. 23, 1923 in Liverpool, Eng. Attended Fordham and Columbia U. Debut 1952 OB in "No Exit," followed by "Hogan's Goat," "Sweeney Todd," "The Fantasticks."

**FOOTE, GENE.** Born Oct. 30, 1936 in Johnson City, TN. Attended ETSU. Bdwy debut 1961 in "Unsinkable Molly Brown," followed by "Bajour," "Sweet Charity," "Golden Rainbow," "Applause," "Pippin," "Chicago," "Celebration" (OB).

**FORBES, BRENDA.** Born Jan. 14, 1909 in London Bdwy debut 1931 in "Barretts of Wimpole Street," followed by "Candida," "Lucrece," "Flowers of the Forest," "Pride and Prejudice," "Storm over Patsy," "Heartbreak House," "One for the Money," "Two for the Show," "Three to Make Ready," "Yester-

day's Magic," "Morning Star," "Suds in Your Eyes," "Quadrille," "The Reluctant Debutante," "Loves of Cass McGuire," "Darling of the Day," "The Constant Wife," "My Fair Lady."

**FORD, SUZANNE.** Born Sept. 22, 1949 in Auburn, NY. Attended Ithaca Col., Eastman Ach. Debut 1973 OB in "Fashion," followed by "El Grande de Coca Cola," "Tenderloin" (ELT).

**FORSLUND, CONNIE.** Born June 19, 1950 in San Diego, CA. Graduate NYU. Debut OB 1972 in "The Divorce of Judy and Jane," followed by "The Cretan Bull," "The Kiss-Off," Bdwy in "The Women" (1973), "Habeas Corpus."

**FRANK, ALLAN.** Born Apr. 5, 1915 in Brooklyn, NY. Bdwy bow 1941 in "Liberty Jones," followed by "I Never Sang for My Father," "Daughter of Silence," "A Shadow of My Enemy," "Skipper Next to God," "A Flag Is Born," "Collector's Item," "Angel Street," OB in "The Boss."

**FRAZIER, RONALD C.** Born Feb. 18, 1942. Graduate Carnegie Tech. Bdwy debut 1970 in "Wilson in the Promise Land," followed by "Enemy of the People," "What Every Woman Knows," "Death Story," OB in "Another Language" (ELT).

**FREED, SAM.** Born Aug. 29, 1948 in York, PA. Graduate Pa. State U. Debut OB 1972 in "The Proposition," followed by "What's a Nice Country Like You . . .," Bdwy 1974 in "Candide."

**FREEMAN, ANN.** Born in Portsmouth, Eng. Bdwy debut 1967 in CC's "Life with Father," followed OB by "Present Laughter," "The Home."

**FREY, LEONARD.** Born Sept. 4, 1938 in Brooklyn. Attended Cooper Union, Neighborhood Playhouse. OB in "Little Mary Sunshine," "Funny House of a Negro," "Coach with Six Insides," "Boys in the Band," "Time of Your Life," "Beggar on Horseback," "People Are Living There," "Twelfth Night," "Troilus and Cressida," on Bdwy in "Fiddler on the Roof," "The National Health," "Knock Knock."

**FUJII, TIMM.** Born May 26, 1952 in Detroit, MI. Attended CalStateU. Bdwy debut 1976 in "Pacific Overtures."

**FULLER, JANICE.** Born June 4 in Oakland, CA. Attended RADA. Debut OB 1975 in "Ice Age."

**FULLER, PENNY.** Born in 1940 in Durham, NC. Attended Northwestern U. Credits include "Barefoot in the Park," "Cabaret," "Richard III," "As You Like It," "Henry IV," "Applause," "Rex."

**GABLE, JUNE.** Born June 5, 1945 in NY. Graduate Carnegie Tech. OB in "MacBird," "Jacques Brel Is Alive and Well and Living In Paris," "A Day in the Life of Just about Everyone," "Mod Donna," "Wanted," "Lady Audley's Secret," "Comedy of Errors," Bdwy 1974 in "Candide."

**GALE, DAVID.** Born Oct. 2, 1936 in England. Debut 1958 OB in "Elizabeth the Queen," followed by "Othello," "White Devil," "Baal," "What Do They Know about Love Uptown," "Joe Egg," "The Trial," "Dumbwaiter," Bdwy 1974 in "Of Mice and Men," "Sweet Bird of Youth."

**GALLAGHER, HELEN.** Born in 1926 in Brooklyn, NY. Bdwy debut 1947 in "Seven Lively Arts," followed by "Mr. Strauss Goes to Boston," "Billion Dollar Baby," "Brigadoon," "High Button Shoes," "Touch and Go," "Make a Wish," "Pal Joey," "Guys and Dolls," "Finian's Rainbow," "Sweet Charity," "Mame," "Cry for Us All," "No, No, Nanette," OB in "Hothouse," "Tickles by Tucholsky."

**GALLEGLY, DAVID.** Born June 2, 1950 in Pampa, TX. Attended WTexState U., NTex State. Debut 1975 OB in "Boy Meets Boy."

**GALLERY, JAMES.** Born in Auburn, NY. Graduate Lemonye Col. Debut 1967 OB in "Arms and the Man," followed by "Shadow of a Gunman," "Where Do We Go from Here," "A Doll's House," "Hamlet," "Bdwy 1970 in "Wilson in the Promise Land."

**GANTRY, DONALD.** Born June 11, 1936 in Philadelphia, PA. Attended Temple U. Bdwy debut 1961 in "One More River," followed by "Ah, Wilderness," OB in "The Iceman Cometh," "Children of Darkness," "Here Come the Clowns," "Seven at Dawn," "Long Day's Journey into Night," "Enclave."

**GARBER, VICTOR.** Born Mar. 16, 1949 in London, Can. Debut 1973 OB in "Ghosts" for which he received a Theatre World Award, followed by "Joe's Opera," "Cracks."

**GARFIELD, JULIE.** Born Jan. 10, 1946 in Los Angeles. Attended UWisc., Neighborhood Playhouse Debut OB 1969 in "Honest-to-God Schnozzola," "East Lynne," "The Sea," followed by "Uncle Vanya" for which she received a Theatre World Award, Bdwy in "The Good Doctor," "Death of a Salesman."

**Kelly Garrett**   **Larry Gates**   **Deborah Geffner**   **Robert Giber**   **Eleanor Cody Gou**

GARNETT, CHIP. Born May 8, 1953 in New Kensington, PA. Attended Indiana U. Debut 1973 OB in "Inner City," followed by Bdwy "Candide" (1974), "Bubbling Brown Sugar" for which he received a Theatre World Award.

GARRETT, BOB. Born Mar. 2, 1947 in NYC. Graduate Adelphi U. Debut OB 1971 in "Godspell," Bdwy in "Grease."

GARRETT, KELLY. Born Mar. 25, 1948 in Chester, PA. Attended Cincinnati Cons. Bdwy debut 1972 in "Mother Earth" for which she received a Theatre World Award, followed by "Words and Music," "The Night That Made America Famous,"

GARRICK, BEULAH. Born June 12, 1921 in Nottingham, Eng. Bdwy debut 1959 in "Shadow and Substance," followed by "Auntie Mame," "Juno," "Little Moon of Alban," "High Spirits," "The Hostage," "Funny Girl," "Lovers," "Abelard and Heloise," "Ulysses in Nighttown," OB in "Berkeley Square."

GATES, LARRY. Born Sept. 24, 1915 in St. Paul, MN. Attended UMinn. Bdwy bow 1939 in "Speak of the Devil," followed by "Twelfth Night," "Bell, Book and Candle," "Taming of the Shrew," "Love of Four Colonels," "Teahouse of the August Moon," "Sing Me No Lullaby," "Carefree Tree," OB in "A Case of Libel," "Carving a Statue," "Hamlet."

GAVON, IGORS. Born Nov. 14, 1937 in Latvia. Bdwy bow 1961 in "Carnival," followed by "Hello, Dolly," "Marat/deSade," "Billy," "Sugar," "Mack and Mabel," "Musical Jubilee," OB in "Your Own Thing," "Promenade," "Exchange," "Nevertheless They Laugh," "Polly," "The Boss."

GAZZARA, BEN. Born Aug. 28, 1930 in NYC. Attended CCNY. Bdwy debut 1953 in "End as a Man" for which he received a Theatre World Award, followed by "Cat on a Hot Tin Roof," "Hatful of Rain," "Night Circus," "Strange Interlude," "Traveller without Luggage," "Hughie," "Duet," "Who's Afraid of Virginia Woolf?"

GEFFNER, DEBORAH. Born in August in West Virginia. Attended Juilliard, HB Studio. Debut 1975 OB in "Tenderloin" (ELT).

GENNARO, MICHAEL. Born Sept. 20, 1950 in NYC. Graduate UNotre Dame, Neighborhood Playhouse. Debut 1975 OB in "The Three Musketeers," followed by "Godspell."

GERSHENSON, SUEANNE. Born Feb. 18, 1953 in Chicago, IL. Attended Indiana U. Debut 1976 OB in "Panama Hattie."

GIBER, ROBERT. Born Oct. 13, 1950 in Youngstown, OH. Graduate UMich., Neighborhood Playhouse. Debut 1975 OB in "The Love Death Plays of William Inge."

GIBSON, JUDY. Born Sept. 11, 1947 in Trenton, NJ. Graduate Rider Col. Bdwy debut 1970 in "Purlie," followed by "Seesaw," "Rachel Lily Rosenbloom," "Rockabye Hamlet," OB in "Sensations," "Manhattan Arrangement," "Two if by Sea," "Let My People Come."

GIBSON, KAREN. (formerly Karen Zenker) Born Jan. 9 in Columbus, OH. Attended Ohio State U. Debut 1975 OB in ELT's "Three Musketeers," followed by Bdwy 1976 in "My Fair Lady."

GILBERT, ALAN. Born Mar. 4, 1949 in Seneca, KS. Graduate USyracuse. Debut 1972 OB in "No Strings," followed by "Follies" (ELT).

GILBERT, JOAN G. Born July 4, 1935 in NYC. Graduate Barnard Col., NYU. Debut OB in "The Rimers of Eldritch."

GILCHRIST, REBECCA. Born June 10, 1948 in Parkersburg, WV. Graduate WVa. U. Debut OB 1972 in "The Proposition," Bdwy debut 1974 in "Grease."

GILLETTE, ANITA. Born Aug. 16, 1938 in Baltimore, MD. Debut 1960 OB in "Russell Patterson's Sketchbook" for which she received a Theatre World Award, followed by Bdwy's "Carnival," "All American," "Mr. President," "Guys and Dolls" (CC), "Don't Drink the Water," "Cabaret," "Jimmy," "Rich and Famous" (OB).

GILMANN LARRY. Born Apr. 3, 1950 in NYC. Graduate Franklin & Marshall Col. Debut OB 1973 in "Tubstrip," Bdwy bow 1975 in "The Ritz."

GISH, LILLIAN. Born Oct. 14, 1896 in Springfield, OH. Bdwy debut 1930 in "Uncle Vanya," followed by "Camille," "9 Pine Street," "Joyous Season," "Hamlet," "Star Wagon," "Dear Octopus," "Life with Father," "Mr. Sycamore," "Crime and Punishment," "Curious Savage," "Trip to Bountiful," "Family Reunion" (OB), "All the Way Home," "Too True to Be Good," "Anya," "I Never Sang for My Father," "Uncle Vanya" (1973), "Musical Jubilee."

GLASER, DAREL. Born Jan. 12, 1957 in Chicago, IL. Bdwy debut 1966 in "Wozzeck," followed by "Tea Party" (OB), "Cry for Us All," "Home Sweet Homer."

GLENN, BETTE. Born Dec. 13, 1946 in Atlantic City, NJ. Graduate Montepelier Col. Debut 1971 OB in "Ruddigore," followed by "Maggie Flynn," Bdwy in "Irene."

GLOVER, JOHN. Born Aug. 7, 1944 in Kingston, NY. Attended Towson State Col. Debut OB 1969 in "A Scent of Flowers," followed by "Subject to Fits," "House of Blue Leaves," "Government Inspector," "Rebel Women," Bdwy in "The Selling of the President," "Great God Brown," "Don Juan," "The Visit," "Chemin de Fer," "Holiday."

GOLDSMITH, MERWIN. Born Aug. 7, 1937 in Detroit, MI. Graduate UCLA. Studied at Old Vic. Bdwy debut 1970 in "Minnie's Boys," followed by "The Visit," "Chemin de Fer," "Rex," OB in "Hamlet as a Happening," "Chickencoop Chinaman," "Wanted," "Comedy," "Rubbers," "Yankees 3, Detroit 0," "Trelawny of the Wells."

GONZALEZ, ERNESTO. Born Apr. 8, 1940 in San Juan, PR. Attended UPR. Bdwy debut 1953 in "Camino Real," followed by "Saint of Bleecker St.," "The Innkeepers," "Cut of the Axe," "Ride the Winds," "The Strong Are Lonely," "Oh, Dad, Poor Dad. . . .," "The Leaf People," OB in "The Kitchen," "Secret Concubine," "Life Is a Dream."

GOODMAN, ROBYN. Born Aug. 24, 1947 in NYC. Graduate Brandeis U. Debut OB 1973 in "When You Comin' Back, Red Ryder?", followed by "Richard III.", "Spelling Bee."

GORBEA, CARLOS. Born July 3, 1938 in Santurce, PR. Graduate Fordham U. Bdwy debut 1964 in "West Side Story," followed by "Fiddler on the Roof," "Cabaret," "Candide," OB in "Time of Storm," "Theatre in the Street."

GORDON, CARL. Born Jan. 20, 1932 in Richmond, VA. Bdwy bow 1966 in "Great White Hope," followed by "Ain't Supposed to Die a Natural Death," OB in "Day of Absence," "Happy Ending," "Strong Breed," "Trials of Brother Jero," "Kongi's Harvest," "Welcome to Black River," "Shark," "Orrin and Sugar Mouth," "A Love Play."

GORDON, PEGGY. Born Dec. 26, 1949 in NYC. Attended Carnegie Tech. Debut OB 1971 in "Godspell."

GORDON, RITA. Born Sept. 9, 1952 in Philadelphia, PA. Attended HB Studio. Debut 1975 OB in "Boy Meets Boy."

GORDON, RUTH. Born Oct. 30, 1896 in Wollaston, MA. Attended AADA. Bdwy debut 1915 in "Peter Pan," followed by "Seventeen," "Clarence," "Saturday's Children," "Serena Blandish," "Hotel Universe," "Church Mouse," "Three Cornered Moon," "Ethan Frome," "Country Wife," "Doll's House," "Three Sisters," "Over 21," "Leading Lady," "Smile of the World," "Matchmaker," "Good Soup," "My Mother, My Father and Me," "A Very Rich Woman," "Loves of Cass McGuire," "Dreyfus in Rehearsal," "Mrs. Warren's Profession" (OB).

GORWIN, PETER. Born June 26, 1948 in Duluth, MN. Attended Loyola U. Bdwy debut 1971 in "Trial of the Catonsville 9," followed by OB "Feast of Flies."

GOULD, ELEANOR CODY. Born in Bradford, PA. Attended Elkins Col., AADA . . . where she became a teacher for many years. Returned to acting and appeared OB in "Ice Age."

GRAY, BRUCE. Born Sept. 7, 1936 in San Juan, PR. Graduate UToronto. Debut 1976 OB in "Who Killed Richard Cory?"

GREEN, MARY-PAT. Born Sept. 24, 1951 in Kansas City, MO. Attended UKan. Bdwy debut 1974 in "Candide."

GREENE, ELLEN. Born Feb. 22 in NYC. Attended Ryder Col. Debut 1973 in "Rachel Lily Rosenbloom," followed by "In the Boom Boom Room." "Threepenny Opera."

GREENE, GAYLE. Born Jan. 22, 1948 in NYC. Graduate Carnegie Tech, NYU. Debut 1975 OB in "The Love Death Plays of William Inge."

GREENFIELD, EDITH. Born Jan. 19 in Poughkeepsie, NY. Graduate NYU, Central Sch. in London. Debut 1974 OB in "The Poseur," followed by "Rites of Passage," "Rimers of Eldritch."

GREENHOUSE, MARTHA. Born June 14 in Omaha, NE. Attended Hunter Col., Theatre Wing. Bdwy debut 1942 in "Sons and Soldiers," followed by "Dear Me, the Sky Is Falling," "Family Way," "Woman Is My Idea," "Summer Brave," OB in "Clerambard," "Our Town," "3 by Ferlinghetti," "No Strings," "Cackle."

GRIFFIS, WILLIAM. Born July 12, 1917 in Hollywood, CA. Debut 1946 OB in "The Would-Be Gentleman," followed by "The Corn Is Green," "Major Barbara," "Babes in Arms," "Capacity for Wines," "No Trifling with Love," "Oklahoma" (LC), Bdwy in "A Pin to See the Peepshow" (1953), "Look after Lulu," "Here's Love," "The Cradle Will Rock," "Never Too Late," "Philadelphia, Here I Come," "Jimmy," "Cry for Us All," "Over Here," "Rex."

GRIMALDI, DENNIS. Born Sept. 30, 1947 in Oak Park, IL. Graduate Goodman Sch. Debut 1970 OB in "Me and Juliet," followed by "Workers," "Apple Pie."

**David Groh**

**Elaine Grollman**

**Gordon Halliday**

**Bara-Cristin Hansen**

**Charles T. Harper**

**GRIMES, TAMMY.** Born Jan. 30, 1934 in Lynn, MA. Attended Stephens Col., Neighborhood Playhouse. Debut 1956 OB in "The Littlest Revue," followed by "Clerambard," Bdwy bow 1959 in "Look after Lulu" for which she received a Theatre World Award, "The Unsinkable Molly Brown," "Rattle of a Simple Man," "High Spirits," "The Only Game in Town," "Private Lives," "Musical Jubilee."

**GRIZZARD, GEORGE.** Born Apr. 1, 1928 in Roanoke Rapids, VA. Graduate UNC. Bdwy bow 1954 in "All Summer Long," followed by "The Desperate Hours," "Happiest Millionaire" for which he received a Theatre World Award, "Disenchanted," "Big Fish, Little Fish," with APA 1961–61, "Who's Afraid of Virginia Woolf?," "Glass Menagerie," "You Know I Can't Hear You . . .," "Noel Coward's Sweet Potato," "Gingham Dog," "Inquest," "Country Girl," "Creation of the World and Other Business," "Crown Matrimonial," "The Royal Family."

**GRODIN, CHARLES.** Born Apr. 21, 1935 in Pittsburgh, PA. Attended UMiami, Pittsburgh Playhouse. Bdwy debut 1962 in "Tchin-Tchin," followed by "Absence of a Cello," "Same Time, Next Year," OB in "Hooray! It's a Glorious Day," "Steambath."

**GROH, DAVID.** Born May 21, 1939 in NYC. Graduate Brown U., LAMDA. Debut OB 1963 in "The Importance of Being Earnest," followed by "Elizabeth the Queen" (CC), "The Hot 1 Baltimore."

**GROLLMAN, ELAINE.** Born Oct. 22, 1928 in The Bronx, NY. Debut 1974 OB in "Yentl the Yeshiva Boy," followed by "Kaddish," "The Water Hen," Bdwy 1975 in "Yentl."

**GUILLAUME, ROBERT.** Born Nov. 30, 1937 in St. Louis, MO. Bdwy debut 1961 in "Kwamina," followed by "Finian's Rainbow," "Tambourines to Glory," "Golden Boy," "Purlie," OB in "Charlie Was Here and Now He's Gone," "Life and Times of J. Walter Smintheus," "Jacques Brel Is Alive . . . ," "Music! Music!," "Miracle Play," "Apple Pie."

**GUITTARD, LAURENCE.** Born July 16, 1939 in San Francisco, CA. Graduate Stanford U. Bdwy debut 1965 in "Baker Street," followed by "Anya," "Man of La Mancha," "A Little Night Music" for which he received a Theatre World Award, "Rodgers and Hart."

**GULACK, MAX.** Born May 19, 1928 in NYC. Graduate CCNY, Columbia U. Debut OB 1952 in "Bonds of Interest," followed by "Warrior's Husband," "Worm in the Horseradish," "Marcus in the High Grass," "Country Scandal," "Song for the First of May," "Threepenny Opera."

**GUNN, MOSES.** Born Oct. 2, 1929 in St. Louis, MO. Graduate TN. AIU, UKan. OB in "Measure for Measure," "Bohikee Creek," "Day of Absence," "Happy Ending," "Baal," "Hard Travelin'," "Lonesome Train," "In White America," "The Blacks," "Titus Andronicus," "Song of the Lusitanian Bogey," "Summer of the 17th Doll," "Kongi's Harvest," "Daddy Goodness," "Cities in Bezique," "Perfect Party," "To Be Young, Gifted and Black," "Sty of the Blind Pig," "Twelfth Night," Bdwy in "A Hand Is on the Gate," "Othello," "First Breeze of Summer," "The Poison Tree."

**GUTIERREZ, GERALD.** Born Feb. 3, 1950 in Brooklyn, NY. Graduate SUNY Stony Brook, Juilliard. Debut 1972 OB in "School for Scandal," followed by "Lower Depths," "U.S.A.," "The Hostage," "The Time of Your Life," Bdwy 1973 in "Measure for Measure," "Beggar's Opera," "Scapin," "Three Sisters."

**HALL, GEORGE.** Born Nov. 19, 1916 in Toronto, Can. Attended Neighborhood Playhouse. Bdwy bow 1946 in "Call Me Mister," followed by "Lend an Ear," "Touch and Go," "Live Wire," "Boy Friend," "There's a Girl in My Soup," "An Evening with Richard Nixon . . . ," "We Interrupt This Program," OB in "The Balcony," "Ernest in Love," "A Round with Ring," "Family Pieces," "Carousel," "Case against Roberta Guardino," "Marry Me! Marry Me!," "Arms and the Man," "The Old Glory," "Dancing for the Kaiser."

**HALL, MARGARET.** Born in Richmond, VA. Graduate Wm. & Mary Col. Bdwy debut 1960 in "Becket," followed by "High Spirits," "Mame," "The Leaf People," OB in "The Boy Friend," "Fallout," "U.S.A.," "Midsummer Night's Dream," "Little Mary Sunshine."

**HALL, PHILIP BAKER.** Born Sept. 10, 1934 in Toledo, OH. Graduate UToledo. Debut OB 1961 in "Donogoo," followed by "The Skin of Our Teeth," "In White America," "The World of Gunter Grass," "The Fantasticks," "Gorky."

**HALLIDAY, GORDON.** Born Apr. 2, 1952 in Providence, RI. Attended RI Col., AADA. Bdwy debut 1975 in "Shenandoah."

**HALPERN, RICHARD.** Born May 18, 1948 in The Bronx, NY. Graduate Columbia U. Debut 1976 OB in "Maggie Flynn."

**HAMILTON, ALMA.** Born Nov. 27, 1886 in Crystal Springs, MS. Attended Goodnight Col. Debut OB 1972 in "Life and Times of Joseph Stalin," Bdwy 1975 in "A Letter to Queen Victoria."

**HAMILTON, ROGER.** Born in San Diego, CA., May 2, 1928. Attended San Diego Col., RADA. OB in "Merchant of Venice," "Hamlet," "Live Like Pigs," "Hotel Passionato," "Sjt. Musgrave's Dance," Bdwy in "Someone Waiting," "Separate Tables," "Little Moon of Alban," "Luther," "The Deputy," "Rosencrantz and Guildenstern Are Dead," "The Rothschilds," "Pippin."

**HANEY, MICHAEL.** Born Dec. 12, 1949 in Annapolis, MD. Graduate Catholic U. Bdwy debut 1976 in "Zalmen or the Madness of God."

**HANLEY, KATIE.** Born Jan. 17, 1949 in Evanston, IL. Attended Carnegie-Mellon U. Debut 1971 OB in "Godspell," followed by "Grease."

**HANSEN, BARA-CRISTIN.** Born Feb. 26, 1955 in NYC. Graduate AADA. Bdwy debut 1975 in "Death of a Salesman."

**HARADA, ERNEST.** Born Oct. 20, 1946 in Honolulu, HI. Attended Syracuse U., LAMDA. Bdwy debut 1976 in "Pacific Overtures."

**HAREWOOD, DORIAN.** Born Aug. 6, in Dayton, OH. Attended UCincinnati. Bdwy debut 1972 in "Two Gentlemen of Verona," followed by "Over Here," "Don't Call Back" for which he received a Theatre World Award, "Streamers."

**HARGER, GARY.** Born Aug. 19, 1951 in New Haven, CT. Ithaca Col. graduate. Bdwy debut 1975 in "Shenandoah."

**HARNEY, BEN.** Born Aug. 29, 1952 in Brooklyn, NY. Bdwy debut 1971 in "Purlie," followed by "Pajama Game," "Treemonisha," "Pippin," OB in "Don't Bother Me, I Can't Cope."

**HARPER, CHARLES THOMAS.** Born Mar. 29, 1949 in Carthage, NY. Graduate Webster Col. Debut 1975 OB in "Down by the River Where Waterlilies Are Disfigured Every Day." "Holy Ghosts."

**HARPER, J. W.** Born Oct. 8, 1948 in Bell, CA. Attended Marin Col., Juilliard. Bdwy debut 1975 in "The Robber Bridegroom," followed by "Edward II," "The Time of Your Life," "Three Sisters."

**HARRELSON, HELEN.** Born in Missouri; graduate Goodman Theatre Sch. Bdwy debut 1950 in "The Cellar and the Well," followed by "Death of a Salesman," OB in "Our Town," "His and Hers," "House of Atreus."

**HARRIS, JULIE.** Born Dec. 2, 1925 in Grosse Point, MI. Attended Yale. Bdwy debut 1945 in "It's a Gift," followed by "Henry V," "Oedipus," "The Playboy of the Western World," "Alice in Wonderland," "Macbeth," "Sundown Beach" for which she received a Theatre World Award, "The Young and The Fair," "Magnolia Alley," "Montserrat," "The Member of the Wedding," "I Am a Camera," "Mlle Colombe," "The Lark," "Country Wife," "Warm Peninsula," "Little Moon of Alban," "A Shot in the Dark," "Marathon '33," "Ready When You Are, C. B.," "Hamlet" (CP), "Skyscraper," "40 Carats," "And Miss Reardon Drinks A Little," "Voices," "The Last of Mrs. Lincoln," "The Au Pair Man" (LC), "In Praise of Love." "Belle of Amherst."

**HARRIS, ROSEMARY.** Born Sept. 19, 1930 in Ashby, Eng. Attended RADA. Bdwy debut 1952 in "Climate of Eden" for which she received a Theatre World Award, followed by "Troilus and Cressida," "Interlock," "The Disenchanted," "The Tumbler," in APA's "The Tavern," "School for Scandal," "Seagull," "Importance of Being Earnest," "War and Peace," "Man and Superman," "Judith" and "You Can't Take It with You," "Lion in Winter," "Old Times," LC's "Merchant of Venice" and "Streetcar Named Desire," "Royal Family."

**HARRIS, TOM.** Born Feb. 17, 1949 in Kingston, PA. Graduate King's Col. Debut 1971 OB in "The Basic Training of Pavlo Hummel," followed by "Fishing," Bdwy bow 1972 in "Grease."

**HARTZ, BEVERLY.** Born Feb. 20 in Pittsburgh, PA. Graduate Ohio U. Debut 1975 OB in ELT's "Tenderloin."

**HARVEY, KENNETH.** Born Dec. 25, 1918 in Montreal, Can. Bdwy debut 1951 in "Top Banana," followed by "John Murray Anderson's Almanac," "Grand Prize," "Pipe Dream," OB in "Phoenix '55," "Augusta," "The Old Glory."

**HATTAN, MARK.** Born Mar. 21, 1952 in Portland, OR. Graduate UVa. Debut 1975 OB in "Our Father," followed by ELT's "Maggie Flynn."

**HAUSMAN, ELAINE.** Born June 8, 1949 in Sacramento, CA. Graduate UCal., Juilliard. Bdwy debut 1975 in "The Robber Bridegroom," followed by "Edward II," "The Time of Your Life," "Three Sisters."

**HAVOC, JUNE.** Born Nov. 8, 1916 in Seattle, WA. Bdwy debut 1936 in "Forbidden Melody," followed by "The Women," "Pal Joey," "Mexican Hay-

**Every Hayes**     **Barbara Heuman**     **Joel Higgins**     **Jane Hoffman**     **John Holly**

ride," "Sadie Thompson," "The Ryan Girl," "Dunnigan's Daughter," "Dream Girl," "Affairs of State," "The Infernal Machine," "Beaux Stratagem," "Warm Peninsula," "Dinner at 8," "Habeas Corpus."

**HAWKINS, TRISH.** Born Oct. 30, 1945 in Hartford, CT. Attended Radcliffe, Neighborhood Playhouse. Debut OB 1970 in "Oh! Calcutta!" followed by "Iphigenia," "The Hot l Baltimore" for which she received a Theatre World Award, "him," "Come Back, Little Sheba," "Battle of Angels," "Mound Builders."

**HAYES, EVERY.** Born Sept. 1, 1949 in Montclair, NJ. OB in "Step Lively, Boys," "Croecus and the Witch," "The Flies," "Ups and Downs of Theophilus Maitland," Bdwy in "Purlie," "Don't Bother Me, I Can't Cope," "All Over Town."

**HAYLE, DOUGLAS.** Born Jan. 11, 1942 in Trenton, NJ. Graduate AADA. OB in "Henry IV," "Romeo and Juliet," "King Lear," "A Cry of Players," "In the Matter of J. Robert Oppenheimer," "The Miser," "Trelawny of the Wells," "Oh, Lady! Lady!," "Desperate Hours," "Panama Hattie" (ELT).

**HAYNES, TIGER.** Born Dec. 13, 1907 in St. Croix, VI. Bdwy bow 1956 in "New Faces," followed by "Finian's Rainbow," "Fade Out—Fade In," "The Pajama Game," "The Wiz."

**HEARN, GEORGE.** Born June 18, 1934 in St. Louis, MO. Southwestern Col. graduate. In NYSF's "Macbeth," "Antony and Cleopatra," "As You Like It," "Richard III," "Merry Wives of Windsor," "Midsummer Night's Dream," "Hamlet," OB in "Horseman, Pass By," Bdwy in "A Time for Singing." "Changing Room."

**HECKART, EILEEN.** Born Mar. 29, 1919 in Columbus, OH. Graduate Ohio State U. Debut OB in "Tinker's Dam." followed by Bdwy in "Our Town," "They Knew What They Wanted," "The Traitor," "Hilda Crane," "In Any Language," "Picnic" for which she received a Theatre World Award, "Bad Seed," "View from the Bridge," "Dark at the Top of the Stairs," "Invitation to a March," "Pal Joey," "Everybody Loves Opal," "And Things That Go Bump in the Night," "Barefoot in the Park," "You Know I Can't Hear You When the Water's Running," "Mother Lover," "Butterflies Are Free," "Veronica's Room."

**HEFFERNAN, JOHN.** Born May 30, 1934 in NYC. Attended CCNY, Columbia, Boston U. OB in "The Judge," "Julius Caesar," "Great God Brown," "Lysistrata," "Peer Gynt," "Henry IV," "Taming of the Shrew," "She Stoops to Conquer," "The Plough and the Stars," "Octoroon," "Hamlet," "Androcles and the Lion," "A Man's a Man," "Winter's Tale," "Arms and the Man," "St. Joan" (LCR), "Peer Gynt" (CP), "Memorandum," "Invitation to a Beheading," "Shadow of a Gunman," "The Sea," Bdwy in "Luther," "Tiny Alice," "Postmark Zero," "Woman Is My Idea," "Morning, Noon and Night," "Purlie," "Bad Habits," "Lady from the Sea," "Knock Knock."

**HEMSLEY, WINSTON DeWITT.** Born May 21, 1947 in Brooklyn, NY. Bdwy debut 1965 in "Golden Boy," followed by "A Joyful Noise," "Hallelujah, Baby," "Hello, Dolly!," "Rockabye Hamlet," "A Chorus Line," OB in "Buy Bonds Buster."

**HENNING, DOUG.** Born May 3, 1947 in Winnipeg, Can. Graduate McMaster U. Bdwy debut 1974 in "The Magic Show."

**HENRITZE, BETTE.** Born May 3 in Betsy Layne, KY. Graduate U. Tenn. OB in "Lion in Love," "Abe Lincoln in Illinois," "Othello," "Baal," "Long Christmas Dinner," "Queens of France," "Rimers of Eldritch," "Displaced Person," "Acquisition," "Crime of Passion," "Happiness Cage," NYSF's "Henry VI," "Richard III," "Older People," "Lotta," Bdwy debut 1948 in "Jenny Kissed Me," followed by "Pictures in the Hallway," "Giants, Sons of Giants," "Ballad of the Sad Cafe," "The White House," "Dr. Cook's Garden," "Here's Where I Belong," "Much Ado about Nothing," "Over Here," "Angel Street."

**HEPBURN, KATHARINE.** Born Nov. 9, 1909 in Hartford, CT. Graduate Bryn Mawr. Bdwy debut 1928 in "Night Hostess," followed by "These Days," "A Month in the Country," "Art and Mrs. Bottle," "Warrior's Husband," "The Lake," "Philadelphia Story," "Without Love," "As You Like It," "The Millionairess," "Coco," "A Matter of Gravity."

**HERLIHY, ED.** Born in Boston, MA. Bdwy debut 1968 in "Mame," OB in "Born Yesterday," "Rubbers," "Yankees 3, Detroit 0."

**HERRMANN, EDWARD.** Born July 21, 1943 in Washington, DC. Graduate Bucknell U., LAMDA. Debut 1970 OB in "Basic Training of Pavlo Hummel," followed by NYSF's "Midsummer Night's Dream," Bdwy 1972 in "Moonchildren," "Mrs. Warren's Profession" (LC).

**HEUMAN, BARBARA.** Born Feb. 24, 1944 in Montrose, PA. Graduate UWash. Debut 1970 OB in "Dames at Sea," followed by Bdwy in "No, No, Nanette," "Something's Afoot."

**HEWETT, CHRISTOPHER.** Born Apr 5 in England; attended Beaumont Col. Bdwy debut 1956 in "My Fair Lady," followed by "First Impressions," "Un-

sinkable Molly Brown," "Kean," "The Affair," "Hadrian VII," OB in "Tobias and the Angel," "Trelawny of the Wells."

**HIGGINS, JOEL.** Born Sept. 28, 1943 in Bloomington, IL. Graduate Mich. State U. Bdwy debut 1975 in "Shenandoah" for which he received a Theatre World Award.

**HIGGINS, MICHAEL.** Born Jan. 20, in Bklyn. Attended Theatre Wing. Bdwy bow 1946 in "Antigone," followed by "Our Lan'," "Romeo and Juliet," "The Crucible," "The Lark," "Equus," OB in "White Devil," "Carefree Tree," "Easter," "The Queen and the Rebels," "Sally, George and Martha," "L'Ete," "Uncle Vanya," "The Iceman Cometh."

**HILL, PARKS.** Born July 26, 1949 in Albemarle, NC. Graduate UNC. Debut 1976 OB in ELT's "Maggie Flynn."

**HILLGARTNER, JAMES.** Born Nov. 14, 1938 in Franklin, NJ. Graduate Lafayette Col., San Francisco State U. Debut OB 1975 in "Bus Stop," followed by "Tenderloin."

**HINCKLEY, ALFRED.** Born Sept. 22, 1920 in Kalamazoo, MI. Graduate NYU. Bdwy bow 1959 in "Legend of Lizzie," followed by "Subways Are for Sleeping," "Man for All Seasons," "Impossible Years," "More Stately Mansions," "That Championship Season," OB in "A Clearing in the Woods," "Long Voyage Home," "Diff'rent," "Rimers of Eldritch," "People vs Ranchman," "Steambath," "Harry Outside."

**HINGLE, PAT.** Born July 19, 1923 in Denver, CO. Graduate Tex. U. Bdwy bow 1953 in "End as a Man," followed by "Festival," "Cat on a Hot Tin Roof," "Girls of Summer," "Dark at the Top of the Stairs," "J. B.," "Deadly Game," "Strange Interlude," "Blues for Mr. Charlie," "A Girl Could Get Lucky," "Glass Menagerie," "Johnny No Trump," "The Price," "Child's Play," "Selling of the President," "That Championship Season," "Lady from the Sea."

**HIRSCH, JUDD.** Born Mar. 15, 1935 in NYC. Attended AADA. Bdwy debut 1966 in "Barefoot in the Park," followed OB by "On the Necessity of Being Polygamous," "Scuba Duba," "Mystery Play," "Hot l Baltimore," "Prodigal," "Knock Knock."

**HOFFMAN, JANE.** Born July 24 in Seattle, WA. Graduate UCal. Bdwy debut 1940 in " 'Tis of Thee," followed by "Crazy with the Heat," "Something for the Boys," "One Touch of Venus," "Calico Wedding," "Mermaids Singing," "Temporary Island," "Story for Strangers," "Two Blind Mice," "The Rose Tattoo," "The Crucible," "Witness for the Prosecution," "Third Best Sport," "Rhinoceros," "Mother Courage and Her Children," "Fair Game for Lovers," "A Murderer among Us," "Murder among Friends," OB in "American Dream," "Sandbox," "Picnic on the Battlefield," "Theatre of the Absurd," "Child Buyer," "A Corner of the Bed," "Someone's Comin' Hungry," "Increased Difficulty of Concentration," "American Hamburger League," "Slow Memories," "Last Analysis," "Dear Oscar," "Hocus-Pocus."

**HOGAN, JONATHAN.** Born June 13, 1951 in Chicago, IL. Graduate Goodman Theatre. Debut OB 1972 in "The Hot l Baltimore," followed by "Mound Builders," "Harry Outside."

**HOLLAND, ANTHONY.** Born Oct. 17, 1933 in Brooklyn, NY. Graduate UChicago. OB in "Venice Preserved," "Second City," "Victim of Duty," "New Tenant," "Dynamite Tonight," "Quare Fellow," "White House Murder Case," "Waiting for Godot," on Bdwy in "My Mother, My Father and Me," "We Bombed in New Haven," "Dreyfus in Rehearsal," "Leaf People."

**HOLLANDER, DONN.** Born June 9, 1946 in Wilkes-Barre, PA. Graduate Hobart Col., Oberlin Col. Debut 1976 OB in ELT's "Panama Hattie."

**HOLLANDER, JACK.** Born Jan. 29, 1918 in Chicago, IL. Graduate Goodman Theatre. Bdwy debut 1959 in "Miracle Worker," followed by "All the Way Home," "Gideon," "Impossible Years," "Man in the Glass Booth," "Inquest," "Birthday Party," "Zalmen, or the Madness of God," OB in "Girl of the Golden West," "Dybbuk," "Journey to the Day," "Titus Andronicus," "Comedy of Errors," "Ergo," "Phantasmagoria Historia . . . ," "Troilus and Cressida."

**HOLLIDAY, POLLY.** Born in Jasper, AL. Attended AL. Col., Fla. State U. Debut 1964 OB in "Orphee," followed by "Dinner on the Ground," "Wedding Band," "Girls Most Likely to Succeed," "Carnival Dreams," Bdwy bow 1974 in "All over Town."

**HOLLY, JOHN.** Born May 6, 1944 in St. Louis, MO. Graduate Ariz. State U. Bdwy debut 1973 in "Grease," OB in "Call Me Madam."

**HOLM, CELESTE.** Born Apr. 29, 1919 in NYC. Attended UCLA, UChicago. Bdwy debut 1938 in "Gloriana," followed by "The Time of Your Life," "Another Sun," "Return of the Vagabond," "Eight O'Clock Tuesday," "My Fair Ladies," "Papa Is All," "All the Comforts of Home," "Damask Cheek," "Oklahoma!," "Bloomer Girl," "She Stoops to Conquer," "Affairs of State," "Anna Christie," "The King and I," "His and Hers," "Interlock," "Third Best Sport," "Invitation to a March," "A Month in the Country" (OB), "Mame," "Candida," "Habeas Corpus."

| Elaine Hyman | Randy Hugill | Anne Ives | Page Johnson | Charlotte Jones |

**HOPKINS, ANTHONY.** Born Dec. 31, 1937 in Port Talbot, South Wales. Attended Cardiff Col. of Music and Drama, RADA. Bdwy debut 1974 in "Equus."

**HORMANN, NICHOLAS.** Born Dec. 22, 1944 in Honolulu, HI. Graduate Oberlin, Yale. Bdwy debut 1973 in "The Visit," followed by "Chemin de Fer," "Holiday," "Love for Love," "Rules of the Game," "Member of the Wedding," OB in "Ice Age."

**HORNE, CHERYL.** Born Nov. 15 in Stamford, CT. Graduate SMU. Debut 1975 OB in "The Fantasticks."

**HOWARD, DAVID.** Born Sept. 10, 1928 in Mr. Kisco, NY. Graduate Cornell U. Debut 1964 OB in "Cindy," followed by "Hamp," "Hamlet."

**HOWARD, JOE.** Born Nov. 24, 1948 in Yonkers, NY. Graduate Hamilton Col. Bdwy debut 1976 in "So Long, 174th Street."

**HOWARD, KEN.** Born Mar. 28, 1944 in El Centro, CA. Yale graduate. Bdwy debut 1968 in "Promises, Promises," followed by "1776" for which he received a Theatre World Award, "Child's Play," "Seesaw," "Little Black Sheep" (LC), "The Norman Conquests," "1600 Pennsylvania Avenue."

**HOXIE, RICHMOND.** Born July 21, 1946 in NYC. Graduate Dartmouth Col., LAMDA. Debut 1975 OB in "Shaw for an Evening," followed by "The Family."

**HUDGINS, WAYNE.** Born June 19, 1950 in Amarillo, TX. Graduate UWash. Bdwy debut 1976 in "Shenandoah."

**HUDSON, TRAVIS.** Born Feb. 2 in Amarillo, TX. Graduate UTex. Bdwy debut in "New Faces of 1962," followed by "Pousse Cafe," "Very good Eddie," OB in "Triad," "Tattooed Countess," "Young Abe Lincoln," "Get Thee to Canterbury," "Golden Apple."

**HUGHES, BARNARD.** Born July 16, 1915 in Bedford Hills, N.Y. Attended Manhattan Col. OB in "Rosmersholm," "A Doll's House," "Hogan's Goat," "Line," "Older People," "Hamlet" "Merry Wives of Windsor," "Pericles," Bdwy in "The Ivy Green," "Dinosaur Wharf," "Teahouse of the August Moon" (CC), "A Majority of One," "Advise and Consent," "The Advocate," "Hamlet," "I Was Dancing," "Generation," "How Now, Dow Jones?," "Wrong Way Light Bulb," "Sheep On The Runway," "Abelard and Heloise," "Much Ado about Nothing," "Uncle Vanya," "The Good Doctor," "All Over Town."

**HUGILL, RANDY.** Born in Olney, IL. Graduate UFla. Bdwy debut 1974 in "Lorelei," followed by OB "Follies."

**HUGO, LAURENCE.** Born Dec. 22, 1917 in Berkeley, CA. Attended UCal., Neighborhood Playhouse. Bdwy bow 1941 in "Distant City," followed by "The Skin of Our Teeth," "I'll Take the High Road," "Decision," "Born Yesterday," "Stalag 17," "Double in Hearts," "There's a Girl in My Soup," "Hamlet," OB in "U.S.A.," "Enclave."

**HULCE, THOMAS.** Born Dec. 6, 1953 in Plymouth, MI. Graduate N.C. School of Arts. Bdwy debut 1975 in "Equus," followed by OB in "A Memory of Two Mondays."

**HUNT, LINDA.** Born Apr. 2, 1945 in Morristown, NJ. Attended Goodman School. Debut 1975 OB in "Down by the River Where the Waterlilies Are Disfigured," followed by Bdwy in "Ah, Wilderness."

**HUNTER, KIM.** Born Nov. 12, 1922 in Detroit, MI. Attended Actors Studio. Bdwy debut 1947 in "A Streetcar Named Desire," followed by "Darkness at Noon," "The Chase," "Children's Hour," "Tender Trap," "Write Me a Murder," "Weekend," "Penny Wars," "The Women," OB in "Come Slowly, Eden," "All Is Bright," "The Cherry Orchard."

**HYMAN, EARLE.** Born Oct. 11, 1926 in Rocky Mount, NC. Attended New School, Theatre Wing. Bdwy debut 1943 in "Run, Little Chillun," followed by "Anna Lucasta," "Climate of Eden," "Merchant of Venice," "Othello," "Julius Caesar," "The Tempest," "No Time for Sergeants," "Mr. Johnson" for which he received a Theatre World Award, "St. Joan," "Hamlet," "Waiting for Godot," "Duchess of Malfi," "Les Blancs," OB in "The White Rose and the Red," "Worlds of Shakespeare," "Jonah," "Life and Times of J. Walter Smintheus," "Orrin," "Cherry Orchard," "House Party," "Carnival Dreams."

**HYMAN, ELAINE.** Born in Detroit, MI. Graduate Columbia U. Bdwy debut 1962 in "General Seeger," followed by "Say Darling," "The Norman Conquests," OB in "Javelin," "Night of the Dunce," "What the Butler Saw," "Children, Children," "Big Fish, Little Fish."

**IACANGELO, PETER.** Born Aug. 13, 1948 in Brooklyn, NY. Attended Hofstra U. Bdwy debut 1968 in "Jimmy Shine," OB in "One Flew over the Cuckoo's Nest," "Moonchildren," "Comedy of Errors."

**ING, ALVIN.** Born May 26, 1938 in Honolulu, HI. Graduate Columbia U. Bdwy debut 1959 in "World of Suzie Wong," followed by "Two Gentlemen of Verona," "Pacific Overtures," OB in "Tenth of an Inch," "Cranes and Peonies," "Coffins for Butterflies," "Six."

**IRVING, GEORGE S.** Born Nov. 1, 1922 in Springfield, MA. Attended Leland Powers Sch. Bdwy bow 1943 in "Oklahoma!," followed by "Call Me Mister," "Along Fifth Avenue," "Two's Company," "Me and Juliet," "Can-Can," "Shinbone Alley," "Bells are Ringing," "The Good Soup," "Tovarich," "A Murderer Among Us," "Alfie," "Anya," "Galileo" (LC), "The Happy Time," "Up Eden" (OB), "4 on a Garden," "An Evening with Richard Nixon and . . . ," "Irene," "Who's Who in Hell," "All over Town," "So Long 174th Street."

**IVES, ANNE.** Born in Providence, RI. Attended Sargent's Sch., AmThWing. Bdwy debut 1906 in "The Chorus Lady," followed by "Point of No Return," "Masquerade," "Uncle Vanya," OB in "The Crucible," "Effect of Gamma Rays . . .," "Good Woman of Setzuan," "The Contractor," "Ice Age."

**JACKSON, ERNESTINE.** Born Sept. 18 in Corpus Christi, TX. Graduate Del Mar Col., Juilliard. Debut 1966 in LC's "Show Boat," followed by "Finian's Rainbow" (CC), "Hello, Dolly!," "Applause," "Jesus Christ Superstar," "Tricks," "Raisin" for which she received a Theatre World Award.

**JAMES, WILLIAM.** Born Apr. 29, 1938 in Jersey City, NJ. Graduate NJ State Teachers Col. Bdwy bow 1962 in "Camelot," followed by "Maggie Flynn," "Coco," "My Fair Lady" (CC & 1976), "Where's Charley?" (CC), OB in "Anything Goes," "Smith."

**JAMROG, JOE.** Born Dec. 21, 1932 in Flushing, NY. Graduate CCNY. Debut OB 1970 in "Nobody Hears a Broken Drum," followed by "Tango," "And Whose Little Boy Are You?," "When You Comin' Back, Red Ryder?," "Drums at Yale," "The Boy Friend," "Love Death Plays."

**JANIS, CONRAD.** Born Feb. 11, 1928 in NYC. Bdwy debut 1942 in "Junior Miss," followed by "Dark of the Moon," "The Next Half Hour," "Brass Ring" for which he received a Theatre World Award, "Time Out for Ginger," "Terrible Swift Sword," "Visit to a Small Planet," "Make a Million," "Sunday in New York," "Marathon '33," "Front Page," "No Hard Feelings," "Same Time Next Year."

**JANSEN, JIM.** Born July 27, 1945 in Salt Lake City, UT. Graduate UUtah. NYU. Debut OB 1973 in "Moonchildren," Bdwy 1974 in "All over Town."

**JAROWSKY, ANDREW.** Born in NYC. Graduate CCNY. Debut OB 1974 in "Festival of Short Plays," followed by "Cakes with Wine," "The Boss."

**JAROSLOW, RUTH.** Born May 22 in Brooklyn, NY. Attended HB Studio. Debut 1964 OB in "That 5 A.M. Jazz," followed by "Jonah," Bdwy in "Mame," "Fiddler on the Roof," "The Ritz."

**JARRETT, JERRY.** Born Sept. 9, 1918 in Brooklyn, NY. Attended New Theatre School. Bdwy debut 1948 in "At War with the Army," followed by "Gentlemen Prefer Blonds," "Stalag 17," "Fiorello," "Fiddler on the Roof," OB in "Waiting for Lefty," "Nat Turner," "Me Candido," "That 5 A.M. Jazz," "Valentine's Day," "Tickles by Tucholsky."

**JEANNETTE, GERTRUDE.** Born Nov. 28, 1918 in Little Rock, AR. Attended New School. Has appeared in "Lost in the Stars," "The Long Dream," "Amen Corner," "Nobody Loves an Albatross," "The Skin of Our Teeth," OB in "This Way Forward," "Deep Are the Roots," "417," "Moon on a Rainbow Shawl," "To Be Young, Gifted and Black."

**JENN, STEPHEN.** Born Mar. 30, 1950 in London, Eng. Graduate RADA. Debut 1976 with Royal Shakespeare Co. in "Henry V."

**JOHNSON, DOTTS.** Born Feb. 3 in Baltimore, MD. Bdwy debut 1950 in "Freight," followed by "Anna Lucasta," "Death of a Salesman," OB in "Freeman."

**JOHNSON, PAGE.** Born Aug. 25, 1930 in Welch, WV. Graduate Ithaca Col. Bdwy bow 1951 in "Romeo and Juliet," followed by "Electra," "Oedipus," "Camino Real," "In April Once" for which he received a Theatre World Award, "Red Roses for Me," "The Lovers," "Equus," OB in "The Enchanged," "Guitar," "4 in 1," "Journey of the Fifth Horse," APA's "School for Scandal," "The Tavern" and "The Seagull," "Odd Couple," "Boys In The Band," "Medea."

**JONES, CHARLOTTE.** Born Jan. 1, in Chicago. Attended Loyola, DePaul U. OB in "False Confessions," "Sign of Jonah," "Girl on the Via Flaminia," "Red Roses for Me," "Night is Black Bottles," "Camino Real," "Plays for Bleecker St.," "Pigeons," "Great Scot!" "Sjt. Musgrave's Dance," "Papers," "Johnny Johnson," "Beggar's Opera," "200 Years of American Furniture," Bdwy in "Camino Real," "Buttrio Square," "Mame," "How Now Dow Jones," "Skin of Our Teeth," "Matter of Gravity."

| Kender Jones | Bunny Kacher | Peter Julian | Mimi Kennedy | Michael Kell |

**JONES, JAMES EARL.** Born Jan. 17, 1931 in Arkabutla, MI. Graduate Mich U. OB in "The Pretender," "The Blacks," "Clandestine on the Morning Line," "The Apple," "A Midsummer Night's Dream," "Moon on a Rainbow Shawl" for which he received a Theatre World Award. "PS 193," "Last Minstrel," "Love Nest," "Bloodknot," "Othello," "Baal," "Danton's Death" (LC), "Boesman and Lena," "Hamlet" (NYSF) "Cherry Orchard," Bdwy in "The Egghead," "Sunrise at Campobello," "The Cool World," "A Hand is on the Gate," "Great White Hope," "Les Blancs," "King Lear," "The Iceman Cometh," "Of Mice and Men."

**JONES, JEFFREY.** Born Sept. 28, 1947 in Buffalo, NY. Graduate Lawrence U., LAMDA. Debut OB 1973 in "Lotta," followed by "The Tempest," "Trelawny of the Wells," "Secret Service," "Boy Meets Girl."

**JONES, KENDER.** Born Sept. 14, 1939 in Equality, AL. Graduate TexChristianU, Cornell U. Debut 1976 OB in ELT's "Rimers of Eldritch."

**JOSLYN, BETSY.** Born Apr. 19, 1954 in Staten Island, NY. Graduate Wagner Col. Debut 1976 OB in "The Fantasticks."

**JOYCE, STEPHEN.** Born Mar. 7, 1933 in NYC. Attended Fordham U. Bdwy bow 1966 in "Those That Play the Clowns," followed by "The Exercise," "The Runner Stumbles," OB in "Three Hand Reel," "Galileo," "St. Joan," "Stephen D" for which he received a Theatre World Award, "Fireworks," "School for Wives."

**JULIA, RAUL.** Born Mar. 9, 1940 in San Juan, PR. Graduate UPR. OB in "Macbeth" "Titus Andronicus" (CP), "Theatre in the Streets," "Life Is a Dream," "Blood Wedding," "Ox Cart," "No Exit," "Memorandum," "Frank Gagliano's City Scene," "Your Own Thing," "Persians," "Castro Complex," "Pinkville," "Hamlet," "King Lear," "As You Like It," "Emperor of Late Night Radio," "Threepenny Opera," Bdwy bow 1968 in "The Cuban Thing," followed by "Indians," "Two Gentlemen of Verona," "Via Galactica," "Where's Charley?"

**JULIAN, PETER.** Born Oct. 23, 1945 in NYC. Graduate CCNY, C.W. Post, HB Studio. Debut 1975 OB in "Pursuit of Happiness."

**JUNG, CALVIN.** Born Feb. 17, 1945 in NYC. Graduate Hillsdale Col. Debut 1972 OB in "Chickencoop Chinaman," followed by "Dawn Song," "Year of the Dragon," "A Memory of Two Mondays," "They Knew What They Wanted."

**KACHER, BUNNY.** Born Mar. 25, 1936 in Chicago, IL. Graduate UWisc. Bdwy debut 1975 in "Sweet Bird of Youth."

**KAGAN, DIANE.** Born in Maplewood, NJ. Graduate Fla. State U. Debut OB 1963 in "Asylum," followed by "Days and Nights of Beebee Fenstermaker," "Death of the Well-Loved Boy," "Madam de Sade," "Blue Boys," "Alive and Well in Argentina," "Little Black Sheep," "The Family," Bdwy in "Chinese Prime Minister," "Never Too Late," "Any Wednesday," "Venus Is," "Tiger at the Gates" (LC).

**KAPEN, BEN.** Born July 2, 1928 in NYC. Graduate NYU. Has appeared OB in "No Trifling with Love," "Good News," "A Memory of Two Mondays," "They Knew What They Wanted," Bdwy in "The Happy Time" (1968), "Man in the Glass Booth," "Penny Wars."

**KARIN, RITA.** Born Oct. 24, 1919 in Warsaw, Poland. Bdwy debut 1960 in "The Wall," followed by "A Call on Kaprin," "Penny Wars," "Yentl," OB in "Pocket Watch," "Scuba Duba," "House of Blue Leaves," "Yentl the Yeshiva Boy."

**KARR, PATTI.** Born July 10 in St. Paul, MN. Attended TCU. Bdwy debut 1953 in "Maggie," followed by "Carnival in Flanders," "Pipe Dream," "Bells Are Ringing," "New Girl in Town," "Body Beautiful," "Bye Bye Birdie," "New Faces of 1962," "Come on Strong," "Look to the Lilies," "Different Times," "Lysistrata," "Seesaw," "Irene," "Pippin," OB in "A Month of Sundays," "Up Eden."

**KASS, ALAN.** Born Apr. 23, 1928 in Chicago, IL. Graduate CCNY. Bdwy bow 1968 in "Golden Rainbow," followed by "Sugar," OB in "Guitar," "Be Kind to People Week."

**KAVA, CAROLINE.** Born in Chicago, IL. Attended Neighborhood Playhouse. Debut 1975 OB in "Gorky," followed by "Threepenny Opera."

**KAYE, STUBBY.** Born Nov. 11, 1918 in NYC. Bdwy debut 1950 in "Guys and Dolls," followed by "Li'l Abner," "Everybody Loves Opal," "Good News," "The Ritz."

**KEEP, STEPHEN.** Born Aug. 24, 1947 in Camden, SC. Attended Columbia, Yale. Bdwy debut 1972 in "Paul Sills Story Theatre" and "Metamorphosis," followed OB in "Clarence," "The Cherry Orchard."

**KELL, MICHAEL.** Born Jan. 18, 1944 in Jersey City, NY. Attended HB Studio. Debut 1972 OB in "One Flew over the Cuckoo's Nest," followed by "Boom Boom Room," "Golden Boy," "Streamers."

**KELLER, JEFF.** Born Sept. 8, 1947 in Brooklyn. Graduate Monmouth Col. Bdwy debut 1974 in "Candide."

**KELLER, MAY.** Born Jan. 25 in Bryn Mawr, PA. Graduate U. Miami. Debut 1976 OB in "Panama Hattie."

**KELLERY, KATE.** Born Aug. 23, 1950 in Washington, DC. Graduate Temple, Catholic U. Bdwy debut 1975 in "The Skin of Our Teeth."

**KELLIN, MIKE.** Born Apr. 26, 1922 in Hartford, CT. Attended Trinity Col., Yale. Bdwy bow in 1949 in "At War with the Army," followed by "Bird Cage," "Stalag 17," "The Emperor's Clothes," "Time of Your Life," "Pipe Dream," "Who Was That Lady," "God and Kate Murphy," "Ankles Aweigh," "Rhinoceros," "Odd Couple," "Mother Courage," "The Ritz," OB in "Taming of the Shrew," "Diary of a Scoundrel," " Purple Dust," "Tevya and His Daughters," "Winkelberg," "Winterset," "Joan of Lorraine," "Bread," "American Buffalo."

**KELTON, RICHARD.** Born Apr. 29, 1943 in Lincoln, NE. Graduate UKan. Bdwy debut 1976 in "Who's Afraid of Virginia Woolf?" for which he received a Theatre World Award.

**KENAN, DOLORES.** Born June 7 in Bellevue, KY. Graduate Xavier U., Goodman Theatre. Debut 1974 OB in "The Killdeer," followed by "Wedding Band," "Summer Brave," "Bus Stop," "Holy Ghosts."

**KENNEDY, MIMI.** Born Sept 25, 1948 in Rochester, NY. Graduate Smith College. Bdwy debut 1975 in "Grease."

**KERT, LARRY.** Born Dec. 5, 1934 in Los Angeles, CA. Attended LACC. Bdwy bow 1953 in "John Murray Anderson's Almanac," followed by "Ziegfeld Follies," "Mr. Wonderful," "Walk Tall," "Look, Ma, I'm Dancin'," "Tickets Please," "West Side Story," "A Family Affair," "Breakfast at Tiffany's," "Cabaret," "La Strada," "Company," "Two Gentlemen of Verona," "Music! Music!," "Musical Jubilee."

**KEYES, DANIEL.** Born Mar. 6, 1914 in Concord, MA. Attended Harvard. Bdwy debut 1954 in "The Remarkable Mr. Pennypacker," followed by "Bus Stop," "Only in America," "Christine," "First Love," "Take Her, She's Mine," "Baker Street," "Dinner at 8," "I Never Sang for My Father," "Wrong Way Light Bulb," "A Place for Polly," "Scratch," "Rainbow Jones," OB in "Our Town," "Epitaph for George Dillon," "Plays for Bleecker Street," "Hooray! It's A Glorious Day!," "Six Characters in Search of an Author," "Sjt. Musgrave's Dance," "Arms and the Man," "Mourning Becomes Electra," "Salty Dog Saga," "Hot l Baltimore."

**KEYS, HENSON.** Born Oct. 7, 1949 in Lincoln, IL. Graduate UOkla., Fla. State U. Debut 1975 OB in "Hamlet."

**KEZER, GLENN.** Born Apr. 2, 1923 in Okemah, OK. Graduate UOkla. Bdwy in "My Fair Lady," "Camelot," "Fade Out—Fade In," "Half a Sixpence," "Little Murders," "Trial of Lee Harvey Oswald," "The Other Man," OB in "Walk in Darkness," "Brigadoon" (CC), "Oh, Say Can You See L.A.," "Firebugs," "The David Show," "Promenade," "Threepenny Opera."

**KILEY, RICHARD.** Born Mar. 31, 1922 in Chicago, IL. Attended Loyola U. Bdwy debut 1953 in "Misalliance" for which he received a Theatre World Award, followed by "Kismet," "Sing Me No Lullaby," "Time Limit!" "Redhead," "Advise and Consent," "No Strings," "Here's Love," "I Had a Ball," "Man of La Mancha" (also LC), "Her First Roman," "The Incomparable Max," "Voices," "Absurd Person Singular," "The Heiress."

**KILLMER, NANCY.** Born Dec. 16, 1936 in Homewood, IL. Graduate Northwestern U. Bdwy debut 1969 in "Coco," followed by "Goodtime Charley," "So Long, 174th Street."

**KIMBROUGH, CHARLES.** Born May 23, 1936 in St. Paul, MN. Graduate Ind. U., Yale, Bdwy bow 1969 in "Cop-Out," followed by "Company," "Love for Love," "Rules of the Game," "Candide," OB in "All in Love," "Struts and Frets," "Troilus and Cressida," "Secret Service," "Boy Meets Girl."

**KIMMINS, KENNETH.** Born Sept. 4, 1941 in Brooklyn, NY. Graduate Catholic U. Debut 1966 OB in "The Fantasticks," followed by "Adaptation," "All My Sons," Bdwy in "Fig Leaves Are Falling," "Gingerbread Lady," "Company," "Status Quo Vadis," "Magic Show."

**KINGSLEY, PETER.** Born Aug. 14, 1945 in Mexico City, Mex. Graduate Hamilton Col., LAMDA. Debut 1974 OB in "The Beauty Part," followed by "Purification."

**Terry Kiser**     **Catherine Henry Lamm**     **Daniel Landon**     **Nancy Lane**     **John Lansing**

KIRK, LISA. Born Sept. 18, 1925 in Brownsville, PA. Bdwy debut 1945 in "Goodnight Ladies," followed by "Allegro," "Kiss Me, Kate," "Here's Love," "Mack and Mabel," "Me Jack, You Jill."

KIRSCH, CAROLYN. Born May 24, 1942 in Shreveport, LA. Bdwy debut 1963 in "How to Succeed . . .," followed by "Folies Bergere," "La Grosse Valise," "Skyscraper," "Breakfast at Tiffany's," "Sweet Charity," "Hallelujah, Baby!," "Dear World," "Promises, Promises," "Coco," "Ulysses in Nighttown," "A Chorus Line."

KISER, TERRY. Born Aug. 1, 1939 in Omaha, NE. Graduate U. Kan. Debut OB 1966 in "Night of the Dunce," followed by "Fortune and Men's Eyes" for which he received a Theatre World Award, "Horseman, Pass By," "Frank Gagliano's City Scene," "The Ofay Watcher," "Castro Complex," "In Case of Accident," "The Children," "More Than You Deserve," Bdwy in "Paris Is Out," "Shelter," "God's Favorite."

KLINE, KEVIN. Born Oct. 24, 1947 in St. Louis, MO. Graduate Ind. U., Juilliard. Debut 1970 OB in "Wars of Roses," followed by "School for Scandal," "Lower Depths," "The Hostage," "Women Beware Women," "Robber Bridegroom," "Edward II," "The Time of Your Life," Bdwy in "Three Sisters," "Measure for Measure," "Beggar's Opera," "Scapin."

KNIGHT, SHIRLEY. Born July 5 in Goessel, KS. Attended Phillips U., Wichita U. Bdwy debut 1964 in "The Three Sisters," followed by "We Have Always Lived in a Castle," "The Watering Place," "Kennedy's Children," OB in "Journey to the Day," "Rooms."

KNUDSON, KURT. Born Sept. 7, 1936 in Fargo, ND. Attended NDState U, Hamline U, UMiami, Debut 1976 OB in "The Cherry Orchard."

KOLBA, MICHAEL. Born Oct. 1, 1947 in Moorhead, MN. Graduate Moorhead U., UHawaii. Debut 1976 OB in "The Cherry Orchard."

KOLOGI, MARK. Born Mar. 23, 1954 in Jersey City, NJ. AADA graduate. Bdwy debut 1975 in "Don't Call Back," followed by "Summer Brave."

KRAUS, PHILIP. Born May 10, 1949 in Springville, NY. Carnegie Tech graduate. Bdwy debut 1973 in "Shelter," followed by "Equus."

KRAMER, JOEL. Born July 1, 1943 in The Bronx, NY. Graduate Queens Coll., UMich. Debut OB 1963 in "St. Joan of the Stockyards," followed by "Playboy of the Western World," "Measure for Measure," "Man Who Corrupted Hadleyburg," "Call Me Madam," Bdwy 1975 in "Candide."

KREITZBERG, DANNY. Born July 2, 1952 in Newark, NJ. Attended NYU. OB in "The Faggot," "The Hot l Baltimore," Bdwy debut 1971 in "The Last Analysis."

KUBIAK, TOM. Born Dec. 29, 1936 in Lackawanna, NY. Attended Actors Studio. Debut 1969 ON in "End of All Things Natural," followed by "Trial of Denmark Vesey," "Primary English Class."

KUHLMAN, RON. Born Mar. 6, 1948 in Cleveland, OH. Graduate Ohio U. Debut 1972 OB in "A Maid's Tragedy," followed by "A Chorus Line" (Bdwy 1975).

KURTZ, SWOOSIE. Born Sept. 6, 1944 in Omaha, NE. Attended USCal., AMDA. Debut 1968 OB in "The Firebugs," followed by "The Effect of Gamma Rays. . . .," "Enter a Free Man.," Bdwy 1975 in "Ah, Wilderness."

LAM, DIANE. Born Mar. 6, 1945 in Honolulu, HI. Graduate UHi., SMU. Bdwy debut 1976 in "Pacific Overtures."

LAMM, CATHERINE HENRY. Born in Washington, DC. Attended IndU, London Actors Workshop. Debut 1976 OB in "The Boss."

LAMONT, ROBIN. Born June 2, 1950 in Boston, MA. Attended Carnegie-Mellon U. Debut 1971 OB in "Godspell," followed by "Thoughts," Bdwy 1976 in "Godspell."

LANCASTER, LUCIE. Born Oct. 15, 1907 in Chicago, IL. Bdwy debut 1947 in "Heads or Tails," followed by "Mr. Pickwick," "The Girl Who Came to Supper," "Bajour," "How Now, Dow Jones," "Little Boxes" (OB), "70 Girls 70," "Pippin."

LANDERS, MATT. Born Oct. 21, 1952 in Mohawk Valley, NY. Attended Boston Cons. Debut OB 1974 in "Godspell," followed by Bdwy 1975 in "Grease."

LANDON, DANIEL. Born Dec. 29, 1950 in NYC. Bdwy debut 1974 in "Mourning Pictures," OB in "Yanks 3, Detroit 0," "Rimers of Eldritch"(ELT).

LANE, NANCY. Born June 16, 1951 in Passaic, NJ. Attended Va. Commonwealth U., AADA. Debut 1975 OB and Bdwy in "A Chorus Line."

LANNING, JERRY. Born May 17, 1943 in Miami, FL. Graduate USCal. Bdwy debut 1966 in "Mame" for which he received a Theatre World Award, followed by "1776," "Where's Charley?," "My Fair Lady," OB in "Memphis Store Bought Teeth," "Berlin to Broadway," "Sextet."

LANSING, JOHN. Born Oct. 16, 1949 in Baldwin, NY. Attended Hofstra Col. Bdwy debut 1972 in "The Sign in Sidney Brustein's Window," followed by "Grease."

LAPKA, BETSY. Born Nov. 14, 1949 in Chicago, IL. Graduate Ill. Wesleyan U. Debut 1975 OB in ELT's "Tenderloin."

LASKY, ZANE. Born Apr. 23, 1953 in NYC. Attended Manhattan Com. Col., HB Studio. Debut OB 1973 in "The Hot l Baltimore," followed by "Prodigal," Bdwy 1974 in "All over Town."

LATHRAM, ELIZABETH. Born Apr. 23, 1947 in Washington, DC. Graduate UOre. Debut 1971 OB in "Godspell," followed by "Moonchildren," Bdwy 1976 in "Godspell."

LAUGHLIN, SHARON. Graduate UWash. Bdwy debut 1964 in "One by One," followed by "The Heiress," OB in "Henry IV," "Huui, Huui," "Mod Donna," "Subject to Fits," "The Minister's Black Veil," "Esther," "Rag Doll," "Four Friends."

LAVIN, LINDA. Born Oct. 15, 1939 in Portland, ME. Graduate William & Mary Col. Bdwy bow 1962 in "A Family Affair," followed by "Riot Act," "The Game Is Up," "Hotel Passionato," "It's a Bird . . . It's Superman!," "On a Clear Day You Can See Forever," "Something Different," "Cop-Out," "Last of the Red Hot Lovers," "Story Theatre," "The Enemy is Dead," OB in "Wet Paint" for which she received a Theatre World Award, "Comedy of Errors."

LAVREN, CHRISTINE. Born Sept. 7, 1944 in Victoria, TX. Bdwy debut 1971 in "Four on a Garden," followed OB by "An Evening with Ma Bell," "Fame," "Patrick Henry Lake Liquors."

LAWLESS, SUE. Born Sept. 26 in Freeport, IL. Graduate DePaul U. Debut 1961 OB in "The Sudden End of Anne Cinquefoil," followed by "Shoemaker's Holiday," "In the Nick of Time," "Don't Shoot, Mabel, It's Your Husband," "Now," "Love Course," "Good Old Fashioned Revue."

LAWRENCE, ELIZABETH. Born Sept. 6, 1922 in Huntington, WV. Graduate UMich., Yeshiva U. Bdwy debut 1954 in "The Rainmaker," followed by "All the Way Home," "Look Homeward, Angel," "A Matter of Gravity."

LAYNE, MARY. Born June 20, 1950 in Colorado, TX. Attended Houston Baptist Col., UHouston. Bdwy debut 1975 in "The Royal Family."

LEA, BARBARA. Born Apr. 10, 1929 in Detroit, MI. Graduate Wellesley, San Fernando State Col. Debut 1961 OB in "The Painted Days," followed by "Do I Hear a Waltz?," "Follies"(ELT).

LEAGUE, JANET. Born Oct. 13 in Chicago, IL. Attended Goodman Theatre. Debut 1969 OB in "To Be Young, Gifted and Black," followed by "Tiger at the Gates," "The Screens," "Mrs. Snow," "Please Don't Cry and Say No," Bdwy debut 1975 in "First Breeze of Summer."

LEE, IRVING. Born Nov. 21, 1948 in NYC. Graduate Boston U. Debut 1969 OB in "Kiss Now," followed by "Ride the Winds," "A Visit with Death," Bdwy in "Pippin"(1973), "Rockabye Hamlet."

LeGALLIENNE, EVA. Born Jan. 11, 1899 in London, Eng./ Bdwy debut 1915 in "Mrs. Boltay's Daughters," followed by "Bunny," "Melody of Youth," "Mr. Lazarus," "Saturday to Monday," "Lord and Lady Algy," "Off Chance," "Lusmore," "Elsie Janis and Her Gang," "Not So Long Ago," "Lilliom," "Sandro Botticelli," "The Rivals," "The Swan," "Assumption of Hannele," "LaVierge Folle," "Call of Life," "Master Builder," "John Gabriel Borkman," "Saturday Night," "Three Sisters," "Mistress of the Inn," "Twelfth Night," "Cradle Song," "Inheritors," "Good Hope," "First Stone," "Improvisations in June," "Hedda Gabler," "Would-Be Gentleman," "Cherry Orchard," "Peter Pan," "Sunny Morning," "Seagull," "Living Corpse," "Romeo and Juliet," "Siegfried," "Alison's House," "Camille," "Dear Jane," "Alice in Wonderland," "L'Aiglon," "Rosmersholm," "Women Have Their Way," "Prelude to Exile," "Madame Capet," "Frank Fay's Music Hall," "Uncle Harry," "Therese," "Henry VIII," "What Every Woman Knows," "Ghosts," "The Corn Is Green"(CC), "Starcross Story," "Southwest Corner," "Mary Stuart," "Exit the King," "The Royal Family."

LEIBMAN, RON. Born Oct. 11, 1937 in NYC. Attended Ohio Wesleyan, Actors Studio. Bdwy debut 1963 in "Dear Me, the Sky Is Falling," followed by "Bicycle Ride to Nevada," "The Deputy," "We Bombed in New Haven" for which he received a Theatre World Award, "Cop-Out," OB in "The Academy," "John Brown's Body," "Scapin," "Legend of Lovers," "Dead End," "Poker Session," "The Premise," "Transfers," "Room Service," "Love Two," "Rich and Famous."

LEIGH, JANET. Born July 6, 1927 in Merced, CA. Attended UPacific. Bdwy debut 1975 in "Murder among Friends."

**Robert Lintner**

**Sara Louise**

**Alvin Lum**

**Debra Lyman**

**Adeyemi Lythco**

**LeMASSENA, WILLIAM.** Born May 23, 1916 in Glen Ridge, NJ. Attended NYU. Bdwy bow 1940 in "Taming of the Shrew," followed by "There Shall Be No Night," "The Pirate," "Hamlet," "Call Me Mister," "Inside U.S.A.," "I Know, My Love," "Dream Girl," "Nina," "Ondine," "Fallen Angels," "Redhead," "Conquering Hero," "Beauty Part," "Come Summer," "Grin and Bare It," "All over Town," OB in "The Coop," "Brigadoon," "Life with Father," "F. Jasmine Addams."

**LeNOIRE, ROSETTA.** Born Aug. 8, 1911 in NYC. Attended Theatre Wing. Bdwy debut 1936 in "Macbeth," followed by "Bassa Moona," "Hot Mikado," "Marching with Johnny,' "Janie," "Decision," "Three's a Family," "Destry Rides Again," "Finian's Rainbow," "South Pacific," "Sophie," "Tambourines to Glory," "Blues for Mr. Charlie," "Great Indoors," "Lost in the Stars," "The Royal Family," OB in "Bible Salesman," "Double Entry," "Clandestine on the Morning Line," "Cabin in the Sky," "Lady Day," LC in "Show Boat," "A Cry of Players," and "Streetcar Named Desire."

**LEON, JOSEPH.** Born June 8, 1923 in NYC. Attended NYU, UCLA. Bdwy debut 1950 in "Bell, Book and Candle," followed by "Seven Year Itch," "Pipe Dream," "Fair Game," "Gazebo," "Julia, Jake and Uncle Joe," "Beauty Part," "Merry Widow," "Henry, Sweet Henry," "Jimmy Shine," "All over Town," OB in "Come Share My House," "Dark Corners," "Interrogation of Havana," "Are You Now or Have You Ever Been."

**LEONARDOS, URYLEE.** Born May 14 in Charleston, SC. Attended Manhattan Sch. of Music. Bdwy debut 1943 in "Carmen Jones," followed by "Shangri-La," "Bells Are Ringing," "Wildcat," "Sophie," "Milk and Honey," "110 in the Shade," "Bajour," "Ilya, Darling," "Dear World," "Billy Noname"(OB), "Desert Song," "1600 Pennsylvania Avenue."

**LEVENE, SAM.** Born Aug. 28, 1905 in NYC. Graduate AADA. Bdwy debut 1927 in "Wall Street," followed by "3 Men on a Horse," "Dinner at 8," "Room Service," "Margin for Error," "Sound of Hunting," "Light up the Sky," "Guys and Dolls," "Hot Corner," "Fair Game," "Make a Million," "Heartbreak House," "Good Soup," "Devil's Advocate," "Let It Ride," "Seidman & Son," "Cafe Crown," "Last Analysis," "Nathan Weinstein, Mystic, Conn.," "The Impossible Years," "Paris Is Out," "A Dream out of Time" (OB), "The Sunshine Boys," "Dreyfus in Rehearsal," "The Royal Family."

**LEYDEN, LEO.** Born Jan. 28, 1929 in Dublin, Ire. Attended Abbey Theatre Sch. Bdwy debut 1960 in "Love and Libel," followed by "Darling of the Day," "Mundy Scheme," "The Rothschilds," "Capt. Brassbound's Conversion," "The Plough and the Stars" (LC), "Habeas Corpus."

**LIDE, MILLER.** Born Aug. 10, 1935 in Columbia, SC. Graduate USC, Am ThWing. Debut 1961 OB in "Three Modern Japanese Plays," followed by "Trial at Rouen," "Street Scene," "Joan of Arc at the Stake," Bdwy in "Ivanov" (1966), "Halfway up the Tree," "Who's Who in Hell," "We Interrupt This Program," "The Royal Family."

**LINDIG, JILLIAN.** Born Mar. 19, 1944 in Johnson City, TX. Debut 1969 OB in "Brownstone Urge," followed by "AC/DC."

**LINTNER, ROBERT.** Born Oct. 21, 1950 in Norfolk, NE. Graduate Midland Col. Debut 1975 OB in "The Three Musketeers," followed by "Panama Hattie."

**LIPSCOMB, DENNIS.** Born Mar. 1, 1942 in Brooklyn, NY. Graduate Clarkson Col., UIowa, LAMDA. Debut 1975 OB in "The Rivals," followed by "The Boss."

**LIPSON, PAUL.** Born Dec. 23, 1913 in Brooklyn. Attended Ohio State, Theatre Wing. Bdwy bow 1942 in "Lily of the Valley," followed by "Heads or Tails," "Detective Story," "Remains to Be Seen," "Carnival in Flanders," "I've Got Sixpence," "The Vamp," "Bells Are Ringing," "Fiorello" (CC), "Sound of Music," "Fiddler on the Roof," OB in "Deep Six the Briefcase," "The Inn at Lydda," "Golden Boy."

**LISTMAN, RYAN.** Born Dec. 30, 1939 in Newark, NJ. With LCRep in "St. Joan," "Tiger at the Gates," and "Cyrano de Bergerac," OB in "Utopia," "Until the Monkey Comes," "Fortune and Men's Eyes," "Spiro Who?," "Blueberry Mountain," "Midsummer Night's Dream."

**LITHGOW, JOHN.** Born in Rochester, NY. Graduate Harvard U. Bdwy debut 1973 in "The Changing Room," followed by "My Fat Friend," OB in "Hamlet," "Trelawny of the Wells," "A Memory of Two Mondays," "Secret Service," "Boy Meets Girl."

**LITTLE, CLEAVON.** Born June 1, 1939 in Chickasha, OK. Attended San Diego State U., AADA. Debut OB 1967 in "MacBird," followed by "Hamlet," "Someone's Coming Hungry," "Ofay Watcher," "Scuba Duba," "Narrow Road to the Deep North," "Great MacDaddy," Bdwy "Jimmy Shine," "Purlie," "All over Town," "The Poison Tree."

**LITTLE, DAVID.** Born Mar. 21, 1937 in Wadesboro, NC. Graduate William & Mary Col., Catholic U. Debut OB 1967 in "MacBird," followed by "Iphigenia in Aulis," "Antony and Cleopatra," "Antigone," "Enemy of the People," Bdwy bow 1974 in "Thieves," "Zalmen, or the Madness of God."

**LITTLE, RON PAUL.** Born Apr. 2, 1949 in New Haven, CT. UConn. graduate. Debut OB 1973 in "Thunder Rock," followed by "Summer Brave," "The Hot 1 Baltimore."

**LIVINGSTON, RUTH.** Born March 25 in New Haven, CT. Graduate UMich., AmThWing. Debut OB 1976 in "The Rimers of Eldritch."

**LoBIANCO, TONY.** Born Oct. 19, 1936 in NYC. Bdwy debut 1966 in "The Office," followed by "Royal Hunt of the Sun," "Rose Tattoo," "90 Day Mistress," "The Goodbye People," OB in "Three-penny Opera," "Answered the Flute," "Camino Real," "Oh, Dad, Poor Dad. . . .," "Journey to the Day," "Zoo Story," "Nature of the Crime," "Incident at Vichy," "Tartuffe," "Yankees 3, Detroit O."

**LONG, AVON.** Born June 18, 1910 in Baltimore, MD. Attended New Eng. Cons. Bdwy debut 1942 in "Porgy and Bess," followed by "Memphis Bound," "Carib Song," "Beggar's Holiday," "Don't Play Us Cheap," "Bubbling Brown Sugar," OB in "Ballad of Jazz Street."

**LOONEY, PETER.** Born Jan. 18, 1937 in Caldwell, ID. Graduate UNev., Neighborhood Playhouse. Debut 1976 OB in ELT's "Missouri Legend."

**LOUISE, SARA.** Born. Apr. 15 in Brooklyn, NY. Attended Northwestern U. RADA. Debut 1969 OB in "Of Thee I Sing," followed by "Show Me Where the Good Times Are," "Lend an Ear," "I'll Die if I Can't Live Forever," "Follies" (ELT).

**LOVETT, MARJORIE.** Born Oct. 4, 1932 in Long Branch, NJ. Debut 1975 OB in ELT's "Another Language."

**LUM, ALVIN.** Born May 28, 1931 in Honolulu, HI. Attended UHawaii. Debut 1969 OB in "In the Bar of a Tokyo Hotel," followed by ELT's "Pursuit o Happiness," Bdwy in "Lovely Ladies, Kind Gentlemen," "Two Gentlemen o Verona."

**LUPINO RICHARD.** Born Oct. 29, 1929 in Hollywood, CA. Attended LACC RADA. Bdwy debut 1956 in "Major Barbara," followed by "Conduct Unbe coming," "Sherlock Holmes."

**LuPONE, PATTI.** Born Apr. 21, 1949 in Northport, NY. Juilliard graduate Debut 1972 OB in "School for Scandal," followed by "Women Bewar Women," "Next Time I'll Sing to You," "Lower Depths," Bdwy in "Thre Sisters," "Measure for Measure," "Next Time I'll Sing to You," "Beggar Opera," "Scapin," "Robber Bridegroom," "Edward II," "The Time of You Life."

**LYMAN, DEBRA.** Born July 17, 1940 in Philadelphia, PA. Graduate Phila Col. Debut 1967 OB in "By Jupiter," Bdwy in "Sugar" (1972), "My Fair Lady."

**LYNCH, RICHARD.** Born Feb. 12, 1940 in Brooklyn, NY. Attended Actor Studio. Bdwy debut 1965 in "The Devils," followed by "Lady from the Sea," OB in "Live Like Pigs," "One Night Stands of a Noisy Passenger," "Thing That Almost Happen," "12 Angry Men," "The Orphan," "Action."

**LYNDECK, EDMUND.** Born Oct. 4, 1925 in Baton Rouge, LA. Graduat Montclair State Col., Fordham U. Bdwy debut 1969 in "1776," followed b "The King and I" (JB), OB in "Mandragola," "A Safe Place," "Amoureuse."

**LYTHCOTT, ADEYEMI.** Born Feb. 19, 1948 in Boston, MA. Graduate Obe lin Col. Debut 1975 OB in "The Taking of Miss Janie."

**MacCAULEY, MARK.** Born Dec. 11, 1948 in NYC. Attended UInd. Deb 1969 OB in "Crimes of Passion," followed by "Anna K," "Godspell."

**MacDONALD, PIRIE.** Born Mar. 24, 1932 in NYC. Graduate Harvard Debut OB 1957 in "Under Milk Wood," followed by "Zoo Story," Bdwy "Shadow and Substance," "Golden Fleecing," "Big Fish, Little Fish," "Dea of a Salesman," "But Not for Me."

**MacMAHON, ALINE.** Born May 3, 1899 in McKeesport, PA. Attend Barnard Col. Bdwy debut 1921 in "Madras House," followed by "Green Ring "Exciters," "Grand Street Follies," "Beyond the Horizon," "Maya," "Once a Lifetime," "Heavenly Express," "Eve of St. Mark," "Confidential Clerk," " Day by the Sea," "I Knock at the Door," "Pictures in the Hallway," "All t Way Home," LC's "The Alchemist," "Yerma," "East Wind," "Galilee "Walking to Waldheim," "Tiger at the Gates," "Cyrano," "Mary Stuart," " Crucible," "Trelawny of the Wells."

**MADAMA, LINDA.** Born July 26, 1947 in Steubenville, OH. Graduate Bost Conserv. Debut 1976 OB in "Panama Hattie."

**MADDEN, SHARON.** Born July 8, 1947 in St. Louis, MO. Debut 1975 ( in "The Hot 1 Baltimore."

Claire Malis

George Maguire

PJ Mann

Terrance McKerrs

Marcia McClain

**TAGGART, BRANDON.** Born Dec. 12, 1933 in Carthage, TN. Graduate U. Penn. OB in "Sing Muse!," "Like Other People," "Put It In Writing" for which he received a Theatre World Award, "Wedding Band," "But Not for Me," Bdwy in "Kelly," "New Faces of 1968," "Applause," "Lorelei," "We Interrupt This Program."

**MAGUIRE, GEORGE.** Born Dec. 4, 1946 in Wilmington, DE. Graduate UPa. Debut 1975 OB in "Polly," followed by "Follies."

**MALIS, CLAIRE.** Born Feb. 17, 1944 in Gary, IN. Graduate UInd., AADA. Debut 1969 OB in "The Man with the Flower in His Mouth," followed by "Berkeley Square."

**MANDIS, RENOS.** Born in Athens, Greece. Attended Hunter Col., HB Studio. Debut 1972 OB in "Tarot," followed by "Ice Age."

**MANN, PJ** Born Apr. 9, 1953 in Pasadena, CA. Bdwy debut 1976 in "Home Sweet Homer."

**MARCH, ELLEN.** Born Aug. 18, 1948 in Brooklyn. Graduate AMDA. Debut OB 1967 in "Pins and Needles," Bdwy 1973 in "Grease."

**MARCH, WILLIAM.** Born Apr. 3, 1951 in St. Paul, MN. Graduate NYU. Debut 1975 OB in "Gift of the Magi."

**MARCUM, KEVIN.** Born Nov. 7, 1955 in Danville, IL. Attended UIll. Bdwy debut 1976 in "My Fair Lady."

**MARGULIES, DAVID.** Born Feb. 19, 1937 in NYC. Graduate CCNY. Debut 1958 OB in "Golden Six," followed by "Six Characters in Search of an Author," "Tragical Historie of Dr. Faustus," "Tango," "Little Murders," "Seven Days Mourning," "Last Analysis," "An Evening with the Poet Senator," "Kid Champion," Bdwy 1973 in "The Iceman Cometh," Zalmen, or the Madness of God."

**MARR, RICHARD.** Born May 12, 1928 in Baltimore, MD. Graduate UPa. Bdwy in "Baker Street," "How to Succeed . . . ," "Here's Where I Belong," "Coco," "The Constant Wife," "So Long, 174th Street," OB in "Sappho," "Pilgrim's Progress," "Pimpernel," "Witness," "Antiques," "Two by Tennessee."

**MARSHALL, LARRY.** Born Apr. 3, 1944 in Spartanburg, SC. Attended Fordham, Xavier, New Eng. Consv. Bdwy debut in "Hair," followed by "Two Gentlemen from Verona," "Midsummer Night's Dream" (LC), "Rockabye Hamlet."

**MARSHALL, NORMAN THOMAS.** Born Apr. 28, 1939 in Richmond, VA. Attended UVa., Hunter Col., CCNY. Debut 1966 OB in "Gorilla Queen," followed by "Boy on the Straight-back Chair," "Charlie Was Here and Now He's Gone," "The Rapists," "Home/Work."

**MARTIN, LYNN.** Born Nov. 13, 1945 in Wilmington, DE. Graduate UDel. Debut 1967 OB in "Shoemaker's Holiday," followed by "Damn Yankees," "The Kid," "Panama Hattie."

**MARTIN, NAN.** Born in Decatur, IL. Attended UCLA, Actors Studio. Bdwy debut 1950 in "A Story for a Sunday Evening," "The Constant Wife," "J. B.," "Great God Brown," "Under the Yum-Yum Tree," "Summer Brave," OB in "Saturday Night Kid," "Sweet Confession," "Lysistrata," "Much Ado about Nothing," "Phaedra," "Merchant of Venice," "Taming of the Shrew," "Hamlet."

**MASIELL, JOE.** Born Oct. 27, 1939 in Bklyn. Studied at HB Studio. Debut 1964 OB in "Cindy," followed by "Jacques Brel Is Alive . . . ," "Sensations," "Leaves of Grass," "How to Get Rid of It," "A Matter of Time," "Tickles by Tucholsky," Bdwy in "Dear World," "Different Times," "Jacques Brel Is Alive"

**MASONER, GENE.** Born Jan. 22, in Kansas City, KS. Attended UKan., HB Studio. Debut OB 1969 in "Your Own Thing," followed by "White Devil," "Sherry," "3 Drag Queens from Datona," Bdwy 1975 in "Shenandoah."

**MASTERSON, PETER.** Born June 1, 1934 in Houston, TX. Graduate Rice U. Debut 1961 OB in "Call Me by My Rightful Name," Bdwy in "Marathon 33," "Blues for Mr. Charlie," "Trial of Lee Harvey Oswald," "Great White Hope," "Poison Tree."

**MATHEWS, WALTER.** Born Oct. 10, 1926 in NYC. Graduate NYU, Ohio U. Bdwy debut 1951 in "St. Joan," followed by "The Long Dream," "King Lear," "Mr. Roberts," "Equus."

**MATHEWSON, JOSEPH.** Born Sept. 22, 1938 in Ashland, KY. Yale graduate. Debut 1969 OB in "Tom Jones," followed by "The Sorrows of Frederick," "The Runner Stumbles."

**MATSUSAKA, TOM.** Born Aug. 8 in Wahiawa, HI. Graduate Mich. State U. Bdwy bow 1968 in "Mame," followed by "Pacific Overtures," OB in "Jungle Cities," "Ride the Winds," "Santa Anita '42."

**MATTHEWS, ANDERSON.** Born Oct. 21, 1950 in Springfield, OH. Graduate Carnegie-Mellon U. Bdwy debut 1975 in "The Robber Bridegroom," followed by "Edward II," "The Time of Your Life."

**MAXWELL, WAYNE.** Born Dec. 22, 1939 in Needesha, KS. OB in "Titus Andronicus," "Boy With a Cart," "Kataki," "Long Voyage Home," "Pictures in a Hallway," "A Whitman Portrait," "Too Close for Comfort," "The Gay Apprentice," "Dog in the Manger," "The Beheading," Bdwy debut 1976 in "Legend."

**MAYER, CHARLES.** Born Apr. 4, 1904 in Germany. Attended State Th. Sch. Debut OB 1944 in "Korbin," followed by "Beavercoat," "Marriage Proposal," "Jacknife," "Boubouroche," "Golden Boy," "The Lawyer," "Flight into Egypt," "Ice Age," Bdwy in "A Bell for Adano," "Red Mill," "Now I Lay Me Down to Sleep," "Springtime Folly," "Thieves."

**MAYER, JERRY.** Born May 12, 1941 in NYC. Graduate NYU. Debut 1968 in "Alice in Wonderland," followed by NYSF productions, "L'Ete," "Marouf," "Trelawny of the Wells," Bdwy in "Much Ado about Nothing" (1972).

**McCALL, NANCY.** Born Jan. 12, 1948 in Atlanta, GA. Graduate Northwestern U. Debut 1975 OB in "Godspell."

**McCARTY, MARY.** Born in 1923 in Kansas. Bdwy debut 1948 in "Sleepy Hollow" for which she received a Theatre World Award, followed by "Small Wonder," "Miss Liberty," "Bless You All," "A Rainy Day in Newark," "Follies," "Chicago."

**McCLAIN, MARCIA.** Born Sept. 30, 1949 in San Antonio, TX. Graduate Trinity U. Debut 1972 OB in "Rainbow," followed by Bdwy bow 1974 in "Where's Charley?" for which she received a Theatre World Award.

**McDERMOTT, KEITH.** Born in Houston, TX. Attended LAMDA. Bdwy debut 1976 in "Equus."

**McDONALD, TANNY.** Born Feb. 13, 1939 in Princeton, IN. Graduate Vassar Col. Debut OB with Am. Savoyards, followed by "All in Love," "To Broadway with Love," "Carricknabauna," "Beggar's Opera," "Brand," "Goodbye, Dan Bailey," "Total Eclipse," "Gorky," Bdwy in "Fiddler on the Roof," "Come Summer," "The Lincoln Mask."

**McGANN, MICHAELJOHN.** Born Feb. 2, 1952 in Cleveland, OH. Graduate Ohio U. Debut 1975 OB in "The Three Musketeers," followed by "Panama Hattie."

**McGILL, EVERETT.** Born Oct. 21, 1945 in Miami Beach, FL. Graduate UMo., RADA. Debut OB 1971 in "Brothers," followed by "The Father," "Enemies," Bdwy 1974 in "Equus."

**McGREEVEY, ANNIE.** Born in Brooklyn, NY. Graduate AADA. Bdwy debut 1971 in "Company," followed by "The Magic Show," OB in "Booth Is Back in Town."

**McINTYRE, BILL.** Born Sept. 2, 1935 in Rochester, NY. Debut 1970 OB in "The Fantasticks," Bdwy 1972 in "Secret Affairs of Mildred Wild," followed by "Legend."

**McKECHNIE, DONNA.** Born in Nov. 1944 in Detroit, MI. Bdwy debut 1961 in "How to Succeed. . . ." followed by "Promises, Promises," "Company," "On the Town," "Music! Music!" (CC), "A Chorus Line."

**McKERRS, TERRANCE.** Born Oct. 11, 1944 in Oakes, ND. Attended St. Cloud Col. Debut 1969 in "Rondalay," followed by "Say When," "Panama Hattie."

**McLERNON, PAMELA.** Born March 1 in Lynn, MA. Graduate Lowell State Col. Debut 1975 OB in "Tenderloin."

**McMILLAN, KENNETH.** Born July 2, 1934 in Brooklyn. Bdwy debut 1970 in "Borstal Boy," OB in "Red Eye of Love," "King of the Whole Damn World," "Little Mary Sunshine," "Babes in the Wood," "Moonchildren," "Merry Wives of Windsor," "Where Do We Go from Here?," "Kid Champion," "Streamers."

**McMILLIAN, LARRY.** Born Jan. 15, 1949 in Birmingham, AL. Graduate UAla. Bdwy debut 1975 in "Very Good Eddie."

**McMURRAY, SAM.** Born Apr. 15, 1952 in NYC. Graduate Washington U. Debut OB 1975 in "The Taking of Miss Janie," followed by "Merry Wives of Windsor," "Clarence."

**McWILLIAMS, CAROLINE.** Born Apr.4, in Seattle, WA. Attended Carnegie Tech, Pasadena Playhouse. Bdwy debut 1971 in "The Rothschilds," followed by "Cat on a Hot Tin Roof," OB in "An Ordinary Man," "Boccacio."

**MEEHAN, DANNY.** Born Feb. 17, 1933 in White Plains, NY. Attended AADA. Bdwy bow 1958 in "Whoop-Up," followed by "Do Re Mi," "Funny Girl," "Ulysses in Nighttown," "Poison Tree," OB in "Smiling the Boy Fell Dead," "Thracian Horses," "O, Oysters," "New Cole Porter Revue."

251

**Dione Messina**  **Jacob Milligan**  **Linda Miller**  **Craig R. Nelson**  **Chi Chi Navarro**

MENDILLO, STEPHEN. Born Oct. 9, 1942 in New Haven, CT. Graduate Colo. Col., Yale. Debut OB 1973 in "Nourish the Beast," followed by "Loot," "Subject to Fits," "Wedding Band," "As You Like It," Bdwy in "National Health," "Ah, Wilderness."

MERENSKY, JOHN. Born Nov. 4, 1943 in NYC. Attended Neighborhood Playhouse. With APA in "Man and Superman," "Judith," "War and Peace," OB in "Something for Kitty Genovese," "The Nun," "Two Gentlemen of Verona," "As You Like It," "Are You Prepared to Be a Marine?," "Disintegration of James Cherry," "Twentieth Century Tar," "The Home."

MERRILL, DINA. Born Dec. 29, 1925 in NYC. Attended AADA. Bdwy debut 1975 in "Angel Street."

MERSON, SUSAN. Born Apr. 25, 1950 in Detroit, MI. Graduate Boston U. Bdwy debut 1974 in "Saturday Sunday Monday," followed by OB "Vanities."

MESSINA, DIONE. Born Jan. 21 in New Orleans, LA. Graduate La.State U. Debut 1976 OB in "Panama Hattie."

METCALF, MARK. Born Mar. 11 in Findlay, OH. Attended UMich. Debut OB 1973 in "Creeps," followed by "The Tempest" (LC), "Beach Children," "Hamlet," "Patrick Henry Lake Liquors," "Streamers."

MILES, JOANNA. Born Mar. 6, 1940 in Nice, France. Attended Actors Studio. Bdwy debut 1963 in "Marathon '33," followed by "Lorenzo," OB in "Walk-Up," "Cave Dwellers," "Once in a Lifetime," "Home Free," "Drums in the Night," "Dylan," "Dancing for the Kaiser."

MILES, ROSS. Born in Poughkeepsie, NY. Bdwy debut 1962 in "Little Me," followed by "Baker Street," "Pickwick," "Darling of the Day," "Mame," "Jumpers," "Goodtime Charley," "Chicago."

MILLER, LINDA. Born Sept. 16, 1942 in NYC. Graduate Catholic U. Debut 1975 OB in "Black Picture Show" for which she received a Theatre World Award.

MILLER, MARTHA. Born Aug. 30, 1929 in New Bedford, MA. Graduate Carnegie-Mellon U. Debut OB 1956 in "House of Connolly," followed by "A Place without Morning," "Julius Caesar," "Major Barbara," "In the Summer House," "Merry Wives of Windsor," "Rimers of Eldritch."

MILLIGAN, JACOB. Born Mar. 25, 1949 in Kansas City, MO. Graduate UKC. Bdwy debut 1976 in "Equus."

MILLS, STEPHANIE. Born in 1959 in Brooklyn, NY. Bdwy debut 1975 in "The Wiz."

MINER, JAN. Born Oct. 15, 1917 in Boston, MA. Debut 1958 OB in "Obligato," followed by "Decameron," "Dumbbell People," "Autograph Hound," Bdwy in "Viva Madison Avenue," "Lady of the Camelias," "Freaking Out of Stephanie Blake," "Othello," "Milk Train Doesn't Stop Here Anymore," "Butterflies Are Free," "The Women," "Pajama Game," "Saturday Sunday Monday," "The Heiress."

MINTUN, JOHN. Born Jan. 16, 1941 in Decatur IL. Princeton graduate. Debut OB 1969 in "Get Thee to Canterbury," followed by "Boys in the Band," "The Rabinowitz Gambit," "Happy Halloween," "Esther," "The Inn at Lydda," "Carnival Dreams," Bdwy 1975 in "The Ritz."

MIRATTI, T. Born Dec. 6 in Santa Barbara, CA. Attended SBCC, Pasadena Playhouse. Debut 1976 OB in "The Shortchanged Review."

MIXON, ALAN. Born Mar. 15, 1933 in Miami, FL. Attended UMiami. Bdwy bow 1962 in "Something about a Soldier," followed by "Sign in Sidney Brustein's Window," "The Devils," "The Unknown Soldier and His Wife," "Love Suicide at Schofield Barracks," "Equus," OB in "Suddenly Last Summer," "Desire under the Elms," "Trojan Women," "Alchemist," "Child Buyer," "Mr. and Mrs. Lyman," "A Whitman Portrait," "Iphigenia in Aulis," "Small Craft Warnings," "Mourning Becomes Electra," "The Runner Stumbles," "Old Glory."

MIZELLE, VANCE. Born Aug. 6, 1934 in Atlanta, GA. Graduate Davidson Col., UGa. Debut 1975 in "Hamlet" (CP & LC).

MOBERLY, ROBERT. Born Apr. 15, 1939 in Excelsior Springs, MO. Graduate UKan. Debut 1967 OB in "Arms and the Man," followed by "The Millionairess," "A Gun Play," "Shadow of a Gunman," Bdwy "A Place for Polly," "A Matter of Gravity."

MOLDOW, DEBORAH. Born Dec. 18, 1948 in NYC. Graduate Sarah Lawrence Col. Debut OB 1958 in "The Enchanted," followed by "The Power and the Glory," "Pursuit of Happiness."

MOORE, JONATHAN. Born Mar. 24, 1923 in New Orleans, LA. Attended Piscator's Sch. Debut OB 1961 in "After the Angels," followed by "Berkeley Square," Bdwy in "Dylan," "1776."

MORENO, RITA. Born Dec. 11, 1931 in Humacao, PR. Bdwy debut 1945 in "Skydrift," followed by "West Side Story," "Sign in Sidney Brustein's Win-

dow," "Last of the Red Hot Lovers," "The National Health," "The Ritz."

MORENZIE, LEON. Born in Trinidad, WI. Graduate Sir George William U. Debut 1972 OB in "Ti-Jean and His Brothers," followed by "The Cherry Orchard," Bdwy in "The Leaf People."

MORFOGEN, GEORGE. Born Mar. 30, 1933 in NYC. Graduate Brown U., Yale. Debut 1957 OB in "Trial of D. Karamazov," followed by "Christmas Oratorio," "Othello," "Good Soldier Schweik," "Cave Dwellers," "Once in a Lifetime," "Total Eclipse," "Ice Age," Bdwy in "The Fun Couple."

MORIARTY, MICHAEL. Born Apr. 5, 1941 in Detroit, MI. Graduate Dartmouth, LAMDA. Debut OB 1963 in "Antony and Cleopatra," followed by "Peanut Butter and Jelly," "Long Day's Journey into Night," Bdwy in "Trial of the Catonsville 9," "Find Your Way Home" for which he received a Theater World Award, "Richard III" (LC).

MORRIS, MARTI. Born June 8, 1949 in Clarksburg, WV. Graduate UWVa. Debut in 1972 OB in "The Fantasticks," followed by "Riverwind" (ELT), Bdwy 1974 in "Candide."

MORSE, ROBERT. Born May 18, 1931 in Newton, MA. Bdwy debut 1955 in "The Matchmaker," followed by "Say, Darling" for which he received a Theatre World Award, "Take Me Along," "How to Succeed in Business . . .," "Sugar," "So Long, 174th Street."

MORSELL, FRED. Born Aug. 3, 1940 in NYC. Graduate Dickinson Col. Debut 1971 OB in "Any Resemblance to Persons Living or Dead," followed by "Enemies," "Merchant of Venice," "Enclave," "Rubbers," "Yankees 3, Detroit 0."

MORTON, JOE. Born Oct. 18, 1947 in NYC. Attended Hofstra U. Debut OB 1968 in "Month of Sundays," followed by "Salvation," "Charlie Was Here and Now He's Gone," Bdwy in "Hair," "Two Gentlemen of Verona," "Tricks," "Raisin" for which he received a Theatre World Award.

MOSS, LELAND. Born Mar. 30, 1948 in NYC. Graduate Harvard, LAMBDA. Bdwy debut 1975 in "Yentl."

MUNSEL, PATRICE. Born May 14, 1925 in Spokane, WA. Made operatic debut 1943 at Met in "Mignon." Bdwy debut in 1964 in "The Merry Widow," followed by "Musical Jubilee."

MUNSON, ESTELLA. Born in Fairfield, CT. Graduate New Eng. Consv. Debut OB 1965 with Am. Savoyards, followed by "Show Boat" (LC), CC's "Carousel" and "Sound of Music," "Open Season on Butterflies," Bdwy "No, No, Nanette," "Musical Jubilee."

MURPHY, PETER. Born Sept. 13, 1925 in Glenarm, Ireland. Attended ULondon, RADA. Debut 1956 OB in "The Comedian," followed by "Macbeth," "Ghosts," "The Fantasticks," "When We Dead Awaken," "Dancing for the Kaiser."

MURRAY, DON. Born July 31, 1929 in Hollywood, CA. Attended AADA. Debut 1948 in "The Insect Comedy" (CC), followed by "The Rose Tattoo," "The Skin of Our Teeth" (1955), "The Hot Corner," "The Norman Conquests."

MUSANTE, TONY. Born June 30, 1936 in Bridgeport, CT. Oberlin Col. graduate. Debut OB 1960 in "Borak," followed by "The Balcony," "Theatre of the Absurd," "Half-Past Wednesday," "The Collection," "Tender Heel," "Kiss Mama," Mme. Mousse," "Zoo Story," "Match-Play," "Night of the Dunce," "A Gun Play," "A Memory of Two Mondays," "27 Wagons Full of Cotton," Bdwy bow 1975 in "P.S. Your Cat is Dead."

NAVARRO, CHICHI. Born June 22, in Puerto Rico. Attended HB Studio. Bdwy debut in 1975 in "The Ritz."

NEILSON, RICHARD. Born Nov. 30, 1924 in London, Eng. Debut 1959 OB in "Heloise," followed by "O Say Can You See," "Tea Party," Bdwy 1964 in "Pickwick," then "Wise Child," "My Fair Lady," "Equus."

NELSON, BARRY. Born in 1925 in Oakland, CA. Bdwy debut 1943 in "Winged Victory," followed by "Light Up the Sky," "The Moon is Blue," "Wake Up, Darling," "Rat Race," "Mary, Mary," "Nobody Loves an Albatross," "Cactus Flower," "Everything in the Garden," "Only Game in Town," "Fig Leaves Are Falling," "Engagement Baby," "Seascape," "Norman Conquests."

NELSON, CRAIG RICHARD. Born Sept. 17, 1947 in Salt Lake City, UT. Attended NYU. Bdwy debut 1972 in "Two Gentlemen of Verona," followed by "The Runner Stumbles."

NETTLETON, DENISE. Born June 9, 1948 in Branford, Can. Bdwy debut 1974 in "Grease."

NETTLETON, LOIS. Born in Oak Park, IL. Attended Goodman Theatre, Actors Studio. Bdwy debut 1949 in "The Biggest Thief in Town," followed by "Darkness at Noon," "Cat on a Hot Tin Roof," "God and Kate Murphy," "Silent Night, Lonely Night," "A Streetcar Named Desire" (LC), "They Knew What They Wanted" (OB).

**Don Nute**     **Mary Ann Niles**     **Ian O'Connell**     **Sylvia O'Brien**     **Thomas O'Rourke**

NEWMAN, STEPHEN D. Born Jan. 20, 1943 in Seattle, WA. Stanford graduate. Debut 1971 OB in Judith Anderson's "Hamlet," followed by "School for Wives," "Beggar's Opera," "Pygmalion," "In the Voodoo Parlour of Marie Leveau," "Richard III," "Santa Anita '42," "Polly," Bdwy in "An Evening with Richard Nixon and . . . ," "Emperor Henry IV," "Habeas Corpus," "Rex."

NICKERSON, SHANE. Born Jan. 29, 1964 in Miami, FL. Bdwy debut 1972 in "Pippin."

NICOL, LESSLIE. Born May 27 in Dundee, Scot. NY debut OB in "Man with Load of Mischief," Bdwy debut 1973 in "Grease."

NILES, MARY ANN. Born May 2, 1933 in NYC. Attended Miss Finchley's Ballet Acad. Bdwy debut in "Girl from Nantucket," followed by "Dance Me a Song," "Call Me Mister," "Make Mine Manhattan," "La Plume de Ma Tante," "Carnival," "Flora the Red Menace," "Sweet Charity," "George M!," "No, No, Nanette," "Irene," OB in "The Boys from Syracuse." CC's "Wonderful Town" and "Carnival."

NOBLE, JAMES. Born Mar. 5, 1922 in Dallas, TX. Attended SMU. Bdwy bow 1949 in "The Velvet Glove," followed by "Come of Age," "A Far Country," "Strange Interlude," "1776," "The Runner Stumbles," OB in "Wilder's Triple Bill," "Night of the Dunce," "Rimers of Eldritch," "The Acquisition," "A Scent of Flowers," "A Touch of the Poet."

NOVY, NITA. Born June 13, 1950 in Wilkes-Barre, PA. Graduate Duke U. Bdwy debut 1960 in "Gypsy," followed by "Sound of Music," OB in "How to Succeed . . . ," "Maggie Flynn!"

NUTE, DON. Born Mar. 13, in Connellsville, Pa. Attended Denver U. Debut OB 1965 in "The Trojan Women," followed by "Boys in the Band," "Mad Theatre for Madmen," "The Eleventh Dynasty," "About Time," "The Urban Crisis," "Christmas Rappings," "The Life of a Man," "A Look at the Fifties."

O'BRIEN, SYLVIA. Born May 4, 1924 in Dublin, Ire. Debut OB 1961 in "O Marry Me," followed by "Red Roses for Me," "Every Other Evil," "3 by O'Casey," "Essence of Woman," "Dear Oscar," Bdwy in "Passion of Josef D," "Right Honourable Geltleman," "Loves of Cass McGuire," "Hadrian VII," "Conduct Unbecoming," "My Fair Lady."

O'CONNELL, IAN. Born Nov. 10, 1945 in Sligo, Ire. Graduate UNC. Debut 1976 OB in 'Maggie Flynn."

O'CONNELL, PATRICIA. Born May 17 in NYC. Attended AmThWing. Debut 1958 OB in "The Saintliness of Margery Kemp," followed by "Time Limit," "An Evening's Frost," "Mrs. Snow," "Electric Ice," "Survival of St. Joan," "Rain," "The Rapists," "Who Killed Richard Cory?," Bdwy in "Crisscrossing," "Summer Brave."

O'DELL, K. LYPE. Born Feb. 2, 1939 in Claremore, OK. Graduate Los Angeles State Col. Debut 1972 OB in "Sunset," followed by "Our Father," "Ice Age."

OH, SOON-TECK. Born June 29, 1943 in Korea. Attended UCLA, Neighborhood Playhouse. Bdwy debut 1976 in "Pacific Overtures."

O'HARA, PAIGE. Born May 10, 1956 in Ft. Lauderdale, FL. Debut 1975 OB in "The Gift of the Magi."

O'NEAL, RON. Born Sept. 1, 1937 in Utica, NY. Attended Ohio State U. Debut 1968 OB in "American Pastoral," followed by "No Place to Be Somebody" for which he received a Theatre World Award, "Dream on Monkey Mountain," Bdwy in "All over Town."

ORBACH, JERRY. Born Oct. 20, 1935 in NYC. Attended Northwestern U. Bdwy debut 1961 in "Carnival," followed by "Guys and Dolls," "Carousel," "Annie Get Your Gun," "The Natural Look," "Promises, Promises," "6 Rms Riv Vu," "Chicago," OB in "Threepenny Opera," "The Fantasticks," "The Cradle Will Rock," "Scuba Duba."

ORFALY, ALEXANDER. Born Oct. 10, 1935 in Brooklyn, NY. Appeared in "South Pacific" (LC), "How Now, Dow Jones," "Ari," "Sugar," "Cyrano," OB "The End of All Things Natural," "Mahogonny," "Johnny Johnson," "Ride the Winds," "Polly," "1600 Pennsylvania Avenue."

O'ROURKE, THOMAS. Born Mar. 28, 1944 in NYC. Attended Goodman Theatre Sch. Debut 1976 OB in "The Old Glory."

ORR, MARY. Born Dec. 21, 1918 in Brooklyn, NY. Attended AADA, Syracuse U. Bdwy debut 1938 in "Bachelor Born," followed by "Jupiter Laughs," "Wallflower," "Dark Hammock," "Sherlock Holmes," "The Desperate Hours," OB in "Grass Widows."

OSBORNE, KIPP. Born Oct. 17, 1944 in Jersey City, NJ. Attended UMich., Neighborhood Playhouse. Bdwy debut 1970 in "Butterflies Are Free" for which he received a Theatre World Award, followed by "Veronica's Room," "Lady from the Sea," OB in "Children's Mass," "Love Gotta Come by Saturday Night."

O'SHEA, MILO. Born June 2, 1926 in Dublin, Ire. Bdwy debut 1968 in "Staircase," followed by "Dear World," "Mrs. Warrens's Profession" (LC).

O'SHEA, TESSIE. Born Mar. 13, 1918 in Caerdydd, GB. Bdwy debut 1963 in "The Girl Who Came to Supper," followed by "A Time for Singing," "Something's Afoot."

OSHEN, GABRIEL. Born Oct. 8, 1950 in NYC. Bdwy debut 1974 in "Equus."

OTTENHEIMER, ALBERT M. Born Sept. 6, 1904 in Tacoma, WA. Graduate UWash. Bdwy debut 1946 in "Affair of Honor," followed by "West Side Story," "Deputy," "Yentl," OB in "Monday's Heroes," "Tiger," "Mother Riba," "A Christmas Carol," "Juno and the Paycock," "Italian Straw Hat," "The Iceman Cometh," "Call It Virtue," "The Immoralist," "The Cat and the Canary," "Exhaustion of Our Son's Love," "Deadly Game," "Brother Gorski," "The Kid," "Holy Ghosts," "Yentl the Yeshiva Boy."

PAGE, GERALDINE. Born Nov. 22, 1924 in Kirksville, MO. Attended Goodman Theatre. OB in "7 Mirrors," "Summer and Smoke" for which she received a Theatre World Award, "Macbeth," "Look Away," Bdwy debut 1953 in "Midsummer," followed by "The Immoralist," "The Rainmaker," "Innkeepers," "Separate Tables," "Sweet Bird of Youth," "Strange Interlude," "Three Sisters," "P.S. I Love You," "The Great Indoors," "White Lies," "Black Comedy," "The Little Foxes," "Angela," "Absurd Person Singular."

PALMER, LELAND. Born June 16, 1945 in Port Washington, NY. Bdwy debut 1966 in "Joyful Noise," followed by "Applause," "Pippin," OB in "Your Own Thing."

PALMIERI, JOSEPH. Born Aug. 1, 1939 in Bklyn. Attended Catholic U. With NYSF 1965-6, "Cyrano de Bergerac" (LCR), OB in "Butter and Egg Man," "Boys in the Band," "Beggar's Opera," "The Family," Bdwy in "Lysistrata," "Candide."

PAPE, PAUL. Born July 17, 1952 in Rochester, NY. Graduate SUNY Brockport. Debut 1976 OB in "The Cherry Orchard."

PARKER, DON. Born Aug. 29 in NYC. Graduate Bard Col. Bdwy debut 1975 in "Kennedy's Children."

PARS, JULIE M. Born Nov. 29, 1949 in Alton, IL. Graduate Monticello Col. Bdwy debut 1971 in "Follies," followed by "Irene," "Musical Jubilee."

PARSONS, ESTELLE. Born Nov. 20, 1927 in Lynn, MA. Attended Boston U., Actors Studio. OB in "Threepenny Opera," "Automobile Graveyard," "Mrs. Dally Has a Lover" for which she received a Theatre World Award, "In the Summer House." "Monopoly," "Peer Gynt," "Mahagonny," "Silent Partner," "Barbary Shore," "Oh Glorious Tintinnabulation," with LCR in "East Wind," "Galileo," "People Are Living There," and "Mert and Phil," Bdwy in "Happy Hunting," "Whoop-Up!," "Beg, Borrow or Steal," "Ready When You Are, C. B.," "Malcolm," "Seven Descents of Myrtle," "A Way of Life," "and Miss Reardon Drinks a Little," "Norman Conquests."

PASEKOFF, MARILYN. Born Nov. 7, 1949 in Pittsburgh, PA. Graduate Boston U. Debut 1975 OB in "Godspell."

PASSELTINER, BERNE, Born Nov. 21, 1931 in NYC. Graduate Catholic U. OB in "Square in the Eye," "Sourball," "As Virtuously Given," "Now Is the Time for All Good Men," "Rain,' "Kaddish," "Against the Sun," "End of Summer," "Yentl, the Yeshiva Boy," Bdwy in "The Office," "The Jar," "Yentl."

PATIK, VICKIE. Born June 14, 1950 in Los Angeles, CA. Graduate Los Angeles State U. Bdwy debut 1976 in "My Fair Lady."

PATTON, LUCILLE. Born in NYC; attended Neighborhood Playhouse. Bdwy debut 1946 in "A Winter's Tale," followed by "Topaze," "Arms and the Man," "Joy to the World," "All You Need Is One Good Break," "Fifth Season," "Heavenly Twins," "Rhinoceros," "Marathon '33." "The Last Analysis," "Dinner at 8," "La Strada," "Unlikely Heroes," "Love Suicide at Schofield Barracks," OB in "Ulysses in Nighttown," "Failures," "Three Sisters, "Yes, Yes, No,No," "Tango," "Mme. de Sade," "Apple Pie," "Follies."

PAULETTE, LARRY. Born Apr. 10, 1949 in Steubenville, OH. Attended UCinn. Debut OB 1974 in "Let My People Come."

PAYTON-WRIGHT, PAMELA. Born Nov. 1, 1941 in Pittsburgh, PA. Graduate Birmingham Southern Col., RADA. Bdwy debut 1967 with APA in "The Show-Off," followed by "Exit the King," "The Cherry Orchard," "Jimmy Shine," "Mourning Becomes Electra," "Glass Menagerie," OB in "Effect of Marigolds . . . ," "The Crucible."

PEACHENA. Born May 15, 1948 in Salisbury, MD. Graduate Morgan State Col. Debut 1974 OB in "Let My People Come."

PEARL, BARRY. Born Mar. 29, 1950 in Lancaster, PA. Graduate Carnegie Tech. Bdwy debut 1961 in "Bye Bye Birdie," "A Teaspoon Every Four Hours," "Oliver," OB in "The Glorious Age."

**Barry Pearl**     **Penny Peyser**     **Jeffrey D. Pomerantz**     **Frances Pole**     **Howard Porte**

**PENN, EDWARD.** Born In Washington, DC. Studied at HB studio. Debut 1965 OB in "The Queen and the Rebels," followed by "My Wife and I," "Invitation to a March," "Of Thee I Sing," "Fantasticks," "Greenwillow," "One for the Money," "Dear Oscar," "Speed Gets the Poppys," "Man with a Load of Mischief." Bdwy bow 1975 in "Shenandoah."

**PERCASSI, DON.** Born Jan. 11 in Amsterdam, NY. Bdwy debut 1964 in "High Spirits," followed by "Walking Happy," "Coco," "Sugar," "Molly," "Mack and Mabel," "A Chorus Line."

**PERKINS, ANTHONY.** Born Apr. 4, 1932 in NYC. Attended Rollins Col., Columbia U. Bdwy debut 1954 in "Tea and Sympathy" for which he received a Theatre World Award, followed by "Look Homeward, Angel," "Greenwillow," "Harold," "Star Spangled Girl," "Steambath" (OB), "Equus."

**PERKINS, PATTI.** Born July 9 in New Haven, CT. Attended AMDA. Debut 1972 OB in "The Contrast," followed by "Fashion," "Tuscaloosa's Calling Me . . . ," Bdwy in "All Over Town."

**PERRIER, MICHAEL.** Born Aug. 6, 1942 In Minneapolis, MN. Graduate UMinn. Debut 1972 OB in "Love Me, Love My Children," followed by "Dancing Picture Show," "New Beginnings," "Follies" (ELT).

**PETERSON, KURT.** Born Feb. 12, 1948 in Stevens Point, WI. Attended AMDA. Bdwy debut 1969 in "Dear World," followed by "Follies," OB in "An Ordinary Miracle," "West Side Story" (LC), "Dames at Sea," "By Bernstein."

**PETRICOFF, ELAINE.** Born in Cincinnati, OH. Graduate Syracuse U. Bdwy debut 1971 in "The Me Nobody Knows," OB in "Hark!," "Ride the Winds," "Cole Porter," Bdwy debut 1973 in "Grease."

**PETTY, ROSS.** Born Aug. 29, 1946 in Winnipeg, Can. Graduate UManitoba. Debut OB 1975 in "Happy Time," followed by "Maggie Flynn" (ELT).

**PEYSER, PENNY.** Born Feb. 9, 1951 in NYC. Emerson Col. graduate. Debut 1975 OB in "Dimaond Studs," followed by "Hot 1 Baltimore," "Lemon Sky."

**PFEIFFER, MARILYN,** Born Nov. 7, 1948 in Houston, TX. Graduate Rice U. Bdwy debut 1976 in "The Runner Stumbles."

**PHELPS, ELEANOR.** Born in Baltimore, MD. Vassar graduate. Bdwy debut 1928 in "Merchant of Venice," followed by "Richard II," "Criminal Code," "Trick for Trick," "Seen But Not Heard," "Flight to the West," "Queen Bee." "We the People," "Six Characters in Search of an Author," "Mr. Big," "Naughty-Naught," "The Disenchanted," "Picnic," "My Fair Lady" (1956 & 76), "40 Carats," "Crown Matrimonial," "Royal Family," OB in "Garden District," "Color of Darkness."

**PICKLES, CHRISTINA.** Born Feb. 17, 1938 in England. Attended RADA. With APA in "School for Scandal," "War and Peace," "The Wild Duck," "Pantagleize," "You Can't Take It with You," "The Seagull," "The Misanthrope," Bdwy in "Inadmissible Evidence," "Who's Who in Hell," "Sherlock Holmes."

**PIERSOL, MORRIE.** Born July 6, 1952 in Philadelphia, PA. Graduate Southampton Col. Bdwy debut 1976 in "The Runner Stumbles."

**PINCUS, WARREN.** Born Apr. 13, 1938 in Brooklyn, NY. Attended CCNY. OB credits: "Miss Nefertiti Regrets," "Circus," "Magician," "Boxcars," "Demented World," "Give My Regards," "Electronic Nigger," "Last Pad," "Waiting for Godot," "In the Time of Harry Harrass," "Yoshe Kolb," Bdwy bow 1976 in "Zalmen, or the Madness of God."

**PITCHFORD, DEAN.** Born July 29, 1951 in Honolulu, HI. Graduate Yale U. Debut 1971 OB in "Godspell," Bdwy 1973 in "Pippin."

**PLUMLEY, DON.** Born Feb. 11, 1934 in Los Angeles, CA. Pepperdine Col. graduate. Debut 1961 OB in "The Cage," followed by "A Midsummer Night's Dream," "Richard II," "Cymbeline," "Much Ado about Nothing," "Saving Grace," "A Whistle in the Dark," "Operation Sidewinder," "Enemy of the People," "Back Bog Beast Bait," "The Kid," Bdwy 1974 in "Equus."

**POLE, FRANCES.** Born June 12, 1907 in St. Paul, MN. Debut 1958 OB in " 'Tis Pity She's a Whore," followed by "Mornings at 7," "Ice Age."

**POLLOCK, GEORGE.** Born May 26, 1937 in NYC. Juilliard graduate. Bdwy debut 1975 in "Lamppost Reunion."

**POMERANTZ, JEFFREY DAVID.** Born July 2, 1945 in NYC. Attended Northwestern U., RADA. Bdwy debut (as Jeffrey David-Owen) 1975 in "The Leaf People," followed by "The Ritz," "Equus."

**PONAZECKI, JOE.** Born Jan. 7, 1934 in Rochester, NY. Attended Rochester U., Columbia. Bdwy bow 1959 in "Much Ado About Nothing," followed by "Send Me No Flowers," "Call on Kuprin,' "Take Her, She's Mine," "Fiddler

on the Roof," "Xmas in Las Vegas," "3 Bags Full," "Love in E-Flat," "90 Day Mistress," "Harvey" "Trial of the Catonsville 9," "Country Girl," "Freedom of the City," "Summer Brave," OB in "The Dragon," "Muzeeka," "Witness," "All Is Bright," "The Dog Ran Away," "Dream of a Blacklisted Actor."

**POOLE, ROY.** Born Mar. 31, 1924 in San Bernardino, CA. Graduate Stanford U. Bdwy in "Now I Lay Me Down to Sleep," "St. Joan," "Bad Seed," "I Knock at the Door," "Long Day's Journey into Night," "Face of a Hero," "Moby Dick," "Poor Bitos," "1776," "Scratch," Ob in "27 Wagons Full of Cotton," "A Memory of Two Mondays," "Secret Service," "Boy Meets Girl."

**PORTER, HOWARD.** Born Oct. 31, 1946 in Gary, WV. Attended WVa. U. AMDA. Bdwy debut 1970 in "Hello, Dolly!," followed by "Purlie," "Two Gentlemen of Verona," OB in "Great McDaddy."

**PREBLE, ED.** Born Nov. 9, 1919 in Chicago, IL. Bdwy bow 1957 in "Inherit the Wind," followed by "Family Way," OB in "Press Cuttings," "Failures," "Krapp's Last Tape," "Marcus in the High Grass," "A Figleaf in Her Bonnet," "Calling in Crazy," "The Family."

**PREECE, K. K.** Born Nov. 14, 1949 in Anna, IL. Graduate Brenau Col. Debut 1976 OB in "Panama Hattie."

**PREMICE, JOSEPHINE.** Born July 21, 1926 in Brooklyn, NY. Graduate Columbia, Cornell U. Bdwy debut 1945 in "Blue Holiday," followed by "Caribbean Carnival," "Mr. Johnson," "Jamaica," "A Hand Is on the Gate," "Bubbling Brown Sugar," OB in "House of Flowers," "Cherry Orchard," "American Night Cry."

**PRENTISS, PAULA.** Born Mar. 4, 1938 in San Tantonio, TX. Graduate Northwestern U. Debut 1969 OB in "Arf" and "The Great Airplane Snatch," Bdwy 1975 in "The Norman Conquests."

**PRESTON, BARRY.** Born May 31, 1945 in Brooklyn, NY. Attended Utah State Col. Bdwy debut 1964 in "Something More," followed by "A Joyful Noise," "Bubbling Brown Sugar."

**PRESTON, WILLIAM,** Born Aug. 26, 1921 In Columbia, PA. Graduate Pa. State U. Debut OB 1972 in "We Bombed in New Haven," followed by "Hedda Gabler," "Whisper into My Good Ear," "A Nestless Bird," "Friends of Mine," "Iphigenia in Aulis," "Midsummer."

**PRICE, GILBERT.** Born Sept. 10, 1942 in NYC. Attended AmThWing. Bdwy bow 1965 in "Roar of the Greasepaint . . . ," followed by "Lost in the Stars," "The Night That Made America Famous," "1600 Pennsylvania Avenue," OB in "Kicks & Co," "Fly Blackbird," "Jerico-Jim Crow" for which he received a Theatre World Award, "Promenade," "Slow Dance on the Killing Ground," "Six," "Melodrama Play."

**PRICE, PAUL B.** Born Oct. 7, 1933 In Carteret, NJ. Attended Pasadena Playhouse. Debut 1960 OB in "Dead End," followed by "Banquet for the Moon," "O Say Can You See," "Dumbwaiter," "Live Like Pigs," "Medea," "4H Club," "Waiting for Godot," Bdwy in "A Cook for Mr. General," "Let Me Hear You Smile," "The Ritz."

**PRIMUS, BARRY.** Born Feb. 16, 1938 in NYC. Attended CCNY. Bdwy debut 1960 in "The Nervous Set," followed by "Oh, Dad, Poor Dad . . . ," "Creation of the World and Other Business," OB in "Henry IV," "Huui, Huui," "The Criminals," "Diary of a Scoundrel," "Jesse and the Bandit Queen."

**PRITCHARD, TED.** Born Sept. 12, 1936 in Lakewood, OH. Graduate Ohio U. Debut 1974 in "Music! Music!" (CC), followed OB 1975 in "Tuscaloosa's Calling Me But I'm Not Going."

**PUMA, MARIE.** Born in Brooklyn, NY. Graduate CUNY. Debut 1969 OB in "Romeo and Jeannette,' followed by "Purification."

**PYSHER, ERNIE.** Born in Youngstown, OH. Graduate Youngstown State U. Bdwy debut 1974 in "Good News," followed by "The Night That Made America Famous," OB in "Carousel," "My Fair Lady,"

**QUARRY, RICHARD.** Born Aug. 9, 1944 in Akron, OH. Graduate UAkron, NYU. Bdwy bow 1970 in "Georgy," followed by "Oh! Calcutta!," "Grease."

**RABB, ELLIS.** Born June 20, 1930 in Memphis, TN. Attended Carnegie Tech. Yale. Debut OB 1956 in "Midsummer Night's Dream," followed by "Misanthrope," "Mary Stuart," "The Tavern," "Twelfth Night," "The Importance of Being Earnest," "King Lear," "Man and Superman," Bdwy in "Look after Lulu," "Jolly's Progress," "Right You Are . . . ," "Scapin," "Impromtu at Versailles," "Lower Depths," "School for Scandal," "Pantagleize," "Cock-a-Doodle Dandy," "Hamlet," "The Royal Family." Founder and director of APA.

254

| ugenia Rawls | John Remme | Antonia Rey | Jess Richards | Elaine Rinehart |

**AITT, JOHN.** Born Jan. 29, 1917 in Santa Ana, CA. Graduate Redlands U. dwy bow 1945 in "Carousel" for which he received a Theatre World Award, llowed by "Magdalena," "Three Wishes for Jamie," "Pajama Game," "A yful Noise," "On a Clear Day You Can See Forever," "Musical Jubilee."

**AMOS, RICHARD.** Born Aug. 23, 1941 in Seattle, WA. Graduate UMinn. dwy debut 1968 in "House of Atreus," followed by "Arturo Ui," OB in Adaptation," "Screens," "Lotta," "The Tempest," "A Midsummer Night's ream," "Gorky."

**ANDELL, RON.** Born Oct. 8, 1920 in Sydney, Aust. Attended St. Mary's ol. Bdwy debut 1949 in "The Browning Version," followed by "A Har-quinade," "Candida," "World of Suzie Wong," "Sherlock Holmes," "Mrs. arren's Profession" (LC).

**AWLS, EUGENIA.** Born Sept. 11. 1916 in Macon, GA. Attended UNC. dwy debut 1934 in "The Children's Hour," followed by "To Quito and Back," ourneyman," "Little Foxes," "Guest in the House," "Man Who Had All the uck," "Strange Fruit," "The Shrike," "Great Sebastians," "First Love," "Case Libel," "Poker Session" (OB), "Sweet Bird of Youth."

**EAMS, LEE ROY.** Born Aug. 23, 1942 in Covington, KY. Graduate U. Cinn. ons. Bdwy debut 1966 in "Sweet Charity," followed by "Oklahoma!" (LC). Applause," "Lorelei."

**EDGRAVE, LYNN.** Born In London Mar. 8, 1943. Attended Central Schl. Speech. Bdwy debut 1967 in "Black Comedy," follwed by "My Fat Friend," Mrs. Warren's Profession" (LC), "Knock Knock."

**EDGRAVE, VANESSA.** Born Jan. 30, 1937 in London, Eng. Attended Cen-al School of Speech and Drama. Bdwy debut 1976 in "The Lady from the ea."

**EED, ALEXANDER.** Born June 9, 1916 in Clearfield, PA. Graduate Colum-a U. Debut OB 1956 in "Lady from the Sea," followed by "All the King's en," "Death of Satan," "The Balcony," "Call Me by My Rightful Name," Studs Edsel," "The Coroner's Plot," on Bdwy in "Witness," "Lost in the ars," "The Skin of Our Teeth."

**EED, BOBBY.** Born Sept. 26, 1956 in NYC. Attended AMDA. Debut OB 975 in "Boy Meets Boy."

**EED, VIVIAN.** Born June 6, 1947 in Pittsburgh, PA. Attend Pittsburgh usical Inst., Juilliard. Bdwy debut 1971 "That's Entertainment," followed by Don't Bother Me, I Can't Cope," "Bubbling Brown Sugar" for which she eceived a Theatre World Award.

**EEHLING, JOYCE.** Born Mar. 5, 1949 in Baltimore, MD. Graduate NC chool of Arts. Debut 1976 OB in "Hot l Baltimore," followed by "Who Killed ichard Cory?"

**EEVE, CHRISTOPHER.** Born Sept. 25, 1952 in NYC. Graduate Cornell U., uilliard. Debut 1975 OB in "Berkeley Square," Bdwy 1976 in "A Matter of ravity."

**EINHARDSEN, DAVID.** Born Jan. 13, 1949 in NYC. Graduate Westmin-er Col. Bdwy debut 1976 in "Zalmen, or the Madness of God."

**EINKING, ANN.** Born Nov. 10, 1949 in Seattle, WA. Attended Joffrey Sch., B Studio. Bdwy debut 1969 in "Cabaret," followed by "Coco," "Pippin," Over Here" for which she received a Theatre World Award, "Goodtime harley," "A Chorus Line."

**EMME, JOHN.** Born Nov. 21, 1935 in Fargo, ND. Attended UMinn. Debut 972 OB in "One for the Money," Bdwy 1975 in "The Ritz," followed by "The oyal Family."

**EPOLE, CHARLES.** Born May 24 in Brooklyn, NY. Graduate Hofstra U. dwy debut 1975 in "Very Good Eddie" for which he received a Theatre World ward.

**EXROAD, DAVID.** Born Jan. 11, 1950 in Parkersburg, WV. Graduate WVa. . Debut OB 1973 in "The Fantasticks."

**EY, ANTONIA.** Born Oct. 12, 1927 in Havana, Cuba. Graduate Havana U. dwy debut 1964 in "Bajour," followed by "Mike Downstairs," "Engagement aby," "The Ritz," OB in "Yerma," "Fiesta in Madrid," "Camino Real" (LC), Back Bog Beast Bait," "Rain," "42 Seconds from Broadway," "Streetcar amed Desire" (LC).

**ICE, SARAH.** Born Mar. 5, 1955 in Okinawa. Attended Ariz State U. Debut 974 OB in "The Fantasticks."

**ICHARDS, JESS.** Born Jan. 23, 1943 in Seattle, WA. Attended UWash. dwy debut 1966 in "Walking Happy," followed by "South Pacific" (LC). Blood Red Roses," "Two by Two," "On the Town" for which he received a heatre World Award, "Mack and Mabel," OB in "One for the Money."

**RICHARDSON, IAN.** Born Apr. 7, 1934 in Edinburgh, Scot. Attended Royal Scottish Acad. Debut 1964 at LC with Royal Shakespeare Co. in "King Lear," "Comedy of Errors," BAM 1975–6 in "Richard II," "Summerfolk," "Love's Labours Lost," "He That Plays the King," Bdwy in "Marat/Sade" (1965), "My Fair Lady" (1976).

**RIDGE, JOHN.** Born May 13, 1924 in Brooklyn, NY. Attended LIU, NYU, Pratt Inst. Debut OB 1969 in "The Triumph of Robert Emmet," Bdwy 1972 in "Mourning Becomes Electra," followed by "Threepenny Opera" (LC).

**RIEGERT, PETER.** Born Apr. 11, 1947 in NYC. Graduate UBuffalo. Debut 1975 OB in "Dance with Me."

**RIFICI, JOE.** Born Nov. 25, 1952 in NYC. Graduate Wagner Col. Bdwy debut 1975 in "Grease."

**RINALDI, JOY.** Born in Yonkers, NY. Graduate Stephens Col., AADA. Debut OB 1969 in "Satisfaction Guaranteed," Bdwy 1973 in "Grease."

**RINEHART, ELAINE.** Born Aug. 16, 1952 in San Antonio, TX. Graduate NC School of Arts. Debut 1975 OB in ELT's "Tenderloin."

**RITCHARD, CYRIL.** Born Dec. 1, 1897 in Sydney, Aus. Attended Sydney U. Bdwy debut 1947 in "Love for Love," followed by "Make Way for Lucia," "The Relapse," "Peter Pan," "Visit to a Small Planet," "The Pleasure of His Com-pany," "Happiest Girl in the World," "Romulus," "Too True to Be Good," "Irregular Verb to Love," "Roar of the Greasepaint . . . ," "Peter and the Wolf," "Sugar," "Musical Jubilee."

**RITTER, KATHRYN.** Born Aug. 1, 1948 in NYC. Attended NYU. Bdwy debut 1974 in "Candide."

**RIVERA, CHITA.** Born Jan. 23, 1933 in Washington, DC. Attended AmSch. of Ballet. Bdwy debut 1950 in "Guys and Dolls," followed by "Call Me Madam," "Can-Can," "Shoestring Revue" (OB), "Seventh Heaven," "Mr. Wonderful," "West Side Story," "Bye Bye Birdie," "Bajour," "Chicago."

**ROBARDS, JASON.** Born July 26, 1922 in Chicago, IL. Attended AADA. Bdwy debut 1947 with D'Oyly Carte, followed by "Stalag 17," "The Chase," "Long Day's Journey into Night" for which he received a Theatre World Award, "The Disenchanted," "Toys in the Attic," "Big Fish, Little Fish," "A Thousand Clowns," "Hughie," "The Devils," "We Bombed in New Haven," "The Country Girl," "Moon for the Misbegotten," OB in "American Gothic," "The Iceman Cometh," "After the Fall," "But for Whom Charlie," "Long Day's Journey into Night."

**ROBBINS, JANA.** Born Apr. 18, 1947 in Johnstown, PA. Stephens Col. graduate Bdwy debut 1947 in "Good News," OB in "Tickles by Tucholsky."

**ROBBINS, REX.** Born in Pierre, SD. Bdwy debut 1964 in "One Flew over the Cuckoo's Nest," followed by "Scratch," "The Changing Room," 'Gypsy," OB in "Servant of Two Masters," "The Alchemist," "Arms and the Man," "Boys in the Band." "A Memory of Two Mondays," "They Knew What They Wanted," "Secret Service," "Boy Meets Girl."

**ROBERTS, BILL.** Born May 25, 1948 in Sealy, TX. Graduate Sam Houston State U. Debut OB 1976 in "Maggie Flynn."

**ROBERTS, RACHEL.** Born Sept. 30, 1927 in Llanelly, Wales. Attended RADA. Bdwy debut 1973 in "The Visit," followed by "Chemin de Fer," "Habeas Corpus."

**ROBERTS, TONY.** Born Oct. 22, 1939 in NYC. Graduate Northwestern U. Bdwy bow 1962 in "Something about a Soldier," followed by "Take Her, She's Mine," "Last Analysis," "The Cradle Will Rock" (OB), "Never Too Late," "Barefoot in the Park," "Don't Drink the Water," "How Now, Dow Jones," "Play It Again, Sam," "Promises, Promises," "Sugar," "Absurd Person Singu-lar."

**ROBERTSON, WILLIAM.** Born Oct. 9, 1908 in Portsmouth, VA. Graduate Pomona Col. Bdwy debut 1936 in "Tapestry in Grey," followed by "Cup of Trembling," "Liliom," "Our Town," OB in "Uncle Harry," "Shining Hour," "Aspern Papers," "Madame Is Served," "Tragedian in spite of Himself," "Ki-bosh," "Sun-Up," "The Last Pad," "Hamlet," "Girls Most Likely to Succeed," "The Petrified Forest," "The Minister's Black Veil," "Santa Anita," "Babylon," "Midsummer Night's Dream," "A Touch of the Poet," "The Zykovs," "Rimers of Eldritch."

**ROBINSON, HAL.** Born in Bedford, IN. Graduate Ind. U. Debut 1971 OB in "Memphis Store-Bought Teeth," followed by "From Berlin to Broadway," "The Fantasticks."

**RODGERS, SHEV.** Born Apr. 9, 1928 in Holister, CA. Attended SF State Col. Bdwy bow 1959 in "Redhead," followed by "Music Man," "Man of La Man-cha" (also LC), "Home Sweet Homer," "Legend." OB in "Get Thee to Canter-bury," "War Games," "Moonchildren."

255

| William Roerick | Judi Rolin | David Russell | Nancy Salis | Craig Schaefer |

**ROERICK, WILLIAM.** Born Dec. 17, 1912 in NYC. Bdwy bow 1935 in "Romeo and Juliet," followed by "St. Joan," "Hamlet," "Our Town," "Importance of Being Earnest," "The Land is Bright," "Autumn Hill," "This Is the Army," "Magnificent Yankee," "Tonight at 8:30," "The Heiress," "Medea," "Macbeth," "Burning Glass," "Right Honourable Gentleman," "Marat/deSade," "Homecoming," "We Bombed in New Haven," "Elizabeth the Queen" (CC), "Waltz of the Toreadors," OB in "Madam, Will You Walk," "Cherry Orchard," "Come Slowly, Eden," "A Passage to E. M. Forster," "Trials of Oz."

**ROLFING, TOM.** Born Sept. 6, 1949 in Cedar Rapids, IA. Carnegie Tech graduate. Debut 1973 OB in "Godspell," Bdwy in "Godspell," "Equus."

**ROLIN, JUDI.** Born Nov. 6, 1946 in Chicago, IL. Bdwy debut 1970 in "40 Carats," followed by "Rodgers and Hart."

**ROLPH, MARTI.** Born March 8 in Los Angeles, CA. Occidental Col. graduate. Bdwy debut 1971 in "Follies," followed by "Good News" for which she received a Theatre World Award.

**ROMAN, ANDREW.** Born Jan. 25, 1939 in Imlay City, MI. Graduate UMich. Debut 1976 OB in ELT's "Follies."

**ROSE, GEORGE.** Born Feb. 19, 1920 in Bicester, Eng. Bdwy debut with Old Vic 1946 in "Henry IV," followed by "Much Ado about Nothing," "A Man for All Seasons," "Hamlet," "Royal Hunt of the Sun," "Walking Happy," "Loot," "My Fair Lady" (CC '68), "Canterbury Tales," "Coco," "Wise Child," "Sleuth," "My Fat Friend." "My Fair Lady."

**ROSEN, ROBERT.** Born Apr. 24, 1954 in NYC. Attended Indiana U., HB Studio. Bdwy debut 1975 in "Shenandoah."

**ROSKAM, CATHRYN.** Born May 30, 1943 in Hempstead, NY. Middlebury Col. graduate. Debut 1970 OB in "Gandhi," followed by "Autumn Garden.," "Maggie Flynn."

**ROSLER, LARRY.** Born Apr. 19, 1951 in Newark, NJ. Graduate Seton Hall U. Debut 1976 OB in "Who Killed Richard Cory?"

**ROSS, HOWARD.** Born Aug. 21, 1934 in NYC. Attended Juilliard, NYU. Bdwy debut 1965 in "Oliver," followed by "1600 Pennsylvania Avenue," OB in "Jacques Brel Is Alive . . . ," "Beggar's Opera," "Philemon."

**ROSS, JUSTIN.** Born Dec. 15, 1954 in Brooklyn, NY. Debut 1974 OB in "More Than You Deserve," Bdwy 1975 in "Pippin."

**ROSSI, GLORIA.** Born Nov. 16, 1946 in San Francisco, CA. Attended SF State, Syracuse U. Bdwy debut 1973 in "The Desert Song," followed by "Gypsy," "The Old Glory" (OB).

**ROSSOMME, RICHARD.** Born Apr. 5, 1936 in Los Angeles, CA. Graduate San Jose State Col., Pasadena Playhouse. Debut OB in 1975 in ELT's "Tenderloin."

**ROUNDS, DAVID.** Born Oct. 9, 1938 in Bronxville, NY. Attended Denison U. Bdwy debut 1965 in "Foxy" followed by "Child's Play" for which he received a Theatre World Award, "The Rothschilds," "The Last of Mrs. Lincoln," "Chicago," OB in "You Never Can Tell," "Money," "The Real Inspector Hound," "Epic of Buster Friend," "Enter A Free Man."

**ROUSSEAU, CAROLLE.** Born Jan. 21 in Belgium. Studied in Paris. NY debut 1976 with Royal Shakespeare Co. in "Henry V" (BAM).

**ROUTLEDGE, PATRICIA.** Born Feb. 17, 1929 in Birkenhead, Eng. Attended ULiverpool, Bristol Old Vic. Bdwy debut 1966 in "How's the World Treating You?," followed by "Darling of the Day," "1600 Pennsylvania Avenue."

**ROWE, HANSFORD.** Born May 12, 1924 in Richmond, VA. Graduate URichmond. Bdwy debut 1968 in "We Bombed in New Haven," OB in "Curley McDimple," "The Fantasticks," "Last Analysis," "God Says There Is No Peter Ott," "Mourning Becomes Electra," "Bus Stop.," "Secret Service," "Boy Meets Girl."

**ROWLES, POLLY.** Born Jan. 10, 1914 in Philadelphia, PA. Attended Carnegie Tech. Bdwy debut 1938 in "Julius Caesar," followed by "Richard III," "Golden State," "Small Hours, " "Gertie," "Time Out for Ginger," "Wooden Dish," "Goodbye Again," "Auntie Mame," "Look after Lulu," "A Mighty Man Is He," "No Strings," "Best Laid Plans," "Killing of Sister George," "40 Carats," "The Women," OB in "Older People," "Mrs. Warren's Profession."

**RUBENSTEIN, BARBARA.** Born in Chicago, IL. Graduate Northwestern U. Debut OB 1969 in "Your Own Thing," followed by "Wings," Bdwy in "Much Ado about Nothing" (1972), "Bubbling Brown Sugar."

**RUBINSTEIN, JOHN.** Born Dec. 8, 1946 in Los Angeles. Attended UCLA. Bdwy debut 1972 in "Pippin" for which he received a Theatre World Award.

**RUDD, PAUL.** Born May 15, 1940 in Boston, MA. OB in "Henry IV," followed by "King Lear," "A Cry of Players," "Midsummer Night's Dream," "An Evening with Merlin Finch," "In the Matter of J. Robert Oppenheimer," "Elagabalus," "Streamers" (LC), "Henry V" (CP), Bdwy in "The Changing Room," "The National Health," "The Glass Menagerie," "Ah, Wilderness."

**RUPERT, MICHAEL.** Born Oct. 23, 1951 in Denver, CO. Attended Pasadena Playhouse. Bdwy debut 1968 in "The Happy Time" for which he received a Theatre World Award, followed by "Pippin."

**RUSKIN, JEANNE.** Born Nov. 6 in Saginaw, MI. Graduate NYU. Bdwy debut 1975 in "Equus."

**RUSSAK, GERARD.** Born Sept. 11, 1927 in Paterson, NJ. Attended NY Col of Music. Bdwy bow 1967 in "Marat/deSade," followed by "Zorba," OB in "The Fantasticks."

**RUSSELL, DAVID.** Born Aug. 9, 1949 in Allenwood, PA. Ithaca Col. graduate. Bdwy debut 1975 in "Shenandoah."

**RYAN, CHARLENE.** Born in NYC. Bdwy debut 1964 in "Never Live over a Pretzel Factory," followed by "Sweet Charity," "Fig Leaves Are Falling," "Coco," "A Funny Thing Happened on the Way to the Forum," "Chicago."

**SABIN, DAVID.** Born Apr. 24, 1937 in Washington, DC. Graduate Catholic U. Debut 1965 OB in "The Fantasticks," followed by "Now Is the Time for All Good Men," "Threepenny Opera" (LC), Bdwy in "The Yearling," "Slapstick Tragedy," "Jimmy Shine," "Gantry," "Ambassador," "Celebration."

**SAKAMOTO, DENNIS.** Born Jan. 23, 1948 in Chicago, IL. Attended SF State Col. Debut 1975 OB in "The Pursuit of Happiness" (ELT).

**SAKATO, ATSUMI.** Born in Japan. Graduate Sophia U., UHawaii. Debut 1976 OB in "The Primary English Class."

**SALATA, GREGORY.** Born July 21, 1949 in NYC. Graduate Queens Col. Bdwy debut 1975 in "Dance with Me," followed by "Equus."

**SALIS, NANCY.** Born Aug. 14, 1952 in Christopher, IL. Graduate UIll. Debut 1976 OB in ELT's "Follies."

**SANDERS, RICHARD.** Born Aug. 23, 1940 in Harrisburg, Pa. Graduate Carnegie Tech., LAMDA. Bdwy debut 1973 in "Raisin," followed by "Hamlet" (LC), "The Boss."

**SANTELL, MARIE.** Born July 8 in Brooklyn, NY. Bdwy debut 1957 in "Music Man," followed by "A Funny Thing Happened on the Way . . . ," "Flora the Red Menace," "Pajama Game," "Mack and Mabel," OB in "Hi Paisano," "Boys from Syracuse," "Peace," "Promenade," "The Drunkard," "Sensations," "The Cast Aways."

**SAPPINGTON, FAY.** Born May 22, 1906 in Galveston, TX. Attended UT, Pasadena Playhouse. Bdwy debut 1950 in "Southern Exposure," followed by "The Cellar and the Well," "Glad Tidings," "J. B.," "The Yearling," "Golden Rainbow," "Pippin," OB in "Campbells of Boston," "In Case of Accident."

**SAUNDERS, LOIS ANN.** Born May 14, 1939 in Toledo, OH. Attended Centenary Col., HB Studio. Debut 1964 OB in "Great Scott," followed by "Man with a Load of Mischief," "Follies."

**SAUNDERS, MARY.** Born Dec. 14, 1945 in Morristown, NJ. Graduate Mt. Holyoke, Middlebury. Debut 1975 OB in "Gift of the Magi."

**SAVADGE, DEBORAH.** Born Apr. 24 in Detroit, MI. Graduate UWisc. Debut 1976 OB in "Rimers of Eldritch."

**SCARDINO, DON.** Born in Feb. 1949 in NYC. Attended CCNY. On Bdwy in "Loves of Cass McGuire," "Johnny No-Trump," "My Daughter, Your Son," "Godspell" OB in "Shout from the Rooftops," "Rimers of Eldritch," "The Unknown Solider and His Wife," "Godspell," "Moonchildren," "Kid Champion," "Comedy of Errors," "Secret Service," "Boy Meets Girl."

**SCHACT, SAM.** Born Apr. 19, 1936 in The Bronx, NY. Graduate CCNY. OB in "Fortune and Men's Eyes," "Cannibals," "I Met a Man," "The Increased Difficulty of Concentration" (LCR), "One Night Stands of a Noisy Passenger," "Owners," Bdwy in "The Magic Show."

**SCHAEFER, CRAIG.** Born Aug. 24, 1953 in San Gabriel, CA. Attended UCLA. Debut 1975 OB in "Tenderloin."

**SCHLEE, ROBERT.** Born June 13, 1938 in Williamsport, PA. Lycoming Col. graduate. Debut 1972 OB in "Dr. Selavy's Magic Theatre," followed by "Hotel for Criminals," "Threepenny Opera."

**SCHMIDT, JACK.** Born Sept. 19, 1927 in San Francisco, CA. Attended UCLA, Mex. City Col. Bdwy debut 1976 in "Something's Afoot."

**SCHRAMM, DAVID.** Born Aug. 14, 1946 in Louisville, KY. Attended Western Ky. U., Juilliard. Debut 1972 OB in "School for Scandal," followed by

| arole Schweid | Steve Scott | Renee Semes | John Sheridan | Corie Sims |

"Lower Depths," "Women Beware Women," Bdwy in "Three Sisters," "Next Time I'll Sing to You," "Edward II," "Measure for Measure," "Robber Bridegroom."

**SCHWEID, CAROLE.** Born Oct. 5, 1946 in Newark, NJ. Graduate Boston U., Juilliard. Bdwy debut 1970 in "Minnie's Boys," followed by "A Chorus Line," OB in "Love Me, Love My Children," "How To Succeed in Business . . ."

**SCOTT, GEORGE C.** Born Oct. 18, 1927 in Wise, Va. OB in "Richard II" for which he received a Theatre World Award, followed by "As You Like It," "Children of Darkness," "Desire under the Elms," Bdwy in "Comes a Day," "Andersonville Trial," "The Wall," "General Seeger,' "Little Foxes," "Plaza Suite," "Uncle Vanya," "Death of a Salesman."

**SCOTT, MARTHA.** Born Sept. 22, 1914 in Jamesport, MO. Graduate UMich. Bdwy debut 1938 in "Our Town," followed by "Foreigners," "The Willow and I," "Soldier's Wife," "Voice of the Turtle," "It Takes Two," "Design for a Stained Glass Window," "Gramercy Ghost," "The Number," "Male Animal," "Remarkable Mr. Pennypacker," "Cloud 7," "A Distant Bell," "Tumbler," "49th Cousin," "Never Too Late," "The Subject Was Roses," "The Skin of Our Teeth."

**SCOTT, STEVE.** Born Oct. 11, 1949 in Denver, CO. Graduate UDenver. Debut 1971 OB in "The Drunkard," followed by "Summer Brave," Bdwy 1975 in "The Ritz."

**SEIDEL, VIRGINIA.** Born July 26 in Harvey, IL. Attended Roosevelt U. Bdwy debut 1975 in "Very Good Eddie" for which she received a Theatre World Award.

**SELDES, MARIAN.** Born Aug. 23, 1928 in NYC. Attended Neighborhood Playhouse. Bdwy debut 1947 in "Medea," followed by "Crime and Punishment," "That Lady," "Tower Beyond Tragedy," "Ondine," "On High Ground," "Come of Age," "Chalk Garden," "The Milk Train Doesn't Stop Here Anymore," "The Wall," "A Gift of Time," "A Delicate Balance," "Before You Go," "Father's Day," "Equus," OB in "Different," "Ginger Man," "Mercy Street," "Candle in the Wind."

**SELL, JANIE.** Born Oct. 1, 1941 in Detroit, MI. Attended UDetroit. Debut 1966 in "Mixed Doubles," followed by "Dark Horses," "Dames at Sea," Bernstein," Bdwy in "George M!," "Irene," "Over Here" for which received a Theatre World Award, "Pal Joey."

**SELTZER, DANIEL.** Born Feb. 13, 1933 in Passaic, NJ. Graduate Princeton, Oxford, Harvard. Bdwy debut 1976 in "Knock Knock" for which he received Theatre World Award.

**SEMES, RENEE.** Born Feb. 27, 1947 in NYC. Attended NYU. Bdwy debut 1974 in "Candide."

**SERANE, HAL.** Born Mar. 17, 1948 in Far Rockaway, NY. Graduate Hofstra U. Bdwy debut 1975 in "Very Good Eddie."

**SHAWHAN, APRIL.** Born Apr. 10, 1940 in Chicago. Debut OB 1964 in "Jo," followed by "Hamlet," "Oklahoma!" (LC), "Mod Donna," Bdwy in "Race of Hairy Men," "3 Bags Full" for which she received a Theatre World Award, "Dinner at 8," "Cop-Out," "Much Ado about Nothing," "Over Here," "Rex."

**SHAWN, DICK.** Born Dec. 1 in Buffalo, NY. Attended UMiami. Bdwy debut 1948 in "For Heaven's Sake, Mother," followed by "A Funny Thing Happened on the Way . . . ," "The Egg," "Peterpat," "Fade Out-Fade In," "I'm Solomon," "Musical Jubilee," OB in "Rebirth Celebration of the Human Race."

**SHEA, JOHN V.** Born in North Conway, NH. Graduate Bates Col., Yale. Debut OB 1974 in "Yentl, the Yeshiva Boy," followed by "Gorky," "Battering Ram," Bdwy 1975 in "Yentl" for which he received a Theatre World Award.

**SHEEN, MARTIN.** Born Aug. 3, 1940 in Dayton, OH. Credits: OB in "The Connection," "Many Loves," "Jungle of Cities," "Wicked Cooks," "Hamlet," "Romeo and Juliet," "Hello and Goodbye," Bdwy in "Never Live over a Pretzel Factory" (1964), "The Subject Was Roses," "Death of a Salesman."

**SHELLEY, CAROLE.** Born Aug. 16, 1939 in London, Eng. Bdwy debut 1965 in "The Odd Couple," followed by "The Astrakhan Coat," "Loot," "Noel Coward's Sweet Potato," "Little Murders" (OB), "Hay Fever," "Absurd Person Singular," "The Norman Conquests."

**SHELTON, REID.** Born Oct. 7, 1924 in Salem, OR. Graduate UMich. Bdwy bow 1952 in "Wish You Were Here," followed by "Wonderful Town," "By the Beautiful Sea," "Saint of Bleecker Street," "My Fair Lady," "Oh! What a Lovely War!," "Carousel" (CC), "Canterbury Tales," "Rothschilds," "1600 Pennsylvania Avenue," OB in "Phedre," "Butterfly Dream," "Man with a Load of Mischief," "Beggar's Opera," "The Contractor," "Cast Aways."

**SHELTON, SLOANE.** Born Mar. 17, 1934 in Asheville, NC. Attended Berea Col., RADA. Bdwy debut 1967 in "Imaginary Invalid," followed by "Touch of the Poet," "Tonight at 8:30," "I Never Sang for My Father," OB in "Androcles and the Lion," "The Maids," "Way of the World," "Dark of the Moon," "Basic Training of Pavlo Hummel," "Felix," "Bits and Pieces," "The Runner Stumbles."

**SHERIDAN, JOHN.** Born May 9, 1947 in Newton, Mass. OB in "Your Own Thing," "Best Foot Forward," "Beggar on Horseback," Bdwy in "No, No, Nanette," "Gypsy" for which he received a Theatre World Award.

**SHIMODA, YUKI.** Born Aug. 10, 1921 in Sacramento, CA. Graduate Sacramento Jr. Col. Bdwy debut 1952 in "Teahouse of the August Moon," followed by "Auntie Mame," "Pacific Overtures."

**SHIMONO, SAB.** Born in Sacramento, Cal. Graduate UCal. Bdwy bow 1965 in "South Pacific" (CC), followed by "Mame," "Lovely Ladies, Kind Gentlemen," "Pacific Overtures," OB in "Santa Anita," "Ride the Winds."

**SHYRE, PAUL.** Born Mar. 8, 1926 in NYC. Attended UFla., AADA. Debut OB 1956 in "Pictures in a Hallway," followed by "Purple Dust," "Cock-a-Doodle Dandy," "U.S.A.," Bdwy in "I Knock at the Door," "Absurd Person Singular."

**SIDNEY, SYLVIA.** Born Aug. 8, 1910 in NYC. Attended Theatre Guild Sch. Bdwy debut 1926 in "Prunella," followed by "The Squall," "Crime," "Mirrors," "The Breaks," "Gods of the Lightning," "Nice Women," "Cross-Roads," "Many a Slip," "Bad Girl," "To Quito and Back," "Gentle People," "We Will Never Die," "Fourposter," "Very Special Baby," "Enter Laughing," "Barefoot in the Park," "Riverside Drive" (OB), "Me Jack, You Jill."

**SIEBERT, CHARLES.** Born Mar. 9, 1938 in Kenosha, WI. Graduate Marquette U., LAMDA. Appeared in "Richard III" (CP), "Galileo" (LC), on Bdwy in "Jimmy Shine," "Gingerbread Lady," "Sticks and Bones," "Lysistrata," "The Changing Room," "Cat on a Hot Tin Roof," OB in "Wilde," "Rubbers."

**SIGNORELLI, TOM.** Born Oct. 19, 1939 in Brooklyn, NY. Attended UCLA. Debut 1960 OB in "Look Back in Anger," followed by "Bury the Dead," "Scapin," "Pretenders," Bdwy debut 1958 in "General Seeger," followed by "Borstal Boy."

**SILLIMAN, MAUREEN.** Born Dec. 3 in NYC. Attended Hofstra U. Bdwy debut 1975 in "Shenandoah."

**SILLS, PAWNEE.** Born in Castalia, NC. Attended Bklyn Col. Debut OB 1962 in "Raisin Hell in the Sun," followed by "Mr. Johnson," "Black Happening," "One Last Look," "NY and Who to Blame It On," "Cities in Bezique," "I'd Go to Heaven if I Was Good," "Oakville, U.S.A.," "Hocus-Pocus," "And So to Bed."

**SILVER, STUART.** Born June 29, 1947 in Hollywood, CA. Attended URochester, AADA. Debut 1969 OB in "Little Murders," followed by "Seven Days of Mourning," "Dance Wi' Me," "Wanted," "The Making of Americans," "Dance with Me."

**SIMMONS, KEITH.** Born June 2, 1955 in Jamaica, NY. Bdwy debut 1973 in "Seesaw," followed by "Raisin."

**SIMS, CORIE.** Born Feb. 23, 1948 in NYC. Graduate Hofstra U. Debut OB 1970 in "You're a Good Man, Charlie Brown," followed by "The Hot l Baltimore."

**SIMS, MARLEY.** Born Feb. 23, 1948 in NYC. Graduate Hofstra U. Debut OB 1971 in "The Me Nobody Knows," followed by "Godspell" OB and Bdwy.

**SINDEN, DONALD.** Born Oct. 9, 1923 in Plymouth, Eng. Attended Webber-Douglas School. After 33 years in the London theatre, made his Bdwy debut 1974 in "London Assurance," followed by "Habeas Corpus."

**SKALA, LILIA.** Born in Vienna; graduate UDresden. Bdwy debut 1941 in "Letters to Lucerne," followed by "With a Silk Thread," "Call Me Madam," "Diary of Anne Frank," "Threepenny Opera" (CC), "Zelda," "40 Carats," OB in "Medea and Jason," "Gorky."

**SLACK, BEN.** Born July 23, 1937 in Baltimore, MD. Graduate Catholic U. Debut 1971 OB in "Oedipus at Colonus," followed by "Interrogation of Havana," "Rain," "Thunder Rock," "Trelawny of the Wells," Bdwy 1976 in "Legend."

**SMALL, NEVA.** Born Nov. 17, 1952 in NYC. Bdwy debut 1964 in "Something More," followed by "Impossible Years," "Henry, Sweet Henry," "Frank Merriwell," "Something's Afoot," OB in "Ballad for a Firing Squad," "Tell Me Where the Good Times Are," "How Much, How Much?," "F. Jasmine Addams," "Macbeth" (LC), "Yentl, the Yeshiva Boy."

| **Marcus Smythe** | **Barbara Spiegel** | **Scott Stevensen** | **June Squibb** | **Mark Syers** |

SMITH, ALEXANDRA. Born Apr. 25, 1944 in Sydney, Aust. Graduate Boston U. Debut 1974 OB in "The Hot l Baltimore."

SMITH, ALEXIS. Born June 8, 1921 in Penticton, Can. Attended LACC. Bdwy debut 1971 in "Follies," followed by "The Women," "Summer Brave."

SMITH, BARREY. Born in Presque Isle, ME. Graduate Wheaton Col., Princeton. Bdwy debut 1973 in "Grease."

SMYTHE, MARCUS. Born Mar. 26, 1950 in Berea, OH. Graduate Otterbein Col., Ohio U. Debut 1975 OB in "Tenderloin."

SNYDER, ARLEN DEAN. Born Mar. 3, 1933 in Rice, KS. Graduate UTulsa, UIowa. Bdwy bow 1965 in "The Family Way," followed by OB's "Benito Cereno," "Hogan's Goat," "Miss Pete," "Open 24 Hours," "Candyapple," "June Moon," "Big Broadcast," "Thunder Rock," "Streamers."

SNYDER, NANCY E. Born Dec. 2, 1949 in Kankakee, IL. Graduate Webster Col., Neighborhood Playhouse. Bdwy debut 1976 in "Knock Knock."

SOIFFER, FREDA. Born Mar. 10, 1950 in NYC. Attended NYU. Bdwy debut 1974 in "Music! Music!" (CC) followed by "So Long, 174th Street."

SOLEN, PAUL. Born Mar. 27, 1941 in Cincinnati, O. Bdwy debut 1964 in "Hello, Dolly!," followed by "Breakfast at Tiffany's," "Dear World," "Pippin," "Chicago."

SORREL, SCOTT. Born Apr. 9, 1964 in Newport Beach, CA. Attended HB Studio. Debut 1976 OB in "The Old Glory."

SPIEGEL, BARBARA. Born Mar. 12 in NYC. Debut 1969 with LCRep in "Camino Real," "Operation Sidewinder" and "Beggar on Horseback," followed by "Feast for Flies."

SPINELLI, LARRY. Born July 20, 1931 in NYC. Debut 1971 OB in "One Flew over the Cuckoo's Nest," followed by "Soon," "The Hot l Baltimore."

SPONSELLER, HOWARD. Born Dec. 30, 1945 in New London, CT. Attended Carnegie-Mellon U. Debut OB 1971 in "Godspell," followed by "Ionescopade,"

SQUIBB, JUNE. Born Nov. 6 in Vandalia, IL. Attended Cleveland Play House, HB Studio. Debut 1956 OB in "Sable Brush," followed by "Boy Friend," "Lend an Ear," "Another Language," Bdwy in "Gypsy" (1960), "The Happy Time."

STADLEN, LEWIS J. Born Mar. 7, 1947 in Brooklyn. Attended Neighborhood Playhouse. Bdwy debut 1970 in "Minnie's Boys" for which he received a Theatre World Award, followed by "Happiness Cage" (OB), "The Sunshine Boys," "Candide."

STANSBURY, HOPE. Born Nov. 23, 1945 in NYC. OB in "Henry and Henrietta," "Just before the War with the Eskimos," "Run to the Sea," "Chocolates," "Couchmates," "Paderefski," "Howies," "Women behind Bars."

STAPLETON, MAUREEN. Born June 21, 1925 in Troy, NY. Attended HB Studio. Bdwy debut 1946 in "Playboy of the Western World," followed by "Antony and Cleopatra," "Detective Story," "Bird Cage," "Rose Tattoo" for which she received a Theatre World Award, "The Emperor's Clothes," "The Crucible," "Richard III," "The Seagull," "27 Wagons Full of Cotton," "Orpheus Descending," "The Cold Wind and the Warm," "Toys in the Attic," "Glass Menagerie," (1965 & 1975), "Plaza Suite," "Norman, Is That You?," "Gingerbread Lady," "Country Girl," "Secret Affairs of Mildred Wild."

STATTEL, ROBERT. Born Nov. 20, 1937 in Floral Park, NY. Graduate Manhattan Col. Debut OB 1958 in "Heloise," followed by "When I Was a Child," "Man and Superman," "The Storm," "Don Carlos," "Taming of the Shrew," NYSFs "Titus Andronicus," "Henry IV," "Peer Gynt," and "Hamlet," LCR's "Danton's Death," "Country Wife," "Caucasian Chalk Circle," and "King Lear," "Iphigenia in Aulis," "Ergo," "The Persians," "Blue Boys," "The Minister's Black Veil," "Four Friends,""Two Character Play," Bdwy in "A Patriot for Me," "Sherlock Holmes."

STENBORG, HELEN. Born Jan. 24, 1925 in Minneapolis, MN. Attended Hunter Col. OB in "A Doll's House," "A Month in the Country," "Say Nothing," "Rosmersholm," "Rimers of Eldrich," "Trial of the Catonsville 9," "Hot l Baltimore," "Pericles," "A Doll's House," "Elephant in the House," Bdwy in "Sheep on the Runway,"

STEPHENS, GARN. Born in Tulsa, OK. Graduate Calif. Western U., Pasadena Playhouse. Debute 1972 OB and Bdwy in "Grease."

STERN, JOSEPH. Born Sept. 3, 1940 in Los Angeles, CA. Graduate UCLA. Debut 1967 OB in "MacBird," followed by "The Homecoming," "Henry IV," "Last Analysis," "Cymbeline," "The Hot l Baltimore."

STERNHAGEN, FRANCES. Born Jan. 13, 1932 in Washington, DC. Vassar Graduate. OB in "Admirable Bashful," "Thieves' Carnival," "Country Wife,"

"Ulysses in Nighttown," "Saintliness of Margery Kemp," "The Room," "A Slight Ache," "Displaced Person," "Playboy of the Western World" (LC) Bdwy in "Great Day in the Morning," "Right Honourable Gentleman," with APA in "Cocktail Party" and "Cock-a-doodle Dandy," "The Sign in Sidney Brustein's Window," "Enemies" (LC), "The Good Doctor," "Equus."

STEVENSEN, SCOTT. Born May 4, 1951 in Salt Lake City, UT. Attended USCal. Bdwy debut 1974 in "Good News" for which he received a Theatre World Award.

STEVENSON, MARGOT. Born Feb. 8, 1918 in NYC. Brearley School graduate. Bdwy debut 1932 in "Firebird," followed by "Evensong," "A Party," "Barretts of Wimpole Street," "Symphony," "Truly Valiant," "Call It a Day," "Stage Door," "You Can't Take It with You," "Golden Wings," "Little Women" (CC), "Rugged Path," "Leading Lady," "The Young and Beautiful," "The Apple Cart," "Triple Play," "Lord Pengo," "Hostile Witness," "The Royal Family," OB in "Autumn Ladies and Their Lovers' Lovers."

STEWART, JEAN-PIERRE. Born May 4, 1946 in NYC Graduate CCNY. Appeared OB in "Henry IV," "King Lear," "Cry of Players," "In the Matter of J. Robert Oppenheimer," "The Miser," "Long Day's Journey into Night," "American Night Cry," "King Lear," "The Old Ones," "Dancing for the Kaiser," "Primary English Class."

STEWART, PATRICIA. Born Aug. 29, 1939 in Bronxville, NY. Graduate St. Lawrence U. Debut OB 1963 in "Best Foot Forward," followed by "The Ginger Man," "Dr. Faustus," "Kid Champion," "Wood Painting," "The Artists," "Elagabalus," "Spelling Bee."

STIERS, DAVID OGDEN. Born Oct. 31, 1942 in Peoria, IL. Attended UOregon, Juilliard. Debut OB 1972 in "School for Scandal," followed by "Lower Depths," "The Hostage," "Women Beware Women," Bdwy in "Three Sisters," "Measure for Measure," "Beggar's Opera," "Scapin," "Ulysses in Nighttown," "The Magic Show."

STILLER, JERRY. Born June 8, 1931 in NYC. Graduate Syracuse U., HB Studio, Debut 1953 OB in "Coriolanus," followed by "The Power and the Glory," "Golden Apple," "Measure for Measure," "Taming of the Shrew," "Carefree Tree," "Diary of a Scoundrel," "Romeo and Juliet," "As You Like It," "Two Gentlemen of Verona," Bdwy 1975 in "The Ritz."

STREEP, MERYL. Born Sept. 22 in Summit, NJ. Graduate Vassar, Yale. Debut 1975 OB in "Trelawny of the Wells," followed by "27 Wagons Full of Cotton" for which she received a Theatre World Award, "A Memory of Two Mondays," "Secret Service," "Henry V," "Measure for Measure" (CP).

STUTHMAN, FRED. Born June 27, 1919 in Long Beach, CA. Attended UCal. Debut 1970 OB in "Hamlet," followed by "Uncle Vanya," "Charles Abbot & Son," "She Stoops to Conquer," "Master Builder," "Taming of the Shrew," "Misalliance," "Merchant of Venice," "Conditions of Agreement," "The Play the Thing," "Ghosts," "The Father," "The Hot l Baltimore," "The Cherry Orchard," Bdwy 1975 in "Sherlock Holmes."

SULLIVAN, IAN. Born Apr. 1, 1933 in NYC. Graduate Boston U. Bdwy debut 1970 in "Man of La Mancha," followed by "Vivat! Vivat! Regina!, "Home Sweet Homer."

SUTORIUS, JAMES. Born Dec. 14, 1944 in Euclid, OH. Graduate Ill. Wesleyan, AMDA. Bdwy debut 1970 in "The Cherry Orchard," followed by "The Changing Room," OB in "Servant of Two Masters," "Hamlet."

SWANSEN, LARRY. Born Nov. 10, 1930 in Roosevelt, OK. Graduate OKU. Bdwy debut 1966 in "Those That Play the Clowns," followed by "Great White Hope," OB in "Dr. Faustus Lights the Lights," "Thistle in My Bed," "A Darker Flower," "Vincent," "MacBird," "Unknown Soldier and His Wife," "Sound of Music," "Conditioning of Charlie One," "Ice Age."

SWEET, DOLPH. Born July 18, 1920 in NYC. Graduate Columbia U. Bdwy debut 1960 in "Rhinoceros," followed by "Romulus," "The Advocate," "Sign in Sidney Brustein's Window," "Great Indoors," "Natural Look," "Billy," "Penny Wars," OB in "The Dragon," "Too Much Johnson," "Sjt. Musgrave's Dance," "Ceremony of Innocence," "Death of J.K.," "Bread," "Streamers."

SYERS, MARK. Born Oct. 25, 1952 in Trenton, NJ. Graduate Emerson Col. Bdwy debut 1976 in "Pacific Overtures."

SYMONDS, ROBERT. Born Dec. 1, 1926 in Bristow, OK. Attended TexU, UMo. With LCRep in "Danton's Death," "Country Wife," "Alchemist," "Galileo," "St. Joan," "Tiger at the Gates," "Cyrano," "Cry of Players," "Inner Journey," "The Miser," "Time of Your Life," "Camino Real," "Disintegration of James Cherry," "Silence," "Scenes from American Life," "Play Strindberg," "Mary Stuart," "Narrow Road to the Deep North," "Enemies," "The Plough and the Stars," "Merchant of Venice," "Streetcar Named Desire," Bdwy 1976 in "The Poison Tree."

Melinda Tanner

David Thomé

Clarice Taylor

William Thomas, Jr.

Virginia Vestoff

**TABORI, KRISTOFFER.** Born Aug. 4, 1952 in Calif. Bdwy debut 1969 in "The Penny Wars," followed by "Henry V," "Habeas Corpus," OB in "Emile and the Detectives," "Guns of Carrar," "A Cry of Players," "Dream of a Blacklisted Actor," "How Much, How Much?" for which he received a Theatre World Award, "The Wager."

**TANNER, MELINDA.** Born Oct. 5, 1946 in Los Angeles, CA. Attended LACC. Debut 1975 in "The Sea," followed by "Godspell."

**TANNER, TONY.** Born July 27, 1932 in Hillingdon, Eng. Attended Webber-Douglas School. Bdwy debut 1966 in "Half a Sixpence," followed by "No Sex Please, We're British," "Sherlock Holmes," OB in "Little Boxes," "The Homecoming."

**TARLETON, DIANE.** Born in Baltimore, MD. Graduate UMd. Bdwy debut 1965 in "Anya," followed by "A Joyful Noise," "Elmer Gantry," "Yentl," OB in "A Time for the Gentle People," "Spoon River Anthology."

**TATE, DENNIS.** Born Aug. 31, 1938 in Iowa City, IA. Attended Iowa U. OB in "Black Monday," "The Blacks," "The Hostage," "Bohikee Creek," "Happy Bar," "Trials of Brother Jero," "Strong Breed," "Goa," "Electronic Nigger," "Black Quartet," "Life and Times of J. Walter Smintheus," "Jazznite," "Cherry Orchard," "Phantasmagoria Historia . . . ," "Merry Wives of Windsor," Bdwy in "Les Blancs." (1970), "The Poison Tree."

**TATUM, BILL.** Born May 6, 1947 in Philadelphia, PA. Graduate Catawba Col. Bdwy debut 1971 in "Man of La Mancha," followed by ELT's "Missouri Legend" (OB).

**TAYLOR, CLARICE.** Born Sept. 20, in Buckingham County, VA. Attended New Theater School. Debut 1943 OB in "Striver's Row," followed by "Major Barbara," "Family Portrait," "Trouble in Mind," "The Egg and I," "A Medal for Willie," "Nat Turner," "Simple Speaks His Mind," "Gold Through the Trees," "The Owl Answers," "Song of the Lusitanian Bogey," "Summer of the 17th Doll," "Kongi's Harvest," "Daddy Goodness," "God Is a (Guess What?)," "An Evening of One Acts," "5 on the Black Hand Side," "Man Better Man," "Day of Absence," "Brotherhood," "Akokawe," "Rosalee Pritchett," "Sty of the Blind Pig," "Duplex" (LC), "Wedding Band," Bdwy 1975 in "The Wiz."

**TEITEL, CAROL.** Born Aug. 1, 1929 in NYC. Attended AmThWing. On Bdwy in "The Country Wife," "The Entertainer," "Hamlet," "Marat/deSade," "All over Town," OB in "Way of the World," "Plough and the Stars," "The Anatomist," "Country Scandal," "Under Milk Wood," "The Bench," "7 Days of Mourning," "Duet," "Trio," "Figures in the Sand," "The Old Ones."

**THACKER, RUSS.** Born June 23, 1946 in Washington, DC. Attended Montgomery Col. Debut 1967 in "Life with Father" (CC), followed OB by "Your Own Thing" for which he received a Theatre World Award, "Dear Oscar," "Once I Saw A Boy Laughing," Bdwy in "Grass Harp," "Heathen," "Music! Music!" (CC), "Home Sweet Homer," "Me Jack You Jill."

**THEODORE, DONNA.** Born July 25, 1945 in Oakland, CA. Debut 1974 OB in "Oh, Lady, Lady," Bdwy 1975 in "Shenandoah" for which she received a Theatre World Award.

**THOMAS, WILLIAM, JR.** Born in Columbus, O. Graduate Ohio State U. Debut OB 1972 in "Touch," followed by "Natural," "Godspell."

**THOMÉ, DAVID.** Born July 24, 1951 in Salt Lake City, UT. Bdwy debut 1971 in "No, No, Nanette," followed by "Different Times," "Good News," "Rodgers and Hart," "A Chorus Line."

**THOMPSON, ERNEST.** Born Nov. 6, 1949 in Bellow Falls, VT. Attended Catholic U., UMd., American U. Bdwy debut 1975 in "Summer Brave."

**THOMPSON, ROBERT E.** Born Oct. 7, 1916 in Kansas City, MO. Graduate North Central Col., UMich, Goodman Theatre. Debut 1941 OB in "Post Mortum," Bdwy bow 1973 in "Status Quo Vadis," followed by "Angel Street."

**TIRELLI, JAIME.** Born Mar. 4, 1945 in NYC. Attended UMundial, AADA. Debut 1975 OB in "Rubbers," "Yanks 3, Detroit O."

**TOLAYDO, MICHAEL.** Born July 23, 1946 in Nairobi, Kenya. Attended Houston Baptist Col., AADA. Bdwy debut 1970 in "The Cherry Orchard," followed by "Robber Bridegroom," "Edward II," "The Time of Your Life," "Three Sisters," OB in "Hamlet."

**TORN, RIP.** Born Feb. 6, 1931 in Temple, TX. Graduate UTx. Bdwy bow 1956 in "Cat on a Hot Tin Roof," followed by "Sweet Bird of Youth," "Daughter of Silence," "Strange Interlude," "Blues for Mr. Charlie," "Country Girl" (CC), "Glass Menagerie," OB in "Chapparal" (1958) for which he received a Theatre World Award, "The Cuban Thing," "The Kitchen," "Deer Park," "Dream of a Blacklisted Actor," "Dance of Death," "MacBeth," "Barbary Shore."

**TORRES, ANDY.** Born Aug. 10, 1945 in Ponce, PR. Attended AMDA. Bdwy debut 1969 in "Indians," followed by "Purlie," "Don't Bother Me, I Can't Cope," "The Wiz," OB in "Billy Noname."

**TOWB, HARRY.** Born July 27, 1925 in Larne, Ire. Attended Belfast Tech. Col. Bdwy debut 1966 in "Under the Weather," followed by "Sherlock Homes," "Travesties."

**TRAPANI, LOU.** Born Dec. 17, 1947 in Brooklyn, NY. Graduate Hofstra U. Debut OB 1970 in "Journey to Bahia," followed by "Hamlet," "She Stoops to Conquer," "Taming of the Shrew," "Misalliance," "Merchant of Venice," "And They Put Handcuffs on Flowers," "Total Eclipse," "Work."

**TRIGGER, IAN J.** Born Sept. 30, 1942 in Eng. Graduate RADA. NY debut OB 1973 in "Taming of the Shrew" followed by "Scapino," "True History of Squire Jonathan . . . ," Bdwy in "Scapino" (1974), "Habeas Corpus."

**TUCCI, MICHAEL.** Born Apr. 15, 1946 in NYC. Graduate C.W. Post Col. Debut 1974 OB in "Godspell," Bdwy 1975 in "Grease."

**TUPOU, MANU.** Born in 1939 in Fiji Islands. Attended San Francisco State U., ULondon. Bdwy bow 1969 in "Indians," followed by "Othello," "Capt. Brassbound's Conversion," OB in "Madwoman of Chaillot," "Passion of Antigona Perez," "Wedding of Iphigenia," "The Old Glory."

**TYRRELL, JOHN.** Born Nov. 24, 1948 in Perth Amboy, NJ. Graduate Marquette U., Neighborhood Playhouse. Bdwy debut 1974 in "Equus."

**UCHIDA, CHRISTINE.** Born Apr. 20, 1952. Bdwy debut 1976 in "Home Sweet Homer."

**URMSTON, KENNETH.** Born Aug. 6, 1929 in Cincinnati, OH. Attended Xavier U. Bdwy debut 1950 in "Make a Wish," followed by "Top Banana," "Guys and Dolls," "John Murray Anderson's Almanac," "Can-Can," "Silk Stockings," "Oh Captain!," "Bells Are Ringing," "Redhead," "Madison Avenue," "Tenderloin," "We Take the Town," "Lovely Ladies, Kind Gentlemen," "Follies," "Pippin."

**VAN BENSCHOTEN, STEPHEN.** Born Aug. 27, 1943 in Washington, DC. Graduate LaSalle Col., Yale. Debut 1967 OB in "King John," Bdwy in "Unlikely Heroes," "Grease."

**VAN VOOREN, MONIQUE.** Born Mar. 25, 1938 in Brussels, Belg. Attended Brussels U., NYU. Bdwy debut 1954 in "John Murray Anderson's Almanac," followed by "Destry Rides Again," "Man on the Moon."

**VARRONE, GENE.** Born Oct. 30, 1929 in Brooklyn, NY. Graduate LIU. Bdwy in "Damn Yankees," "Take Me Along," "Ziegfeld Follies," "Goldilocks," "Wildcat," "Tovarich," "Subways Are for Sleeping," "Bravo Giovanni," "Drat! The Cat!," "Fade Out—Fade In," "Don't Drink the Water," "Dear World," "Coco," "A Little Night Music," "So Long, 174th Street," OB in "Promenade."

**VERDON, GWEN.** Born Jan 13, 1926 in Culver City, CA. Bdwy debut 1950 in "Alive and Kicking," followed by "Can-Can" for which she received a Theatre World Award, "Damn Yankees," "New Girl in Town," "Redhead," "Sweet Charity," "Children, Children," "Chicago."

**VESTOFF, VIRGINIA.** Born Dec. 9, 1940 in NYC. Bdwy bow 1960 in "From A to Z," followed by "Irma La Duce," "Baker Street," "1776," "Via Galactica," "Nash at 9," "Boccaccio," OB in "Boy Friend," "Crystal Heart," "Fall Out," "New Cole Porter Revue," "Man with a Load of Mischief," "Love and Let Love," "Short-changed Review."

**VICKERS, LARRY.** Born June 8, 1947 in Harrisonburg, VA. Attended Howard U. Bdwy debut in "Purlie," followed by "Shirley McLaine at the Palace."

**VITA, MICHAEL.** Born in 1941 in NYC. Studied at HB Studio. Bdwy debut 1967 in "Sweet Charity," followed by "Golden Rainbow," "Promises, Promises," "Chicago," OB in "Sensations," "That's Entertainment."

**VITELLA, SEL.** Born July 7, 1934 in Boston, MA. Graduate San Francisco Inst. of Music. Debut 1975 OB in "Merchant of Venice," Bdwy 1976 in "Something's Afoot."

**VON FURSTENBERG, BETSY.** Born Aug. 16, 1931 in Westphalia, Ger. Attended Neighborhood Playhouse. Bdwy debut 1951 in "Second Threshold," followed by "Dear Barbarians," "Oh, Men! Oh, Women!," "Chalk Garden," "Child of Fortune," "Nature's Way," "Wonderful Town," "Mary, Mary," "Paisley Convertible," "Gingerbread Lady," "Absurd Person Singular," OB in "The Making of Moo," "Season of Choice," "Measure for Measure."

**259**

| Chet Walker | Cynthia Wells | Stuart Warmflash | Patricia Wheel | Jim Weston |

VON SCHERLER, SASHA. Born Dec. 12. in NYC. Bdwy debut 1959 in "Look after Lulu," followed by "Rape of the Belt," "The Good Soup," "Great God Brown," "First Love," "Alfie," "Harold," "Bad Habits," OB in "Admirable Bashville," "The Comedian," "Conversation Piece," "Good King Charles' Golden Days," "Under Milk Wood," "Plays for Bleecker Street," "Ludlow Fair," "Twelfth Night," "Sondra," "Cyrano de Bergerac," "Crimes of Passion," "Henry VI," "Trelawny of the Wells," "Screens," "Soon Jack November," "Pericles," "Kid Champion," "Henry V."

WAITE, JOHN THOMAS. Born Apr. 19, 1948 in Syracuse, NY. Attended Syracuse U. Debut 1976 OB in "The Fantasticks."

WALKEN, CHRISTOPHER. Born Mar. 31, 1943 in Astoria, NY. Attended Hofstra U. Bdwy debut 1958 in "J. B.," followed by "High Spirits," "Baker Street," "The Lion in Winter," "Measure for Measure" (CP), "Rose Tattoo" (CC'66) for which he received a Theatre World Award, "Unknown Soldier and His Wife," "Rosencrantz and Guildenstern Are Dead," "Scenes from American Life," (LC), "Cymbeline" (NYSF), LC's "Enemies," "The Plough and the Stars," "Merchant of Venice," "The Tempest," "Troilus and Cressida," and "Macbeth," "Sweet Bird of Youth," OB in "Best Foot Forward," "Iphigenia in Aulis," "Lemon Sky," "Kid Champion."

WALKER, CHET. Born June 1, 1954 in Stuttgart, AR. Bdwy debut 1972 in "On the Town," followed by "Ambassador," "Pajama Game," "Lorelei," "Pippin."

WALKER, DOUGLAS W. Born Oct. 18, 1951 in NYC. Attended AMDA. Debut 1976 OB in "Godspell."

WALKER, KATHRYN. Born in Jan. in Philadelphia, PA. Graduate Wells Col., Harvard, LAMDA. Debut 1971 OB in "Slag," followed by "Alpha Beta," "Kid Champion," "Rebel Women," Bdwy 1973 in "The Good Doctor," "Mourning Pictures."

WALKER, MICHAEL. Born Mar. 11, 1950 in Kenya. Bdwy debut 1974 in "Sherlock Holmes."

WALKER, PETER. Born July 24, 1927 in Mineola, NY. Studied with Stella Adler. Bdwy debut 1955 in "Little Glass Clock," followed by "Dear World," "Follies," "Where's Charley?", OB in "Dancing for the Kaiser."

WALLACE, LEE. Born July 15, 1930 in NYC. Attended NYU. Debut OB 1966 in "Journey of the Fifth Horse," followed by "Saturday Night," "An Evening with Garcia Lorca," "Macbeth," "Booth Is Back in Town," "Awake and Sing," "Shepherd of Avenue B," "Basic Training of Pavlo Hummel," Bdwy in "Secret Affairs of Mildred Wild," "Molly," "Zalmen, or the Madness of God."

WALLACE, TIMOTHY. Born July 24, 1947 in Racine, WI. Graduate UWisc, Penn State U. Debut 1976 OB in "The Rimers of Eldritch" (ELT).

WALSH, THOMAS J. Born Mar. 15, 1950 in Auburn, NY. Attended Boston Consv. Bdwy debut 1973 in "Seesaw," followed by "Rachel Lily Rosenbloom," "Music! Music!," "A Chorus Line."

WARD, DOUGLAS TURNER. Born May 5, 1930 in Burnside, LA. Attended UMich. Bdwy bow 1959 in "A Raisin in the Sun," followed by "One Flew over the Cuckoo's Nest," "Last Breeze of Summer," OB in "The Iceman Cometh," "The Blacks," "Pullman Car Hiawatha," "Bloodknot," "Happy Ending," "Day of Absence," "Kongi's Harvest," "Ceremonies in Dark Old Men," "The Harangues," "The Reckoning," "Frederick Douglass through His Own Words," "River Niger."

WARD, JANET. Born Feb. 19 in NYC. Attended Actors Studio. Bdwy debut 1945 in "Dream Girl," followed by "Anne of a Thousand Days," "Detective Story," "King of Friday's Men," "Middle of the Night," "Miss Lonelyhearts," "J. B.," "Cheri," "The Egg," "Impossible Years," "Of Love Remembered," OB in "Chapparal," "The Typists and The Tiger," "Summertree," "Dream of a Blacklisted Actor," "Cruising Speed 600MPH," "One Flew over the Cuckoo's Nest," "Love Gotta Come by Saturday Night," "Home Is the Hero," "Love Death Plays."

WARFIELD, MARLENE. Born June 19, 1941 in Queens, NY. Attended Actors Studio. Bdwy debut 1968 in "The Great White Hope" for which she received a Theatre World Award, OB in "The Blacks," "All's Well That Ends Well," "Volpone," "Taming of the Shrew," "Who's Got His Own," "Elektra," "2 by Cromwell," "Midsummer Night's Dream," "So Nice They Named It Twice."

WARMFLASH, STUART. Born June 27, 1949 in NYC. Graduate NY Debut 1970 OB in "The Lady from Maxim's," followed by "Secret Service "Boy Meets Girl."

WARREN, JENNIFER. Born Aug. 12, 1941 in NYC. Graduate UWisc. Deb 1967 OB in "Scuba Duba," followed by "Trees in the Wind," Bdwy 1972 in Rms Riv Vu" for which she received a Theatre World Award, followed by "P Your Cat Is Dead."

WASHINGTON, VERNON. Born Aug. 10, 1927 in Hartford CT. Attend Wholter School of Drama. OB in "Cabin in the Sky," "The Strong Breed "Trials of Brother Jero," "Scuba Duba," "Hocus-Pocus," Bdwy 1976 in "Bu bling Brown Sugar."

WATERSTON, SAM. Born Nov. 15, 1940 in Cambridge, MA. Graduate Ya Bdwy bow 1963 in "Oh, Dad, Poor Dad . . . ," followed by "First One Asle Whistle," "Halfway up the Tree," "Indians," "Hay Fever," "Much Ado abo Nothing," OB in "As You Like It," "Thistle in My Bed," "The Knack," "Fitz "Biscuit," "La Turista," "Posterity For Sale," "Ergo," "Muzeeka," "R Cross," "Henry IV," "Spitting Image," "I Met a Man," "Brass Butterfly "Trial of the Catonsville 9," "Cymbeline," "Hamlet," "A Meeting by t River," "The Tempest," "A Doll's House," "Measure for Measure."

WATSON, DOUGLASS. Born Feb. 24, 1921 in Jackson, GA. Graduate UN Bdwy bow 1947 in "The Iceman Cometh," followed by "Antony and Cleop tra" for which he received a Theatre World Award, "Leading Lady," "Richa III," "Happiest Years," "That Lady," "Wisteria Trees," "Romeo and Julie "Desire under the Elms," "Sunday Breakfast," "Cyrano de Bergerac," "Con dential Clerk," "Portrait of a Lady," "Miser," "Young and Beautiful," "Litt Glass Clock," "Country Wife," "Man for All Seasons," "Chinese Prime Min ter," "Marat/deSade," "Prime of Miss Jean Brodie," "Pirates of Penzance NYSF's "Much Ado about Nothing," "King Lear," and "As You Like I "Over Here," OB in "The Hunter," "Dancing for the Kaiser," "Money."

WEAVER, FRITZ. Born Jan. 19, 1926 in Pittsburgh, PA. Graduate UChicag Bdwy debut 1955 in "Chalk Garden" for which he received a Theatre Wor Award, followed by "Protective Custody," "Miss Lonelyhearts," "All Ame can," "Lorenzo," "The White House," "Baker Street," "Child's Play," "A surd Person Singular," OB in "The Way of the World," "White Devi "Doctor's Dilemma," "Family Reunion," "The Power and the Glory," "Gre God Brown," "Peer Gynt," "Henry IV," "My Fair Lady" (CC).

WEBB, ROBB. Born Jan. 29, 1939 in Whitesburg, KY. Attended Ohio Sta U. Debut 1976 OB in "Who Killed Richard Cory?"

WEINER, ARN. Born July 19, 1931 in Brooklyn, NY. Attended Pratt, LAC Bdwy debut 1966 in "Those That Play the Clowns," followed by "Yentl," ( in "Come Walk with Me," "Saving Grace," "Come Out, Carlo," "Evenin with Chekhov," "Sunset."

WELCH, CHARLES C. Born Feb. 2, 1921 in New Britain, CT. Attend Randall Sch., AmThWing. Bdwy debut 1958 in "Cloud 7," followed by "Don Brook," "Golden Boy," "Little Murders," "Holly Go Lightly," "Darling of t Day," "Dear World," "Follies," "Status Quo Vadis," "Shenandoah," OB "Half-Past Wednesday," "Oh, Lady! Lady!"

WELLER, PETER. Born June 24, 1947 in Stevens Point, WI. Gradua AADA. Bdwy bow 1972 in "Sticks and Bones," followed by "Full Circl "Summer Brave," OB in "Children," "Merchant of Venice," "Macbeth "Rebel Women."

WELLS, CYNTHIA. Born Mar. 6, 1942 in Jackson, MN. Graduate Macales Col, UMinn. Bdwy debut 1975 in "Very Good Eddie."

WENTZ, EARL. Born Mar. 22, 1938 in Charlotte, NC. Attended Charlot Wingate, Queens Cols. Debut 1976 OB in ELT's "Missouri Legend."

WESTON, JIM. Born Aug. 2, 1942 in Montclair, NJ. Attended Manches Col. AADA. Bdwy bow 1969 in "Red, White and Maddox," followed "Lovely Ladies, Kind Gentlemen," "Grease," "Over Here," OB in "She Lov Me," "Ballad of Johnny Pot," "A Gun Play."

WHEEL, PATRICIA. Born in NYC. Has appeared in "Cyrano," "The Te pest," "Arms and the Man," "Little Brown Jug," "Stars Weep," "Brown Version," "Cry of the Peacock," "Gertie," "Sacred Flame," "Soldiers," "B terflies Are Free," "Voices," "The Women," "Grass Widows" (OB).

WHITEHEAD, PAXTON. Born in Kent, Eng. Attended Webber-Doug Drama Sch. Bdwy debut 1962 in "The Affair," followed by "Beyond t Fringe," "Candida," "Habeas Corpus," OB in "Gallows Humour," "One W Pendulum," "A Doll's House," "Rondelay."

argaret Whitton     J. Thomas Wierney     Elizabeth Wilson     Jerrold Ziman     Madonna Young

WHITMORE, CHRISTINEA. Born Dec. 24, 1952 in Derby, CT. Attended AB Studio. Debut 1972 OB in "Trelawny of the Wells," Bdwy in "The National Health" (1974), "Ah, Wilderness."

WHITTON, MARGARET. (formerly Peggy) Born Nov. 30, 1950 in Philadelphia, PA. Debut 1973 OB in "Baba Goya," followed by "Arthur."

WIERNEY, J. THOMAS. Born Jan. 11, 1953 in Honolulu, HI. Graduate Syracuse U. Debut 1976 OB in ELT's "Panama Hattie."

WILCOX, RALPH. Born Jan. 30, 1951 in Milwaukee, WI. Attended UWisc. Debut 1971 OB in "Dirtiest Show in Town," followed by "Broadway," "Miracle Play," Bdwy in "Ain't Supposed to Die a Natural Death," "The Wiz."

WILKINSON, LISA. Born in NYC. Graduate NYU. Debut OB 1970 in "Slave Ship," followed by "Don't Fail Your Lovin' Daddy, Lily Plum," Bdwy 1974 "Candide."

WILLIAMS, CURT. Born Nov. 17, 1935 in Mt. Holly, NJ. Graduate Oberlin Col., UMiami. Debut 1964 OB in "The Fantasticks," followed by "Pinafore," "Mikado," "Night Must Fall," "The Hostage," "Macbeth," "Ice Age," Bdwy 1970 in "Purlie."

WILLIAMS, DICK ANTHONY. Born Aug. 9, 1938 in Chicago, IL. Debut 1968 OB in "Big Time Buck White," followed by "Jamimma," "What the Winesellers Buy," Bdwy in "Ain't Supposed to Die a Natural Death," "We Interrupt This Program," "The Poison Tree."

WILLIAMS, SAMMY. Born Nov. 13, 1948 in Trenton, NJ. Bdwy debut 1969 in "The Happy Time," followed by "Applause," "Seesaw," "A Chorus Line."

WILLISON, WALTER. Born June 24, 1947 in Monterey Park, CA. Bdwy debut 1970 in "Norman, Is That You?," followed by "Two by Two" for which he received a Theatre World Award, "Wild and Wonderful," "Pippin."

WILSON, ELIZABETH. Born Apr. 4, 1925 in Grand Rapids, MI. Attended Neighborhood Playhouse. Bdwy debut 1953 in "Picnic," followed by "Desk Set," "Tunnel of Love," "Big Fish, Little Fish," "Sheep on the Runway," "Sticks and Bones," "Secret Affairs of Mildred Wild," OB in "Plaza 9," "Eh?," "Little Murders," "Good Woman of Setzuan," "Uncle Vanya," "Threepenny Opera."

WILSON, MARY LOUISE. Born Nov. 12, 1936 in New Haven, CT. Graduate Northwestern. OB in "Our Town," "Upstairs at the Downstairs," "Threepenny Opera," "A Great Career," "Whispers on the Wind," "Beggar's Opera," Bdwy in "Hot Spot," "Flora, the Red Menace," "Criss-Crossing," "Promises, Promises," "The Women," "Gypsy," "The Royal Family."

WINDE, BEATRICE. Born Jan. 6 in Chicago, Ill. Debut 1966 OB in "In White America," followed by "June Bug Graduates Tonight," "Strike Heaven on the Face." Bdwy 1971 in "Ain't Supposed to Die a Natural Death" for which she received a Theatre World Award.

WINTERS, NEWTON. Born in Henderson, NV. Bdwy debut 1976 in "Bubbling Brown Sugar."

WINTERS, WARRINGTON. Born July 28, 1909 in Bigstone County, MN. Graduate UMinn. Debut OB 1975 in ELT's "Another Language."

WISE, WILLIAM. Born May 11, 1940 in Chicago, IL. Attended Bradley U. Northern Ill. U. Debut 1970 OB in "Adaptation/Next," followed by "Hot l Baltimore."

WISEMAN, JOSEPH. Born May 15, 1919 in Montreal, Can. Attended CCNY. Bdwy in "Journey to Jerusalem," "Abe Lincoln in Illinois," "Candle in the Wind," "Three Sisters," "Storm Operation," "Joan of Lorraine," "Antony and Cleopatra," "Detective Story," "That Lady," "King Lear," "Golden Boy," "The Lark," "Zalmen, or the Madness of God," OB in "Marco Millions," "Incident at Vichy," "In the Matter of J. Robert Oppenheimer," "Enemies," "Duchess of Malfi," "Last Analysis."

WITHAM, JOHN. Born Apr. 3, 1947 in Plainfield, NJ. Graduate AMDA. Debut 1972 OB in "Two if by Sea," followed by "Comedy," Bdwy 1976 in "1600 Pennsylvania Avenue."

WOLFE, JOEL. Born Sept. 19, 1936 in NYC. Graduate CCNY. Debut 1968 OB in "Ergo," followed by "Room Service," "The Co-op," Bdwy 1975 in "All over Town."

WOLFSON, ROB. Born Dec. 3, 1953 in NYC. Debut 1974 OB in "The Hot l Baltimore."

WOOD, JOHN. Born in 1931 in Derbyshire, Eng. Attended Jesus Col. Oxford. Bdwy debut 1967 in "Rosencrantz and Guildenstern Are Dead," followed by "Sherlock Holmes," "Travesties."

WOODS, RICHARD. Born May 9, 1921 in Buffalo, NY. Graduate Ithaca Col. Bdwy in "Beg, Borrow or Steal," "Capt. Brassbound's Conversion," "Sail Away," "Coco." "Last of Mrs. Lincoln," "Gigi," "Sherlock Homes," "Murder among Friends," OB in "The Crucible," "Summer and Smoke," "American Gothic," "Four-in-One," "My Heart's in the Highlands," "Eastward in Eden," "The Long Gallery," "The Year Boston Won the Pennant" and "In the Matter of J. Robert Oppenheimer" (LC), with APA in "You Can't Take It with You," "War and Peace," "School for Scandal," "Right You Are," "The Wild Duck" "Pantagleize," "Exit the King," "The Cherry Orchard," "Cock-a-Doodle Dandy," and "Hamlet."

WORONOV, MARY. Born Dec. 8, 1946 in Brooklyn, NY. Graduate Cornell U. Debut OB 1968 in "Kitchenette," followed by "Clearing House," "Queen of Greece," "Two Noble Kinsmen," "Boom Boom Room" for which she received a Theatre World Award, "Women behind Bars."

WORTH, IRENE. Born June 23, 1916 in Nebraska. Graduate UCLA. Bdwy debut 1943 in "The Two Mrs. Carrolls," followed by "The Cocktail Party," "Mary Stuart," "Toys in the Attic," "King Lear," "Tiny Alice," "Sweet Bird of Youth."

WRIGHT, TERESA. Born Oct. 27, 1918 in NYC. Bdwy debut 1938 in "Our Town," followed by "Life with Father," "Dark at the Top of the Stairs," "Mary, Mary," "I Never Sang for My Father," "Death of a Salesman," "Ah, Wilderness," OB in "Who's Happy Now," "A Passage to E. M. Forster."

WRIGHT, WILLIAM. Born Jan. 21, 1943 in Los Angeles, CA. Graduate UUtah, Bristol Old Vic. Debut 1973 OB in "Merchant of Venice" (LC), Bdwy 1976 in "Equus."

WYMAN, NICHOLAS. Born May 18, 1950 in Portland, ME. Graduate Harvard. Bdwy debut 1975 in "Very Good Eddie."

WYNKOOP, CHRISTOPHER. Born Dec. 7, 1943 in Long Branch, NJ. Graduate AADA. Debut 1970 OB in "Under the Gaslight," followed by "And So to Bed," "Panama Hattie" (ELT).

WYNNE, JONATHAN. Born Mar. 7, 1947 in Los Angeles, CA. Graduate LACC. Bdwy debut 1975 in "Hello, Dolly!"

YANCY, EMILY. Born in 1947 in NYC. Attended Bklyn Col. Bdwy debut 1967 in "Hello, Dolly!," followed by "Man of La Mancha," "Your Own Thing" (OB), "1600 Pennsylvania Avenue."

YATES, CRAIG. Born Feb. 13, 1948 in Harvey, IL. Attended UCLA, LACC. Bdwy debut 1971 in "On the Town," followed by "Mame," "A Musical Jubilee."

YATES, JOHN ROBERT. Born Sept. 12, 1948 in Chicago, IL. Graduate UIll. Debut OB 1976 in "Medal of Honor Rag."

YOSHIDA, PETER. Born May 28, 1945 in Chicago, IL. Graduate UIll., Princeton U., AmThWing. Debut 1965 OB in "Coriolanus," followed by "Troilus and Cressida," "Santa Anita '42," "Pursuit of Happiness."

YOUNG, MADONNA. Born July 16 in Lackawanna, NY. Graduate NYU, AADA. Debut 1972 OB in "DuBarry Was a Lady," followed by "Brainwashed."

ZACHAR, GLENN. Born Nov. 30, 1961 in NYC. Bdwy debut 1975 in "Ah, Wilderness."

ZAKS, JERRY. Born Sept. 7, 1946 in Germany. Graduate Dartmouth, Smith Col. Bdwy debut 1973 in "Grease," OB in "Death Story," "Dream of a Blacklisted Actor," "Kid Champion," "Golden Boy."

ZANG, EDWARD. Born Aug. 19, 1934 in NYC. Graduate Boston U. OB in "Good Soldier Schweik," "St. Joan," "Boys in the Band," "The Reliquary of Mr. and Mrs. Potterfield," "Last Analysis," "As You Like It," "More Than You Deserve," "Polly," "Threepenny Opera."

ZIMAN, JERROLD J. Born in Colorado. Graduate UChicago. Debut OB 1969 in "Brass Butterfly," followed by "The Screens," "Kaddish," "Beggars Opera," "Sunset," "Lotta," "Universal Nigger," "Ice Age," Bdwy in "The Beauty Part" (1962)

ZORICH, LOUIS. Born Feb. 12, 1924 in Chicago, IL. Attended Roosevelt U. OB in "Six Characters in Search of an Author," "Crimes and Crimes," "Henry V," "Thracian Horses," "All Women Are One," "Good Soldier Schweik," "Shadow of Heroes," "To Clothe the Naked," "Sunset," "A Memory of Two Mondays," "They Knew What They Wanted," Bdwy in "Becket," "Moby Dick," "The Odd Couple," "Hadrian VII," "Moonchildren," "Fun City," "Goodtime Charley."

ZWICK, JOEL. Born Jan. 11, 1942 in Brooklyn, NY. Graduate Bklyn Col. Debut 1967 OB in Macbird!," followed by "Dance with Me."

261

# OBITUARIES

John Baragrey (1971)

Larry Blyden (1966)

Pamela Brown (1960)

**SIG ARNO,** 79, German-born stage and film character actor, died in Los Angeles Aug. 17, 1975 from complications of Parkinson's disease. He came to the U.S. in 1939 and appeared in films before making his Broadway debut in 1940 in "Victoria Regina." Subsequently he appeared in "Song of Norway," "The Play's the Thing," "Time Remembered" (for which he received a Tony nomination), "The Cold Wind and the Warm," and the 1964 revival of "The Merry Widow." Surviving are his widow, and a son by his first wife.

**MARGARET BANNERMAN,** 83, Canadian-born actress, died Apr. 25, 1976 in Englewood, NJ. After her London stage debut in 1915, she rose to stardom in 1923 in "Our Betters." Her first Bdwy role was in 1942 in "By Jupiter," followed by "Our Betters," "One Touch of Venus," "Rebecca," "The Deep Mrs. Sykes," "John Loves Mary," "Getting Married," "Starcross Story," "Thor with Angels," "Garden District," and "My Fair Lady." She was twice married and divorced. There are no survivors.

**JOHN BARAGREY,** 57, Alabama-born actor, died Aug. 4, 1975 in his NYC home. Made his Bdwy debut 1943 in "Sons and Soldiers," followed by "A Flag Is Born," "The Enchanted," "The Royal Family" (CC), "One Eye Closed," "The Crucible," "The Devils," "Elizabeth the Queen" (CC), "The Grass Harp," and "Murderous Angels." He also appeared in several films and many tv productions. Surviving is his widow, actress Louise Larabee.

**ALAN BAXTER,** 67, Ohio-born actor died of cancer, May 8, 1976 in Woodland Hills, CA. Made Bdwy debut in 1933 in "Lone Valley," followed by "Men in White," "Gold Eagle Guy," "Black Pit," "Winged Victory," "Home of the Brave," "The Hallams," "Jenny Kissed Me," and "South Pacific" (CC). He also appeared in over 60 films and on many tv shows. He is survived by his second wife, actress Christy Palmer.

**EARL BENHAM,** 89, former actor, died Mar. 21, 1976 in his home in Northport, NY. Began his career at 17 traveling with the Primrose Minstrels. He later appeared in many Bdwy musicals, including "The Little Millionaire," "Winsome Widow," "Carnival," "Very Good Eddie," and "Hitchy-Koo." In 1920 he went into business as a custom tailor for entertainers. He was a trustee of the Actors Fund. His son James survives.

**LARRY BLYDEN,** 49, versatile performer who also produced, and directed for stage, film and tv, died June 6, 1975 while on vacation in Agadir, Morocco, from injuries received in an automobile accident. He had just completed 250 performances in "Absurd Person Singular" and was vacationing before beginning his tv game show "The Showoff." His Bdwy debut was in 1948 in "Mr. Roberts," followed by "The Miser," "Wish You Were Here," "Oh! Men! Oh! Women!," "Italian Straw Hat," "Who Was That Lady I Saw You With?," "Flower Drum Song," "Foxy," "Blues for Mr. Charlie," "Luv," "The Apple Tree," "Mother Lover," "You Know I Can't Hear You When the Water's Running," "A Funny Thing Happened on the Way to the Forum." He was divorced from the late Carol Haney. A son and daughter survive.

**CHARLES BROKAW,** 77, actor, died in a NYC hospital Oct. 23, 1975. His Bdwy appearances include "The Road to Rome," "The Decoy," "Elizabeth the Queen," "Jenny," "The Squall." He also had roles in several films. A brother and stepson survive.

**JOSEPHINE BROWN,** 84, Chicago born actress, died Apr. 26, 1976 at her home in Ibiza, Spain, where she had been in retirement for 10 years. Made her debut at 11 with Lillian Russell, and subsequently appeared with William Gillette, John Barrymore, Arnold Day, and George Fawcett. Her most recent appearances were in "Bachelor Born," "I Remember Mama," "Gigi," "Anniversary Waltz," and off-Bdwy in "Diary of a Scoundrel." She was painted by Augustus John, sculpted by Auguste Rodin, and rejected Caruso's proposal of marriage. Her daughter, Wauna Paul, died in 1973.

**PAMELA BROWN,** 58, a prominent British actress, died Sept. 18, 1975 in London. She made her Bdwy debut in 1947 in "The Importance of Being Earnest," and subsequently returned for roles in "Love for Love," "The Lady's Not For Burning," "The Country Wife," and "Heartbreak House." She was divorced from actor Peter Copley.

**ANGUS CAIRNS,** 65, actor, died in NYC Oct. 14, 1975. He made his NY debut in "Othello," followed by "Henry VIII," "What Every Woman Knows," "Androcles and the Lion," "Yellow Jack," "Alice in Wonderland," "Mock Turtle," "Brigadoon," "Kiss Me, Kate," "Paint Your Wagon," "Threepenny Opera," "The Engagement Baby," and "Soon." He is survived by his brother and sister.

**FRANK CARRINGTON,** 73, co-founder, producer and director of the Paper Mill Playhouse, Millburn, NJ, died July 3, 1975 in his Millburn home. In 1938, with Antoinette Scudder, he opened the Playhouse and in 1972 it was proclaimed the State Theater of New Jersey. No reported survivors.

**JACQUES CHARON,** 55, director and leading actor of the Comedie Francaise, died of a heart attack in his Paris home Oct. 15, 1975. His last NY appearance with the company was in February 1970 at City Center. No reported survivors.

**EDWARD CHOATE,** 67, producer and manager, died in a NYC hospital July 23, 1975. He was a member of the Shubert staff for 12 years, serving as producer and casting director, and also produced independently. He had been in retirement for 6 months. Surviving are his second wife, a daughter, and 3 sons.

**AGATHA CHRISTIE,** 85, a tremendously successful writer, died Jan. 12, 1976 at her home in Wallingford, Eng. Among her many works are 14 plays, including "Ten Little Indians," "Appointment with Death," "Hidden Horizons," "Witness for the Prosecution," and "The Mousetrap" which has been running in London since 1952. She was made a Dame of the British Empire in 1956. She is survived by her second husband, Sir Max Mallowan, and a grandson.

LEE J. COBB, 64, actor, died Feb. 11, 1976 in his home in Woodland Hills, CA. He was born Leo Jacob in NY's Lower East Side, and studied to become a violinist. His Bdwy debut was in "Crime and Punishment" (1935), followed by "Till the Day I Die," "Waiting for Lefty," "Mother," "Bitter Stream," "Johnny Johnson," "Golden Boy," "The Gentle People," "The Fifth Column," "Thunder Rock," "Clash by Night," "Jason," "Death of a Salesman," "The Emperor's New Clothes," and "King Lear" (LC). He was well known for his tv series "The Virginian," and had appeared in over 80 films. Surviving are his second wife, a daughter, and two sons.

BARBARA COLBY, 35, actress, was shot and killed July 24, 1975, by unknown gunmen as she left an acting class in Venice, CA. She made her Bdwy debut in 1965 in "The Devils," and appeared Off-Bdwy in "Under Milkwood," "Six Characters in Search of an Author," "Murderous Angels," and Lincoln Center productions of "Richard III" and "A Doll's House." No reported survivors.

CLANCY COOPER, 68, actor, died in Hollywood, June 14, 1975, of a heart attack while driving his car on Mulholland Drive. He made his Bdwy debut in 1938 in "Casey Jones," and subsequently had roles in over 35 plays, including "The Fabulous Invalid" and "Juno and the Paycock." He also appeared in over 60 films. He is survived by his authoress wife, Elizabeth Cooper, and a son.

KEVIN COUGHLIN, 30, stage, film and tv actor, died Jan. 19, 1976 of multiple injuries resulting from a hit-and-run accident in North Hollywood, CA. He was struck while cleaning his car. Before going to Hollywood, he had appeared on Bdwy in "Frogs of Spring," "The King and I," "Life with Mother," and "The Square Root of Wonderful." He was a regular on tv's "Horn and Hardart Children's Hour" and "I Remember Mama." Surviving are his wife and mother.

GEORGE CURZON, 77, British actor, died May 10, 1976 in London. He made his Bdwy debut in 1935 in "Parnell," subsequently appearing in "Hitch Your Wagon," "Black Lime-light," "Yes, M'Lord," and "The Little Glass Clock." No reported survivors.

DOLORES, 83, British-born "Ziegfeld girl," died Nov. 7, 1975 in Paris. She was one of the most publicized and beautiful girls from Ziegfeld's "Follies," and appeared in them for several years beginning in 1917. She was "The Empress of Fashion" and "The Peacock Girl." She also appeared in the musical "Sally." She was born Kathleen Mary Rose and became a prominent London model before Ziegfeld offered her a spot in the "Follies." In 1923 she sailed for France to marry Tudor Wilkinson, a millionaire art collector, and from then on lived a quiet life in Paris. During WWII she was arrested by the Germans on a charge of aiding the Resistance and kept in jail until Paris was liberated in 1944. There are no reported survivors.

VINCENT J. DONAHUE, 58, Actors Equity Assistant Executive Secretary, and former actor, was found stabbed to death Feb. 10, 1976 in his NYC hotel room. Before joining Equity's staff he had appeared in numerous Broadway productions, including "20th Century," "Stalag 17," "The Andersonville Trial," City Center productions of "Cyrano de Bergerac," "The Shrike," and "Charley's Aunt," and his last Bdwy play in 1961 "Daughter of Silence." A sister survives.

EDDIE DOWLING, 81, singer, dancer, actor, playwright, songwriter, director, and producer, died Feb. 18, 1976 in Smithfield, RI. He was born Joseph Nelson Goucher in Woonsocket, RI, and made his Bdwy debut in 1919 in "The Velvet Lady" singing two songs he had composed. Subsequently he appeared in "Ziegfeld Follies," "Sally, Irene and Mary" which he co-authored, and co-produced, and co-directed, "Honeymoon Lane," "Sidewalks of New York," "Thumbs Up!," "Here Come the Clowns," "The Time of Your Life," "Magic," "Hello Out There," "The Greatest of These," "Manhattan Nocturne," "The Glass Menagerie," "The Home Life of the Buffalo," "Minnie and Mr. Williams," "Angel in the Pawnshop," and "Paint Your Wagon." He retired in the early 1960's. He leaves his widow, dancer-comedienne Rae Dooley whom he married in 1914, and a daughter.

JOE DOWNING, 71, actor, died during February 1976. Among his many Broadway appearances were roles in "Garrick Gaieties," "Farewell to Arms," "Shooting Star," "Heat Lightning," "Page Miss Glory," "Ceiling Zero," "Dead End," and "Ramshackle Inn." No survivors reported.

ROBERT DOWNING, 61, drama critic for the Denver Post, and former actor and manager, died June 14, 1976 following abdominal surgery in Denver, CO. After several years in stock and touring companies, he made his Bdwy debut in 1940 with the Lunts in "The Taming of the Shrew," followed by "There Shall Be No Night," "The Naked Genius," "Wake Up, Darling," "Say, Darling," "Butter and Egg Man." He was stage manager for more than 26 Bdwy productions, and a book reviewer for Variety. No survivors reported.

ROBERT ECKLES, 55, singer-actor, died of a heart attack Aug. 9, 1975 in his NYC home. He appeared in numerous Gilbert and Sullivan revivals, and in "The Lady's not for Burning," "Cyrano de Bergerac," and "Becket." No survivors reported.

CHARLES ELLIS, 83, an abstract painter and former actor, died Mar. 11, 1976 in Pittsfield, Mass. In NY he had appeared in "The Rope," "Moon of the Caribbees," "Desire under the Elms," "Show Boat" (1932), "Valley Forge," "Key Largo," "The Eve of St. Mark," "Joan of Lorraine," and "Anne of the Thousand Days." He leaves his wife, former actress Norma Millay.

PAUL FORD, 74, retired actor, died Apr. 12, 1976 in Mineola, NY. Born Paul Ford Weaver in Baltimore, he did not become an actor until his late 30's. He made his Bdwy debut in 1944 in "Decision," and subsequently appeared in "Lower North," "Kiss Them for Me," "Flamingo Road," "On Whitman Avenue," "Another Part of the Forest," "As We Forgive Our Debtors," "Command Decision," "Brass Ring," "Teahouse of the August Moon," "Good as Gold," "Whoop-Up," "Music Man," "A Thurber Carnival," "Never Too Late," "3 Bags Full," "What Did We Do Wrong?," "3 Men on a Horse," "Front Page," and "Fun City." For 5 years he was Col. Hall on tv's "Sgt. Bilko" show. Surviving are his widow, two sons and two daughters.

Lee J. Cobb (1970)

Robert Downing (1960)

Paul Ford (1966)

Frieda Inescort (1937)

Margaret Leighton (1973)

Tilly Losch (1936)

CHARLES GAYNOR, 66, writer of sketches, music and lyrics, died of a heart attack Dec. 19, 1975 in Washington, D.C. He was the creator of "Lend an Ear" and "Show Girl" starring Carol Channing. He wrote additional numbers for the 1973 revival of "Irene." No reported survivors.

PAUL KIRK GILES, 80, retired actor, died Apr. 23, 1976 in NYC. Among his Broadway appearances were roles in "Born Yesterday," "Ah, Wilderness" and "Pillar to Post." Surviving are his widow and two daughters.

RUTH GILLMORE, former actress and teacher, died Feb. 12, 1976 at her home in Nantucket, Mass. She made her debut in 1918 in "The Betrothal," subsequently appearing in "No More Frontier," and "The Farmer Takes a Wife." Surviving are her husband and son, and a sister, actress Margalo Gillmore.

FERNANDO GRAHAL, 32, Puerto Rican-born dancer and choreographer, was killed Sept. 4, 1975 in San Juan, P.R., when an armed fugitive tried to use him as a shield. On Bdwy he had appeared in "Carnival," "Bajour," "Man of La Mancha," "Guys and Dolls," and "Around the World in 80 Days" at Jones Beach. He is survived by his mother, a brother and sister.

ETHEL GRIFFIES, 97, British actress, died of a stroke Sept. 9, 1975 in London. She was the oldest working actress in the English-speaking theatre, and began her career as a child in 1881. She made her Bdwy debut in 1924 in "Havoc," followed by "Interference," "Pygmalion," "Mariners," "Loose Ends," "Old English," "The Cherry Orchard," "Lady Dedlock," "Criminal Code," "The Druid Circle," "The Hallams," "The Leading Lady," "Shop at Sly Corner," "Miss Liberty," "Legend of Sarah," "The Royal Family" (CC), "Autumn Garden," "Write Me a Murder," "A Very Rich Woman," "Ivanov," "Billy Liar," and "The Natural Look" in 1967. She also appeared in over 100 films. Her first husband, actor Walter Beaumont, died in 1910, and her second, actor Edward Cooper, died in 1956. There were no immediate survivors reported.

WILLIAM HANSEN, 64, character actor, died June 23, 1975 in Woodland Hills, CA. He made his Bdwy debut in 1934 in "My Heart's in the Highlands," subsequently appearing in "Night Music," "Medicine Show," "Twelfth Night," "Macbeth," "The Assassin," "Brigadoon," "Montserrat," "The Member of the Wedding," "Barefoot in Athens," "Golden Boy," "Teahouse of the August Moon," and "Lorenzo." He also appeared in films. No reported survivors.

FRIEDA INESCORT, 75, Scottish-born actress, died of multiple sclerosis Feb. 21, 1976 in Motion Picture Country Hospital where he had been a patient since 1969. She made her Bdwy debut in 1922 in "The Truth about Blayds," followed by "Escape," "Merchant of Venice," "Major Barbara," "Pygmalion," "When Ladies Meet," "False Dreams, Farewell," "Soldier's Wife," "Mermaids Singing," and "You Never Can Tell." She also appeared in many films. A sister survives.

ROBERTA JONAY, 54, singer-actress, died of cancer Apr. 19, 1976 in Tarzana, CA. Her Bdwy credits include "Allegro" and "As You Like It." She is survived by her husband, actor Judson Pratt, and two sons.

ANNETTE KELLERMANN, 87, "Australia's million dollar mermaid," died Nov. 5, 1975 in Southport, Aust. After winning international fame as a swimmer, she became the sensation of Bdwy and vaudeville in an aquatic act. She was arrested in Boston for wearing her original one-piece bathing suit. A sister survives.

MARGOT KELLY, 82, English-born retired actress, died Mar. 10, 1976 in Summit, NJ. She came to NY in 1916 to make her debut in "A Little Bit of Fluff," followed by "Pierrot the Prodigal," "Carnival," "Deburreau," "Floradora," "The Second Mrs. Tanqueray," and "The Pearl of Great Price." She was the widow of NY deputy police commissioner James Sinnott. She is survived by her daughter, actress Patricia Sinnott.

JAMES KIERNAN, 35, actor, was shot and killed July 24, 1975 as he was leaving an acting class in Venice, CA. A native of Brooklyn, he had appeared Off-Broadway in "Colette" and "When You Comin' Back, Red Ryder?"

HYMAN KRAFT, 76, playwright, died in NYC July 29, 1975. He wrote "Mr. Papavert," "Ten Percent," "Cafe Crown," "Thank You, Svoboda," "Hot-Cha," "Cue for Passion" with Edward Chodorov, and "Top Banana." His widow survives.

MARGARET LEIGHTON, 53, British-born actress, died of multiple sclerosis Jan. 13, 1976 in Chichester, Eng. Her Bdwy debut in 1946 was with the Old Vic in "Henry IV Parts I & II," and "Uncle Vanya." She subsequently appeared on Bdwy in "Separate Tables," "Much Ado about Nothing," "The Night of the Iguana," "Tchin-Tchin," "The Chinese Prime Minister," "Homage to Shakespeare," "Slapstick Tragedy," and "The Little Foxes." She received "Tony" awards for "Separate Tables" and "Night of the Iguana." Surviving is her third husband, actor Michael Wilding.

DAVID LIGHT, 71, Polish-born director and former Yiddish actor, died of a heart attack in NYC July 31, 1975. He came to the U. S. in 1945 from Buenos Aires, and for 30 years was associated with the Folksbiene. In 1973 he received an "Obie" for his direction of "Hard to Be a Jew." His widow survives.

TILLY LOSCH, an internationally recognized Vienna-born dancer, actress, choreographer and painter, in her 70's, died of cancer Dec. 24, 1975 in a NY hospital. After becoming a prima ballerina in Europe, she made her Bdwy debut in 1927 in Max Reinhardt's "A Midsummer Night's Dream," followed by "Everyman," "Danton's Death," "Servant of Two Masters," "This Year of Grace," "Wake Up and Dream," "The Band Wagon," "The Miracle," and "Topaze." Two marriages to prominent Britons ended in divorce. She had no immediate survivors.

**MARTY MAY,** 77, comedian, singer and actor, died of a heart ailment Nov. 11, 1975 in Las Vegas. After a career in vaudeville, he appeared in such Bdwy productions as "Roberta," "Walk with Music," "Best Foot Forward," "Artists and Models," "Annie Get Your Gun," "Sons o' Fun," "Funzapoppin," and "Pardon Our French." In 1962 he moved to Las Vegas where he entertained in and helped produce hotel-casino shows. Surviving are his widow, actress June Johnson, and a son.

**RUTH McDEVITT,** 80, character actress, died May 27, 1976 in her Hollywood home. After the death of her husband Patrick J. McDevitt, she turned to acting, and made her Bdwy debut 1940 in "Young Couple Wanted." She subsequently appeared in "Goodbye in the Night," "Arsenic and Old Lace," "Meet a Body," "Harvey," "Sleepy Hollow," "Picnic," "Solid Gold Cadillac," "Diary of a Scoundrel," "Clerambard," "The Best Man," "Save Me a Place at Forest Lawn," and "Absence of a Cello." She was the mother of Wally Cox in the popular tv series "Mr. Peepers." No survivors reported.

**Ruth McDevitt (1963)**

**JOHN McGIVER,** 62, a Bronx high school teacher who became a noted character actor, died of a heart attack Sept. 9, 1975 at his home in West Fulton, NY. After his Bdwy debut in 1956 in "Little Glass Clock," he had roles in "Cloud 7," "Drink to Me Only," "God and Kate Murphy," "A Thurber Carnival," "A Cook for Mr. General," "Happiness Is Just a Little Thing Called a Rolls Royce," "A Way of Life," "Front Page," and "Our Town." He appeared in films and many tv roles. He is survived by his wife, six sons and four daughters.

**DORO MERANDE,** Kansas-born character actress in her 70's, died Nov. 1, 1975 in Miami, Fla., where she had gone to act in a Jackie Gleason "Honeymooners" tv special. She first appeared on Bdwy in 1935 in "Loose Moments," followed by "One Good Year," "Fulton of Oak Falls," "Red Harvest," "Angel Island," "Our Town," "Love's Old Sweet Song," "Beverly Hills," "The More the Merrier," "Junior Miss," "Hope for a Harvest," "Three's a Family," "Naked Genius," "Pick-up Girl," "Violet," "Hope for the Best," "Apple of His Eye," "The Silver Whistle," "Rat Race," "4 Twelves Are 48," "Lo and Behold!," "Diary of a Scoundrel," and "Front Page" (1969). No reported survivors.

**JO MIELZINER,** 74, versatile and imaginative scenic designer, collapsed in a NYC taxicab of a massive stroke and was dead on arrival at the hospital Mar. 15, 1976. He had created the settings, and usually the lighting, for more than 300 plays, musicals, operas and ballets. Born of American parents in Paris, he came to the U. S. in 1909. He began his theatrical career in 1923 as an actor and stage manager, but changed to scenic design a year later, creating the set for the Lunts' production of "The Guardsman." Among his most memorable designs are "South Pacific," "Winterset," "Guys and Dolls," "Death of a Salesman," "Streetcar Named Desire," "Pal Joey," "Carousel," "Annie Get Your Gun," "The King and I," "Can-Can," "Gypsy," "Strange Interlude," "Street Scene," "Glass Menagerie," "Summer and Smoke," "Cat on a Hot Tin Roof," "Barretts of Wimpole Street," "Tea and Sympathy," and "Picnic." His designs received 5 "Tony" Awards, 5 Donaldson Awards, and an Academy Award for the film "Picnic." Surviving are two sons and a daughter, and his wife from whom he had been separated for many years.

**John McGiver (1965)**

**SAL MINEO,** 37, actor, was stabbed to death by an unknown assailant Feb. 12, 1976 as he was returning to his Hollywood home from a rehearsal. He made his Bdwy debut at 11 in "The Rose Tattoo," followed by "The King and I," "Something about a Soldier." He appeared in many tv roles, and in films. He is survived by his mother, a sister, and two brothers.

**KARL NIELSEN,** 85, retired stage manager, died Sept. 8, 1975 in West Palm Beach, Fla., where he had been living for several years. Before his retirement in 1970, he had managed over 100 productions, and for 34 years was associated with the Theatre Guild. No reported survivors.

**PATRICIA O'CONNELL,** 73, Alabama-born singer-actress, died Dec. 24, 1975 in New Haven, Conn. She had appeared in the original companies of "The Student Prince," "The Desert Song," "The Great Waltz," and "Rosalie." She also sang with the Chicago Opera and the New York Opera Comique. The widow of journalist Angus Shaw McCabe, she is survived by two sisters.

**DONALD M. OENSLAGER,** 73, scenic designer and teacher, died June 21, 1975 in his summer home near Bedford, NY. Among the more than 250 productions he designed are "The Emperor Jones," "The Farmer Takes a Wife," "First Lady," "Stage Door," "You Can't Take It With You," "I'd Rather Be Right," "Of Mice and Men," "The Man Who Came to Dinner," "Pygmalion," "Born Yesterday," "Sabrina Fair," "Major Barbara," "The Pleasure of His Company," "Good News," "A Doll's House," and "A Majority of One." For 46 years he was on the faculty at Yale. His widow survives.

**REX O'MALLEY,** 75, British-born actor, died May 1, 1976 in the Mary Manning Walsh Home in NYC. He came to the U. S. in 1926 to appear in "The Strange Prince," subsequently he had roles in "The Comic," "The Marquise," "Bachelor Father," "The Apple Cart," "Lost Sheep," "Wonder Bar," "Experience Unnecessary," "The Mad Hopes," "The Best Sellers," "No More Ladies," "The Red Cat," "Revenge with Music," "Simpleton of the Unexpected Isles," "Matrimony Pfd.," "Merely Murder," "You Never Know," "The Man Who Came to Dinner," "Naked Genius," "The Cherry Orchard," "Many Happy Returns," "Devils Galore," "Lute Song," "Lady Windermere's Fan," "Charley's Aunt," "The Sleeping Prince," "The Lady of the Camellias," and "Say Nothing." No known survivors.

**SANTOS ORTEGA,** 76, stage, tv and radio actor, died Apr. 10, 1976 while visiting Fort Lauderdale, Fla. He began his career at 17 singing at the Hippodrome Theatre. His most important stage role was in "Jeb" in 1946. He was skilled in accents and played in many radio serials, including "Ellery Queen," "Perry Mason," "Charlie Chan," and "Boston Blackie." He was probably best known as Grandpa Hughes on the tv serial "As the World Turns." He leaves a son and daughter.

**Doro Merande (1964)**

Paul Robeson (1933)

Ethel Shutta (1963)

Arthur Treacher (1949)

**B. IDEN PAYNE,** 94, British-born actor-director-teacher and Shakespearean authority, died Apr. 6, 1976 in Austin, Tex., where he had been on the faculty of the Univ. of Tex. He made his Bdwy bow in 1915 in "The Critic," followed by "The Great Broxoff," "Candida," and directed numerous other plays with some of the great stars of the theatre. During the latter part of his life, he adopted university theatre as his metier, and was a visiting professor at several universities and colleges. He is survived by his second wife, a son and a daughter.

**LOU POLAN,** 71, Russian-born character actor, died Mar. 3, 1975 in Freeport, ME. He made his Bdwy debut in 1922 in "R.U.R.," followed by "The Bootleggers," "The Jolly Roger," "Cyrano de Bergerac," "Othello," "Hamlet," "Goat Song," "Immortal Thief," "Electra," "Henry V," "Merchant of Venice," "The Firebird," "Yoshe Kalb," "Sweet Mystery of Life," "Haiti," "Night Music," "Liberty Jones," "Walk into My Parlor," "Cafe Crown," "The Whole World Over," "Gentleman from Athens," "Golden State," "Desire under the Elms," "Bus Stop," and "Hamlet." No reported survivors.

**RONALD RADD,** 47, British-born actor, died of a brain hemorrhage Apr. 23, 1976 in Toronto, Can., where he was appearing in "Great Expectations." He made his Bdwy debut in 1957 in "Hotel Paradiso," followed by four years in "My Fair Lady" as successor to Stanley Holloway, "Ivanov," and "Abelard and Heloise." His widow and three children survive.

**PAUL ROBESON,** 77, singer and actor, died of a severe cerebral vascular disorder Jan. 23, 1976 in Philadelphia, Pa. After graduating from Rutgers U. as an All-American football player with a Phi Beta Kappa key, he decided to turn to acting and singing. He made his stage debut in 1921 in "Simon the Cyrenian," and subsequently appeared in "Taboo," "All God's Chillun Got Wings," "Emperor Jones," "Black Boy," "Porgy," "Show Boat" (NY, London, and 1930 NY revival), and "Othello" in 1945. He became an international concert favorite and film star. He had been in retirement since 1963. He leaves a son and a sister

**SHIMEN RUSKIN,** 69, Polish-born character actor, died of cancer Apr. 23, 1976 in Los Angeles. His Bdwy debut in 1937 in "Having Wonderful Time," was followed by "Saturday Night," "Little Murders," "7 Days of Mourning," "The Corner Bar," and "The Last Analysis." Surviving are his widow and a son.

**EVELYN RUSSELL,** 49, actress, died Jan. 28, 1976 in her Sherman Oaks, Cal., home. She began her career at 5 in radio serials, and made her Bdwy debut in 1961 in "Sail Away," followed by "Nobody Loves an Albatross," "A Warm Body," "A Place for Polly," and "Lysistrata" with Melina Mercouri. In an off-Bdwy revival of "On the Town" she came to the attention of choreographer Joe Layton who became her husband. He and a son survive.

**ETHEL SHUTTA,** 79, singer-actress, died Feb. 5, 1976 in NYC. She began her career at 7 in vaudeville as "The Little Girl with the Big Voice" with her family. Her Bdwy debut was in "The Passing Show of 1922," followed by "Louie the 14th," several "Ziegfeld Follies," "Whoopee," "Marjorie," "My Dear Public," "Jennie," and "Follies." She was the singer with the George Olsen Band and became a radio favorite. Two sons survive. She was divorced from George Olsen.

**SYBIL THORNDIKE,** 93, versatile British-born actress, died June 9, 1976 after a heart attack in her London home. Began her career in 1904 and gave her last performance in 1969, after playing every possible type of role in a list of plays that would be too lengthy to enumerate. After George Bernard Shaw saw her play "Candida," he wrote "St. Joan" for her and she performed it over 2000 times to great acclaim. She toured the U.S. for four years (1904–08) playing Shakespeare with the Ben Greet Co., and subsequently appeared on Bdwy in "Smith," "The Distaff Side," "Time and the Conways," and "The Potting Shed." She met and married actor-producer Lewis Casson in 1908 and until his death in 1969 they formed one of the great partnerships of the theatre. In 1931 George V made her a Dame of the British Empire. Two daughters and two sons survive, all actors: John, Christopher, Mary and Ann Casson.

**ARTHUR TREACHER,** 81, British-born character actor, died from a heart ailment Dec. 14, 1975 in Manhasset, NY. He made his stage debut in London as a chorus boy in 1919 and performed steadily until he came to the U. S. in 1926 for his Bdwy debut in "Great Temptations." He subsequently appeared in "A Night in Paris," "The Madcap," "The Silent House," "Colonel Satan," "Wonder Bar," "School for Scandal," "The Cat and the Fiddle," "Panama Hattie," "Ziegfeld Follies," "Caesar and Cleopatra," "Getting Married," "Back to Methuselah," "The Fighting Cock," and "Camelot." He appeared in over 40 films, usually as snobbish butler, and was a regular for several years on Merv Griffin's tv show. His widow survives.

**FRANCES UPTON,** 71, retired comedienne, died Nov. 27, 1975 in Philadelphia. Pa. She had been featured in several musicals, including "Little Jesse James," "Ziegfeld Follies" for three years, "Twinkle, Twinkle," and "You Said It." She gave up her career in 1934 when she married the late Bert Bell, NFL commissioner. Surviving are two sons and a daughter.

**HOWARD D. WENDELL,** 67, Pennsylvania-born character actor, died Aug. 11, 1975 at his home in Oregon City, Ore. After beginning his career at the Cleveland Play House, and performing in many stock companies, he appeared on Bdwy in "The Curious Savage," "Julius Caesar," "Arms and the Man," and "Make a Wish." He went to Hollywood in 1950 and played many films and tv roles. His widow, three sons and a daughter survive.

**LEIGH WHIPPER,** 98, character actor, and the first black member of Actors Equity, died July 26, 1975 in NYC. He retired in 1972 after 65 years in the theatre, and 21 Broadway productions. His credits include "Those Who Walked in Darkness," "Stevedore,' "In Abraham's Bosom," "Three Men on a Horse," "Of Mice and Men," "Volpone," "Set My People Free," "Lysistrata," "Porgy," "The Shrike." He was a founder of the Negro Actors Guild. A son and a daughter survive.

**THORNTON WILDER,** 78, actor, novelist, and Pulitzer-Prize-winning playwright, died Dec. 7, 1975 in his sleep in his home in Hamden, Conn. He received three Pulitzer prizes: for his novel "The Bridge of San Luis Rey," and his plays "Our Town" and "The Skin of Our Teeth." His other plays include "The Trumpet Shall Sound," "The Happy Journey from Trenton to Camden," "The Long Christmas Dinner," "Love and How to Cure It," "Lucrece," "The Merchant of Yonkers" which he re-worked and re-titled "The Matchmaker" and eventually became the musical "Hello, Dolly!" Three sisters and a brother survive.

# INDEX

Aaron, Bob, 213
Aaron, Jack, 69, 127, 235
Aaron, Richard, 235
Abajian, John, 209, 224
Abaldo, Joseph, 62, 224
Abatemarco, Tony M., 190, 204
Abbott, Bruce, 182
Abbott, Charles, 117
Abbott, George, 8, 12, 54, 116
Abbott, Jane, 224
Abbott, Loretta, 169
Abbott, Ron, 27
Abe, Frank, 189
Abe Lincoln in Illinois, 228
Abel, Walter, 128, 235
Abelew, Alan, 200
Abels, Gregory, 106, 145, 235
Abigail Adams: The Second First Lady, 199
Abode, Peter, 126
Abraham, F. Murray, 57, 235
Abrahams, Doris Cole, 22, 63, 155, 163
Abrams, Alan, 116, 235
Absurd Musical Revue for Children, 186
Absurd Person Singular, 66
Abuba, Ernest, 39, 235
Achorn, John, 209
Achziger, L. B., 214
Ackerman, Loni, 52, 62, 235
Ackroyd, David, 129, 208, 235
Act: A Contemporary Theatre, 186
Act Without Words 1, 78
Acting Company, The, 8, 91
Actman, John, 62
Actors Equity Association, 8
Actors Theatre of Louisville, 187
Adair, Naola, 235
Adams, Edie, 234
Adams, Elise, 200
Adams, Frank, 179
Adams, J. Edwards, 55
Adams, John, 188
Adams, Mason, 130, 235
Adams, Molly, 235
Adams, Polly, 45, 235
Adams, Ray, 210
Adams, Samuel Hopkins, 116
Adams, Sheila K., 21, 235
Adams, Wayne, 58, 74
Adamson, Frank, 213
Adding Machine, The, 202
Addis, David, 226
Addison, Nancy, 148
Addy, Mark, 215
Ade, George, 46
Adinaro, Barbara, 180
Adler, Alisa Jill, 47
Adler, Bruce, 68
Adler, Christopher, 51, 54, 126
Adler, Ernest, 61
Adler, Gil, 209
Adler, Jerry, 47, 172
Adler, Philip, 47
Adler, Richard, 51, 54
Adnerson, Evelyne, 213
Adorante, Joseph, 75
Adshead, Patricia, 33, 63
Adu, Frank, 97
Adzima, Melissa, 75, 136
Affoumado, Sam, 127
Afiche, 150
Agrell, Lewis, 191
Agress, Ted, 65, 235
Aguado, Harry, 197
Aguilar, Tommy, 41, 160
Aguirre, Bela, 150
Ah, Wilderness!, 8, 13, 223
Ahrens, John, 110
Aidus, Hillary, 194
Aiello, Danny, 8, 16, 229, 232, 235
Aiken, Michael Blue, 52
Ainsley, Paul, 197
Akalaitis, JoAnne, 104
Akers, Andra, 196
Akselrod, Sherry, 113
Alabama Shakespeare Festival, 173
Alaimo, Marc, 196
Alamo, Sadel, 150
Alann, Lloyd, 60, 235
Alaskey, Joseph, 126
Albano, Joseph, 110
Albee, Edward, 48, 207
Albers, Ken, 199
Albert, Edward, 218

Albert, Wil, 127
Alda, Alan, 234
Aldredge, Theoni V., 14, 128, 131, 133, 136, 156, 160, 161
Aldredge, Tom, 17, 51, 235
Aldrich, Keith, 151
Alechnowicz, Todd, 174
Alexander, Adrienne, 182
Alexander, Barry, 190
Alexander, Bob, 190
Alexander, C. K., 133, 235
Alexander, J., 116, 117
Alexander, Jane, 8, 50, 129, 234, 235
Alexander, Jason, 190
Alexander, Leon, 207
Alexander, Robert, 190
Alexander, Terry, 132, 235
Alexander, Wayne, 176, 189
Alexander, Zoe, 213
Alexander-Willis, Hope, 189
Alexandrine, Dru, 47, 68, 235
Alex-Cole, Steven, 153
Alexis, Alvin, 123
Alexis, Connie, 121, 143
Alford, Lamar, 205
Alice in Wonderland, 100
Alison, Barbi, 180
Alison's House, 228
All My Sons, 228
All Over, 207
All Over Town, 66, 158
All the Way Home, 228
Allan, Douglas, 184
Allan, Richie, 127
Allen, Arthur, 200
Allen, Betty, 18
Allen, Billie, 97
Allen, Deborah, 155, 235
Allen, Gary, 105, 235
Allen, Guy, 25
Allen, Jayne Meadows, 196
Allen, Jonelle, 234
Allen, Lee, 137
Allen, Louise, 211
Allen, Malcolm, 47, 86
Allen, Peter, 182
Allen, Rae, 223
Allen, Ralph, 211
Allen, Ralph G., 200
Allen, Rasa, 70
Allen, Richard, 39
Allen, Ross, 168
Allen, Scott, 14, 235
Allentuck, Katharine, 40, 55
Allentuck, Max, 63, 163
Allert, Richard, 143
Alley Cats, 79
Alley Theatre, 188
Allinson, Michael, 33, 235
Allison, Jack, 123
Allison, Jay, 190
Allman, Robert, 178, 199
All's Well That Ends Well, 182, 204
Allsopp, Clarence J., 10, 58, 71, 74, 124, 125, 159, 162
Allyn-Raye, Mary, 151
Almquist, Gregg, 174
Almquist, Jane, 206
Alper, Jonathan, 144, 204
Alper, Linda, 198
Alperin, David, 200
Alpert, Barbara, 114, 126
Alpert, Michael, 18, 30, 44, 49, 56, 69, 81, 158, 171
Alphonse, Raoul, 190
Altman, Jane, 74, 235
Altman, Richard, 28
Alton, Walter George, 73
Altvater, Alice, 176
Alvins, Fern, 146
Alzado, Peter, 121
Amaral, Barbara, 195
Amaral, James, 61
Amaral, Marilyn, 16
Amarino, Michael, 170
Ambros, Julio, 115
American Buffalo, 80, 206
American Conservatory Theatre, 189
American Experiment, The, 192
American Place Theatre, 95
American Shakespeare Theatre, 174
American Theatre Wing, 228
Amerling, Victor, 74
Ames, Dorothy, 90
Amick, John, 218
Ammann, Vincent L., 215

Ammirati, Frank, 113
Ammon, Clifford, 187
Ammon, Richard, 47
Amor De Don Perlimplin Con Belisa En Su Jardin, 150
Amorous Flea, The, 201
Amoureuse, 127
Amud, Jorge, 150
And So To Bed, 74
And Where She Stops Nobody Knows, 196, 197
Anderman, Maureen, 8, 48, 129, 232, 234, 235
Andersen, Tobias, 186
Anderson, Arthur, 152, 235
Anderson, Daryl, 186
Anderson, Frank, 169
Anderson, George, 188
Anderson, Haskell V. III., 126, 127
Anderson, John, 172
Anderson, Kent, 114
Anderson, Louisa, 111
Anderson, Maxwell, 208
Anderson, Mia, 184
Anderson, Paul, 159
Anderson, Russell, 68
Anderson, Sonja, 47
Anderson, Stanley, 190
Anderson, William D., 122, 123, 145
Andes, Keith, 234
Andor, Paul, 122, 126
Andreas, Christine, 8, 33, 47, 54, 229, 232, 235
Andreozzi, Beverly, 225
Andres, Barbara, 51, 235
Andrews, Ann, 36
Andrews, David, 73
Andrews, George Lee, 123
Andrews, Jessica L., 207
Andrews, Julie, 47, 234
Andrews, Linda, 75
Andrews, M. S., 75
Andrews, Marnie, 221
Andrews, Nancy, 68, 234
Andrews, Tod, 234
Andrisano, Gui, 77
Androcles and the Lion, 183, 221
Andros, Douglas, 67, 151
Andrus, Dee, 202
Angel, Adrienne, 198
Angel Street, 93
Anglim, Philip, 198
Aniston, John, 34
Anka, Paul, 8
Anlyan, Peter, 126
Anna Christie, 228
Another Language, 117
Another Part of the Forest, 225
Anouilh, Jean, 112, 146
Anselmo, Andy, 44
Anson, Edith N., 191
Antalosky, Charles, 173
Antaramian, Anna, 83
Anthony, Bert, 51
Anthony, Eugene J., 206
Anthony, Robert, 57, 235
Anthony, Steve, 41
Antoinette Perry (Tony) Award Productions, 228
Antone, Ronald, 137, 149
Antonelli, Donald, 158, 165
Antonio, Lou, 234
Antoon, A. J., 128
Anuli, My, 20
Aoki, Yoichi, 201
Apocalypse According to J J (Rousseau), The, 110
Apollonio, Mario, 110
Apostoleris, Lee, 19
Appelt, Joseph, 217
Applause, 228
Apple Pie, 137
Applegate, Steven, 170
April, 127
April Fish, 121
Apter, Harold, 78
Aranco, Eduardo, 150
Aranguren, Alfonso, 150
Aranha, Ray, 207, 216
Arbeit, Herman O., 20, 235
Archer, David L., 221
Archer, Lynn, 119
Archer, Richard, 209
Archibald, John, 143
Arden, Daniel, 177
Arden, Eve, 203
Ardrey, Robert, 121
Are You Now or Have You Ever Been, 205
Arena Stage, 8, 190
Arenal, Julie, 27

Argo, Allison, 46, 235
Ariel, 126
Aristides, John, 37
Aristophanes, 178
Arkin, Adam, 208
Arkin, Alan, 208, 234
Arkin, Matthew, 208
Arkin, Tony, 208
Arlt, Lewis, 8, 34, 235
Arluck, Neal, 143
Armenian, Raffi, 184
Armistead, Robert, 208
Armour, Mary, 211
Arms and the Man, 187, 209, 215
Armstrong, Alan, 173, 177
Armstrong, Ann, 195
Armstrong, C. W., 186
Armstrong, Curtis J., 215
Armstrong, Louise, 166
Arnaz, Desi, 54
Arndt, Denis, 182
Arner, Gwen, 197
Arno, Sig, 262
Arnold, Barry, 43, 74, 154
Arnold, Deborah, 208
Arnold, Richard, 186
Arnold, Richard E., 221
Arnone, John, 85, 143, 144, 214
Arnstein, David, 174
Aronis, Tom, 107
Aronson, Boris, 39
Aronstein, Martin, 24, 38, 56, 129, 131, 156, 165, 181, 205
Arrangers, The, 221
Arrick, Larry, 208
Arrington, Don, 114
Arrow, Jerry, 90, 107
Arsenault, Sue, 180
Arthur, Jean, 199
Arthur, Phil, 234
Artichoke, 212
Arvold, Mason, 56, 171
As You Like It, 176, 178, 185
Asbell, Ronnie, 113
Asbury, Claudia, 52
Aschmann, Timothy, 218
Asher, Sara, 206
Ashes, 196, 197
Ashley, Barbara, 234
Ashley, Elizabeth, 8, 12, 54, 57, 234, 235
Ashley, Mary Ellen, 20, 117, 235
Ashworth, Jack, 182
Askew, Maggie, 181
Askin, Frank, 98
Asolo State Theater, 191
Assad, James, 217
Assaid, Sam, 120
Assante, Armand, 27, 121, 235, 236
Astley, Joan, 207
Aston, Tom, 215
Astredo, Humbert Allen, 163, 180
Atha, Steve, 27, 66, 91, 102, 174, 211
Atherton, William, 8, 136, 211, 212, 232, 234, 235
Atkins, Eileen, 196
Atkins, Irwin, 45
Atkins, Sarah, 187
Atkins, Tom, 220
Atkinson, Clinton J., 126
Atkinson, David, 166
Atkinson, Linda, 209, 227
Atlee, Howard, 10, 58, 71, 74, 124, 125, 159, 162
Attles, Joseph, 43, 235
Atwell, Rick, 116
Auclair, Len, 112
Auerbach, Hope, 143
Augusztiny, Eric, 186
Auletta, Robert, 227
Aulisi, Joseph G., 34, 41
Aumont, Jean-Pierre, 56, 235
Austin, Clayton, 192
Austin, Ernest, 129, 165, 181
Austin, Ivy, 100
Austin, Michael, 160
Austin, Ned, 151
Austin, Paul, 16
Austrian, Marjorie, 121
Avallone, Rose, 11
Avcollie, David, 151
Avedisian, Edward, 82
Avedon, Doe, 234
Avery, Brian, 186
Avery, Burneice, 215
Averyt, Bennett, 191, 192

Avian, Bob, 14, 160, 161
Awake and Sing!, 207, 214
Axelrod, George, 156
Axler, George, 214
Ayckbourn, Alan, 28, 199
Ayers, Allen, 135
Ayers-Allen, Phylicia, 64
Ayler, Ethel, 10, 124
Aylward, John, 186, 221
Aylward, Tony, 120, 220
Aysta, Joyce, 119, 183
Azar, Ted, 41, 52
Azenberg, Emanuel, 19, 38, 59, 64, 155, 160, 161
Azito, Antonio, 133, 235, 236

Babatunde, Obba, 194
Babcock, Richard, 35
Bacigalupi, Robert, 91, 92, 93, 94, 235
Backer, Andy, 143, 221
Backus, Richard, 8, 13, 174, 214, 234, 235
Backus, Sally, 174, 214
Bacon, Constance, 158
Badvi Hamar (For the Sake of Honor), 110
Baer, Marian, 111
Baff, Regina, 123, 149, 235, 236
Baggett, Jim, 195
Bagley, Henrietta, 107
Bagnold, Enid, 40
Bagwell, Marsha, 8
Bahr, Joseph, 213
Bailey, Dennis, 198
Bailey, G. W., 196
Bailey, Julian, 147
Bailey, Larry, 218
Bailey, Patricia, 192, 204
Bailey, Pearl, 25, 235
Bailey, Peter John, 206
Baines, Robert, 114, 198
Bair, Tom, 121, 126
Baird, Bil and Susanna, 100
Baird, Mary E., 95, 97, 98
Baird, Peter, 100
Baizley, Doris, 197
Baker, Bob, 184
Baker, David, 51
Baker, Douglas C., 37, 161
Baker, Earl L., 18
Baker, Gregg, 169
Baker, Henry Leon, 171
Baker, Jim, 187
Baker, Lenny, 122, 141, 142, 235
Baker, Mark, 30, 234, 235
Baker, Paul, 201
Baker, Richard, 177
Baker, Robert, 149
Baker, Ronnie B., 179
Baker, Sunny, 120
Baker, Terence, 215
Baker, Word, 152, 225
Bakkon, James R., 213
Baksa, Anthony, 144
Bal, Henry Kaimu, 110, 209
Balaban, Robert, 208
Balcony, The, 223
Balderston, John L., 67
Baldo, Jo-Ann, 55
Baldwin, Brooks, 91, 92, 93, 94
Balestrino, Richard, 224
Balin, Ina, 234
Ball, David, 213
Ball, Leland, 203
Ball, William, 189
Ballard, Larry R., 182
Balthrop, Carmen, 18
Balzaretti, Phyllis, 150
Bamford, George, 35, 235
Bancroft, Anne, 234
Banever, Carol, 111
Banister, Henry, 185
Bankhead, Tallulah, 12
Banks, Renee Y., 220
Bannerman, Guy, 213
Bannerman, Margaret, 262
Bar, Dan C., 215
Baragray, John, 262
Baranski, Christine, 194
Barbeau, Adrienne, 60, 234
Barber, Lorie, 122
Barber, Nancy, 126
Barbour, Eleanor, 119, 235
Barbour, Thomas, 107, 128, 185
Barcelo, Randy, 17, 62, 81, 204
Barclay, Dean, 180
Barcos, George, 170
Barger, Robert, 144
Bari, L., 71
Barilla, John J., 78
Barkdull, Les, 113
Barker, Christine, 160

Barker, John, 116
Barnes, Cheryl, 62, 155
Barnes, Clayton, 218
Barnes, Irving, 169
Barnes, Kay, 169
Barnes, Polita, 200
Barnes, Thea Nerissa, 18, 64
Barnett, Nate, 169
Barney, David, 114
Barnhurst, Linda, 110
Baron, Evalyn, 215
Baron, Joanne, 153, 235
Baron, Roger, 50, 235, 236
Baron, Sheldon, 152
Barone, Carl, 123
Barr, Julia, 127, 224
Barr, Richard, 48, 224
Barr, Sue, 180
Barrault, Jean-Louis, 56
Barre, Shelley, 60
Barrett, Alice, 78
Barrett, Bill, 235
Barrett, Candace, 189
Barrett, Clyde-Jacques, 18, 55
Barrett, Frank, 206
Barrett, Gene, 72
Barrett, James Lee, 65
Barrett, Joe, 70, 235
Barrett, John, 190
Barrett, Laurinda, 127, 174, 224
Barrie, J. M., 212
Barrie, Virginia, 88
Barrios, Eduardo, 150
Barroquillo, Jimmie, 221
Barrows, Diana, 117, 235
Barrows, Mark, 117
Barry, Bill, 81
Barry, Bob, 34
Barry, Diane, 123
Barry, Ellen, 180
Barry, Linda, 143
Barry, Paul, 180
Barry, Philip, 121
Barry, Ray, 137
Barry, Raymond J., 17
Barry, Robert, 52, 235
Barter Theatre, 192
Bartholomae, Phillip, 32
Bartlett, Dan, 120
Bartlett, D'Jamin, 27, 232, 234, 235
Bartlett, Peter, 143
Bartlett, Robin, 20
Bartolotta, Pat, 122
Barton, Daniel, 38, 235
Barton, Donald, 36, 214, 235
Barton, Gloria, 218
Barton, Lee, 70
Barton, Samuel, 207
Barton, Virginia, 119
Bartonn, Edward, 82
Bascari, Rita, 113
Basement, The, 122
Basie, Count, 8
Bass, Gary, 112
Bassler, Dale, 218
Bastard Son, 225
Bastone, Elsa, 208
Batchelder, William H., 155
Bates, Andrew, 114
Bates, Joseph E., 206
Bates, Kathy, 85, 143, 144, 235
Bates, Kenneth, 18
Batson, Susan, 17
Batten, Keith, 184
Battis, Emery, 212
Battista, Lloyd, 95, 235
Battle, Hinton, 64
Battle, Kathleen, 18
Battle, Lettie, 64
Bauer, Bruce, 235
Bauer, Richard, 27, 45, 190
Baughman, Renee, 14, 15, 161
Baum, Marlyn, 109
Baum, Susan J., 86
Baumann, K. T., 114, 128, 145, 235, 236
Baumann, Steve, 160
Baumhauer, Charles, 195
Bavar, Tony, 234
Bavan, Yolande, 199
Bawtree, Michael, 76, 198
Baxley, Barbara, 44, 211, 235
Baxter, Alan, 262
Baxter, Dwight, 18
Baxter, Keith, 234
Bay, Frances, 105
Bay, Howard, 37, 63
Bayer, Frank, 30
Bayer, Gary, 190
Bayer, Louise, 214
Bayless, Anita, 121
Bayne, Richard Cooper, 119, 235
Baysinger, Hugh A., 218
Bazemore, Raymond, 18, 55

B/C, 210
Be Kind to People Week, 154
Beach Children, The, 127
Beach, Gary, 59, 147, 235
Beachner, Louis, 212
Beals, Margaret, 90
Bean, Orson, 234
Bean, Reathel, 121
Beard, Betsy, 63
Beard, Charles, 52, 236
Beard, Danny, 64
Beard, Robert, 138, 140, 141, 142
Bearden, Dale, 195
Beary, John, 208
Beasley, Russ, 32
Beatey, Patrick, 144, 204
Beatey, Robert, 198
Beato, Christine, 195
Beaton, Cecil, 47
Beattie, Kurt, 186, 221
Beattie, Rod, 184
Beatty, Ethel, 43
Beatty, John Lee, 42, 107, 108, 109, 122, 190, 221
Beatty, Max A., 217
Beatty, Ned, 190
Beatty, Talley, 205
Beatty, Warren, 234
Beaty, Kim, 52
Beaufort, Fred, 210
Beaux' Stratagem, The, 192
Beavers, Virgil, 201
Beck, Annette, 227
Beck, Barbara, 119
Beck, Kenneth G., 113
Beck, Mary, 172
Beckel, Graham, 127, 181, 211, 223
Becker, Bill, 40
Becker, Gene, 113
Becker, Phillip, 151
Becker, Randy, 113, 114
Becker, Zoa, 151
Becket, 228
Beckett, Samuel, 78, 213
Beckham, Willard, 59, 235
Beckler, Steven, 50
Bedbug, The, 114
Beddeau, Andrew, 194
Bede, Claude, 213
Bedelia, Bonnie, 234
Bedford, Brian, 163, 184, 235
Bedford, Cal, 188
Bedford, Hi, 173
Beebe, Hank, 77
Behan, Brendan, 73, 208
Beim, Norman, 120
Beirne, Michael, 235, 236
Bel Geddes, Barbara, 234
Belafonte, Harry, 234
Belanger, Jo-Anne, 107
Belden, Ursula, 183, 227
Belin, Steve, 117
Bell, Gail, 154
Bell, Glynis, 91, 93, 94, 235
Bell, Jay, 177
Bell, Joan, 8, 235
Bell, Joe, 203
Bell, Kenneth, 144
Bell, Marion, 234
Bell, Richard, 43
Bell, Robert, 183
Bell, Susan, 64
Belle of Amherst, The, 8
Bellin, Toby, 121
Bellomo, Joe, 235
Beloff, Jim, 55
Benavente, Jacinto, 150
Bence, Amelia, 150
Bendall, Gordon, 11, 13, 31, 46
Bender, Jack, 193
Bender, Jim, 180
Benedict, Paul, 149
Benemann, Linda, 200
Benet, Stephen Vincent, 180
Benetsky, R. Bennett, 47
Bengston, Paul, 171
Benguria, Xonia, 150
Benham, Earl, 262
Benito Cereno, 98, 206, 221, 222
Benjamin, Allan, 224
Benjamin, Paul, 98
Benjamin, Richard, 28, 29, 234, 235
Benjamin, Robert, 64
Benkoe, Jeffrey, 195
Bennett, Alan, 30
Bennett, Fred, 202
Bennett, Joe, 14, 15
Bennett, Meg, 60, 235
Bennett, Michael, 14, 160, 161
Bennett, Paul, 71, 73
Bennett, Robert Russel, 47, 116
Benoit, Patricia, 234

Benoit, Sally, 25, 47
Benschoten, Stephen Van, 60
Bensen, Carle, 159
Benson and Cissy, 113
Benson, Joanne, 118, 120, 121
Benson, Jon Peter, 149, 221
Benson, Mary, 215
Benson, Raymond, 127
Benson, Robert, 213
Bentley, Eric, 146, 205
Bentley, Jeff, 221
Bentley-Fisher, Pat, 184
Benton, Charles, 176
Bercu, Barbara, 186
Berel, Avrom, 120
Berendt, Charles, 171
Berenson, Stephen, 208
Berezin, Tanya, 109, 123, 235
Berg, Barry, 127
Berg, Lisa, 68
Berg, Tony, 197
Bergen, Norman, 153
Berger, Carole, 220
Berger, Jacqueline, 114
Berger, Lauree, 14
Berger, Stephen, 215
Berger, Susan, 114
Berggren, Art, 176
Bergman, Brenda, 88
Bergman, Sandahl, 14
Bergqvist, Jeff, 196
Bergren, Peter, 200
Bergsman, Rolfe, 215
Bergstrom, John, 74
Berk, David, 52, 237
Berkeley, Alexander H., 180
Berkeley, Edward, 83, 223
Berkeley Square, 67
Berkman, John, 61
Berkowsky, Kevin B., 84
Berkowsky, Paul B., 20, 81, 84
Berlind, Roger, 51
Berliner, Charles, 197
Berliner, Joan, 190
Berlinger, Warren, 234
Berman, David, 127, 199
Berman, Norm, 199
Berman, Norman L., 76, 181
Bernache, Virginia, 210
Bernard, Bob, 51
Bernardi, James, 11, 13, 31, 46
Bernardoni, John, 195
Bernau, Christopher, 35
Bernecky, Jean, 224
Bernhard, Karen, 114
Berning, Victoria, 135
Berns, Vincent, 184
Bernstein, Ira, 8, 28, 61
Bernstein, Leonard, 55, 76
Bernstein, Linda, 127
Berring, H. Douglas, 169
Berrings, Hank, 71
Berry, Donald, 112
Berry, Eric, 61, 237
Berry, Fred, 112
Berry, Marie, 47
Berthrong, Dierdre, 200
Bertram, Diane, 195
Bertrand, Jacqueline, 108, 237
Beruh, Joseph, 62, 154
Beseda, Robert, 174
Bessell, Ted, 66
Best, Edna, 50
Best, Michael, 114
Betancourt, Guido, 115
Beth, Leona, 180
Betsko, Kathleen, 122
Bettenbender, John, 113
Bettis, Valerie, 234
Beven, John, 27, 131
Bever, Darleen, 112
Bew, Andy G., 161
Bewley, Susan, 180
Bey, Marki, 97
Bey, Rafic, 221
Bey, Richard, 227
Bey, Salome, 205
Beyond the Horizon, 228
Beyond Words, 213
Bibb, Leon, 186
Bichel, Ken, 27
Bicknell, Sharon, 199
Bieri, Ramon, 11
Bigelow, Dennis, 182
Bigelow, Roger, 61
Bigley, Isabel, 234
Bil Baird's Marionettes, 100
Bilheimer, Robert, 213
Bill, Mary, 178
Billett, Don, 60
Billington, Ken, 12, 35, 102, 172, 174, 211
Billington, Lee, 114, 237
Biltgen, Bill, 203
Bimson, Wanda, 40, 143

Bindiger, Emily, 65
Bingo, 199
Bingo: Scenes of Money and Death, 199
Binkley, Lane, 126
Binns, Edward, 209
Binus, Judy, 151
Biography, 192
Birch, Patricia, 39, 60, 155
Bird, Joseph, 179, 189
Birk, Ray, 189
Birk, Tom, 206
Birmbaum, Adrien, 189
Birney, David, 234
Birney, Reed, 123
Birthday Party, The, 218, 219
Biser, Jack, 120
Bishop, Andre, 98, 143
Bishop, Carole (Kelly), 14
Bishop, D., 71
Bishop, Joyce, 218
Bishop, Kathleen, 177
Bishop, Kelly, 8, 15, 232, 237
Bishop, Ronald, 171
Bisk, Brad, 203
Biskup, Bill, 22
Bissell, Ted, 66
Bittner, Jack, 76, 237
Black Comedy, 194, 209
Black, G. David, 225
Black, George, 192
Black, Gerry, 135
Black, Robert, 225
Black, Stephen, 123
Black Woman Speaks, A, 210
Blackburn, Darlene, 202
Blackburn, Dorothy, 50, 237
Blackburn, Richard, 186
Blackburn, Robert, 206
Black-Eyed Susan, 82
Blackfeather, Francisco, 17
Blackman, Robert, 189
Blackmore, Michael, 218
Blackton, Jay, 51, 68
Blackwell, Charles, 38
Blacque, Taurean, 135
Blahnik, Jeremy, 197
Blair, Kerin, 154
Blair, Pamela, 8, 14, 15, 161, 237
Blair, Tom, 216
Blaisdell, Brad, 116, 237
Blaisdell, Nesbitt, 206
Blake, Mervyn, 184
Blake, Sydney, 52, 237
Blake, Warner, 178
Blakely, Mike, 218
Blakely, Ronee, 57
Blalock, Adrienne, 195
Blanchford, Esther, 113
Blanco, Antoineta, 115
Bland, Steve, 176
Blank, Larry, 172
Blank, Lawrence J., 172
Blank, Rhoda Butler, 172
Blank, Tom, 128
Blankfield, Mark, 209
Blanks, Gertrude, 207
Blanton, Jeremy, 47, 68
Blase, Linda, 201
Blaser, Cathy, 30, 171
Blau, Eric, 88
Blausen, Whitney, 55, 220
Bleezarde, Gloria, 234
Blier, Steven, 123
Bliss, George, 208
Blithe Spirit, 194
Blitzstein, Marc, 212
Bloch, Andrew, 34, 123, 145
Blocher, Walter, 166
Block, Barbara Jean, 60
Block, James D., 226
Block, Larry, 181, 237
Blood Knot, The, 122, 123
Bloodworth, Susan, 180
Bloom, Claire, 155
Bloom, Dvida, 220
Bloom, Sidney S., 218
Bloom, Susan, 172
Bloom, Verna, 149, 237
Bloomgarden, John, 163
Bloomgarden, Kermit, 63, 163
Blossom, Roberts, 105
Blount, Helon, 32
Bluebeard, 154
Blum, Baruch, 68
Blum, Doris, 55
Blum, Harry, 79
Blum, Mark, 149, 237
Blumenfeld, Alan, 182
Blunt, Joseph, 111
Bly, Joe, 146
Bly, Joseph, 146
Blyden, Larry, 262
Boardman, Robert, 126
Bobbie, Walter, 60, 237
Boccaccio, 27

Boccaccio, Giovanni, 27
Boccia, Arthur, 11
Boccio, Nico, 226
Bock, Jerry, 116
Bock, Joseph, 220
Boddy, Richard, 167
Bodie, Scott, 123
Bodry, Penelope, 133
Bodtke, Shirley, 119
Boen, Earl, 189
Boese, Jody, 209
Boettrich, Matthias, 110
Bogard, Mitchell, 70
Bogen, Laurel, 200
Bogert, William, 208, 237
Bogosian, Eric, 75
Bohdan, Serhij, 224
Bolcom, William, 227
Bolick, Liz, 159
Boller, James, 177
Bolt, Jonathan, 199
Bolton, Greg, 189
Bolton, Guy, 32
Bolton, Jane, 189
Bond, Edward, 199, 227
Bond, Paula, 199
Bond, Philip, 64
Bond, Raleigh, 130
Bond, Sudie, 60, 149, 190, 237
Bondor, Rebecca, 100
Bonds, Robert, 117, 145, 237
Bonehill, Anne, 103
Bonenfant, Denise, 81
Bongiorno, Frank, 16
Bonifay, Randy, 201
Bonine, Marsha, 73
Bonnell, Donald, 68, 69
Bonnell, Jay, 113
Bonnell, Mary Lynn, 215
Bonner, Beverly, 88
Boockvor, Steve, 237
Boonstra, Michael, 111
Bookwalter, Deveren, 177
Booth, Daniel, 220
Booth, Eric, 187
Booth, James, 22, 23
Boothby, Victoria, 143, 144
Boothe, Powers, 174, 214
Borak, Andrea, 82
Borders, 113
Bordman, Paul, 177
Bordo, Edwin, 45, 186, 237
Borelli, Emil, 170
Borelli, Jim, 60
Borelli, Vincent, 180
Borger, Anne Marie, 67
Borgman, Frank, 174, 214
Borha, Tricia, 206
Borio, Gene, 70
Borjas, Elias Perez, 150
Born Yesterday, 203, 207, 215, 217
Borneman, Susan, 217
Borod, Robert, 163
Borod, Robert L., 63, 163
Boros, Frank J., 224
Borovicka, Anthony, 110
Borrelli, Jim, 237
Borrie, Alexandra, 54
Borsay, Tom, 180
Borstal Boy, 228
Bosboom, David, 151
Bosche, Peter, 211
Boscia, Monica, 19
Bosco, Philip, 131, 237
Boss, The, 106, 145
Bostick, Cynthia, 123
Bostwick, Barry, 60, 140, 237
Boswell, William, 202
Both Your Houses, 228
Bott, John, 22, 23, 237
Bottom, James, 176
Bouchard, Bruce, 98, 99
Boudrot, Mel, 117
Boulton, Sarah, 177
Bourke, Peter, 103
Bourne, Jonathan, 175
Boushey, Carmi, 182
Boushey, David L., 182, 237
Boussom, Ronald, 189
Boutsikaris, Dennis, 117, 237
Bowden, Richard, 200
Bowen, Bobby, 70, 237
Bower, Tom, 205
Bowes, Geoffrey, 184
Bowlin, Ted, 201
Bowmer, Angus L., 182
Boxes, 113
Boxes Going to Salem, 113
Boy Meets Boy, 70
Boy Meets Girl, 141, 142, 191
Boyd, Guy, 114, 204
Boyd, Julianne, 123
Boyden, Peter, 67, 71
Boyer, Tricia, 130, 237
Boykin, Nancy, 190
Boyle, Marilyn, 213

Boyle, Michael R., 178
Boys, Barry, 216
Braca, Elia, 110
Brack, Philip, 103
Bradbury, Ray, 190, 206
Braddell, Maurice, 121
Braden, John, 13
Bradford, Alex, 205
Bradford, Lonnie, 210
Bradley, Dai, 163
Bradley, William W., 38
Brady, Arthur, 82
Brady, Barbara, 234
Brady, Jim, 204
Braet, James, 41, 198
Braha, Herbert, 130, 237
Brailsford, Renee, 18
Brainwashed Witness, 120
Bramble, Mark, 83, 153
Bramlet, Christiana, 176, 177
Brand, Gibby, 71
Brando, Marlon, 234
Brandon, Alan, 221
Brandon, Peter, 215
Brandstein, P., 71
Brandt, Geoffrey M., 180
Brandt, Robert C., 145
Brannigan, Bernard J., 220
Branyon, Nell, 120
Brasington, Alan, 126, 224
Bratt, Bengt, 114
Braun, Roger, 117
Braunstein, Alan, 145
Braunstein, Steven, 145
Braxton, Robin, 126
Bray, Jane, 186
Bray, Make, 98
Brazeau, Jay, 213
Breaux, Marc, 172
Brecher, Leah, 114
Brecht, Bertolt, 133, 216
Brecht, Mary, 82
Brecka, Katherine Donohoe, 179
Breedlove, Joella, 55
Bremseth, Lloyd, 237
Brene, Jose R., 115
Brengel, George, 198, 199
Brenmark, Erik, 197
Brennan, Eileen, 196, 197, 234
Brennan, James, 52
Brennan, Maureen, 234, 237
Brennan, Peggy Lee, 190
Breslin, Tommy, 123
Brestoff, Richard, 126, 129, 181
Breuer, Lee, 104
Brewer, Sandra, 8
Brewer, Sharon, 127
Brice, George, 123
Briceno, Rafael, 150
Brick, James, 208, 227
Bridge at Belharbour, The, 206
Bridges, Kenith, 127
Bridgewater, Dee Dee, 64
Brigadoon, 228
Briggs, Charles, 169
Bright, Fred, 220
Bright, Michael, 147
Brighton, Bruce, 156
Brigleb, Annabel, 120
Brill, Fran, 212
Brindisi, Michael, 121
Brink, Robert, 116
Brinkley, Ritch, 191
Brisbane, Ruth, 64
Brisson, Frederick, 52
Bristol, Alyson, 47
Bristow, Cecilia, 218
Brito, Silvia, 115
Britt, Rod, 112, 146
Brittan, Robert, 169
Britton, Barbara, 148
Britton, Christopher, 213
Britton, Patricia, 74
Britton, Ronnie, 76
Broaddus, Jim, 144, 198
Broadway, 192
Broat, Neil, 122
Brocato, Thomas, 196
Brochu, James, 67, 237
Brockman, Lance, 215
Brockmeier, William, 76
Brockmeyer, John D., 82
Brocksmith, Roy, 17, 133, 208, 237
Broderick, George, 162
Broderick, James, 190
Brody, Stanley J., 172
Brokaw, Charles, 262
Brome, Rawle, 112
Bromka, Elaine, 123, 145, 206
Bronte, Blanche, 197
Brook, Jeremy, 112
Brook, Melody, 218
Brook, Pamela, 220
Brooke, Sarah, 175, 226
Brookes, Jacqueline, 237

Brooklyn Academy of Music, The, 8, 101, 103
Brooks, Alan, 208, 226
Brooks, Donald, 21
Brooks, Jack, 100
Brooks, Jacqueline, 234
Brooks, Jeff, 90, 182
Brooks, Joel, 127, 145, 199
Brooks, Martin, 234
Brooks, Randall, 11, 31, 44, 46
Brooks, Sharon, 205
Brooks, Sydney, 11, 13, 31, 67
Brotherson, Eric, 47, 237
Brouwer, Peter, 144
Brown, Arvin, 13, 212
Brown, Barry M., 21, 36
Brown, Bernard, 103
Brown, Blair, 133, 181, 212
Brown, Candy A., 8, 237
Brown, Carl, 112
Brown, Charles, 10, 38, 125
Brown, Christopher J., 237
Brown, Daniel, 37, 237
Brown, DeLoss, 137
Brown, Dorothy J., 202
Brown, Elizabeth, 224
Brown, Forman, 37
Brown, Frederick Norman, 226
Brown, Garrett M., 72
Brown, Graham, 124, 238
Brown, Gwendolyn, 114, 141, 142, 238
Brown, Josephine, 262
Brown, Joyce, 169
Brown, Kermit, 224
Brown, Lisa, 25
Brown, Martha J., 191
Brown, Max, 32
Brown, Morris, 176
Brown, Pamela, 262
Brown, Patrika, 27, 85, 119
Brown, Pendleton, 133
Brown, Richard C., 217
Brown, Roger, 152, 210
Brown, Sharon, 43
Brown, Shirley, 124, 238
Brown, Steve, 71
Brown, Tom, 218
Brown, Walter P., 169, 238
Brown, Wendell, 126
Brown, William F., 64
Brown, William R., 183
Brown, Zack, 227
Browne, Coral, 159
Browne, Harry, 127, 238
Browne, Roscoe Lee, 98
Brownfield, Clint, 104
Browning, Dolph, 146
Browning, John Christian, 214
Browning, Robert, 117, 238
Browning, Susan, 234, 238
Brownlee, Brian, 171
Brownstone, Doreen, 213
Broyles, Jeff, 195
Brubach, Robert, 62
Bruce, Brenda, 103
Bruce, John Q., Jr., 217
Bruce, Katherine, 48, 221, 224
Bruce, Mary Aiello, 185
Brudny, Stanislaw, 104, 224
Bruguiere, Ronald, 156
Bruhns, Marian, 114
Brumer, Larry, 75
Brumfield, Linda, 69, 78
Brumley, Keith, 209
Brummel, David, 152, 166, 185, 238
Bruneau, Ralph, 152, 238
Brunjes, Hank, 8
Bruno, Jean, 238
Brustein, Norma, 227
Brustein, Robert, 227
Brute, The, 112
Bruton, Susan, 195
Bryan, George B., 175
Bryan, James, 153
Bryan, Maureen, 126
Bryan, Shirley, 13, 36
Bryan, Wayne, 238
Bryant, Bilo, 113
Bryant, David, 43
Bryant, Hazel, 194
Bryant, Mary, 39
Bryant, Yolande, 192
Bryce, Edward, 234
Brydon, W. B., 238
Bryggman, Larry, 123
Brynner, Yul, 37, 238
Bryon, Lisa, 143
Bubbling Brown Sugar, 8, 43, 229, 230
Buccos, Daniel, 184
Buch, Rene, 150
Buchan, Marck, 221

Buchman, Jeff, 67
Buchner, Georg, 137
Buchs, Sharon, 70
Buck, Ed, 197
Buck, John, Jr., 199
Buckley, Betty, 61, 238
Buckman, Forrest, 36, 179, 214
Budd, Barbara, 184
Buell, William, 218
Buff, Janell, 196
Bulasky, David, 177
Bulifant, Joyce, 234
Bull, Sally, 195
Bullard, Thomas, 122, 123
Bullins, Ed, 123
Bullshot Crummond, 201, 209
Buloff, Joseph, 72
Bulos, Yusef, 194, 223
Bundock, Donald, 174
Bunn, Evelyn, 151
Bunse, Elaine, 55
Bunson, Deborah, 173
Buonassissi, John, 82
Burch, Cynthia, 189
Burdick, Steve, 144
Burdick, Frances, 122
Burge, Gregg, 64
Burge, James C., 36, 214, 238
Burgess, Gerald, 221
Burk, Claudia, 27
Burk, Terence, 63, 238
Burke, Gary, 74
Burke, James, 105
Burke, James L., 189
Burke, Jobai, 202
Burke, Karen G., 8, 18
Burke, Mary Louise, 144
Burke, Michael, 143, 145
Burke, Robert, 130, 143, 144
Burks, Donny, 155, 234
Burland, Bob, 64
Burlesque, 115
Burmester, Leo, 187
Burnell, Peter, 108, 224, 234, 238
Burnett, Carol, 234
Burnett, Jim, 120
Burnham, Linda, 191
Burns, Art, 156
Burns, Catherine, 232, 234
Burns, Douglas G., 197
Burns, John, 203
Burns, Mary, 117, 145
Burns, Ralph, 8, 61
Burns, Traber, 189
Burr, Charles, 37
Burr, Robert, 129, 181, 238
Burrell, Deborah, 64
Burrell, Pamela, 67, 106, 145, 234, 238
Burroughs, Jackie, 184
Burrus, Bob, 183, 187
Burstyn, Ellen, 66, 238
Burt, Michael, 173
Burtoff, Elliot, 143
Burton, Richard, 8, 63, 234, 238
Busada, Jean, 68
Busby, Barbara, 204
Bush, Thommie, 86
Busheme, Joseph, 34, 41, 47
Bushore, Lucy, 192
Bussert, Meg, 59
Bustamente, Agustin, 155
Busy Bee Good Food All Night Delicious, 194
Busy Dyin', 190
Butler, Henry, 221
Butler, J. J., 203
Butler, Leslie, 64
Butler, Paul, 206
Butler, Rhoda, 238
Butley, 224
Buttkus, Glenn, 186, 221
Button, Jeanne, 75, 91, 214, 227
By Bernstein, 76
Bye Bye Birdie, 228
Bye, Dianne, 204
Bye, Robert, 205
Byers, Bill, 14, 160, 161
Byers, Catherine, 63, 200, 238
Byers, Ralph, 143, 211
Byrd, Anne Gee, 197
Byrd, Bob, 111
Byrd, Carolyn, 43
Byrde, Edye, 64, 238
Byrne, Linda, 37
Byrne, Terrence, 79
Cabaret, 228
Cabman, 86
Cabrona, 190
Cacharel, Jean, 150
Cacy, Patricia, 218
Caesar and Cleopatra, 199

Cage, Ruth, 37
Cahill, James, 181, 221, 222, 224, 238
Cahill, Tim, 74
Cahn, Cathy, 172
Cahn, Lawrence Scott, 68
Cahn, Sammy, 172, 234
Cain, William, 187, 225
Caine, Daniel, 122
Cairns, Angus, 262
Cakes with the Wine, 145
Calamoneri, Alfred, 17, 130, 132, 181
Calderisi, David, 213
Calderon, Ian, 128, 147, 148, 194, 207
Caldwell, Elizabeth, 18, 171
Caldwell, Erskine, 191
Caldwell, John A., 182
Caldwell, Zoe, 8, 102, 211, 234, 238
Calhoun, Mary, 143
Calhoun, Robert, 196
California Actors Theatre, 193
Call, Edward Payson, 190
Callahan, Bill, 234
Callahan, Bob, 208
Callahan, Kristina, 127
Callan, Chris, 155
Callario, Maria, 143
Callejo, Bobjack, 82
Callman, Nancy, 55
Calloway, Northern J., 8, 38, 61
Calloway, Terry, 41
Calomee, Gloria, 210
Caltabiano, Sandy, 46
Cambridge, Edmund, 124
Camera, John, 113, 167
Cameron, Ellen, 127
Cameron, Faye, 67
Cameron, Holly, 192
Cameron, Trudy, 213
Cameron-Webb, Gavin, 149
Camp, Helen Page, 196
Campanella, Philip, 147, 148
Campbell, Alan, 175
Campbell, Gar, 200
Campbell, George, 124
Campbell, Graeme, 184
Campbell, J. Kenneth, 184, 185
Campbell, Larry, 81
Campbell, Le-Von, 169
Campbell, Nancy, 129, 133, 181
Campbell, Sally, 14
Campisi, Tony, 145
Camus, Albert, 115
Canary, Evan, 121
Canary, John, 127
Candide, 66, 228
Canning, James J., 60, 238
Cannon, A. D., 145
Cannon, Alice, 123
Cantor, Arthur, 100, 156
Cantor, Murray, 127
Capecce, Vittorio, 122, 123
Capelli, Joseph, 163
Capers, Virginia, 126, 127, 169, 238
Capodice, John C., 209
Capone, Clifford, 36, 59, 141, 142
Capone, Joseph, 227
Capozzoli, Geanine Michele, 17, 238
Capozzoli, Ron, 17, 238
Cappa, Ron, 110
Cappa, Rona, 117
Cappelli, Joseph, 163
Cappiello, Lawrence, 183
Caprice, 82
Caprichovna, Claudette, 82
Cara, Christopher, 24, 69, 78
Carden, William, 122
Cardona, Annette, 155
Caretaker, The, 209
Carey, David, 72
Carey, Mary-Pat, 68
Carhart, Jackie, 137
Cariou, Len, 213, 234
Carlin, Chet, 206
Carlin, Joy, 189
Carlin, Leo, 220
Carlisle, Thomas, 175
Carlisle, Ward, 200
Carlsen, Allan, 204, 218
Carlson, Dinah, 114
Carlson, Harry, 118, 238
Carlson, Linda, 138, 140, 144
Carmichael, Fred, 114
Carmichael, Pat, 114
Carnett, Dana, 218
Carnevale, Cathy, 72
Carney, Mary, 192, 204
Carney, Patricia, 14
Carnival, 228

Carnovsky, Morris, 174, 214
Carole, Bette, 207
Caroli, Victor, 199
Carousel, 228
Carpenter, Barbara, 193
Carpenter, Carleton, 113, 238
Carpenter, John, 131, 156
Carpenter, Larry, 41, 174
Carpetas, Jim, 195
Carr, Larry, 144
Carr, Mimi, 188
Carr, Russell, 190
Carr, Ruth, 192
Carra, Lawrence, 178
Carradine, David, 234
Carrellas, Barbara, 138, 140, 141
Carrere, Tedd, 65
Carricart, Robertson, 180
Carrick, Chris, 106, 145
Carrington, Frank, 262
Carrington, James, 57, 137
Carroll, Barbara, 73
Carroll, Beeson, 205
Carroll, David James, 54, 206
Carroll, Leo G., 33
Carroll, Mary Beth, 147, 149
Carroll, Patrick, 179
Carroll, Vinnette, 162, 205
Carroll, Winston J., 184
Carruthers, James, 121, 221
Carson, Jean, 234
Carson, Jeannie, 221
Carson, Terri, 197
Carson, Thomas, 220, 223
Carson, Wayne, 48
Carssons, Ben, 195
Cartaya, Mirtha, 150
Carter, Bent, 65
Carter, Bettina R., 180
Carter, Debbie, 121
Carter, Dixie, 8, 134, 229, 232, 238
Carter, Mary, 143, 145, 238
Carter, Maryce, 205
Carter, Myra, 207
Carter, Patricia, 120
Carter, Ralph, 234
Carter, Rosanna, 125, 207, 209
Carter, Steve, 124
Cartier, Jacques, 194
Cartmell, Tiina, 192
Caruso, Barbara, 127, 190, 200
Caruso, John, 22, 52
Carver, Mary, 196
Cascio, Frank, 121
Case, Channing, 123
Case, Mary, 100
Caseworker, The, 145
Casey, Eileen, 61
Casey, Ellen Sullivan, 69
Casey, Lawrence, 174, 214
Casey, Warren, 60
Casnoff, Philip, 41, 60
Casquelourd, Malonga Auguste, 194
Cass, James, 223
Cass, Lee, 68, 69
Cass, Leslie, 190
Cass, Peggy, 234
Cassel, Leonard, 111
Cassidy, Frank, 211
Cassidy, Jack, 34, 238
Cassidy, Tim, 54, 161
Cassity, Kraig, 189
Cassmore, Judy, 196
Cast Aways, The, 71
Castang, Veronica, 122
Castillo, Mario, 115
Castle, Amanda, 116
Castle, Marc, 75
Castle, Michael, 197
Cat on a Hot Tin Roof, 228
Catch Me If You Can, 218
Catch-22, 208
Cates, Madlyn, 67
Cathedral of Ice, 225
Cathey, Dalton, 207
Catlin, Faith, 127, 145
Cauley, Harry, 120
Caulkins, Jon, 191
Cavaliere, Al, 25
Cavanagh, Garry, 75
Cavander, Kenneth, 27, 227
Cavey, George, 185
Caworrie, Kwabena, 202
Cellario, Maria, 36, 143, 238
Center Stage, 194
Center Stage Theatre, 195
Center Theatre Group, 196
Cento, Frank, 145
Chace, Dorothy, 221
Chadman, Christopher, 8, 41, 61

269

Chagrin, Claude, 63, 163
Chaikin, Joseph, 137, 197
Chaikin, Judy, 197
Chaikin, Shami, 197
Chalbaud, Roman, 150
Chaleff, James, 143
Chalfant, Kathleen, 143
Chalfy, Sima, 111
Chamberlain, Bill, 195
Chamberlain, Douglas, 184
Chamberlain, Howland, 190
Chambers, David, 84, 122,
    190, 204
Chambers, Jane, 197
Chambers, Marilyn, 86
Chambers, Michael, 129,
    133
Champagne, Mike, 144,
    204
Champion, Gower, 25, 41
Champion, Marge, 196
Champlain Shakespeare
    Festival, 175
Chandler, David, 214
Chandler, Jack, 74
Chandler, John, 218
Chandler, Kathy, 173
Chandler, Leah, 198
Chaney, Frances, 207
Changing Room, The, 228
Channing, Carol, 25, 234,
    238
Chapel, Robert, 177
Chapin, Miles, 21, 238
Chapin, Samuel, 144
Chaplin, Sydney, 234
Chapman, David, 62, 71,
    86, 204, 207, 220
Chapman, Graham, 87
Chapman, Lonny, 31
Chapman, Roger, 109, 239
Chapman, William, 65, 224
Chappell, Cathy S., 191
Chappell, Richard, 55
Chappell, William, 22
Charbonneau, Dianne, 73
Charin, Robin, 153, 239
Charisse, Zan, 234, 239
Charles, David, 218
Charles, Keith, 133
Charles, Marlin, 196
Charles, Paul, 161
Charles, Walter, 55, 60,
    239
Charlesworth, John D., 190
Charley's Aunt, 159, 182
Charlton, Leigh, 196
Charmoli, Tony, 49
Charon, Jacques, 262
Charter, Garry, 218
Chartoff, Melanie, 123
Chase, Amy, 144
Chase, Jo Flores, 121, 123
Chase, Norman Michael, 12
Chase, Susan, 43
Checco, Al, 196
Chekhov, Anton, 69, 94,
    112, 144, 149, 180,
    194, 196
Chekhov Comedies, The,
    144
Chekhov Portfolio, A, 112
Chelsea Theater Center of
    Brooklyn, 105, 106
Cherin, Robert, 24
Cherry, Harold, 143
Cherry Orchard, The, 149,
    194, 217
Cherry, Stephen F., 193
Chester, Nora, 191
Chestnutt, Jim, 191
Chianese, Dominic, 206
Chiang, Dawn, 197
Chicago, 7, 8, 206
Chick, Les, 218
Chidnoff, Hal, 179
Children, 226
Children of Darkness, 112
Childs, Casey, 176
Childs, James, 195
Childs, Paul, 171
Ching, Tisa, 116
Chinn, Lori, 239
Chiurnoi, Minda, 112, 144
Chisholm, Anthony, 194
Chmielewska, Krystyna, 104
Choate, Edward, 262
Chock, Cindy, 35, 45
Chocron, Isaac, 150
Choder, Jill, 27, 239
Chomont, Kenneth L., 114
Chorus Line, A, 4, 7, 8, 14,
    160, 161, 228
Christakos, Candice, 82
Christensen, Bonnie, 128
Christensen, Michael, 221
Christiaens, Daniel J., 239
Christian, Robert, 122, 123,
    126, 239
Christiansen, Eric R., 208
Christianson, Bob, 154, 155
Christie, Agatha, 262
Christie, Alfred, 123

Christman, Kermit, 196
Christmas Carol, A, 188,
    213
Christmas, David, 32, 239
Christmas Show, The, 186
Christofer, Michael, 196
Christopher, Barbara, 18
Christopher Columbus, 223
Christopher, Jordan, 234
Christopher, Ron, 206
Christopher, Thom, 218,
    234
Christy, Al, 217
Chuma, Natalia E., 121
Churchill, Mark L., 180
Churchman, Calvin, 117
Churgin, Neil, 190
Ciesla, Diane Jean, 206
Cifalo, Jo-Ann, 32
Cilento, Diane, 234
Cilento, Wayne, 14, 15, 239
Cimino, Leonardo, 138,
    140, 181
Cincinnati Playhouse in the
    Park, 198
Cinelli, Rocko, 127
Cinema Soldier, 111
Cinko, Paula, 239
Cioffi, Charles, 129, 239
Ciplet, Carolyn, 60
Cipolla, Tom, 143
Circle Repertory Company,
    107, 108, 109
Circle Repertory Theatre, 8
Cissel, Charles, 14, 15, 232,
    239
Citronbaum, Jene, 166
Claflin, Rick, 75, 79
Clair and the Chair, 143
Clanton, Ralph, 191
Claps, Louise, 75
Clare, Susan, 203
Clarence, 148
Clarence Brown Theatre,
    200
Clark, Cheryl, 8
Clark, David, 168
Clark, David M., 76
Clark, Dick, 155
Clark, Douglas, 95
Clark, Elizabeth, 197
Clark, Geoffrey, 206
Clark, Gwynne, 190
Clark, James A., 209
Clark, James Nisbet, 88
Clark, Janice, 191
Clark, Josh, 98, 239
Clark, Katherine, 126
Clark, Liam, 190
Clark, Peggy, 100
Clark, Peter, 68, 69
Clark, Wayne, 76
Clark, William, 190
Clarke, Burton, 191
Clarke, Constance, 114
Clarke, David Ulysses, 126,
    216
Clarke, Diana, 179
Clarke, Jane, 208
Clarke, Katherine, 126, 220
Clarke, Keith, 103
Clarke, Lydia, 234
Clarke, Marian, 148
Clarke, Michael, 151
Clarke, Richard, 98, 239
Clarke, Stephen, 57
Clarkson, John, 22, 47, 239
Classic Theatre, The, 110
Clauss, Karen, 123
Clay, Isaac, 169, 206
Clay, Louise, 239
Clayburgh, Jill, 61
Clayton, Curtiss, 218
Cleese, John, 87
Clemons, Bill, 207
Clemons, Maryellen, 197
Clennon, David, 84, 204
Clerk, Clive, 14, 15
Clester, Sam, 91, 92, 93,
    94
Cleveland, Carol, 87
Cleveland, Jerry, 10
Cleveland Play House, 199
Clift, Montgomery, 12
Clifton, Melissa J., 218
Clinton, Mildred, 148
Clive, David, 205
Clontz, Johnny, 11, 13
Close, Glenn, 51, 216, 239
Cloud, Douglas, 95
Cloutier, Tom, 195
Clow, Dave, 107, 109
Clytemnestra, 196
Coates, Alan, 146
Coates, Carolyn, 190, 234,
    239
Cobb, Lee J., 11, 262, 263
Cobb, Mel, 226
Cobbs, Bill, 10, 221
Coble, Tom, 79
Cocktail Party, The, 188,
    228
Cocteau, Jean, 123

Coddington, Jack, 71
Codron, Michael, 28, 30
Coeyman, Karol, 32, 81
Coffeen, Peter, 143
Coffey, Charles, 189
Coffin, Frederick, 141, 142,
    186, 239
Coffin, Stanton, 121
Coggin, Barbara, 126, 127
Cohan, Blossom, 224
Cohan, George M., 13, 123,
    199
Cohen, Alexander H., 8, 234
Cohen, Barbara, 127
Cohen, Bruce, 14, 134,
    135, 136, 137
Cohen, Edward M., 145
Cohen, Jason Steven, 132,
    136, 181
Cohen, Larry, 200
Cohen, Leo K., 39, 51
Cohen, Lynn, 217
Cohen, Margery, 76, 123,
    239
Cohen, Martin, 66
Cohen, Pattee, 152
Cohen, Paul, 155
Cohen, Paula, 78
Cohen, William C., 25, 50,
    51, 158
Cohn, Al, 169
Colavecchia, Franco, 18
Colbert, Ray, 153
Colbin, Rod, 174
Colby, Barbara, 262
Colby, Robert, 24, 155,
    239
Cole, Andrew, 179, 197
Cole, Kay, 14, 161, 239
Cole, Liza, 217
Cole, Megan, 189
Cole, Olivia, 196
Cole, Steven, 18
Cole, Tom, 84, 204
Coleman, Bert, 176
Coleman, Charles H., 64
Coleman, Cy, 49
Coleman, Don, 25
Coleman, George, 112
Coleman, Gwendolyn, 224
Coleman, James, 119, 217
Coleman, L. C., 221
Coleman, Nancy, 215
Colitti, Rik, 133, 239
Colker, Jerry, 61, 116, 239
Collamore, Jerome, 145,
    221
Collected Works of Billy The
    Kid, The, 204, 213,
    221
Collens, Gina, 120, 239
Collinge, Patricia, 50
Collins, Ed, 209
Collins, Kathleen, 208
Collins, Ken, 185
Collins, Pat, 133, 137
Collins, Patrick, 208
Collins, Paul, 239
Collins, Rise Cherylyn, 145
Collins, Stephen, 239
Collins, Suzanne, 123, 128,
    239
Collison, Willson, 143
Colmar, Andrew, 108
Colodner, Joel, 122, 138,
    139, 140, 212, 239
Colombi, Licia, 204
Colombo, Gary T., 168
Colonel Montana, 197
Colonna, Robert J., 225
Colonnades Theatre Lab,
    111
Colorado, Vira, 88
Colton, Chevi, 145, 239
Columbus, Tobie, 239
Coluntino, Robert, 120
Colyer, Austin, 118, 239
Combs, David, 63, 239
Combs, Deborah, 118, 185,
    239
Comden and Green, 76
Comden, Betty, 54, 76, 234
Comedy of Errors, The,
    181, 183, 184, 204
Comenzo, Ron, 143
Commings, Katina, 58, 208
Common Garden Variety,
    The, 197
Commons, Milt, 28
Company, 213, 228
Company Theatre, 200
Conaway, Jeff, 60, 239
Concern, Wartoke, 87
Condon, Michael, 74
Cone, Randi, 56, 81
Confidence Game, The, 203
Conger, Eric, 192
Conklin, John, 17, 51, 174,
    211, 214
Conkling, Diana, 110
Conlow, Peter, 234
Conn, William, 11, 13, 31,
    46

Connell, David, 221
Connell, Gordon, 196
Connelly, Bruce, 154
Connelly, Joe, 203
Connelly, R. Bruce, 239
Conner, Bruce, 145
Connolley, Denise, 239
Connolly, Mark E., 220
Connolly, Michael, 171
Connor, Linda, 189
Connor, Whitfield, 234
Connors, Brian, 113
Connors, Chuck, 203
Connors, Marc, 184
Connors, Matthew, 180
Connors, Michael, 38
Conroy, Jarlath, 212
Constant, Kevin, 123
Consul, The, 228
Contact: Fred Coffin, 186
Contractor, The, 228
Contrast, The, 198, 226
Conversations with an Irish
    Rascal, 73
Converse, Frank, 212
Conway, Bill, 98
Conway, Kevin, 102, 122,
    211, 239
Conway, Shirl, 234
Conwell, Charles, 106
Conwell, Patricia, 149, 239
Cook, Barbara, 234
Cook, Elisha, Jr., 13
Cook, Gail, 74
Cook, James, 152
Cook, Jane, 143
Cook, Jill, 52
Cook, Linda, 120
Cook, Michael A., 194
Cook, Nancy, 11
Cook, Nathan, 196, 197
Cook, Ray, 160
Cook, Roderick, 188, 207
Cook, Wayne Darby, 220
Cooke, Thomas, 200
Cookson, Peter, 234
Cooley, Dennis, 65, 239
Coonan, Sheila, 143
Cooney, Dennis, 208, 234,
    239
Cooper, Clancy, 262
Cooper, Donny, 65
Cooper, Edwin, 221
Cooper, Neil, 76
Cooper, Pamela, 197
Cooper, Paul, 143, 145
Cooper, Peggy, 146
Cooper, Robert M., 43
Cooper, Sara Lou, 147
Cooper, Thelma, 10, 58
Coote, Robert, 47, 239
Copani, John, 81
Copani, Peter, 81
Copeland, Joan, 240
Copeland, Maurice, 127
Copelin, David, 197
Copland, Laurie, 144
Copley, Johnathan, 86
Coppola, Tom, 123
Corben, Rima, 107, 108,
    109
Corbet, Lee, 194, 221
Corbin, Albert, 204, 220
Corbin, Barry, 187
Corbin, Clayton, 194
Corcoran, Tom, 179
Cordes, Kathryn, 198
Cordon, Susan, 22
Corenthal, Amy, 146
Corey, Wendell, 234
Corkill, John, 169
Corley, Hal, 190
Corley, Pat, 35, 155
Corman, Paul A., 118, 240
Corn is Green, The, 228
Cornell, Allen, 209
Corner, Gerald, 184
Corno, Lyn, 70
Corpora, Robert, 8
Correia, Donald, 54, 161
Corridor, The, 126
Corrigan, James, 215
Corsaro, Frank, 18
Cortese, Carole, 208
Corti, Jim, 75
Cortland, Nicholas, 189
Corwen, Carol, 144
Corwin, Norman, 199
Corzatte, Clayton, 186,
    199, 221
Cosco, Nicholas, 224
Cosentino, Michael, 195
Costa, Joe, 192
Costello, Pamela, 35
Costello, Tom, 135
Costen, Russell, 110
Coster, Nicholas, 240
Coster, Nicolas, 98
Costigan, Ken, 191
Costley, Guy, 55
Cothran, John, Jr., 217
Cothran, Robert, 200, 211
Cotner, Stefan, 177

Cotsirilos, Stephanie, 123,
    137
Cotter, Kevin, 180
Cotterell, Lee, 113
Coughlin, Kevin, 262
Coulette, Yvonne, 103
Coulston, Candace, 146
Coulter, Clare, 213
Council, Richard, 36, 240
Councill, Christopher, 190
Counterpoint Theatre
    Company, 112
Country Girl, The, 223
Court, Geraldine, 144, 240
Covey, Elizabeth, 194, 216
Covey, Shan, 127
Coward, Noel, 207, 213
Cowboys #2, 151
Cowgill, Douglas, 126
Cowles, Fred, 176
Cowles, Matthew, 35, 240
Cowles, Peggy, 80, 216
Cowley, Eric R., 82
Cox, Barbara A., 188
Cox, Maggie, 195
Cox, Raymond, 55
Cox, Richard, 121
Cox, William, 89
Coyle, Clay, 126, 127
Cracked Tokens, 123
Cracks, 81
Craddock, Carol, 180
Craig, Jack, 25
Craig, Joel, 32, 240
Craig's Wife, 228
Crampton-Smith, Howard,
    91, 92, 93, 94
Crane, Warren, 66
Cravens, Rutherford, 188
Craver, William, 105, 106
Crawford, Cheryl, 20
Crawley, Robert, 78, 190
Crawley, Tom, 223
Cray, Patricia, 223
Crea, Patrick, 180
Creamer, Linda, 143
Crean, Jan, 70
Crean, Patrick, 184
Creatore, Luigi, 118
Creeps, 213
Cremeans, Jan, 190
Cresson, James, 8, 28
Creswell, Saylor, 70
Crinkley, Richmond, 12, 21,
    36, 50, 211
Crisp, Jim, Jr., 191
Cristensen, Sam, 62
Cristofer, Michael, 196, 197
Crofoot, Ron, 25
Croft, Paddy, 194
Cromar, James, 98
Cromwell, David, 204
Cromwell, J. T., 55, 240
Cronin, Jane, 240
Cross Country, 196
Cross, Murphy, 43
Cross, Richard, 234
Crossley, Jim, 224
Crossley, Karen, 32, 240
Crouse, Lindsay, 102, 211,
    240
Crow, Laura, 35
Crowder, Jack, 234
Crowe, Timothy, 225
Crowell, McLin, 145
Crowley, Ann, 234
Crowley, Ed, 112, 114
Croxton, Darryl, 98, 240
Crucible, The, 184, 226,
    228
Crudup, Carl, 10
Crumb, Ann, 218
Crumlish, Cynthia, 107,
    207
Cruse, Kimothy, 211
Cruse, Sandy, 186
Cruz, Louis, 145
Cryer, Bruce, 152
Cryer, David, 234
Crystal, Hattie, 120
Cubiculo, The, 113
Cuervo, Alma, 227
Cuff, Tom, 143
Cuka, Frances, 22
Cullinan, Francis J., 217
Cullison, Barry, 209
Cullum, John, 8, 65, 232,
    234, 240
Culman, Peter W., 194
Culver, Carol, 60
Cumming, Richard, 225
Cummingham, John, 145
Cummings, Gretel, 82, 133
Cummings, Kay, 123
Cuneo, Fred J., 171
Cunningham, Billy, 153
Cunningham, Derek, 209
Cunningham, Geoffrey T.,
    187
Cunningham, Robert, 221
Cuomo, James, 110
Curnock, Richard, 184
Curran, Mark, 113

Currie, Richard, 82
Currier, Terrence, 190
Currin, Brenda, 133, 209
Curry, Christopher, 122, 145, 149, 240
Curry, Julia, 114, 120
Curry, Tim, 22, 23
Curry, Virgil, 137
Curtin, Theresa, 158
Curtis, Robbi, 119, 240
Curzon, George, 262
Cushman, Nancy, 224
Custer, John, 225
Custer, Marianne, 200, 211
Cutler, Lisa, 196
Cutt, Michael, 118, 129, 181
Cwikowski, Bill, 240
Cymbeline, 177
Cypherd, Jim, 200
Cyrano de Bergerac, 177, 213, 221, 222
Cyrus, Jim, 226
Czaykowski, Anne-Marie, 180
Czerwinski, E. J., 104
Daarlin' Juno, 212
DaCosta, Morton, 118, 157
Dafgek, Nancy, 160
Dahlmann, J. L., 215
Dahlstrom, Robert, 221
Dale, Elaine, 216
Dale, Grover, 62, 224
Dale, Jim, 199, 224
D'Alessio, Carlos, 56
Daley, John Edward, 120
Daley, Ronald, 112
Dall, John, 50
Dallas, Scotty, 218
Dallas Theater Center, 201
Dalley, Nick, 201
D'Aloia, Betty, 169
Dalton, Diane, 199
Daly, James, 31, 234
Daly, Joseph, 123, 126
Daly, Tyne, 196, 197
Dalzell, Michael, 192
Damadian, Jevan, 121
Damashek, Barbara, 208
Damask, Donald, 54
D'Amato, Anthony, 60
Dames at Sea, 176
Damkoehler, William, 225
Damn Yankees, 228
Damon, Bruno, 75
Damon, Cathryn, 35, 240
Damon, Stuart, 234
Dana, Barbara, 208
Dana, F. Mitchell, 189, 196
Dana, Leora, 190, 240
Dana, Mildred, 117, 240
Dance, Charles, 103
Dancer without Arms, 210
Dancing for the Kaiser, 108
Dancy, Virginia, 75
Dandelion Wine, 190, 206
Daneel, Sylvia, 234
Dangcil, Linda, 197
D'Angelo, Beverly, 41
Dangler, Anita, 128, 181, 240
Daniel, Pat, 79
Daniele, Graciela, 8, 240
Daniele, Graziela, 52
Danielewski, Tad, 178
Danielle, Martha, 51, 172
Daniels, Billy, 25
Daniels, David, 234
Daniels, Dennis, 51
Daniels, Edgar, 196
Daniels, James, 182
Daniels, Paul, 207
Daniels, Ron, 227
Daniels, Stan, 52
Dann, Elonzo, 133, 156
Dann, Sam, 77
Danneman, Jeffrey, 44
Dannenbaum, David, 217
Danner, Blythe, 234
Dannevik, William, 200
Danson, Randy, 78
Danson, Ted, 181
Dante, 104
Dante, Nicholas, 14, 160, 161
Dantuono, Mike, 118, 127, 199
Danzi, Diane, 198
Danziger, Maia, 127
DaPrato, William, 120, 121
D'Aprile, Robert, 180
Darby, Prudence, 41, 162
Darby, Ra Joe, 197
Darby, Richard B., 218
D'Arc, Victor, 28, 41
Dardaris, Janis, 143
Dare, Daphne, 184
Darion, Joe, 166
Dark at the Top of the Stairs, The, 199
Dark Lady of the Sonnets, 183
Darke, Rebecca, 112

Darkness at Noon, 228
Darlin' Juno, 212
Darlow, Cynthia, 114
Darlow, David, 192
D'Arms, Ted, 182, 221
Darnay, Toni, 50, 240
Darr, Deborah, 204
Darwall, Barbara, 107
Darzin, Daina, 240
Das Lusitania Songspiel, 90
DaSilva, Howard, 54
Davalos, Dick, 234
Davenport, Tiv, 30, 171
David, Carol, 149
David, Jeanne, 96
David, Jeff, 205
David, John, 63
David, Michael, 75, 76, 105
David, Regina, 190
Davidow, Ellen, 168
David-Owen, Jeffrey, 17
Davids, S. Spencer, 22
Davidson, Gordon, 196
Davidson, Jack, 240
Davidson, Jeannie, 182
Davidson, Jez, 123
Davidson, John, 234
Davidson Judi, 161
Davidson, Lorraine, 153, 240
Davidson, Philip, 188
Davies, Harry, 163
Davies, Joseph C., 12, 240
Davies, Lane, 225
Davies, Victor, 213
Davila, Diana, 37, 240
Davis, Ali, 125
Davis, Allen, III, 127
Davis, Andrew, 227
Davis, Barry, 75
Davis, Brenda, 197
Davis, Buster, 59
Davis, Carl, 188
Davis, Clifton, 234
Davis, Clinton Turner, 18, 124
Davis, Colleen, 202
Davis, Daniel, 189, 216
Davis, Edward H., 25, 50, 51, 60, 158
Davis, Edythe, 98
Davis, Fred, 191
Davis, Gail, 86
Davis, Harold, 113
Davis, Humphrey, 207
Davis, Jeff, 8
Davis, Jeff, 88
Davis, John H., 42
Davis, Judith, 201
Davis, Kenneth, 240
Davis, Lance, 212
Davis, Larry, 213
Davis, Linda Ann, 180
Davis, Michael, 117
Davis, Montgomery, 216
Davis, Patti, 195
Davis, Paula, 118
Davis, Richard, 234
Davis, Thelma, 157
Davis, Tracy, 204
Davison, Deborah, 111
Dawson, Curt, 214, 240
Dawson, Mark, 234
Dawson, Robert, 216
Day, Connie, 224
Daykin, Judith E., 101
Days in the Trees, 56
D'Beck, Patti, 61
De Banzie, Lois, 218
de Barbieri, Mary Ann, 204
De Beer, Gerrit, 240
de Boer, Lodewijk, 75
De Castro, Francisco, 96
de Cervantes, Miguel, 150
de Filippo, Eduardo, 201
De Fonte, Tony, 196
de Hartog, Jan, 203
De Hetre, Katherine, 11
de la Paz, Danny, 210
De Lany, Robert, 183
de Lavallade, Carmen, 227
de Luce, Virginia, 234
De Martin, Imelda, 234
De Matteo, Donna, 148
de Maupassant, Guy, 80
De Mello, Gaudencio Thiago, 150
de Onis, Carol, 146
de Pietri, Stephen, 241
De Rigault, Jean, 96
de Rosier, G. Philippe, 217
De Rousie, Pat, 211
de Rueda, Lupe, 150
De Salvio, Joseph, 182
De Sanctis, Juan, 155
De Shields, Andre, 64, 122
Deakin, Ian, 213
Dean, Arlen, 38
Dean, Gerri, 19
Dean, Hannah, 197
Dean, Jacque, 95, 240
Dean, James, 234
Dean, Mary Jennings, 143

Dean, Phillip Hayes, 97
Deane, Tina, 177
DeAngelis, Judy, 41
Deangelo, Vivian, 150
Dear Liar, 187
Dear Mr. G, 148
Dearborn, Dalton, 171
Dearing, Judy, 16, 38, 97
Dearinger, Kevin Lane, 47, 240
Dearle, Bronia, 177
Dearly Beloved, 123
Deary, Carol, 103
Death of a Salesman, 8, 11, 190, 198, 228
DeBaer, Jean, 187
DeBatto, David, 218
DeBlaise, Colleen, 81
DeBlase, Justin, 224
DeBuskey, Merle, 11, 13, 14, 17, 31, 38, 44, 46, 65, 128, 129, 130, 131, 132, 133, 135, 136, 161, 181
Decameron, The, 27
DeChalus, Allyne, 55
Decker, Lee, 65
Deckert, Patricia, 123
DeCof, Bethany, 180
DeCroes, Eliza, 114
Dee, Blanche, 20, 240
Dee, Dottie, 151, 191, 226
Dee, Peter, 126
Dee, Ruby, 181, 240
Dee, Sandra, 203
Dee, Victor, 209
Deering, Martha, 117, 240
Deese, Carl, 153
DeFabees, Richard, 12, 21, 127, 240
DeFilipps, Rick, 117, 240
DeFrank, Bob, 122
Dehn, Fredric, 117
Deitch, Dan, 143, 240
Deitrich, Robert, 186
DeKoven, Roger, 105, 149, 221, 240
Del Medico, Michael A., 71
Del Monte, Adrienne, 116
Delahanty, Richard, 156
Delapenha, Denise, 17, 114
DeLaurier, Peter, 145
Delgado, Carlos, 70
Delgado, Rafael, 115
D'Elia, Chet, 41
Dell, Gabriel, 16, 241
Dell, Kathryn, 173
Dell, Yvonne, 82
Della-Grotte, Linda, 180
Dellasala, Gerald, 135
DeLorenzo, Peter, 175
DeMaat, Martin, 151
DeMaio, Arthur, 143
DeMaio, Peter, 10, 66, 122, 241
Demas, Carole, 60, 241
DeMastri, Tom, 179
DeMattis, Ray, 60
Demenkoff, Tom, 88, 154
Democracy, 216
DeMone, Richard, 123
Dempsey, Jerome, 98, 128, 241
DeMunn, Jeffrey, 113, 114, 175
Dench, Jeffery, 103
Dengel, Jake, 137, 145, 241
DeNicola, Peter, 138, 140, 141, 142
Dennis, Alfred, 177
Dennis, John, 196, 197
Dennis, Robert, 149, 190
Dennis, Ronald, 14, 161, 241
Dennis, Sandy, 66, 241
Dennis, Shirley, 221
Dennison, Susan, 143, 145
Denton, Scot, 213
DePass, Paul, 78, 113
dePauw, Joseph, 217
DePietri, Stephen, 20
DePree, Molly, 191
Derl-Davis, William, 203
DeRose, Victor, 127
Derr, Richard, 234
Derrington, Richard, 103
DeSantis, John, 196
DeSantis, Tony, 57
DeShields, Andre, 64, 241
Desiderio, Robert, 180
Design for Living, 223
Desmond, Daniel, 199
Desnoo, Deborah, 221
deSouza, Michael, 113
DeSpain, Rick, 218
Desperate Hours, The, 228
Destazio, Brian, 37
DeSylva, B. G., 117
Detroit Repertory Theatre, 202

Devane, William, 205
deVelder, Anne, 151
Devereaux, Diana, 201
Devils and Diamonds, 123
Devil's Disciple, The, 192, 206
Devin, Richard, 221
Devine, Jerry, 201
Devine, Mary E., 114
DeVito, Danny, 181
Devitt, Sydnee, 172
Devlin, Jay, 123
Devlin, Lisa M., 175
Devon, Alexandra, 113
Dewhurst, Colleen, 8, 48, 212, 232, 234, 241
Dexter, John, 63, 163
Di Dia, Maria, 89
Di Filia, Frank, 129, 133
Di Paolo, Tonio, 123
Di Sesa, Leonard, 144
Dia, Dick, 155
Diamond, Dan, 218
Diamond Studs, 154
Diamonds in the Rough, 197
DiAngelo, James, 200
Diaries of Adam and Eve, 151
Diary of Anne Frank, The, 192, 218, 228
Diaz, Horace, 155
Diaz, Idalia, 115
Diaz, Paul, 54
Diaz, Rafael, 81
Diaz, Tony, 150
Dick, Bill, 195
Dick, Paul, 73, 86
Dickason, Cynthia, 91, 92, 93, 94
Dickens, Charles, 213
Dickerson, Wyatt, 52
Dickey, Carolelinda, 199
Dicterow, E. Marcy, 197
diDario, Linda, 147
Diehl, Crandall, 47
Diener, Joan, 37, 234, 241
Dietz, J. Robert, 208
Diffen, Ray, 37
DiFilia, Frank, 181
Diggles, Dan, 198
Dighton, Jeffrey, 180
DiLeone, Leon, 33
Dilker, Barbara, 223
Dillchay, Kaylyn, 119
Dille, Karen, 60
Dillehay, Kaylyn, 119, 241
Dillingham, Charles, 189
Dillman, Bradford, 234
Dillon, Denny, 12, 224, 241
Dillon, John, 190, 191, 206, 216
Dillon, Melinda, 48, 234
Dillon, Mia, 130
Dimple, Alvin, 135
Dinan, Andrew C., 146
Dineen, Tom-Patrick, 106, 145
Dinerman, Barry, 186
Dinkins, Elbert, 146
Dirickson, Barbara, 189
Dirlam, Jim, 208
DiStefano, Chelsey, 224
Ditman, Walter, 72
Divine, 88
Dix, Richard, 174, 214
Dixon, Beth, 120
Dixon, Bob, 117
Dixon, Dianne Oyama, 241
Dixon, Ed, 76, 241
Dixon, MacIntyre, 113, 190, 241
Dixon, Nedra, 43
Doby, Kathryn, 8
Dodd, Richard, 25
Dodd, Rory, 41
Dodds, William, 55
Dodge, Jimmy, 172
Dodge, Renee, 110
Dodrill, Marji, 199
Doerr, James, 117
Dogim, Isaac, 72
Dolby, Cheryl Sue, 8
Dolin, Kenneth, 199
Doll's House, A, 224
Dolores, 262
Dompe, Peter, 143
Don, Carl, 45, 241
Don Juan, 27
Dona Rosita, la Soltera, 150
Donahue, Timothy, 225
Donahue, Vincent J., 262
Donat, Peter, 189, 234
Donkin, Eric, 184
Donlevy, Martin L., 184
Donley, Robert, 186, 208, 221, 222
Donnelly, Jamie, 60, 241
Donnelly, Kathleen, 25
Donnelly, Peter, 221
Donnenberg, Marilyn, 194
Donner, Clive, 24, 165
Donner, Jack, 209

Donohue, Morgan, 69
Donohue, Nancy, 58, 208, 241
Donovan, King, 211
Donovan, Nancy, 147
Don't Bother Me, I Can't Cope, 162
Doolin, John B., 218
Doolin, Richard B., 218
DoQui, Bob, 197
D'Orazzi, Vikki, 170
Dorcy, Gloria, 177
Dorfman, Richard H., 180
Dorge, Claude, 213
Dorn, Franchelle Stewart, 189
Dorner, Francoise, 56
Dorrin, John, 68
Dorsey, Billy, 205
Dorst, Tankred, 105
Doscher, Carole, 143
Doty, Cynthia, 192
Douglas, Melvyn, 199
Douglas, Michael, 234
Douglas, Paul, 234
Douglas, Randi, 182, 187
Douglass, Charles, 38
Douglass, Pi, 64, 158, 241
Dour, Daniel, 224
Dourif, Brad, 107
Dovey, Mark, 160
Dowell, Madelyn, 221
Dowling, Eddie, 31, 262
Dowling, Peter, 192, 206
Dowling, Vincent, 225
Downe, Edward R. Jr., 51
Downer, Herb, 123
Downing, David, 207, 241
Downing, Joe, 262
Downing, Robert, 262, 263
Downing, Virginia, 119, 241
Downs, Peter, 185
Downs, Stephen, 200
Doyen, Robert, 159
Doyle, Arthur Conan, 171
Doyle, Jay, 200, 211
Doyle, Kathleen, 204
Doyle, Martin, 213
Doyle, Mary, 63
Doyle, Ray, 79
Dr. Hero, 114
Dr. Jekyll and Mr. Hyde, 199
Drake, Alfred, 8, 12, 208, 241
Drake, Donna, 14, 232
Drama Desk Awards, 8
Draper, Ruth, 80
Dream on Monkey Mountain, 194, 207
Dremak, W. P., 224
Dressler, Roger, 213
Drew, Camelia, 198
Drew, Dennis, 123
Drexel, Todd, 118
Drexler, Rosalyn, 82
Dreyfoos, David, 198
Drischell, Ralph, 13, 133, 241
Driscoll, Ann, 177
Drisin, David, 18
Drivas, Robert, 57, 234, 241
Driver, John, 60, 234
Drucker, Paula, 173
Drummond, Alice, 21, 138, 141, 142, 241
Drummond, Joseph, 206
Drummond, Roger, 218
Drury Lane North Theatre, 203
Drylie, Patricia, 161
du Rand, le Clanche, 182, 241
DuBois, Ronald, 69
Dubov, Stephen, 65
DuBrock, Neal, 224
Duchess of Malfi, The, 196
Duckens, Dorceal, 18
Duckworth, Dortha, 61
Dudich, John, 113, 114, 167
Dudley, Bambi, 164
Duell, William, 133, 241
Duets of Drama, 114
Duff, Jonathan, 188
Duff-MacCormick, Cara, 157, 234, 241
Duffy, Diane, 95
Duffy, Marty, 153
Duffy, Patrick, 179
Duffy, Robert, 201
Duffy, Steve, 145
Dugan, Dan, 179
Dugan, Dennis, 194
Duke, Patty, 234
Dukes, David, 22, 127, 241
Dulin, Michael, 76
Dullaghan, Edward, 81
Dumas, Debra L., 180
Dume, Herberto, 115
Dume Spanish Theatre, 115
Dunaway, Faye, 234

Dunbar, Philip, 103
Duncan, Alexe, 213
Duncan, Bill, 200
Duncan, Cameron, 82
Duncan, Ron, 226
Duncan, Sandy, 234
Duncan, Scott, 210
Duncan, Stuart, 154
Dunfee, Nora, 126
Dungan, Joseph, 133
Dunham, Clarke, 43, 135, 143
Dunham, Ronald, 64
Dunlap, Gina, 208
Dunlap, Roy E., 218
Dunlop, Frank, 30, 199, 224
Dunlop, Susan, 175
Dunn, Candy, 120
Dunn, James, 193
Dunnavant, Mary, 82
Dunning, Janis, 213
Dunnock, Mildred, 11, 212
DuPois, Starletta, 135
Dupree, Paul, 188
DuPuis, Betty, 202
Duquet, Wally, 119
Durang, Christopher, 90
Duras, Marguerite, 56
Durbian, Ron, 217
Durham, Joe, 176
Durning, Charles, 242
Durrell, Michael, 11, 34, 242
Dussault, Nancy, 234
Dutton, Nancy, 45, 242
DuVal, Herbert, 192
Dvorak, Wayne C., 196
Dvorsky, Peter, 91, 92, 93, 94, 242
Dworkin, Andy, 200
Dworkin, Susan, 145
Dyas, Kathy, 180
Dybas, James, 39, 155, 242
Dye, Lyle Jr., 218
Dyer, David, 123
*Dynamite Tonite!,* 227
Dzundza, George, 57
Eagon, Joel, 123
Eames, John, 106, 145, 194, 242
Earl, Paris, 210
Earley, Candice, 60, 242
Early, Dan, 84
*Earnest in Love,* 193
Easley, Holmes, 147, 148, 149, 191
Easley, Richert, 144
East, Therese Dean, 195
Easterbrook, Leslie, 242
Eastman, Charles, 194
Easton, Edward, 156, 242
Easton, Richard, 234
Eaton, Dan, 223
Eaton, William B., 179
Ebb, Fred, 8, 49, 54, 123
Ebeling, George, 171
Eberle, Fred, 206
Ebersole, Christine, 33
Ebert, Joyce, 212
Eck, Marsha L., 130
Eckert, Doug, 200
Eckhouse, James H., 206
Eckles, Robert, 262
*Economic Necessity,* 82
Economos, John, 206
eda-Young, Barbara, 123
Ede, George, 46, 194, 242
Edelman, Stan, 143, 145
Edelson, Alan, 165
*Eden,* 124
Eden, Tom, 197
Edens, Joseph P., 192
Edgerton, Earle, 187
Edloe, 210
Edmead, Wendy, 64, 242
Edmonds, Louis, 198
Edmondson, James, 182
Edmonson, James, 188
*Edward II,* 92
Edwards, Ben, 40, 102, 211
Edwards, Brandt, 14, 242
Edwards, Cathy, 189
Edwards, Derrel, 126
Edwards, Edward, 111
Edwards, Eugene, 68
Edwards, Maurice, 110
Edwards, Susan, 123
*Effect of Gamma Rays on Man-in-the-Moon Marigolds, The,* 228
Efron, Morry, 197
Egan, Michael, 80, 242
Egan, Suzanne, 214
Eggert, Ann, 203
Ehler, Ursula, 105
Ehlinger, Dominique, 56
Ehrlich, Janice, 116, 242
Eichel, Paul, 172
Eichelberger, Ethyl, 82

Eichler, Alan, 82, 88, 110, 113
Eifert, Karen L., 91, 93
Eigsti, Karl, 20, 35, 60, 87, 190
Eikenberry, Jill, 21, 83, 208
Eikleberry, Dean, 218
Eiland, Kenneth S., 39, 155
Einenkel, Robert, 105, 119, 143, 242
Einhorn, Susan, 45
Eisen, Max, 16, 32, 43, 45, 72, 79, 169
Eisenberg, Barry S., 176
*El Grande De Coca Cola,* 209
*El Malentendido,* 115
*El Teatro Campesino,* 210
*El Viejo Celoso,* 150
Elbert, Wayne, 125
Elder, Eldon, 221
Elder, Judyann, 205
Eldridge, Florence, 12
*Eleanor,* 205
*Electra,* 197
*Elephant in the House, The,* 107
Elgh, Mona, 68
Eliasberg, Jan P., 107
Eliot, Marge, 97
Elkind, Susan, 17
Elkow, Margo Bruton, 123
Elkow, Richard, 91, 93
Ellington, Mercedes, 54
Elliot, Gregory, 177, 186
Elliot, Marge, 97
Elliott, Alice, 143, 185
Elliott, Cheryle, 185
Elliott, Patricia, 76, 234, 242
Elliott, Robert, 209, 217
Ellis, Antonia, 61, 196, 242
Ellis, Catherine, 73, 74
Ellis, Charles, 262
Ellis, Joshua, 18, 30, 44, 69, 78, 81, 171
Ellis, Sam, 43
Ellison, Art, 217
Elmer, George Allison, 88, 89
Elrod, Susan, 31, 46
Elrod, Tom, 203
Elterman, Sam, 56
Elterman, Samuel, 44
*Elusive Angel, The,* 127
Emanuel, Terrence, 25
Emery, John, 36
*Emlyn Williams as Charles Dickens,* 78
Emmanuel, Donna, 122, 123
Emmert, Lynn, 173
*Emperor Jones, The,* 226
Empry, Gino, 160
En Yu Tan, Victor, 119, 135
*Enchanted Hudson, The,* 126, 127
*Endecott and the Red Cross,* 99
Endes, Joe, 69
*Endgame,* 213
*Endcott and The Red Cross,* 98
Endy, Michael, 177
*Enemy of the People, An,* 190
Eney, Woody, 120, 151, 242
Engel, Bernard, 200
Engel, Bernerd, 191, 211
Engstrom, Jon, 32, 242
Enik, Ted, 114
Ennis, Flloyd, 35, 242
Enos, Leann, 208
*Enrico IV,* 193
Enriquez, Mercedes, 115
Enriquez, Rene, 155
Enserro, Michael, 242
Enten, Boni, 242
*Enter Laughing,* 52
Enterline, Alicia, 35
Enters, Warren, 27, 171
*Entertaining Mr. Sloane,* 221
*Envoi Messages, The,* 209
Epstein, Alvin, 227
Epstein, Dasha, 59, 66
Epstein, Pierre, 138, 139, 140, 143, 181, 242
Epstein, Robert, 123, 177
Epstein, Sabin, 189
Equity Library Theater, 119
Equity Library Theatre, 8, 116, 117, 120, 204
*Equus,* 7, 8, 63, 163, 189, 213, 224, 228
Erdman, Dennis, 63, 163
Erdman, Wendy, 12
Erhard, Bernard, 206
Eric, David, 20, 242
Erickson, Maury, 226
Erickson, Mitchell, 156, 211

Ericson, Christian, 208
Ertelt, Jeannette, 17
Eskew, Donna, 186, 221
Espel, Paul, 242
Esposito, Carlos, 135
Esselstein, Rob, 177
Estabrook, Christine, 227
*Estate, The,* 207
Esterman, Laura, 122, 123, 127, 206, 242
Estes, Steve, 218
Estwick, Pat, 64
Etchison, Greg, 143, 145
Etheridge, Rose Mary, 173
Ettinger, Heidi, 227
Euba, Femi, 207
Eubanks, Shannon, 177
Eure, Ella, 18
*Eustace Chisholm and the Works,* 225
Evanko, Ed, 51, 54, 234, 242
Evans, Alice, 166
Evans, Bill, 12, 20, 25, 28, 34, 41, 75, 76, 155
Evans, David, 47
Evans, Gary, 207
Evans, Gwyllum, 192, 223
Evans, Harvey, 68
Evans, Norman, 127
Evans, Peter, 132, 143, 212
Evans, R. Paul, 88
Evans, Steve, 147
Evelyn, John, 33
*Even The Window is Gone,* 127
*Evening of Sholom Aleichem, An,* 123
*Evening of Tennessee Williams, An,* 208
Everard, David M., 123
Everett, Tim, 234
Everett, Tom, 30, 174
Everhart, Rex, 8, 9, 242
Everson, John, 242
*Every Night When the Sun Goes Down,* 97
*Everyman,* 78, 200
Evett, Ben, 199
Ewer, Donald, 186, 209, 215
Eyen, Tom, 88
Faber, Ron, 137
Fabricant, Gwen, 197
Factor, Diane, 147, 148
Faga, Gary, 63, 242
Fagan, J. B., 74
Fagin, Gary, 227
Fahey, Lee Anne, 187
Fairbank, Spring, 32, 242
Faison, Frankie, 125
Faison, George, 55, 64
Faison, Margaret, 10
Faison, Sandy, 204
Falabella, John M., 119
Falana, Lola, 234
Falk, Kathy, 208
Fallis, Mary Lou, 184
Falls, Gregory A., 186
*Family, The,* 75
Fann, Albert, 64, 242
*Fanshen,* 216
*Fantasticks, The,* 152, 168, 185
Farbman, Jamie, 127
Farentino, James, 8, 11, 234, 242
Farinella, Rosalyn R., 208
Farley, James A. III, 151
Farnworth, Ralph, 55
*Far-Off Sweet Forever, The,* 127
Farquharson, James, 177
Farr, Gary, 156
Farr, Kimberly, 46, 242
Farrah, 103
Farran, Ellen, 74
Farrand, Jan, 198
Farrell, Agnes, 52, 68
Farrell, Brian, 234
Farrell, Scott, 153
Farris, Jon, 175
Farwell, Jonathan, 199
Faso, Laurie, 181, 242
Faso, Nina, 154
*Father Uxbridge Wants to Marry,* 126
Faulks, Barton, 195
Faust, Vincent, 187
Fawcett, Harry, 51
Fay, Patricia, 211
Fayad, Dameon, 143, 144
Faye, Elli, 122
Faye, Joey, 54
Fearl, Clifford, 47, 242
Fearnley, John, 68
Fearon, Abigail, 227
Featherstone, Joanna, 17, 135
Federico, Robert, 150
Feidner, Edward J., 175
Feiffer, Jules, 42, 108

Feingold, Bob, 188
Feinstein, Martin, 211
Feist, Gene, 147, 148
Fejer, Cordis, 206
Felcher, Sarah Philips, 119
Felder, Clarence, 122, 138, 139, 140, 180, 212, 242
Feldman, Joseph H., 182
Feldman, Laurence, 173
Feldner, Sheldon, 144
Feldshuh, David, 213
Feldshuh, Tovah, 8, 20, 230, 232, 242
Felgemacher, Olga, 100
*Fellowship,* 184
Fennessy, John, 60
Ferber, Edna, 36, 211, 214, 218
Ferenchak, Joan, 109, 111
Ferguson, Colin, 40, 50
Ferguson, John, 200
Ferguson, Patrick, 179
Fergusson, Denise, 184
Fermina, Maria, 166
Fernandes, Yuye, 12, 243
Fernandez, Jay, 186
Fernandez, Jose, 155
Fernandez, Roberto, 11, 13
Ferncheck, Joan, 168
Ferrand, Chuck, 127
Ferrand, Katherine, 221
Ferrara, Vivien, 171
Ferraris, Claire, 207
Ferraro, Dolores, 201
Ferraro, John, 135
Ferreira, Maria, 150
Ferrell, Conchata, 107, 190, 234, 243
Ferrell, Nate, 124
Ferrentino, Henry, 121
Ferrer, Jose, 33, 220
Ferrero, Martin, 193
Ferrier, James, 212
Ferris, Paul A., 203
Ferris, Perrin, 114
Ferriter, William, 189
Ferro, Talya, 210
Ferro, Vincent, 151
Ferstenberg, Bernard, 11, 31, 46
Fetterly, Ralph, 193
Feuer, Kurt K., 204
Feuer, Rhoda, 127
Fevrier, Lawrence, 96
Feydeau, 173
Fezelle, Deborah, 211
Fichandler, Thomas C., 190
Fichandler, Zelda, 190
Fichman, Joel S., 43
Fickett, Mary, 234
*Fiddler on the Roof,* 228
Field, Robert, 200
Fielding, Dorothy, 146
Fielding, Henry, 208
Fields, Chip, 25
Fields, Fred, 155, 200
Fields, Herbert, 117
Fields, Joe, 186, 212
Fields, John H., 183, 187
Fields, Judy, 69, 243
Fierson, Andrea, 126
*Fifth Season, The,* 72
Figimiller, John, 201
Fillet, Carol-Lynn, 197
Finamore, Roy, 82
Fineman, Vivian, 243
Fingerhut, Arden, 109, 122, 123, 134, 136, 143, 145, 149, 197, 204, 207
Fingesten, Faye, 107
Finkel, Fyvush, 95, 243
Finkelstein, Niri, 61
Finkle, Eliott, 146
Finlayson, Michael, 176
*Finn Mackool the Grand Distraction,* 71
Finn, Nancy T., 116
Finnegan, Jack, 119, 243
Finnerty, Michael, 185
*Fiorello!,* 228
Fiorentine, Myke, 111
*Fire,* 186
*Fire of Flowers,* 83
Firment, Marilyn, 117
*First Breeze of Summer, The,* 10
*First Monday in October,* 199
Firth, Peter, 63, 234, 243
Fisch, Craig, 177
Fischer, Stefan, 196
Fishbaugh, Arni, 197
Fishburne, Laurence 3d, 124
Fishel, Anne, 107
Fisher, Douglas, 12, 144, 206
Fisher, Jules, 8, 41, 61
Fisher, Linda, 27, 207, 212
Fisher, Mary Helen, 168
Fisher, Michael, 47

Fishler, Franceska, 72
Fiske, Ellen, 36
Fitch, Herb, 177
Fitch, Ken, 82
Fitch, Robert, 243
*Fitting for Ladies,* 173
Fitzgerald, Ella, 8
Fitzgerald, Fern, 8
Fitzgerald, Geraldine, 8, 13, 44, 174, 212, 218, 219, 243
Fitzgerald, Larry, 195
Fitzgerald, T. Richard, 147
Fitzpatrick, Aileen, 196
Fitzpatrick, Bettye, 188
Fitzpatrick, Kelly, 143, 191
Fitzpatrick, Lynn, 47, 243
Fitz-Simons, Haskell, 188
*Five Finger Exercise,* 228
Flacks, Niki, 243
Flagg, Tom, 57, 152, 243
Flagg, Wendie, 221
Flaherty, Lanny, 35
Flanagan, Flossie, 82
Flanagan, Michael, 144, 220
Flanagan, Neil, 42, 107, 108, 167, 243
Flanagan, Walter, 211
Flanders, Richard, 65
Flannery, Daniel, 75, 105
Flannery, Gary, 49
Flato, Malou, 200
Flatt, Robyn, 201
Flaxman, John, 118
Fleckman, Neil, 90
Fleenor, Georgie, 143
Fleischman, Mark, 36, 243
Fleisig, Alan, 123
Fleming, Conn, 127
Fleming, Gus, 116
Flender, Rodman, 45, 145
Fletcher, Allen, 189
Fletcher, Bramwell, 217
Fletcher, Julia, 189
Fletcher, Michael, 184
Flinchum, Doug, 226
Flippin, Lucy Lee, 144, 243
Flood, Peter, 127
Flora, Becky, 58, 71, 74, 159
Flores, Paul, 68
Flower, Wayne, 151
Fludd, Quitman, III., 61
Flynn, John, 177
Flynn, Maryellen, 108, 243
Fogarty, Anne, 172
Fogarty, Jack, 152, 243
Fogarty, Mary, 212
Folden, Lewis, 227
Foley, Paul A., 200
Foley, Robert, 180
Foley, Terence, 107
Folger Theatre Group, 204
*Follies,* 8, 119, 228
Foltz, Richard, 75
Fond, Miriam, 72
Fonda, Jane, 234
Fonda, Peter, 234
Fonner, Fred, 215
Fontaine, Luther, 194
Fontana, Jana, 82
Fontane, Char, 60
Foose, Robert, 120
Foote, Gene, 8, 61, 243
Footman, Fish, 100
Forbes, Brenda, 47, 188, 243
Forbes, Kathleen, 185
Ford, Chip, 65
Ford, Larry, 188
Ford, Paul, 262, 263
Ford, Spence, 119, 226
Ford, Suzanne, 116, 243
Ford-Davies, Oliver, 103
Forde, Larry, 57
Ford's Theatre, 205
Forella, Michael, 27
Foreman, Richard, 133
Forman, Arthur Ed, 156
Forman, John, 172
Forrest, Milton Earl, 200
Forrest, Paul, 51
Forrester, Bill, 186
Forrester, Julian, 200
Forslund, Connie, 30, 243
Forslund, Sinden, 30
Forste, Paul, 198
Forster, Robert, 187
Forward, Jeffrey G., 176
Forward, William, 177
Foss, Loren, 221
Fosse, Bob, 8, 61
Fosser, William, 203
Foster, Christopher, 179
Foster, Frances, 10, 125
Foster, Gloria, 234
Foster, Herb, 197
Foster, Kathleen, 12, 22, 32, 155
Foster, Norah, 73
Foster, Stephen, 185
Foster, Suzanne, 120

Founding Father, 113, 114
Fourposter, The, 203, 228
Fouse, Thomas Jefferson, Jr., 205
Fowkes, Conrad, 214
Fowler, Beth, 55
Fowler, Clement, 204
Fowler, John, 120
Fowler, Keith, 226
Fox, Alan, 86
Fox, Dorothi, 126
Fox, Erika, 146
Fox, Florence, 208
Fox, Jay, 62, 224
Fox, Maxine, 60
Fox, Sonny, 148
Fox-Brenton, David, 200, 211
Foxworth, Robert, 234
Foy, Kenneth, 212
Foy, Nancy, 127
Fradrich, James, 70, 75, 76
Fraina, Robert, 123
Franceschina, John, 113, 114, 168
Francesco, Nick, 126, 127
Franciosa, Anthony, 234
Francis, Arlene, 54
Francis, Paul W., 152
Frand, Harvey, 35
Frangione, Nancy, 146
Frank, Allan, 106, 145, 243
Frank, Barbara Joan, 72
Frank, David, 88
Frank, Gerri-Ann, 72
Frank, Mary K., 126
Frank, Michael J., 154
Frankel, Kenneth, 192, 212, 214
Franken, Rose, 117
Frankfather, William, 177
Franklin, Bonnie, 234
Franklin, Nancy, 126, 127
Franklin, Robert, 82, 226
Franklin, Roger, 162
Franklin, Sandi, 126
Franks, Geri, 114
Franks, Penny, 155
Franz, Elizabeth, 209
Franz, Gina, 189
Franz, Joy, 61
Fraser, Jean, 160
Fraser, Pat, 206
Fratti, Mario, 73
Frawley, Bernard, 208
Frazier, David O., 73
Frazier, Grenoldo, 25
Frazier, Hank, 135
Frazier, Ronald C., 117, 194, 243
Frederick, Marcia, 193
Frederick, Vickie, 14
Fredericks, David, 41
Fredericks, William, 86
Fredericksen, Erik, 129, 181
Fredricks, Rita, 27
Fredricksen, Erik, 129, 213
Fredrik, Burry, 21, 22, 36
Fredrix, Paul, 177
Free Southern Theatre, 210
Freed, Les, 37
Freed, Sam, 243
Freedman, Gerald, 91, 131, 156
Freedman, Ginny, 85, 105
Freedman, Glenna, 62
Freedman, Robert, 169
Freeman, Al, Jr., 165, 207
Freeman, Ann, 82, 114, 243
Freeman, David, 134, 213
Freeman, Kenneth, 114
Freeman, Steven, 132
Freeman, Yvette, 153
Freitag, Dorothea, 30, 169
Frelich, Phylis, 127
French, Arthur, 11, 38
French, Bruce, 197
French, Dorothy, 163
French, Mark A., 98
French, Valerie, 71, 171
Freudenberger, Daniel, 138, 141
Frey, Leonard, 42, 211, 218, 219, 243
Freydberg, James B., 218
Fried, Martin, 190, 223
Fried, Michael, 147
Friedheim, Eric, 156
Friedlander, Jane, 159
Friedlander, Sylvia, 72
Friedman, David, 70
Friedman, Jane, 87
Friedman, Joan, 208
Friedman, Joel, 112
Friedman, Phil, 8
Friedman, Shelly, 70, 118, 119
Friel, Jack, 169
Frierson, Andrea, 155
Frimet, Adrienne, 86

Fripp, Amy, 76
Frisari, Joseph, 110
Frissell, Robert, 24, 59, 87
Frogs, The, 178
From Sholom Aleichem With Love, 79
Front Page, The, 188, 190
Frost, Cynthia, 145
Frounfelter, Earl, 193
Frumkin, Marla, 217
Fry, Christopher, 180
Fry, Ray, 187
Frye, Dwight, 37
Fryer, Robert, 8, 28
Fuentes, Carmelita, 114, 145
Fugard, Athol, 123
Fuhrman, Ben, 224
Fujii, Timm, 39, 243
Fujimoto, Haruki, 39
Fulginetti, Michael, 221
Fuller, Dale, 82
Fuller, Janice, 105, 143, 145, 243
Fuller, Penny, 51, 243
Fuller, Sally, 223
Fuller, Sandra, 173
Fullum, Clay, 76
Funky Monkeys, The, 64
Funny Thing Happened on the Way to the Forum, A, 228
Furth, George, 213
Gabbert, Timothy, 82
Gabel, Cyprienne, 119
Gabel, Donna, 127, 144
Gabel, Martin, 54
Gabis, Stephen, 69
Gable, Christopher, 88
Gable, June, 181, 243
Gaffney, Warren, 200
Gage, Gary, 59
Gage, Jeremy, 204
Gage, Patricia, 194, 215
Gagliano, Frank, 126, 127
Gagne, Wayne, 188
Gagnon, Roland, 15
Gaige, Truman, 157
Gaines, Mervyn Jr., 126
Gaisford, Kimberly, 207
Galban, Margarita, 197
Gale, David, 35, 223, 243
Galiber, Doris, 68
Gallagher, David, 143
Gallagher, Helen, 89, 243
Gallagher, Jamie, 212, 223
Gallardo, Sandra, 155
Gallegly, David, 70, 243
Gallegos, Lawrence, 82
Gallery, James, 129, 181, 243
Gallo, Fred, 154
Gallo, Paul, 183, 227
Gallogly, John, 95
Gallon, Richard G., 191
Galloway, Don, 234
Galloway, Jane, 85, 143, 144
Galloway, Leata, 41
Galloway, Pat, 184
Gallu, Samuel, 164
Gallup, Bonnie, 193
Galuppi, Richard, 200, 211
Galvin, James, 118
Galvin, Timothy, 118
Gamble, Duncan, 197
Gammell, Robin, 196
Gandy, Sue, 134
Gann, John, 200
Gannaway, Lynn, 78
Gant, Richard, 123
Gantry, Don, 13, 212, 224
Gantry, Donald, 243
Garber, Victor, 81, 212, 227, 234, 243
Garcia, Janice, 189
Garcia, Pilar, 70
Garcia, Robert, 206
Gardner, Cliff, 213
Gardner, Craig R., 188
Gardner, Dean, 186
Gardner, Gregory, 18
Gardner, Jonathan, 209
Gardner, Louanna, 114
Gardner, Marilyn, 213
Gardner, Mark, 199
Garfield, Julie, 11, 123, 234, 243
Garfield, Kurt, 186, 208
Gargan, Kathleen, 89
Gargiulo, Ted, 180
Garland, Geoff, 171
Garland, Patricia, 14, 161
Garner, Florene Merrit, 218
Garner, Larry, 143
Garner, Peggy Ann, 36
Garnett, Chip, 8, 43, 229, 232, 244
Garnett, Gale, 81, 184
Garnett, George Carr, 192
Garofalo, Joe, 16
Garr, Rick, 196
Garrabrandt, Ed, 177

Garraty, Tri, 204
Garrett, Bob, 60, 244
Garrett, Davidson, 121
Garrett, Frederick, 121, 124, 125
Garrett, Kelly, 234, 244
Garrett, Maureen, 218
Garrett, Michael, 209
Garrick, Beulah, 67, 244
Garrick, John, 225
Garrison, David, 190
Garrison, Sean, 234
Garry, Joseph J., 73
Garza, Rudy, 73
Garza, Troy, 160
Gasbarre, Roberta, 190
Gascon, Jean, 178, 213
Gass, Marc Jordan, 123
Gassell, Sylvia, 112, 186
Gatchell & Neufeld, 34
Gatchell, R. Tyler, Jr., 34
Gates, Diane, 182
Gates, Larry, 129, 181, 244
Gatto, Peter, 208
Gaughan, Jack, 90
Gauthier, Guy, 144
Gavin, Matt, 65
Gavon, Igors, 106, 145, 244
Gawryn, Myrna, 200
Gayford, Susan, 203
Gaynes, Edmund, 86
Gaynor, Charles, 264
Gazzara, Ben, 8, 48, 232, 234, 244
Gear, Valorie, 190
Gebhard, Fran, 213
Gebhard, Penny, 134
Gee, Richard, 170
Geer, Faith, 128, 129, 130, 131, 132, 133
Geer, Kevin, 107
Geffner, Deborah, 116, 244
Gehrels, Royce, 195
Geidt, Jan, 227
Geidt, Jeremy, 227
Geier, Paul, 144
Geis, Cynthia Ann, 143
Geiser, Linda, 112
Gelb, Susan, 200
Gelb, Victor A., 119
Gelblum, Peter B., 98
Geld, Gary, 65
Gelfman, Shelly, 67
Gemignani, Paul, 39
Gendel, Max, 33
Gendell, Gary, 8
Gene, Terry, 25
General Gorgeous, 189, 227
Genest, Ed, 127
Genest, Edmond, 207
Genise, Livia, 60, 147
Genke, John, 106, 145
Gennaro, Michael, 244
Genovese, Margaret, 188
Genovese, Mike, 206
Gentles, Avril, 206
Gentry, Bob, 234
Gentry, Minnie, 125
Geoffries, K. W., 146
Geography of a Horse Dreamer, 122
George Abbott . . . A Celebration, 54
George, David, 69, 144, 145
George, Hal, 128, 129
George Washington Slept Here, 145
George, William, 201
Geraci, Frank, 177, 196
Geraci, Leslie, 216
Gerald, Kimo, 169
Gerb, Lynn, 123
Gere, Richard, 30, 214
Gerety, Anne, 227
Gerety, Peter, 225
Gerhard, Bruce, 189
Gerlach, Robert, 59
Geronemus, David, 90
Gerringer, Robert, 218, 219
Gersh, Ellyn, 197
Gershenson, Sueanne, 117, 244
Gerstein, Bailie, 62
Gersten, Bernard, 14, 17, 128, 137, 160, 161, 181
Gertrude og Ophelia, 221
Get-Rich-Quick Wallingford, 199
Getting Gertie's Garter, 143
Getz, John, 98, 110
Getzov, Ramon, 24, 165
Gevanthor, Norman, 190
Ghoston, Karen, 206
Giambalvo, Louis, 81, 111
Giannini, Cheryl, 215
Giannini, Christina, 89, 121, 147, 148, 149

Giardina, Tony, 143
Gibberson, William, 50
Gibbons, June, 199
Gibbs, Richard, 82
Giber, Robert, 69, 244
Gibson, Anne A., 187
Gibson, B. G., 41
Gibson, Judy, 41, 153, 244
Gibson, Karen, 47, 244
Gibson, Michael, 155
Gibson, William, 145
Gideon, Pat, 25, 51
Gifford, Alan, 207
Gift of the Magi, 76
Giglio, Allison, 206
Giglio, Gino, 20, 155
Gilbert, 143
Gilbert, Alan, 119, 226, 244
Gilbert, Alyce, 14
Gilbert, Edward, 106, 145, 213
Gilbert, Joan G., 119, 244
Gilbert, John, 221
Gilbert, Pia, 156
Gilbert, Ray, 244
Gilbert, Ruth, 194
Gilborn, Steven, 143, 214
Gilchrist, Denise, 221
Gilchrist, Rebecca, 60, 244
Gile, Bill, 32
Giles, Paul Kirk, 264
Gilford, Jack, 54
Gilhooley, Jack, 126, 127
Gillett, Julia, 75, 194
Gillette, Anita, 8, 136, 234, 244
Gillette, Priscilla, 234
Gillette, William, 141, 171, 196
Gilliam, Terry, 87
Gillies, David, 213
Gillmore, Ruth, 264
Gillotte, Tony, 206
Gilmann, Larry, 244
Gilvezan, Dan, 177
Gimenez, Juan Carlos, 115
Gin, Raymond, 189
Gingold, Alfred, 143
Ginty, E. B., 118
Ginza, Joey, 39
Giordano, Tony, 81
Giovanetti, Antony, 90, 110
Giovanni, Paul, 224
Giraldo, Esther, 150
Giraldo, George, 41
Giraud, Claude, 234
Giroux, Laurent, 8, 61
Gish, Lillian, 26, 244
Gisondi, John, 123, 143, 144, 145
Gitlin, Amy Idell, 58
Gitlin, Murray, 102, 165, 211
Giunta, Aldo, 127
Give 'Em Hell Harry!, 164
Givens, Jack, 220
Givin, Ann, 25
Gladstone, Brooke, 175
Gladstone, Dana, 120, 143
Glance of a Landscape, 143
Glanville, Maxwell, 209
Glaser, Darel, 37, 244
Glaser, Kathy, 182
Glass, Joanna, 212
Glass Menagerie, The, 8, 31, 218, 219, 220, 228
Glass, Philip, 104
Glass, Ralph, 213
Glassco, Bill, 184
Glassman, Seth, 123
Glaze, Susan, 211
Gleason, James, 172
Gleason, John, 25, 36, 47, 87, 151, 155, 158, 196, 211, 214
Gleason, Paul, 82
Glenn, Barbara, 43, 45, 72
Glenn, Bette, 118, 244
Glenn, David M., 180
Glenn, Scott, 197
Glick, Linda, 123
Globe of the Great Southwest, 176
Globe Playhouse, The, 177
Glover, John, 174, 218, 219, 244
Glynn, Carlin, 82
Gochman, Len, 77
Godby, Jack, 147
Goddard, Wesley, 193
Godfrey, Lynnie, 88
Godines, Ronald Joseph, 197
Godkin, David S., 175
Godspell, 154, 179, 195
Goeddertz, Charles, 25
Goetz, Augustus, 50, 211, 214
Goetz, Ruth, 50, 211, 214
Goggin, Dan, 57
Gogol, Nikolai, 208

Going Ape, 191
Going, John E., 192, 198, 220
Gold, Alice, 67
Gold, Harvey, 200
Gold, Lloyd, 214
Gold, Robert Alan, 152
Gold, Russell, 188
Goldberg, Jeanette, 206
Goldberg, Mort, 200
Goldberg, Robert I., 49
Golden Apple, The, 228
Golden Boy, 122
Golden, Kevin, 126
Golden, Louis, 89
Golden, Tony, 16
Goldman, Byron, 32
Goldman, Charles, 177
Goldman, James, 119
Goldman, Lorry, 196
Goldmund, David, 193
Goldring, Danny, 206
Goldsborough, Randy, 143
Goldsmith, Merwin, 51, 128, 244
Goldsmith, Ted, 55, 76, 88
Goldstein, Ira, 206
Goldstein, Judy, 120
Goldstein, Steven, 25
Golub, Peter, 137
Golyn, Rudi, 71
Gomer, Steven, 107, 108
Gomes, Enrique, 115
Gomez, Mateo, 115
Gonzalez, Ernesto, 17, 244
Gonzalez, Ofelia, 150
Gooch, Jenny, 123
Good, Karen, 224
Good Old-Fashioned Revue, 113
Good Old-Fashioned Revue, A, 113
Good Time Dolly Dee, 123
Goode, Joe, 82
Goodin, John C., 184
Goodman, Arlene Wolf, 73
Goodman, Diana, 195
Goodman, Dody, 196
Goodman, Douglas F., 147, 148, 149
Goodman, Frank, 73
Goodman, Lee, 52
Goodman, Margaret, 119
Goodman, Martha Robinson, 201
Goodman, Pegi, 123
Goodman, Robyn, 145, 244
Goodman Theatre Center, 206
Goodridge, Ted, 25
Goodson, Ann, 87
Goodwin, Cliff, 127
Goodwin, Geena, 145
Goodwin, Mark, 218
Goossen, Lawrence, 204
Gorbea, Carlos, 39, 244
Gorbea, Rafael, 150
Gordean, Meg, 10, 71, 74, 159
Gordon, Betty, 208
Gordon, Carl, 244
Gordon, Gail, 180
Gordon, Gayle, 209
Gordon, Haskell, 208
Gordon, Kathleen, 65
Gordon, Lewis, 184
Gordon, Peggy, 244
Gordon, Rita, 70, 244
Gordon, Ruth, 131, 244
Gordon, Stephanie, 107
Gore, Christopher, 48
Gorfein, Henry R., 190
Goring, Jack, 203
Gorky, 95
Gorman, Madeleine, 121, 123, 144
Gorman, Mari, 234
Gorman, Pat, 41
Gorman, Patricia, 122
Gorney, Walt, 128
Gorrin, Michael, 45
Gorwin, Peter, 244
Gosse, Van, 107
Gosselin, David, 223
Gossett, Lou, 196, 197
Gottlieb, Morton, 66
Gott-Lin, Brad, 225
Gould, Eleanor Cody, 105, 121, 244
Gould, George, 199
Gould, Harold, 196
Gould, Richard, 199
Gould, Tom, 208
Goulding, William R., 156
Goulet, Robert, 234
Government Inspector, The, 208
Gowans, John D., 196
Grace, Dan, 200
Grace, Michael L., 172
Graden, David, 172
Grady, Richard, 177
Graeber, Ted, 207

Graff, Hank, 220
Graff, Ilene, 60, 155
Graff, Tom, 183
Grahal, Fernando, 264
Graham, Elaine, 207
Graham, Lou Ann, 189
Graham, R. H., 216
Graham, Richard, 180
Graham, Ronny, 234
Graham, Ross, 189
Grammer, Gerri, 177
Grammis, Adam, 49
Granat, Carla, 108
Granata, Dona, 55
Grandin, Isabel, 159
Granfield, Suzanne, 114
Granger, Farley, 165, 221, 222
Granger, Michael, 208
Grannum, Karen, 43
Grant, Barra, 196, 197
Grant, Carol, 82
Grant, Charles E., 169
Grant, Diane, 184
Grant, Grayce, 174, 190
Grant, J. Lloyd, 43
Grant, James R., 147, 148, 149
Grant, Micki, 162
Grant, Randy, 194
Grant, Wesley, 221
Grant, William, III, 210
Grant-Green, Charles, 194
Grant-Greene, Charles, 207
Graphenreed, Timothy, 64
Grassilli, Ann B., 116
Grassilli, John, 209
Grauer, Ben, 54
Grave Undertaking, A, 214
Graves, Ernest, 102
Gray, Amlin, 82, 114
Gray, Bruce, 109, 244
Gray, Douglas, 100
Gray, John, 191
Gray, Kathleen, 143
Gray, Kenneth, 200
Gray, Liebe, 197
Gray, Margery, 100
Gray, Sam, 112, 198
Gray, Simon, 224
Grayson, Laura, 195
Grayson, Milton, 169
Grayson, Rod, 195
Grayton, Lisa, 223
Graziano, Richard J., 134
Great Lakes Shakespeare
  Festival, 178
Great Potato Famine, The,
  197
Great White Hope, The, 228
Greek, James, 206
Green, Adolph, 54, 76
Green, Darren, 169
Green, Howard, 112
Green, Kay, 103
Green, Mary-Pat, 244
Green, Mitchell, 70
Green, Nancy L., 146
Green Pastures, The, 228
Green, Paul, 202
Green, Richard, 114
Green, Rodney, 64
Green, Romaine, 8
Greenbaum, Susan, 151
Greenberg, Albert, 197
Greenberg, Charles L., 109
Greenberg, Edward M., 90
Greenberg, Rocky, 210
Greene, Ellen, 133, 244
Greene, Gayle, 69, 244
Greene, James, 212
Greene, Loretta, 123
Greene, Richard, 127, 204
Greene, Schuyler, 32
Greene, Theodore, 221
Greenfeld, Josh, 205
Greenfield, Edith, 119, 126,
  244
Greenhouse, Martha, 21,
  244
Greenwald, Robert, 19, 196,
  197, 205
Greenwood, Deanna, 72
Greenwood, Jane, 40, 48,
  66, 71, 102, 174,
  205, 211, 214, 218
Greer, Ann, 177
Gregg, Julie, 234
Gregorio, Rose, 196
Gregory, Andre, 135
Gresham, Gloria, 157
Greth, Roma, 143
Grey, DeMarest, 64
Grey, Janet, 12
Grey, Joel, 232
Gribetz, Gabriel, 82
Grifasi, Joe, 138, 141, 142,
  227
Griffen, Joyce, 75
Griffies, Ethel, 36, 264
Griffin, Dwight, 213
Griffin, Kristin, 211
Griffin, Linda, 55

Griffin, Sean, 13, 212
Griffin, Tom, 225
Griffis, William, 51, 244
Griffith, Andy, 234
Griffith, Gwendolyn, 176
Griffith, Kristin, 211
Grigas, John, 39
Grignon, Monica, 70
Grill, Gary, 82
Grillo, Robert, 143
Grimaldi, Dennis, 244
Grimes, Tammy, 26, 234,
  245
Grise, Emmy Nance, 156
Grizzard, George, 8, 31, 36,
  48, 101, 214, 234,
  245
Grober, Douglas, 61
Grober, Steve, 65
Grodin, Charles, 66, 245
Groener, Harry, 222
Grogan, B. J., 177
Groh, David, 244, 245
Grollman, Elaine, 20, 244,
  245
Groom, Bill, 123
Gropman, David Lloyd, 227
Grose, Anna, 221
Gross, Kit, 193
Gross, Michael, 187
Grossman, Bill, 116, 137
Grossman, Hal, 157
Grossman, Iris, 146
Grossman, Larry, 172
Grossman, Robert, 215
Grossman, Shirley, 120
Grossman, Terry, 48, 78
Grosvenor, Lucie D., 43,
  135
Group, Merlin, 19
Grove, Barry, 122
Grover, Barbara, 200
Groves, Jane, 206
Groves, Robin, 31, 46
Grubar, Justine, 121
Gruet, Allan, 187
Grun, Otto, Jr., 88
Grynheim, Joel, 119
Guarascio, Louis, 74
Guardino, Larry, 122
Guare, John, 136
Gubner, Heather, 82
Guc, David, 147
Gudell, Ileane, 119
Guerra, Lynn, 60
Guerrasio, John, 143, 209
Guglielmina, Monica, 58
Guilbeault, Melanie, 195
Guilfoyle, Richard, 177
Guillaume, Robert, 137,
  206, 245
Guillory, Bennett, 189
Guilmartin, Ken, 95
Guinn, David, 70
Guiterrez, Lolina, 150
Guittard, Laurence, 234,
  245
Gulack, Max, 133, 191,
  245
Gullison, Liesha, 145
Gunas, Gary, 62
Gundersen, Arne, 72
Gunn, Moses, 8, 10, 38,
  245
Gunnersen, Mickey, 68
Gunther, William, 177
Gurney, A. R., Jr., 109, 226
Gustafson, Carol, 209
Gustafson, Otis, 78
Gusti, 73
Guthrie, Tyrone, 94
Gutierrez, Gerald, 92, 93,
  94, 245
Gutierrez, Lolina, 150
Gutierrez-Soto, Ben, 86
Gutter, Lynn, 71, 80
Guttman-Iranyi, Miriam, 110
Guy Gauthier's Ego Play,
  144
Guys and Dolls, 191, 226,
  228
Gwenver, Margaret, 143,
  145
Gwillim, Jack, 200, 214
Gwillim, Sarah-Jane, 214
Gwynne, Fred, 174, 211
Haas, Amelia, 145
Haas, Nathan, 189
Habeas Corpus, 30
Hackady, Hal, 172
Hacker, Christopher, 145
Hacker, Sander, 45
Hackett, Jim, 146
Hackett, Joan, 234
Hadary, Jonathan, 123
Hadge, Michael, 82
Hageman, Jessye, 210
Hagen, Robert, 204
Hagen, Uta, 38, 48
Hagman, Larry, 234
Haid, Charles, 154
Hailey, Oliver, 196
Haimsohn, George, 176

Haines, Howard, 39
Haines, Mervyn Jr., 131,
  136
Haire, James, 189
Halbert, Bill, 188
Halbert, Jean, 80
Hale, Birdie M., 25
Halfway Tree Brown, 126
Hall, Adrian, 225
Hall, Alan, 22
Hall, Cardell, 205
Hall, Carl, 55
Hall, Dale, 218
Hall, Dan, 110
Hall, Davis, 194
Hall, Delores, 205
Hall, Demene, 215
Hall, Ed, 208, 225
Hall, George, 98, 108, 245
Hall, Grayson, 17
Hall, Harriet, 206
Hall, J. F., 12
Hall, Joanna, 159
Hall, Lisa, 86
Hall, Margaret, 17, 221,
  222, 245
Hall, Mary Porter, 131
Hall, Michael Keys, 182
Hall, Nick, 191
Hall, Philip Baker, 95, 245
Hallahan, Charles, 189
Hallaren, Jane, 109
Halliday, Gordon, 65, 244,
  245
Halliday, William, 215
Hallow, John, 215
Halperin, Sandra, 91, 92,
  93, 94
Halpern, Jonas, 49
Halpern, Mortimer, 52, 69
Halpern, Richard, 118, 245
Halverson, Richard, 199
Hama, Larry, 39
Hambleton, T. Edward, 138
Hamerman, Marc, 86
Hamilton, Alma, 245
Hamilton, Dan, 227
Hamilton, Frank, 38, 122,
  149, 206, 211
Hamilton, James, 157, 164
Hamilton, Kenneth, 218
Hamilton, Mitzi, 160
Hamilton, Patricia, 213
Hamilton, Patrick, 33
Hamilton, Rick, 189
Hamilton, Roger, 61, 245
Hamilton, Samantha S., 148
Hamlet, 8, 41, 129, 177,
  181
Hamlet Syndrome, The, 221
Hamlin, Harry, 189
Hamlin, Jeff, 14, 161
Hamlisch, Marvin, 14, 160,
  161, 232
Hammack, Warren, 196
Hammer, Arthur, 126
Hammer, Mark, 190
Hammerstein, James, 77
Hammerstein, Oscar, 2nd,
  68
Hammett, Gordon, 122
Hammil, John, 111
Hammill, Nancy, 167
Hammond, Dorothea, 190
Hammond, Jacqueline, 191
Hammond, John, 215
Hampton, Jim, 218
Hampton, Roger, 177
Hancock, John, 187
Hancock, Tom, 161
Handley, Oliver, 195
Handman, Wynn, 95
Hands, Terry, 103
Handy, James, 127
Haney, Carol, 234
Haney, Michael, 45, 245
Haney, Russell, 209
Hanft, Helen, 145, 194
Hanks, Mark, 163
Hanley, Ellen, 234
Hanley, Katie, 60, 245
Hanley, Valli, 119
Hanlon, Mary-Ellen, 70
Hanmer, Don, 234
Hanna, Edna K., 186
Hannigan, Patricia, 111
Hansberry, Lorraine, 169
Hansen, Bara-Cristin, 11,
  212, 244, 245
Hansen, George, 42, 107,
  108, 122, 123
Hansen, June, 204
Hansen, William, 264
Happy Days, 116
Hara, Mary, 163
Harada, Ernest, 39, 245
Haraldson, Marian, 120
Harbison, Lawrence, 110,
  113
Harburg, E. Y. (Yip), 79

Harden, Ernest, Jr., 126
Harden, Richard, 120
Harder, James, 32
Hardin, Joseph, 114
Hardin, Lo, 174, 205
Harding, Harvey, 213
Harding, June, 234
Harding, Paul, 40
Harding, Wayne, 120
Hardstark, Michael, 110
Hardy, John W., 202
Hardy, Lynne, 67
Hardy, Thomas, 80
Hardy, William, Jr., 205
Hare, David, 216
Hare, Eugene, 199
Harewood, Dorian, 8, 132,
  234, 245
Harger, Gary, 65, 245
Hargreaves, William, 177
Harker, Jeanne, 208
Harker, Wiley, 206
Harkins, Paul, 114
Harkness, Sam, 64
Harley, Margot, 91
Harmel, Richard, 119
Harmful Effects of Tobacco,
  The, 188
Harmfulness of Tobacco,
  The, 112
Harmon, Lewis, 70, 81,
  116, 117, 118, 119
Harney, Ben, 18, 61, 245
Harnick, Sheldon, 51, 100,
  116
Harper, Bob, 190
Harper, Charles, 114, 143
Harper, Charles Thomas,
  107, 244, 245
Harper, J. W., 91, 92, 93,
  94, 245
Harper, Ken, 64
Harper, Richard, 81
Harper, Wally, 52
Harrell, Gordon Lowry, 41
Harrelson, Helen, 11, 245
Harrington, Margaret, 82
Harrington, Nancy, 116
Harrington, Ron, 113
Harris, Albert, 200
Harris, Alison, 212
Harris, Barbara, 234
Harris, Barbara A., 203
Harris, Baxter, 211
Harris, Catherine, 213
Harris, Charlise, 43
Harris, Cynthia, 196
Harris, David, 141, 142
Harris, Donald, 19, 200,
  205
Harris, Gary, 111
Harris, Herbert, 181
Harris, James, 187
Harris, James Berton, 58,
  225
Harris, Jeffrey, 203
Harris, Jeremy, 77
Harris, Joseph, 8, 28, 61
Harris, Joyce, 209
Harris, Julie, 8, 53, 232,
  234, 245
Harris, Keith, 64
Harris, Linda, 151
Harris, Margaret, 169
Harris, Michael, 210
Harris, Neil, 135
Harris, Patricia, 195
Harris, Renee, 64
Harris, Ron, 8, 59, 64, 89,
  101, 214, 232, 234,
  245
Harris, Sandra, 98
Harris, Sarah, 122
Harris, Ted, 45
Harris, Timmy, 93
Harris, Tom, 60, 245
Harris, Wes, 155
Harrison, Alphanzo, 88
Harrison, Eric, 63
Harrison, Ford, 155
Harrison, Rex, 47
Harry Outside, 154
Hart, Cecilia, 50
Hart, Dana, 199
Hart, David, 182
Hart, Dolores, 234
Hart, Floyd, 221
Hart, John Raymond, 123
Hart, Joseph, 113
Hart, Louisa, 209
Hart, Michael, 82
Hart, Michel, 96
Hart, Moss, 47, 145, 146,
  196
Hart, Richard, 234
Hart, Roxanne, 181
Hart, Stan, 120
Hart, William, 144
Hartenstein, Frank, 14, 161
Hartford Stage Company,
  207
Hartle, Sherie, 195

Hartley, Mariette, 197
Hartman, Dylan, 70
Hartman, Elek, 110, 112
Hartman, Stefan, 90
Hartman Theatre Company,
  208
Harty, Stephen, 126
Hartz, Beverly, 116, 245
Harum, Eivind, 160
Harvey, 228
Harvey, Dyane, 64
Harvey, Kenneth, 98, 99,
  245
Harvey, Laurence, 234
Harvey, Michael, 24, 35,
  165
Harvey, Patricia, 177
Harvey, Peter, 191, 194
Harvey's Bazaar, 14
Harwood, Jill, 113
Hase, Marilyn, 208
Haseltine, Fred, 226
Hash, Burl, 75, 76, 105
Haskell, David, 214
Haskell, Judy, 113
Haskell, Paul, 151
Haskins, Paul, 151
Hasnain, Arif, 213
Hastie, S. C., 191
Hastings, Edward, 189
Hastings, Karen Sue, 195
Hastings, Margot, 113
Hattan, Mark, 118, 245
Hattendorf, Delia, 209
Hattub, Beth, 158
Haugan, Kristine, 74
Hausman, Elaine, 91, 92,
  93, 94, 245
Haverinen, Richard, 183
Havoc, June, 30, 54, 245
Havrilla, Jo Ann, 146
Hawke, Sindy, 197
Hawken, Victoria, 208
Hawkins, Cynthia, 221
Hawkins, Maureen, 221
Hawkins, Trish, 109, 194,
  234, 246
Hawthorne, Myrenna, 202
Hay, Richard L., 182
Haydon, Julie, 31
Hayes, Every, 246
Hayes, Gardner, 221
Hayes, Helen, 1, 2, 31, 54
Hayes, John, 184
Hayes, Lois, 64
Hayle, Douglas, 117, 246
Haynes, Cynthia, 73
Haynes, Jayne, 127, 143
Haynes, Michael, 113
Haynes, Neal, 153
Haynes, Tiger, 64, 246
Haynie, Charles, 202
Haynie, Susan A., 201
Hays, Rex D., 145
Hays, Stephen E., 223
Hayter, Louise, 197
Hayter, Pearl, 192
Hayward, Henry, 126
Hazell, Jan, 205
Head, Eric, 198
Head, Helaine, 36, 214
Healy, Christine, 182
Healy, David, 201
Heaney, Kathleen, 40
Heard, John, 123, 129,
  181, 212
Hearn, George, 129, 212,
  246
Heartbreak House, 190,
  191
Heath, Bob, 55
Heath, Louise, 55
Heaton, Michael, 122, 144,
  145
Heavenrich, Jill, 216
Hebert, Gail, 186
Hecht, Lawrence, 189
Heckart, Eileen, 174, 205,
  234, 246
Hedaya, Dan, 122
Hedda Gabler, 218, 219
Hedges, David, 40
Hedison, David, 234
Heffner, David Kerry, 122
Heffelfinger, Shanley, 185
Heffernan, John, 46, 246
Heflin, Nora, 200
Hegedus, Michael, 180
Heifner, Jack, 85, 143, 144
Heikin, Nancy, 113
Heim, Michael, 196
Heineman, Laurie, 143, 246
Heiner, Barta, 189
Heinz, Rosalind, 212
Heiress, The, 8, 50, 211,
  214
Heiss, Christie, 143
Heit, Sally-Jane, 120
Heitmanek, John, 206
Helfond, Susie, 197
Helitzer, Deborah Lynne,
  112
Helland, Eric, 221

Helland, J. Roy, 50, 131, 133, 140
*Hell-Bent fer Heaven*, 228
Hellend, Roy J., 128
Heller, Jack, 203
Heller, Joseph, 208
Heller, Randee, 60
Helliker, Steve, 89
*Hello, Dolly!*, 8, 25, 228
Helm, Thomas, 116, 117, 118
Helpmann, Max, 184
Helsing, Raili, 192
Helton, Shaun, 211
Helward, Dale, 188
Hemmer, John, 166
Hemphill, Lisa, 198
Hemsley, Gilbert V., Jr., 194, 205
Hemsley, Winston DeWitt, 14, 41, 246
Henderson, Forsythe, 209
Henderson, Jo, 198
Henderson, Luther, 52
Henderson, Marcia, 234
Hendrickson, Benjamin, 91, 92, 93, 94
Hendry, David, 103
Henley, Ken, 51
Henner, Marilu, 60
Hennessy, Noreen, 197
Henning, Doug, 62, 224, 246
Henritze, Bette, 33, 174, 214, 246
Henry, Edward, 204
*Henry IV, Part I*, 180
*Henry IV, Part II*, 180
Henry, Martha, 184, 234
*Henry V.*, 8, 103, 204
*Henry VI*, 182
Hensel, Karen, 193
Henshaw, Anne, 87
Henshaw, Wandalie, 200
Hensleigh, Jimmy, 173
Henson, John, 201
Hepburn, Audrey, 234
Hepburn, Katharine, 8, 40, 246
Herb, Mark S., 180
Herbert, Dawn, 51
Herbert, Diana, 234
Herbert, Robin, 32
Herbin, Jean, 96
Herbst, Judy, 206
Hergault, Roland, 96
Herlihy, Ed, 246
Herlihy, James Leo, 113
Herman, Bill, 191
Herman, Gloria Hayen, 192
Herman, Jeffrey, 114
Herman, Jerry, 25
Herman, Louise, 143, 144, 145
Hermann, Edward, 8
Hermon, Michel, 96
Herndon, Bill, 224
Herndon, Wayne, 37
Herritt, Keith, 182
Herrmann, Edward, 131, 190, 246
Herrmann, Steven W., 186
Herron, Robert J., 143
Herron, Rose, 216
Hershcopf, Jane, 86
Herter, Al, 69
Herz, Shirley, 21, 36
Herzer, Martin, 12, 19, 160
Hess, Benton, 123
Heston, Charlton, 234
Heuman, Barbara, 59, 246
Hewett, Christopher, 128, 246
Hewgill, Roland, 213
Hewitt, Frankie, 205
Heyer, Bill, 77
Heyer, Rome, 77
Heyman, Barton, 214
Hibbard, Allen, 201
Hicken, Tana, 194
Hickey, Michael P., 226
Hickey, Nancy, 200
Hickey, William, 71
Hicks, Israel, 198
Hicks, Kenneth, 18
Hicks, Lee, 218
Hicks, Munson, 27, 57, 67, 123
Hicks, Peter, 215
Higdon, Don, 177
Higgins, James, 159, 186
Higgins, Joel, 65, 234, 246
Higgins, Michael, 63, 246
Higgins, Steve, 218
*High Tor*, 228
Highland, James, 221
Highstein, Jene, 104
Higley, Susie, 195
Hilbrandt, James, 123
Hild, Dan, 35, 42, 108
Hilferty, Susan, 121
Hill, Arthur, 48
Hill, Jeffrey, 187

Hill, Joseph, 156
Hill, Melanie, 121
Hill, Michael, 193
Hill, Michael J., 182
Hill, Parks, 118, 246
Hill, Tom, 227
Hiller, Bernardo, 198
Hiller, Wendy, 50
Hillgartner, James, 116, 191, 246
Hillock, Jeffrey, 171
Hilton, Margaret, 199, 221
Himberg, Philip, 143
Himberg, Philip J., 144
Himelsbach, James, 112
Himes, David, 196
Hinckley, Alfred, 209, 246
Hindman, Earl, 145
Hines, Patrick, 211
Hingle, Jody, 118, 127
Hingle, Pat, 31, 46, 214, 246
Hippodrome Theatre, 209
Hirsch, Gregory A., 37
Hirsch, Jeffrey, 182
Hirsch, Judd, 42, 108, 246
Hirsch, Philip, 114
Hirson, Roger O., 61
Hitchcock, L. Joyce, 75
Hitchcock, Sam, 173
Ho, Alvin, 151
Hoad, Marianna, 202
Hoard, Bruce, 173
Hobson, I. M., 198
Hoch, Timmy, 218
Hochman, Dyanne, 21, 102, 211
Hodapp, Ann, 72, 113
Hodge, Willie, 202
Hodges, Dale, 63, 122
Hodges, David Earl, 218
Hodges, Eddie, 234
Hodges, Frenchy, 202
Hodin, Cynthia, 180
Hoefler, Charles E., 77
Hoff, Robin, 51
Hoffman, Anne, 90
Hoffman, Dustin, 158, 234
Hoffman, Henry, 186, 196, 197
Hoffman, Jane, 34, 246
Hoffman, Jay S., 72
Hoffman, Jerry, 196
Hofmann, Gert, 123
Hofsiss, Jack, 102, 211
Hogan, Frank, 71
Hogan, Jonathan, 107, 246
*Hogan's Goat*, 191
Hogarth, Meg, 184
Holamon, Ken, 123
Holbrook, Ruby, 212
Holden, Vicki S., 218
Holder, Geoffrey, 64
*Hole in the Wall Click*, 120
Holgate, Danny, 43, 162
Holiday, Leila, 72
Holladay, Cleo, 192
Holland, Anthony, 17, 246
Holland, Beth, 126
Holland, Patrick, 160
Hollander, Donn, 117, 246
Hollander, Jack, 45, 114, 246
Hollander, Owen, 113
Hollander, Sylvia, 122
Holley, Marietta, 80
Holley, Robert Bruce, 162
Holliday, David, 224, 234
Holliday, Judy, 234
Holliday, Kene, 132
Holliday, Mark, 166
Holliday, Polly, 215, 246
Hollinger, Sharon, 114, 167, 168
Hollis, John, 190
Holloman, Elaine, 162
*Hollow Crown*, 103
Holloway, Stanley, 47
Holly, John, 60, 246
Holm, Celeste, 30, 246
Holm, Hanya, 47
Holman, Bryce, 156
Holmes, Edward, 147
Holmes, Lois, 207
Holmes, Prudence Wright, 226
Holms, John P., 135
Holsclaw, Doug, 127
Holt, Fritz, 21, 36
Holt, Will, 19, 54, 89
*Holy Ghosts*, 113, 114
Holzer, Adela, 18, 44, 81, 155, 158, 171
Holzer, Carlos, 81
*Home*, 228
*Home Sweet Homer*, 8, 37
*Home, The*, 114
*Homecoming, The*, 74, 228
Homewood, Bill, 103
Honor, Jack, 185
Hood, John Robert, 227
Hooks, Bebe Drake, 10
Hooks, Robert, 124, 234

Hoot, Fred, 90
Hopkins, Anthony, 63, 247
Hopkins, Bernard, 184
Hopkins, John, 82
Hopkins, Linda, 8, 19
Hopkins, Terrence, 126
Hopwood, Avery, 143
Horen, Bob, 114, 145, 191
Horgan, Patrick, 47
Hormann, Nicholas, 105, 247
Horn, Jim, 126
Horn, John, 186, 208
Horn, Lew, 179
Horne, Cheryl, 152, 247
Horne, Geoffrey, 82
Horne, J. R., 146
Horne, Kathi, 82
Horne, Marjorie, 109, 122
Horne, Nat, 226
Horner, Pamela, 190, 204
Hornish, Rudy, 147
Horovitz, Israel, 83, 114, 206
Horowitz, Jeffrey, 207
Horrigan, Patrick, 37, 52
Horstman, Del, 54
Horton, Cindy, 120
Horton, Karl M., 55
Horton, Michael, 182
Horvath, Joe, 213
horvath, Miklos, 132, 134
Horwitz, David, 76
Horwitz, Murray, 123
Hosken, Dianne, 203
Hoskins, Fred, 207
Hoskins, Jim, 191
Hosmer, George, 192
Hossack, Grant, 22
*Hostage, The*, 208
*Hot I Baltimore, The*, 154, 187, 218, 228
Hotchkis, Joan, 197
Hotopp, Michael, 78, 113
Hoty, Dee, 199
Houghton, Katharine, 187, 234
Houlihan, Michael, 174, 204, 212, 214
House, Eric, 198
House, Jane, 194
*House of Blue Leaves, The*, 228
*House of Mirth, The*, 212
*House of Solomon, The*, 127
House, Ron, 209
Houseman, John, 91
Houser, John, 188
Houston, Gary, 206
Hovis, Joan, 234
*How to Succeed in Business without Really Trying*, 228
Howard, Alan, 103
Howard, Bette, 126
Howard, David, 129, 180, 191, 247
Howard, Dennis, 71, 226
Howard, Jason, 121
Howard, Joe, 52, 247
Howard, Ken, 8, 28, 55, 234, 247
Howard, Peter, 8
Howard, Rebecca, 84
Howard, Sidney, 140
Howell, Kay, 197
Howell, Steven T., 193
Hoxie, Richmond, 70, 75, 114, 247
Hoyt, J. C., 180
Hrkach, Joanne, 204
Hubbard, Bruce A., 55
Hubbard, Elizabeth, 121
Hubbard, Karen, 25
Hubbard, Merle, 54
Huber, Kathleen, 120
Huddle, Elizabeth, 189
Huddleston, John, 195
Huddleston, Will, 182
Hudgins, Joe, 197
Hudgins, Wayne, 65, 247
Hudson, Travis, 32, 247
Huffman, David, 196
Huffman, Dianne, 113
Huffman, Linda, 184
Hughes, Allen, 190
Hughes, Bernard, 247
Hughes, Earl, 49, 107, 108
Hughes, M. Patrick, 133
Hugill, Randy, 119, 247
*Hugo*, 223
Hugo, Laurence, 156, 247
Hugo, Victor, 110
Hulce, Thomas, 63, 138, 139, 247
Hull, Bryan, 59, 198
Hull, Katherine, 86
Hulter, Christine, 220
*Human Voice, The*, 123
Humble, Gwen, 25, 120
Hume, Michael J., 71
Hummert, James, 122, 212

Hunt, Annette, 110
Hunt, Betty Lee, 12, 20, 28, 34, 37, 41, 48, 50, 57, 60, 85, 90
Hunt, Linda, 13, 247
Hunt, Marguerite, 146
Hunt, Neil, 171
Hunt, Peter, 207
Hunt, Peter H., 164
Hunt, Ruth, 105
Hunter, Kevin, 86
Hunter, Kim, 149, 247
Hunter, Marie Goodman, 226
Hunter, Ronald, 129
Hunter, Terry, 110
Huntley, Paul, 106, 147, 148, 158
Huntress, Steve, 218
Hurband, David, 213
Hurd, Hugh L., 143
Hurdle, James, 129
Hurley, Millard, 43
Hurley, Pat, 191
Hurt, Marybeth, 128, 141, 142
Hurt, William M., 182
Husinko, Greg, 72
Husmann, Ron, 234
Hussein, Waris, 212
Hussey, Ruth, 36
Hussung, Will, 155
Hutchings, Geoffrey, 103
Hutchings, Jeannine, 217
Hutchins, Charles, 177
Hutt, Jack, 184
Hutt, Peter, 184
Hutt, William, 184
Hutter, Mark, 206
Hutton, Susan B., 223
Hyland, Frances, 213
Hyman, Charles H., 189
Hyman, Earle, 200, 226, 234, 247
Hyman, Elaine, 28, 247
Hyman, Larry, 41
Hyslop, Jeff, 160

*I Am a Camera*, 228
*I Hate the Situation More Than I Love You*, 114
*I Have a Dream*, 205
*I Knock at the Door*, 86
*I Paid My Dues*, 88
Iacangelo, Peter, 181, 247
Iagnocco, Ray, 47
Ianni, Richard, 86
Ibsen, Henrik, 46, 218, 224
*Icarus*, 221
*Ice Age*, 105
*Icebound*, 228
*Idiot's Delight*, 228
Idle, Eric, 87
Idoine, Christopher M., 216
Igdalsky, Zviah, 45
Iglesias, Loida, 160
Ignacio, Jose, 150
Ilene, Luzary, 127
Ilg, Paul, 209
*Imaginary Invalid, The*, 193
Imbarrato, Valerie Laura, 110
*Importance of Being Earnest, The*, 143, 184
*In Abraham's Bosom*, 202, 228
*In the Boom Boom Room*, 78
*In the Well of the House*, 217
*In the Wine Time*, 123
Indiana Repertory Theatre, 209
*Indians*, 188
Inescort, Frieda, 264
Ing, Alvin, 39, 247
Ingalls, James F., 227
Inge, William, 21, 199, 211
Ingham, Robert, 216
Ingram, Cheri, 218
*Inherit the Wind*, 218
Inneo, Anthony, 224
Inner City Repertory Theatre, 210
Innes, John, 184
Innes, Neil, 87
Insinnia, Albert, 60
Insull, Sigrid, 223
*Interview, The*, 220
Iovanne, Tom, 113
Iowa Theater Lab, 210
Irby, Dean, 124, 125
Ireton, Kathleen, 204
Irizarry, Gloria, 157
Irvine, Daniel, 109
Irving, George S., 52, 54, 100, 208, 247
Irwin, Wynn, 205
Isaac, Al J., 154
Isaacson, Donna, 131, 156
Isbell, Stephen, 188
Isekeit, Nelson, 199
Itkowitz, Harry, 145
Ito, Genji, 39

Itzin, Gregory, 189
*Ivanov*, 69
Ivanov, Peter, 191
Ives, Anne, 105, 247
Ives, Elizabeth, 187
Ivey, Judith, 206
*J. B.*, 228
*Jack Street*, 197
Jacklin, Joan, 98
Jacksina, Judy, 32, 45, 72
Jackson, Anne, 54
Jackson, Bonita, 169
Jackson, C. Bernard, 210
Jackson, Chequita, 207
Jackson, Ernestine, 234, 247
Jackson, George, 188
Jackson, Gregory, 98
Jackson, John C., 119
Jackson, Mary, 197
Jackson, Nagle, 216
Jackson, Reggie, 18
Jackson, Veda, 18
Jacob, Abe, 8, 14, 41, 54, 61, 71, 87, 160, 161
*Jacobowsky and the Colonel*, 228
Jacobs, Craig, 8
Jacobs, Jim, 60, 206
Jacobs, Sally, 196, 197
Jacobs, Sheldon, 70
Jacobsen, John W., 145
Jacobson, Eugene, 218
Jacobson, Sol, 70, 116, 117, 118, 119
Jacobus, Jacqueline, 11
Jacoby, Billy Jayne, 211
Jacoby, Gordon A., 123
Jacoby, Susan Jayne, 211
Jaffe, Bob, 105, 106, 114, 145
Jaffe, Monte, 95
Jakeman, Clint, 20
James, Bob, 92
James, Clark, 25
James, David, 85, 126, 144, 170
James, Debbie, 206
James, Douglas J., 119
James, Emrys, 103
James, Judith, 123
James, Katherine, 182
James, Lisa, 200
James, Mary, 234
James, Rex, 211
James, Stanley, 43, 64, 169
James, William, 47, 172, 247
Jameson, Adair, 177
Jameson, Colin, 177
Jameson, Jo Anne, 183
Jampolis, Neil Peter, 98, 171, 198
Jamrog, Joseph, 69, 126, 214, 247
Janda, Donald, 195
Janek, James, 162, 166, 172
Janis, Conrad, 66, 234, 247
Janney, Ben, 18
Jansen, Christine, 143
Jansen, Jim, 247
Jarkowsky, Andrew, 106
Jaroschy, Michel, 195
Jaroslow, Ruth, 127, 247
Jarowsky, Andrew, 145, 247
Jarret, Bella, 188
Jarrett, Bella, 190
Jarrett, Jerry, 89, 207, 247
Jarus, Tom, 110
Jason, Mitchell, 52
Jason, Rick, 234
Jasper, Zina, 225
Jay, Roger, 17
Jay, William, 135, 191, 207
*Jazz Babies*, 123
Jeakins, Dorothy, 196
Jeannette, Gertrude, 12, 247
Jeans, Joan M., 67
Jebens, Jennifer Herrick, 121
*Jeff Peters Photos*, 126
Jefferson, Emily, 117
Jefferson, Herbert, Jr., 212
Jellison, John B., 45
Jemima, 143
Jenkins, Carol Mayo, 209, 220, 224
Jenkins, David, 95, 174, 194, 212, 214
Jenkins, Ken, 187
Jenkins, Mark, 197
Jenkins, Marvin, 54
Jenkins, Richard, 225
Jenkins, Timothy, 204
Jenkins, Trent, 188
Jenn, Stephen, 103, 247
Jennifer, John, 232
Jennings, Brent, 135

Jennings, Byron, 196
Jennings, Eulaula, 25
Jennings, Gwen, 130
Jennings, Kathy, 25
Jennings, Robert W., 164
Jensen, David, 179
Jensen, Don, 88, 89
Jensen, John, 194
Jensen, Mary Ann, 179
Jernigan, Vernon, 151
Jerome, Timothy, 62
*Jesse and the Bandit Queen*,
   8, 134, 229
Jessup, Reginald, 103
Jestin, Jennifer, 207
Jillson, Joyce, 234
Jines, Lee, 122
*Jinxs Bridge*, 135
Jobin, Peter, 213
Jockers, Bob, 153
Joe, Jeanne, 210
Johanson, Don, 51
Johanson, Robert, 65, 183
*John*, 121
*John Brown's Body*, 180
John, Carl, 224
John F. Kennedy Center for
   the Performing Arts,
   211
John, Flozanne, 191
John, Michael, 51
John, Tom H., 64
Johns, David, 224
Johns, Everett, 126
Johnson, Alan, 49, 52
Johnson, Bernard, 43, 169
Johnson, Bill, 195
Johnson, Bosha, 143
Johnson, Cora, 18
Johnson, Dan, 193
Johnson, David Cale, 65
Johnson, Don, 51, 187
Johnson, Dotts, 11, 247
Johnson, Edguard, 179
Johnson, Greg, 145
Johnson, Janet, 196, 197
Johnson, Jorge, 126
Johnson, Jory, 136
Johnson, Ken, 195
Johnson, Kurt, 41, 119
Johnson, Kwame, 64
Johnson, Louis, 18
Johnson, Mel, Jr., 158, 207
Johnson, Michael, 210
Johnson, Nunnally, 208
Johnson, Page, 63, 234,
   247
Johnson, Patricia, 69
Johnson, Reginald Vel, 129,
   181
Johnson, Richard Beeson,
   122
Johnson, Richard M., 197
Johnson, Robert, 198
Johnson, Sarita, 180
Johnson, Sheri L., 180
Johnson, Stephen, 191
Johnson, Susan, 234
Johnson, Tabby, 213
Johnstad, Randy, 186
Johnston, Gail, 224
Johnston, J. J., 206
Johnston, Lanni, 198
Johnston, Ron, 143
Johnstone, Chris, 190
Jonah, Dolly, 89
Jonas, Darrell, 62
Jonas, Joanne, 11
Jonay, Roberta, 264
Jones, B. J., 203
Jones, Barbara O., 210
Jones, Carolyne A., 43
Jones, Charlotte, 12, 40,
   247
Jones, Cheryl, 135
Jones, Cliff, 41
Jones, David C., 184, 225
Jones, Dennis, 73
Jones, Douglas, 198
Jones, Eddy, 145
Jones, Franz, 120
Jones, Gary, 109
Jones, James Earl, 234,
   248
Jones, Jeffrey, 80, 128,
   141, 181, 190, 248
Jones, Jen, 113
Jones, John Christopher,
   181, 224
Jones, John Frederick, 179
Jones, Jonathan Howard,
   86, 224
Jones, Kathy, 133
Jones, Keith, 218
Jones, Kender, 119, 248
Jones, Lauren, 234
Jones, Llewellyn, 98
Jones, Margaret, 173
Jones, Mary Sue, 201
Jones, Marzetta, 124
Jones, Melanie, 225
Jones, Nina, 183

Jones, Philip L., 182
Jones, Preston, 199, 201,
   206, 211
Jones, Robbee, 143
Jones, Shami, 208
Jones, Terry, 87
Jones, Tom, 152, 168
Jones, Walt, 227
Jones, Wanda Jean, 151
Jones-DeBroux, Lee, 197
Jones,Jeffrey, 142
Joplin, Scott, 18
Jordan, Alan, 180
Jordan, Eddie, 169
Jordan, John, 234
Jordan, Marc, 59
Jordan, Melvin, 18
Jory, Jon, 182, 187, 189
Jory, Terrill, 37
Jory, Victor, 187
Joseph, Irving, 171
Joseph Jefferson Theatre
   Company, 121
Joseph, Meryl, 126
Joseph, Michael, 202
Joseph, Stephen, 191
Joslyn, Betsy, 152, 248
Joslyn, Donald, 89
Joy, Toni, 179
Joyce, Dorothea, 137
Joyce, Elaine, 234
Joyce, Robert, 41
Joyce, Shelley, 209
Joyce, Stephen, 58, 208,
   234, 248
Joyce, Timothy K., 209
*Judas-Pax*, 210
Judge, Don, 32
Judge, Ian, 103
Julia, Raul, 133, 248
Julian, Emile, 119
Julian, Peter, 116, 248
Juliano, Frank, 123
*Julius Caesar*, 143
*Jumpers*, 221
Jun, Irena, 104, 224
Jun, Rose Marie, 100
Jung, Calvin, 138, 139,
   140, 248
Jung, Philipp, 117
Jung, Rose H., 180
Jung-en, Liu, 206
Junkin, Don, 184
*Juno and the Paycock*, 188
Jurado, Katy, 155
*Just Between Us*, 80
Kachadoorian, Zubek, 202
Kacher, Bunny, 35, 248
Kadaster, Mustafa, 167
Kadison, Luba, 72
Kafka, Franz, 110
Kagan, Diane, 75, 126, 248
Kahl, Jean, 220
Kahn, Michael, 174, 205,
   214
Kahn, Stan, 116
Kaikkonen, Gus, 63, 69,
   206
Kaine, Paul, 82, 123, 143,
   144
Kaiser, Kevin, 172
Kalcheim, Lee, 191, 199
Kaledin, Nicholas, 183
Kalem, Toni, 110, 122,
   123, 127
Kalfin, Robert, 20, 75, 76,
   105
Kallan, Randi, 172
Kallman, Dick, 234
Kalman, Bruce, 195
Kaminsky, Joe, 111
Kaminsky, Stanley F., 52,
   155, 156
Kamlot, Robert, 129, 132,
   133, 135, 136, 137
Kampley, Linda, 18
Kampmann, Ears, 151
Kan, Lilah, 116
*Kander & Ebb Cabaret, A*,
   123
Kander, John, 8, 54, 123,
   146
Kane, Michael, 185
Kanin, Garson, 54, 203,
   207
Kanter, David Robert, 215
Kapen, Ben, 138, 140,
   212, 248
Kapilow, Susan, 213
Kaplan, Ellen, 146
Kaplan, Herbert, 98, 126,
   136
Kaplan, Jeanne, 127, 155
Kaplan, Jordan, 114
Kaplan, Nicki, 123
Kaplan, Randy, 39
Kaplan, Stan, 120
Kaplan, Wendy, 76
Karam, Elena, 35
Karcher, Jack, 47
Karen, James, 48
Karin, Rita, 20, 248
Karl, Alfred, 33, 155

Karlowski, Kris, 55
Karnes, Lee, 199
Karniewich, A. T., 61
Karnilova, Maria, 54
Karnowsky, Bill, 143
Karp, Arthur, 174, 214
Karpen, Pat, 190
Karpova, Tamara, 82
Karr, Patti, 61, 248
Karzynska, Aleksandra, 104
Kasarda, John, 218
Kass, Alan, 248
Kassul, Art, 203
Kates, Bernard, 209
Katsaros, Douglas, 41
Katt, William, 196
Katz, Stephen P., 180
Kaufman, Alan, 91
Kaufman, Charles, 207
Kaufman, Don, 157
Kaufman, George S., 36,
   145, 146, 196, 211,
   214, 218
Kava, Caroline, 95, 133,
   248
Kavanagh, Joseph, 106
Kavanaugh, Richard, 225
Kavanaugh, Tony, 88
Kavy, Linda, 117
Kavy, Lynda, 119
Kay, Hershy, 14, 55, 160,
   161
Kay, Lloyd, 110, 180
Kayahara, Lauren, 14
Kaye, Irma, 153
Kaye, Lloyd, 110
Kaye, Robert R., 157
Kaye, Stubby, 248
Kazoo, Bessie Lou, 69
Keal, Anita, 194
Kean, Norman, 27, 89
Keane, George, 234
Keane, Teri, 107
Kearsley, Barry, 63
Kearsley, Kimberly Francis,
   187
Keathley, George, 50, 206,
   211
Keating, Barry, 143
Keaton, Diane, 83
Keck, John W., 68
Kedrick, Geraldine, 113
Kee, Elizabeth, 94
Keefe, Anne, 212
Keeler, Mark, 114
Keen, Clinton, 41, 169
Keen, Elizabeth, 174, 181
Keen, Stan, 186
Keenan, Michael, 221
Keene, Jay B., 114
Keep, Stephen, 148, 149,
   248
Keever, Tom, 127
Kehr, Donald, 57
Keitel, Harvey, 11
Kell, Michael, 122, 132,
   212, 248
Keller, Jeff, 248
Keller, Karen, 117
Keller, May, 117, 248
Keller, Susan, 218
Kellermann, Annette, 264
Kellery, Kate, 12, 248
Kelley, James, 176
Kelley, Peter, 234
Kelley, Trueman, 114
Kellin, Mike, 80, 248
Kellner, Peggy, 179
Kellogg, Marjorie, 11, 38,
   122, 207, 212, 214
Kellstrom, Gail, 123
Kelly, Christopher, 64
Kelly, Danny, 190
Kelly, Ellen, 110
Kelly, Frank, 122, 143, 144
Kelly, George, 212
Kelly, Grace, 234
Kelly, K. C., 165
Kelly, Margot, 264
Kelly, Mark M., 146
Kelly, Steven, 12
Kelly, Terence, 184
Kelton, Gene, 71
Kelton, Richard, 8, 48, 230,
   232, 248
Kemmerling, Michael, 75
Kemp, Brandis, 209
Kemp, Emme, 43
Kemp, Sally, 196
Kenan, Dolores, 114, 143,
   248
Kendrick, Henry, 186
Kenne, Jay, 114
Kennedy, Arthur, 11
Kennedy, Dennis, 206
Kennedy, Harold J., 44
Kennedy, Judith, 182
Kennedy, Kathleen, 73
Kennedy, Laurie, 196
Kennedy, Mimi, 60, 248
*Kennedy's Children*, 8, 24,
   165, 184, 221
Kennison, Gail, 144

Kennon-Wilson, James, 25
Kent, Daryn, 180
Kenyon, Neal, 191
Kerman, David, 110
Kermizian, Keith, 113
Kern, Daniel, 189
Kern, Jerome, 32
Kern, Teddy, 75
Kerns, Jane, 73
Kerr, Berrilla, 107
Kerr, Charles, 187
Kerr, Deborah, 156
Kerr, Elaine, 214
Kerr, John, 234
Kerr, Philip, 214, 227
Kert, Larry, 26, 248
Kessler, Howard, 113
Kessler, Woody, 52
Kessler, Zale, 196
Keter, Shanit, 67
Ketron, Larry, 123
Kettermaster, John, 203
Kevin, Michael, 187
Key-Aberg, Sandro, 114
Keyes, Daniel, 234
Keyes, Earl, 199
Keys, Chip, 149
Keys, Henson, 129, 191,
   208, 248
Keysar, Franklin, 95, 97,
   98, 211
Keyser, Andy, 61, 160, 161
Keys-Hall, Michael, 189
Kezer, Glenn, 133, 248
Khabeera, Aisha, 205
Khan, Faizul, 126
Khanzadian, Anita, 143,
   145
Kheel, Lee, 120
Kibbe, Alan, 217
Kibbee, Roland, 37
Kidder, Ruth, 186
Kiernan, James, 264
Kiker, Dorothea, 195
Kikuchi, Susan, 39
Kilberg, Richard, 108
Kilburn, Terence, 215
Kilden, Elaine, 112
Kiley, Richard, 8, 50, 234,
   248
Killam, Tracy, 107
Killmer, Nancy, 52, 248
Kilpatrick, Empress, 153
Kim, Randall Duk, 227
Kim, Willa, 98
Kimbrough, Charles, 141,
   142, 248
Kimmins, Kenneth, 62, 248
Kindl, Charles, 156, 211
*King and I, The*, 228
King, Buddy, 170
King, Catherine, 191
King, Elizabeth, 215
King, John Michael, 234
King, Lawrence, 223
King, Lawrence, 44, 75, 76,
   106, 145
*King Lear*, 174, 183, 191,
   216
King, Mabel, 64
King, Ramona, 124
King, Richard, 70
*King Richard III*, 177
King, Terri, 181
King, Woodie, Jr., 10, 84
Kingery, Larry, 86
Kingsley, Evelyn, 72
Kingsley, Peter, 248
Kingsley, Susan Cardwell,
   187
Kingwill, Jay, 24, 35, 83,
   153, 165
Kinne, David, 177
Kinney, Debbie, 86
Kinney, Jean Marie, 221
Kinsella, Marion, 18
Kinser-Lau, Patrick, 39
Kinter, Richard, 185
Kipness, Joseph, 41, 83
Kipnis, Leonard, 94
Kirby, John Mason, 59, 155
Kirchner, Liza, 133
Kiriakos, Jack, 173
Kirk, Lisa, 44, 249
Kirkham, Willi, 114
Kirkland, James, 226
Kirkland, Molly, 87
Kirkland, Sally, 165
Kirkpatrick, Bill, 82
Kirksey, Dianne, 135
Kirkwood, Diana, 171
Kirkwood, James, 14, 160,
   161
Kirsch, Carolyn, 14, 249
Kirsch, Dan, 185
Kirsch, Rick, 180
Kirwin, Frederick, 143
Kiser, Terry, 234, 249
Kisley, Douglas, 180
*Kismet*, 228
Kisner, Meribeth, 52
*Kiss Me, Kate*, 228

*Kiss the World Goodbye*,
   114
Kissel, David, 107
Kitchen, Heather, 184
Kitchings, Margaret, 120
Kitzrow, Richard, 196
Kizziah, K. C., 249
Kladitis, Mannie, 91, 92,
   93, 94
Klassel, Barry, 191
Kleban, Edward, 14, 160,
   161, 232
Klein, I. W., 121
Klein, Louise, 145
Klein, Marjie, 143, 144,
   145
Klein, Neal, 224
Klein, Ricki, 146
Klein, Ron, 114
Klein, Stewart, 232
Kleinman, Sheldon, 193
Kleman, Vic, 220
Klenck, Margaret, 175
Kline, Kevin, 91, 92, 93,
   94, 249
Kline, Richard, 198, 204
Kling, Irene Frances, 114
Klinghoffer, Rona, 110
Klitzkie, Linn, 190
Klotz, Florence, 39, 57
Klotz, Jeffrey H., 180
Klunis, Tom, 185
Kneebone, Tom, 184
Kneeland, Richard, 225
Knickel, Wayne, 205
Knight, Gary, 146
Knight, Martha, 135, 164
Knight, Shirley, 8, 24, 165,
   249
Knill, Paul, 221
Knittel, Wolfgang, 89
Knoblauch, M. T., 76
*Knock Knock*, 8, 42, 108,
   231
Knode, Charles, 87
Knowlton, Warren, 18, 49,
   56, 77, 81
Knox, John, 202
Knudson, Kurt, 149, 158,
   249
Koch, William, 118, 121
Koehler, D. W., 129, 133
Koetting, Daniel, 128, 148,
   149
Kohn, Marvin, 157
Kolb, Greg, 208
Kolba, Atsumi, 31, 46
Kolba, Michael, 113, 149,
   249
Kolberg, Sharon, 31, 46
Kolo, Krystyna, 104
Kolodziejczyk, Krystyna,
   104
Kologi, Mark, 21, 78, 249
Kon, George, 210
Konowitz, Arlene, 24
Kootsher, Alan Lee, 86
Kopelman, Charles, 144,
   145
Kopp, Fred, 170
Kopp, Lee, 193
Koppmeier, Keith, 51
Korb, Marsha, 187
Kordos, Richard S., 203
Koren, Daniel V., 213
Kornbluth, Jerry, 97, 151
Kornfeld, Lawrence, 227
Kornman, Cam, 74
Korol, Taras, 213
Korthaze, Richard, 8, 61
Kossez, Robes, 44
Kostal, Irwin, 51
Kotlisky, Marge, 206
Kovacevich, Glenn, 206
Kozak, Ellen M., 216
Kozik, Peter, 127
Kozlovska, Ewa, 104, 224
Krafchick, David, 180
Kraft, Barry, 179
Kraft, Hyman, 264
Kraft, Leonard, 206
Kramer, Joel, 249
Kramer, Terry Allen, 42
Kranz, Ben D., 157
Krasna, Norman, 203
Kraus, Philip, 63, 249
Krause, Mark, 159, 214
Krauss, Marvin A., 38, 59
Kravat, Annie, 112
Krawczyk, Michael, 216
Krawitz, Patricia McLean,
   40, 47, 55, 88
Krawitz, Seymour, 40, 47,
   55, 73, 88, 174
Krebs, Susan, 69
Kreindel, Mitch, 209
Kreitzberg, Danny, 249
Krell, Sally, 120
Krempetz, Ronald E., 193
Kreppel, Paul, 77, 181
Kresley, Edmond, 162
Kressyn, Miriam, 72
Krider, Dik, 10, 124, 125

Kristen, Ilene, 60
Krizman, Greg, 199
Kroeger, Perry, 180, 196
Kron, Gustaw, 104
Krone, Gerald S., 10
Krug, John, 152
Kruger, Otto, 36
Krupska, Dania, 51
Kruse, Bert, 167
Kruse, Carolyn, 144
Kubiak, Ted, 69
Kubiak, Tom, 83, 249
Kuczewski, Ed, 75
Kudelka, Jan, 184
Kuhlman, Ron, 14, 161, 249
Kuhni, Chris, 177
Kulok, Peter T., 156
Kulukundis, Eddie, 22, 171
Kupfer, Fritz, 220
Kuratomi, Lynn, 210
Kurland, Rachel, 208
Kurowski, Ron, 160
Kurt Weill Cabaret, A, 89
Kurth, Peter, 175
Kurtz, Mitchell, 90, 214
Kurtz, Swoosie, 13, 122, 212, 218, 249
Kurz, Stephanie, 21
Kuss, Richard, 35
Kutee, 210
Kutz, Dawn, 218
Kux, William L., 186
Kuypers, C. V., 114
Kvares, Don, 151
Kwiat, David, 191
La Caratula, 150
La Compania De Marionetas De Bogota, 150
La Malquerida, 150
La Noche De Los Asesinos, 115
La Padula, Nick, 82
La Padura, Jason, 21
La Relacion, 115
La Revolucion, 150
La Ronde, 146, 192
La Senorita Julia, 115
La Tirenta, Paul, 155
Lacey, Margo, 86
LaChapelle, Carol, 194
Lack, John, 143
LaCourse, Michael, 67, 71
Ladd, Diane, 211
Ladd, Margaret, 123, 218
Laden, David, 135
Ladson, Rick, 71
Lady from the Sea, The, 8, 46
Lady, Robb, 60
Lady's Not for Burning, The, 180, 228
LaFerla, Sandro, 147
Lafferty, Thom, 137
LaFortune, Felicity, 206
Lagerfelt, Carolyn, 148
LaGioia, John, 127
LaGrange, Eileen, 117
LaGue, Michael, 217
Lahm, Rosalie, 30
Lahti, Christine, 70
Laing, Alan, 184
Lalli, Richard, 16
Lam, Diane, 39, 249
Lamagna, Gary, 207
Lamb, Larry, 184
Lamb, Myrna, 137
Lambert, Sherry, 65, 68, 69
Lambert, William, 114
Lamm, Catherine Henry, 106, 145, 249
Lamont, Robin, 249
Lampel, Bob, 167
Lamppost Reunion, 8, 16, 229
Lancaster, Burt, 234
Lancaster, Lucie, 61, 249
Lanchester, Robert, 216
Landers, Matt, 60, 249
Landis, Jeanette, 198, 220
Landon, Daniel, 119, 249
Landon, Hal, Jr., 197
Landon, Sofia, 118
Landow-Lewis, Brett, 69
Landrin, Lori, 200
Landron, Jack, 187
Lane, Dickson, 173
Lane, Ernie, 203
Lane, Nancy, 14, 161, 249
Lane, Robin, 67
Lang, Barbara, 52
Lang, Bernard, 49
Lang, Charles, 234
Lang, Pat, 205
Lang, Phil, 47
Lang, Stephen, 129, 181
Langan, Dan, 78
Lange, John, 150
Langner, Armina Marshall, 116
Langner, Lawrence, 116

Langston Hughes Said, 210
Lankester, Michael, 171
Lanning, Jerry, 8, 47, 214, 232, 234, 249
Lansbury, Angela, 232
Lansbury, Edgar, 62, 154
Lansden, Sarah Fairfax, 180
Lansing, John, 60, 249
Lanwehr, Hugh, 207
Lanzaroni, Bhen, 195
LaPadula, Nick, 16
LaPadura, Jason, 21
Lapka, Betsy, 116, 249
LaPlount, Craig, 149
Large, Graham, 49
Larkin, Christopher, 70
Larkin, James, 69
Larkin, Peter, 81
Larkin, Sheena, 184
Larkins, Grady, 187, 190
LaRosa, William, 180
Larrea, Joseph, 173
Larsen, Lance, 200
Larsen, William, 174, 214
Larson, Andrea, 146
Larson, Duncan, 209
Larson, Paul, 214
Larson, Peter M., 59
Larson, Philip, 196, 197
Larsson, Scott, 206
LaRusso, Louis II, 16
Las Aceitunas, 150
Lasky, Zane, 249
Last Christians, The, 126
Last Meeting of the Knights of the White Magnolia, The, 187, 188, 199, 206, 211, 217, 218, 221, 222
Last Meeting of the White Magnolia, The, 187
Last of the Red Hot Lovers, 67, 203
Latella, Denise, 203
Latesa, Dick, 122
Latessa, Dick, 122
Lathan, Bill, 135
Latham, Elizabeth, 154, 249
Lathrop, Alton, 43
Latimer, Kathleen, 201
Latimer, Ken, 201
Latouche, John, 76
Lauck, Joe Dalton, 167
Laughlin, Sharon, 50, 127, 143, 249
Lauren, Amelia, 177
Laurence, Gil, 200
Laurence, James Howard, 209
Laurence, Paula, 224
Laurencelle, Hank, 79
Laurie, Fern, 86
Laurie, Piper, 31
Laurie, Sallie, 201
Lauter, Linda, 198
LaVallee, Sandra, 36
Laveau, Albert, 194
Laveau, Lynette, 194
LaVelle, Pat, 143
Lavin, Linda, 181, 227, 234, 249
Lavin, Ric, 17, 114
Lavine, W. Robert, 47
Lavren, Christine, 123, 249
Lawder, Anne, 189
Lawless, Sue, 113, 249
Lawlor, Barbara, 213
Lawlor, David, 36
Lawlor, Eileen, 98
Lawner, Mordecai, 11, 224
Lawrence, Anna, 151
Lawrence, Carol, 234
Lawrence, Darrie, 113, 114
Lawrence, Delphi, 163
Lawrence, Elizabeth, 40, 249
Lawrence, James, 180
Lawrence, Jeremy, 187
Lawrence, Jerome, 199
Lawrence, Peter, 74
Lawrence, Vera Brodsky, 18
Lawson, David, 41
Lawson, Peter, 195
Layne, Mary, 36, 101, 179, 214, 249
Lazarus, Bruce, 126
Lazarus, Joe, 143
Le Bellybutton, 86
Le Brun, Barbara, 98
Le Gallienne, Eva, 3, 8, 36
Le Massena, William, 211
Le Relacion, 115
Lea, Barbara, 72, 119, 249, 72Me
Leach, William, 191, 208
Leachman, Cloris, 234
Leaf, Paul, 100
Leaf People, The, 17
League, Janet, 10, 249

League of New York Theatre Owners and Producers, The, 8
Leahy, Jeannette, 203
Leary, David, 63, 122, 123, 190
Leatherman, Allen, 199
Leatherman, Barbara, 199
Leavee, Kenneth, 200
Lebow, Will, 78
Lebowitz, Marilyn, 133
Lebowsky, Stanley, 8
LeBrun, Barbara, 98
Lederer, Richard, 171
Lederer, Suzanne, 13, 212
Ledet, Shana, 218
Lee, Angela, 126
Lee, Baayork, 14, 161
Lee, Bobby, 154
Lee, Charles, 221
Lee, Eugene, 12, 194, 225
Lee, Evan, 176
Lee, Franne, 12
Lee, Irving, 41, 61, 249
Lee, Jae Woo, 39
Lee, Jason, 179
Lee, Jennifer Ann, 160
Lee, Kaiulani, 24, 165
Lee, Leslie, 10
Lee, Linda, 43
Lee, Ming Cho, 31, 190
Lee, Nora, 205
Lee, Paul, 199
Lee, Robert E., 199
Lee, Wayne, 182
Lee, Will, 207
Leempoor, Xantheus Roh, 17
Lees, Carol, 227
Lefevbre, Larry, 213
Leffingwell, Laurie, 151
LeGallienne, Eva, 7, 36, 101, 214, 249
Legend, 57
LeGrand, Lissa, 173
LeGrande, John Bryson, 206
Lehane, Gregory, 178
Lehmann, Jo Ann, 49, 153
Lehne, John, 205
Lehrman, Mike, 208
Leib, Russell, 218
Leiber, Jerry, 76
Leibick, Laine, 195
Leibick, Sandy, 195
Leibman, Ron, 8, 136, 249
Leicester, Bridget, 109
Leigh, Christian, 189
Leigh, Dan, 72
Leigh, Janet, 34, 249
Leigh, Mitch, 37, 166
Leighton, Betty, 218
Leighton, Margaret, 264
Lema, Julia, 78
Lemans, Cheryl, 202
LeMassena, William, 158, 215, 218, 219, 250
Leming, Warren, 206
Lemon, Dianemarie, 153
Lenard, Mark, 145
Lenert, Marguerite, 225
Lenhart Leanna, 164
Lenk, Vivian, 167
Lenk, Vivienne, 167
Lennon, Fritz, 201
LeNoire, Rosetta, 36, 43, 214, 250
Lenz, Richard, 196, 214
Leo, Jamie, 210
Leo, Tom, 112
Leob, Eric, 35
Leon, Dorothy, 60
Leon, Joseph, 206, 218, 250
Leonard, Bob, 188
Leonard, Lu, 59
Leonard, Michael, 60
Leonard, Richard, 172
Leonardos, Urylee, 55, 250
Leone, William A., 167
Leonelli, Leslie, 67
Leontovich, Eugenie, 74
Leopold, Thomas, 13
LePlat, Ted, 17
Lepsinger, Debbie, 100
Lerner, Alan Jay, 47, 55
Lerner, Melanie, 166
LeRoux, Madeleine, 221
LeRoy, Zoaunne, 221
Lerstrom, Marjorie, 226
Leschin, Luisa, 150
Lesis, Edwina, 153
Lesko, John, 52
Leslie, Bob, 190
Leslie, Charles, 72
Leslie, Karen, 148
Lessac, Michael, 111
Lessane, Leroy, 207
Lesser, Gene, 190
Lesser, Robert, 122, 208
Lester, Barbara, 214, 218
Lester, Carl Blackwell, 226
Lester, Hugh, 190, 204
Lester, Ketty, 234

Leston, Ernesto, 112
LeStrange, Philip, 191
Let My People Come, 153
Letner, Ken, 226
Letta, 11
Levan, Frank, 69
Leveen, Amy F., 116, 118
Levene, Sam, 8, 36, 54, 101, 214, 250
Leveridge, Lynn Ann, 20
Leversee, Loretta, 234
Levian, Lauren, 187
Levin, Charles, 227
Levin, Herman, 47
Levin, Peter, 212
Levine, David M., 204
Levine, Elliot, 79
LeVine, Marilynn, 18, 30, 44, 49, 56, 81, 171
Levine, Peggy, 114
Levine, Susan, 180
Levinsky, Walt, 27
Levitin, Nicholas, 127
Levition, Stewart, 103
Levitt, Harriet, 217
Levitt, Robert Jeffrey, 180
Levy, Jacques, 122
Levy, Jay, 21
Levy, Marty, 151
Levy, Ned, 152
Levy, Owen, 10
Lewellen, Kirby, 79
Lewis, Allan, 174
Lewis, Bobo, 165
Lewis, Claudia, 64
Lewis, E. Bonnie, 182
Lewis, Edwina, 153
Lewis, Irene, 207
Lewis, Jeremy, 143
Lewis, Laura May, 74
Lewis, Mark, 220
Lewis, Norman, 73
Lewis, Pamela, 191
Lewis, Richard, 197
Lewis, Ron, 125
Lewis, Steven Pamela, 143
Lewis, Sydney, 169
Lewis, Tarina, 180
Lewis-Jones, Nick, 221
Leyden, Leo, 30, 250
L'Heureux, Judith, 123
Liberatore, L., 166
Liberman, Bill, 102
Libertini, Richard, 83
Libin, Paul, 11, 13, 31, 44, 46
Licht, David, 185
Lichtefeld, Michael, 55
Lichtenberg, Andrew, 199
Lichtenstein, Harvey, 101
Lichtenstein, Todd, 117
Lide, Miller, 36, 214, 250
Lieber, Paul, 143, 144
Lieberman, Richard, 207
Liebman, Laura, 198
Liebman, Ron, 234
Life Class, 122
Life Is Like a Musical Comedy, 123
Life of Christ, The, 176
Lifschitz, Alan, 83
Light, David, 264
Light, Judith, 134, 208
Light, Karl, 214
Light, Laverne, 183
Light Up the Sky, 192
Ligon, Tom, 126
Lihamba, Amandina, 78
Lilla, David, 58
Lillard, Chenault, 209
Lilly, Joy, 71
Lilly, Terry, 42, 86
Lily and the Rose, The, 120
Lincoln, Donald, 81
Lincks, Beth, 191
Lincoln, Steve, 67
Lincoln, Tony, 206
Lindbloom, Ron, 144
Lindell, Marion, 127
Linden, Robert, 28
Linderman, Ed, 59
Lindhart, Rachael, 226
Lindig, Jillian, 110, 156, 208, 250
Lindner, Richard, 137
Lindo, Delroy, 213
Lindsay, George, 227
Lindsay, Philip, 12, 35
Lindsay, Priscilla, 209
Lindsay, Randy, 221
Lindsay, Vachel, 80
Lindsey, Jonathon, 221
Lindsey, Kathleen, 190
Lindstrom, William C., 188
Link, Peter, 128, 181
Link, Ron, 88
Linke, Paul, 200
Linker, Chuck, 196
Linn, Bambi, 234
Linn, Steve, 176
Linn, Steven, 176
Linney, Romulus, 114

Lintner, Robert, 117, 250
Linton, John-Peter, 213
Lipari, Joanna, 123
Lipp, Frieda, 126
Lippman, Petder, 42
Lippman, Sidney, 155
Lipscomb, Dennis, 106, 145, 175, 185, 250
Lipson, Clifford, 62
Lipson, Paul, 122, 127, 250
Lisa, Luba, 234
Lischner, Rose, 119, 121
Liscinsky, Michael, 184
Listman, Ryan, 250
Lithgow, John, 128, 138, 139, 141, 142, 181, 250
Littell, Philip, 20, 223
Litten, Jim, 51
Little, Cleavon, 8, 38, 250
Little, David, 45, 250
Little, Eugene, 64
Little Foxes, The, 198, 215, 225
Little Night Music, A, 224, 228
Little, Ron Paul, 250
Littleman, Anita, 18
Litton, Rita, 175
Liu, Frank Michael, 210
Livin' Fat, 125
Living Together, 28
Livingston, Barry, 12
Livingston, Robert H., 143
Livingston, Ruth, 119, 250
Llowell, Odysseus, 177
Lloyd, Christopher, 81, 212
Lloyd, George, 121
Lloyd, James, 221
Lloyd, Sherman, 36, 214
Lo Presto, Charles, 40
Lobban, Lynn, 67
Lobdell, Peter, 63
Lobenstein, Drew, 197
Loblanco, Tony, 250
Local Stigmatic, The, 206
Locke, Sally, 82
Locker, Janet, 206
Lockhart, June, 234
Lockhart, Warren, 172
Loden, Barbara, 69, 234
Lodge, Linda, 127
Lodick, Michael, 88
Loeb, Eric, 35
Loewe, Frederick, 47
Logan, John, 201
Logan, Joshua, 211
Logan, Rebecca, 201
Logan, Susan, 35
Logan, Susan Kay, 35
Logue, Dolores, 220
Logue, Spain, 137
Lombardo, Guy, 8
Lombino, Norman, 214
Lombo, Bobby, 162
London, Charles, 42, 107, 108, 122, 123
London, Howard, 225
Londono, Victoria, 150
Lonergan, Michael, 197
Long, Avon, 8, 43, 250
Long, Bob, 98
Long Day's Journey into Night, 8, 102, 182, 190, 209, 211, 228
Long, Glenn, 195
Long, John, 220
Long, Ronald, 179
Long, Sue, 218
Long Wharf Theatre, 212
Longbottom, Robert, 117
Look Back in Anger, 228
Look Homeward, Angel, 191, 228
Looney, Peter, 118, 250
Lopata, Andy, 137
Loper, Robert B., 186
Lopez, Lillian, 43
Lopez, Pedro Del, 150
Lopez, Priscilla, 8, 14, 61, 161
Lopez, Rafael, 197
Loquasto, Santo, 24, 34, 57, 129, 165, 181, 190, 207
Lorberbaum, Larry, 127
Lorca, Federico Garcia, 150
Lord, Gloria, 78
Lord, Jack, 234
Lorden, Joe, 50, 166
Loring, Rande, 173
Loring, Estelle, 234
Lorring, Joan, 214
Lortel, Lucille, 84
Los Habladores, 150
Los Soles Truncos, 150
Losch, Tilly, 264
Lothe-Stanislawska, Wanda, 104
Loti, Elisa, 234
Lott, Larry C., 214
Loudon, Dorothy, 234

Louise, Mary, 25
Louise, Sara, 119, 250
Love and Intrigue, 149
Love, Andre, 36
Love Death Plays of William Inge, The, 69
Love of Four Colonels, The, 228
Lovejoy, Robin, 201
Love's Labours Lost, 177
Lovett, Marjorie, 117, 250
Lovett, Steve, 201
Lowe, John H., Ill., 61
Lowell, Joan, 143, 145
Lowell, Robert, 98, 206
Lowman, Jay, 224
Lownds, Peter, 98
Lowry, Jane, 81, 223
Lowther, Michael, 186
Lowy, Donald Bondy, 227
Lu Ann Hampton Laverty Oberlander, 211
Lubin, Harold, 8
Lucas, Christopher, 62
Lucas, Craig, 51, 65
Lucas, J. Frank, 143
Lucas, Jeremy, 81
Lucas, John, 164
Lucas, Jonathan, 234
Lucia, Chip, 106, 145
Luciano, Bob, 145
Luckacovic, John Philip, 224
Luckenbach, Trey, 88
Luckinbill, Laurence, 196
Ludlam, Charles, 82
Ludlow, Susan, 186, 221
Lugenbeal, Carol Jo, 51
Luhrman, Henry, 42, 86
Luiken, Carol, 190
Lukaszewicz, Richard, 198
Lukather, Suzanne, 41
Lum, Alvin, 116, 250
Luman, David Stanley, 198
Lumley, Terry, 196
Lumsden, Mary, 79
Lund, John, 234
Lundell, Kert F., 41, 55, 69, 97, 194, 214
Luneeta, Sam, 208
Lunsford, Margaret, 192
Lupino, Richard, 250
LuPone, Patti, 91, 92, 93, 94, 250
LuPone, Robert, 7, 14, 62, 161
Lurie, Victor, 18, 30, 171
Lust, 127
Lustberg, Arch, 76
Lutes, Betty, 224
Lutzky, Dan, 110
Lydiard, Robert, 126
Lyman, Debra, 47, 250
Lyman, Dorothy, 212
Lymann, Libby, 126
Lymworth Millions, The, 143
Lynch, Charles O., 194, 196
Lynch, Claudia, 224
Lynch, Richard, 46, 250
Lynch, Skipp, 44
Lynd, Betty, 12
Lyndeck, Edmond, 126
Lyndeck, Edmund, 131, 156, 250
Lyndon, Nicholas Wolff, 137
Lynley, Carol, 234
Lynn, Anne, 207
Lynn, Gloria, 203
Lynn, Paula, 41
Lynner, Brian, 180
Lyon, Eve, 185
Lyon, Milton, 193
Lyon, Wendy, 113
Lythcott, Adeyemi, 250
M. Gorky: A Portrait, 71
Mabry, Mary, 221
MacAdam, Adam, 82
MacArthur, Charles, 208
MacArthur, James, 234
Macbeth, 167, 195, 200
Macbeth, Robert, 123
MacBeth, Toby, 135
MacCauley, Mark, 250
MacDonald, Cathy, 179
MacDonald, Jane, 127
MacDonald, Joyce, 55
MacDonald, Pirie, 11, 207, 250
MacDonald, Saundra, 113
MacEnulty, David, 74, 185
MacFarland, Dorothea, 234
MacGregor, Barry, 184
Machado, Josevaldo, 17
Machlis, Joseph, 123
Machray, Robert, 143, 180, 209
Macht, Stephen, 184
Maciejewski, Zygmunt, 104
MacIntyre, Kate, 102, 103, 104
MacIver, Jane, 206
Mack, Andrew, 175

Mack, C. K., 127
Mackay, Lizbeth, 199
MacKaye, Percy, 211
Mackenroth, Steven, 201
MacKenzie, Julia, 174
MacKenzie, R. Duncan, 182
Mackey, Bill, 37
Mackey, Keith, 178, 198
MacLaine, Shirley, 8, 49, 54
MacLean, Peter, 71
MacLeod, Beatrice, 183
MacMahon, Aline, 128, 250
MacMath, Dennis, 215
MacMillan, Barry, 204
MacNeill, David, 208
MacNeille, Dennis, 206
MacRae, Heather, 226
MacRae, Sheila, 203
Macy, William H., 206
Madama, Linda, 117, 250
Madden, Donald, 127, 174, 234
Madden, Sharon, 107, 109, 250
Maddison, John, 217
Maddox, Diana, 179
Maddox, Gloria, 192
Made for TV, 221, 222
Madmen, 190
Madrid, Pinocchio, 60, 143
Madurga, Gonzalo, 112
Mad-woman of Chaillot, The, 221, 228
Maffei, Dorothy, 204
Magbee, Linda, 218
Magdalany, Philip, 144, 214
Magerman, Leslie H., 147
Maggart, Brandon, 234, 251
Maggie D. Mouse Meets De Dirdy Rat Fink, 210
Maggie Flynn, 118
Maggiore, Charles, 72, 72
Me
Magic Show, The, 62, 224
Magidson, Herman, 61
Magnifico, Jack, 71
Magnuson, Jim, 143
Magradey, Jack, 52
Magritte Skies, 145
Maguire, George, 119, 251
Mahaffey, Valerie, 51, 126
Mahard, Thomas, 177
Maharis, George, 234
Maher, James, 36
Maher, Joseph, 36, 101, 214
Mailer, Ralph Lev, 197
Maines, Mike, 127
Mainguy, Rene, 98
Major, Frederic, 127, 166, 200
Makman, Michael, 116
Mako, 8, 39
Malafronte, Albert, 204
Malandra, Lou, 209
Male Animal, The, 192
Maleczech, Ruth, 104
Malekos, Nick, B, 157
Maleski, Nadine, 175
Maley, Peggy, 234
Malis, Claire, 67, 144, 251
Malizia, Lester, 173
Mallow, Tom, 162, 166
Malof, Peter, 195
Maloney, Bill, 114
Maloney, James, 207
Maloney, Peter, 127
Maltby, Richard, Jr., 44, 123, 212, 218
Mamet, David, 80, 206
Man for All Seasons, A, 228
Man of La Mancha, 166, 195, 228
Man Who Drew Circles, The, 127
Man with the Flower in his Mouth, The, 209
Mandel, Howard, 100
Mandel, Jane, 137
Mandel, Oscar, 120
Mandel, Robert, 122, 149
Mandela, Sandra, 30, 171
Mandell, Alan, 82
Mandis, Renos, 105, 251
Manente, Mina, 225
Manfugas, Zenaida, 150
Mangravite, Ron, 180
Manhattan Theatre Club, 122
Manheim, Richard, 20
Manitoba Theatre Centre, 213
Manley, Sandra, 59, 64, 84, 89
Manley, Sandy, 19
Mann, Jack, 39
Mann, Michael, 37
Mann, P. J., 37, 251
Mann, Patrick, 120
Mann, Theodore, 11, 13, 31, 44, 46
Manne, Noah, 98, 99

Mannheim, Ralph, 133
Manning, Dick, 72
Manning, Katharine, 192
Manno, Dana, 123
Manny, 201
Manosalvas, Alfonso, 150
Mansfield, Jayne, 234
Mansfield, John, 216
Mansfield, Scott, 86
Mansfield, Wendy, 160
Mantel, Bernard, 143
Mantel, Michael, 190, 192
Manuel, Robert, 145
Manwaring, David, 181
Manzi, Tony, 41
Manzur, Jaime, 150
Mao, Freddy, 39
Maraden, Frank, 184
Maraden, Marti, 184
March, Ellen, 60, 251
March, Fredric, 12
March, William, 76, 251
Marchand, Nancy, 31, 127
Marcovicci, Andrea, 181
Marcum, Kevin, 47, 251
Marcus, Arthur, 107
Mardirosian, Tom, 178, 198, 224
Marfield, Dwight, 121
Margolin, Janet, 234
Margolis, Debra, 221
Margulies, David, 45, 251
Marie, Julienne, 234
Marin, Paul, 207
Marinaro, Martin, 127
Marino, Frank, 87, 151, 158
Marinyo, Tony, 39
Marion, Richard, 179
Mark, Anthony, 114
Markham, Monte, 234
Markle, Lois, 194
Markovich, Terrence, 218
Marks, Barbara, 70
Marks, Bebe, 200
Marks, Jack R., 129, 181
Marks, Jonathan, 227
Marks, Peggy, 133
Marks, Richard Lee, 225
Marks, Sandi, 122
Markson, Edith, 189
Markus, Tom, 226
Marletto, Don, 112
Marley, Susanne, 118, 180
Marlin-Jones, Davey, 180
Marlowe, Christopher, 92
Marlowe, Gloria, 234
Marmy, Mae, 215
Maron, Jeff, 143
Marques, Rene, 150
Marquez, Yolanda, 210
Marquis, Marjorie, 13
Marr, Richard, 52, 121, 251
Marre, Albert, 37
Marrero, Tony, 22, 155
Marriner, Gregg, 126
Marriott, John, 211
Marrow, Esther, 64
Marsden, Howard, 190
Marsh, Granvill, 167
Marsh, Jean, 30
Marsh, Lynn, 213
Marshall, Bette, 127
Marshall, Eric, 151
Marshall, Ken, 181
Marshall, Larry, 41, 251
Marshall, Norman Thomas, 251
Marshall, Patricia, 234
Marshall, Richard, 163
Marshall, Sarah, 234
Marshall, Susan, 127
Marshall, Will Sharpe, 137
Marsolais, Ken, 12, 48
Marsters, Richard, 192
Marston, David, 182
Marston, Don, 203, 206
Martenson, Edward A., 214
Martin, Adam, 224
Martin, Barney, 8
Martin, Betty, 74, 89
Martin, Bruce R., 118
Martin, Christopher, 150
Martin, Clyde, 218
Martin, Elliot, 22
Martin, Ernest, 151
Martin, Gary, 113
Martin, George, 39, 208, 225
Martin, Guy, 11
Martin, Jean, 56
Martin, John J., 112
Martin, Kent, 215
Martin, Leila, 22, 224
Martin, Lewis, 177
Martin, Linda, 35
Martin, Lynn, 117, 251
Martin, Mary, 12
Martin, Nan, 21, 251
Martin, Norman, 190
Martin, Sandy, 208
Martin, Stephen, 200

Martin, Tom, 212
Martin, W. T., 102, 211
Martinez, Frank C., 155
Martinez, Rafael, 150
Martinez, Rosemary, 210
Martini, Richard, 166
Martinuzzi, John, 143, 144
Martorella, Michael, 60, 120
Marvin A. Krauss Associates, 21
Marvin, Mel, 20, 95, 106, 122
Marvin's Garden, 122
Mary, Mary, 218
Mary Tudor, 110
Maryan, Charles, 192
Marymont, Jerry, 177
Marzecki, Tomasz, 104
Mas, Graciela, 150
Mascolo, Joseph, 207
Masiell, Joe, 89, 251
Masked Choir, The, 200
Maskow, Harro, 213
Masnica, Denise, 216
Mason, Cameron, 14, 15
Mason, Clifford, 126
Mason, Jack, 208
Mason, Jan, 208
Mason, Judi Ann, 125
Mason, Marshall W., 42, 107, 108, 109
Mason, T. Richard, 144, 208, 209
Masoner, Gene, 65, 251
Masques, 221
Mass Murder in the Balcony of the Old Ritz-Rialto, A, 75
Masters, Ben, 206
Masters, Patricia, 68
Masterson, Peter, 38, 251
Mastrodonato, Lee, 45, 211
Mastrosimone, William, 113
Matchmaker, The, 25, 189
Mather, Ada Brown, 185
Mather, Jack, 213
Mathews, Carmen, 226
Mathews, Diana, 50
Mathews, Mary Ellen, 113, 114
Mathews, Quinn, 201
Mathews, Walter, 63, 251
Mathews, Yvette, 160
Mathewson, Joseph, 58, 211, 251
Mathis, Sherry, 155
Matlock, Norman, 97
Matsusaka, Tom, 39, 251
Matt, the Killer, 143
Matt, the Killer, 143
Matter of Gravity, A, 8, 40
Matthaei, Konrad, 40, 174
Matthews, Anderson, 91, 92, 93, 94, 251
Matthews, Dakin, 193
Mauck, Joseph, 173
Mauer, Judy, 81
Maung, Kevin, 39
Maurita, Albert, 75
Mauthe, Denise, 52
Max, Ron, 57
Maxmen, Mimi Berman, 116, 117
Maxon, Richard, 25, 47
Maxwell, Douglas, 114
Maxwell, Janie, 78
Maxwell, Roberta, 63, 218, 219
Maxwell, Wayne, 57, 251
May, Beverly, 187
May, Curt, 114
May, Deborah, 189
May, Lenora, 82
May, Marilynn, 208
May, Marty, 265
May, Monica, 151
May, Val, 34
Mayakovsky, Vladimir, 114
Maybaum, Robert, 155
Mayer, Charles, 105, 251
Mayer, Edwin Justus, 112
Mayer, Jerry, 128, 223, 251
Mayer, Jo, 91, 92, 93, 94
Mayer, Jody, 98
Mayer, Valentine, 57
Mayfield, Cindee, 76
Maylond, Sara, 147
Maynig, Scott, 195
Maze, Steven A., 182, 221
Mazy, Duane F., 153
McAdams, Stacy, 169
McAnuff, Desmond, 204, 213
McAuliffe, Jason, 74
McBride, Vaughn, 187, 199
McBroom, Joyce, 217
McCain, Frances Lee, 196, 197
McCall, Nancy, 154, 251
McCallin, Clement, 103
McCallum, Sandy, 193
McCally, Brett Elise, 176
McCally, Charles David, 176

McCally, Regina Walker, 176
McCalman, Macon, 207
McCann, Christopher, 137
McCann, Eva, 221
McCarren, Fred, 198
McCarroll, Earl, 183
McCarter Theatre Company, 214
McCarthy, Lillah, 126, 127, 223
McCarthy, Michael, 114
McCarthy, Molly, 69
McCarty, Mary, 8, 234, 251
McCaughan, Charles, 181
McCaughan, Chuck, 145
McCauley, Judith, 68
McCauley, Robbie, 135
McClain, Marcia, 234, 251
McClane, G. Warren, 32
McClaskey, Glen, 166
McCleister, Thom, 181
McClelland, Lee, 183
McClure, J. Shane, 218
McClure, John, 55
McClure, Marc, 197
McClure, Michael, 189, 200, 227
McColl, Ian, 123, 143, 144, 145
McCombas, Wendell, 208
McCormick, Cara-Duff, 147
McCormick, James E., 218
McCormick, Parker, 69
McCoy, Dennis, 221
McCoy, Eleanor, 64
McCracken, Peggy, 176
McCray, Ivy, 123
McCready, Tom, 143
McDaniel, Druce, 180
McDaniel, William F., 152
McDermott, James T., 206
McDermott, Keith, 8, 63, 122, 144, 251
McDermott, Patricia, 18
McDermott, Tom, 108
McDevitt, Ruth, 265
McDonald, Bob, 16
McDonald, Durward, 216
McDonald, J. Perry, 146
McDonald, James, 59
McDonald, Joyce, 68
McDonald, Perry, 146
McDonald, Rodger, 188
McDonald, Tanny, 95, 112, 127, 186, 251
McDonald, Tom, 206
McDonough, Ann, 128, 141, 142
McDonough, Charles, 146
McDonough Edwin J., 122
McDowall, Roddy, 159
McDowell, John Herbert, 82
McDowell, Richard, 195
McDowell, Stephen, 187
McDuffie, Alvin, 64
McElroy, David, 218
McElroy, Evie, 199
McElroy, Judith, 218
McElroy, Margo, 188
McErlane, Thomas J., 164
McFarland, R. Lorne, 184
McFarland, Robert, 143, 144
McGaha, James, 128, 181
McGann, Duncan, 195
McGann, Michaeljohn, 117, 251
McGeary, Maura, 207
McGee, Jerry, 127
McGhee, Albert, 221
McGhee, Johnn Ray, 197
McGill, Bruce, 129, 181
McGill, Everett, 63, 211, 251
McGinn, Walter, 211
McGinnis, Kathi, 200
McGiver, John, 265
McGlade, Robert, 179
McGourty, Patricia, 83, 137
McGrath, George, 133
McGrath, Janet, 209
McGreen, Brian, 193
McGreevey, Annie, 62, 211, 251
McGregor-Stewart, Kate, 22, 90
McGuire, Linda, 212
McGuire, Mitchell, 155
McGuire, Steve, 176
McHattie, Stephen, 155, 212
McHenry, Andrea, 200, 211
McHugh, David, 81
McIlrath, Patricia, 217
McIlwaine, Robert, 123
McInerney, Bernie, 224
McIntyre, Bill, 57, 126, 251
McIntyre, Marilyn, 190
McIntyre, Roger, 107
McIntyre, Spencer, 199
McKay, Anthony, 10, 148
McKay, Brian, 213
McKay, Gardner, 122

McKay, Kent, 213
McKay, Sindy, 179
McKayle, Donald, 169
McKearnan, Betsey, 110
McKechnie, Donna, 7, 8, 14, 161, 251
McKeehan, Catherine, 184
McKeever, Jacqueline, 234
McKenna, Mark, 147
McKenzie, James B., 189
McKenzie, Julia, 198
McKeon, Doug, 155
McKeon, Thomas, 206
McKereghan, William, 216
McKerrs, Terrance, 117, 251
McKie, Jim, 221
McKim, Marie, 114
McKinley, Galen, 17
McKinney, Mark, 215
McKinney, Thomas, 68
McKnight, Michael, 210
McLain, John, 17, 179, 205, 208, 214
McLaughlin, Ira, 218
McLaughlin, Jeffrey B., 207
McLaughlin, Karen, 177
McLaughlin, Vickie, 113
McLean, Doug, 213
McLellan, Nora, 213
McLerie, Allyn Ann, 234
McLernon, Pamela, 116, 251
McMahan, David, 186
McMahon, Eileen, 134, 135, 137
McMahon, Helen, 140, 141, 174
McMahon, Michael, 194
McMartin, John, 234
McMillan, Kenneth, 132, 212, 251
McMillian, Larry, 32, 251
McMinn, Mari, 47
McMinn, Patrick, 179
McMurray, Sam, 148, 251
McNab, Horace Greeley, 171, 172
McNamara, Pat, 38
McNeeley, Gale, 192
McNeil, Lonnie, 43
McNeilly, Michael, 197
McPhee, Carole, 113
McPhee, Clarkston, 207
McRay, Terri, 215
McWilliams, Caroline, 27, 251
Me and Bessie, 19
Me Jack, You Jill, 44
Meacham, Paul, 120, 121
Mead, Lewis, 147, 148, 149
Meade, Lou, 147
Meader, Derek, 225
Meadow Brook Theatre, 215
Meadow, Howard, 82
Meadow, Lynne, 122, 123
Meadows, Jayne, 196
Meadows, John, 187
Meagher, Madonna T., 223
Meares, Jim, 90
Measure for Measure, 179, 184, 187
Meat Loaf, 41
Meconi, Kevin, 175
Medal of Honor Rag, 84, 204
Medalis, Joseph G., 196
Medeiros, John, 221
Medford, Kay, 234
Medina, Julio, 197
Medley, Jack, 213
Meecham, Gregory, 193
Meehan, Danny, 38, 251
Meek, Barbara, 225
Meek, Joseph Edward, 186
Meeker, Ralph, 234
Meeker, Roger, 208
Mefford, Heidi, 205, 208
Megna, John, 177, 197
Meiners, Barry, 210
Meisle, Kathryn, 183
Meisle, William, 183
Meister, Brian, 143
Meister, Philip, 113, 114, 167, 168
Melang, Dean, 221
Mellender, Mark Dennis, 119
Mellor, Steve, 190
Mellors, Constance, 200
Melvin, Robert, 162
Member of the Wedding, The, 226, 228
Memoirs of Charlie Pops, The, 113
Memory of Two Mondays, A, 138
Men in White, 228
Mencher, Hy, 108
Mendenhall, Francie, 25
Mendillo, Stephen, 13, 212, 252

Menefee, Pete, 19, 196
Menke, Richard, 224
Mennen, James, 12, 34
Menz, Thomas, 193
Merande, Doro, 265
Mercado, Hector Jaime, 55, 166
Mercado, Nereida, 150
Mercer, Marian, 179, 234
Mercer, Sally, 113, 114
Meredith, Lee, 157
Meredith, Martin, 185
Merensky, John, 110, 114, 252
Merigold, Jack, 184
Merin, Eda Reiss, 147
Merkel, Ken, 71
Merkel, Virginia, 31, 46, 67
Merkey, Ryland, 201
Merlin, Joanna, 114
Merrick, David, 22, 32, 155
Merrifield, Gail, 181
Merrifield, Randall, 143, 198
Merrill, Bill, 60
Merrill, Dina, 33, 252
Merrill, Paul, 127
Merrill, Scott, 234
Merritt, Larry, 61
Merritt, Theresa, 64
Merry Wives of Windsor, The, 189
Merryman, Monica, 198
Mersky, Kres, 177
Merson, Susan, 85, 144, 252
Mertz, Michael, 190
Meryl, Cynthia, 47
Messina, Dione, 117, 252
Metaxas, Jason, 185
Metcalf, Alexander, 190
Metcalf, Mark, 123, 127, 132, 181, 190, 252
Metoyer, Ciel, 175
Mette, Nancy, 114
Metter, Laurie, 200
Metzman, Irving, 114
Metzo, William, 143
Meulener, Maria, 150
Meyer, Carla, 204
Meyer, David, 199
Meyer, Donna, 119
Meyer, Edgar, 206, 215
Meyer, Leo B., 159
Meyer, Peter, 173
Meyer, Susana, 107
Meyers, Bruce, 218
Meyers, David, 177, 179
Meyers, Kimberly, 90
Meyers, Marilyn, 221
Meyers, Nicholas, 137
Meyrich, Victor, 191
Miazga, Francis Carmine, 120, 121
Michelovitch, Bill, 151
Michaels, Bruce, 90
Michaels, Dennis, 191
Michaels, Drew, 197
Michaels, Fred, 203
Michaels, Jerryn, 76
Michaels, Joshua, 119
Michaels, Laura, 155
Michaels, Mary Ann, 113
Michalski, John, 110, 156
Michener, Curtis, 218
Middlebrook, Leslie, 143
Midsummer Night's Dream, A, 146, 193, 215, 227
Mielziner, Jo, 265
Mihok, Andrew, 130, 132, 133, 136, 181
Mikado, The, 143
Mikelson, Ivars, 186
Miklojcik, Donna, 113
Miklojcik, Joseph, 113
Milder, Josh, 121
Milder, Rachael, 121
Milder, Rifka, 121
Miles, Joanna, 108, 252
Miles, Julia, 95
Miles, Noanna, 108
Miles, Ross, 8, 252
Milewska, Anna, 104
Milford, Kim, 41
Milford, Penelope, 65
Milgrim, Lynn, 198
Milikin, Paul, 204
Millan, Bruce E., 202
Millar, Douglas, 213
Millard, Vincent, 110
Miller, Allan, 205
Miller, Alton, 190
Miller, Arthur, 11, 138, 141, 142, 213
Miller, Betty, 48
Miller, Daniel B., 208
Miller, Eric Booth, 182
Miller, Frank, 203
Miller, I. Mitchell, 43
Miller, Jason, 180
Miller, Jeanie, 218
Miller, Ken, 61

Miller, Linda, 234, 252
Miller, Marilyn S., 138, 140, 141
Miller, Martha, 119, 252
Miller, Michael, 190, 223
Miller, Mitch, 25, 50, 51, 169
Miller, Robin, 176
Miller, Samuel, 98
Miller, Sharron, 62
Miller, Susan, 196
Miller, Timothy, 137
Miller, William F., 173
Miller, Wynne, 234
Millett, Joe, 123
Milligan, Jacob, 63, 252
Milligan, John, 175, 223
Millman, Henry, 95, 97, 98
Millman, Howard J., 191
Mills, Alison, 143
Mills, Fred, 207
Mills, Stephanie, 64, 252
Millstein, Carol, 180
Milne, A. A., 100
Milo, Christopher, 166
Milton, Frank, 63, 163
Milton, Robert, 110, 114
Milwaukee Repertory Theater, 214
Mime for a Summer Night, 70
Mineo, John, 14, 61
Mineo, Rose Anna, 224
Mineo, Sal, 265
Miner, Jan, 50, 212, 252
Minkow, Gene S., 190
Minnelli, Liza, 8, 54, 234
Minnis, Marjorie, 143
Minor, Candy, 207
Minor, Robert, 155
Minot, Anna, 126, 127
Minton, T. A., 218
Mintun, John, 127, 252
Mintzer, William, 20, 106, 145, 169, 190
Mirabella, George, 143
Miracle Worker, The, 228
Miranda, Lou, 120, 151
Miranda, Sylvia, 81
Miratti, T., 130, 252
Mirras, Diana, 55
Mirror Mirror, 200
Misalliance, 144
Miser, The, 178, 218, 219
Miss Julie, 112
Miss Lulu Bett, 228
Mississippi Moonshine, 143
Missouri Legend, 118
Missouri Repertory Theatre, 217
Mister Roberts, 228
Mistretta, Sal, 59
Mitchell, Cameron, 11, 234
Mitchell, David, 128, 131, 137
Mitchell, Delores, 189
Mitchell, James, 234
Mitchell, John, 122
Mitchell, Loften, 43
Mitchell, Sally, 116, 198
Mitchell, Stevie Ann, 177
Miterko, Julie, 225
Mixon, Alan, 63, 98, 252
Miyori, Kim, 39
Mizell, Danny, 80, 123
Mizelle, Vance, 129, 143, 181, 252
Moberly, Robert, 40, 252
Moby Dick, 210
Mockus, Tony, 203, 206, 215
Modlin, Marilyn, 121
Moeser, Patricia, 122, 123
Moldow, Deborah, 116, 252
Moliere, 178, 194, 218
Moller, Pam, 110
Mollien, Roger, 234
Molnar, Carin, 110
Molyneaux, Thom, 118, 127
Monahan, Roz, 155
Monette, Richard, 184
Mongoven, Danna, 179
Monitor, James W., 186
Monk, Robby, 121, 151
Monosalvas, Alfonso, 150
Monte, Camille, 118, 145
Monte-Britton, Barbara, 14
Monteil, Robert, 68, 69
Montel, Michael, 21, 206, 211, 215
Montero, Luis, 166
Montez, Mario, 82
Montgomery, Barbara, 10, 24, 124
Montgomery, Bruce, 201
Montgomery, Charles, 204
Montgomery, Elizabeth, 234
Montgomery, Jack, 221
Montgomery, John, 119
Montgomery, Lynn, 116
Montgomery, Reginald, 210
Montgomery, Robert, 122, 197

Month in the Country, A, 111
Monti, Mary Elaine, 81
Monty Python Live!, 87
Moody, Janette, 18, 55
Moody, Michael Dorn, 130
Moon, Mary, 127
Mooney, Daniel, 216
Mooney, Deborah, 146, 147
Mooney, R. Joseph, 215
Moor, Bill, 190
Moore, Benjamin, 189
Moore, Cheryl, 183
Moore, Christina, 199
Moore, Donald C., 119, 215
Moore, Edward J., 109
Moore, Jeff, 200
Moore, John J., 39
Moore, Jonathan, 67, 252
Moore, Marion, 18
Moore, Melba, 234
Moore, Michael Dennis, 120
Moore, Michael Kevin, 182
Moore, Norma, 201
Moore, Randy, 201
Moore, Richard, 103
Moore, S. A., 93
Moore, Tom, 60, 190
Moore, Vera, 18
Moore, Wendy, 78
Moose, G. Eugene, 51
Moose 100, 122
Moran, Jay, 221
Moran, John, 114
Moran, Michael, 135
Mordden, Ethan, 123
Mordecai, Benjamin, 209
Mordecai, Sherry Lynn, 209
More, Robert G., 184
Morea, Gabor, 214
Moreing, William, 182
Moreno, Belita, 197
Moreno, Donato, 111
Moreno, Rita, 252
Moreno, Soni, 17
Morenzie, Leon, 17, 252
Moreton, Patrik D., 121
Morey, Charles, 143, 204
Morfogen, George, 105, 194, 252
Morgan, Danny, 72, 144
Morgan, David, 111
Morgan, Ethel A., 75
Morgan, Frances, 64
Morgan, James, 153
Morgan, Roger, 95, 194
Morgan, Sandra, 200
Morgan, Sonny, 123
Morgan, Willard, 58, 74
Morgan Yard, The, 217
Moriarty, Michael, 8, 102, 211, 234, 252
Morin, A. J., 223
Morin, Francisco, 150
Moritz, Dwayne, 147
Moritz, Louisa, 196
Morley, Carol, 214
Morley, Ruth, 105
Morning's At Seven, 121, 202
Morrell, Valerie, 120
Morrill, Warren, 57
Morris, Anita, 62, 248
Morris, Beth, 22, 23
Morris, Duane, 121
Morris, Garry, 180
Morris, John, 129
Morris, Linda Robin, 145
Morris, Marilyn, 218
Morris, Matt, 123, 252
Morris, Nat, 162
Morris, Terry, 200
Morrison, David, 203
Morrison, Michael, 176
Morrison, Sharon, 31
Morrow, Byron, 205
Morrow, John W., Jr., 192
Morrow, Karen, 234
Morse, Ken, 50
Morse, Richard, 70
Morse, Robert, 52, 234, 252
Morsell, Fred, 126, 127, 234
Mortenson, Louise, 186
Morton, Joe, 88, 234, 252
Morton, Joy Venus, 75
Morton, Winn, 65, 68
Mortorella, Michael, 158
Moses, Gavin, 98
Moses, Gerard, 175
Moses, Gilbert, 55, 97
Moses, Miriam, 111
Mosher, Gregory, 80, 206
Mosher, Susan, 179
Mosley, Louise, 201
Mosley, Milledge, 226
Moss, Barry, 69
Moss, Jeffery B., 72
Moss, Kathi, 60
Moss, Lawrence John, 52, 122

Moss, Leland, 20, 143, 145, 252
Moss, Paula, 194
Moss, Robert, 143, 144
Moss, Stephanie, 191
Mosse, Spencer, 16, 89, 123, 145, 218
Most Happy Fella, The, 228
Mostel, Josh, 211
Mott, Will, 169
Motter, Marcina, 200
Motyka, William, 113
Mourning Becomes Electra, 206
Moyer, Libby, 208
Mrozek, Slawomir, 207
Mrs. Warren's Profession, 8, 131
Mucciolo, Kathleen, 126, 127
Much Ado About Nothing, 167, 175, 176, 179, 201, 217
Muchmore, Dale, 68
Muchmore, JoAnn, 218
Muellerleile, Marianne, 121, 126, 215
Muenz, Richard, 55
Mufson, Ken, 67
Muhleisen, Arthur, 135
Mulgrew, Kate, 174
Mulhern, Leonard A., 44, 71, 73, 77, 81
Mulholland, Barry, 182
Mullen, Michele, 215
Muller, Romeo, 157
Mullette, Gilda, 108
Mulligan, Richard, 234
Munch, Allen, 143
Munchow, William, 206
Munday, Penelope, 234
Mundy, Meg, 234
Munier, Leon, 113
Munro, Ray, 181
Munsel, Patrice, 26, 252
Munson, Estella, 252
Muramoto, Betty, 210
Murawski, C., 65
Murcelo, Karmin, 197
Murch, Robert, 191, 206
Murder Among Friends, 34
Murdock, David, 120
Murdock, Frances, 123
Murney, Christopher, 187
Murphey, Mark, 182, 188
Murphy, Barbara, 143
Murphy, Charles Thomas, 196
Murphy, Dan, 218
Murphy, Donald, 234
Murphy, Drew, 5
Murphy, Eileen MacRae, 186
Murphy, Mark, 188
Murphy, Melissa, 197
Murphy, Michael V., 220
Murphy, Peter, 108, 114, 252
Murphy, Rosemary, 206
Murphy, Thomas, 212
Murray, Anne, 145
Murray, Brian, 80, 98, 206, 212, 218
Murray, Don, 28, 29, 252
Murray, Ellen, 145
Murray, Jeremiah, 146
Murray, Michael, 198
Murray, Michelle, 205
Murray, Patricia, 186
Murray, Paul, 191
Murray, Peg, 36
Murray, Timothy J., 206
Musante, Tony, 138, 139, 156, 252
Murri, Mark, 202
Music Man, The, 228
Musical Evening with Fred Coffin and Dorothea Joyce, A, 122
Musical Merchant of Venice, A, 147
Musser, Tharon, 14, 19, 39, 55, 64, 66, 160, 161, 196, 232
My Fair Lady, 8, 47, 228, 229
My Kinsman, Major Molineux, 98, 99
My Sister, My Sister, 216
My Three Angels, 203
Myers, Annette Brafman, 39
Myers, Barbara, 146
Myers, Bill, 186
Myers, Brook, 90
Myers, Fran, 143
Myers, Lorna, 18
Myers, Lou Leabengula, 10
Myers, Pamela, 172
Myers, Rozanne, 148
Myers, Timothy, 60
Myers, William, 198
Mylenski, Katherine, 143
Myles, Lynda, 143, 226

Myles, Meg, 81, 217
Mylett, Jeffrey, 62
Myrvold, Paul, 65
Nabel, Bill, 14, 37
Nader, Michael, 69
Nadir, Robert, 183
Nagel, Maryann M., 186
Nagle, Tom, 118
Nagrin, Lee, 90
Nahrwold, Thomas M., 179
*Naming, The,* 210
Nance, Sam, 201
Nangle, Scott, 180
Nanus, Sasha, 180
*Naomi,* 120
Napier, John, 63, 163
Napierala, John, 193
Napolin, Leah, 20
Napolitan, Neil, 207
Nash, David, 211
Nash, Murray, 206
Nash, Ron, 73, 86
Nash, Steven D., 120
Nastasi, Frank, 148
Nasuta, Stephen, 174, 211
Nathan, Amy, 192
Nathan, Fred, 69, 153
*National Lampoon Show,*
154
National Shakespeare
Company, 167
National Shakespeare
Festival, 179
Natker, Leon, 221
Natzke, Andrew, 146
Naughton, David, 129
Naughton, James, 208, 234
Nause, Allen, 182
Navarre, Max, 146
Navarre, Pam, 179
Navarro, Chi Chi, 252
Naylor, Anthony, 103
Naylor, Ian, 153
Neal, Candy, 182
Neal, Charles, 25
Neal, Joseph, 89, 137
Neal, Patricia, 234
Neal, Sally, 8
Nealie, Mary, 158
Nederlander, James, 18, 30,
171
Needles, William, 184
Neeley, Ralph, 199
Neeley, Ted, 197
Neelon, Michael, 185
Neely, Anthony, 169
Neeson, Peggy, 198
Negin, Louis, 213
Negin, Mark, 213
Negro Ensemble Company,
The, 10, 124
Negro, Mary Joan, 214
Negro, Mary-Joan, 92, 93,
94
Nehmer, Sherry, 204
Neil, Norman, 173
Neilson, Richard, 47, 63,
252
Neipris, Janet L., 206
Nelken, Harry, 213
Nelki, Nicki, 113
Nelson, Al, 186
Nelson, Barry, 28, 29, 252
Nelson, Bruce, 76
Nelson, Craig Richard, 58,
197, 252
Nelson, Ed, 164
Nelson, Gail, 186
Nelson, Gene, 234
Nelson, Jolly, 13, 31, 46
Nelson, Marjorie, 186, 221,
222
Nelson, Richard, 45, 52,
62, 71, 97
Nelson, Saidah, 135
Nelson, Toby, 120
Nemetz, Lenora, 8, 9
Nemiroff, Robert, 169
Nesbitt, Cathleen, 47
Nesladek, Pat, 203
Nettleton, Denise, 60, 252
Nettleton, Lois, 140, 252
Netzel, Sally, 201
Neu, Georgia, 198
Neu, Robert, 215
Neufeld, Eric, 197
Neufeld, Jane E., 137
Neufeld, Peter, 34, 161
Neuman, Gayle Stuwe, 182
Neuman, Joan, 75
*Never a Snug Harbor,* 126,
216
Neville-Andrews, John, 74,
148, 209, 227
New Dramatists Inc., The,
126
New Jersey Shakespeare
Festival, 180
New York Drama Critics
Circle, 8
New York Drama Critics
Circle Awards, 228
*New York Idea, The,* 191

New York Shakespeare
Festival, 128, 181
New York Theatre Company,
168
Newcomb, Steve, 182
Newell, Veronica, 176
Newman, Alyse, 78
Newman, Bill, 147
Newman, Paul, 35, 234
Newman, Stephen D., 30,
51, 253
Newman, William, 147
Newmar, Julie, 197
Newton, Jesse, 202
Newton, Jim, 196
Newton, John, 221
*Nice Girl Like You, A,* 127
Nicholas, Bryan, 61
Nichols, Allan, 197
Nichols, Harriet, 200
Nichols, Josephine, 12, 114,
216
Nichols, Lindie, 176
Nichols, Mike, 132, 212
Nichols, Nancy, 225
Nichols, Robert, 198
Nick, 117
Nickerson, E. Lynn, 43
Nickerson, Helen L., 22, 32,
155
Nickerson, Shane, 61, 253
Nickleson, Janis, 213
Nickless, Eleanor, 184
Nicoli, Lesslie, 253
Niederjohn, Clark, 191
Nielsen, Karl, 265
Nieminski, Joseph, 191
Nigh, Douglas, 221
*Night of the Iguana, The,* 91
Nigro, Donna, 166
Niles, Mary Ann, 253
Niles, Richard, 127
Nilsson, Gun-Marie, 209
Nimoy, Leonard, 171, 203,
220
*Nino Roger In Hombre, Grito
Y Guitarra,* 150
Nivelt, Barbara, 126
*No Exit,* 228
*No Place to Be Somebody,*
228
Noble, Eulalie, 71
Noble, James, 58, 208,
212, 253
Noble, Sharon, 213
Nobles, Gerald, 218
*Noel Coward Cabaret, A,*
123
Noel, Craig, 179
Noel, Tom, 155
Noh, David, 75
Nolan, Jim, 188
Noland, Nancy, 234
Nolte, Charles, 215, 234
Noone, Bill E., 111
Norgard, Richard, 226
*Norman Conquests, The,* 8,
28
Norman, Maria, 150
Norowicz, Helena, 104
Norris, E. E., 174
Norris, Kenneth, 107
Norris, Lenard, 206, 221
North, Sheree, 234
*Not to Worry,* 107
Nothmann, Karen E., 121
Noto, Lore, 152
Noto, Thad, 152
Novak, Michael, 174
Novelli, Steve, 192
Novick, Saul, 159
Novy, Nita, 118, 121, 253
Nowak, Achim, 190
Nowicki, D. Michael, 179
Nowicki, Steven D., 227
Nugent, Nelle, 18, 30, 171
Nugent-Head, Marie, 220
Nuland, Victoria, 174
Nunez, Orlando, 150
Nunn, Robin J., 184
Nunn, Trevor, 103
Nute, Don, 123, 253
Nute, Wendy, 110
Nuti, Al, 203
Nutt, Paul, 218
Nutter, Mark, 206
Nuyen, France, 234
Nyberg, Peter, 193
Nye, Gene, 143
Nype, Russell, 234
Oakes, Michael, 74, 118
Oakland, Simon, 196
Oakley, Gilbert, 190
Oas-Heim, Gordon, 206
Oates, Richard, 206
Oberbroeckling, Anne, 11
Oberjat, Suzanne, 123
Oberlin, Richard, 199
Oberman, Mark, 127
Obituaries, 262
O'Brien, Adale, 187
O'Brien, Bill, 208
O'Brien, Carmel, 208

O'Brien, Jack, 93, 179
O'Brien, Michael, 183
O'Brien, Richard, 170
O'Brien, Ruthmary, 175
O'Brien, Seamus, 152
O'Brien, Sylvia, 47, 253
O'Brien, Vince, 157
O'Callaghan, Kathy, 226
O'Casey, Sean, 86
*Ocean Walk,* 144
O'Connell, Deirdre, 221
O'Connell, Ian, 118, 253
O'Connell, Jerry, 54
O'Connell, Patricia, 21, 109,
224, 253, 265
O'Connor, Dennis, 117
O'Connor, Donald, 157
O'Connor, James-Ivers, 78
O'Connor, Kevin, 134
O'Connor, Lois, 102, 211
O'Connor, Sara, 216
O'Connor, Terrence, 179
O'Connor, Thomas, 174
O'Creagh, John, 223
O'Dell, K. Lype, 105, 226,
253
Odenz, Leon, 75
Odets, Clifford, 112, 122,
207, 214
Oditz, Carol, 84, 204
O'Donnell, Ann, 198
O'Donnell, Patti, 201
O'Donoghue, Noel, 212
Odsley, Robert, 175
Odums, Rick, 18
*Oedipus at Colonus,* 197
*Oedipus the King,* 182, 187
Oenslager, Donald M., 265
Oesterman, Phil, 153
Oetken, Patricia, 191
*Of Mice and Men,* 186,
199, 213, 228
*Of Thee I Sing,* 228
Offner, Deborah, 107, 214
Ogawa, Joann, 41
Oglesby, Marshall, 107,
108
*Oh Coward!,* 186, 207
Oh, Soon-Teck, 39, 253
*Oh Speakies,* 114
O'Hara, Edith, 70
O'Hara, Jill, 234
O'Hara, Paige, 76, 253
O'Hara, Riggs, 30
O'Hare, Brad, 206
O'Haughey, M., 8
M'Horgan, Tom, 17
Oka, Zoe, 67
O'Karma, Alexandra, 111
Okarski, Dave, 77
O'Keefe, Michael-Raymond,
212
O'Keefe, Paul, 211
O'Kelley, Maureen, 226
*Oklahoma!,* 8, 68
Oklahoma Theater Center,
218
O'Kleshen, James, 177
*Old Glory, The,* 98
*Old Maid, The,* 228
*Old Times,* 188, 194
*Oldest Living Graduate, The,*
211
Olesen, John, 208
Olesen, Oscar E., 40, 55,
211
Oleson, Todd, 182
Olich, Michael, 178
Olim, Dorothy, 152
Olive, Marcy, 73
Oliver, Bette, 191
Oliver, D. Jule, 110
Oliver, Donald, 86
Oliver, Douglas J., 177
Oliver, Lynn, 227
Oliver, Rochelle, 66
Oliver, Susan, 234
Oliveri, Patricia, 215
Olon-Scrymgeour, John,
114, 216
Olshin, Iris, 145
Olson, Joan, 182
Olson, Jon, 172
Olster, Fredi, 189
O'Malley, Etain, 204
O'Malley, Rex, 265
Ommerle, Stephen, 126
O'Morrison, Janet, 157
O'Morrison, Kevin, 143
Oms, Alba, 127, 203
*On the Inside,* 212
*On the Outside,* 212
*Once in a Lifetime,* 146,
190, 196
Ondaatje, Michael, 204,
213
*Ondine,* 220
*One Flew over the Cuckoo's
Nest,* 220
O'Neal, Cleveland, III, 181
O'Neal, Mary Ann, 173
O'Neal, Ron, 158, 234, 253
O'Neal, Tricia, 234

O'Neil, Brad, 182
O'Neil, Danny, 75
O'Neil, F. J., 12, 21
O'Neil, Madlyn, 208
O'Neil, Sara, 175
O'Neil, Tricia, 57
O'Neill, Annie, 118
O'Neill, Eugene, 13, 102,
206, 211
O'Neill, Gene, 38
Onyango, Akki, 73
Ooms, Richard, 91, 92, 93,
94
O'Oonnell, Sam, 200
O'Quinn, Terrance, 194,
204
Oram, Frederic-Winslow,
191
Orbach, Jerry, 8, 253
Orchard, Robert J., 227
Orcutt, Sandi, 41
Oregon Shakespeare
Festival, 188
O'Reilly, James D., 215
O'Reilly, Mary Ann, 161
Orfaly, Alexander, 55, 253
Oringer, Jaqui, 120
Orion, Elisabeth, 215
Orkeny, Istvan, 190
Orman, Roscoe, 97
Ormond, Dan, 65
Ornbo, Robert, 22
*Orner, Fredric H.,* 216
O'Rourke, Robert T., 24, 47
O'Rourke, Theresa, 190
O'Rourke, Thomas, 98, 99,
253
Orr, Mary, 253
Orsborn, Carol, 170
Orson, Barbara, 225
Ortega, Santos, 265
Osato, Sono, 54
Osborn, Paul, 121, 202
Osborne, Kipp, 46, 234,
253
Osborne, Suzanne, 121
Oscar, Gail, 72, 72 *Me*
*Oscar Remembered,* 184
O'Shea, Michael Sean, 157
O'Shea, Milo, 131, 212,
253
O'Shea, Tessie, 59, 253
Oshen, Gabriel, 63, 253
Oshins, E. J., 11
Ossenfort, Robert, 162
Oster, Ed, 118
Osterhoff, Ned, 173
Osterman, Curt, 113, 217
Osterman, Georg, 82
Ostrow, Stuart, 61
O'Sullivan, Anne, 78
O'Sullivan, Maureen, 54
O'Sullivan, Michael, 234
Ott, Suzan, 218
Ottenheimer, Albert M., 20,
253
Otto, Richard, 172
*Our Father's Failing,* 206
*Our Town,* 174, 175, 178,
190, 193, 206, 228
Ousley, Roubert, 175
*Out,* 216
*Out at Sea,* 216
Overpeck, Helen, 218
Owen, Edith, 199
Owen, Mary Lou, 187
Owen, Meg Wynn, 22, 23
Owen, Paul, 187
Owens, Edwin, 145
Owens, Jill, 61
Oyster, Jim, 224
Ozker, Eren, 126, 208
Pace, Atkin, 108
Pace, Robert, 86
Pacht, Joelle, 120
*Pacific Overtures,* 8, 39,
228
Pacino, Al, 234
Packard, Deborah, 143
Packer, Eve, 151
Padgett, Billy, 86
Pagano, Giulia, 24
Page, Anthony, 174
Page, Geraldine, 35, 234,
253
Page, Michael, 68
Page, Stan, 47, 68, 69,
116
Pagent, Robert, 68
Pagliaro, Sam, 69
Paige, Adele, 60
Paige, Autris, 169
Paine, Bruce, 41
*Pajama Game, The,* 228
*Pal Joey,* 228
Palance, Jack, 234
Paley, Jane, 128
Palin, Michael, 87
Paliotti, Michael, 163
Pally, Steven, 98
Palmer, Betsy, 185, 224
Palmer, Byron, 234
Palmer, Elizabeth, 194

Palmer, Jim, 111
Palmer, Joni, 64
Palmer, Leland, 61, 253
Palmer, Liz, 200
Palmer, Mack, 202
Palmer, Peter, 234
Palmer, Ruthe, 202
Palmer, Suzanne, 227
Palmieri, Joseph, 75, 253
Palmissano, Larry, 206
Palo, Jon, 177
*Panama Hattie,* 117
Panchot, D. H., 186
Pancirov, Rose, 180
Pandolfo, Antonio, 121,
144, 204
Pankin, Stuart, 95
Pannullo, Gary, 180
Paolucci, Anne, 110
Pape, David, 218
Pape, Joan, 190
Pape, Paul, 149, 253
Papenfuss, Tony, 197
Papp, Joseph, 14, 17, 128,
137, 181
Pappas, Ardeth, 187
Pappas, Theodore, 75
Pappas, Victor, 193
Paquette, Mark, 123
Paquin, Gilles, 213
Parady, Ronald, 183
Paredes, Felipe, 150
Parham, Glover, 18
Parichy, Dennis, 42, 107,
108, 109
Parker, Blaine, 184
Parker, Don, 24, 165, 253
Parker, Harry, 218
Parker, John, 218
Parker, Oren, 220
Parker, Paula, 118
Parker, Ron, 28, 190
Parker, Salli, 191
Parkin, Judd, 182
Parks, Andrew, 200
Parks, John, 64, 98
Parlakian, Nishan, 110
Parone, Edward, 196
Parrinello, Richard, 65
Parrish, Elizabeth, 212, 223
Parry, George, 57
Parry, William, 17, 41, 114
Pars, Julie M., 253
Parsons, Estelle, 8, 28, 29,
232, 234, 253
Parsons, Joel, 121
Parsons, Sally Ann, 90, 114
Partington, Rex, 192
Partington, Richard, 184
Partington, Tony C., 192
Pascal, Stephen, 122, 123
Pasco, Don, 226
Pasekoff, Marilyn, 154, 253
Pashalinski, Lola, 82
*Pasos Y Entremeses,* 150
Pasqualini, Tony, 190
Pasquin, John, 181, 190
Passeltiner, Berne, 20, 253
Pastene, Robert, 190, 223
Paterson, William, 189, 199
Pates, Patricia, 18
Patik, Vickie, 47, 253
Patinkin, Mandy, 128, 129
Patnaude, Greg, 175
Patrick, Dennis, 234
*Patrick Henry Lake Liquors,*
221
Patrick, Julian, 54
Patrick, Robert, 24, 165,
221
*Patriots, The,* 191, 228
Patron, Elias, 72
Patten, Carmichael, 143
Patten, Moultrie, 141, 142
Patterson, Chuck, 11
Patterson, George, 126
Patterson, John, 218
Patterson, Mary S., 218
Patterson, Portia, 111
Patterson, Robin, 213
Patterson, William, 199
Patton, JoAnn Johnson, 182
Patton, John, 175
Patton, Kristin Ann, 182
Patton, Lucille, 119, 137,
253
Patton, Pat, 182
Patton, Shirley, 182
Patton, William, 182
Paul, Alan, 60
Paul, Don, 144, 145, 151
Paul, Sid, 120
Paul, Vicki, 80
Paula III, 95, 97
Paulette, Larry, 88, 253
Paulus, Kristin, 214
Pavone, Lou, 79
Payne, B. Iden, 266
Payne, Ben, 25
Payne, Jim, 70
Payne, Julie, 196, 197
Payton-Wright, Pamela, 31,
134, 253
Peachena, 253

Peacock, Michon, 8
Peacock, Trevor, 103
Peakes, John L., 215
Pearcy, Patricia, 194
Pearl, Barry, 153, 254
Pearl, Matthew, 176
Pearle, Gary, 123
Pearlman, Nan, 62
Pearlstein, Dennis, 144
Pearson, Beatrice, 234
Pearson, David, 195
Pearson, Donna, 44
Pearson, Randolf, 201
Pearson, Rush, 180
Pearson, Scott, 161
Peaslee, Richard, 27, 46
Peate, Patricia, 151
Pechar, Tom, 224
Peck, William, 189
Peckham, Margaret, 220
Pecknold, Adrian, 213
Peek, Brent, 63
*Peer Gynt*, 189
Pelc, Donna, 191
Pelikan, Lisa, 107
Pell, Amy, 119
Pell, Pat, 146
Pell, Reet, 154
Pellaton, Roger I., 180
Pellegrino, Susan, 189
Penderecki, Krzysztof, 104
Pendleton, Austin, 58, 98, 208, 211
Pendleton, David, 194
Pendleton, Wyman, 147, 174, 214
Peniston, Pamela S., 124
Penn, Edward, 65, 254
Penn, Leo, 234
Penn, Polly, 183
Penn, William, 18, 204
Pennell, Nicholas, 184
Penney, Hannibal, Jr., 129, 181
Pennington, Cleveland, 55, 169
Pennyfeather, Carol, 43
Pentecost, Jim, 120
Penzner, Jonathan, 141, 142
Penzner,Jonathan, 138, 140, 141
*People from Division Street*, 113
Percassi, Don, 14, 161, 254
*Perched on a Gabardine Cloud*, 145
Percy, Dwight, 200
Peretti, Hugo, 118
Peretz, Susan, 181
Perez, Severo, 197
Perez, William, 115
Perkins, Anthony, 7, 8, 63, 232, 234, 254
Perkins, Anthony William, 155, 160
Perkins, Michael, 221
Perkins, Patti, 71, 77, 254
Perley, William, 116
Perlman, Ken, 208
Perlman, Rhea, 111
Perman, Mark, 65
Pernas, Teresa, 115
Perrier, Michael, 119, 254
Perry, Antoinette (Tony), 8
Perry, Bob, 114
Perry, Elizabeth, 143
Perryman, Al, 55
Perryman, Stanley, 205
*Persecution and Assassination of Marat, The*, 228
Persky, Lisa Jane, 88
Persons, Fern, 203, 206
Pesaturo, George, 14, 68
Petchey, Brian, 174
Peter, Frances, 221
Peters, Anne L., 120
Peters, Bernadette, 234
Peters, Claude, 143
Peters, Jeff, 126
Peters, Lauri, 234
Peters, Leonard, 109, 117, 145
Peters, Susanne, 215
Peters, Suzanne, 82
Petersen, David O., 207
Petersen, Erika, 178
Petersen, Robert, 95
Petersen, Roi, 12
Peterson, David, 207
Peterson, Kurt, 76, 254
Peterson, Nora, 74
Peterson, Peggy, 58
Peterson, Rico, 208
Peterson, Sarah, 174, 214
Petlock, Martin, 191
Petricoff, Elaine, 60, 254
*Petrified Forest, The*, 182
Petronia, 10

Petrucelli, Rick, 133, 144
Pettet, Joanna, 234
Pettey, Jack, 143
Petty, Ross, 118, 254
Peyser, Penny, 254
Pezzulo, Ted, 121
Pfiederer, Marge, 117
Pfeiffer, Marilyn, 58, 69, 78, 254
Pfenning, Wesley, 203, 206
Pflanzer, Howard, 143, 144
*Phedre*, 96
Phelan, Karol, 195
Phelan, Tony, 199
Phelps, Dwayne, 18
Phelps, Eleanor, 36, 47, 214, 254
Philadelphia Drama Guild, 218
Philips, Norrine, 177
Phillips, Andy, 63, 163
Phillips, Barbara, 175
Phillips, Eddie, 54
Phillips, Florence, 208
Phillips, Jeff, 51
Phillips, Joe, 114
Phillips, Lacy, 169
Phillips, Linda, 123, 144
Phillips, Louis, 209
Phillips, Margaret, 50, 234
Phillips, Margie A., 79
Phillips, Owen, 192
Phillips, Paul, 8
Phillips, Peter, 227
Phillips, Robin, 184
Phillips, Sandra, 169
Phoenix Company, The, 8
*Phoenix Theatre*, 138
*Piano Bar*, 210
Piazza, Ben, 234
Picardo, Robert, 83
Pichette, David, 226
Pickard, Joan, 218
Pickard, John C., Jr., 218
Pickering, James, 216
Pickles, Christina, 254
*Picnic*, 21, 228
Picq, Olivier, 96
Picus, Stan, 226
Piday, Louie, 200
Piedrahita, Francisco, 150
Piegaro, Frank, 60
Pierce, Verna, 61
Pierce, Wanda, 195
Piering, Mary, 170
Piersol, Morrie, 58, 208, 254
Pierson, Edward, 18
Pierson, Thomas, 76
Pietropinto, Angela, 135
Pietrucha, Bill, 79
Pike, Rick, 191
Pilato, Joseph, 221
Pilditch, Charles, 150
Pilloud, Rod, 186, 221
*Pimienta Pancakes, The*, 151
Pinckney, Serge, 115
Pincus, Stan, 47
Pincus, Warren, 32, 45, 145, 254
Pine, Larry, 135
Pinero, Arthur Wing, Sir., 128
Pines, Carolyn, 201
*Pink Helmet, The*, 200
Pint, Mark, 177
Pinter, Harold, 74, 122, 194, 218
Pipes, Nona, 123
*Pippin*, 61
Pippin, Don, 14, 71, 160, 161
Pippin, Roger, 126
Piretti, Ron, 110
Piriz-Carbonell, Lorenzo, 115
Pirkle, Joan, 193
Piro, Phillip, 215
Pistone, Charles, 208
Pitchford, Dean, 61, 254
Pitilli, Lawrence, 81
Pitkin, William, 156
Pitney, Christopher, 123, 143
Pittman, Demetra, 221
Pitts, William, 226
Pittsburgh Playhouse, 220
Pittsburgh Public Theater, 220
Place, Dale, 199
*Place on the Magdalena Flats, A*, 201
Place, Richard, 145
Plachy, William J., 145
Plakias, Leigh, 223
Platt, Martin, 173, 177
Platt, Samuel E., 130
Playten, Alice, 234
Playwrights Horizons, Inc., 143
Plessner, Anita, 96
Plonka, Liz, 123

Plumbtree, Rusty, 218, 219
*Plume de Ma Tante, La*, 228
Plumley, Don, 63, 254
Plummer, Christopher, 234
Poggi, Gregory, 213
Poindexter, H. R., 196
*Poison Tree, The*, 8, 38
Pojawa, Jerry, 200
Pokas, Ewa, 104
*Pokey, The*, 123
Polan, Lou, 266
Polan, Nina, 120
Poland, Albert, 35
Pole, Frances, 105, 121, 254
Polekoff, Marsha, 200
Polenz, Robert, 137
Polito, Philip, 158
Polizos, Vic, 122, 123
Polk, Cindy, 121
Polk, Ivson, 18
Pollack, Daniel, 190
Pollard, Thomas M., 19
Polley, Nora, 184
Pollock, Bernard, 69, 127
Pollock, Faye, 180
Pollock, George, 16, 254
Pollock, Kate, 66
Pollock, Steve, 227
Pollux, 96
Poloway, Merel, 41
Polseno, Robin, 166
Pomerantz, Jeffrey David, 63, 254
Pomerantz, Steve, 143
Ponazecki, Joe, 21, 254
Pontillo, Larry J., 76
Ponzini, Anthony, 148
Poole, Roy, 11, 138, 139, 141, 142, 254
Poor, Harold, 89
Porazzi, Arturo E., 65
Porcher, Nananne, 18
Porter, Cole, 117
Porter, David, 180
Porter, Howard, 25, 254
Porter, Kenneth, 25
Porter, Mary Ed, 69, 78, 113
Porter, Rand, 188
Porter, Stan, 72
Porter, Stephen, 140, 224
Porter, Tom, 44
Porto, Gary, 80, 126, 127, 180
Poser, Linda, 198
Post, Lu Ann, 218
Potamkin, Mrs. Victor H., 20
Potash, Paul, 197
Potashnick, Barry, 34
Potter, Betsey, 225
Potter, Don, 172
Potter, Mark, 32, 40
Potts, Ann, 159
Potts, Anne, 177
Potts, Nancy, 92, 93, 194
Poulenc, Francis, 123
Poulos, George, 21
Poulos, Michael, 153
Pounder, C. C. H., 187
Powell, Bruce, 206
Powell, Ed, 114
Powell, Missy, 121
Power, Geraldine, 203
Powers, David, 24, 35, 74, 152
Powers, Sharon, 55
Prados, Emilio, 155
*Prague Spring, The*, 199
Prange, Laurie, 155
Pratt, Jack Sterling, 254
Preble, Ed, 65, 75, 254
Predovic, Dennis, 187
Preece, K. K., 117, 254
Premice, Josephine, 43, 254
Prendergast, Alan, 173
Prentiss, Paula, 28, 29, 254
Prescott, James, 220
Presler, Dusty, 218
Pressman, Lawrence, 206, 234
Prestia, Vincent, 47, 71
Preston, Barry, 43, 54, 254
Preston, Edward, 54
Preston, William, 127, 149, 180, 218, 254
Previous Theatre World Award Winners, 234
Price, Barbara, 147, 148
Price, Elisabeth, 98, 99
Price, Gilbert, 8, 55, 232, 234, 254
Price, Paul B., 254
Price, Peggity, 192
Price, Phillip, 89
Price, Roger, 254
*Price, The*, 213
Price, Vincent, 33, 159
Prichard, Michael, 200
Prideaux, George, 110

Priest, Natalie, 20, 107
*Primary English Class, The*, 83
Primus, Barry, 134, 227, 254
Prince, Harold, 39, 54
Prinyz-Pahlson, Goran, 114
Prinz, Rosemary, 224
Pritchard, Ted, 77, 254
Pritchett, James, 143
*Private Lives*, 213, 221, 222
Priwieziencew, Eugeniusz, 104
Procter, Ray, 190
Proctor, Charles, 234
Proctor, Philip, 234
Professional Performing Company, 221
*Professor George*, 143
*Profile of Benjamin Franklin, A*, 199
*Promenade, All!*, 201
Prosky, Robert, 190
Prosser, William, 82
Pshena, Lewis, 122, 143
Pszoniak, Antoni, 104, 224
*Public Good, The*, 145
Public Players, Inc, 146
Public Theater, 8
Pucci, Maria Cristina, 12, 20, 25, 28, 34, 37, 41, 48, 50, 57, 60, 85, 90, 155, 160
Pucklis, Lee, 82, 122, 151
Pugh, Trish, 187
Pugliese, Joseph, 41
Pulis, Janell, 172
Pulitzer Prize, 8
Pulitzer Prize Productions, 228
Pulles, Nidia, 150
Pulliam, Zelda, 169
Pulvino, Louis, 30
Puma, Marie, 254
*Pup*, 145
Purcell, Dennis, 107, 108, 109
*Purgatory*, 188
Purins, Janus, 220
Purinton, Craig, 175
Pursley, Mona, 201
*Pursuit of Happiness, The*, 116
Pusilio, Robert, 25
Putnam, Deborah, 180
Putnam, Marilyn, 54
Puzo, Madeline, 196
*Pygmalion*, 47
Pyle, Roxann, 193, 200
Pyle, Russell, 193, 200
Pysher, Ernie, 47, 254
Pyskacek, June, 206
Quaglia, Jonn, 94
*Quality of Mercy, A*, 143
Quarry, Richard, 60, 254
Quayle, Anthony, 200, 211
Quebleen, Rodolfo C., 150
*Quibbletown Recruits, The*, 191
Quick, Louise, 86
*Quiet Caravans*, 186
Quigley, Frances K., 211
Quigley, Robert E., 151
Quillici, Angelo, 37
Quillin, Kim, 195
Quimby, Gerald, 191
Quimby, Thomas, 191
Quinault, Nick, 120
Quincy, George, 69
Quinn, Anthony, 155
Quinn, Frank, 16
Quinn, J. J., 57, 82
Quinn, Patricia, 11
Quintero, Jose, 12, 211
Quiyou, Lynn, 57, 141
Rabb, Ellis, 36, 92, 179, 211, 214, 254
Rabe, David, 78, 132, 212
Rabold, Rex, 188
Rachman, Lee, 114
Racine, 96
Rackmil, Gladys, 57
Rackoff, Louis, 128, 130, 181
Radano, Gene, 127
Radd, Ronald, 266
Radford, Sylvia, 151
Radka, William, 225
Radosh, Stephen, 122
Rae, Sheilah, 27
Rafalowicz, Mira, 137, 197
Raff, Leslie H., 180
Raffaello, Nino, 45
Ragey, Joseph, 182
Raggio, Lisa, 62
Ragno, Joseph, 82, 127
Rago, Bartholomeo, 189
Raiken, Lawrence, 168
Railsback, Steve, 12
Rain, Jeramie, 157
Raines, Cristina, 197
*Rainmaker, The*, 217

Rainone, San, 155
*Raisin*, 66, 169, 228
*Raisin in the Sun, A*, 228
Raitt, John, 26, 234, 255
*Ralph Roister Doister*, 173
Ralph, Sheryl-Lee, 124
Ralph, Stacey, 57
Ralston, James, 177
Ralston, Rick, 33
Ralston, Teri, 208
Rambal, Virginia, 150
Ramey, Cathy, 109
Ramin, Sid, 55
Ramirez, Tom, 179, 193
Ramone, Phil, 62
Ramos, Israel, 115
Ramos, Ramon, 180
Ramos, Richard, 95, 190, 255
Rampino, Lewis D., 221
Ramsel, Gina, 47
Ramsey, Barbara, 113
Ramsey, David, 63
Ramsey, Gordon, 113
Ramsey, John, 122, 155
Ramsey, Mack, 182
Ramsey, Marion, 205
Ramsey, Stanley, 43
Rand, Amy, 146
Randall, Bob, 62, 224
Randall, Marilyn, 123
Randell, Ron, 131, 255
Randolph, Leah, 55
Randolph, Robert, 28
Ranelli, J., 127, 199
Rankin, Arthur, 195
Rankin, Steven J., 191
Ransom, Dwight, 18
Ranson, Camille, 25, 60
Rantapaa, Ray, 114
Rao, Katherine, 191
Raphael, Gerrianne, 114
Rapkin, David, 141, 142
Raposo, Joe, 100
Rapp, Leslie, 199
Rasche, David, 121
Rasemus, Anthony, 152
Rasmuson, Judy, 212, 223
Rasmussen, Tom, 196
Rathbone, Basil, 50
Rathburn, John, 180
Rathbun, Roger, 226, 234
Ratkevich, Paul, 70
Raven, Elsa, 128
Raven, Yolanda, 41
Rawls, Eugenia, 35, 255
Ray, James, 196
Rayam, Curtis, 18
Rayvid, Bruce, 180
Raywood, Maggie, 119
Reagan, Dean, 213
*Real Inspector Hound, The*, 194, 209
Reams, Lee Roy, 198, 255
Rearden, Brad, 196
Reardon, Dennis J., 17
Reardon, Nancy, 123
Reavey, Elizabeth, 127
Rebhorn, James, 123
Rech, Annie, 110
Recht, Raymond C., 84, 123, 204, 213
Rechtzeit, Jack, 72
Red, Buryl, 87
*Red Devil Battery Sign, The*, 155
*Red Horse Animation, The*, 104
Redd, Veronica, 135
Redding, Robert, 177
Redfield, Dennis, 200
Redfield, Liza, 137
Redford, Robert, 234
Redgrave, Lynn, 8, 131, 255
Redgrave, Vanessa, 8, 46, 255
*Redhead*, 228
Redmond, Barbara, 226
Redmond, Marge, 196
Redmond, Morgan, 208
Redpath, Ralph, 90
Reece, Randy, 195
Reece, Richard, 166
Reed, Alaina, 122
Reed, Alexander, 12, 255
Reed, Bobby, 70, 255
Reed, Carolyn, 193, 197
Reed, Darrell, 160, 166
Reed, Jozella, 64
Reed, Larry A., 215
Reed, Pamela, 187
Reed, Penelope, 216
Reed, Richard, 188
Reed, Steve, 210
Reed, T. Michael, 62, 160
Reed, Vivian, 8, 43, 230, 232, 255
Reeds, Robin, 221
Reehling, Joyce, 109, 255
Reese, Gloria, 177
Reese, Greta, 176
Reese, Jim, 176

Reese, Lance, 218
Reeve, Christopher, 40, 67, 255
*Reflections*, 111
Regalbuto, Joseph, 126, 198, 221
Regan, Sylvia, 72
Reggiardo, Carl, 193
*Rehearsal, The*, 112
Rehner, H. Adrian, 221
Reich, John, 193
Reichenbach, Todd, 182
Reichert, James, 126
Reid, Barbara, 191
Reid, John, 73, 86
Reilly, F. Jackson, 215
Reilly, Jacqueline, 88
Reimueller, Ross, 37
Reineke, Gary, 221
Reinglas, Fred, 76
Reinhardsen, David, 45, 255
Reinhardt, Ray, 189
Reinhardt, Stephen, 62, 154
Reinking, Ann, 14, 15, 234, 255
Reisman, Jane, 44
Reit, Sally Faye, 175
Reiter, Dean, 71
Reiter, Dean H., 67, 180
Reiter, Nita, 145
Reiter, Val, 81
Reitman, Ivan, 62
*Relatively Speaking*, 198, 199, 215
Relyea, David, 44, 71, 73, 77, 81
Remme, John, 36, 214, 255
Renaud, Madeleine, 8, 56
Renensland, Ellen, 199
Renensland, Howard, Jr., 199
Renforth, John, 186, 221
Rennagel, Marilyn, 155
Rennich, Cathy, 107
Renz, Mary Ann, 146
*Replika*, 104, 224
Repole, Charles, 8, 32, 147, 230, 232, 255
*Report to an Academy, A*, 110
*Report to the Stockholders*, 143
Reseen, Robin, 70
*Resistible Rise of Arturo Ui, The*, 186
Resnick, Melanie, 215
Resnikoff, Bob, 127
Restaino, Phyllis, 10
Restrepo, Omar, 150
*Resurrection of Jackie Cramer, The*, 127
Revelle, Harry, Jr., 218
Revelle, Phoebee, 218
*Rex*, 8, 51
Rexite, Seymour, 72
Rexroad, David, 152, 255
Rey, Antonia, 255
Reyer, Avner, 145
Reyno, 10
Reynolds, Bryant J., 201
Reynolds, Chris, 206
Reynolds, Nette, 149
Reynolds, Paulene, 112
Reynolds, Robert, 170
Reznikoff, Peter, 143
Rhodes, Tran William, 79
Rhodes, Walter, 217, 226
Rhys, William, 199
Ribalow, Meir Zvi, 144, 181
Ribman, Ronald, 38
Rice, Aramide Pamela, 194
Rice, Catherine, 47
Rice, Ed, 208
Rice, Elmer, 202
Rice, Frank, 206
Rice, Herb, 126
Rice, Jon, 195
Rice, Rebecca, 190
Rice, Sarah, 152, 224, 255
Rich, Alan, 67
*Rich and Famous*, 8, 136
Rich, Jim, 153
Rich, Stephen, 197
Rich, Susan, 210
Rich, Sylvester, 121
*Richard II*, 173
"Richard III", 177
Richards, Beah, 210, 234
Richards, Gillian, 210
Richards, Helen, 65
Richards, James, 199
Richards, Jeffrey, 51
Richards, Jess, 234, 255
Richards, Jon, 211
Richards, Lisa, 35, 126
Richards, Martin, 8, 28, 41
Richards, Reve, 75
Richards, Sebastian, 173
Richards, Tim, 103
Richardson, Brian, 213
Richardson, Claibe, 36

Richardson, Dorene, 169
Richardson, Douglas E., 180
Richardson, Ian, 8, 47, 232, 255
Richardson, Lee, 174, 211
Richardson, Sally, 186
Richardson, Tony, 46
Richart, Bradley G., 114
Richie, Chuck, 143
Richie, Cornel, 18, 55
Richman, Saul, 69, 153
Richmond, Charles, 179
Rickner, Robert H., 111
Ricks, Ann, 221
Ridge, John, 133, 255
Ridge, John David, 94
Rieben, Robert, 173
Riegert, Peter, 204, 255
Riehle, Richard, 215
Rieth, Nancy K., 180
Rifici, Joe, 60, 255
Rifkin, Ron, 196
Riford, Lloyd S., III, 227
Rigby, Harry, 42
Rigg, Jonathan, 123
Riggs, James, 223
Rigley, Robert, 98
Rigby, Kent, 143
Riley, James, 52
*Rimers of Eldritch, The*, 119
Rimmer, Rod, 197
Rinaldi, Elicia, 57
Rinaldi, Joy, 60, 255
Rinehart, Elaine, 116, 255
Ring Round the Moon, 146
Ringland, Byron, 208
Ringwood, Susan, 200
Rinklin, Ruth, 206
Rios, Linda, 88
*Rip Van Winkle*, 200, 211
Rippe, Mark, 225
Riscol, Randolph, 55
Riseman, Naomi, 180
Rish, Oliver, 75
Riskin, Susan, 209
Risso, Richard, 216
Ritch, Rozanne, 143
Ritchard, Cyril, 26, 255
Ritchie, Lynn, 75
Ritco, Penelope, 184
Ritman, William, 45, 48, 66
Ritter, Kathryn, 255
Rittman, Trude, 47, 211
*Ritz, The*, 66
*River Niger, The*, 228
Rivera, Chita, 7, 8, 9, 255
Rivera, Esther, 115
Rivera, Gloria, 37
Rivera, Jose, 180
Rivera, Martin, 75
Rivera, Walter, 102, 103
Rivers, Jimmy, 25
Robards, Jason, 8, 102, 211, 234, 255
Robb, Jon, 203
*Robber Bridegroom, The*, 8, 91
Robbins, Carrie, 211
Robbins, Carrie F., 20, 60, 106, 145, 155
Robbins, Gil, 143, 144
Robbins, Jana, 89, 255
Robbins, Jerome, 54
Robbins, Linda, 143
Robbins, Mary Ann, 147
Robbins, Randall, 74
Robbins, Rebecca, 182
Robbins, Rex, 138, 139, 140, 141, 142, 212, 255
Robbinson, James F., 218
Roberson, Virgil, 185
Robert, Eve, 186
Robertiello, Mary Jo, 114
Roberts, Bill, 118, 255
Roberts, Brennan, 224
Roberts, Chapman, 43
Roberts, Dana, 113
Roberts, Howard, 97, 169
Roberts, J. W., 86
Roberts, Jack, 184
Roberts, Jerri, 198
Roberts, Les, 97, 132
Roberts, Patricia, 108
Roberts, Peter, 184
Roberts, Rachel, 8, 30, 255
Roberts, Ralph, 211, 220
Roberts, Stephen, 205
Roberts, Tom, 76
Roberts, Tony, 255
Robertson, Cliff, 234
Robertson, Kerry, 218
Robertson, William, 105, 107, 119, 121, 145, 255
Robeson, Paul, 266
Robey, Kathleen, 68
Robinette, Dale, 180
Robinsin, Leslie, 217
Robinson, Barry, 205
Robinson, Betsy Julian, 78
Robinson, Dyann, 43

Robinson, Hal, 255
Robinson, James, 88
Robinson, John, 218
Robinson, Leslie, 209
Robinson, Mabel, 18
Robinson, Mark, 204
Robinson, Robin, 173
Robison, David V., 201
Robles-Arena, Humberto, 197
Robman, Steven, 122
Rocco, Alex, 208
Roche-Zujko, Kathleen, 79
*Rockabye Hamlet*, 8, 41
Rockoff, Rena, 123
*Rocky Horror Show, The*, 170
Rodd, Marcia, 196
Roddick, John, 197
*Rodgers & Hart*, 66
Rodgers, Chev, 57
Rodgers, Gaby, 234
Rodgers, Richard, 51, 68
Rodgers, Shev, 37, 255
Rodgers, Valerie, 221
Rodin, Brina, 206
Rodman, Elizabeth, 19, 64, 84
Rodman, Sarah, 107
Rodriguez, Edward, 88
Rodriguez, Emilio, 115
Rodriguez, Jose, 150
Rodriquez, Patricia, 115
Roe, Patricia, 211
Roebling, Paul, 234
Roefaro, Francis, 121
Roerick, William, 122, 149, 256
Roetter, Carl, 209
Rogan, Peter, 208
Roger, Belinda, 115
Rogers, Gil, 127, 221
Rogers, Irma, 68, 69
Rogers, Jonathan D., 194
Rogers, Ken, 25, 160
Rogers, Patricia, 18
Rogers, Robert, 55
Rogers, Synthia, 201
Roggensack, David, 95, 97, 98
Rohrbach, Frank, 35, 114
Rohrbacker, Jacquiline, 166
Rohrer, Andrew, 120, 194
Rohs, Pamela, 198
Rojas, Dana, 218
Rolenz, Robert, 137
Rolf, Frederick, 149
Rolfing, Tom, 163, 256
Rolin, Judi, 256
Rollins, Howard E., Jr., 84, 204
Rolph, Marti, 198, 234, 256
Roman, Andrew, 119, 256
Romann, Susan, 211
Rombola, Ed, 205
Rome, Harold, 123
*Romeo and Juliet*, 182
Romer, Dennis, 199
Romilly, Chris, 223
Romoff, Colin, 54
Ronglin, Skip, 150
Rongstad, William, 221
Rooney, Sherry, 116
Roop, Reno, 156
Roos, Casper, 65
Rorke, Richard, 188
Rorvik, Alice, 193
Rosa, Dennis, 95
Rosalba, 41
Rosario, Terry, 80
Rosato, Mary Lou, 91, 92, 93, 94
Rose, Cristine, 188
Rose, George, 8, 47, 256
Rose, Jill P., 60
Rose, Philip, 65
Rose, Renee, 55
Rose, Reva, 234
Rose, Robin, 147
Rose, Robin Pearson, 147, 209
*Rose Tattoo, The*, 228
Roseborough, Charles R., 202
Roseman, Ralph, 52
Rosen, Gene, 197
Rosen, Lewis, 187
Rosen, Robert, 65, 256
Rosenak, David, 187
Rosenberg, Alan, 114, 143
Rosenberg, Amy, 180
Rosenberg, Ben, 66
Rosenberg, David, 114, 119, 121, 143, 145
Rosenblatt, Marcell, 227
Rosenblum, M. Edgar, 212
*Rosencrantz and Guildenstern Are Dead*, 228
Rosenfeld, Hilary M., 130, 134

Rosenkak, David S., 123
Rosenthal, Carl, 158
Rosenthal, Mark, 227
Roskam, Cathryn, 118, 121, 143, 256
Rosler, Larry, 109, 256
Rosner, Jo, 164
Rosno, Rea, 204
Rosofsky, Iris, 145
Rosqui, Tom, 196
Ross, Anthony, 31
Ross, Duncan, 221
Ross, Hank, 135
Ross, Howard, 55, 256
Ross, Jack, 195
Ross, John, 143
Ross, Justin, 14, 61, 256
Ross, Kimberly, 221
Ross, Larry, 207
Ross, Linda, 88
Ross, Mark, 166
Ross, Sandra L., 10, 124, 125
Ross, Ted, 64
Rossi, Alfred, 177
Rossi, Gloria, 98, 256
Ross-Oddo, Michael, 177
Rossol, Monona, 79
Rossomme, Richard, 116, 256
Rosson, Paul, 212
Rostand, Edmond, 213
Roston, Ronald, 123, 127
Rotblatt, Steven, 116
Roth, Ann, 36, 50, 214
Roth, Wolfgang, 105
Rothenberg, Laurence, 116
Rothman, Stephen, 208
Rothpearl, Harry, 71
Rothstein, Norman E., 25
Rothwell, Brian, 114
Rottman, Ann, 113
Roulet, Bill, 127
Roumain, Marial, 55
Roumain, Martial, 18
*Round and Round the Garden*, 28
Roundabout Theatre Company, 147
Rounds, Dan, 70
Rounds, David, 214, 234, 256
Rousseau, Carolle, 103, 256
Routledge, Patricia, 55, 256
Roveta, Sandy, 160
Rowan, Michael, 176
Rowe, Hansford, 141, 142, 256
Rowe, Jack, 200
Rowe, John, 181
Rowe, Stephen, 227
Rowe, Thomas A., 123
Rowles, Polly, 256
Roy, Will, 68
*Royal Family, The*, 7, 8, 36, 101, 211, 214, 218, 219
Royal Shakespeare Company, 8, 22, 103
*Rubbers/Yanks 3 Detroit O*, 154
Ruben, Paul, 121
Rubenstein, Barbara, 43, 256
Rubes, Jan, 184
Rubin, David, 170
Rubin, Steven, 13, 123, 179, 212
Rubinate, Dan, 110
Rubinstein, Arthur, 161
Rubinstein, Arthur B., 211
Rubinstein, John, 61, 234, 256
Rubinstein, Tedd, 196
Rubio, Carrie, 127
*Ruby's Place*, 122
Rudd, Paul, 8, 13, 31, 132, 232, 256
Rudin, Scott, 63
Rudkin, David, 196
Rudman, Michael, 129, 181
Rudman, William, 178
Rudner, Rita, 52
Rudney, Edward, 180
Rudolph, Ron, 197
Rudy, Martin, 214
Rue, Joan, 191
Rue, Vickie, 196, 197
Rule, Charles, 51
Rule, Colter, 98
Rulon, Kent, 218
Runge, Cathleen Gregory, 176
Runge, D. Arthur, 176
Runge, Dennis Arthur, 176
Runge, Kathleen Gregory, 176
*Runner Stumbles, The*, 58, 208
Rupert, Michael, 61, 234, 256
Rupp, Craig, 133

Rupprecht, David, 203
Rush, Barbara, 165
Rush, Lucy, 221
Rush, Marc, 221
Ruskin, Ellin, 212
Ruskin, Jeanne, 63, 126, 127, 256
Ruskin, Shimen, 266
Rusoff, Carol, 200
Russ, Jean E., 224
Russ, Sebastian, 143
Russ, William, 126, 130
Russak, Gerard, 256
Russel, Tony, 188
Russell, A. J., 100
Russell, Betty, 127
Russell, Brad, 74
Russell, Cindy, 112
Russell, David, 65, 256
Russell, Evelyn, 266
Russell, Forbesy, 120
Russell, Peter H., 172
Russell, Ruth, 60
Russell, Stephen, 184
Russiyan, Nicholas, 47, 63, 163
Russom, Leon, 212
Rutherford, Florence L., 209
Rutland, Robert E., Jr., 192
Rutter, Barrie, 103
Ruvolo, Danny, 14, 51
Ruymen, Ayn, 234
Ryan, Charlene, 8, 161, 256
Ryan, Charles, 143
Ryan, Gail, 113
Ryan, Greg, 188
Ryan, Irene, 61
Ryan, John, 223
Ryan, Kenneth, 227
Ryan, Ron, 16
Ryan, Steven, 191, 209
Ryane, Melody, 184
Ryder, Richard, 122, 144, 146
Rye, Judy, 200
Ryland, Jack, 174, 190
Rymer, James M., Jr., 176
Sabin, David, 133, 256
Sacharoff, Hope W., 121
Sackeroff, David, 67, 70, 143
Sackler, Howard, 196
Sacks, Bonnie, 225
Sacks, Michael, 24, 165
Saddler, Donald, 54, 91
Sadler, William, 69, 225
*Safe Place, A*, 127
Sager, Edward, 146
Sahl, Anne, 114
Sahl, Michael, 114
Saidenberg, Theodore, 47
Saifer, Steffen, 210
Saint, Eva Marie, 234
*Saint Joan*, 184
*Saint of Bleecker Street, The*, 228
Saint Subber, 55
Sakakeeny, Kaleel, 221
Sakamoto, Dennis, 116, 220, 256
Sakato, Atsumi, 83, 256
Saks, Gene, 66
Salata, Gregory, 63, 256
Saldana, Theresa, 147
Salerno, George, 112
Salis, Nancy, 119, 256
*Salt*, 200
Salt, Jennifer, 234
Saltus, Sarah, 158
Salvio, Robert, 234
Salzman, Eric, 114
Sambolin, Raymond, 123
*Same Time, Next Year*, 66
Sammler, Bronislaw, 227
Sammon, Patrick B., 179
Sample, Norman, 110
Sampson, Avis LaVelle, 206
Samrock, Carl, 16, 49, 56
Samrock, Victor, 54
Samuelson, Amy Margaret, 114
Samuelson, Tim, 206
Sanchez, Jaime, 234
Sanchez, Rene, 150
Sanchez, Roland, 10
Sand, Jonathan, 78
Sander, Peter, 105
Sanders, Albert, 158, 224
Sanders, Alvin Lee, 186, 221
Sanders, Elizabeth, 67
Sanders, Paulette, 86
Sanders, Peter, 59
Sanders, Richard, 129, 256
Sanders, Richard K., 106, 145
Sanderson, Alan, 54
Sandoe, Anne, 191
Sandre, Didier, 96
Sands, Diana, 234
Sandstroem, Yvonne, 114

Sandusky, Jerry, 88
Sanford, Beth, 188
Sanford, Jane, 144, 165
Sankowich, Lee D., 71
Sannes, Loyd, 62
*Santa Camila ...*, 115
*Santa Camila De La Habana Vieja*, 115
Santana, Jose Angel, 175
Santaniello, A. E., 107
Santell, Marie, 71, 256
Santiago, Ramona, 215
Santiago, Susan, 31, 46
Santoro, Tony, 143, 144, 145
Santos, Cecile, 37
Santucci, Bob, 75
Sanz, Nikki, 210
Sappington, Fay, 61, 256
Saracino, Frank, 123
Sarandon, Chris, 214
Sardella, Al, 113
Sargent, Meg, 120
Sarno, Janet, 130
Saroyan, William, 93
Sassen, Steven, 177
Sasso, Dick, 203
Satie, Stephanie, 121
Sato, Isao, 8, 39
Satterfield, Steve, 149
*Saturday Sunday Monday*, 201
Saucier, Claude Albert, 175
Sauer, Peter, 218
Saunders, Jessie, 216
Saunders, Lanna, 206
Saunders, Lois Ann, 119, 256
Saunders, Mary, 76, 256
Saunders, Susan, 179
Savadge, Deborah, 119, 256
Savage, Lesley, 157
Savage, Neil A., 182
Saveriano, Lori, 88
Saville, Carol, 198
Saxon, Don, 157
Sbano, James, 17, 86
Scadura, Laurie Ann, 68
Scafa, Alexander J., 119
Scales, Robert R., 184, 213
Scalici, Gillian, 14, 32
Scannell, J. Kevin, 65, 95
*Scapino!*, 187, 199, 224
Scardino, Don, 141, 142, 181, 256
Scardino, Frank, 8
*Scarecrow, The*, 211
Scarlata, Estela, 197
Scassellati, Vincent, 217
Searcry, Steve, 217
*Scenes from American Life*, 188
Schacht, Sam, 62
Schact, Sam, 256
Schaded, Maurice, 17, 160
Schadt, Ellie, 88
Schaefer, Craig, 116, 256
Schaefer, Kate, 107
Schaefer, Michael, 75
Schaeffer, Carl, 82
Schaeffer, David, 190
Schafer, Lawrence, 213
Schafer, Reuben, 20
Schaffer, Boguslaw, 104
Schaffer, Craig, 256
Schaffner, Billy, 200
Schak, John, 120, 131
Schaller, Diane R., 224
Shapiro, Kate, 121
Schatz, Neil, 44
Schear, Robert, 54, 83
Schechter, Debra, 147
Schechter, Howard, 147
Schecter, Amy, 109, 122, 123
Scheeder, Louis W., 204
Scheerer, Bob, 234
Scheffler, John, 121, 145, 191
Scheider, Maxmillia, 82
Scheinblum, Rafe, 113
Scheine, Raynor, 177
Schelble, William, 24, 35, 52, 74
Schenk, Robert, 177
Schenk, Terry, 218
Schere, Louis, 143
Schermer, Phil, 186
Schertler, Nancy Jean, 185
Scherzer, Wayne, 123
Schevill, James, 225
Schieffer, Rosemarie, 81
Schierhorn, Paul, 227
Schifter, Peter, 90
Schill, William, 17, 63
Schilling, William, 145
Schirner, Laurie, 215
Schisgal, Murray, 158
Schissler, Jeffrey, 116, 145
Schlee, Robert, 133, 256
Schlegel, Jeanne, 113, 114, 118

Schlissel, Jack, 83
Schlitten, Tiana Jo, 180
Schlossberg, Jerry, 76
Schlosser, Ira, 143, 144
Schmeider, Jana, 88
Schmidt, Douglas W., 33, 60, 91, 92, 93, 94, 133, 155
Schmidt, Harvey, 152, 168
Schmidt, Jack, 59, 256
Schmidt, Mary, 180
Schmidt, Steven, 218
Schneider, Alan, 45, 190, 211
Schneider, Bill, 41
Schneider, Eric, 200
Schneider, Harlan, 181
Schneider, Jana, 88
Schneider, Lorri, 143
Schneider, Paul, 123, 143
Schneider, Peter, 98
Schneider, Rick, 47, 68
Schneider, Schorling, 96
Schnetzer, Stephen, 189
Schnitzer, Sunny, 204
Schnitzler, Arthur, 146
Schoaff, Eric, 218
Schoditsch, Peggy, 193
Schoen, Walter, 209
Schoenbaum, Milly, 61, 66, 83
Schofield, Scott, 190
*School for Wives*, 216
Schooley, B. Jaye, 177
Schoonover, Holly, 179
Schramm, David, 91, 92, 93, 94, 257
Schroder, William, 205
Schroeder, Gregory, 173
Schroeder, Ronald, 224
Schuck, Peter, 189
Schudson, Ruth, 216
Schuette, Elizabeth, 173
Schulfer, Arlene, 206
Schuller, Gunther, 18
Schulman, Susan L., 11, 13, 31, 44, 46
Schulte, Sally, 200
Schultz, Dwight, 188
Schultz, Rhona, 206
Schuman, Edward L., 66
Schurmann, David, 215
Schuster, Matthew, 78
Schwadron, Patricia, 225
Schwartz, Aaron, 213
Schwartz, Jan Ian, 180
Schwartz, Stephen, 61, 62, 154, 177, 179, 224
Schwartz, Vernon R., 203
Schwatz, Carole, 14, 232, 257
Schweitzer, Thomas, 184
Schweppe, Marla, 118
Schwinn, Ron, 8
Sclan, Shellie, 208
Scofield, Pamela, 70
Scogin, Robert, 209
Scolari, Peter, 111
Scott, Alan, 86
*Scott and Zelda*, 187
Scott, Bessye Ruth, 25
Scott, David M., 218
Scott, George, 124, 125
Scott, George C., 8, 11, 234, 257
Scott, Gloria, 210
Scott, Harold, 145, 221
Scott, James, 177
Scott, Joel, 86
Scott, John, 18
Scott, Kenneth, 64
Scott, Lea, 124
Scott, Les, 39
Scott, Martha, 8, 12, 257
Scott, Mike, 78
Scott, Pippa, 234
Scott, Seret, 207, 216
Scott, Stacy, 123
Scott, Steve, 257
Scott, Timothy, 160
Scott/Bloom, 12
Scoullar, John, 155
Scurria, Anne, 208
*Sea Horse, The*, 187, 209
*Sea Marks*, 122
*Sea, The*, 191
Seacat, Sandra, 82
Seale, Douglas, 218
Seales, Franklyn, 181, 223
Seamon, Ed, 123
Seamon, Edward, 75
Sears, Michael, 78
Sears, Sally, 21, 36
*Seascape*, 228
Seasongood, Eda, 12
Seatle, Dixie, 213
Seattle Repertory Theatre, 221
*Second Wind*, 111
Secrest, James, 223
*Secret Service*, 141
Secretario, Dingo, 39
*Section Nine*, 214

*See the Players*, 186
Seeger, Sanford, 45
Seely, Nina, 13, 132, 212
Seff Associates, 56
Seff, Richard, 28
Segal, David F., 21, 50, 91, 92, 93, 94, 211, 224
Segal, Eric, 143
Segal, Mark, 208
Seger, Richard, 59
Segovia, Isabel, 115
Sehrt, Ann, 151
Seidel, Virginia, 8, 32, 231, 232, 257
Seidman, John, 131
Seignious, Juliet, 55
Seitz, John, 147, 171, 181
Seitz, Karen, 120
Selby, Anne, 184
Selby, David, 50, 75
Selby, James, 178
Selden, Barbara, 183
Seldes, Marian, 63, 257
Self, Kas, 181
Selig, Susan, 175
Sell, Janie, 76, 234, 257
Sellers, Barry, 173
Sellin, Nancy, 223
Sellon, Kim, 30
Selman, Linda, 151, 209
Seltzer, Daniel, 8, 42, 108, 231, 232, 257
Selzer, Milton, 213
Semer, Neil, 120
Semes, Renee, 257
Semien, Steiv, 162
Semonin, David, 69
Senack, Marsha, 214
Sender, Henry, 100
Seneca, Joe, 97
Sennett, Jo, 180
*Separate Checks, Please*, 120
Septee, Moe, 20, 45
Serafin, S. R., 180
Serbagi, Roger, 126, 127
*Serenading Louie*, 109, 223
Serino, Frederic, 199
Serpe, Richard, 196
Serrecchia, Michael, 14
Sertner, Bob, 195
Setzer, Dell, 88
Setzer, Milton, 166
Seubert, Evelyn, 71
*Seven Keys to Baldpate*, 221
*1776*, 228
*1776 ... And All That Jazz*, 191, 244, 245
Sevra, Robert, 221
Sewali, Roger, 224
Sewell, Danny, 122, 147, 163
Sexton, Anne, 123
Seymour, James, 224
Seymour, Mary, 169
Shackelford, John, 123
Shackelford, Ted, 34
*Shadow and Substance*, 228
*Shadow Box, The*, 196
Shaffer, Louise, 106, 145
Shaffer, Peter, 63, 163, 194, 213, 224
Shakar, Martin, 145, 205
Shakespeare, William, 103, 129, 143, 146, 147, 167, 174, 175, 176, 178, 179, 180, 181, 201, 204, 214, 220, 227
Shakespearean Theater of Maine, 183
Shaktman, Ben, 220
Shaler, Anna, 145
Shallat, Phil, 221
Shallo, Karen, 127
Shalwitz, Howard, 224
Shane, Hal, 32, 257
Shannon, Mark, 163
Shapiro, Dan, 206
Shapiro, Jon, 176
Shapiro, Joseph, 65
Shapiro, Leonardo, 137
Shapiro, Mel, 136
Shapiro, Sparky, 51
Sharkey, Susan, 123, 211, 212
Sharkey, Tom, 203
Shatner, William, 234
Shattil, Arlene, 169
*Shaw for a Summer Night*, 70
Shaw, George Bernard, 47, 131, 144, 206, 221
Shaw, Madeline, 20
Shaw, Margery, 180
Shaw, Philip W., 167
Shaw, Steven, 38, 64
Shaw, Vanessa, 169
Shaw, Zola, 205
Shawhan, April, 51, 234, 257

Shawn, Dick, 26, 208, 257
Shawn, Marvin G., 218
Shawnasey, Camille, 180
Shay, Michele, 174
Shaye, Lin, 144, 145
Shayne, Sharron, 145
*She Who Was He*, 82
Shea, Joe, 203
Shea, John V., 8, 20, 231, 232, 257
Sheahan, Steve, 123
Shear, Pearl, 196
Shearin, John, 143, 144, 149
Shearman, Alan, 201, 209
Shearwood, James, 143
Sheehan, John, 109, 146
Sheehan, Michael, 227
Sheehan, Nadya Grushetzka, 208
Sheehan, Thomas, 218
Sheen, Martin, 11, 257
Sheffer, Jonathan, 137
Sheiness, Marsha, 143, 145
Shelby, Ken, 74
Shelby, Lillian, 51
Sheldon, Anne, 214
Sheldon, Edward, 106, 145
Shelley, Barbara, 51
Shelley, Carole, 8, 28, 29, 257
Shelley, Mary, 70
Shelton, Louise, 120
Shelton, Ray, 75
Shelton, Reid, 55, 71, 257
Shelton, Sloan, 8, 208, 211, 257
Shen, Freda Foh, 39
*Shenandoa*, 65
Shendell, Earl, 19, 37, 59, 64, 155
Shepard, Joan, 126
Shepard, Karen, 37
Shepard, Sam, 122, 151, 206
Shepard, Tina, 197
Shepherd, Haig, 205
Shepherd, John, 180
Sheppard, Gene, 43
Sher, Gloria, 65
Sher, Louis K., 65
Sherer, Werner, 51, 55, 65
Sheridan, Bobby, 146
Sheridan, John, 234, 257
Sheridan, Liz, 59
Sheridan, Roseann, 114
Sherin, Edwin, 35, 51, 155, 211
*Sherlock Holmes*, 66, 171
*Sherlock Holmes in Scandal in Bohemia*, 214
Sherman, Arthur, 82
Sherman, Lee, 12
Sherman, Martin, 81
Sherman, Wende, 110
Shermer, Phil, 221
Sherrer, Hugh, 95, 143
Sherwood, Anthony, 196
Sherwood, John, 177
Sherwood, Robert, 151
Shevelove, Burt, 52, 196
Shevelove/Sondheim, 178
Shewer, Kenneth, 119, 121
Shields, Thom, 177
Shimerman, Armin, 133, 175
Shimizu, Sachi, 25
Shimoda, Yuki, 39, 257
Shimono, Sab, 39, 257
Shirvanzade, Alexandre, 110
Shlansky, Steven P., 117
Shnider, Marshall, 174, 204, 214
Shockley, Robert, 121
Shookhoff, David, 123
Shores, Charles, 166
Shorr, William, 143
*Short Eyes*, 228
*Shortchanged Review, The*, 130
Shorte, Dino, 226
Short-Goldsen, Martha, 10, 123
Shotwell, Sandra, 189
Shovestull, Thom, 204
*Show-off, The*, 188, 212
*Shrike, The*, 228
Shropshire, Anne, 207
Shub, Lauren, 143
Shub, Vivienne, 194
Shubb, Jason, 197
Shulman, Alan, 75
Shumaker, David, 143
Shumlin, Lola, 61
Shutta, Ethel, 266
Shutter, Nancy, 13
Shyre, Paul, 86, 257
Sibella, Barbara, 183
Sibert, Roderick, 169
Sica, Louis, 63, 163
Sicari, Sal, 86
Sick, Mark, 151

Siders, Irving, 38
Sidney, Sylvia, 44, 257
Siebert, Charles, 257
Siebert, Ron, 212
Sieck, Barbara, 208
Siegal, Gerald, 147, 148
Siegal, Janet, 114
Siegel, Harvey, 127
Siegel, June, 72
Siegel, Robin, 113
Siff, Ira, 143
Siff, Iris, 188
Sigley, Marjorie, 223
Signore, Don, 81
Signore, Norma, 81
Signorelli, Tom, 16, 257
Sigrist, Susan, 116
Silbert, Larry, 208
Silbert, Peter, 182, 187
Sileika, Gintare, 224
Siletti, Mario, 167
Silk, Geri, 113
Silliman, Maureen, 65, 257
Sills, Pawnee, 74, 257
Silver, Alf, 213
Silver, Dorothy, 82
Silver, Robert, 143
Silver, Robert B., 123
Silver, Scott, 208
Silver, Stanley D., 208
Silver, Stuart, 257
Silver, Tim, 114
Silvestri, Marty, 78
Silvey, Frank, 193
Simeone, Jerry, 120
Simione, Donn, 160
Simmonds, Stanley, 54
Simmons, Keith, 257
Simmons, Nancy, 28, 61
Simmons, Stanley, 52
Simms, George Cecil, 199
Simon, Alfred, 142
Simon, Cliff, 121, 143, 151
Simon, Cyril, 121
Simon, Joel, 145
Simon, Marion, 225
Simon, Neil, 67, 203
Simonds, Al, 81
Simpler, Norman, 179
Simpon, George, 98
Simpson, Peter, 143, 144
Simpson, Steve, 220
Sims, Corie, 78, 257
Sims, Marley, 257
Simson, George, 98
Sinatra, Frank, 8
Sinclair, Eric, 221, 234
Sinclair, Paulette, 143
Sinclair, Richard, 218
Sinden, Donald, 8, 30, 257
Singer, Barry, 16
Singer, Isaac Bashevis, 20
Singlar, James, 112, 114
Singleton, Dorothy, 221
Singleton, Janyse M., 64
Singleton, Katherine, 18
Singleton, Sam, 126, 194
Sirasky, Fred, 113
Sirchia, Jerry, 48, 79
Sirianni, E. A., 197
*Sister Sadie*, 126, 127
*1600 Pennsylvania Avenue*, 8, 55
Skal, Dave, 207
Skala, Lilia, 95, 257
Skelton, Thomas, 10, 11, 31, 40, 46, 57, 65, 68, 157
*Skin of Our Teeth, The*, 8, 12, 211, 228
Skinner, Margo, 225
Sklar, Warren, 186
Sklaroff, Michael, 143
Skorton, Ronald, 180
Slack, Ben, 57, 127, 128, 257
Slade, Bernard, 66
Slade, Betsy, 197
Slade, Loraine, 226
Slaiman, Marjorie, 45, 190
Slane, Stephan, 185
Slater, Jack, 202
Slater, Shirley, 197
Slater, Stewart, 187
Slavin, Fredda, 83, 223
Slavin, John, 123
*Sleuth*, 186, 192, 228
Slez, Tony, 68, 69
*Slight Ache, A*, 122
Sloan, Gertrude, 85
Sloan, Roberta, 218
Slotnick, Barbara, 158
Small, Marya, 60
Small, Neva, 59, 257
*Small War on Murray Hill*, 151
Smalls, Charlie, 64
Smallwood, Tucker, 127
Smart, Jean, 182
Smiley, Brenda, 234
Smith, Adrian, 206
Smith, Alan, 191
Smith, Alexandra, 258

Smith, Alexis, 21, 258
Smith, Alison, 195
Smith, Allan, 79
Smith, Anna Deavere, 189
Smith, Barrey, 60, 258
Smith, Barry, 159, 200
Smith, Caroline, 189
Smith, Charlotte, 208
Smith, Chris, 200
Smith, Dana, 146
Smith, Delos V., Jr., 196
Smith, Dick, 202
Smith, Donald P., 77
Smith, Donegan, 28
Smith, Douglas, 225
Smith, Ernie, 90, 123
Smith, Garnett, 62
Smith, Gay Beale, 180
Smith, Geddeth, 207
Smith, Gladys, 127
Smith, Glenn Allen, 201
Smith, Guy J., 126
Smith, Howlett, 19
Smith, J. W., 135
Smith, Jeremy, 227
Smith, Jim, 147, 218
Smith, Joy, 208
Smith, Kurtwood, 193
Smith, Lane, 17, 69, 190
Smith, Lawrence, 224
Smith, Lemmie, 200
Smith, Lionel, 206
Smith, Lois, 31
Smith, Michael, 169, 221
Smith, Mimi, 179
Smith, Nancy Johnston, 211
Smith, Nick, 135
Smith, Oliver, 25, 36, 47, 50, 158, 214
Smith, Polly, 175
Smith, Rodger W., 218
Smith, Roy, 54, 161
Smith, Sandra, 234
Smith, Sheila, 163, 234
Smith, Stephen Lawrence, 98
Smith, Sydney, 21, 49, 59
Smith, T. Schuyler, 60, 155
Smith, Thomas C., 50
Smith, Timothy, 47, 54, 68, 206
Smith, Tom, 13, 31, 46
Smith, Walter Barrett, 200
Smith-Lee, Jacqueline, 162
Smithwrick, Jarett, 98, 126
Smoking Pistols, 151
Smothers, William, 234
Smythe, Marcus, 116, 175, 258
Snair, Joseph, 194
Sneed, Maurice, 126
Snell, David, 220
Snodgrass, Wanda, 176
Snook, Robert, 199
Snoopy!!!, 172
Snow, Norman, 91, 92, 93, 94
Snow, Steven, 221
Snowdon, Ted, 144
Snyder, Arlen Dean, 132, 258
Snyder, Beverly, 165
Snyder, Bill, 218
Snyder, Dan, 136
Snyder, Drew, 214
Snyder, Nancy, 8, 42, 108, 223
Snyder, Nancy E., 258
So Long, 174th Street, 52
So Nice, They Named It Twice, 135
Sobechanskaya, Ekathrina, 82
Sobek, Allan, 21
Soboloff, Arnold, 196
Soiffer, Freda, 52, 258
Sokoll, Zelig, 73
Sol, 115
Solen, Paul, 8, 61, 258
Solly, Bill, 70
Solomon, Renee, 72
Soloway, Leonard, 12, 41, 42, 48
Someone sort of Grandish, 79
Somerville, Phyllis, 190
Something's Afoot, 59
Somkin, Steven, 127
Sommer, Elke, 203
Sommer, Josef, 207, 208, 214
Sommers, T. J., 218
Sommer, Pearl, 65
Son, The, 123
Sondheim, Stephen, 39, 76, 119, 146, 213, 224
Song of the Whip-Poor-Will, The, 202
Songs from Pins and Needles, 123
Songs of Quincy-Burch, 123
Songs of the Street, 44
Soodik, Trish, 200

Soon, Terence Tam, 205, 210
Sophocles, 197
Sopyla, Ronald S., 173
Sorel, Eve, 117
Sorel, Theodore, 174, 214
Sorrel, Scott, 98, 258
Sorrells, Vance B., 190
Sorrels, Roy, 151
Sosenko, Anna, 54
Sosnowsky, Bonnie, 199
Soto, Anibal, 150
Soubirou, Genevieve, 56
Soule, Robert D., 225
Soules, Dale, 62, 75, 122
Sound of Music, 228
Sousa, Pamela, 8
South Pacific, 228
Southcotte, Georgia, 118, 149
Southern, Richard, 130
Souvenir, 156
Spackman, Thomas C., 215
Spangler, David, 62
Spanish Theatre Repertory Company, 150
Sparer, Paul, 45, 127
Spear, Kathy, 78
Special Theatre World Award, 8
Spector, Arnold, 68
Spector, Mary, 167, 168
Spector, Renee, 68
Speer, Alexander, 187
Spelling Bee, The, 145
Spelman, Jeffery, 218
Spelman, Leon, 120, 158
Spelman, Sharon, 221
Spencer, Christine, 18
Spencer, Clint, 212
Spencer, Frank, 143
Spencer, John, 192
Spencer, Vernon, 117
Speros, Jo, 51
Spewack, Bella, 142, 191, 203
Spewack, Sam, 142, 203
Spiegel, Barbara, 258
Spiegel, Laurie, 114
Spielberg, David, 205
Spielman, Jeff, 41
Spiller, Jo, 204
Spiller, Marshall S., 84
Spiller, Tom, 186
Spinelli, Larry, 258
Spiner, Brent, 75
Spinetti, Victor, 234
Spitz, Alan, 120
Spitz, Sharon, 144
Spivey, Richard, 211
Sponseller, Howard, 154, 258
Sponsler, Suzanne, 37
Spoon River Anthology, 168
Spratt, Nadyne, 135
Springer, Ashton, 16, 43, 74
Springer, John, 163
Spring's Awakening, 107
Spritzer, Lorraine, 148
Squibb, June, 117, 145, 258
St. Clair, Robert, 38
St. George, Dick, 180
St. John, Kelly, 170
St. John, Larry, 179
St. John, Marco, 31, 207
St. John, Michael, 95
St. Louis, Louis, 60, 155
Stabler, Stephen, 208
Stadd, Arlene, 205
Stadlen, Lewis J., 234, 258
Stadtmore, Neil, 180
Staetter, Michael, 179
Stafford, Ronald, 62
Stag at Bay, 208
Stage I Theatre Lab, 221
Stage/West, 223
Stahlnecker, Pennye, 149
Staley, James, 211, 221
Staller, David, 25
Stallings, Bill, 121
Stallings, Rex, 144
Stallworth, Robert, 191
Stancil, William, 226
Stanford, Gully, 190
Stanford-Grant, Kathleen, 43
Stanley, Alvah, 171, 174
Stanley, Andrey, 182
Stanley, Kim, 234
Stanley, Robert, 68
Stansbury, Hope, 258
Stanton, Janice, 200, 211
Stanton, Katharine, 147
Stanton, Thomas J., 55
Stapleton, Jean, 54
Stapleton, Katharine, 189
Stapleton, Maureen, 8, 31, 54, 234, 258
Star Spangled Girl, The, 218
Stark, Douglas, 127, 145
Starkey, Jack, 47

Starr, John, 180
Starwalt, David Carl, 203
Stashick, Brian, 100
State of the Union, 228
Stathis, Nicholas John, 110
Stattel, Robert, 190, 258
Statues, 206
Staub, Gerd, 110
Staudt, Christian, 81
Stauf, 114
Stavola, Charlie, 111
Stechschulte, Tom, 35
Stecko, Bob, 88
Stedham, Michael, 173
Steele, M. Jonathan, 109
Steele, Walter, 123
Steelman, Ronald, 180, 198
Steenburgen, Mary, 123
Steere, James, 116
Stefan, Marina, 112
Stefani, Michael, 200
Steffe, Edwin, 55
Steiger, Robert, 193
Steiker, Giselle, 51
Stein, Daniel, 80
Stein, Gary, 16
Stein, Joseph, 52
Stein, Julian, 152
Stein, Vicki, 8
Steinbeck, John, 199, 213
Steinberg, Elvira, 111
Steinberg, Lillian, 218
Steinberg, Robert, 126, 127
Steinke, Carole, 82
Steinkellner, Hans, 193
Steinlauf, Steven, 83
Steisel, Steve, 109
Steisel, Steven, 145
Stenborg, Helen, 107, 258
Stender, Douglas, 181, 200, 212
Stephen, Garn, 60
Stephen, Prima, 75
Stephens, Allan, 195
Stephens, Garn, 196, 258
Stephens, Mary Lou, 195
Stephens, Nicki, 127
Stephens, Norman, 89
Stephens, Robert, 171
Stephenson, Colleen, 184
Stern, Artie, 180
Stern, Daniel, 98
Stern, Deborah Ann, 190
Stern, Edward, 209
Stern, Joseph, 258
Stern, Leo, 17, 38, 65
Stern, Pat, 116
Sternhagen, Frances, 63, 258
Stevens, Connie, 234
Stevens, E. Allan, 65
Stevens, John R., 201
Stevens, John Wright, 208
Stevens, Maura, 143
Stevens, Roger L., 12, 21, 36, 40, 50, 57, 211
Stevens, Roy K., 91, 92, 93, 94, 149
Stevens, Scott, 206
Stevens, Susan, 208
Stevens, Tony, 8, 41
Stevensen, Scott, 234, 258
Stevenson, Clay, 84
Stevenson, Florence, 120
Stevenson, Margot, 36, 258
Stevenson, Robert, 209
Stevlingson, Edward, 178, 209
Stewart, Benjamin, 197
Stewart, Billie Anita, 178
Stewart, Dixie, 68
Stewart, Gordon, 134
Stewart, Jean-Pierre, 83, 108, 258
Stewart, Jim, 143
Stewart, John, 57, 234
Stewart, Louis, 116
Stewart, Mary Lou, 189
Stewart, Michael, 25
Stewart, Patricia, 145, 258
Stewart, Thomas A., 206
Stewart, William, 174
Stickler, Sam, 89
Stickney, Dorothy, 61
Sticks and Bones, 228
Stiegel, William, 150
Stiers, David Ogden, 62, 179, 196, 258
Stifel, David, 197
Stiller, Jerry, 258
Stillsong, 201
Stillwell, Diane, 60, 126
Stimac, Anthony, 67, 71
Stings, 90
Stinnette, Dorothy, 198
Stitt, Milan, 58, 208
Stivender, Regina, 207
Stockley, Mada, 186
Stockton, Charles, 223
Stockton, Dai, 145
Stockwell, Guy, 215
Stoddart, Alexandra, 13, 171

Stoehr, Joel, 173
Stokes, Diane, 36
Stone, Anne, 204
Stone, Fredric, 158
Stone, Harold, 206
Stone, Jay, 194
Stone, Michael, 166
Stoney, Yvonne, 64
Stonorov, Andrea, 224
Stoppard, Tom, 22, 194
Storch, Frank, 13
Storey, David, 122
Storey, Francine, 113, 114
Storey, Howard, 213
Storm, Michael, 109, 146, 147
Storrow, James, 51
Story, 86
Stott, Ken, 103
Stough, Raymond, 113, 114
Stout, Stephen, 216
Stovall, Count, 207
Straiges, Tony, 143, 226, 227
Strait, Ralph, 155
Strane, Robert, 191
Strange, Clayton, 55
Strange Interlude, 228
Strasberg, Lee, 228
Strasser, Robin, 196, 197
Stratford Festival of Canada, 184
Stratford, Michael James, 20
Stratton, Charlotte, 218
Straub, John, 178
Straus, Barnard S., 34
Straus, Robert V., 21
Strauss, Marilyn, 41
Strauss, Suzy, 172
Streamers, 8, 132, 212, 228
Streater, Susan, 226
Streep, Meryl, 8, 128, 138, 139, 141, 231, 232, 258
Street Scene, 228
Streetcar Named Desire, A, 191, 217, 228
Strickland, Cynthia, 225
Strickler, Susan, 208
Stricklyn, Ray, 234
Stride, John, 234
Strimling, Arthur, 137
Strindberg, August, 112, 115
Striptease, 207
Strobach, Ben, 40
Strong, Sidney, 98
Stronger, The, 112
Strozier, Henry, 217
Stuart, Laura, 28
Stuart, Michel, 14, 21
Stuart, Rosana, 84
Stuart, Sebastian, 57
Stuart, Sonja, 47
Stubbs, Louise, 141, 142
Stubbs, Michelle, 41
Stuckmann, Eugene, 155
Studer, Hal, 144
Studio Arena Theatre, 224
Sturges, Patricia, 196
Sturgis, Craig, 143
Stuthman, Fred, 149, 258
Styne, Jule, 54
Suarez, Regina, 150
Subject Was Roses, The, 228
Subreal, 192
Suda, Rocky, 153
Sudert, Susan, 144
Sudol, Kim, 177
Sudrow, Irving, 159
Sues, Alan, 171
Suffin, Jordan, 65
Sulka, Elaine, 113, 114, 167, 168
Sullivan, 143
Sullivan, Brad, 204
Sullivan, Frank, 100
Sullivan, Ian, 37, 258
Sullivan, Jeremiah, 209, 224
Sullivan, Jim, 60
Sullivan, Owen, 203
Sullivan, Pat, 86
Summer and Smoke, 147
Summer Brave, 21, 211
Summer in the Country, 112
Summer, Marnel, 155
Summerhays, Jane, 160
Summers, Caley, 207
Summers, Michelle, 194
Summers, Tuesday, 153
Sumner, Marnel, 55
Sumter, Gwen, 81
Sunday in New York, 203
Sundsten, Lani, 155
Sunrise at Campobello, 228
Sunshine Boys, The, 187
Surerus, Gerard, 146

Surovy, Nicolas, 91, 92, 93, 94, 234
Surviving the Barbed Wire Cradle, 113
Susa, Conrad, 123, 179
Sutherland, Esther, 203
Sutherland, Steven, 215
Sutorius, James, 129, 258
Sutter, Maury, 205
Sutton, J. D., 199
Suzuki, Pat, 234
Swaine, Jim, 143
Swan Dive, 143
Swan, Jon, 123
Swan Song, 112
Swansen, Larry, 105, 258
Swanson, Britt, 196
Swanson, Sara, 68
Swartz, Gary, 114
Sweeney, John, 184
Sweet Bird of Youth, 7, 8, 35, 101, 180, 211
Sweet, Dolph, 132, 212, 258
Sweet William, 88
Sweetbird, 210
Sweigart, Charles, 174
Swenson, Inga, 234
Swenson, Linda, 111
Swenson, Swen, 234
Swerdfager, Bruce, 184
Swetland, William, 13, 212
Swiggard, William, 52
Swire, R. Derek, 45
Swit, Loretta, 66
Switkes, Willy, 145
Swope, Rusty, 218
Sydnor, Earl, 206
Sydow, Jack, 186
Syers, Mark, 39, 258
Sylbert, Paul, 196
Sylvain, Virginia, 16
Sylvest, Donovan, 122
Sylvester, Joyce, 125
Symonds, Robert, 38, 188, 258
Szablya, Helen, 210
Szajna, Jozef, 104, 224
Szarabajka, Keith, 206
Szatanski, Jania, 212
Szelag, Dan, 194
Szogyi, Alex, 69
Szykulska, Ewa, 104
Szymkowicz, Cyndee, 143
Table Manners, 28
Tabor, David, 208
Tabor, Eron, 41
Tabor, Richard, 24
Tabori, Kristoffer, 8, 30, 234, 259
Tacker, Francine, 189
Tackey, Bill, 170
Tackus, Sallyanne, 98
Taffee, Beth, 173
Taft, Mary Gordon, 218
Tagliente, Robin, 108
Tait, Dean, 123
Takcus, Sallyanne, 98
Taking of Miss Janie, The, 154, 228
Talayco, Lucille, 73
Talbert, Katherine, 122, 123, 132
Talbot, Lyle, 188
Talbot, Sharon, 74
Tallman, Randolph, 201
Talmadge, Edward Lee, 220
Tamaroff, Marsha, 68
Tambor, Jeffrey, 216
Taming of the Shrew, The, 189
Tamm, Daniel, 40
Tammi, Paavo, 111
Tammi, Tom, 111
Tampoya, Sam, 161
Tan Chinn, Lori, 83
Tango, Donald, 166
Tania, 73
Tanner, Melinda, 154, 259
Tanner, Tony, 59, 147, 224, 259
Tanzania, War Hawk, 135
Tapper, Max, 213
Tarallo, Barry J., 60
Tarbuck, Barbara, 190, 223
Tarkington, Booth, 148
Tarleton, Diane, 20, 259
Tarrant, Larry, 199
Tartuffe, 191, 194
Task, Maggie, 40
Taste of Honey, A, 228
Tate, Dennis, 38, 145, 259
Tato, Bernard, 146
Tatum, Bill, 118, 120, 121, 259
Tauber, Eleanor, 33
Tauber, Joy, 190
Tauber, Richard, 90
Taulane, Gina, 201
Tavaris, Eric, 180, 215
Tavern, The, 209
Taylor, Alwin, 64, 205
Taylor, Billy, 205

Taylor, Clarice, 64, 259
Taylor, Clay, 203
Taylor, Corliss, 169
Taylor, Danny, 161
Taylor, David, 12, 41, 160, 218
Taylor, E. J., 39
Taylor, George, 194
Taylor, Glenn, 190
Taylor, Greg, 42
Taylor, Holland, 34
Taylor, Horacena J., 10, 125
Taylor, Laurette, 31
Taylor, Mark, 208
Taylor, Melissa, 173
Taylor, Noel, 28
Taylor, R. Thad, 177
Taylor, Robert U., 16, 27, 111, 169
Taylor, Samuel, 57
Taylor, Theda, 185
Taylor, Thomas, 176
Taylor, Vern, 186
Teacher's Room, The, 144
Teague, Anthony S., 189
Teahouse of the August Moon, 228
Tebelak, John-Michael, 154
Tebesli, Ilsebet Anna, 137
Teeter, Lara, 218
Teijelo, Gerald R., 51
Teitel, Carol, 102, 220, 259
Teller, Deborah, 114
Temchin, Jack, 209
Tempest, The, 167, 173, 179, 183, 223
Temple, Renny, 77
Temptation, Tammy, 113
Ten Little Indians, 187
Tenderloin, 116
Tennenbaum, Cindy, 143, 144
Tenney, Chris, 149
Tenney, Del, 208
Tenney, Margot, 208
Ter-Arutunian, Rouben, 46
Terkel, Studs, 113
Terrell, Gloria P., 217
Terrible Jim Fitch, 113
Terry, Lee, 155
Terry, Paul, 121
Tesich, Steve, 95
Tesney, Steven B., 218
Tessier, Claude R., 161
Testa, Mary, 127
Tewkesbury, Joan, 197
Texas Trilogy, A, 211
Tezla, Michael, 206
Thacker, Cheryl, 58, 130, 143
Thacker, Russ, 37, 44, 232, 234, 259
Thalenberg, David, 145
Thanksgiving July 2, 120
That Championship Season, 180, 195, 201, 209, 228
Theatre Off Park, 151
Theatre Venture '76, 185
Theodore, Donna, 8, 65, 234, 259
There Shall Be No Night, 228
There's One in Every Marriage, 191
Therriault, Daniel, 188
Thesing, James J., 183
They Knew What They Wanted, 140, 228
Thigpen, Lynne, 62
Thigpen, Martha, 55, 143
Thirkield, Rob, 107
This Is (An Entertainment), 189
Thomas, Brandon, 194
Thomas, Brent, 195
Thomas, Cal, 177
Thomas, Chris, 144
Thomas, David E., 55
Thomas, Eberle, 191, 217
Thomas, Ernest, 126
Thomas, Evelyn, 64
Thomas, Gwen, 213
Thomas, Henry, 194
Thomas, Isa, 191
Thomas, Jacque, 201
Thomas, Marshall, 65
Thomas, Paul C., 102, 194, 221
Thomas, Robert, 14, 160, 161
Thomas, Roy, 126
Thomas, Scott, 208
Thomas, Tasha, 64
Thomas, Tom, 220
Thomas, William, Jr., 259
Thomason, Ruth, 110
Thome, David, 14, 54, 259
Thompson, Ann, 127
Thompson, Cameron A., 149

Thompson, Edmonstone, Jr., 102, 211
Thompson, Eric, 28, 126, 127
Thompson, Ernest, 21, 259
Thompson, Evan, 152
Thompson, Fred, 215
Thompson, Jeffery V., 209
Thompson, Jeniffer, 121
Thompson, John, 218
Thompson, Liz, 174
Thompson, Marina, 127
Thompson, Michael, 187, 220
Thompson, Molly, 208
Thompson, Nancy, 215
Thompson, Neal, 116, 198
Thompson, Robert E., 33, 259
Thompson, Tazewell, 82
Thompson, Tony, 78
Thompson, Trinity, 194
Thomson, Margaret, 207
Thorndike, Sybil, 266
Thorne, Joan, 211
Thorne, Richard, 82
Thornton, Clark W., 67, 71
Thorpe, John C., 210
Thorpes, Chuck, 169
Three Plays of the Yuan Dynasty, 206
Three Sisters, 193, 196
Three Sisters, The, 94, 193
Threepenny Opera, 133
Threepenny Opera, The, 8
Thrush, Bradley, 177
Thunder Rock, 121
Thurn, Jane, 114, 167
Thurston, James, 18
Tiano, Lou, 127
Tibbles, George, 203
Tickles By Tucholsky, 89
Tidwell, Brian, 218
Tiffin, Pamela, 234
Tigar, Ken, 143
Tiger at the Gates, 228
Tiller, Monica, 8
Tillinger, John, 212
Tilton, James, 138, 141, 142
Time of Your Life, The, 93, 228
Timm, Charles C., 121
Timmers, Jack, 51
Timon of Athens, 175
Tims, Gareth, 112
Tiny Alice, 188, 189
Tipton, Jennifer, 30, 34, 51
Tirabassi, Donald, 10, 45
Tiraco, Joseph, 76
Tirelli, Jaime, 259
Titanic, 90
Titus, Rawle, 180
To See the Elephant, 197
Tobacco Road, 191
Tobia, Ricardo, 39
Tobin, Francis, 155
Toguri, David, 184
Tokuda, Marilyn, 210
Tolan, Robert W., 198
Tolaydo, Michael, 91, 92, 93, 94, 259
Tolbert, Gayle, 221
Tolbert, Leonard R., 220
Toler, Ronald F., 122
Toles, Paul, 218
Tolkan, James, 190
Tolson, Pat, 34
Tom Jones, 208
Toman, Alan, 207
Tomei, Concetta, 188
Tomfohrde, Anne, 47
Tomko, Michael, 113
Tomlin, Lily, 190
Tomlin, Robert, 143
Tommon, Marie, 158
Tompkins, Claudia, 19
Tompkins, Joe, 197
Toms, Carl, 22, 30, 171
Tone, Ben, 186
Toner, Thomas, 158, 211
Tony, 8
Tonys, 8
Too Much Johnson, 196
Toombs, Lee, 200
Top of the Seventh, 154
Topping, Ann H., 186
Topping, Susan, 113
Torchia, Lee, 73
Tore, Alberto, 150
Tores, Gil, 114
Torn, Rip, 8, 31, 234, 259
Torok, Frank S., 227
Torres, Andy, 64, 259
Torres, Donald, 196
Torres, Mariana, 51
Tortora, Ozzie, 121, 127
Toser, David, 32
Tost, William, 100
Tot Family, The, 190
Total Recall, 190
Toth, Betsy, 204
Touers, Charles, 175

Touliatos, George, 190
Toupou, Manu, 98
Tovar, Candace, 8, 51, 68, 69
Towb, Harry, 22, 259
Towbin, Marion Fredi, 121
Townley, Edward, 70
Toys in the Attic, 228
Trachtenberg, Harriett, 8, 59, 89
Tracy, Ed, 175
Tracy, John, 234
Tracy, Matt, 201
Trainer, Sirin Devrim, 216
Trammell, Lynn, 201
Transformations, 123
Trapani, Lou, 259
Traube, Lenny, 33
Traube, Shepard, 33
Travers, James, 19
Travers, Sy, 152
Travesties, 7, 8, 22, 228
Travis, Douglas, 24, 143
Travis, Priscilla, 113
Treacher, Arthur, 266
Treat, Martin, 114
Treemonisha, 8, 18
Trelawny of the 'Wells', 8, 128
Trenkle, Tom, 62, 91, 92, 93, 94, 138, 140, 141, 142, 154
Trenner, Donn, 49
Treyz, Russell, 119, 185
Triana, Jose, 115
Triana, Patricia, 145
Tribach, Augie, 177
Tribush, Nancy, 122
Trigger, Ian J., 30, 214, 259
Trinity Square Repertory Company, 225
Triplett, Lee, 86
Troilus and Cressida, 176, 227
Trolls and Bridges, 191
Troob, Daniel, 39
Troobnick, Eugene, 227
Trotman, William, 188
Trott, Pat, 32
Trotta, Ed, 154
Trotta, Francie, 82
Troutman, Ron, 70
Troutman, William, 188
Troy, Louise, 63, 218, 219
Troyano, Rosemary, 65
Truckload, 155
Trumpets and Drums, 184
Trumpler, Alan, 218
Tsoutsouvas, Sam, 92, 93, 94
Tsu, Susan, 118, 154
Tucci, Maria, 174, 214
Tucci, Michael, 60, 259
Tuckho, Les, 210
Tucker, Betsy, 223
Tucker, Brooke, 203
Tucker, Courtney, 208
Tucker, Dane, 224
Tucker, Forrest, 203
Tucker, Michael, 128, 181, 208
Tucker, Robert, 65
Tucker, Tommy N., Jr., 223
Tuider, Herman, 183
Tullman, Erv, 34
Tumarin, Boris, 94
Tunick, Jonathan, 14, 39, 160, 161
Tupou, Manu, 98, 259
Turenne, Louis, 127, 208
Turet, Maurice, 20, 25, 57, 155
Turgenev, Ivan, 111
Turley, Myra, 121
Turnbull, Walter, 18
Turner, Charles, 207
Turner, Dan, 210
Turner, Gloria, 18
Turner, Jake, 220
Turner, James, 30
Turner, Jerry, 182
Turner, Lily, 88, 89
Turner, Mary, 182
Turner, Mary M., 220
Turner, Stewart, 180
Turner, Valeda, 179
Turner, William, 182
Turnham, Ruthmary, 176
Turque, Michael, 55
Turque, Mimi, 121
Turtz, Evan, 61
Tuscaloosa's Calling Me . . . But I'm Not Going!, 77
Tuthill, Bob, 81
Twelfth Night, 143, 173, 184, 220
27 Wagons Full of Cotton, 138, 231
Two for the Seesaw, 145
Two Gentlemen of Verona, 180, 184, 225, 228

Two McClures Sunnyside UP: 'The Pink Helmet,' 'The Masked Choir', 200
Two on an Island, 192
Two See Beside the Sea, 113
Twyford, Pepper, 218
Tymus, Tina, 79
Tyndall, Charles, 143
Tyrrell, John, 63, 259
Tyrrell, Lark Lee, 228
Tyrrell, Susan, 197
U. S. A., 218
Uchida, Christine, 37, 259
Uchima, Diane, 200
Udell, Peter, 65
Udoff, Yale M., 145
Uggams, Leslie, 234
Uhler, Eric, 218
Uhry, alfred, 65
Ullius, Mark, 203
Ullman, Bob, 14, 54, 134, 135, 136, 137
Ulloa, Martha, 150
Ullrick, Sharon, 196, 197
Ulmer, Joan, 119
Ulmer, John, 191, 208
Ulrickson, John, 51
Umbras, Peter, 167
Uncle Vanya, 180
Under Milk Wood, 215
Under Papa's Picture, 203
Unger, Charles, 218
Unger, Deborah, 191
Unger, Sally, 218
Unruh, Dell, 218
Uprooted, 197
Upton, frances, 266
Urbanski, Kazimierz, 104
Urmston, Kenneth, 61, 259
Urquhart, Deems, 221
Ursin, Marya, 144
Vaccaro, Brenda, 234
Vachon-Coco, LizaGrace, 75
Vail, Bishop, 224
Valance, Nikos, 208
Valente, J. P., 178, 198
Valentine, James, 218, 219
Valle, Freddy, 115
Van Ark, Joan, 234
Van Benschoten, Stephen, 191, 259
Van der Noot, Emile, 110
Van Dine, Louise, 8, 28
Van Dyke, Dick, 234
Van Dyke, Marcia, 234
Van Goeye, Ray, 177
Van Hunter, William, 114
Van Lieu, Ron, 143
Van Norden, Peter, 181
Van Patten, Joyce, 66
Van Vooren, Monique, 259
Van Zandt, Porter, 91
Vanase, Paul, 75
Vance, Kay, 37
Vance, Nina, 188
Vandergriff, Robert, 25
VandeSande, Bill, 224
Vanities, 8, 85, 144
Vann, David, 65
Vannutt, Robert P., 22
VanOver, Pat, 198
VanZandt, Christopher, 218
Vargas, Yasmin, 113
Vari, John, 123
Varian, Mark, 173
Varner, Jennifer, 173, 177
Varon, Susan, 144
Varrone, Gene, 52, 259
Vartorella, Rick, 196, 197
Vaughan, Anne, 127
Vaughan, Melanie, 51
Vaughan, Stuart, 127
Vazquez, Cookie, 14
Vega, Jose, 38, 64, 155
Vehr, Bill, 82
Velez, Henry, 38
Velton, Leslie, 182
Venable, Ronald, 200, 211
Vennema, John C., 36, 122, 171
Ventura, Paul, 193
Venus Observed, 228
VerBerkmoes, Robert, 208
Verbit, Helen, 128
Verbit, Larry, 204
Verdery, James, 182
Verdesca, Albert, 147
Verdi, Guiseppe, 146
Verdon, Gwen, 7, 8, 9, 234, 259
Vereen, Ben, 61, 234
Vernon, Richard, 151, 204
Vernon, Wall, 218
Very Gentle Person, A, 193
Very Good Eddie, 8, 32, 230, 231
Vestoff, Virginia, 27, 130, 259
Viator, Alma, 205
Viccini, Juan, 150

Vichiola, John, 208
Vickers, Larry, 49, 259
Vickland, Eric, 190
Victor, Lucia, 29
Vidnovic, Martin, 37
Vieira, Jelom, 17
Viertel, Peter, 156
Vigod, Robert, 184
Villaire, Holly, 30
Villar, Braulio, 150
Villechaize, Herve, 197
Vilvas, Emma, 115
Vincent, Irving Harrison, 208
Vincent, Paul, 198
Vines, William, 206
Vinovich, Steve, 126, 214
Viola, Richard S., 128, 137, 181
Viola, Rik, 218
Viracola, Fiddle, 138, 212
Virgin and the Unicorn, The, 120
Virginia Museum Theatre Repertory Company, 226
Visco, Philip, 113
Visions of Simone Machard, The, 216
Visit, The, 228
Vita, Michael, 8, 259
Vitale, Bill, 75
Vitella, Sel, 59, 147, 259
Vitelli, Ronald, 44
Voelpel, Fred, 32
Vogel, David, 152
Vogel, Ed, 81
Vogel, Gini, 193
Vogler, Herb, 62
Vogt, Peter, 194
Vohs, Frank, 114
Voice of the Turtle, The, 123
Voices Inc., 210
Voight, Jon, 234
Voland, Rex, 195
Vollano, George W., 208
Von Bargen, Danie, 225
Von Dohln, Christine, 83
Von Furstenberg, Betsy, 259
Von Hartz, John, 121
von Mayrhauser, Jennifer, 42, 107, 108, 109
von Mayrhauser, Peter, 136, 181
von Mayrhouser, Jennifer, 122
von Scherler, Sasha, 128, 208, 260
von Schiller, Friedrich, 149
Vos, David, 59
Voss, Gary, 193
Vucci, Ralph, 68, 69
Waaser, Carol, 122
Waddy, Gyle, 79
Wade, Janet, 206
Wadley, Steve, 75
Wadsworth, Don, 220
Wager, Douglas C., 190
Wager, Michael, 220
Wagner, Art, 8
Wagner, Gerard, 98
Wagner, Janyce Ann, 205
Wagner, Paula, 227
Wagner, Robin, 14, 155, 160, 161
Wagner, Ruth, 155
Wagner, Thomas, 70
Wahlquist, Carol D., 112
Wainer, Sherrill, 111
Wainscott, Ronald, 173
Waissman, Kenneth, 60
Waite, John Thomas, 147, 152, 260
Waiting for Godot, 190
Wakefield, Jo Marie, 62
Walcott, Derek, 194, 207
Wald, Joel, 105, 106
Waldman, robert, 91
Waldman, Susan, 89
Waldrip, Mack, 195
Walk the Dog, Willie, 227
Walken, Christopher, 7, 8, 35, 101, 232, 234, 260
Walker, A. J., 210
Walker, Arnetia, 169
Walker, Bill, 13, 132, 212
Walker, Bobby, 18
Walker, Bonnie, 47
Walker, Chet, 61, 260
Walker, Deborah Dean, 68, 69
Walker, Don, 65
Walker, Douglas W., 154, 260
Walker, Jaison, 154
Walker, Kathryn, 260
Walker, M. Burke, 186
Walker, Michael, 260
Walker, Patti, 71
Walker, Peter, 108, 260
Walker, Renate, 202

Walker, Robert, 234
Walker, Scott, 213
Walker, Sullivan, 194
Walker, Susan, 121
Walker, Suzanne, 86
Walker, Sydney, 189
Walker, W. Bradford, 175
Wall, John C., 191
Wall, Lawrence, 126
Wall, Vernon, 218
Wallace, Bradford, 191
Wallace, Chikita, 176
Wallace, Ian, 184
Wallace, Jack, 206
Wallace, Lee, 45, 260
Wallace, Marian, 191
Wallace, Marie, 215
Wallace, McClelland, 188
Wallace, Mimi B., 55
Wallace, Ronald, 13, 132,
212, 223
Wallace, Steve, 201
Wallace, Timothy, 119, 260
Wallach, Eli, 54, 234
Wallack, Daniel, 82
Wallman, Ronetta, 217
Wallman, Ruth, 111
Wallowitz, Howard, 110
Walsh, David, 184
Walsh, James, 55
Walsh, J. T., 80, 98
Walsh, M. Emmet, 205
Walsh, Thomas J., 14, 15,
260
Walston, Ray, 199
Walter, Bob, 200
Walter, Tracey, 121, 127,
134
Walters, Donald, 224
Walters, Marrian, 189
Walther, Deborah, 204
Walton, Mary Lou, 190
Walton, Russ, 218
Walton, Tony, 8, 61, 132,
212
Waltz of the Toreadors, The,
228
Wandrey, Donna, 28
Wanetik, Ric, 199
Wang, Ingrid, 126
Ward, Bethe, 19, 41
Ward, Brendan Noel, 191
Ward, David, 225
Ward, Donald, 70
Ward, Douglas Turner, 10,
124, 125, 260
Ward, Janet, 69, 260
Ward, Kelly, 155
Ward, Michael, 176
Ward, Phylis, 147
Ward, Richard, 97, 126
Ward, Robin, 213
Ward, Sheila, 78
Ward, Tim, 78
Ward, Vera, 203
Warden, James Jr., 124
Wardenburg, Mark, 182
Wardwell, John, 206, 211
Ware, Herta, 196
Warfel, William, 227
Warfield, Donald, 204
Warfield, Marlene, 234, 260
Warik, Josef, 48
Warmbash, Stuart, 141,
142, 260
Warncke, Margaret, 123
Warner, Annie Peacock, 198
Warner, Elise, 51
Warner, Eugene, 223
Warner, Rick, 122
Warner, Russell, 32, 65
Warner, Sherman, 105
Warner, Sturgis, 88
Warner, Valerie, 147, 148
Warrack, David, 72 Me
Warren, Allan, 121
Warren, Harold, 178
Warren, Jennifer, 234, 260
Warren, Joel, 220
Warren, Joseph, 126, 215
Warren, Lesley Ann, 234
Warren, Mary Mease, 10,
125
Warren, Renee, 169
Warren, Tim, 208
Warrick, Richard, 196
Warrilow, David, 104
Warriner, Frederick, 227
Warwick, Margaretta, 47
Washburn, David, 144
Washburn, Dede, 74
Washburn, Robert, 200
Washington, Glen, 221
Washington, John-Ann, 224
Washington, Vernon, 43,
260

Waterston, Sam, 129, 181,
260
Watkins, Maurine Dallas, 8
Watkins, Patrick, 163, 178
Watkins, Toney, 64
Watson, Ann, 220
Watson, Craig, 207
Watson, Douglass, 108,
234, 260
Watson, Edna, 124
Watson, John, 137
Watson, Lawrence, 126
Watson, Maurice, 126
Watson, Michael, 82, 226
Watson, Richard, 186
Watson, Walter, 59
Watt, Billie Lou, 144
Watts, Jefferson, 177
Waxman, Debbie, 180
Way Back When . . ., 207
Wayne, Anthony, 98
Wayne, David, 234
We Three, 185
Wear, Benjamin, 195
Weary, A. C., 186
Weatherhead, Chris, 143
Weathersbee, Gary, 151
Weaver, Carl, 64
Weaver, Fritz, 234, 260
Weaver, Rose, 225
Weaver, Sigourney, 90
Webb, Elmon, 75
Webb, Geoffrey, 112
Webb, John, 218
Webb, Robb, 69, 109, 260
Webber, Lloyd, 190
Weber, Carolyn, 123
Weber, Fredricka, 234
Weber, Lynne, 137
Weber, Patricia, 224
Webster, Byron, 196
Webster, John, 196
Webster, Kate, 158
Webster, Peter, 183
Wechsler, Gil, 213
Weddle, Vernon, 193
Wedekind, Frank, 107
Wedgeworth, Ann, 82, 165
Weeden, Robert, 59
Weekend With Feathers,
157
Weeks, 113
Weeks, Alan, 41, 64, 137
Wehle, Deedee, 82
Weholt, Michael, 186
Weidman, Jerome, 116
Weidman, John, 39
Weidner, Paul, 207, 216
Weigel, Jean, 136
Weiler, Norman, 86, 224
Weill, Kurt, 133
Weiman, Kate, 135, 145,
149
Wein, Tony, 127
Weinberg, Anne, 69
Weinberg, Jon, 190
Weiner, Arn, 145, 158, 260
Weiner, Zane, 122
Weingast, Arnold, 204
Weinstein, Arnold, 227
Weinstein, Gerald, 121
Weinstock, Richard, 155
Weintraub, Carl, 179
Weisgal, Jonathan, 45
Weisman, Sari, 122, 127
Weismann, Chris, 195
Weiss, Belle, 127
Weiss, Douglas, 203
Weiss, George D., 118
Weiss, Hedy, 74
Weiss, Jim, 145
Weiss, Julie, 196, 197
Weiss, Marc B., 76, 81,
223
Weissberger, L. Arnold, 126
Weitz, Bruce, 11, 190
Weitz, Eric, 190
Weitzenhoffer, Max, 89
Welch, Charles C., 65, 260
Welch, Don, 113
Welch, Miriam, 160
Welch, Ron, 113
Weldon, Charles, 205
Weller, Peter, 21, 132, 260
Welles, Jack, 166, 172
Welles, Joan, 67
Wellington, Jasper, 208
Wells, Bob, 49
Wells, Cynthia, 32, 260
Wells, Marion, 120
Wells, Ruth A., 145
Wells, Steven, 197
Welsh, Kenneth, 206
Welty, Eudora, 91
Weltz, T. Louis, 167
Welzer, Irving, 83, 169
Wendell, Howard D., 266
Wenrich, Douglass, 116
Wentz, Earl, 118, 260
Weppner, Christina, 114
Werner, Ken, 86
Wertheim, R. E., 180
Wessler, Rick, 224

Wesson, Craig, 11
West, Alvy, 100
West, Brooks, 203
West, Jennifer, 234
West Side Story, 195
Westman, Bud, 22, 52, 70,
83
Weston, Celia, 151
Weston, Jim, 60, 260
Weston, Steve, 213
Weterick, Fred, 158, 166
Wetherill, Elkins, 218
Wexler, Peter, 220
Weygandt, Sandra, 203
Weylock, Bill, 120, 126
Weyte, Stephan, 126
Wharton, Edith, 212
What Every Woman Knows,
212
What Price Glory?, 193
What the Babe Said, 190
What the Butler Saw, 198
Wheat, Tammy, 218
Wheel, Patricia, 260
Wheeler, Harold, 64
Wheeler, Hugh, 155, 224
Whelan, Richard, 184
When You Comin' Back, Red
Ryder?, 186, 218
Where's Charley?, 198
Whipper, Leigh, 266
Whipple, Winnie, 69
Whitaker, David, 203
White, Al, 189
White, Alice, 143
White, Billie, 18, 171
White, Diane, 209
White, Diz, 201, 209
White, Erik, 177
White, J. Steven, 189
White, Janet, 174
White, Joseph, 127
White, Justin, 194
White, Maryanne, 110
White, Richard C., 218
White, Sally, 182
White Steed, The, 228
White, Stuart, 88
White, Terri, 153
White, Willard, 18
Whitehead, Paxton, 30,
191, 260
Whitehead, Peter, 18
Whitehead, Robert, 40, 211
Whitehill, Brian T., 224
Whitehill, Kelli, 170
Whitehouse, Anthony, 43
Whitelaw, Arthur, 172
Whitfield, Arthur, 68
Whitmarsh, Roger, 79
Whitmore, Christinea, 13,
261
Whitmore, George, 145
Whitmore, James, 234
Whittemore, Robert B., 143
Whitton, Margaret, 117,
261
Whitton, Peggy, 224
Who Killed Richard Cory?,
109
Who's Afraid of Virginia
Woolf?, 8, 48, 228,
230
Why Marry?, 228
Whybrow, Arthur, 103
Whyte, Ron, 122
Widdoes, Kathleen, 184
Wideman, Beverly, 113
Widerman, Steven, 100
Widman, Sharon, 170
Widney, Stone, 52
Wieben, Michael, 63
Wieczorek, Jozef, 104, 224
Wiegert, Rene, 61
Wiener, Sally Dixon, 151
Wierney, J. Thomas, 117,
261
Wiesel, Elie, 45
Wiesel, Marion, 45
Wiest, Dianne, 190
Wietrzychowski, Stanley, 44
Wigfall, James, 64
Wilcock, Edgar, 207
Wilcox, Anne, 208
Wilcox, Ralph, 64, 261
Wilde, Oscar, 143
Wilder, Clinton, 48
Wilder, Thornton, 12, 25,
174, 175, 178, 206,
211, 266
Wilds, Rob, 195
Wiley, Bill, 118
Wiley, Flow, 123
Wiley, Ricardo, 225
Wilhelm, Kurt, 187
Wilhelm, Sheldon, 218
Wilkenfeld, H., 188
Wilkerson, John, 114
Wilkinson, Kate, 211, 214
Wilkinson, Lisa, 261
Wilkinson, Marc, 63, 163
Wilkof, Lee, 143

Wilks, Terry, 202
Will, Lennie, 37
Willard, C. George, 100,
156
Willett, John, 133
William, Noel, 40
Williams, Arthur, 18
Williams, Bill, 213
Williams, Billy Dee, 205
Williams, Clarence, III, 234
Williams, Curt, 105, 261
Williams, David, 178
Williams, Deborah Ann, 102
Williams, Dennis, 41
Williams, Dick Anthony, 8,
38, 261
Williams, Earl Christopher,
221
Williams, Ellwoodson, 126
Williams, Emlyn, 78
Williams, Grace, 123
Williams, Heathcote, 206
Williams, Jack Eric, 74, 133
Williams, Jerry, 186, 221
Williams, John R., 72
Williams, Joyce, 202
Williams, Lisette, 200
Williams, Louise, 145
Williams, Paulette, 221,
222
Williams, Richard, 121, 143
Williams, Richard B., 118
Williams, Robert, 202
Williams, Samm-Art, 10,
124
Williams, Sammy, 8, 14, 15,
161, 261
Williams, Steven, 206
Williams, Sundra Jean, 126,
135
Williams, Teddy, 25
Williams, Tennessee, 31,
35, 138, 147, 155,
180, 189, 211, 218,
220
Williams, Valerie, 154
Williams, Van Photos, 140
Williams, Yolanda, 202
Williamson, Cris, 197
Williamson, Kate, 126
Williamson, Laird, 189
Williamson, Nicol, 51
Willinger, Kathy, 70
Willis, Greg, 127
Willis, Horton, 143
Willis, Penelope, 163
Willis, Susan, 178
Willison, Walter, 54, 234,
261
Willson, Parker, 86
Wilson, Andrea, 83
Wilson, Bill, 203
Wilson, Billy, 43
Wilson, David, 122
Wilson, Earl Jr., 153
Wilson, Eleanor D., 190
Wilson, Elizabeth, 133, 261
Wilson, K. C., 133
Wilson, Kevin, 65
Wilson, Lanford, 107, 109,
119
Wilson, Laurel Ann, 45
Wilson, Lee, 161
Wilson, Lester, 19
Wilson, Mary Louise, 36,
101, 214, 261
Wilson, Pamela, 18
Wilson, Randal, 41
Wilzak, Crissy, 14
Wimsatt, James, 175
Win with Wheeler, 191
Winberry, T., 114, 122
Winbush, Marilynn, 114,
168
Winde, Beatrice, 126, 127,
198, 216, 234, 261
Wines, Halo, 199
Winfield, James, 215
Wing, Virginia, 210
Wingate, Peter, 213
Wingate, William P., 196
Winge, Violette, 210
Wingerter, Patricia, 145
Winker, James R., 189
Winkle, Fred Van, 211
Winkler, James R., 189
Winkler, Richard, 49, 54,
59, 69, 86
Winkworth, Mark, 147, 204
Winn, Cal, 182
Winn, Ellene, 111
Winner Take All, 144
Winnie the Pooh, 100
Winslow Boy, The, 228
Winston, Dan, 221
Winston, Hattie, 125
Winston, Lee, 5
Winters, Marian, 234
Winters, Newton, 43, 261
Winters, Shelley, 165
Winters, Susan Arleen, 218
Winter's Tale, The, 174,
178, 182, 214

Winters, Warrington, 69,
117, 261
Winterset, 228
Winton, Don, 196
Wirth, David, 206
Wischhusen, Marsha, 145
Wise, Steve, 173
Wise, William, 261
Wiseman, Joseph, 45, 261
Witham, John, 15
Witness for the Prosecution,
215, 228
Witt, Andrew M., 186
Witt, Howard, 190
Witt, Marilyn, 59
Witt, Peter, 75
Witter, William C., 186
Wittstein, Ed, 152, 205
Wiz, The, 64, 228
Wludarski, Tadeusz, 104
Wojewodski, Robert, 194,
204
Wojewodski, Stan, Jr., 194
Wojtasik, George, 116
Woldin, Judd, 169
Wolf, Ben, 188
Wolf, Catherine, 218
Wolf, Michael, 209
Wolf, Terry, 197
Wolfe, Joel, 261
Wolfe, Richard, 184
Wolfe, Skip, 208.
Wolfe, Timothy, 194
Wolfe, Wendy, 88
Wolff, Ann, 123
Wolfinger, Kirk, 114, 168
Wolfson, John, 127
Wolfson, Rob, 261
Woliver, Patrick, 211
Woll, Cynthia, 200
Wolsk, Eugene V., 64
Wolsky, Albert, 138, 158,
181
Wolves and the Lambs, The,
126
Womack, George, 206
Women Behind Bars, 88
Wonderful Town, 228
Wood, Angela, 127, 213
Wood, Bert, 169
Wood, Durinda, 197
Wood, G., 179, 186, 196
Wood, Helen, 234
Wood, John, 7, 8, 22, 23,
184, 261
Wood, Kent, 144
Wood, Nancy, 160
Wood, Peter, 22
Wood, Raymond, 70
Wood, Victoria, 190
Wood, Walter, 62, 107
Woodard, Alfre, 19, 135
Woodard, Charlaine, 164
Woodard, Grace, 114, 116
Woodard, Paul, 207
Woodbridge, Pat, 123
Woodbridge, Patricia, 58
Woodman, William, 191,
206
Woodruff, Eleanora, 218
Woods, James, 234
Woods, Richard, 34, 36,
261
Woods, Ron, 122
Woodville, Kate, 197
Woodward, Charles, 79
Woody, Stephen, 227
Wooing of Lady Sunday,
The, 121
Wooley, Steve, 49
Woolfenden, Guy, 103
Wootten, Robert, 218
Words and Music, 172
Workman! Whoever You Are
. . ., 207
World of Carl Sandburg,
The, 199
Woronov, Mary, 234, 261
Worsley, Joyce, 30
Worth, Irene, 7, 8, 35, 101,
261
Worthington, Barbara, 123
Woyzeck, 51
Wozniak, Maria Alexandra,
200, 211
Wray, Daniel, 197
Wray, Jeanne Adams, 218
Wright, Amy, 119, 127,
220
Wright, Garland, 85, 143,
144
Wright, Haidee, 36
Wright, Kathrynann, 14
Wright, Mark, 24, 35, 48
Wright, Mary, 122, 216
Wright, Max, 190, 221
Wright, Pam, 180
Wright, Samuel E., 61
Wright, Teresa, 8, 11, 13,
261
Wright, Wendell W., 190
Wright, William, 63, 261
Wrobleski, Marianne, 114

Wulp, John, 98
Wurst, David, 188
Wurtzel, Stuart, 21, 204
Wurz, Gregory, 176
Wyant, Shelley, 149, 224
Wycisk, Paul, 183
Wyckoff, Craig, 110
Wyeth, Zoya, 130
Wyler, David, 21, 49
Wyler, Hillary, 143
Wylie, John, 145, 194,
    221, 222, 226
Wylton, Tim, 103
Wyman, Dan, 200
Wyman, Nicholas, 32, 261
Wymore, Patrice, 234
Wynkoop, Christopher, 74,
    117, 185, 261
Wynne, David, 214
Wynne, Jonathan, 25, 261
Xifo, Ray, 133
Yaffee, Stephen, 143
Yakim, Moni, 89
Yale Repertory Theatre, 227
Yama, Conrad, 39
Yancy, Emily, 55, 261
Yanez, Robert, 107, 108

*Yankee Ingenuity*, 215
Yankee, Luke, 174
Yanowitz, Edward, 113
Yarnell, Bruce, 234
Yates, Craig, 261
Yates, John, 127
Yates, John Robert, 84, 261
Yder, Loretta, 209
Yeargan, Michael H., 44, 76,
    227
Yellen, Sherman, 51
Yenque, Teresa, 115
*Yentl*, 8, 20, 230, 231
Yeo, Leslie, 184, 188
Yesckas, Manuel, 115
York, Rebecca, 14, 161
York, Y Yve, 180
Yoshida, Fusako, 39
Yoshida, Peter, 116, 261
Yoshimura, Leo, 80
Yossiffon, Raquel, 72
*You Can't Take It with You*,
    228
Youens, Frederic, 178
Young, Barbara, 18
Young, Bryan, 52
Young, Edward, 204

Young, Edwin, 114
Young, Fay, 48
Young, Janice Kay, 113
Young, Janis, 223
Young, Kate, 178
Young, Madonna, 120, 261
Young, Ronald, 160
Young, Vikki, 179
Young, Wendy, 32
Young-Smith, Otis, 123
Younger, Carolyn, 218
Younger, Charles, 221
Yount, Kenneth M., 122,
    123, 145
*Your Arms Too Short to Box
    with God*, 205
*Your Own Thing*, 228
*You're a Good Man, Charlie
    Brown*, 218
Yovino, Rita, 172
Zaccaro, Michael Zeke, 116,
    118
Zacek, Dennis, 206
Zachar, Glenn, 13, 261
Zagal, Wilfredo, 115
Zahn, Claudia, 198
Zakian, Haig, 180

Zakkai, J., 122, 123
Zakrzewski, Maria, 137
Zaks, Jerry, 60, 122, 261
Zaldivar, Gilberto, 150
Zaleski, Anthony, 123
Zalk, Ellen, 118, 143, 145
*Zalmen or the Madness of
    God*, 45
Zalon, Paul, 214
Zaloom, Joe, 196, 197
Zaltzberg, Charlotte, 169
Zambrana, Haydee, 150
Zamora, Romulus E., 191
Zampedri, Josephine, 38,
    55, 155
Zampese, Alan, 221
Zang, Edward, 133, 261
Zank, Ric, 210
Zapata, Carmen, 197, 210
Zaragoza, Rolando, 115
Zaslove, Arne, 105, 221
Zaslow, Michael, 27
Zavaglia, Richard, 121
Zeigler, Eloise, 226
Zelaya, Nikki, 203
Zemenick, Michael, 203
Zenobia, 88

Zentis, Robert, 196, 197
Zheutlin, Cathy, 197
Ziegler, Darrell, 74
Zien, Chip, 77, 148, 158
Ziff, Charles, 102, 103,
    104
Ziman, Jerrold, 105, 122,
    261
Zimet, Paul, 197
Zimmerman, Edward, 68
Zimmerman, Ken, 196
Zippi, Daniel, 189
Zippin, Louis, 75
Zipprodt, Patricia, 8, 61
Ziskie, Dan, 206
Zivetz, Carrie, 197
Zobel, Richard, 113
Zomina, Sonia, 105
Zorich, Louis, 140, 261
Zupancic, Tim, 199
Zweigbaum, Steve, 65
Zwick, Joel, 261